I0890978

SOUND JUDGMENT

The essays in *Sound Judgment* span the full career of Richard Leppert, from his earliest to work that appears here for the first time, on subjects drawn from early modernity to the present concerning music both popular and classical, European and North American. Noted for his path-breaking interdisciplinary scholarship on music and visual culture, the collection includes key essays on music's visualization in art practices in virtually all visual media, including film. The fourteen essays comprising this volume demonstrate Leppert's many contributions to critical musicology, particularly in the areas of aesthetics as well as social and intellectual history, all of it grounded in a heterodox body of critical and cultural theory, with the work of Theodor W. Adorno particularly noteworthy. The collection is preceded by an introduction in which Leppert traces his intellectual development, defined in large part by the social, cultural, and political upheavals of the 1960s and their aftermath both in the academy and in society at large.

ASHGATE CONTEMPORARY THINKERS ON CRITICAL MUSICOLOGY SERIES

The titles in this series bring together a selection of previously published and some unpublished essays by leading authorities in the field of critical musicology. The essays are chosen from a wide range of publications and so make key works available in a more accessible form. The authors have all made a selection of their own work in one volume with an introduction which discusses the essays chosen and puts them into context. A full bibliography points the reader to other publications which might not be included in the volume for reasons of space. The previously published essays are published using the facsimile method of reproduction to retain their original pagination, so that students and scholars can easily reference the essays in their original form.

Titles published in the series

Critical Musicology and the Responsibility of Response
Lawrence Kramer

Music and Historical Critique
Gary Tomlinson

Taking Popular Music Seriously
Simon Frith

Music, Performance, Meaning
Nicholas Cook

Reading Music
Susan McClary

Sound Judgment

Selected Essays

RICHARD LEPPERT
Regents Professor and Morse Alumni Distinguished Teaching Professor, University of Minnesota, USA

ASHGATE CONTEMPORARY THINKERS ON CRITICAL MUSICOLOGY SERIES

Routledge
Taylor & Francis Group
LONDON AND NEW YORK

First published 2007 by Ashgate Publishing

2 Park Square, Milton Park, Abingdon, Oxfordshire OX14 4RN
711 Third Avenue, New York, NY 10017

Routledge is an imprint of the Taylor & Francis Group, an informa business

First issued in paperback 2018

ISBN 978-0-7546-2683-1 (hbk)
ISBN 978-1-138-38354-8 (pbk)

British Library Cataloguing in Publication Data
Sound judgment : selected essays. - (Ashgate contemporary thinkers on critical musicology)
1. Music - Philosophy and aesthetics 2. Music - history and criticism
I. Leppert, Richard D.
780

US Library of Congress Cataloging-in-Publication Data
Leppert, Richard D.
Sound judgment : selected essays / by Richard Leppert.
p. cm. – (Ashgate contemporary thinkers on critical musicology)
Includes index.
ISBN 978–0–7546–2683–1 (alk. paper)
1. Music–Philosophy and aesthetics. 2. Music–History and criticism. I. Title.

ML3800.L614 2007
780–dc22

2007015774

Contents

Acknowledgments

By Theodor W. Adorno

'Four Hands, Once Again', Translated by Jonathan Wipplinger. *Cultural Critique,* **60**, 2005, pp. 1–4.

By Richard Leppert

'*Concert in a House*: Musical Iconography and Musical Thought', *Early Music*, **7**, 1979, pp. 3–17.

'"Everybody's Lonesome for Somebody": Age, the Body, and Experience in the Music of Hank Williams', Co-authored with George Lipsitz, *Popular Music,* **9**, 1990, pp. 259–74.

'Four Hands, Three Hearts', Commentary on T.W. Adorno 'Four Hands, Once Again', *Cultural Critique*, **60**, pp. 5–22.

'Imagery, Musical Confrontation and Cultural Difference in Early Eighteenth-Century London', *Early Music*, **14**, 1986, pp. 323–45.

'Male Agony: Awakening Conscience', in *The Sight of Sound: Music, Representation, and the History of the Body*, pp. 188–211, 275–81. © 1993 The Regents of the University of California. Published by the University of California Press.

'Music and the Body: Dance, Power, Submission', in *Music and Image: Domesticity, Ideology and Socio-Cultural Formation in Eighteenth-Century England*, pp. 71–106, 230–32. Cambridge: Cambridge University Press, 1988.

'Music "pushed to the edge of existence" (Adorno, Listening, and the Question of Hope)', *Cultural Critique*, 60, 2005, pp. 92–133.

'Music Teachers of Upper-Class Amateur Musicians in Eighteenth-Century England', in *Music in the Classical Perieod: Essays in Honor of Barry S. Brook*, edited by Allan Atlas, pp. 133–58. New York: Pendragon Press, 1985.

'The Musician of the Imagination', in *The Musician as Entrepreneur, 1700-1914: Managers, Charlatans, and Idealists*, edited by William Weber, pp. 25–58. Bloomington and Indianapolis: Indiana University Press, 2004.

'Nature and Exile: Adorno, Mahler and the Appropriation of Kitsch', in *Frispel: Festskrift till Edström*, edited by Alf Björnberg, Mona Hallin, Lars Lilliestam, and Ola Stockfelt, pp. 448–63. Gothenburg: Skrifter från Institutionen för musikvetetenskap, Göteborgs universitet, 2005.

'On Reading Adorno Hearing Schubert', Commentary on Theodor W. Adorno, 'Schubert', *Nineteenth-Century Music*, **29**, pp. 55–62. © 2005 The Regents of the University of California. Published by the University of California Press.

'Opera, Aesthetic Violence, and the Imposition of Modernity: *Fitzcarraldo*', in *Beyond the Soundtrack: Representing Music in Cinema*, edited by Daniel Goldmark, Lawrence Kramer, and Richard Leppert, pp. 99–119. © 2007 The Regents of the University of California. Published by the University of California Press.

'The Prodigal Son: Teniers and Ghezzi', *Minneapolis Institute of Arts, Bulletin*, **61**, 1974, pp. 80–91.

Introduction

I don't suppose that, as children, many people grow up intending to become musicologists. Until my mid-twenties or so the profession was not in the forefront of my mind, and thereafter, especially during my graduate studies in musicology, while it was certainly on my mind a good deal, I sometimes wondered why, which over time led me to the work that gradually emerged in the years following the PhD.

My parents were farmers, and I was one in training. In truth, I loved it, though crops and cattle on the northern plains were a long way from a life in the academy. That said, my parents, children of the depression, were passionate about education. Alas, school came too easily for me, and until I was seventeen I was something of a goof-off, until a high school music teacher took me under wing. Over a two-year period, he mentored me on the principle of intellectual challenge, figuring out that through music it would be possible to put some other forms of knowledge into my head as well. One-on-one, via tutorials, he assigned me books on art, architecture, literature, philosophy, and music history.

In college, in no small part on account of the interests he developed in me, I finished three major field concentrations: music, English literature, and German literature; I likewise studied art history. Upon graduation, I was undecided between Musicology and English Literature; I applied to graduate school in both fields. Musicology offered me funding; Literature didn't. Having undergone several years of total crop failures (from hail to drought), my parents' savings had been wiped out; becoming a musicologist was an easy choice. I don't regret the outcome, though the story has a few twists and turns along the way.

My graduate training occurred between 1966 and 1970, after which I spent two years in Brussels researching and writing my dissertation, earning my degree in 1973. This is to say that my training overlapped, more or less precisely, the worst years of the Vietnam War. By the good fortune of a deferment and an educationally-sympathetic local draft board, I was safe, unlike some of my friends who were sent over, some never to return. Musicology offered me a four-year fellowship, paid for by the federal government under the quaint idea that the nation was producing far too few PhDs to staff the colleges and universities in the near future; the program, ironically, was called the National Defense Education Act. (It was ended a year or so into my graduate studies and there has never been anything like it since.)

I've incorporated these biographical details in order to explain a few things about the way my work has shaped itself. As an undergraduate my focus in music was voice. I completed that major, before moving on to study literature and visual art. I pursued subjects beyond music principally because of frustration, though less with my music professors and more with fellow students who for the most part only wanted to discuss technical questions about whatever pieces they were struggling to learn. Music was notes. Just notes. What one talked about was how to make them. Music existed in a realm wholly separate from ideas.

I certainly didn't feel superior to my colleagues; I did however feel like a stranger in their presence, no doubt in part because of what I'd had the privilege to learn from my high school teacher: a de facto insistence that music was part of a larger set of mutually informing cultural discourses. The English literature students, whatever the pretensions we all promoted, wanted to talk about ideas—and, of course, politics. For my musician friends, by contrast, the outside world beyond notes seldom seemed to intrude. Thus when Kennedy was killed (I was twenty), I hung out with my literature friends trying to make sense of it; I seriously doubt we had all that much to say to one another worth remembering (I remember none of it, in any event), but we absolutely knew we had to discuss it and did so endlessly over many weeks. Not much of this seemed to penetrate the practice rooms. The disconnect was dramatic, almost as though the notes could shut out the nastiness of modern life.

Later, in graduate school, the degree of privilege we enjoyed as students was increasingly apparent, insulated as we were from the social and political realities at our metaphorical doorstep—the worsening war, of course, and closer by the civil rights struggles acting out within a day's drive of the campus; literally on our doorstep, to complete the picture, there was a protracted strike at a local major-appliance assembly plant. In particular, some guilt set in among many of us who had been spared making the difficult choices of Vietnam, on the one hand, or Sweden or Canada, on the other. Unlike some other white kids who stood with the marchers in Selma and elsewhere, we pretty much kept to our books, if only with some sense of shame. And what we discovered about town–gown realities became quickly evident for those who tried to join the strike picket lines: we were not welcomed, and for the simple reason that the working stiffs from town read the situation, probably correctly, as involving a bunch of middle class guys slumming for an afternoon. I'll return to some of this shortly.

My graduate training in musicology was uneventful and typical for the period. We learned notes: theory and standard repertory, most of it German; we learned how to deal with Renaissance notation, this being the heyday of Reese-inspired studies; we were assigned to undertake minor researches on very minor composers, the 'good' ones having already been 'done' by our forebears. In brief, our education was largely positivist and formalist. Thus a friend of mine who had enrolled in a semester-long seminar on the Bartók quartets spent fourteen grueling weeks at a single task, namely, to label every vertical note concurrence, movement by movement, of all six compositions. That's all. Six miniature scores with pencil marks under each beat. That was Bartók. Nothing—nothing—else.

As graduate students in those days, we called our professors by their surnames only, and we didn't question what they were doing and certainly not what they asked us to do. So to speak, we labeled chords and we memorized. Regarding memorization: one part of every qualifying exam was 'sing the tune.' A member of the examining committee would call out a theme (say, the B theme of the Beethoven Quartet Whatever, first movement), and we were expected to perform it. I spent six months, seven days a week, memorizing themes. Like all of my colleagues, and something like a trained seal, I could give back hundreds of them on the spot, though to what purpose no one ever had the temerity to ask and no justification was ever offered. After some years at such tasks, we became musicologists (or theorists). There's some hyperbole here, of course, but not too much. So far as I know, this is how it was pretty much anywhere. As Leonard B. Meyer once aptly remarked in relation to the state of musicological inquiry at the time: musicology went in search of rigor; it achieved rigor mortis.

Meanwhile, a war raged on, more bloody with each passing week. Nightly at 5:30, the graduate students in my housing unit would gather in the basement TV room to catch Walter Cronkite and the CBS Evening News. The body counts he reported were staggering; some weeks on the American side they reached 500 and more, that horror offset—or so it was reported—by the still higher body counts on the other side. The same newscasts reported on the beatings and worse among civil rights workers. Meanwhile, we dutifully labeled Bartók harmonies. Or to state the matter differently, during the daytime we labeled chords, but at night we went to our rooms or to the bars and listened to the music that wasn't admitted at all, under any circumstances, to the hallowed halls. What I remember most of this music was its direct, explicit, and often forceful commitment to engage with a world that seemed increasingly dystopian; that much was evident even from the play lists of the local Top-40 stations, never mind college radio. The music came with several labels; for convenience, if lacking precision, we called it rock or folk or jazz, depending. This music *meant*, and its meanings went beyond the lyrics. That much we figured out, however tentatively. But any further application of the insight that music could mean anything beyond itself stopped at the door to the School of Music.

For a lot of young graduate students the contradictions of our life experience—privilege and personal safety especially—were not entirely containable. Life outside the academy intervened, whether in the jungles of Southeast Asia, the graveled back roads of Alabama and Mississippi, or the picket lines a couple of miles away. Life, and death, beyond the campus seemed increasingly to demand a place in our thinking about what it was we were doing—studying musicology—and, not least, what the way we were studying it had to do with anything beyond the positivist-formalist protocols that organized its practice. In brief, the troubling issue was less musicology in principle and more the apparent social and cultural limitations of its established practice.

To skip some of the story, fast forward to May 1970 and Kent State, the moment when external reality penetrated the campus perimeter, actual and metaphoric, in a way never since equaled. Kent State was pretty close by, making the killings seem all the more real, visceral. We marched en masse (and then went home). A friend and I, in the same musicology course, told our professor that we were staying away for the next couple of classes, in response to a call for a general campus strike—at least minimally inconvenient to us because of a scheduled exam. We didn't ask to make up the test; in truth, I don't remember how that was worked out in the end. He was an understanding man, absolutely decent. He didn't support our action, nor—and this is the point—did he understand it. The only part I remember of the conversation we had with him to explain ourselves was his response: he didn't see what Vietnam, Kent State, or our actions had to do with studying to be musicologists. In a fundamental sense, to be sure, he was right and that, precisely, was the problem. I'm not sure why, but his response shocked us.

In looking back at this history, indeed, perhaps reconstructing it in ways to make myself feel somehow morally superior, this twenty-minute exchange was something of a turning point. It came after four years in graduate school and in the last semester I was taking classes. Essentially, the lesson it taught me was this: if I hoped to justify spending my life teaching and writing about music, I needed to figure out why I really thought music was important. Was I embarking on a life of self-delusion and self-entertainment? Or did music matter as much as I thought (or hoped) it did, but was unable to articulate? Was music more than its notes? Did it mean something, and, if so, did those somethings really matter?

I returned from Europe in 1972 without a job, though not for wont of trying. (Any national fears of there being too few humanists to stock the nation's faculties by then had been laid entirely to rest by the economic realities that tracked the effects of the Vietnam debacle.) Of the seventy positions I applied for—some ranging well beyond musicology—I received a follow up from just two, a remotely located community college and another from a second-tier research university, which, times being tough, offered me an on-campus interview, provided I could travel at my own expense from Brussels. I couldn't, and that was the end of the prospect. Instead, that summer I moved back to the farm to help with the harvest. A few weeks later, and entirely out of the blue, I had the good fortune to be offered a contract research appointment at the Graduate Center of The City University of New York. Barry Brook phoned me with the offer. I owe him a great deal for the confidence he showed in me. Having written a dissertation principally organized around iconographical sources, later published (*The Theme of Music in Flemish Paintings of the Seventeenth Century* [1977]), Barry asked me to help establish a new center at CUNY to serve as a clearing house for an international effort at gathering data concerning the visual traces of music history (RidIM, The International Repertory of the Iconography of Music). I developed the cataloguing system for RIdIM, based on the protocol I produced for my dissertation. Unfortunately, the CUNY position didn't involve teaching, and I was keen to teach. The following year I got the opportunity; I was hired on a tenure-track appointment at the University of Minnesota, where I've spent the balance of my career.

I was hired into what was then an undergraduate humanities program, which later evolved into a department, developed a PhD track, and eventually merged with Comparative Literature: Cultural Studies and Comparative Literature, with twin PhD tracks, Comparative Studies in Discourse and Society, essentially where I reside, and Comparative Literature. Apart from my first term at Minnesota, during which I commuted weekly to New York to teach a graduate seminar at Columbia, I've never been part of a music or musicology department. Early in my career, Columbia's generosity notwithstanding, I couldn't imagine how I'd fit in. That has changed with the advent of Cultural Musicology in the late 1980s, to be sure, but the change came slowly.

Susan McClary was hired by the School of Music at Minnesota four years after my arrival, though we were actually introduced only some months later in Chicago by Howard Mayer Brown. We became fast friends from the start, and interlocutors. Whatever alienation I experienced looking in from the outside at what then constituted established musicology, Susan experienced rather more of it and at first hand. We had many discussions about our chosen discipline in those early years, among other things, duly comparing notes over whose rejection letters were the nastiest (a few of them were very unpleasant indeed). We did nonetheless keep at it, and in 1985, we put together a small conference at the University, *Music and Society: The Politics of Composition, Performance, and Reception*. Two years later, Cambridge University Press published the papers under the same title. After a decade of teaching and post-doctoral reading, the project was our attempt to state what we wanted to be as scholars. Many of the participants, it turned out, shared our frustrations with established musicological inquiry. It's not an accident that we were all nearly the same age, late 30s to early

40s. We had all been thinking a lot about how to rethink thought and talk about music. We had read the voices of an older generation whose work spoke forcefully to us, people like Joseph Kerman (I'd read *Opera as Drama* when I was a high school student; it was my first piece of musicological reading), Leonard B. Meyer (like Kerman, a scholar keenly interested in music and meaning), Christopher Small (a high school teacher in England, who concerned himself with music as a material practice), and, a bit later, Jacques Attali (the French economist, writing on music as an agent of political economy). And we'd started to read people who, though they had been around a long time, had no voice whatever in American musicology: Barthes (on musical semiotics read through the erotics of the musical body), and of course, Adorno (of whom more presently), as well as a number of other scholars working beyond the parameters of musical discourse, household names now in our field, from the disciplines of history, literature, and philosophy in particular.

Early on in my academic career, and to some degree in a panicked effort to find my way, I started to read beyond my discipline: popular culture studies (Frith, Hall, Hebdige), literary theory (sampling among the several dozen volumes in the Theory and History of Literature series, published by the University of Minnesota Press, and to this day unquestionably the single most influential collection of its kind), philosophy (principally the German idealist tradition and its aftermath in Marx, Gramsci, Benjamin, Bataille, Althusser), qualitative sociology (Veblin, Weber, Horkheimer, Marcuse, Elias, Bourdieu), discourse theory (Baudrillard, de Certeau, Foucault, Kittler, Said), and visual culture (Alpers, Barrell, Bürger, Bryson, Clark, Crary, Mulvey, Nochlin, Silverman). Eventually, I found my way to Adorno, principally through Susan's urgings and Rose Rosengard Subotnik's now-classic essays; my interest in his work has kept me busy for the last decade and more.

For many colleagues of my generation, myself included, the years since 1985 have been rather more fulfilling than those that preceded. Musicology changed. Music studies joined the other human sciences. Qualification met quantification head on. Criticism engaged formalism. Positivism backed off a little. What was assigned the unfortunate nomenclature of New Musicology, more aptly called Cultural (or Critical) Musicology, gained a foothold in the North American academy, and ever less as an interloper and more as a partner of sorts with the dominant paradigms that had long prevailed, having taken their heritage from (principally) German musicology three or so generations previously.

• • •

The Theme of Music in Flemish Paintings of the Seventeenth Century (1977) began as an empirical study of 770 paintings with musical subjects. I proposed the topic to my dissertation committee as a study in performance practice; it evolved into something else entirely. The project was positivist in outline; each chapter was organized around particular groups of musical instruments, each employed for more or less distinct and non-overlapping purposes in high and popular culture including domestic life, public entertainment, civic and ecclesiastical affairs, hunting, and war. But the result was something different from what the chapter titles implied. In the end, I wrote about musical representation as a series of discursive tropes, reflecting less precisely on the music made in the Flemish Low Countries than on the ideas and investments associated with and/or assigned to music of this time and place. In other words, the study was essentially a contribution to cultural history, investigated through the material remains of music now more or less entirely silenced apart from its visual traces (notated survivals the exception). An early essay, '*Concert in a House*: Musical Iconography and Musical Thought' (1979), included in this collection, complements this book, addressing the question of music and morality as perceived in early modernity in Flanders.

Thereafter, but in keeping with *The Theme of Music*, my work turned more directly to the study of music as a phenomenon of social class articulation and the subjectivities that class and music together anchored. This started with two journal essays devoted to paintings on musical subjects by the prolific seventeenth-century Fleming David Teniers the Younger, 'The Prodigal Son: Teniers and Ghezzi' (1974), in this collection, and 'David Teniers the Younger and the Image of Music' (1978); and by my second book, *Arcadia at Versailles* (1978), addressing one aspect of musical life at the French court (c. 1660-1789), namely, the bizarre adoption and adaptation by courtiers of two musical instruments previously associated solely with peasants (the bagpipe) and beggars (the hurdy-gurdy). My interest was to make sense of why such a radical upheaval could occur, especially at a time when the social-class based hierarchies among musical instruments were so rigidly observed. What had to happen for the bagpipe, popular as a lower-class dance instrument, and the hurdy-gurdy, almost uniquely associated with destitute blind men, to become court favorites? *Arcadia at Versailles*, while grounded in iconographical survivals, led me in other directions as well: organology (the history and design of musical instruments), musical treatises, instruction manuals ('how to play' books), and contemporaneous pamphlets inviting nobility to recuperate these instruments from their lowly rank. I regarded this project as social history, hoping to clarify something about 'the sorts of relationships that exist between music as a human activity and social class as a human fact' (p. 1). What got my attention to investigate the question was the suddenness with which—however temporarily—a long dominant musical order had been upended.

In these early studies, I struggled to find my voice within the context of Marxian cultural analysis, much of it indebted to the social–historical work of art historian Arnold Hauser (*The Social History of Art* [1951]), and the sociology of composer Elie Siegmeister [*Music and Society* [1938]). I came to Adorno shortly thereafter, and his work took me much farther and more directly into a dialectical, and more nuanced, relationship that defines music both as a social practice and an aesthetic discourse. Indeed, Adorno helped teach me how to think about music and society, even—perhaps especially—when I most resisted him.

Music and Image (1988), appeared three years after *Music and Society;* it concerned the gender politics of domestic musical life in eighteenth-century England, and was the first work that showed the impact of my reading Adorno, though the references to him in this volume are few: an epigraph on page one, and one other, concerning music and social class, near the end. Nonetheless, his *Dialectic of Enlightenment* [co-authored with Horkheimer] and *Introduction to the Sociology of Music* had helped me to refine my sense of how music produced history. In introducing *Music and Image*, I explained the project in a way that has organized much of my work, both before and since:

> [*Music and Image*] is not a social history of music, nor of performance practice, nor of the history of musical instruments; it is least of all a history of music in pictures. Rather it is a history of an ideology of music—yet one anchored in actual musical practice, which is to say that I do not view

> the book specifically (or only) as a contribution to the history of ideas. I have tried to understand how music, as shaped by social-cultural forces, itself contributes to socio-cultural formation. In other words, I am not interested in demonstrating how music *mirrors* anything, but rather in how, in what ways and why music is an agent [pp. 2–3].

Music and Image, as the title stresses, is fundamentally organized around the visual representation of musical practices; that said, the sources beyond imagery are in fact as important: period music histories, philosophical tracts about music, musical instruction manuals, dance treatises, books on education, travel literature, poetry, fiction, advertising, and courtesy and conduct literature. While limited to domestic music making among the English upper classes, the presence of the lower and middling social orders and their musics inevitably shadows, and even haunts, the musical identities and subjectivities of the privileged. And as I discovered in the course of the research for this book, music's hold on ideological investments surrounding sexuality, sex, and gender difference often seemed to trump all other issues of the place—and practice—of music in this society. The chapter 'Music and the Body: Dance, Power, Submission,' is included in this volume, as is a related free-standing essay, 'Music Teachers of Upper-Class Amateur Musicians in Eighteenth-Century England' (1985).

Journal essays written around the same time took up complimentary issues embedded in opera ('Imagery, Musical Confrontation and Cultural Difference in Early 18th-Century London' [1986], in this volume), looking at gender in relation to cultural chauvinism and xenophobia; and colonialism ('Music, Domestic Life and Cultural Chauvinism: Images of British Subjects at Home in India' [1987]), looking at gender within the context of racial difference.

The Sight of Sound (1993) broadened the geographical and chronological domain of my inquiry on music, gender, and sexuality to incorporate the 300 years following the advent of early modernity, emphasizing music's relation to the materiality of the body and its cultural history. Incorporated into the fabric of this project, always in relation to gender and sexuality, is violence: music's sometime protest against it, and music's sometime acquiescence and even participation in it. Above all, the book is focused on music as a means in modernity of ordering society through sound and the practices to make and experience it. *The Sight of Sound* concerns itself with the history of ideas—as well as the history of bodies in action—some aestheticized and utopian, others de-aestheticized and dystopian. *The Sight of Sound*, perhaps to a greater extent than any of my previous work, organizes itself around the social tensions and contradictions that lie at the heart of Western modernity, with respect to which the title of the second chapter duly characterizes the whole: 'Desire, Power, and the Sonoric Landscape.' One chapter, 'Male Agony: Awakening Conscience,' is reproduced in this collection.

All of my work to this point was anchored in both the written and visual record of music, understood as a social or socialized activity. My interest in the iconographical record of Western music's history deviated from the established practice of such research, which was almost exclusively concerned with performance practice and organology. Indeed, the relevance of visual history for the study of performance practice in particular is far more fraught than the appropriation of images for that purpose invites. Simply stated, visual art is not analogous to the snapshot; there is no necessary indexical relationship between images and reality. Visual representation's relation to the facts of history—or what might more aptly be described by the concept of historical truth—is indirect at best, and without regard to the truism all facts require interpretation.

What the record of visual culture offers above all to the history of music is a remembrance of things past. The representation of music in visual culture, like music itself, is invariably highly selective in its tropes. Music's representation to some uncertain degree mirrored what was; at least as important, it also projected that which is to be. It functioned as a record of qualification and assessment; it made judgments, right or wrong, about what seemed to matter. What mattered, and how it mattered in sound, has always been up for grabs. Music's purpose, in part, in other words, has been to assess reality: to pass judgment.

All art reveals; the trouble is, of course, it also hides. What music's representation reveals is both direct and indirect. That which is indirect tempers any and all surface claims; what is 'said' also serves to disguise or even silence what is not said. In other words, the 'facts' of history inhabit the realm of highly partial truths. Rarely simply objective, cultural facts are assuredly always *interested.* Responsible history attempts to unmask what lies in shadow or has otherwise been shoved aside; responsible history, in Benjamin's words, brushes history against the grain.[1] Music itself, and whatever beyond sound that remains as history's trace music, are ways to gain access to judgments about what musical sound was asked to do, whether to challenge or to perpetuate certain ways of living—to urge, to praise, to control, to condemn. Throughout my career, I have wanted to learn about music perceived as a set of concerns, investments, and ideas set in practice—sound as a discourse of estimable historical agency, organized and experienced as an aesthetic phenomenon.

Aesthetic discourses engage the present in order to organize the future through the construction of memory. As such, they *profess*. The historian's role is at once to recognize the professing while discerning as well that to which these discourses need to *confess*. All futures the terrains of contestation. The cultural battles fought over music in the past, as in our own time, whether virtual or actual, link to the wars over society. Music entertains and pleases. It also instructs; sometimes it assaults. And as a (potentially) utopian discourse, music itself is often assaulted: 'Music is realized in musical life, but that life conflicts with music'.[2] My interest in the visual record of music history was not to discern how music 'looked,' but to learn how it was *made* to look, and for what purpose. Stated succinctly, my interest was musical practice as informed by the *idea* of music that directed people towards (or away from) music and in turn helped to organize the practices that responded to the urge. This has led me to questions of subjectivity, class, race, gender, and national identity. In sum, then, my work addresses less musical practices themselves and more what lay behind them.

• • •

In several recent essays I have turned to historical discourses about musicians, public performers and virtuosos in particular, that prevailed during the course of the eighteenth

1 Walter Benjamin, "Theses toward a Philosophy of History," in *Illuminations*, ed. Hannah Arendt, trans. Harry Zohn (New York: Schocken, 1969), p. 257.

2 Theodor W. Adorno, *Introduction to the Sociology of Music*, trans. E. B. Ashton (New York: Continuum, 1976), p. 119

and nineteenth centuries. One of these studies, 'The Musician of the Imagination' (2004), is included in this volume. Much of my concern (evident especially in 'Cultural Contradiction, Idolatry, and the Piano Virtuoso: Franz Liszt' [2000]; and 'The Social Discipline of Listening' [2002]) was to understand the paradoxical, often contradictory cultural meanings attached by audiences to these figures—men (principally) who articulated deep-set societal antagonisms. Increasingly self-defined as artists, performers were also often people of business commonly heavily invested in calculated, even manipulative, self-marketing. The virtuosos among them, and here Liszt is the perfect exemplar, seemed at once and contradictorily to proclaim and undercut increasingly rigid definitions of gender (as simultaneously masculine and feminine), and class (hyper bourgeois in lifestyle and anti bourgeois in their proclamations about aesthetic practice). Musicians, put simply, were at once strikingly 'real' and also the vehicle of an affective cultural imaginary onto whom audiences projected obsessive, sometimes fetishized, attention, whether to praise or to blame.

I have addressed the interface between music and gender in essays on country music included in this collection, '"Everybody's Lonesome for Somebody": Age, the Body and Experience in the Music of Hank Williams' (1990), co-authored with George Lipsitz, and 'Gender Sonics: The Voice of Patsy Cline' (2008). My effort in both essays was to think through how gender was articulated through the voices of these artists. In particular I sought to consider how Hank and Patsy musically repositioned themselves in opposition to established conventions of both country music and pop for projecting male and female identities—sonic traces of personal experience that mark and make history.

Two other essays likewise address gender in sound, but in these instances gender questions are interfaced with musical discourses concerning nature and natural beauty in tension with the discourses surrounding aesthetics: 'Opera, Aesthetic Violence, and the Imposition of Modernity: *Fitzcarraldo*' (2007), included in this volume; and 'Paradise, Nature, and Reconciliation, or, a Tentative Conversation with Wagner, Puccini, Adorno, and The Ronettes' (2002). Both essays address music's articulation of nature as an acoustic sublime projecting a utopian cultural–social imaginary, an otherness of hopeless hope, set within the lies of modernity's mythologies of progress.

• • •

At an Adorno session I organized for the AMS Toronto 2000 meeting a prominent musicologist, not much amused with the proceeding, announced to the assembled that, he 'had read Adorno' and—unlike the panel (Lydia Goehr, Susan McClary, Rose Rosengard Subotnik, Rob Walser, and I)—had 'gotten over him', this spoken with an air of triumph. I can't confess to this accomplishment. Whatever the ways that I disagree with Adorno, no other aesthetician/musicologist has taught me more about how to think either about music *tout court*, or about music in its relation to culture and society—whether as a practice necessarily infected with modern society's sad realities, or as an aesthetic discourse informed by a utopian imaginary, the *promesse de bonheur*, that Stendahl recognized,[3] and a phrase

3 Stendahl [Henri Beyle], *Life of Rossini*, trans. Richard N. Coe (Seattle: University of Washington Press, 1972), p. 347.

that Adorno repeated numerous times during his career with respect to art in general and music in particular. There's irony here, to the extent that Adorno has long—and carelessly, even vulgarly—been designated pessimist nonpareil. The essays occupying the last section [*Utopia*] in this collection all concern Adorno: 'Nature and Exile: Adorno, Mahler and the Appropriation of Kitsch' (2005), 'Four Hands, Three Hearts: A Commentary' (2005), and 'Music "pushed to the edge of existence" (Adorno, Listening, and the Question of Hope)' (2005), as does the volume's first essay, 'On Reading Adorno Hearing Schubert' (2005). These pieces follow from the volume I edited, introduced, and annotated, *Theodor W. Adorno: Essays on Music* (2002), twenty-seven Adorno essays on music in modernity: art music, popular music; aesthetics and the philosophy of music; music on radio and record; the social conditions of modern composition, performance, listening, and reception; the nature and social impact of the culture industries; the challenge to imagine in late modernity a music responsible to the demands of history; and the composers whose work Adorno most favored (Beethoven, Mahler, Berg, Schoenberg) and most critiqued (Wagner, Stravinsky). What I have sought to do in all of this writing is at once to understand, and in turn help to realize, one of Adorno's most insistent claims that determine his own life's work: 'I believe in the strict knowability of music—because music is itself knowledge, and in its way very strict knowledge',[4] this from his never-completed career-long project to make sense of Beethoven, an effort whose fragmentary nature nonetheless aptly and repeatedly demonstrates Adorno's struggle to know, precisely because he believed the stakes to be high. Adorno held that art's ultimate social responsibility was to preserve the trace of something better, especially at those critical moments in history when anything better seemed the most remote. He expressed the idea succinctly in the final sentence of his unfinished last book, *Aesthetic Theory*: 'But what then would art be, as the writing of history, if it shook off the memory of accumulated suffering.'[5]

Along the way, I've learned from many people whose work I deeply admire, and none more than that of Susan, already mentioned, Larry Kramer, Rose Rosengard Subotnik and Lydia Goehr. Whatever I've contributed to the discipline, I owe these colleagues a good deal more than I can easily acknowledge.

4 Theodor W. Adorno, *Beethoven: The Philosophy of Music*, ed. Rolf Tiedemann, trans. Edmund Jephcott (Stanford: Stanford University Press, 1998), p. 180

5 Adorno, *Aesthetic Theory*, ed. Gretel Adorno and Rolf Tiedemann, trans. Robert Hullot-Kentor (Minneapolis: University of Minnesota Press, 1997), p. 261.

Published Writings

1. Books

a) Concerning Music

Beyond the Soundtrack: Representing Music in Cinema. Edited by Daniel Goldmark, Lawrence Kramer and Richard Leppert. Berkeley and Los Angeles: University of California Press, 2007.

Theodor W. Adorno: Essays on Music. Berkeley and Los Angeles: University of California Press, 2002.

The Sight of Sound: Music, Representation, and the History of the Body. Berkeley and Los Angeles: University of California Press, 1993, 1995.

Music and Image: Domesticity, Ideology, and Socio-Cultural Formation in Eighteenth-Century England. Cambridge: Cambridge University Press, 1988, 1993.

Music and Society: The Politics of Composition, Performance, and Reception. Co-edited with Susan McClary. Cambridge: Cambridge University Press, 1987, 1989.

Arcadia at Versailles: Noble Amateur Musicians and Their Musettes and Hurdy–gurdies at the French Court (c. 1660–1789). A Visual Study. Amsterdam and Lisse: Swets and Zeitlinger, 1978.

The Theme of Music in Flemish Paintings of the Seventeenth Century. Musik und Musiker im Bild: Ikonologische Studien, 1. Series edited by Walter Salmen. 2 vols. Munich: Musikverlag Emil Katzbichler, 1977.

b) Concerning Art

The Nude: The Cultural Rehtoric of the Body in the Art of Western Modernity. Boulder: Westview, 2007.

Art and the Committed Eye: The Cultural Functions of Imagery. Boulder: Westview/HarperCollins, 1996.

Turkish translation: *Sanatta Anlamin Görüntüsü: Imgelerin Toplumsal Islevi.* Istanbul: Ayrinti, 2002.

2. Journal Issue

Special Issue, co-edited with Bruce Lincoln. 'Discursive Practices and the Economy of Prestige.' *Cultural Critique* 12 (Spring 1989).

3. Journal Articles and Book Chapters

'The Civilizing Process: Music and the Aesthetics of Time–Space Relations in *The Girl of the Golden West*'. In *Musical Meaning and Human Values,* edited by Keith Chapin abd Lawrence Kramer. Fordham: Fordham University Press 2008 forthcoming.

'Gender Sonics: The Voice of Patsy Cline.' In *Musicological Identities: Essays in Honor of Susan McClary*, edited by Raymond Knapp, Steven Baur, and Jacqueline Warwick. Aldershot, UK: Ashgate, 2008, forthcoming.

'Temporal Interventions: Music, Modernity, and the Presentation of the Self.' In *Structures of Feeling in Seventeenth-Century Cultural Expression*, edited by Susan McClary. Toronto: University of Toronto Press, 2008, forthcoming.

'Opera, Aesthetic Violence, and the Imposition of Modernity: *Fitzcarraldo.*' In *Beyond the Soundtrack: Representing Music in Cinema*, edited by Daniel Goldmark, Lawrence Kramer, and Richard Leppert, pp. 99–119. Berkeley and Los Angeles: University of California Press, 2007.

'On Reading Adorno Hearing Schubert.' Commentary on Theodor W. Adorno, 'Schubert.' *Nineteenth-Century Music* 29 no. 1 (Summer 2005): 55–62.

'Nature and Exile: Adorno, Mahler and the Appropriation of Kitsch.' In *Frispel: Festskrift till Edström*, edited by Alf Björnberg, Mona Hallin, Lars Lilliestam, and Ola Stockfelt, pp. 448–63. Gothenburg: Skrifter från Institutionen för musikvetetenskap, Göteborgs universitet, 2005.

'Knowledge, Self, and the Aurality of the Immaterial.' Review essay of Michael P. Steinberg, *Listening to Reason: Culture, Subjectivity, and Nineteenth-Century Music* (Princeton, 2004). *Beethoven Forum* 12 no. 2 (2005): 177–95.

'Four Hands, Three Hearts.' Commentary on T.W. Adorno, 'Four Hands, Once Again.' Special Adorno issue. *Cultural Critique* 60 (Spring 2005): 5–22.

'Music 'pushed to the edge of existence' (Adorno, Listening, and the Question of Hope).' Special Adorno issue. *Cultural Critique* 60 (Spring 2005): 92–133.

'The Musician of the Imagination.' In *The Musician as Entrepreneur, 1700–1914: Managers, Charlatans, and Idealists*, edited by William Weber, pp. 25–58. Bloomington and Indianapolis: Indiana University Press, 2004.

'The Social Discipline of Listening.' In *Le concert et son public: Mutations de la vie musicale en Europe de 1780 à 1914 (France, Allemagne, Angleterre)*, edited by Hans Erich Bödeker, Patrice Veit, and Michael Werner, pp. 459–95. Paris: Éditions de la Maison des sciences de l'homme, 2002. Reprinted in *Aural Cultures*, edited by Jim Drobnick, pp. 18–35. Toronto: YYZ Books, and Walter Phillips Gallery Editions, 2004.

'The Male Nude: Identity and Denial' (excerpt from *Art and the Committed Eye: The Cultural Functions of Imagery)*. In *Critical Perspectives on Art History*, edited by John C. McEnroe and Deborah F. Pokinski, pp. 134–38. Upper Saddle River, NJ: Prentice Hall, 2002.

'Paradise, Nature, and Reconciliation, or, a Tentative Conversation with Wagner, Puccini, Adorno, and The Ronettes.' *Echo* [online journal] 4 no. 1 (Fall 2002).

'On Music and Dance' (excerpt reprinted from *Music and Image: Domesticity, Ideology and Socio-Cultural Formation in Eighteenth-Century England*). In *Music, Culture, and Society: A Reader*, edited by Derek B. Scott, pp. 100–03. Oxford: Oxford University Press, 2000.

'Cultural Contradiction, Idolatry, and the Piano Virtuoso: Franz Liszt.' In *Piano Roles: Three Hundred Years of Life with the Piano*, edited by James Parakilas, pp. 252–81, 425–27. New Haven: Yale University Press, and Washington: Smithsonian Institution, 2000.

'Representing Girls: Modernity, Cultural Anxiety, and the Imaginary.' In *The Body Aesthetic: From Fine Art to Body Modification*, edited by Tobin Siebers, pp. 75–106. Ann Arbor: University of Michigan Press, 2000.

'Desire, Power, and the Sonoric Landscape (Early Modernism and the Politics of Musical Privacy).' In *The Place of Music*, co-edited by Andrew Leyshon, David Matless, and George Revill, pp. 291–321. London: Guilford, 1998. Reprinted from *The Sight of Sound: Music, Representation and the History of the Body*.

'Social Order and the Domestic Consumption of Music (The Politics of Sound in the Policing of Gender Construction in 18th–Century England).' In *The Consumption of Culture 1600–1800: Image, Object, Text*, edited by Ann Bermingham and John Brewer, pp. 514–34. London: Routledge, 1995.

'The Post Modern Condition and Musicology's Place in Humanistic Studies.' Review Essay of *The Last Post: Music after Modernism*, edited by Simon Miller (Manchester, 1993). *Journal of Musicological Research* 14 nos. 3–4 (1995): 235–50.

'From Robespierre to the Ryman: Hank Williams and History.' Co-authored with George Lipsitz. In *1789–1989: Musique, histoire, democratie*, edited by Antoine Hennion, vol. 3, pp. 753–64. Paris: Maison des Sciences de l'Homme, 1995.

'Sexual Identity, Death, and the Family Piano.' *Nineteenth-Century Music* 16 no. 2 (Fall 1992): 105–28.

Review Essay: Lawrence Kramer, *Music as Cultural Practice, 1800–1900*. (Berkeley and Los Angeles, 1990). *Journal of Musicological Research*, 12 Supp (1992): 99s–108s.

'Vision and the Sonoric Construction of Reality (Private Pleasure and Social Order).' In *Musica Privata: Die Rolle der Musik im privaten Leben: Festschrift für Walter Salmen*. Edited by Monika Fink, Rainer Gstrein, and Günter Mössmer, pp. 67–78. Innsbruck: Edition Helbling, 1991. Reprinted from *The Sight of Sound: Music, Representation and the History of the Body*.

'Music as a Sight in the Production of Music's Meaning.' In *Metaphor: A Musical Dimension*. Edited by Jamie C. Kassler, pp. 69–88. Sydney: Currency, 1991. Reprinted from *The Sight of Sound: Music, Representation and the History of the Body*.

'"Everybody's Lonesome for Somebody": Age, the Body, and Experience in the Music of Hank Williams.' Co-authored with George Lipsitz. *Popular Music* 9 no. 3 (October 1990): 259–74. Reprinted in (1) *All that Glitters: Country Music in America*, edited by George H. Lewis, pp. 22–37. Bowling Green: Bowling Green State University Press, 1993. (2) *Reading Pop: Approaches to Textual Analysis in Popular Music*, edited by Richard Middleton, pp. 307–28. Oxford: Oxford University Press, 2000.

'Introduction.' *Reader: Essays in Reader-Oriented Theory, Criticism, and Pedagogy*, 23 (Spring 1990): 1–9.

'Music, Representation and Social Order in Early Modern Europe.' *Cultural Critique*, 12 (Spring 1989): 25–55.

'Discursive Practices and the Economy of Prestige: Introduction,' co-authored with Bruce Lincoln. *Cultural Critique*, 12 (Spring 1989): 5–23.

'Music, Domestic Life and Cultural Chauvinism: Images of British Subjects at Home in India.' In *Music and Society: The Politics of Composition, Performance, and Reception*, co-edited by Richard Leppert and Susan McClary, pp. 63–104. Cambridge: Cambridge University Press, 1987.

'Imagery, Musical Confrontation and Cultural Difference in Early Eighteenth-Century London.' *Early Music*, 14 no. 3 (August 1986): 323–45.

'Men, Women and Music at Home: The Influence of Cultural Values on Musical Life in Eighteenth-Century England.' *Imago Musicae* 2 (1985): 51–133.

'Music Teachers of Upper-Class Amateur Musicians in Eighteenth-Century England.' In *Music in the Classic Period: Essays in Honor of Barry S. Brook*, edited by Allan Atlas, pp.133–158. New York: Pendragon, 1985.

'Johann Georg Plazer: Music and Visual Allegory.' In *Music East and West: Essays in Honor of Walter Kaufmann*, edited by Thomas Noblitt, pp. 209–224. New York: Pendragon, 1981.

'*Concert in a House*: Musical Iconography and Musical Thought.' *Early Music* 7 no. 1 (January 1979): 3–17. Reprinted in [Japanese translation] *Recorder* (1979) no. 4: 2–7, and (1980), no. 1: 17–27.

'David Teniers the Younger and the Image of Music.' *Koninklijk Museum voor Schone Kunsten* [Antwerpen] *Jaarboek* (1978): 63–154.

'Viols in Seventeenth-Century Flemish Paintings: The Iconography of Music Indoors and Out.' *Journal of the Viola da Gamba Society of America* 15 (December 1978): 5–40.

'Musical Iconography and Visual Perception: Knowledge as the Delimiter of Expectation.' *Répertoire International d'Iconographie Musicale, Newsletter* 2 no. 2 (Spring 1977): 12–15.

'The Prodigal Son: Teniers and Ghezzi.' *The Minneapolis Institute of Arts, Bulletin* 61 (1974): 80–91.

'The Research Center for Musical Iconography of The City University of New York: Description of an International Research Project in Musicology.' In collaboration with Barry S. Brook. *Symposium of the College Music Society* 13 (Fall 1973): 106–13.

4. Reviews

Margaret Myers, *Blowing Her Own Trumpet: European Ladies' Orchestras and Other Women Musicians (1870–1950) in Sweden*. Göteborg, 1993. *Svenska Tidskrift för Musik* (November 1993): 114–20.

W. L. Braekman, ed. *Christiaen van Vaerenbrakens Conste von musike oft vanden Sanghe. De oudste musiekleer in het Nederlands (1535)*. Brussels, 1981. *Speculum: A Journal of Medieval Studies* 58, no. 2 (1983): 548–49.

Phillip T. Young. *The Look of Music: Rare Musical Instruments, 1500–1900*. Seattle: University of Washington Press, and Vancouver: Douglas and McIntyre, 1980. *Winterthur Portfolio: A Journal of American Material Culture* 17, no. 4 (1982): 274–77.

A.P. de Mirimonde, *L'Iconographie musicale sous les rois Bourbons: la musique dans les arts plastiques (XVIe–XVIIIe siècle)*. 2 vols. Paris, 1975, 1977. *American Musical Instrument Society Journal* 5–6 (1979–80): 166–71.

Walter Salmen. *Musikleben in 16. Jahrhundert*. Musikgeschichte in Bildern, vol. III/9. Musik des Mittelalters und der Renaissance. Leipzig, 1976. *Journal of the American Musicological Society* 32, no. 2 (Summer 1979): 339–43.

Tilman Seebass, *Musikdarstellung und Psalterillustration im früheren Mittelalter. Studien ausgehend von einer Ikonologie der Handschrift Paris, Bibliothèque Nationale, fond latin 1118*. Bern, 1973. *Speculum: A Journal of Medieval Studies* 52, no. 1 (January 1977): 165–71.

Miscellaneous

Editor of commissioned series for *The Minnesota Composers Forum Newsletter*: (1) Robert Walser. 'The Premises of Composition' (January 1989): 5–7; (2) Stephen Houtz. 'Coming Out: The Acknowledgment of a Gay Experience in Music' (April 1989): 4, 6–7; (3) Georgina Born. 'IRCAM, Legitimation, Post Modern Music Policy: Some Thoughts from Europe' (December 1989): 2–5; (4) Barbara Engh. 'Utopia at Hand? Composition and Cultural Studies' (June 1990): 3–6.

'Musical Iconography and Visual Perception: Knowledge as the Delimiter of Expectation.' Panel Report: Present State of Iconographical Research. *Congress Report: International Musicological Society, Twelfth Congress* (Berkeley, 1977), edited by Daniel Heartz and Bonnie Wade, pp. 806–08. Kassel: Bärenreiter, 1981.

Part One

Aurality

CHAPTER 1

On Reading Adorno Hearing Schubert

> Art is the semblance of what is beyond death's reach.
> —Adorno, *Aesthetic Theory*

I

By age twenty-five, Adorno had been publishing commentaries on music—specifically, performance reviews of concerts and operas in Frankfurt—for seven years. He was already an old hand at it.[1] His "Schubert" essay, however, was something entirely new and different: a sustained, if still brief, foray that attempts to make sense of the *œuvre* of a major composer. The essay's condensation is notable, but not much less so than are his "mature" (was Adorno ever immature?) single-composer essays; indeed, even his monographs (Berg, Mahler, Wagner) are brief, and no less idiosyncratic than "Schubert." The brevity of "Schubert" is striking, but it is not accidental, and this despite the essay's considerable ambition. Not only was Adorno out to explain Schubert, he did so—just as he was always to do—by means often well outside the conventions and intellectual sympathies of the musicological community. Indeed, he stayed outside the evolving reach of the discipline pretty much his entire life. "Schubert" in that regard is wholly symptomatic of a shot he kept firing across the bow of the musical establishment (not that it invariably chose to notice, either then or now). Perhaps more to the point, Adorno's music studies, this early one included, consistently resisted the ever-tightening binds of intellectual specialization characteristic of "scientific" humanities research in general. The essay is as much philosophy and sociology as musicology; it's also fundamentally literature in the form of aesthetic critique that is immanently self-reflexive, not only in how the argument is advanced, but also by means of the rhetorical

[1]See Adorno, *Gesammelte Schriften*, vol. 19, ed. Rolf Tiedemann, et al. (Frankfurt am Main: Suhrkamp, 1970–86), pp. 11–139.

impact of the aesthetic form through which its argument unfolds.

The essay form, which defines the bulk of Adorno's writing, permits spontaneity and even (intellectual) play; thought and writing that in their own form replicate both the spirit of emancipation and a constitutive part of the realized subject. Anti-dogmatic, the essay's "method" is to proceed "unmethodically."[2] As a structure for philosophical thought, the essay is not predetermined by a philosophical first principle; the thought it reflects arises more directly from the material it studies, and less from the concepts that precede the material and always threaten to overwhelm it. The essay—in a sense *ideally* unsystematic, spontaneous, fragmented—formally constitutes itself less as a magnifying-glass, more as a splinter in the eye.[3] Its tendency is critical, its purpose "to move culture to become mindful of its own untruth."[4] Terry Eagleton comments that "Every sentence of [Adorno's] texts is thus forced to work overtime; each phrase must become a little masterpiece or miracle of dialectics, fixing a thought in the second before it disappears into its own contradictions."[5]

The trick Adorno manages here, and honed throughout his writing life, is that the essay textually reenacts what it recognizes in Schubert's music. Like the music, the essay repeats itself but with subtle differences, as though Adorno were holding up a cut gem to light and turning it to see the differences manifested in its facets. And what's "there," in Adorno and in Schubert, bears repeating; indeed, it begs for it. Adorno's ideas about this music, like so many things in Schubert's music itself, are less developed than juxtaposed, often paratactically, so as to constitute what Benjamin termed a constellation, closely related to Adorno's concept of a force field (*Kraftfeld*), the more effectively to reveal the "truth content" of Schubert's music.

Adorno's essay is evidently inorganic, at least as regards conventional scholarship; it surveys an acoustic landscape that is in turn internalized: philosophically, subjectively, formally. Adorno listens to the familiar otherness of Schubert and finds mutuality—empathy. The result is joy, but also tears. Can music ever be cheerful, asks Schubert? And Adorno, with tears in his eyes, answers the rhetorical question with an emphatic "no, at least not now, in good conscience": "The injustice committed by all cheerful art, especially by entertainment, is probably an injustice to the dead; to accumulated, speechless pain."[6] The world's misery doesn't evoke smiles, let alone laughter. (Laughter is sometimes tried on for size in music, but Adorno regards its modern manifestations with particular bitterness; consider thus his scathing comments about *Petrushka*.)[7] Still, though music of good conscience isn't happy, it can assert joy; it can bring forth a *promesse de bonheur*.

That richly evocative phrase, drawn from Stendahl, is one that Adorno kept pretty much at the forefront of his mind for decades, repeating it a number of times in writing about art generally and music especially to the very end of his life; indeed, the phrase more or less defines what might be called his insistent pessimistic optimism. What matters dearly to Adorno is that Stendahl penned the phrase in specific reference to music. Music, Stendahl wrote, "as an art, suffuses the soul of man with sweet regret, by giving it *a glimpse of happiness;* and a glimpse of happiness, even if it is no

[2]Adorno, "The Essay as Form," in *Notes to Literature*, ed. Rolf Tiedemann, trans. Shierry Weber Nicholsen (New York: Columbia University Press, 1991), I, 13.

[3]Adorno, *Minima Moralia: Reflections from Damaged Life*, trans. E. F. N. Jephcott (London: Verso, 1978), p. 50: "The splinter in your eye is the best magnifying-glass."

[4]Adorno, "The Essay as Form," p. 20. David Martin ("Dr. Adorno's Bag of Tricks" [review of *Minima Moralia*], *Encounter* 47 [1976], 70) refers to Adorno's writing as a process of unmasking, achieved not least by his fragmentary form of writing. "Nothing is as it seems, and truth is paradoxically layered. You can only break through to truth by exposing the paradoxes and masquerades at each layer and setting them against other masquerades and paradoxes."

[5]Terry Eagleton, "Art after Auschwitz: Theodor Adorno," in *The Ideology of the Aesthetic* (Oxford: Blackwell, 1990), p. 342.

[6]Adorno, *Aesthetic Theory*, ed. Gretel Adorno and Rolf Tiedemann, trans. Robert Hullot-Kentor (Minneapolis: University of Minnesota Press, 1997), p. 40.

[7]Adorno, *Philosophy of Modern Music*, trans. Anne G. Mitchell and Wesley V. Blomster (New York: Continuum, 1985), pp. 143–45, and pp. 157–58, n. 18. He regards the humor in *Petrushka* to be sadomasochistic.

more than a *dream* of happiness, is almost the dawning of hope."[8] Schubert's heavily mediated joy, as Adorno envisioned it, emerged in the surroundings of death's Everywhere: death, to be sure, as an ontological ("natural") fact, but even more as the product of subjectivity drained of happiness, wherein the loss of happiness is at once historical and social. Modernity carries the mark of Cain, the stakes increasingly raised by the technological efficiencies for producing pain and worse. The damage is somatic and psychological at the same time; it is individual and it is general. So where, in all this, comes Schubert?

Schubert looks to the horizon while gazing inward. He surveils a scene: lived life (his own and those of his imagination). Brooks babble. Trout swim. Millwheels turn. Wanderers wander. It's all in his head (how modern is that?), and it's outside him as well. It's all there in a landscape. But just what *is* Schubert's landscape? For starters, if it really involves land/ nature, that's not what's interesting. Whatever it is, it's out *there:* it's an other, but it's also partly the otherness of the self (the "me," alike of Schubert and Adorno). In Schubert, Adorno hears the reciprocity that emerges when the subject recognizes in the object not difference but, however disconcertingly, sameness.

Landscape by definition marks distance, the extreme otherness. We see a landscape specifically at a remove from ourselves, literally as a kind of fata morgana. The closer we approach, the more the landscape disconcertingly at once becomes more real *and* less of what it first appeared to be. Put differently, landscape is *not* whatever we take into our line of vision when we're outdoors and in the country; landscape is something special that we choose to see as such. Thus landscape paintings make special particular sights of certain geographies. It's hardly accidental that painted landscapes don't often "look" like the "real" ones, because, in point of fact, there aren't any. Landscape involves the realm of the imaginary, typically scenes of striking beauty (but also some that strike terror, as in the early-Romantic visions of Vernet and Friedrich) in which the gaze finds itself locked onto something so mesmerizing that the sense of sight falters. Landscape, in short, is cultural; it is a product of the soma and the psyche; and yet it exists outside of both.[9] The "magic" of landscape ultimately can be held onto by one of two (impossible) means: by suspending time-as-progress—we stop to stare; we halt our future for the look of the scene; or, alternatively, by holding the scene in our mind's eye afterwards as an afterimage.

Landscape is like music to the extent that it is at once material and ethereal. Neither can really be grasped; both are invariably just out of reach.[10] What matters is the instant of their realization, which can be retained (by repeating the gaze, by replaying the piece, or in memory) but never more than fleetingly. In an age defined not simply by the myth of progress but, concomitantly, by the ideology of objective possession, landscape and music alike refuse their cooperation. In that refusal Adorno hears articulated the possibility of an alternative, a momentary hint of reconcilation between subject and object:

> As indeterminate, as antithetical to definitions, natural beauty is indefinable, and in this it is related to music, which drew the deepest effects in Schubert from such nonobjective similarity with nature. Just as in music what is beautiful flashes up in nature only to disappear in the instant one tries to grasp it. Art does not imitate nature, not even individual instances of natural beauty, but natural beauty as such.[11]

From childhood, Adorno was deeply attuned to the natural world; the metaphor of landscape

[8]Stendhal [Henri Beyle], *Life of Rossini*, trans. Richard N. Coe (Seattle: University of Washington Press, 1972), p. 347 (original emphasis).

[9]Adorno, *Aesthetic Theory*, p. 68: "For in every particular aesthetic experience of nature the social whole is lodged."

[10]The poignancy of this fact appears when music expresses something of the material quality of objective reality (hence, opposed to mere "copying" of natural sounds, like bird songs); as such it is the product of a subject (the composer) who at once acknowledges and respects the otherness of the natural object. Adorno, *Beethoven: The Philosophy of Music*, ed. Rolf Tiedemann, trans. Edmund Jephcott (Stanford: Stanford University Press, 1998), p. 8: "Images of the objective world appear in music only in scattered, eccentric flashes, vanishing at once; but they are, in their transience, *of music's essence*" (original emphasis).

[11]Adorno, *Aesthetic Theory*, p. 72.

in reference to Schubert's music is for him a declaration of love. What we choose to see as a landscape is selected for what we variously determine as its perfection, its *desirable difference* from our here and now. In other words, landscape defines a terrain whereupon difference engenders embrace, not domination. (Little wonder we choose to fence off the "best" of landscapes into park "preserves," literally to protect them from ourselves. Ironically, little wonder that our often desperate "embrace" of these increasingly rare and special places is now commonly smothering.)

II

Our relationship to the other-yet-us of nature remains ambivalent at best. Accordingly, Adorno once noted, the very concept of natural beauty "rubs on a wound."[12] Art responds to this hurt. Art is not nature, "but art does want to keep nature's promise."[13] The "perfect" Schubert melody is like the imagined perfection of landscape[14]—as though, like "nature," it were always already complete. The C-minor Andante of the Piano Trio in E♭ (op. 100, D. 929) is, in this sense, perfect. The opening melodic statement from the cello and the folklike second theme from the violin for the most part can only be repeated, not improved upon, though Schubert tries. The tunes are fragmented, modulated, and passed among the three voices, sometimes impatiently, as though not one of the three wants to let go of the melodic material. In the end, the homophonic enterprise (and here Schubert had no real rival), nicely infects any real effort at the counterpoint that convention assigns to development processes. The "counterpoint," such as it is, seems to accomplish very little more than to comment by default on the perfection of the themes' first statements. How can perfection be elaborated? The three voices gradually acknowledge that it can't. It's as though they engage the tunes, passing bits of them back and forth, as if to say, "Can you believe how beautiful this is? What happiness it gives me to sing the sadness."[15]

The opening statement, almost literally "sung" by the cello, is repeated immediately by the piano, thereafter to be played in its entirety only once more, toward the middle of the movement, following the initial statement of the second theme. The second theme provides the material for initial fragmenting, but less as a "development" and more as the means by which to enact a series of momentary modulations culminating in a gradual increase in dynamics and harmonic rhythm, all three instruments working toward a dramatically stated eighth-note G-major chord, played *sforzando,* and then: silence. A full measure of nothing. And then, as if in acknowledgment of the dilemma of "now what do we do?," there follow two measures of transition back to C minor and a full restatement by the piano of the opening, but now set against small bits of the second theme in both the violin and cello. (Something similar occurs with the second theme later in the movement.)

The point, I think, is that only the initial statement at the movement's beginning really matters, but this becomes evident only as the movement unfolds. That is, the perfection of the opening statements, the first theme especially, becomes unambiguously evident only when the movement ends. We need everything that follows the initial statements to realize what we first heard: a melody (more than a theme) complete in itself, perfect, and on that account acoustically utopian—the semblance of happiness embedded in the sad honesty of C minor's pensive melancholy. To be sure, the movement's opening tries to return at the very end, but there's nothing left of it but a distant echo, a fading memory of something already

[12]Adorno, *Aesthetic Theory*, pp. 61–62.
[13]Adorno, *Aesthetic Theory*, p. 65.
[14]Theodor Adorno and Hanns Eisler, *Composing for the Films* (London: Athlone Press, 1994), pp. 6–7: "The concept of melody first gained ascendancy in the nineteenth century in connection with the new *Kunstlied*, especially Schubert's. Melody was conceived as the opposite of the 'theme' of the Viennese classicism of Haydn, Mozart, and Beethoven. It denotes a tonal sequence, constituting not so much the point of departure of a composition as a self-contained entity that is easy to listen to, singable, and expressive."

[15]Adorno, *Beethoven: The Philosophy of Music*, pp. 23–24: "Schubert's sadness results not just from the expression . . . but from the liberation of the particular. The liberated detail is abandoned, exposed, just as the liberated individual is also alone, sorrowful—the negative."

lost but treasured all the more for it. And then . . . the final silence, and an apt close for what Adorno once referred to as Schubert's "romanticism of disillusion."[16] Lost, but remembered. And one thing more: the opening themes of the Andante never quite become part of the whole. Ultimately, they remain solitary in their isolation from what comes after their initial statements (very unlike what happens in Beethoven). In this resides their truth, the fractured relation of part to whole that marks modernity and its subjects.

The truth content [*Wahrheitsgehalt*] that Adorno pursued in "Schubert" as a young man, and in *Aesthetic Theory*[17] left unfinished at his death, constitutes the stakes of art. That truth is less encompassed by the expression of things as they are, and more by the appearance of what they might be. In Beethoven, the utopian moment emerges through an intense and prolonged engagement with the musical materials dominated by the composer's will, shaped and reshaped until the truth-potential of the materials not so much emerges (as though it were always already "there") as it gradually takes shape. The "moment" in Beethoven is a long one, a process, manifesting a kind of patently self-reflexive acoustic philosophy. In Schubert it's different. The truth of Schubert doesn't emerge through development, at least not one that we'd term "Beethovenian," except, ironically perhaps, in the "successful" failure of his developments. Instead, more or less, it's articulated in a virtual instant, as in the shape and turn of a melody (and distinctly not in its working out).

The truth of Schubert's music lies in the actual *absence* of what it "glimpses": happiness. Put differently, the happiness (however sad) of Schubert is boxed in by history, and Schubert knows it. The would-be reality of happiness can manage not more than its acoustic trace—an aural moment, a present absence. The Schubert of Adorno's "Schubert" responds—intellectually, emotionally, spiritually, and not least somatically—to the demands of the history that he cannot eschew. Indeed, even (or perhaps especially) his subjective reactions are objectively tied to reality. The music that emerges when he puts fingers to keyboard or pen to paper may already have been "there." These tunes, whatever their kinetic status in Schubert's inmost being, were certainly already there to the extent that they "exist," even in embryonic form, in response to experience, which itself embeds a history more complex than any human subject can begin to fathom, even as that history makes him what he is. Schubert's reality was not "simply" his own; it was his present, his past and *the* past. He could never live outside it. And thus a tune's gestation was long prepared, no matter the "moment" it got to make its first appearance, becoming initially audible to Schubert himself.

The truth content of artworks is not something poured into them from without; instead, as Adorno always insisted, it emerges—immanently—from the technical manipulation of the musical materials, that is, in the attempt by the composer literally to dominate the materials. The "crystalline" [23] truth of Schubert's music emerges from the extreme degree to which the materials—Schubert's melodies-qua-themes, for example—"resist" him every inch of the way. If Beethoven constructs themes ripe for their own reworking, Schubert's are close to freestanding. Their truth emerges in the composer's "failure" to do more with them, at least the "more" that history expects of a Viennese contemporary of Beethoven. The truth (hence worth) of Schubert's music, Adorno suggests, is the result of what it accomplishes, but also in what it fails to accomplish. Aesthetic failure for Adorno was a mark of saving grace to the extent that failure revealed truths that an untrue modernity strove relentlessly to shove under the carpet. Thus Adorno's considerable admiration for the "failures" of the late quartets of Beethoven. Not for nothing does he describe them via the poetic imagery of a decaying nature: "The maturity of the late works . . . does not resemble the kind one finds in fruit. They are, for the most part, not round, but furrowed, even ravaged. Devoid of sweetness,

[16]Adorno, *Minima Moralia*, p. 116, from the opening of aphorism 75, "Chilly hospitality," in reference to *Winterreise*, no. 21, "Das Wirtshaus." Concerning the return of the opening theme of the Andante in the trio's finale, see Lawrence Kramer, *Franz Schubert: Sexuality, Subjectivity, Song* (Cambridge: Cambridge University Press, 1998), pp. 157–60, 171–72.

[17]Adorno, *Aesthetic Theory*, pp. 126–33.

bitter and spiny, they do not surrender themselves to mere delectation."[18] And not for nothing does Adorno here likewise invoke landscape:

> No longer does [Beethoven] gather the landscape, deserted now, and alienated, into an image. He lights it with rays from the fire that is ignited by subjectivity, which breaks out and throws itself against the walls of the work, true to the idea of its dynamism. . . . Objective is the fractured landscape, subjective the light in which—alone—it glows into life. He does not bring about their harmonious synthesis. As the power of dissociation, he tears them apart in time, in order, perhaps, to preserve them for the eternal. In the history of art late works are the catastrophes.[19]

So Schubert's failure, at once real and not, is, precisely, Schubert's "success." Put differently, the "completeness" of the Schubertian melody produces its quality of having a remainder, a "something" that is beyond both Schubert's ultimate reach and, not less important, Schubert's listener. This alone helps explain the poetic imagery that Adorno employs in his effort to say what matters in this music. Ordinary "analysis" comes up short as mere data collecting. (Poetry exists, after all, in recognition of the shortcoming of language.) Adorno argued that the enigmatical character of art is not its failure but an essential component of its being art in the first place. Further, the residue of the uncertain is all the more critical under the prevailing circumstances that define the long trajectory of modernity, already encompassing the modernity of early Romanticism, to the extent that it constitutes a resistance to music's instrumental utilization.[20]

III

Adorno clung to the memories of his childhood happiness throughout his life, while acknowledging adulthood as a permanent condition of exile from his past. His own literal exile during the war years overdetermined the urgency of the loss. As he commented near the end of his life:

> At no moment during my emigration did I relinquish the hope of coming back [to Germany]. . . . I simply wanted to go back to the place where I spent my childhood, where what is specifically mine was imparted to the very core. Perhaps I sensed that whatever one accomplishes in life is little other than the attempt to regain childhood.[21]

Schubert for Adorno is something like a childhood memory. He moved on—to Beethoven and, in a word, to development—yet without ever quite surrendering the joy he recalls from hearing repeated what is already perfect.[22] To be sure, Adorno does not regard Schubert as a musical child, a case of arrested musical development. Indeed, he hears in Schubert's music

[18]Adorno, "Late Style in Beethoven," in *Essays on Music*, ed. Richard Leppert, trans. Susan H. Gillespie (Berkeley and Los Angeles: University of California Press), p. 564; these are the opening lines of the essay.

[19]Ibid., p. 567.

[20]Adorno wryly emphasizes that music's character is at once enigmatical and "emphatically contingent. . . . Art as a whole is probably not amenable to this context of immanent explanations that asks everything that exists to show its passport" ("On the Contemporary Relationship of Philosophy and Music," in *Essays on Music*, p. 138); he later clarified the sentiment in *Aesthetic Theory*: "The enigmaticalness of artworks remains bound up with history. It was through history that they became an enigma; it is history that ever and again makes them such, and, conversely, it is history alone—which gave them their authority—that holds at a distance the embarrassing question of their raison d'être" (p. 120). Richard Wolin, "Utopia, Mimesis, and Reconciliation: A Redemptive Critique of Adorno's *Aesthetic Theory*," *Representations* 32 (1990), 39: "Art's mode of articulation relies on images, sounds, and colors rather than the clarity of discursive argument. Consequently as vehicles of truth works of art are inherently 'enigmatic' (*rätselhaft*). And it is precisely this enigmatic quality that beseeches, implores, and requires the *philosophical interpretation* of art" (original emphasis).

[21]Adorno, "On the Question: 'What is German?'" in *Critical Models: Interventions and Catchwords*, trans. Henry W. Pickford (New York: Columbia University Press, 1998), pp. 209–10. Adorno is, of course, playing off the title of Wagner's essay "What is German?" in *Richard Wagner's Prose Works*, trans. William Ashton Ellis (1895; rpt. New York: Broude Brothers, 1966), IV, 149–69.

[22]In *Composing for the Films*, Adorno and Eisler succinctly mark the fundamental distinction between Schubert and Beethoven. In the former, "the whole [of a composition] is derived from the details, conceived as musical germs, and developed blindly under the compulsion of their inherent drive." In the latter, the inverse of the former, "all the details are derived from the whole" (p. 94). Adorno fleshed out the point in *Beethoven: The Philosophy of Music*, p. 24: "Beethoven's achievement lies in the fact that in his work—and in his alone—the whole is never external to the particular but emerges solely from its movement, or, rather, is this movement. In Beethoven there is no mediation *between* themes, but, as in Hegel, the whole, as pure becoming, is itself the concrete mediation."

something profound: the self-reflexivity of a composer whose music all too well recognizes the condition of the modern subject, subjected and not least subject to his own damaged subjectivity; but music that at the same time remembers what was, or at least what might have been, namely, the utopian perfection of (lost) joy, or what Adorno once termed the "subjectively lyrical."[23] The real point for Adorno is that Schubert's music incorporates both what was and what might be. He doesn't "work it out."[24] What I think Adorno hears, and valorizes, in Schubert is something like an adult memory of childhood: a social, cultural, and reconciled imaginary of what might have been. But after Beethoven—after Beethoven's music and the history it engages—only a hapless semblance of reconciliation, at best, remains. Schubert provides it, but as "schöne Stellen."

Mahler, Schönberg, and Berg addressed the question of utopia under circumstances quite different from what Schubert could have experienced, amid the increasingly dystopian historical trajectory of modernity's self-immolation. The fact that they "took it further," especially in light of the alarming increased urgency of terrestrial *Götterdammerung*, led Adorno after 1928 to pay them a great deal more heed. Never once after age twenty-five, an age by which time childhood has been lost at the same time it remains sharply remembered,[25] did Adorno write about Schubert again, except in passing. But just as we characteristically grasp childhood memories as their distance from us increases, Adorno repeatedly invoked his early thoughts about Schubert and Schubert's music, although often via an admiration tinged with the shadow of critique regarding what Schubert's music "wasn't." To be sure, Adorno admired Schubert's refusal to kowtow to convention: the points at which he "uninhibitedly introduces a general pause and breaks off where good musicianship stipulates continuous developments"[26] (the general pause at m. 81 of the E♭ Trio's Andante is a perfect example). But he likewise saw the price to be paid, as when he lumped Schubert together with composers for whom he had little more than grudging admiration (Chopin, Debussy) or near contempt (Strauss):

> Again and again composers of the stature of Schubert, Chopin, Debussy and Richard Strauss were seduced into sacrificing integrity of structure to the need to conciliate. The repugnance aroused by these insinuating, ingratiating gestures, which have wormed their way into even the greatest works, forms part of the pathos of a qualitatively new music.[27]

IV

The Schubert of the operetta *Lilac Time* (1915, originally *Das Dreimäderlhaus*, music adapted by Heinrich Berté) emerges in a potpourri of biographical and musical prettiness. Yet Adorno does not on that account conclude either that such a fate is wholly undeserved or that the "real" Schubert has disappeared in what results. Quite the opposite. The kitschification of Schubert, as Adorno sees it, reveals a general truth about art: "Kitsch is not, as those believers in erudite culture would like to imagine, the mere refuse of art, originating in disloyal accommodation to the enemy; rather, it lurks in art, awaiting ever recurring opportunities to spring forth."[28] (One might say that kitsch is art's bad conscience.)

In "Music in the Background" (1934), an aphoristic essay addressing everyday, utterly ordinary, and clichéd live entertainment music of 1930s cafés and pubs, Adorno returned to the popular arrangements of (if I may) "once-classical" music, now rearranged, and played pot-

---

[23]Adorno, "Little Heresy," in *Essays on Music*, p. 319.

[24]Adorno, *Beethoven: The Philosophy of Music*, p. 39: "Even in Schubert, the commodity character of music is indicated by a shop-soiled, shabby, slipshod element, which emerges most clearly where the music seems most Beethovenian."

[25]The impact of Adorno's childhood happiness was significantly inflected by the centrality of music in his home, the memories of which remained fresh even as he approached thirty, in the traumatic year of 1933, concerning which he published an aphoristic essay, "Vierhändig, noch einmal"; the essay is available in a new English translation ("Four Hands, Once Again") by Jonathan Wipplinger, together with my commentary ("Four Hands, Three Hearts") in *Cultural Critique* 60 (2005).

[26]Adorno, "Vienna," in *Quasi una Fantasia: Essays on Modern Music*, trans. Rodney Livingstone (London: Verso, 1992), p. 212.

[27]Adorno, "Music and New Music," in *Quasi una Fantasia*, p. 261.

[28]Adorno, *Aesthetic Theory*, p. 239.

pourri- or medley-style. Its "gaudy" sound, Adorno says, "has something splendidly shabby about it. It is as bright as tinsel; but it tears in your hand. . . . The ruins of their [original] sound have been joined together in a second, strangely transparent form. . . . The truly noble melody will shine like a star against the background: one hears it as music."[29] Or, as he puts it in "Schubert," the old music—shopworn, stripped down, rearranged—gets "a new lease of life" [21]; adding that "potpourris seek to reclaim the lost unity of works of art on the off-chance, simply by putting bits of music together" [22]. The result is "crystalline" [23], at once fragmentary *and* truthful; the potpourri kitsch reveals that Schubert's landscape is one of death.

Of Schubert's landscape, Adorno says that "dried flowers are its mournful bloom" [24], an image he repeated in "Music in the Background," where "the café arranges bouquets of dead flowers." And here's the point:

> The cafés are the site of potpourris. The latter are constructed out of the fragments of the work, its best-loved melodies. But they awaken the ruins to new, ghostly life. If our art music lingers in the comforting realm of Orpheus—here its echo sounds from Euridice's mournful region. Its glow is netherworldly. It can remain unnoticed because it is unreal. But it is not a black shadow, rather a bright one, like milk glass. One can, as it were, hear vaguely through this music, through to the next room. This is why it shines.[30]

Schubertian kitsch, the reduction of his music to its most obvious few common denominators (pretty tunes, nifty modulations), thrusts into the foreground for Adorno what we (desperately) seek to find in his music, if only by making it into something it at once is and is not. Potpourri-Schubert promises comfort, compensation. But in so doing, potpourri-Schubert has the disconcerting knack of reminding its listener of the ontological reality, as well as the historical instantiations, of death. Potpourri-Schubert provides a shortcut to "a gateway to the underworld" [29]. Or, as Adorno polemically expressed it elsewhere, "the positive element of kitsch lies in the fact that it sets free for a moment the glimmering realization that you have wasted your life."[31]

[29]Adorno, "Music in the Background," *Essays on Music*, p. 508.
[30]Adorno, *Essays on Music*, p. 509.

[31]Adorno, "Commodity Music Analysed," in *Quasi una Fantasia*, p. 50.

Abstract.
Adorno's "Schubert" textually reenacts what he recognizes in Schubert's music, repeating himself but with subtle differences, as though he were holding up a cut gem to light and turning it to see the differences manifested in its facets. Adorno's ideas about this music are less developed than juxtaposed, often paratactically, so as to constitute what Benjamin termed a constellation. What Adorno hears in Schubert is a kind of reciprocity toward otherness. Schubert's "landscape," for Adorno, is grounded in the realm of the cultural imaginary; it represents for him a declaration of love, defined by the difference between subject and object that engenders embrace, rather than domination. The aesthetic truth of Schubert's music doesn't emerge through development, except, ironically perhaps, in the "successful" failure of his developments. Instead, it's articulated in a virtual instant, as in the shape and turn of a melody (and distinctly not in its working out).

The Schubert melody is like the imagined perfection of landscape—as though, like "nature," it were always already complete. The C-minor Andante of the Piano Trio in E♭ (op. 100, D. 929) is a case in point. The opening melodic statement in the cello and the folklike second theme in the violin, for the most part, can only be repeated, not improved upon, though Schubert tries—the melodic perfection of the opening statements, the first theme especially, becomes unambiguously evident only when the movement ends. We need everything that follows the initial statements to realize what we first heard: a melody (more than a theme) complete in itself, perfect, and on that account acoustically utopian—a semblance of happiness embedded in the sad honesty of C-minor's pensive melancholy.

CHAPTER 2

Opera, Aesthetic Violence, and the Imposition of Modernity: *Fitzcarraldo*

I consider opera a universe all its own. On stage an opera represents a complete world, a cosmos transformed into music.

Werner Herzog

The operatic world is, whatever else, a world of magic invocations.

Siegfried Kracauer

Werner Herzog's *Fitzcarraldo* (1982), set in the Peruvian Amazon sometime near the turn of the last century, tells the story of an Irishman of uncertain class standing, a passionate lover of opera who wants to build an opera house in the frontier town of Iquitos—a theater to rival the opera house in Manaus, the product of European rubber-baron largesse.[1] Fitzcarraldo intends for Caruso to inaugurate his theater. First, however, he's got to make some money. In the remote jungle, far from Iquitos, there lies a vast and heretofore inaccessible tract of land rich in rubber trees. One impediment stands in his way of reaching it: the wickedly impassable Pongo das Mortes rapids, deep in a gorge of the Ucayali River, an Amazon tributary. Fitzcarraldo hopes to overcome this challenge by first traveling upstream on the Pachitea River, another Amazon tributary that closely parallels the Ucayali; indeed, at one point the two rivers virtually meet, save for a steep hill separating them. Fitzcarraldo will pull his riverboat up this hill and down the other side, thereby reaching the Ucayali. By this means having bypassed the rapids, he will then steam downstream to his rubber-tree tract and its awaiting fortune. The engineering challenge of moving a 350-ton riverboat overland[2] is surpassed by the challenge of pacifying a dangerously hostile indigenous population. The raison d'être of the endeavor is opera, and the means to this end is opera as well, not only because it provides the inspiration for meeting the engineering challenge, but also, and more important, because it is the means by which the Indians are subdued.

There are four kinds of music employed in the film, two of which are used nondiegetically and two diegetically, with virtually no overlap between the pairs. The principal nondiegetic music is provided by a purpose-composed score by Florian Fricke and his ensemble, Popol Vuh, a team that is also responsible for the music in several of Herzog's other films, including *Aguirre, der Zorn Gottes* (1972) and *Nosferatu—Phantom der Nacht* (1979). Popol Vuh's music comes off as a kind of ambient wall of sound whose acoustic vastness is matched by the vagueness of its cultural sources. The rampantly hybrid (not to say pastiche) quality of the music, something like New Age meets Orff, has an air of the ritualistic tempered with an off-the-shelf mysteriousness that is at once worldly and not. The music affects timelessness, if only on account of the mix of sounds that cancel out historical and cultural specificity. Throughout the film Herzog uses Popol Vuh's music as a discursive accompaniment to nature, nearly always represented in dire opposition to culture.

The only other nondiegetic music in the film is heard only fleetingly. When the riverboat heads upriver for its fateful encounter with "nature"—setting out for, and later departing from, the last European settlement, a missionary outpost—brief excerpts from Richard Strauss's *Tod und Verklärung* play softly as background accompaniment.[3] The choice is apt, to the extent that Fitzcarraldo has now entered into the lived space of the Indians. As Fitzcarraldo proceeds, the threat of physical *Tod* (death) becomes increasingly real; but the actual *Tod* will be that of Fitzcarraldo's dream, which becomes the inadvertent vehicle for the *Verklärung* (transfiguration) of the Indians' dream, one entirely different from his. As the riverboat leaves the mission outpost, and hence approaches the last remnant of "civilization," Strauss's music is accompanied by a thunderstorm and lightening as the sky darkens and the sun sets. In short, the trope announced by the composition's title is both aurally and visually overdetermined.

Throughout the film, Fricke's nondiegetic score is often abruptly intercut with the diegetic music principally provided by Italian opera. These two sound masses, radically different from one another, establish an acoustic binary that in turn underscores the design of the film's nature/culture narrative. Herzog also uses small bits of indigenous and pseudo-indigenous music, but it's opera that matters most. Opera determines the narrative, defines the antiheroic hero, and, not least, provides a commentary to the story of which it is a determinant. Opera is staged, "live" ("live" in scare quotes), at the beginning and end of the film. At six other points opera is referenced, and almost exclusively so as part of the narrative action, via a windup, lotus-horn gramophone. (There is only one instance where the diegetic use of gramophone briefly morphs towards the nondiegetic, and only one instance, also brief, where operatic music is used nondiegetically.) For the purposes of this chapter, I will say nothing more about Popol Vuh's music, though there's a good deal to be said; I will comment on Herzog's use of nativelike music. Most of what I have to say will concern Herzog's use of opera in *Fitzcarraldo*, concerning which I'll restrict the discussion to the live-action staged scenes that open and close the film, and to just two of the six episodes where the gramophone is employed.

Herzog's story for *Fitzcarraldo* connects the Peruvian Amazon to an incomplete, timeless space seemingly caught in the ahistoric moment of its creation. The film's first visual is a static distance shot of the jungle, darkly green, functioning like a curtain that is about to be raised on the epic stage of the Amazon basin, where a romantic parable will be played out in quasi-documentary style. The first "event" is acoustic—audible but invisible: thunder, in sonic allusion to trouble and change. The electrical discharge has no visual referent; we can hear what we cannot see, a hint that the film is literally about acoustic realities. Visual stasis is succeeded by a slow pan of the jungle shrouded in fog; the curtain, as it were, becomes a scrim. We see enough to know that we're not seeing what is there to be seen. The camera moves from the pan to a slow zoom into the "face" of the jungle, only to confirm its visual impenetrability, an effect that overdetermines the sense of the invisibility that plagues seeing.[4] Herzog then cuts to the façade of the Manaus opera house, shot from below from the bottom of a long stairway. The opera house sits high like a gigantic altar, a site of art worship, whereupon the sacrifice of nature to culture will be celebrated.

The logical impossibility that lies at the heart of opera organizes the film's logic. Opera is the film's form and its content. Opera as both an institution and sonic manifestation defines the film's narrative structure, particularly its overtly exaggerated situations, as well as the character of its principal protagonist. Fitzcarraldo himself is operatically larger than life, and a man obsessed to hear life sung; every narrative element in the film revolves around this urgent need. As Fitzcarraldo puts it, "Opera gives expression to our greatest feelings."[5] Indeed, the function of spoken language in the film is wholly instrumental; its purpose is to lead to song.[6]

As the action begins, Fitzcarraldo, together with his lover Molly, is furiously paddling his small boat into Manaus, after traveling 1,200 miles on the river, including two days at the end with a broken-down motor. He reaches the opera house and begs his way in, just in time to see the performance conclude. It's *Ernani*. Caruso is performing the title role, and it's Caruso whom Fitzcarraldo came to hear, and for the first time in his life. It's obviously a special performance, all the more so because the role of Elvira is performed by none other than Sarah Bernhardt, who mimes her part.[7]

(The "soprano," whose voice Bernhardt lip syncs, is visible, in concert attire, well off to the side, though she too attracts some attention with her gesturing.)[8]

This scene was staged for Herzog by Werner Schroeter, who, besides being a filmmaker, already had experience with directing opera, unlike Herzog at the time. Schroeter created a surreal, multiply overdetermined dream world on a stage illuminated in luridly saturated colors, and peopled by actors who perform with intense emotion the ridiculous text Verdi has assigned them.

Ernani (1844) is early Verdi, his fifth opera, premiered five years after his first. Herzog's original plan had called for *Un ballo in maschera* (1859), a mature work, whose plot—itself fairly ridiculous—is nonetheless positively Shakespearean by comparison with the abundantly ludicrous goings-on of *Ernani*. For that matter, the plot of Bellini's *I Puritani*, used for the film's final scene, is equally absurd.[9] Indeed, epic-quality improbability constitutes the film's cultural logic, a point Herzog is keen to establish from the very start.[10] *Ernani*'s tragic story is a triumph of nearly cosmic absurdity, no less than its score is often stunningly beautiful, and a perfect vehicle for a great singer—here Caruso—but one whose acting abilities are limited to stock gestures signaling the intensity of his passions. The now-ancient nonsinging Bernhardt, who not incidentally lip-synchs atrociously (hinting that she barely knows her part), does everything within her powers of pantomime to draw attention to herself and away from Caruso.[11] She grandiosely performs the part of Elvira, a would-be bride, many decades after any amount of lighting and cosmetics could achieve her credibility. Bernhardt, in life rail-thin and just over five feet tall, here physically dominates the short Caruso. In sum, Schroeter represents her as a consummate ham, a character more fit for music hall than a star of the legitimate stage.[12]

The mute actor playing the aged Bernhardt is a cross-dressed male,[13] poorly disguised, and that's exactly the point. Bernhardt essentially proclaims her transvestism, as it were, as the open secret of the surface foundation of opera's dream world.[14] Opera, especially as staged here, drives home the point that what we see (real fakery) claims little authority over what we can hear (the centrality of song). Thus the performance of *Ernani* is live, but all of it is *obviously* in playback. Bernhardt's mouth doesn't come close to fitting the text she purportedly sings (this is part of the diegesis); but then neither does the mouth of Caruso or that of the "real soprano" performing Elvira's role offstage. (The ventriloquism of Caruso and the offstage soprano is nondiegetic, to be sure, yet plainly visible and hence discursive.) To complete the point, an actor plays Caruso playing Ernani; the actor's voice is neither Caruso's nor his own, but that of another singer whose performance he mimes.

We have our first look at the performance, in medias res, as the aged Bernhardt, portraying one half of a romantic couple, missing her cue, enters the scene too soon at the top of a very long and curved staircase; she checks herself, backs out of sight momentarily, and then reappears, but with arms outstretched as though she were confusing Elvira with Lucia and about to do a mad scene for the benefit of its heightened dramatic impact. Bernhardt's right leg was amputated in 1914, a biographical fact that Schroeter vigorously exploits. On the way down the stairs she moves haltingly, nearly stumbling, troubled by her prosthesis, but averting disaster, if barely. Her exaggerated clumsiness visually degrades to near slapstick the overwrought drama of the approach to her lover, where, shortly thereafter, she will enact her own death. Verdi gives Elvira a faint at the end of *Ernani*, but Bernhardt, not to be upstaged by Caruso's text-authorized death scene, seizes his exceedingly large dagger after he stabs himself and impales herself in his footsteps, in a free adaptation that better serves her purposes. As if that weren't sufficient, she tries to upstage him during the curtain calls—to Caruso's obvious irritation, as Schroeter is careful to represent.

Managing to gain admittance to *Ernani* just before the opera's conclusion, Fitzcarraldo witnesses the operatic hero's self-inflicted death, a matter of profoundly misplaced homosocial, hypermasculine honor. On his wedding day, with a masked ball in progress, and at the last possible moment, rival Silva sounds the hunting horn that signals to Ernani that he must kill himself to keep a promise, made in the second act for reasons too foolish to require detailing here. Suffice it to say that Silva blows the horn, and Ernani, true to his word, kills himself as his bride-to-be stands by helplessly (though not, of course, silently).[15]

When Ernani/Caruso dies, he reaches out his hand toward the audience, a stock gesture that Fitzcarraldo, with Molly's help, reads as being directed at him alone: he interprets it as the passing of Ernani's torch to the dream-beguiled Irishman. From that point forward Fitzcarraldo recognizes no worldly impediment to his goal of bringing Caruso to his own personal part of the jungle.

Fitzcarraldo is a man in the middle. He hates the established bourgeois colonizers, if only because he regards them as vulgar. They're interested in rubber for money; he wants rubber for opera—just as he wants opera for the "natives," and the children especially. To bring opera to the Indians, he will colonize them, as it were for their own good. He'll become a rubber baron for art's sake. Fitzcarraldo's quest, driven by opera, is no less absurd than the heroics of *Ernani*, and no less credible than the sonorous passion of the hapless lovers singing their hearts out. It's all mad, *and* it's all perfectly congruent with that which it defines and simultaneously aestheticizes: atavistic romanticism in deep denial of what its own denials of rapacious modernity in turn help to authorize, stabilize, and reproduce. The very Indians who will benefit from Caruso in the wilderness are the ones Fitzcarraldo sarcastically calls "bare asses," picking up the lingo of the colonial Europeans he otherwise despises. The Indians are the laborers who will build his aesthetic pyramid, one that is constructed on what, to all *appearances* at least, is a foundation of cultural kitsch.[16] That is, Schroeter's staging of *Ernani* fundamentally comes off as a good deal less than the high art Fitzcarraldo himself assigns it. In Schroeter's account, it's on a par with music hall—overwrought, and borderline camp—but at the same time utterly sincere in its multiple levels of exaggeration. The point, obviously enough, is that Schroeter and Herzog stage opera as a carnival-mirror reflection of modernity whose truth lies precisely in distortion.[17] Thus, the apparent *lack* of synchronous sound, produced by the consistently bad lipsynching by everyone purporting to sing, produces a yawning gap between image and soundtrack. The discursive indexicality that might emerge from the synchronicity of sound and vision is denied, and obviously so.

The role of technology, as a fundamental constituent of modernity, helps to organize the film's narrative; technology, as a component part of the narrative, accounts in part for the documentary look of *Fitzcarraldo*. Herzog lavishes visual and sonoric attention on equipment and how, by means of equipment, things get done, in particular, of course, the lifting of the boat over the hill, a conceit that becomes literally real, since Herzog eschewed special effects in making this happen. (Herzog has stated that the scene was intended to have the quality of farce, specifically *despite* its actuality. He has referred to the scene as "having the quality of Italian Opera.")[18] However crucial engineering know-how is to the success of Fitzcarraldo's endeavor, the technology of sound recording is, if anything, still greater. As the riverboat, christened *Molly Aida*, steams deeper into country seldom visited by Europeans, the signs of acute danger from hostile Indians increase, culminating in the sounds of mass chanting and drumming—though in fact it's African and not low-land Peruvian drumming that Herzog employs.[19] Fitzcarraldo refuses to answer with the boat's cannon, the usual acoustic certificate of authority and overwhelming power, to silence the unseen Indians' drums and voices, thereby overwhelming them. Instead, he sets up the gramophone on the roof of the pilothouse. Herzog briefly shoots the gramophone in a close-up, stationary and secure, set against the shifting green backdrop of the passing jungle. "Now," Fitzcarraldo says, "it's Caruso's turn"—and the turntable is put in motion. The voice insistently wafts onto the water, and, apparently, penetrates the jungle, spiritlike, reaching the ears of the Indians who, though they can be plainly heard, cannot be seen. The acoustic claim of the Indians is answered by "Il sogno" from Massenet's *Manon*,[20] the second-act aria in which des Grieux relates to Manon a dream he's had of happiness in the country. In the dream he is surrounded by beautiful nature, but his happiness is nonetheless incomplete because Manon herself is absent.

The aria fits the scene. Caruso, as Fitzcarraldo's alter ego, calls out to a Euro-feminized Nature, the woman of the forest and the Indians, which he is prepared to make his own.[21] As Michel Chion once put it, referring to speech, "The presence of a human voice structures the sonic space that contains it."[22] In this instance, the *singing* voice raises the stakes of Chion's insight not least by the illogic of both the look of the gramophone taking the place of the boat's warning whistle, and by the sounds that emanate from it—sounds whose volume Herzog significantly exaggerates. For a few moments, the two musics compete, while Fitzcarraldo stands next to his gramophone, shot from behind as he looks into the green curtain of the jungle. Gradually, however, the sounds of chanting and drumming cease.[23] The mood of Fitzcarraldo, standing next to the revolving turntable, shifts from anxiety to confidence; he puts his hands on his hips in a kind of self-satisfied gloat, while Caruso reaches his melodic, and authoritative, climax. Thus the gramophone, built for and suited to the domestic parlor, merges into the public realm of Eden, with a voice that "speaks" with the authority of the Word made musical. The claim of music—of the Western variety—as the universal "language" plays out here, if only in Fitzcarraldo's lunatic dream, as acoustic conquistador.

Melody and harmony conquer rhythm. Culture, serviced by technology, trumps nature—or so Fitzcarraldo thinks. Caruso silences the Indians, and then pulls them into visibility, out of the jungle and onto the river in their dugouts, in a kind of watery Pied Piper story. (In this regard Fitzcarraldo's gramophone shares a functional relation with the stereo system onboard Kilgore's attack helicopter in *Apocalypse Now*, except that Caruso attracts, whereas the acoustic blasts of *Die Walküre* repel and terrify.) The impact of Caruso is driven by technology, and, indeed, it is impossible in technology's absence. In the modern era, the voice is invariably mediated; it is never "natural"—not even when "live" in the opera house, as I have already suggested. In *Fitzcarraldo*, the social agency of opera is dialectically twinned with the social agency of the machine.

Throughout the narrative, Fitzcarraldo evokes only Caruso's name, despite the fact that the music he plays on his gramophone is for the most part Caruso in ensemble, as is the case in the staged opera scenes that begin and end the film. The other ensemble voice parts are prominently those of women. They don't seem to matter much to Fitzcarraldo; he never once refers to them, though he does of course name his boat after an ancient operatic princess, as well as Molly, a brothel keeper. When all is said and done, he hears only Caruso. Indeed, the women's vocal presence marks the absence of women in the film generally (Molly's rather small supporting role notwithstanding), except to the extent that embodied women serve as iterations of the feminine-nature trope—that is, as the foil that Fitzcarraldo both figuratively and literally penetrates.[24] In short, the feminine is displaced as nature, but as well the feminine is imagined *in* music and *as* music. It is the feminine "voice" of music on which Fitzcarraldo focuses his most urgent desires (the desires he has for Molly, on the other hand, are barely bothered with). The real point is that music, which long played the role of the eternal feminine in European consciousness, makes itself heard through the gender-colonized agency of a man's voice. The singing women are there to fill in the harmonies, or, perhaps better stated, to make things harmonious.

Caruso's voice competes with the background noise common to shellac discs, the effect of which is to remind us of the modern technology upon which latter-day art worship rests, a worship that for Fitzcarraldo otherwise functions as a profound critique of that very modernity for which Caruso acts as antidote. In particular, the singer's muffled voice, the tinny-sounding wind orchestra accompanying him, and the disc noise, not to mention the riverboat's engine (alternately subdued or heightened, as demanded by the context), together emphasize the technological authority brought to bear against mere nature, including the "natural" folk of the jungle. For Fitzcarraldo, that is, Caruso on shellac is His Master's Voice to the Irishman's Nipper; and what's good enough for Nipper will do fine for anyone else within earshot.[25] Whatever Fitzcarraldo introjects will in turn be shared by an uncompromising projection/transference, as it were, on waves of music.

This is to suggest that the cultural hegemony claimed by Caruso on the gramophone in the "wilderness" is overdetermined (if, in the end, oversubscribed by Fitzcarraldo himself). The Indians hear a voice from somewhere, but it is from nowhere they can recognize; the singing voice makes strange claims as it bares its soul in order to colonize theirs. Caruso's singing foretells, with the authority of an untranslated secular scripture, the Indians' future, and whether or not they recognize it matters only insofar as it concerns Fitzcarraldo's immediate instrumental need for their giving him safe passage and, subsequently, their labor.

After the *Molly Aida* is safely back in the water on the other side of the hill, and following a long night's drunken celebration by crew and Indians alike, the Indians cut the mooring lines: the Indians have their own dream, namely, the sacrifice of the riverboat to the gods of the rapids. The boat tumbles helplessly toward disaster, careening through the rock-strewn gorge, while the hungover Fitzcarraldo and the few of his diminished crew on board are thrown about sufficiently to awaken from their stupor—but much too late to do anything but hang on for dear life. In the midst of all this, so we're given to believe, the boat's movement sets the gramophone into motion and it gives us Caruso in the sextet from *Lucia,*[26] with its various commentaries on love and its myriad complications, disillusionments, betrayals, and failures, made gloriously ironic by the interweaving of voices that produce a rampant degree of melodiousness underwritten by the harmonic envelope in which the tunes are wrapped. Even if one knows the language, it's impossible to follow the words, and here in the jungle no one knows Italian, nor likely even the opera's plot, which narrates not only disaster, but also the end of dreams. The unexpected entrance of Edgardo, triggering the sextet, mirrors the cutting of the mooring lines. Nothing will be the same thereafter. A mad scene, and deaths, will follow. Musically, however, the *Lucia* sextet *celebrates* disaster in its immensely pleasurable sonorities. Better said, the sextet "speaks" in its own way of hopeless hope—not through its dystopian text, but in its music, all those splendid thirds, sixths, unisons, and octaves.

As the boat careens through the rapids (figure 6.1), Caruso and his confederates serenade, and the needle never skips. The logically impossible diegetic incongruity—the diegesis confirmed at least at the start by means of a quick close-up of the spinning turntable—sets two sounds in dire conjunction: an operatic ensemble and a riverboat crashing into rocks in a raging rapids, the boat, like the shellac discs, turning in circles, a favorite visual effect found in other Herzog films. Our eyes inform us of disaster and the violent triumph of nature; the soundtrack, however, describes the triumph of culture by means of the harmonies of intertwined voices, never mind the crisis that brought these voices together in song. As if to make the matter clear, Herzog gradually eliminates all sound except that of the sextet. The now-silenced diegesis, visually dramatic, demands acoustics, but hardly opera, except of course in the illusory reality of a film about dreams.[27] The beauty of Donizetti's acoustic wave, undisturbed by the chaos and turbulence surrounding it, is in fact matched by the sublime visual beauty of the

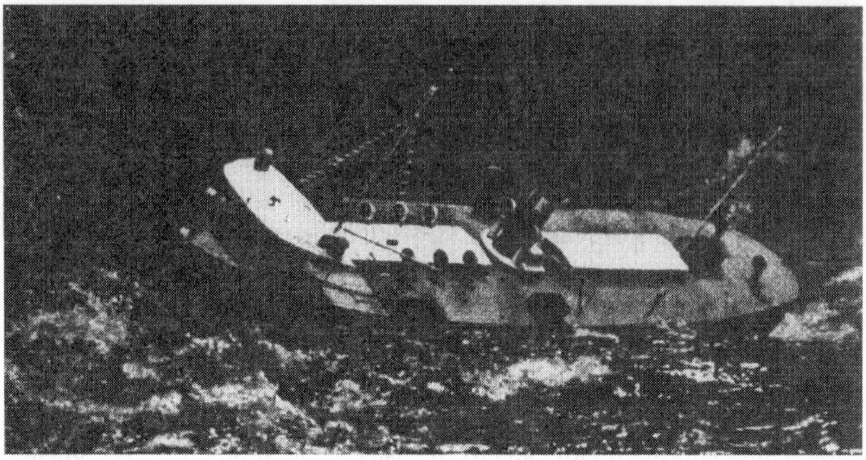

Figure 6.1 *Lucia* in the rapids, in *Fitzcarraldo.*

riverboat rebounding helplessly from one side to the other of the roaring river. The violence of the putatively "real" event, by being completely silenced, reverts to the indexical aesthetics of romanticized nature, the raw energy Goethe fixed on in *Werther,* an unfeeling nature that his psychotic-neurotic and narcissistic young hero at once abhorred and found himself mesmerized by: nature meant nothing, and nature meant more than he could imagine.[28]

Caruso's arias give Fitzcarraldo's ears what his eyes deny him. If the gaze, filmic and otherwise, is intended to penetrate, throughout the film Fitzcarraldo's eyes hit a wall of impenetrable green that acts on him in a way analogous to a blue screen, in front of which he acts out his dream, with the keen assistance of a crucial prop that helps suture him into a narrative that he's trying desperately to write. The narrative is informed by psychic introjection via acoustic displacement. Metaphorically, if hardly literally, the ethereality of music, its ethereality underscored by the reproductive apparatus from which it emanates, drowns out the visually noisy but acoustically "silenced" enemy: nature and the "bare-ass" culture Fitzcarraldo includes under the term. All this notwithstanding, Fitzcarraldo acknowledges nature's agency, but as an amorphous fiend. Caruso, ever at his beck and call, provides him—and not just us—what Adorno and Eisler claimed generally for film music, namely, that it corresponded to the "whistling or singing child in the dark."[29] In short, that is to say, the film's music addresses fear, and is its antidote. Put differently, the sublime visuality of the riverboat in the rapids demands the acoustic hermeneutics of opera for sense to be made of it.

Fitzcarraldo names his boat after two women, Molly and Aida. Aida marks what matters about opera to Herzog. The singing voice makes sensible the utopian desire of perfect expressibility. Opera, as it were, finds the way to name the Name, the imaginary Absolute, the hoped-for Spirit. Aida voluntarily entombs herself so that she can sing to the end (or maybe forever) with her lover. If opera is "about" singing—singing understood to "say" what speaking desperately seeks to convey but can't—then being entombed and ending life in a love duet is not the worst way to go. Indeed, it's possibly the ultimate form of peace (and "*Pace*" is the word that Amneris intones repeatedly in her blessing from outside the sealed chamber). What I'm suggesting is that *Aida* is about its ending, its *sense* of an ending. To die in love is good; to die in love and in song is to accomplish in death that for which life is lived, namely, once and for all time to be able to express love absolutely, exceeding the hopeless inadequacy of mere language.

Aida plays out its final scene in the metaphorical total darkness of a smothering tomb. The eyes can no longer see. Only sound conveys what must be said and before it's too late; those words must be sung—and, to be sure, sung in harmony, a sonoric oneness for all time. *Aida* ends in a dream world; its last scene, in effect if not in staged practice, is a long blackout. All we have is music conveying utterly selfless love. It's there to be heard; seeing it is utterly irrelevant. And just as *Aida* ends, so also does *Fitzcarraldo.* Herzog closes his film with a sustained blackout. The visual sense is denied, while the auditory sense is offered the privilege of a cadence. And this brings me to my own conclusion, via the film's final scene.

Earlier in the film, in a scene involving a conversation with missionaries living in the remote bush and ministering to the Indians, Fitzcarraldo hears a priest's complaint that "We can't seem to cure [the Indians] of the idea that everyday life is only an illusion behind which lies the reality of dreams." Fitzcarraldo replies, simply, "Actually, I'm very interested in these ideas. I specialize in opera myself."

Fitzcarraldo's scheme for a rubber plantation whose proceeds would fund an opera house in Iquitos fails, but in failing he manages a momentary triumph by realizing a substitute dream in the form of live opera on water. He sells the damaged *Molly Aida* and invests the proceeds to hire a small itinerant opera troupe. The absurdity of the mise-en-scène is extreme. Ten small boats pull alongside the riverboat loaded down, variously, with singers in costume, orchestra musicians with instruments in hand and wearing full formal attire—never mind the midday heat and choking humidity—and paltry scenery rather badly representing a castle atop a cliff and a cutaway of battlements. The musicians disembark on shore, welcomed by Fitzcarraldo, and shortly thereafter take their places aboard the riverboat turned opera theater. During this disembarkation, the French horn players acknowledge Fitzcarraldo, however incongruously (and ironically), by playing the horn motif from the opening movement of Beethoven's "Emperor"[30] Concerto (first heard at measures 48–52). Fitzcarraldo, so it seems, is king for a day, as sonically confirmed by the king of all music that really matters (figure 6.2).

Shortly thereafter, the boat approaches Iquitos for the last time, making a grand entrance, in mid-performance, with a staged scene from *I Puritani* (1835) in progress on its top deck and pilothouse roof.[31] The scene is part of act 1, scene 3, beginning with Arturo's aria "A te, o cara, amor talora," and involves the love duet between Arturo and Elvira, with the chorus performed by mestizo musicians.[32] The Puritan costumes worn by brown-skinned people is perhaps visually jarring to our eyes, but no such discomfort is evident among the singers or orchestra. Like opera itself, the hybridization is for them naturalized, indeed comfortable. And all of them seem uncannily happy, even celebratory. Herzog edits the scene to show, alternately, distance and close-up shots of Fitzcarraldo, who, despite the economic ruin facing him, is in a splendid mood. Proud as punch, and smoking what he describes as "the biggest cigar in the world," he takes it all in, and invites us to do the same by means of a grandly sweeping gesture that would fit nicely on any opera stage.

The operatic lovers express their delight and passion with the usual stock moves (figure 6.3). But their happiness is ventriloquized: they lip-synch badly to the playback. The fakery is as obvious as the castle scenery is low budget. Nothing is what it seems, apart from the sublime happiness apparent everywhere, including on the faces of the large crowd on shore hearing opera for the first time. The *Puritani* lovers recall old torments, now convinced—mistakenly—that joy is at hand (after subsequent trials and tribulations the opera eventually has a happy ending). And then the screen goes black. The music continues for a few seconds, after which the volume is cut quickly to silence at a cadence. We're at a full stop, but not at closure. We have the sense, however momentary, of an ending—indeed, an insistence on it, since the film is literally over at this point, for which reason Herzog placed the credits at the beginning. The reality of the dream meets the alternate reality of the film's end: the house lights return us to the here and now. The dream is kept going only so long as music, which exceeds reality, plays against the perverted rationalities embedded in the film's visual narrative. Herzog sets music in striking dialectical tension with the indexical character of the film image itself, which Herzog constantly inflects with

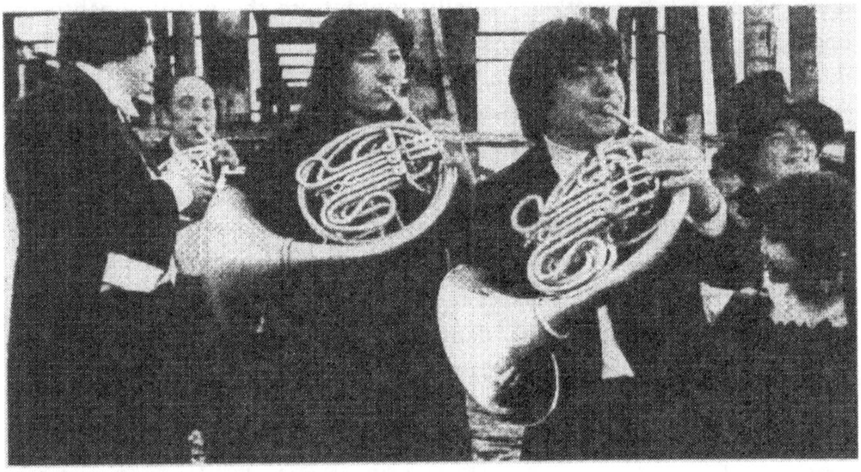

Figure 6.2 Saluting the "emperor" of opera (*Fitzcarraldo*).

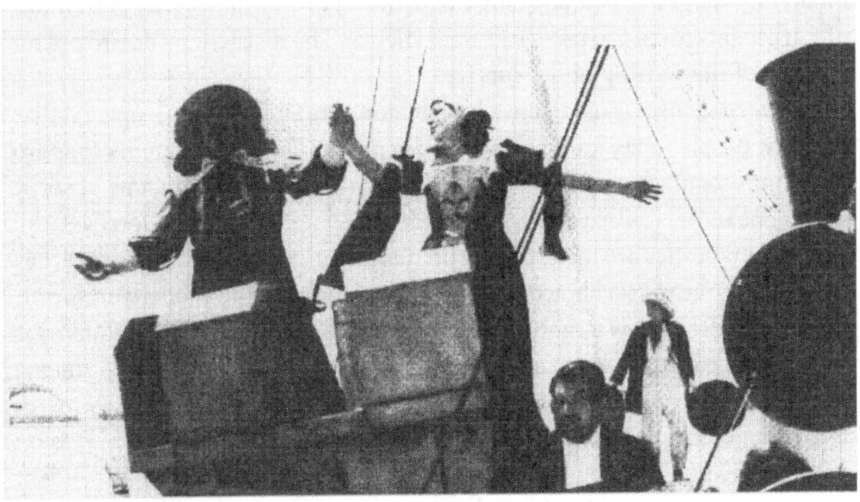

Figure 6.3 The *I Puritani* love duet aboard the *Molly Aida* (*Fitzcarraldo*).

both the resonance and actuality of the documentary. Yet what is documented is at once both more and less than the "reality" available to the eyes. For that matter, the aria and ensemble texts themselves relate *only* fictions. The truth, so to speak, is there nonetheless, but in the sonorous notes, in the evanescent reality of music.

The utopian charge of opera in *Fitzcarraldo* is anchored in the insistence to hear life sung—and notwithstanding the myriad instrumentalities of opera's own material-institutional foundations. This much is acknowledged in repeated shots throughout the film of the gramophone and the shellac discs, which, taken together, visually concentrate the institutionality of opera into the commodity forms associated with mechanical sound reproduction.[33] In *Fitzcarraldo* music gives life to sight; life musically determined, however, includes nothing of the mundane: recitative is barred. What matters is life heightened in aria form, the acoustic sublime. The reality of Fitzcarraldo's dream life is defined by assorted operatic fragments torn from their narrative context. What he chooses to hear, in other words, is a phonograph album of sonic snapshots. His utopian acoustic is constituted from fragile bits of treasured musical detritus inscribed on brittle shellac, which with every playing is damaged by the heavy tone arm tipped by a steel needle. Every hearing takes away from what he desires most, bringing closer to the foreground what Adorno once named the "hear-stripe" (in reference to radio broadcast interference), and the increasing static of the worn and damaged disc, technology's calling card, the noisy sign of the modernity that Fitzcarraldo at once depends upon and abhors. Each audition of Caruso promises Caruso's ultimate silence. The disc will be destroyed by the love of the writing on its surface.

Fitzcarraldo uses music from a long bygone era and of a sort—opera—that very few people today know or care much about. The musical quotations are likely unrecognizable to most viewers; figuring them out is a game of sorts, since none of the Caruso recordings is identified in the credits. Moreover, the staged opera scenes are made to play off distinctly exaggerated popular clichés about opera, the most characteristically overwrought of all modern art forms. Opera, in short, is now largely strange and estranged. For Herzog, I think, this strangeness constitutes its saving grace in late modernity, for which cinema commonly serves as an aesthetic proponent. In one sense, in other words, in *Fitzcarraldo* Herzog has made a film that functions in acute dialectical tension with the medium through which he speaks. In a film so visually dependent upon turning, and turning in circles, the "visual turn" of modern culture is called into question by the aural, not as supplement of the image, but as the foundation for the insight by which to critique it.

For Herzog, opera foregrounds the ever-widening gap between the mundane, perversely hyper-rationalized, and duly fetishized love affair with facts as the sole legitimate index of the real, on the one hand, and the reality of the unreal, on the other. Whatever Herzog's complicated relation to nature and to the Others without whom his film would have been impossible, he clearly valorizes the principle of otherness, just as he recognizes the refusal embedded in what Attali, paraphrasing Adorno, called "residual irrationality," which for both men was a form of principled alternative to "*Mitmachen*,"[34] to going with the flow. The old operas, as employed in this film, in spite of everything about them that is otherwise objectionable, still have a truth to tell about the social struggle embedded in the changing hierarchy of human sensing. But to get at this truth we have to look and to hear backwards, so to speak. The film begins with an ending (*Ernani* and death), and it ends with a mirthful beginning (the act 1 scene from *I Puritani*) that, against the odds, celebrates another ending (the collapse of Fitzcarraldo's dream). Herzog thus sets the linearity of narrative historicism akimbo; the usual truths, here of narrative closure and pictorial indexicality, fail in the confusion.

Herzog's point, in a way, is to mark the fallibility of seeing in order to make audible the truths of hearing: hearing music. The advantage of opera is that it accomplishes both tasks at once.[35] All of its fallibilities and, indeed, its absurdities do not overwhelm the truths of the singing voice, the simple fact that people literally *need* to sing. One might say, I suppose, that it's precisely in opera's lie through which its truth is revealed: that truth is at once acoustic, sublime, and in part utopian. Herzog's film, in tension with its own visually determined documentary excess, points to this alternative—and it's there for the hearing.

NOTES

I wish to express my gratitude to Hisham Bizri for his careful reading and thoughtful criticism of an earlier draft of this essay.

1. Manaus is in western Brazil. The first performance in the lavishly decorated Teatro Amazonas took place on New Year's Eve, 1896. The rubber boom lasted from 1880 to 1914. See Lester Caltvedt, "Herzog's *Fitzcarraldo* and the Rubber Era," *Film & History* 18.4 (December 1988), pp. 74–84. According to Richard Collier, *The River That God Forgot: The Story of the Amazon River Rubber Boom* (New York: Dutton, 1968), p. 56, Caruso was in fact invited to sing at the Manaus opera house but never did so; the closest he got was Rio de Janeiro for performances in 1903 and again in 1914. The historical character on whom Herzog loosely based his film was Carlos Fermin Fitzcarrald (1862–97), a rubber baron and merchant. Like Herzog's character, Fitzcarrald brought a boat over a hill—a much higher one than Herzog's—but only by first disassembling it. For the basic biographical details, see Ronald H. Dolkart, "Civilization's Aria: Film as Lore and Opera as Metaphor in Werner Herzog's *Fitzcarraldo*," *Journal of Latin American Lore* 11.2 (1985), p. 129.

2. *Fitzcarraldo* is not the first film to document such a feat. The French documentary *La Croisière jaune* (1934), directed by André Sauvage, a promotional record of an expedition sponsored by Citroën intended to advertise the advanced technology of their automobiles, includes scenes involving the feat of taking the cars across the Himalayas. The vehicles were disassembled and their parts toted by Sher-

pas through the mountain passes. The use of native labor to facilitate the penetration of Western technology into other worlds, a hoary trope, to be sure, is used in both films. See Charles Musser, "Engaging with Reality: Documentary," in *The Oxford History of World Cinema*, ed. Geoffrey Nowell-Smith (Oxford: Oxford University Press, 1996), p. 322. Thanks to Hisham Bizri for telling me about this film.

3. A very brief quotation from another piece of classical instrumental music occurs, this time diegetically, near the film's end; see below.

4. Herzog, in his original story for *Fitzcarraldo*, described his opening shot as follows in his *Fitzcarraldo: The Original Story*, trans. Martje Herzog and Alan Greenberg (San Francisco: Fjord Press, 1982), p. 23:

> As immense as an ocean extending to the edge of the universe, the jungle stretches out, steaming, as on the morning of Creation, still indistinct, full of animal noise. A music swells up, magnificent, breathtaking, and measured, as a hundred million birds awaken far below our feet. The earth lies in wait, calmly and patiently, but the sky begins to quiver as if this were some painful quaking of the heavens, something like the birth throes of heaven.

5. Oscar Hammerstein I held similar views. The following is quoted from an interview in Vincent Sheean, *Oscar Hammerstein I: The Life and Exploits of an Impressario* (New York: Simon and Schuster, 1956), pp. 252–53, as cited by Dolkart, "Civilization's Aria," p. 131:

> Grand opera is, I truly believe, the most elevating influence upon modern society, after religion. . . . I sincerely believe that nothing will make better citizenship than familiarity with grand opera. *It lifts one so out of the sordid affairs of life and makes material things seem so petty, so inconsequential, it places one for the time being, at least, in a higher and better world. . . .* [Opera] will establish a brotherhood of art which knows not race or creed and makes all the civilized world akin; that will erect a shrine of beauty in form, color, and tone, before which all may bend the knee. [emphasis added]

To be sure, Hammerstein seems oblivious of the material reality that makes grand opera possible, and which in turn preserves it as elite entertainment.

6. Opera has long been linked to film, beginning in the silent era. See Joengwon Joe and Rose Theresa, eds., *Between Opera and Cinema* (New York: Routledge, 2002); Jeremy Tambling, *Opera, Ideology and Film* (New York: St. Martin's Press, 1987); and Marcia J. Citron, *Opera on Screen* (New Haven, CT: Yale University Press, 2000).

7. Sarah Bernhardt (1844–1923) was the most famous actress of her age; her career spanned six decades. She toured widely in Europe and the United States, and in 1886 she made one trip to South America, including a visit to Lima, her closest approach to the film's setting. In 1877, Bernhardt had performed in Victor Hugo's *Hernani,* the source for Verdi's opera. Cross-dressed, she played the title role in *Hamlet* in 1899, and she toured across Europe in this role for two years. Interested in modern technology, she recorded her voice and, late in her career, she made eight films, of which five were hits. She also made a number of home movies between 1913 and 1915. Bernhardt starred in several films whose subjects had been used for opera, including *La Tosca* (1908; reprising a stage role she first performed in 1887); *La Dame aux camélias* (1911), the source for *La traviata;* and *Adrienne Lecouvreur*

(1913). At the time of her death at age seventy-eight, she was at work on the film *La Voyante* (The Fortune), completed with a stand-in. Bernhardt, after seeing the final cut of her greatest film hit, the seven-reel *La Reine Elizabeth* (1912), is reputed to have exclaimed, "I am immortal! I am film!" On Bernhardt's film career, see Ruth Brandon, *Being Divine: A Biography of Sarah Bernhardt* (London: Secker & Warburg, 1991), pp. 433–35. In real life, Caruso and Bernhardt only once performed at the same event, though not together, at a war benefit at the Metropolitan Opera House on 17 April 1917, together with Frances Alda. See Francis Robinson, *Caruso: His Life in Pictures* (New York: Studio Publications in association with Thomas Y. Crowell, 1957), pp. 90–91, which reproduces the program.

8. The film's consistent dependence on the displaced singing voice is mirrored in the fact that *Fitzcarraldo* was actually filmed with dialogue spoken in English; the German "original" is dubbed.)

9. Herzog, *Fitzcarraldo: The Original Story*, pp. 11–14, 17–18. Numerous differences exist between Herzog's original story and the finished film.

10. Paul Cronin, ed., *Herzog on Herzog* (London: Faber and Faber, 2002), p. 188. Indeed, for Herzog, it is precisely the plausible within the implausibility of opera that attracts him. "It matters little that most of the libretti are bad or . . . [even] a true catastrophe. In fact, so many of the opera plots are not even within the calculus of probability; it would be like winning the lottery jackpot five consecutive times over. And yet, when the music is playing, the stories do make sense. Their strong inner truths shine through and they seem utterly plausible" (p. 259). Since making *Fitzcarraldo*, Herzog has directed a number of opera productions throughout Europe, as well as in Japan and the United States. For a list, current to 2002, see Beat Presser, ed. and photographer, *Werner Herzog* (Berlin: Jovis Verlag and Arte Edition, 2002), p. 119.

11. The situation is similar to an operatic drag-act performed by Larry, Moe, and Curly in The Three Stooges' short *Micro-Phonies* (1945). The music they attempt to lip-synch is the sextet from *Lucia* or, as they would have it, the sextet from *Lucy*.

12. Theodor W. Adorno, "On the Contemporary Relationship of Philosophy and Music," in *Essays on Music*, ed. Richard Leppert, trans. Susan H. Gillespie (Berkeley and Los Angeles: University of California Press, 2002), p. 136, comments on the Marx Brothers film *A Night at the Opera* (1935), which involves a performance of *Il trovatore*, the scenery for which the boys manage to destroy. Adorno notes the singers' "clumsily grandiloquent, old- fashioned gestures," which contribute to exposing the ridiculousness of opera as an icon of elite art, replete with its affectations and its insistence on the "dignity of music." Even so, Adorno suggests, the comedy reveals a utopian truth about music: "Music that has merely to begin in order to define itself as an exception to normalized life, as a more elevated extreme, places itself, by dint of its always already potential perceptible and nowadays complete integration into the average normalcy of a false life, in contradiction to the claim that its mere sounding inevitably makes." Adorno, in an earlier essay alluding to this same film, compliments his later insight with the following: "Music has become comic in the present phase primarily because something so completely useless is carried on with all the visible signs of the strain of serious work. By being alien to solid

[*tüchtig*] people, music reveals their alienation from one another, and the consciousness of alienation vents itself in laughter." Theodor W. Adorno, "On the Fetish-Character in Music and the Regression of Listening," in *Essays on Music*, p. 314. The "work" of Fitzcarraldo to make opera, involving pulling a riverboat over a small mountain, is—obviously enough—absurdly comic, all the more given the extraordinary seriousness, utterly nonironic, with which he engages in his harebrained scheme. The act is also operatic, a fact not lost on Herzog: "I pulled the ship [sic] over the mountain not for the sake of realism. . . . What you actually see is a very stylized thing. It looks like an operatic event, like a dream-event, and that's what's so strange about it. It's not really a paradox." Quoted by Guido Henkel, "Werner Herzog the Real Fitzcarraldo," *DVD Review* (1 November 1999), online review at http://www.dvdreview.com/html_dvd_Werner_Herzog.shtml.

13. The French actor Jean-Claude Dreyfuss plays the part of Bernhardt, whom he had previously impersonated. (Herzog's commentary accompanying the DVD release of *Fitzcarraldo* refers to the actor as a transvestite.) See further Dolkart, "Civilization's Aria," p. 132; and Presser, ed. *Werner Herzog*, p. 38. For more on Herzog's opera directing, see Cronin, ed., *Herzog on Herzog*, pp. 253–54, 258–60.

14. There are historical antecedents to the cross-dressing, as in an 1865 production of an English burlesque of *Ernani* by William Brough, *Ernani, or, the Horn of a Dilemma*, in which the two male characters, including Ernani himself, were played by women. See Roberta Montemorra Marvin, "Verdian Opera Burlesqued: A Glimpse into Mid-Victorian Theatrical Culture," *Cambridge Opera Journal* 15.1 (March 2003), p. 47. Marvin points out that *Ernani* was the Verdi opera most subjected to burlesquing, though *Il trovatore* and *La traviata* were also popularly mocked. On the extraordinary popularity of *Ernani* in the United States for several decades beginning in 1847, only three years after the opera's premiere, see George Martin, "Verdi Onstage in the United States: *Ernani*," *Opera Quarterly* 20.2 (Spring 2004): 171–96. In short, there is good historical reason for Herzog's choice of this opera. Not the least sign of *Ernani*'s popularity at the time of *Fitzcarraldo*'s setting is evident in the fact that the Victor Talking Machine Company by 1912 had released no fewer than forty-five recordings of its arias and choruses (p. 183).

15. See also the discussion of this scene in Roger Hillman, *Unsettling Scores: German Film, Music, and Ideology* (Bloomington: Indiana University Press, 2005), pp. 141–44.

16. Dolkart, "Civilization's Aria," p. 125: "The most significant and enduring lore embraced by elites in Latin America is the division between civilization and barbarism. The separation into two Latin Americas, one civilized, that is positive and progressive, another barbaric, that is negative and regressive, has shaped the foreigner's views, as well as the self-image of the region, as has no other concept." Dolkart explains that opera in particular constituted a sign of civilization among nineteenth-century Latin American elites, concerning which see by the same author, "Elitelore at the Opera: The Teatro Colón of Buenos Aires," *Journal of Latin American Lore* 9.2 (1983), pp. 231–50.

17. Werner Herzog, "The Minnesota Declaration: Truth and Fact in Documentary Cinema," in Cronin, ed., *Herzog on Herzog*, p. 301: "There are deeper strata of

truth in cinema, and there is such a thing as poetic, ecstatic truth. It is mysterious and elusive, and can be reached only through fabrication and imagination and stylization."

18. Herzog, in his commentary to the DVD release of *Fitzcarraldo.*

19. Herzog, in his commentary accompanying the DVD release of *Fitzcarraldo,* indicates that the music is "authentic," but it was recorded in Burundi. Acknowledging that African drumming is "totally different" from the kind of drumming employed by the Indians native to the rain forest, he says he chose it because of what he terms the "certain danger" and "certain menace" he associates with its sound.

20. Caruso recorded the aria in 1904. See J. Freestone and H. J. Drummond, *Enrico Caruso: His Recorded Legacy* (London: Sidgwick and Jackson, 1960), p. 27.

21. Theodor W. Adorno, "The Curves of the Needle," in *Essays on Music,* p. 274: "What the gramophone listener actually wants to hear is himself, and the artist merely offers him a substitute for the sounding image of his own person, which he would like to safeguard as a possession. The only reason that he accords the record such value is because he himself could also be just as well preserved. Most of the time records are virtual photographs of their owners, flattering photographs—ideologies."

22. Michel Chion, *The Voice in Cinema,* ed. and trans. Claudia Gorbman (New York: Columbia University Press, 1999), p. 5. Chion adopts his insight from a remark by Christine Sacco ("The presence of a body structures the space that contains it").

23. Martin Scherzinger, in a private communication:

> One reason the Burundi segment synchronizes so easily—too easily—with the photograph's song fragment is because both are hyperbolic indexes of contrasting culture: "Western" music as individualized expressive song, primarily harmonic-melodic in construction (mechanically produced even); non-Western music as functional, primarily rhythmic, collectivist (apparently not mechanically produced, but of course the latter music stops like a recording stops, not like a group of performers stops—an indication that mischief of another sort is afoot). This extreme, almost mannerist, presentation of dualized musical worlds must work well musically because the one fills the obvious inadequacy of the other. This is why the phonograph sounds so isolated when the drumming is switched off.

24. The penetration of the jungle by the riverboat, traveling where no white man has ventured previously, anticipates the resolutely male enterprise of creating the deep gash in the jungle, a literal deflowering, clearing the way for the boat to, as it were, mount the mountain. The scene resonates with the iconography of Watteau's *Embarkation from the Isle of Cythera,* in which a boatload of would-be lovers has penetrated a landmass whose form is analogous to the shape of two legs. At the shoreline stands a small hill, replete with a Venus figure atop the mound. Lutz P. Koepnick, "Colonial Forestry: Sylvan Politics in Werner Herzog's *Aguirre* and *Fitzcarraldo,*" *New German Critique* 60 (Fall 1993), especially pp. 133–59, referring to Herzog's "green essentialism" (p. 157), argues that, in the name of filmic authenticity, he clear-cuts forest and levels hills for the land journey of the riverboat. Lutz regards Herzog as "a master in the jargon of authenticity" (p. 158), summing up, "Herzog, in other words, uses the diegetic text of *Fitzcarraldo* to exercise his own

colonial practice, an exercise that cannot but forfeit its alleged aspiration to obliterate the grounds and politics of what I call here colonial forestry" (p. 158). See also John E. Davidson, "Contacting the Other: Traces of Migrational Colonialism and the Imperial Agent in Werner Herzog's Fitzcarraldo," *Film & History* 24, 3–4 (1994), pp. 66–83; and by the same author, "As Others Put Plays upon the Stage: *Aguirre*, Neocolonialism, and the New German Cinema," *New German Critique* 60 (Fall 1993), pp. 101–30. See also Les Blank and James Bogan, eds., *Burden of Dreams: Screenplay, Journals, Reviews, Photographs* (Berkeley: North Atlantic Books, 1984). For Herzog's response, see Cronin, ed., *Herzog on Herzog*, pp. 169–70, 177–84, 188–89.

25. The trademark based on the painting *His Master's Voice* was established in 1902. See Friedrich A. Kittler, *Gramophone, Film, Typewriter*, trans. Geoffrey Winthrop-Young and Michael Wutz (Stanford, CA: Stanford University Press, 1999), p. 69; and Barbara Engh, "After His Master's Voice," *New Formations* 38 (Summer 1999), pp. 54–63. For an illustrated account of the logo, see Leonard Petts, *The Story of "Nipper" and the "His Master's Voice" Picture Painted by Francis Barraud* (Bournemouth, UK: The Talking Machine Review International, 1973/1983).

26. Caruso recorded the sextet three times, in 1908 (with Marcella Sembrich, Antonio Scotti, Marcel Journet, Gina Severina, and Francesco Daddi), 1912 (with Luisa Tetrazzini, Pasquale Amato, Journet, Angelo Bada, and Josephine Jacoby), and 1917 (with Amelita Galli-Curci, Minnie Egener, Journet, Giuseppe De Luca, and Bada). The film seems to use the 1917 recording. See Freestone and Drummond, *Enrico Caruso: His Recorded Legacy*, pp. 40–41, 75, and 104. For a photograph of the ensemble taken the day of the recording session in January 1917, see Robinson, *Caruso: His Life in Pictures*, p. 99. The *Lucia* sextet, performed as an instrumental, was often used to accompany scenes in silent films—in other words, films made at the same time of *Fitzcarraldo*'s setting.

27. Michel Chion, *Audio-Vision: Sound on Screen*, ed. and trans. Claudia Gorbman (New York: Columbia University Press, 1994), p. 54: "The cinema is a realist art: but it remains that this realist art has progressed only by means of straining against its own principle, through forceful doses of unrealism." On Herzog's obsession with dreams, dreamers, and dreaming, see also Michael Goodwin, "Up the River with Werner Herzog," in *Burden of Dreams: Screenplay, Journals, Reviews, Photographs*, ed. Les Blank and James Bogan (Berkeley: North Atlantic Books, 1984), pp. 212–34.

28. Johann Wolfgang von Goethe, *The Sorrows of Young Werther, and Selected Writings*, trans. Catherine Hutter (New York: New American Library, 1962), p. 63: "My heart is undermined by the consuming power that lies hidden in the Allness of nature, which has created nothing, formed nothing, which has destroyed neither its neighbor nor itself. Surrounded by the heavens and the earth and the powerful web they weave between them, I reel with dread. I can see nothing but an eternally devouring, eternally regurgitating monster."

29. Theodor W. Adorno, Hanns Eisler, and Theodor W. Adorno, *Composing for the Films* (London: Athlone Press, 1994), p. 75. The text for this monograph was revised for its appearance in a German edition. The somewhat clumsy sentence, as rendered in the original English, cited above, is rearranged and simplified in Adorno's *Gesammelte Schriften*, ed. Rolf Tiedemann et al. (Frankfurt am Main: Suhrkamp

Verlag, 1976), vol. 15, p. 75: "Kinomusik hat den Gestus des Kindes, das im Dunkeln vor sich hinsingt."

30. On the *Molly Aida* riverboat "configured to be suggestive of an opera house," as well as a brief comment concerning the Beethoven citation, see Hillman, *Unsettling Scores*, pp. 144–45.

31. Herzog, *Fitzcarraldo: The Original Story*, pp. 155–59, calls for an unspecified scene from *Die Walküre.*

32. See, on this point, Dolkart, "Civilization's Aria," p. 141. Susan Sontag, "Notes on 'Camp,' " in *Against Interpretation and Other Essays* (New York: Noonday Press / Farrar, Straus & Giroux, 1966), writes, "The essence of Camp is its love of the unnatural: of artifice and exaggeration" (p. 275). Sontag provides a shopping list of canonic camp that includes among its musical artifacts *Swan Lake*, Strauss operas (she cites *Der Rosenkavalier*), and, among the Italian works, *Il trovatore* and "Bellini's operas" (pp. 277, 280, 286).

33. Alexander Kluge, in his 1983 film *The Power of Emotion [Die Macht der Gefühle]*, took on the institutionality of opera in a scathing critique. See also the book with numerous stills by Alexander Kluge, *Die Macht der Gefühle* (Frankfurt am Main: Zweitausendeins, 1984). Caryl Flinn has devoted an excellent essay to this film, "Undoing Act 5: History, Bodies, and Operatic Remains: Kluge's *The Power of Emotion*," in *The New German Cinema: Music, History, and the Matter of Style* (Berkeley and Los Angeles: University of California Press, 2004), pp. 138–69. As she explains, "Kluge turns to [opera] productions, focusing on the material *behind* the fantasies and *underneath* the spectacle, blasting them out in so many directions" (p. 139). For Kluge, she continues, opera "is an industry that capitalizes on human misery, glorifies defeat, and disguises the material aspects of its production. Especially cruel is how tragic opera encourages audiences to buy into its fatalistic worldview, and Kluge aggressively directs his line of fire in that direction" (p. 141).

34. Jacques Attali, *Noise: The Political Economy of Music*, trans. Brian Massumi (Minneapolis: University of Minnesota Press, 1985), p. 6. Attali's insight is indebted to Adorno, whose work he knows well. See Theodor W. Adorno, *Aesthetic Theory*, ed. Gretel Adorno and Rolf Tiedemann, trans. Robert Hullot-Kentor (Minneapolis: University of Minnesota Press, 1997), pp. 53–54 and 228.

35. Holly Rogers, "Fitzcarraldo's Search for Aguirre: Music and Text in the Amazonian Films of Werner Herzog," *Journal of the Royal Musical Association* 129 (2004), p. 98, points out that Fitzcarraldo's operatic music is "supported by the pillars of Western tonality, a music that constantly drives towards closure," which she appropriately contrasts with the acoustic circularity of the music provided by Popol Vuh against which Caruso is heard. And yet such sonic closure is repeatedly set in opposition to the failure textually narrated by the arias and ensembles. In other words, the dream-claims of the operatic excerpts employed in the film are consistently mediated by their own internal dialectics: outright failure (the narrative) and apparent success (musical climax/closure). This fact notwithstanding, opera serves in the film as a protest against the overdetermined inadequacy of modern life.

CHAPTER 3

'Everybody's Lonesome for Somebody': age, the body and experience in the music of Hank Williams

'He was so ordinary he merges with the crowd in my memory.' (Mrs Lilly McGill, teacher, Georgiana, Alabama, on her former pupil, Hank Williams.)

Houston Baker locates the blues at the crossroads of lack and desire, at the place where the hurts of history encounter determined resistance from people who know they are entitled to something better (Baker 1984, pp. 7, 150). Like the blues singers from whom he learned so much, Hank Williams (1923 to 1953) spent a lot of time at that particular intersection. There he met others whose own struggles informed and shaped his music. Williams's voice expressed the contradictions of his historical moment – post Second World War America – a time when diverse currents of resistance to class, race and gender oppressions flowed together to form a contradictory, but nonetheless real, unity of opposites. Standing at a crossroads in history, at a fundamental turning point for relationships between men and women, whites and blacks, capital and labour, Williams's songs about heartbreak and failed personal relations indentified the body and the psyche as crucial terrains of political struggle in the post-war era.

Hank Williams was an extraordinary artist, a songwriter with a gift for concise yet powerful expression, and a singer with exceptional phrasing and drama. Yet we miss the point if we view Williams solely as an individual genius who rose above the crowd; the real story of Hank Williams is how he remained part of the crowd by letting its diverse currents flow through him. His extraordinary popularity, his success at introducing country music to new audiences, and his influence on an astonishingly diverse range of popular musical artists and genres all stem from Williams's ability to understand and articulate the blasted hopes and repressed desires of his audience.

Above all, Hank Williams understood that the profound changes in American family life during the 1930s and 1940s had ushered in a new era, fundamentally altering old categories of age, gender and romance. His songs soared to popularity in the early 1950s, a time often hailed as the 'golden age' of the family (see May 1988; Mintz and Kellogg 1988). Yet Williams's narratives exuded a fatalism and despair about personal relationships. They resisted romantic optimism, and also avoided the kinds of closure and transcendence historically associated with male subjectivity. In this way, they expressed what Tania Modleski has described as a refusal to be oedipalised (Modleski 1982, p. 74), and what Fred Pfeil calls the 'de-oedipalisation of American society' (Pfeil 1988, pp. 395–6).[1]

This is not to argue that Hank Williams found his way to an emancipatory political programme or even to a cultural vision completely free from dominant constructions of gender, sexuality and romance. Far from it. But it is to claim that Williams's music and lyrics represented a significant refusal to accept dominant cultural narratives, and that they gave voice to potentials for resistance that remain important to this day. People can be imprisoned by cultural stories as easily as by iron bars and stone walls. Indeed, the core insight of contemporary cultural studies has been the understanding that people are more frequently contained within cultural narratives than within jail cells. In this context, all refusals are important because they represent a challenge to the prisons of mind and spirit that repress emancipatory hopes. Our exploration of the music of Hank Williams focuses on the ways in which he gave an individual voice to collective fears and hopes about the body, romance, gender roles and the family. We wish to locate these issues variously in the site/sight of his physical body, his voice, his lyrics and his music.

Age and historicisation of the body

Hank Williams began his career as a child prodigy and ended it as a still young man who appeared years older than his age. At thirteen, he won an 'amateur hour' contest in Montgomery, Alabama with a song protesting against the conditions facing labourers for the federal Works Progress Administration. Williams's singing and songwriting immediately earned him a spot as 'The Singing Kid' on a local radio show featuring 'Dad' Cryswell and his band (Caress 1979, p. 25). But his first recording session did not come until 11 December 1946 and he attained his first hit record in 1947 (Kingsbury and Axelrod 1988, p. 247). His last recording session occurred on 23 September 1952, slightly more than three months before his death in the early morning hours of 1 January 1953. Thus his career as a country singer spanned only six years, beginning when he was twenty-three and ending with his death at twenty-nine. Despite Williams's short life and the relative brevity of his career, among the more striking aspects of his work as a lyricist, composer and performer were the multiple and complex encodings of both age and experience as played out on the ground of the individual human body, both physically and psychically. Significantly, he located his work within a context that invariably posited that body not in the transcendence of timeless/universal humanism, but in the history of rural southern poor and working class America in the mid-twentieth century.

The concept of youth is largely taken as a 'natural' – and not constructed – category in American middle-class culture today. But in the early post-war years (especially among the rural poor) the concept had little bearing on life as it was lived, as Williams's own typical experience as a child labourer illustrates. To be young was essentially to be an even less reliable wage slave than one's parents, in a setting when obtaining work at all ages was a necessity for survival. Hank Williams lived out his short life within this larger reality; he lived out his decade as an 'official' of-age adult under still more complex circumstances, during a decade of traumatic post-war change in America in general, and in the rural south in particular. In this respect, his experience paralleled that of a generation of young men – and women – who came of age during the war (where, in the field, a twenty-six-year-old might commonly be referred to as the Old Man) and who confronted the jolting realities of an atomic peace immediately re-defined in terms of Cold War and economic upheaval, massive migrations from the land to the emerging suburbs, and changing prescriptions for family life and for relations among races, classes and genders.

Hank Williams was heard as 'authentic' at a time when authenticity was a prime determinate in the success of in-person and radio performers. (Like other country singers of his time, Williams never pulled back from the live-performance circuit; audiences were built and maintained by visual contact and live radio, without which recording careers could not develop, and 'in his prime, Hank was doing two hundred one-nighters a year' (Koon 1983, p. 88; see also p. 93).) There are several interlocking reasons why this is so, among which the 'age' of the experiences his lyrics described and the 'age' of his voice were of special importance. At a more immediate – and pre-musical – level, his appearance played a part as well.

At twenty-three, as at twenty-nine, Williams was a chronologically young man long past youth – indeed, a man who seemingly never experienced youth, as was borne out by his physical appearance. At six feet in height he was not especially tall, but his thin body (140 lbs), and the hats he perpetually wore (to cover his thinning hair about which he was sensitive [Williams 1981, p. 144]), made him look taller: he stood out. Toward the end of his life he was haggard, gaunt, physically wrecked. He began drinking by the time he was eleven (*ibid.*, p. 15), a habit he continued with few interruptions for the rest of his life, compounded by drug use in his later years (amphetamines and Seconal, the sedative chloral hydrate, and morphine). He had a form of spina bifida which exacerbated his chronic back pain and, near the end, hepatitis and a heart condition; and he suffered from malnutri-

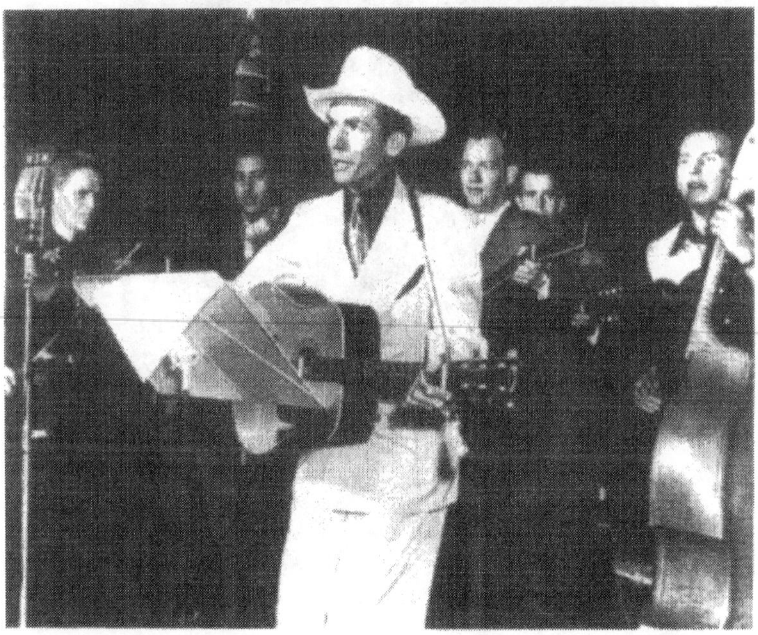

Hank Williams in performance. Photographs courtesy of the Country Music Foundation Inc.

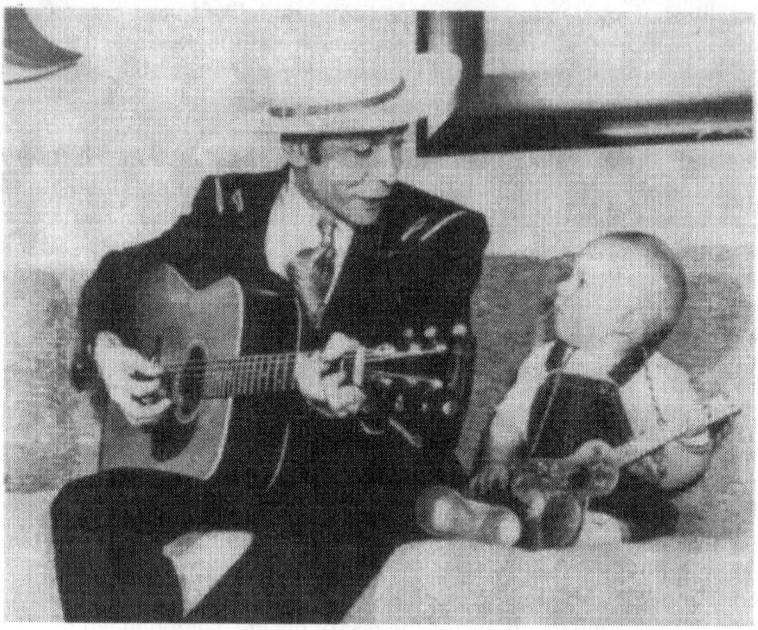

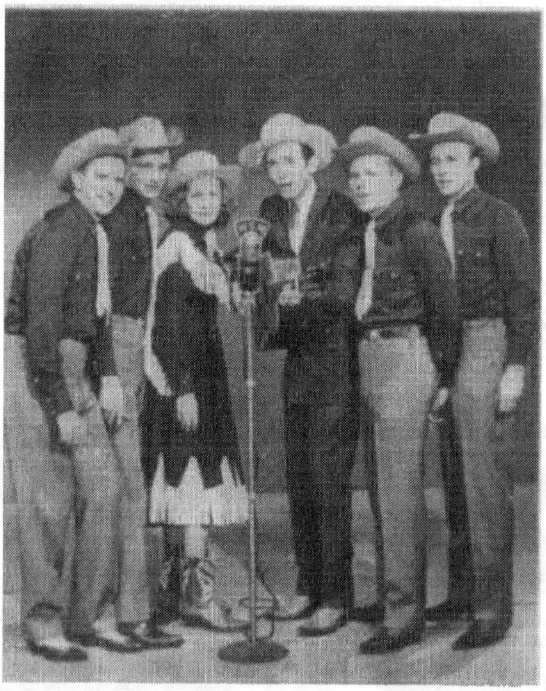

Hank Williams in performance. Photographs courtesy of the Country Music Foundation Inc.

tion – when drinking heavily he did not eat, sometimes for days on end (*ibid.*, pp. 175, 205, 207; Koon 1983, p. 50). His body could never properly fill out his expensive tailor-made suits (evident even in the posed publicity shots).

The appearance of Williams's body marked the urgency of age as a central category in his work, especially in a culture where increasingly prescriptive post-war expectations of bodily and behavioural propriety were being forged. It was well known that Hank Williams lived his life on the edge. His music masked none of it. His songs about failed love followed closely the dismal history of his marriages – and his innumerable one-night stands – just as his obsession with death and repentence (of which more follows) confirmed that he knew the price he was paying both in this life and, unless he was careful, likewise the next. Williams referred to himself as 'ole Hank' both on the air and in private.[2]

Audiences were by no means amused by or even tolerant of his most drunken performances, especially when he failed to remember lyrics (see Williams 1981, p. 180). His increasingly debilitating alcoholism culminated in his being thrown off the Grand Ole Opry in 1952 (*ibid.*, pp. 172–3, 191, 196–8); his trips to sanitariums for drying out 'became almost routine' (*ibid.*, p. 194). Nevertheless, audiences 'loved Hank partly *because* of his problems', according to Frank Page, associated with Shreveport's KWKH Louisiana Hayride (*ibid.*, p. 198).[3] For those who saw his live performances, drunk or sober, his physical vulnerability was both obvious and affecting. In body he confounded the model of the self-reliant, self-contained in-shape and battle-tested post-war male ('He'd come slopping and slouching out on stage, limp as a dishrag' [*ibid.*, p. 140, quoting *Montgomery Advertiser* columnist Allen Rankin]).

Hank Williams's lyrics and music, like his physical appearance, reflect age and the historicisation of the body in love songs and gospel numbers alike. In the first instance, his subjects invariably exude a spoken or unspoken history. His upbeat love songs ('If You'll be a Baby (to Me)') characteristically refer to a rural timelessness, a pastoral imagery that pulls back from post-war futurism ('I can plow and milk the cow . . . [You] keep the homefires burnin' ') but which, by recalling agrarian cyclical chronology, confront the sense of the real (not imagined) loss of that way of life.[4] To be sure, images of the man in the field and the woman in the kitchen correspond roughly to the Levittown ideal of suburban social organisation, but only to an urban/suburbanite. The rural reality encoded here is one of shared labours: the woman is not kept cosy by her man's work; she is a labourer as well. She heats her cookstove with wood and coal, and she does the wash with her bare knuckles. In this way Williams's lyrics, built on traditional domestic rural social organisation, incorporate simultaneously an ancient and recent past that his listeners clearly recognised, that most had lived or were still living, but which they also knew was ending in favour of a future that was profoundly uncertain. In this regard, Williams when he sang about love, voiced more than the desire for partnership: he voiced the pain of loss for a way of life that could already be described with the anxiety of ending.

As regards gospel, the fact that a young man in the 1940s might sing of Jesus (and in 20 per cent of his repertory [Koon 1983, p. 81]) is not in itself particularly surprising, at least in the rural south, though the numbers of Williams's gospel tunes may be unusual (some were recorded under his own name, others under the pseudonym of his alter-ego Luke the Drifter). In many respects a tune like 'How Can You Refuse Him Now?' is quite an ordinary, even conventional piece of white gospel. But in other ways, this song and others like it exceed conventions. Unlike contemporaneous southern black gospel, his tunes are seldom upbeat; neither musically nor lyrically do they convincingly encode happiness, let alone ecstasy. Instead, they fixate on death (as in 'We're Getting Closer to the Grave Each Day', recorded when he was twenty-six, and 'Mother is Gone') and on death rituals ('The Funeral'; in this instance that of a black child[5]). Williams's religious lyrics speak to life's suffering and failures, often without recourse to the promise of an afterlife. As such they tend to exceed and politically subvert the generic passivity encoded especially into much white gospel music. (The musical and performative vitality of black gospel, by contrast, acts to undercut the otherworldly fixation of the lyrics, re-establishing the physical present, as well as the spiritual future, in the lives of believers.) That is, once the hope of afterlife is pushed aside, the terrain that matters is located in the concrete personal and social body, not in the abstract soul. Thus even in 'I Saw the Light', perhaps his best known gospel song – but certainly not his best – the most Williams can offer for accepting Jesus fails to exceed this life, as it vaguely conjures up the rather tired imagery of smiling in the face of adversity (as the phrase now runs: 'Don't worry, be happy'). The text proffers consolation, and consolation is the only reward; the reserve with which Williams sings the words only confirms the limits of hope offered, all the more given his 'biological' youth from which conventional 'idealism' and future directedness are already stripped.

'Men with Broken Hearts', a Luke the Drifter (non-gospel) recitation (recorded 21 December 1950), locates the terrain of failure in particularly dismal (and unrelenting) fashion, calling forth rhetorically to God at the end, but without hope for redress. The text speaks of defeat in the metaphor of men's broken bodies – stooped shoulders, heads 'bowed low', vacantly staring eyes – walking allegories of what Williams calls 'living death', relief from which can only come via death itself.

At the level of an unconscious politics lies the gesture of recognition that to have failed in this life is to have failed: it carries its own punishment and there is nothing more beyond it, or at least nothing one can safely predict. In 'We're Getting Closer to the Grave Each Day', Williams reiterates the theology of Christ's redemptive death and, to be sure, he makes passing reference to the Judgement Day. But the image that incessantly repeats is that of the approach to the grave. In 'How Can You Refuse Him Now?', the image of Christ crucified is not that of the redeemer, but of a man suffering. It is His suffering that should trigger our response, not our own fear of death or a hope for afterlife. Christ, in essence, becomes one of us, a man in trouble.

Hank Williams's singing voice registers differently from his [FM!-] radio-perfect speaking voice. There is an aura of careworn exhaustion even in his quasi-upbeat tunes. Thus in the 56 second fragment 'If You'll Be a Baby (to Me)', a lyric essentially proposing marriage, Williams does not sound like a teenager in love, nor even a twenty-year-old. There is no sense of passionate sensuality in either the words or the voice. There is instead a textual promise of peace ('no quarrellin' ') and a vocal – explicitly timbral – expression of hope for refuge. That is, the putative subject of the tune has all the naivete of uncomplicated first-love-and-family aspirations ('I'll be your baby/ And I don't mean maybe'), but Williams's voice encodes something more complex. The delivery is subdued, the words slightly swallowed, the overall acoustical affect establishing associations less of first love than of trying-once-more. It is a voice of knowing, not anticipating, confined to a narrow range (a major sixth), middle register (the high note is A below middle C), and a middling dynamic. The enthusiasm presumed by the lyrics is undercut by the doubtfulness of the delivery.

In 'A House without Love is Not a Home', the narrative plays off a long-time relationship now failed, its imagery repeatedly referring to the passage of time and loss. The timbral difference from Williams's deep, resonant speaking voice is striking. The voice is thin – and, characteristically, his pitch wavers on held notes, especially in the upper half of his narrow register. It is a voice lacking certainty – but gaining thereby in credibility. The melodic structure produces a different affect from that of 'If You'll Be a Baby (to Me)'. In the earlier tune, Williams's upper register is not called upon and most of the intervallic relationships are seconds, apart from the major/minor thirds and a single perfect fourth. In 'A House Without Love' the range extends over a tenth (to E above middle C), and the tune is largely constructed around the interval of a fourth: that is, it is far more disjointed, providing the opportunity/necessity for him to connect the two pitches of the interval with a slurred slide (in instances where the interval is falling, as the majority of them do). And though, to be sure, this is a musical gesture characteristic to much country music, it is a musical practice – outside country music – more commonly located in the singing of women than men. Combined with the other vocal features we have described, it registers uncertainty, vulnerability, and – given the lyrics – the sorts of failure that only age can produce.

Both tunes are in the key of C and neither uses any chromatic inflection: the melodies are musically straightforward, 'guileless'. Indeed, Williams characteristically keeps melodic, rhythmic and harmonic surprises to a minimum – the arch-shape of his melodies is sufficiently predictable that committing the tunes to memory is easily accomplished on one or two hearings. All of this affects the reception of Williams's music. Taken together, the appeal is that of a boy–man; the musical vocabulary encodes a simplicity on the verge of the child-like; contrarily, the voice is marked by uncertain age. The contradiction results in the ambiguity and complexity of audience reactions, especially when combined with his physical performance image. He is to be mothered, but also to be erotically loved, and above all to be heard as one's own: a capsulised history of a self-consciously regionally-ghettoised people.

If we look at Williams's gospel tunes, the same features are found ('We're Getting Closer to the Grave Each Day', 'How Can You Refuse Him Now?'); indeed, the distinctions between these two primary genres of his work are few.[6] Notable among them are the frequent shift from the duple time characteristic of the secular tunes to a lilting 3/4 in gospel; in the religious tunes, he uses a more pronounced slur-slide on downward moving intervals; and here too the famous vocal 'tear' (as in both weeping and pulling apart) appears: the voice momentarily breaks, in a convention of pathos which Williams perfected (this device occurs repeatedly in 'We're Getting Closer to the Grave Each Day').

There was a considerable rift between Williams's deep, resonant speaking voice and the thinner, more nasal, crooning quality of his singing, a rift notably widened by the accompanying change in his physical appearance when, from standing before the microphone conversing, he shifted into song: 'It was like a charge of electricity had gone through him' (Allen Rankin, quoted in Williams 1981, p. 140). (Between songs Williams enjoyed folksy bantering with his audiences; indeed such contacts were conventional in gigs and radio shows alike. And many Luke the Drifter bits were essentially monologues with musical accompaniment.) Minnie Pearl was struck by his stage presence from the first time she encountered it: 'He had a real animal magnetism. He destroyed the women in the audience.' (*ibid.*, p. 144)[7] He knew how to use his body; hunching forward into the mike, 'He'd close his eyes and swing one of those big long legs, and the place would go wild' (*ibid.*, p. 145, quoting Don Helms).[8] He played on a sexuality that was exciting precisely because of the contradictions it contained. Minnie Pearl suggests that Williams appealed to women's maternal instincts. Others suggest a far more sensual dimension, though both reflected his true character – a womaniser nevertheless dominated by his strong mother. This contradiction engenders an ambiguity of a simultaneously exciting but politically dangerous sort. It constitutes a partially masked refusal to adhere to standards of propriety established for a post-war culture of re-domestication, a culture built on self-contradictory and increasingly complex erotic economies of controlled role-playing. Williams – like Elvis soon after him – marked with his bodily gestures a language of difference and demand, just as one might expect (or hope for) in the young – thereby accounting for the insistence then, as now, that youth be tightly controlled, especially physically. Yet his speaking and singing voices also referenced acoustics culturally characteristic of middle age and beyond, just as his love songs consistently dealt with the failures of middle age, and his gospel tunes with death. In sound and sight alike, he encompassed the experiences of life's full range of contradictions, hopes and failures for a society which unquestionably recognised in him both what they loved and hated of themselves.

Gender difference and social class: identity by alienation

America as a social and political organization is committed to a cheerful view of life. (Film critic Robert Warshow)

That's just it, Minnie, there ain't no light. (Hank Williams to Minnie Pearl)

Kent Blaser points out that forty-five of Williams's fifty most important songs deal with relationships between men and women, and that fifteen of these complain about being abandoned by one's partner (Blaser 1985, p. 23). From 'Lovesick Blues' to 'Your Cheatin' Heart', his most popular songs articulate loneliness, frustration and despair as necessary parts of the search for love. This pessimism made a break with the traditional romantic optimism of popular music as crafted in Tin Pan Alley, but in the context of post-Second World War America it held special significance.

After the Second World War, Americans married earlier and in greater numbers and had more children than had been true in the past. This extraordinary increase in marriages and births brought with it an unprecedented focus on the family by both private capital and the state. The nuclear family emerged as the primary social unit, a unit whose true home was the suburban shopping mall (see Leo 1988, p. 31), and everything from the Cold War to the growth of suburbs to increases in private debt and consumer spending drew justification from uncritical celebrations of the nuclear family and heterosexual romance (see May 1989, p. 155). In that context, Hank Williams's fatalism and existential despair rebuked dominant social narratives and spoke directly to the internal psychic wounds generated by the gap between lived experience and an ideology that promised universal bliss through the emergence of romance and the family as unchallenged centres of personal life.

Hank Williams's own life experience allowed him precious few illusions about the nuclear family, and in that respect he exemplified a broader social and historical experience. The Great Depression of the 1930s had undermined both the theory and the practice of the nuclear family. Unemployed fathers deserted their families in large numbers; by 1940 1,500,000 married women lived apart from their husbands. Many families formed extended households by moving in with relatives, but in the mid-1930s an estimated 200,000 vagrant children roamed the country. Women and children once again entered the workforce in large numbers, and their earning power undercut the previously unchallenged authority of male breadwinners (Mintz and Kellogg 1988, pp. 137–8). Mobilisation for the Second World War accelerated these trends. During the war, six million women workers entered high-paying production jobs in industry. Sixteen million Americans left their homes to join the armed forces, and another fifteen million travelled to new jobs in war production centres. Under these conditions, old ties of family and community broke down, and Americans experimented with new gender and family roles (*ibid.*, p. 155).

Hank Williams's family life reflected these larger social trends. His father had suffered shell shock in combat during the First World War and, after a series of short-term jobs in the late 1920s, was committed in 1930 to the Veterans Administration Hospital in Biloxi, Mississippi where he stayed ten years. Thus for most of the time between his sixth and sixteenth birthday, Hank Williams was raised by his mother and his sister. His mother assumed an awesome presence in his life and career, supporting her children with her own labour during the hard years of the Great Depression, and managing her son's entry into show business. Like many working class children, he also spent considerable time with relatives outside his nuclear family, living for a year when he was six with his cousin J. C. in Monroe County, Alabama, so that J. C.'s sister could go to school in Georgiana by living with Hank's mother and sister (Caress 1979, p. 12). Lilly Williams moved her family to Montgomery in 1937 when Hank was fourteen, and she ran a boarding house there that exposed her son to yet another extended household.

There was little in Hank Williams's personal experience that conformed with the reigning cultural optimism about the nuclear family. He started dating Audrey Mae Sheppard, a married woman with a daughter at home and a husband overseas, in 1942. Sheppard's father threatened to kill Hank over the relationship, and when Hank first brought Audrey home to meet his mother, Lilly asked 'Where'd you get this whore?', a comment that provoked a fistfight between mother and son (*ibid.*, pp. 35–6, 38). In a culture that increasingly lauded motherhood in the abstract while imposing ever-greater burdens on it in practice, not every son could use the words Hank Williams employed to speak about his mother to Minnie Pearl, 'Minnie, there ain't nobody in the world I'd rather have alongside me in a fight than my mama with a broken beer bottle in her hand' (Pearl 1980, p. 213). Hank married Audrey in 1944 before a Justice of the Peace in a Texaco station in Andalusia, Alabama, but the marriage was illegal because it came too soon after Audrey's separation from her husband to satisfy the requirements of Alabama law (Koon 1983, p. 19). Hank and Audrey were divorced in 1948, but reconciled after the birth of their son Randall Hank (Hank Williams, Jr) in 1949 (*ibid.*, pp. 29–30). The tempestuous relationship led to another divorce, and his remarriage (in 1952) to Billie Jean Eshlimar (who had been abandoned by her first husband) led to constant bickering among Williams, his mother and both his wives (Caress 1979, p. 189).

Biographer Jay Caress locates the roots of Williams's personal problems in the singer's distance from the experience of a nuclear family, arguing that Williams 'never made the normal psychological transfer from what psychologists call dependent mother love to assertive, independent (father emulating) mother love' (*ibid.*, p. 12). Yet Hank Williams's experiences with strong-willed and competent women left him with a deep respect for women and a powerful desire for connection to them. His 'failure' to make the oedipal break led him to remain in dialogue with all of the significant women in his life, and led him away from the dominant 'heroic' image of masculinity.

In an age when cultural voices ranging from the masculinist rhetoric of Mickey Spillane novels and John Wayne films to the conformist and paternalistic pressures of outer-directed corporate culture to the hedonistic appeals of *Playboy* magazine all encouraged men to widen the distance between themselves and women, Williams presented a masculine voice that longed for reconnection with the feminine, that refused the oedipality of the dominant culture in favour of an almost pre-oedipal craving for intimacy, pleasure and reconnection with women (see Modleski 1982, pp. 72–9). Of course, even this refusal could be channelled into the kind of flight from the family and responsibility that Barbara Ehrenreich describes as an important factor in sexualising and engendering male consumer desire in the 1950s (Ehrenreich 1984). The pre-oedipal stage might be seen as the perfect model for the needy narcissism vital to consumer desire. As Fred Pfeil explains, 'the increasing number of de-Oedipalized middle-class male subjects, even ostensibly politically progressive ones, in no way guarantees any decrease in their fear of and hostility toward women' (Pfeil 1988, p. 396). But the rise of a de-oedipalised subjectivity does constitute the body and psyche as sites for political meaning, and it also evidences a kind of subjectivity that seeks connection rather than separation, that disconnects ego and identity from hatred of a (proximate) mother and identification with a (distant) father. Collective social problems can never be solved by purely individual responses, but individual predispositions can often disclose contradictions and interruptions in dominant ideology that prefigure the sites where resistance might emerge. In Hank Williams's case, resistance to the oedipal narrative reveals structural weaknesses within the idealised nuclear family and its promises of happiness, as well as the existence of a popular desire for something better.

Hank Williams not only refused a narrowly oedipal definition of masculinity, but in fact he spent most of his life as a fugitive from nearly any stable identity. As a child he attached himself to black street singers Rufus Payne (known as Tee Tot) and Connie McKee (known as Big Day) who became his first strong adult male role models. Before deciding on a life as a musician, he tried out for the rodeo, and while working as a shipfitter's helper in Mobile, Alabama took a secret trip to Portland, Oregon in 1944 to try his luck in the Kaiser shipyards in that city. Even after achieving stardom, he went to work under the pseudonym Herman P. Willis for Dallas nightclub owner (and later assassin of Lee Harvey Oswald) Jack Ruby (Koon 1983, p. 34). As a young musician, he formed a country and western band with 'Indian Joe' Hatcher on lead guitar and 'Mexican Charlie' Mayes on fiddle. He adopted the pseudonym 'Luke the Drifter' for a series of recitations, and repeated the 'drifting' theme by naming his band of Alabama-born musicians the 'Drifting Cowboys' (Caress 1979, pp. 20, 22, 26, 17; Koon 1983, p. 34). While on tour with his band, he loved to listen to baseball games on the car radio, but had no favourite team (Williams 1981, p. 135). He sang religious hymns to his audiences, but lived a decidedly non-religious life.[9] This refusal to accept any permanent identity also characterized Williams's view of class which he interpreted through the frame of gender. As Dorothy Horstman notes,

> The farmers and labourers who made up the original market for country music were for the most part dirt-poor, bypassed by the American dream and the means of achieving it. Burdened with poor land, a poor economy, and hostile natural forces beyond their control, many felt they were, indeed 'born to lose'. . . . A tragic love affair, then, is the final insult – and perhaps the focus for economic and social frustrations it would be unmanly to admit. (Horstman 1975, p. 140)

Country musicians in general, and Hank Williams in particular, locate the politics of gender on the terrain of social class difference, but less on the overt ground of society and its institutions than on the privatised body, particularly its psyche. In the process, Williams gives sight to the unseen, especially in love song laments about infidelity and failed relationships.

Marital cheating was a taboo subject in country music recordings prior to the social upheavals of the 1940s, so that Hank Williams's 'Your Cheatin' Heart', among the classics of the genre (recorded in his last session – 23 September 1952 – together with another tune of the same sort, 'Take These Chains from My Heart', and two others), was a type of song having a very short history. When Williams wrote these tunes, their subject rang true, not as repetitious or timeless commentaries, but as expressions of profound and shattering change. They caught on precisely because he was able to locate the societal in the most personal and private terrain of sexual love. It was not that infidelity never occurred in the rural south prior to Williams's generation; it was rather that infidelity was admitted for the first time among the expressible catalogue of failures. By inscribing the rising stakes of societal suffering in infidelity, by locating that suffering in the psyche, he undercut the final refuge for resistance. The soul of the privatised body could no longer be separated, refuge-like, from the larger social economy: cheating songs confirmed devolutionary change.[10]

Similarly, songs of unrequited love ('I'm So Lonesome I Could Cry'; 'Cold, Cold Heart'), though excluding the sin of adultery, preserve the political essentials of songs about cheating, even if they accomplish their politics of emotion in a slightly different fashion. By emphasising a love that is never responded to, as opposed to a love that once was but is now lost, unrequited love songs fundamentally account for an equally defeating – if not necessarily worse – sort of failure: the inability to find love in the first place, to love but not be loved in return, to be rejected. It is in songs of unrequited love that the work of Hank Williams approaches black music most directly, and where it crosses gender lines into emotional ground more commonly occupied by women, and notably by women who are black (e.g. Billie Holiday, Nina Simone). As Billie Holiday, dying, gravel-voiced, movingly – and pathetically – sang in 'Glad to Be Unhappy', one of her last recorded songs, when someone you adore fails to love you back, 'It's a pleasure to be sad'.

The emotional intensity that Billie Holiday accorded to this topic,[11] via her vocal/timbral inscription of failure (as well as by the words), bears a distinct similarity to that achieved by Hank Williams, though musically by quite different means. The difference can be stated quite simply: the musical and cultural traditions that would allow a black woman to produce this lament generally affect men in a quite dissimilar way. For a man to utter similar sentiments, in this society, reflects a more extreme degree of failure and frustration. The fact that Williams wrote and sang such tunes, in other words, produces affect by collapsing the distinction not only between genders, but between races as well (southern whites, after all, heard blues music). Not only with subject matter, but also with what might be termed the politics of timbre, an acoustic solidarity is implicitly forged: between genders, between the races, and among the poor. Black audiences recognised elements of their own culture in Williams's music, and in large numbers attended the Louisiana Hayride when he was on the bill.[12] Blues singer B. B. King remembers paying special attention to the songs by Hank Williams that he heard on the radio while working on a Mississippi plantation because:

> Like Hank Williams, man, when he wrote 'Cold, Cold Heart', tunes like that, that carried me right back to my same old blues about 'don't answer the door' and all that kind of stuff. 'Cause this is a guy hurting. He's hurting from inside. And 'Your Cheating Heart', many things of this sort are just to me another form of blues sung by other people. (Redd 1974, p. 97)

The sound of a white man's voice singing about these subjects, hence crossing gender and racial boundaries, inscribes a socio-cultural disruption of the most encompassing finality, at precisely the instant that it offers the specifically *acoustic* opportunity to establish a relationship of resistance with another socially alienated group.

Finally, even in tunes of courtship or proposal, like 'If You'll Be a Baby (to Me)', conventional romantic love is not part of the equation;[13] instead there is an offer of a partnership for mutually-supporting labour, and the extent of the male singer's love is promised in terms of the work appropriate to her that he's willing to shoulder: if she cooks, he'll plow and *even* do the churning. He loves her and considers doing 'women's' work a gesture of his devotion.[14] This may not be in the depoliticised tradition of romantic love, but it *is* romantic love of the most meaningful and committed sort. It openly recognises the mutuality of marital labour and the urge to take on more than what society conventionally identifies as the man's share. (It is arguable that, under these conditions, what otherwise passes for romantic love might flourish past the stages of passion characterising young relationships.) Lyrics of this sort are all the more striking given the national phenomenon in the early post-war years of a return to 'traditional' pre-war gender divisions, articulated especially in the domestication of the suburb with its removal of women from the labour force, as well as in a broad range of popular cultural expressions built upon the assumption of innate antagonisms between men and women, ranging from commercial television programmes and film noir motion pictures to the lyrics of most popular songs.

Yet for all his shifting subjectivities, a remarkable consistency characterises Williams's voice, and that consistency is connected to his class and regional identity. There is no discernible difference between his earliest recordings and his last, and the same holds for his unsophisticated, elementary, essentially three-chord guitar strumming. The voice is common, untrained. The delivery is inevitably straightforward, without pretence, without acrobatics or tricks – unless one counts the country-conventional vocal 'tear' mentioned earlier. The upper range, which Williams uses to good effect in producing acoustic tension, is thin and often strained, the latter quality exacerbated by a notable and fast vibrato; the low and middle range is both rich and firm, like his speaking voice. Together these variant timbres produce a comfort in the latter, inevitably undercut by the vulnerability of that comfort in the former. Moreover, he typically gives accentual and dynamic emphasis to his high voice, that is, to that part of his range that semiotically undercuts the culturally coded paternal assuredness of the deeper male sounds.

Williams's slightly nasal twang is especially obvious in the higher register – the locus of tension – thus most evident in precisely the acoustic space that best identifies pain and its politics. The country twang, in other words, locates him as one of his listeners' own, a man who shares their experiences. Nasality in other circumstances provides the southern rural poor with subcultural/community identity, like any other accentual or dialectical effect. But in extra-regional popular culture (notably the movies, often in grotesquely exaggerated burlesques like *Ma and Pa Kettle*, and in later television shows like *Beverly Hillbillies*) that effect becomes a weapon for derision, a fact never lost on any poor person. Hank Williams exploited that sound in a timbral expression of class and regional solidarity, though to be sure he was not unique in this regard. To similar, if more obvious, purpose is his swallowing of word endings at phrase ends ('quarrellin' ', 'churnin' '), and regional pronounciations ('yer' for 'your' and so on). In his Luke the Drifter recitation 'Beyond the Sunset' (recorded 10 January 1950), he tells of a man's vigilant loyalty to a woman preceding him in death; it is his memory of her that gives him the strength to go on. The recitation depends on an implicit understanding of the uses of memory as regards its connection to history, issues that go far beyond the narrower topic of this small piece. As 'Beyond the Sunset' has it: 'Memory is a gift from God that death cannot destroy'. The politics embedded here grow from the fact that Williams recognised less that songs are social constructions and more that society itself is constructed by the songs we sing, the stories we tell, and the *sounds* we voice in the narration.

Everybody's Lonesome for Somebody

I'm so lonesome I could cry. (Hank Williams lyric)

What prepares men [*sic*] for totalitarian domination in the non-totalitarian world is the fact that loneliness, once a borderline experience usually suffered in certain marginal social conditions like old age, has become an everyday experience of the ever-growing masses of our century. (Hannah Arendt in *The Origins of Totalitarianism*)

Goodbye Hank Williams, my old friend, I didn't know you but I've been the places you've been. (Tim Hardin lyric)

Hank Williams you wrote my life. (Moe Bandy lyric)

The extraordinary popularity of Hank Williams's songs in the late 1940s and early 1950s played a crucial role in transforming country music from a regional and class-bound genre to a staple of mass popular culture. Along with related developments in popular speech, dress and dance, the rise to national prominence of country music reflected the emergence of a prestige from below in which cultural hybrids emanating from intersections of race, class and gender articulated a new basis for American commercial culture.

Class, race and gender all contributed to the grounding of Williams's music in oppositional cultures and practices. His songs resonated with the materials memory forged in previous popular struggles against hierarchy and exploitation. But as a creation of a distinct historical moment, he added a new element to the historic struggle for the good life. In an age of renewed racism, he created a music that underscored the connections between whites and blacks. At a time of upward mobility and cultural assimilation for much of the working class, he affirmed his standpoint as a worker and an ordinary citizen. In an age of resurgent patriarchy, he lamented the schisms between men and women, resisted the dominant oedipal narrative, and sought closer connections to women. Finally, he foregrounded existential despair in an age of exuberant and uncritical 'progress', countering ubiquitous romantic invocations of the superiority of the nuclear family with honest words and deep emotions drawn from the hurts of history and the experiences of everyday life. As modern life became increasingly characterised by 'the policing of families' as part of capital's project to colonise the psyche and the body, Williams constituted his own voice and body as sites of resistance. Millions of fans could feel that he 'wrote their lives', because even when they did not know him, they could feel that he knew the places they had been.

Endnotes

1 We use psychoanalytic language here as a shorthand way of describing our culture's dominant narratives about the construction of subjectivity, not because we believe in any innate or transcendent human personality.

2 See the examples quoted by Williams's second wife Billy Jean in Horstman 1975, p. 194.

3 His chronic back problem, for example, was explained on a pre-recorded-for-broadcast apology that Williams produced from his hospital bed when he had to miss a December 1951 appearance in Baltimore. It is reproduced as the final cut on *Hank Williams: I Won't Be Home No More (June 1952–September 1952)*, Polydor 833 752-1 Y-2, volume 8, and the last, of Polydor's comprehensive, retrospective series of Williams's recordings.

4 The loss of home through the upheavals of war and migration are a recurrent theme in Southern culture beginning with the Civil War, and become more intense after each of this century's two world wars. One price paid for migration was guilt for not remaining to 'share the common burden'. See Horstman 1975, pp. 3–5.

5 See further Hume 1982, pp. 94–6, 'Dead Kids and Country Music'.

6 The other genres being the Luke the Drifter accompanied monologues, and the occasional novelty songs like the slightly bizarre 'Indian' love song 'Kaw Liga' or the famous 'Jambalaya'.

7 On Williams's securing of women following show dates, see *ibid.*, p. 164. Nor was his stage presence effective only on women: 'He quickly became the favorite act on a military entertainment entourage to Europe in 1951. [Moreover, o]n a celebrity-studded touring show known as the Hadacol Caravan he upstaged such luminaries as Jack Benny, Milton Berle, and Bob Hope, and eventually took over the closing spot.' (Blaser 1985, p. 17, n. 18) For details of the Caravan tour, see Williams 1981, pp. 150–5; Koon 1983, pp. 36, 38.

8 Cf. Frank Page: 'He was just electrifying on stage. . . . He had the people in the palm of his hands from the moment he walked out there'. (*ibid.*, p. 74) See also Koon 1983, p. 28.

9 His contradictory relationship to religion is encapsulated in what is probably an apocryphal story about a young fan who admitted to not being a 'God-fearing boy', and found Hank piping up 'Don't let it trouble you none. I ain't afraid of God, either' (Caress 1979, pp. 81–2). Koon quotes the very authoritative Bob Pinson as saying that the Shestack interview, from which this story is taken, is 'all fiction; it never happened' (Koon 1983, p. 94). Yet the quotation seems to capture correctly something about Williams's view of religion. Roger M. Williams notes, 'Hank, after his childhood, never demonstrated an interest in organized religion. But he had flashes of intense personal feeling about spiritual matters, which led to some of the finest songs he ever wrote. Further, he knew that "sacred songs" always find a ready market in country music' (Williams 1981, p. 57).

10 'Inevitably, in the upheaval of a wartime society, with women working, husbands and wives separated, easy social and geographical mobility, and honky tonks no longer populated exclusively by women of easy virtue, country writers began to flirt with, then to address directly, the subject of cheating.' (Horstman 1975, p. 182; see also Hume 1982, pp. 84–5)

11 See also the work of Nina Simone, ten years Hank Williams's junior, for example, on her live album, *Little Girl Blue*, especially 'He Needs Me (He doesn't know it but he needs me)'.

It is worth noting the correspondences and,

especially, the differences between Hank Williams's songs of failed love and some of the early recordings of Patsy Cline (all songs written by others, whereas Williams mostly performed his own material). 'If I Could Only Stay Asleep' moves slowly, underscoring the sense of loss inscribed by a vocal line repeatedly leaping to high notes only to slide back as if in defeat. 'I'm Blue Again' registers the vocal 'tear' – perfected by Williams – to help mark a text entirely about loss, but this effect (and others) acts in contrast to the tempo, oddly upbeat, and to Cline's vocal delivery which breathes an air of confidence seriously undercutting the text's defeatism. Indeed, time and again in Cline's work, discrepancies occur between the putative subjects of the lyrics and her delivery of them. Among the reasons Patsy Cline is such an exciting singer is that, like Hank Williams, she pushed hard against the margins of musical conventions – stretching semiotic possibilities, introducing contradictions and unexpected tensions, and, in particular, refusing to be bound by conventional expectations of vocal delivery located in gender distinction. Thus whereas Williams voices a feminine identity, mediating traditional masculine vocal qualities, Patsy Cline voices a masculine identity, notably by mediating the passivity that tunes of loss commonly inscribe lyrically and often musically. The loss of a man may be getting her down, so her words go, but she won't be down for long, so her voice encodes. She subscribes to the potential joys of men and women relating to each other but she refuses (not textually but vocally) to be overwhelmed by the absence or failure of the experience. It is very difficult to listen to 'I've Loved and Lost Again' and really believe that the pain will be permanent. She will be up and dancing soon, playing a profoundly (vocally) liberated role: her vocal-gutteral growls on 'Gotta Lot of Rhythm (In My Soul)', a thoroughly upbeat number, echo an effect heard commonly in early rock 'n' roll singers (both male and female).

12 On these shows Williams typically included one or two Luke the Drifter recitations that specifically addressed black subjects, such as 'The Funeral'. This recitation, to the accompaniment of Hammond organ and steel guitar (recorded 10 January 1950), tells of the narrator, a white man, coming upon a humble country church and witnessing the funeral service for a black child. To be sure, Williams repeats racial stereotypes and dialogue embedded in southern racism (the child is described as having 'curly hair, protruding lips'; the black preacher's speech includes 'sho 'nough'); on the other hand, Williams in effect absents himself as narrator almost from the start, giving sole voice to the preacher whose sermon he repeats at length. That is, a white man takes a pew to witness a funeral and thereafter tells his story: he tells his (primarily white) audience that he has learned something from what he describes as the 'wisdom and ignorance of a crushed, undying race'. (See Williams 1981, pp. 74–5.) Hank Williams's own funeral, held in Montgomery auditorium, included about two hundred blacks – seated in the segregated balcony – among the three thousand mourners who managed to squeeze inside; moreover, the music was provided in part by a black quartet, the Southwind Singers, in addition to various white country music luminaries (see Koon 1983, p. 54).

13 Indeed, romantic love is generally in short supply in the country music of Williams's day, precisely because it could have had little ring of credibility in the circumstances of its hearers. See Horstman 1975, p. 119.

14 Occasionally Williams confronted the politics of class more directly; perhaps the best example is 'A Mansion on the Hill' (recorded 7 November 1947). Audrey Williams has said that (Chicago, urban-bred) Fred Rose gave Hank the title and sent him off to see what he could do with it. The result was an explicit articulation of high–low class hierarchy invited by Rose's title – the lyrics employ a binary opposition between the mansion on a hill and the narrator's cabin in a valley. (See Horstman 1975, p. 165.)

References

Baker, H. 1984. *Blues, Ideology, and Afro-American Literature: a Vernacular Theory* (Chicago)

Blaser, K. 1985. ' "Pictures from Life's Other Side": Hank Williams, country music, and popular culture in America', *The South Atlantic Quarterly*, 84 (1), pp. 12–26

Caress, J. 1979. *Hank Williams: Country Music's Tragic King* (New York)

Ehrenreich, B. 1984. *The Hearts of Men: American Dreams and the Flight from Commitment* (Garden City, NY)

Horstman, D. 1975. *Sing Your Heart Out, Country Boy* (New York)

Hume, M. 1982. *You're So Cold I'm Turnin' Blue: Martha Hume's Guide to the Greatest Country Music* (New York)

Kingsbury, P. and Axelrod, A., eds. 1988. *Country: The Music and the Musicians. Pickers, Slickers, Cheatin' Hearts & Superstars* (New York)
Koon, G. 1983. *Hank Williams: A Bio-Bibliography* (Westport, CT)
Leo, J. 1988. 'The familialism of man in American television melodrama', *The South Atlantic Quarterly*, 88 (1), pp. 31–51
May, E.T. 1988. *Homeward Bound* (New York)
May, E.T. 1989. 'Explosive issues: sex, women, and the bomb', in *Recasting America*, ed. L. May (Chicago), pp. 154–70
Mintz, S. and Kellogg, S. 1988. *Domestic Revolutions* (New York)
Modleski, T. 1982. 'Film theory's detour', *Screen*, 23 (5), pp. 72–9
Pearl, M., with Dew, J. 1980. *Minnie Pearl: An Autobiography* (New York)
Pfeil, F. 1988. 'Postmodernism as a "structure of feeling"', in *Marxism and the Interpretation of Culture*, ed. L. Grossberg and C. Nelson (Champaign), pp. 381–405
Redd, L. 1974. *Rock is Rhythm and Blues* (East Lansing)
Williams, R.M. 1981. *Sing a Sad Song: The Life of Hank Williams*, 2nd edn (Urbana)

Discography

Cline, P. 1985. 'Gotta Lot of Rhythm (In My Soul)', 'If I Could Only Stay Asleep' and 'I've Loved and Lost Again', *Patsy Cline: Today, Tomorrow & Forever*, MCA-1463 (all songs first released 1955–9)
Holiday, B. 1987. 'Glad to Be Unhappy', *Lady in Satin*, Columbia CK 40247 (first released 1958)
Simone, N. 1958. 'He Needs Me', *Little Girl Blue-Nina Simone*, Bethlehem BCP 6028
Williams, H.

Note: All Hank Williams's songs mentioned in this article are available in the eight-volume comprehensive series issued on Polydor (PolyGram Records) between 1985 and 1988. The discography, drawn exclusively from Polydor's retrospective, indicates the date of the original release, when we could establish it, or instead lists the date of the recording session. In the years immediately following Williams's death, many home recordings (Williams accompanying himself on guitar without back-up) were released in over-dubbed versions. A number of years sometimes intervened between the original recording date and the over-dubbed issue. The Polydor set makes available for the first time many of Williams's home recordings in their original, undubbed state. For additional information see the discographies in Williams 1981 (compiled by Bob Pinson), and Koon 1983.

1985. 'I Saw the Light' (recorded 21 April 1947), *Hank Williams: I Ain't Got Nuthin' But Time (December 1946–April 1947)*, Polydor 825 548-2
1985. 'Lovesick Blues' (first released 1949) and 'A Mansion on the Hill' (recorded 7 November 1947), *Hank Williams: Lovesick Blues (August 1947–December 1948)*, Polydor 825 551-2
1986. 'A House without Love is Not a Home' (recorded 30 August 1949), 'How Can You Refuse Him Now' (first released in 1954; over-dubbed home recording), 'If You'll be a Baby (to Me)' (first release of original home recording; over-dubbed version released previously), 'I'm So Lonesome I Could Cry' (first released 1949) and 'We're Getting Closer to the Grave Each Day' (first release of original home recording; over-dubbed release in 1957), *Hank Williams: I'm So Lonesome I Could Cry (March 1949–August 1949)*, Polydor 825 557-1 Y-2
1987. 'Cold, Cold Heart' (first released 1951), 'Beyond the Sunset' (by Luke the Drifter; recorded 10 January 1950), 'The Funeral' (by Luke the Drifter; first released 1950), *Hank Williams: Long Gone Lonesome Blues (August 1949–December 1950)*, Polydor 831 633-4
1987. 'Men with Broken Hearts' (by Luke the Drifter; recorded 21 December 1950), *Hank Williams: Hey, Good Lookin' (December 1950–July 1951)*, Polydor 831 634-1
1987. 'Kaw Liga' (first released 1953), 'Mother is Gone' (first released 1955; over-dubbed), 'Take These Chains from My Heart' (first released 1953), 'Your Cheatin' Heart' (first released 1953), *Hank Williams: I Won't Be Home No More, June 1952–September 1952*, Polydor 833 752-1 Y-2
1988. 'Jambalaya' (first released 1952), *Hank Williams: Let's Turn Back the Years (July 1951–June 1952)*, Polydor 833 749-1

CHAPTER 4

Gender Sonics: The Voice of Patsy Cline

The basic facts about the life and career are well established and can be quickly rehearsed.[1] Patsy Cline, né Virginia Patterson Hensley, was born on 8 September 1932; she died on 5 March 1963, in the crash of a private plane piloted by her manager Randy Hughes, returning from a benefit concert in Kansas City, together with two musician friends, Hawkshaw Hawkins and Cowboy Copas. She was thirty years old. Patsy learned to play the piano by ear from the time she was eight. She never learned to read music. Patsy was first heard on local radio in 1948, at age sixteen. Following a number of gigs on national radio hookups beginning in 1953, she signed a record contract with Four Star Records in the fall of 1954 to terms strikingly not in her favor, as regards either compensation or control of material.[2] The first fifty-one of her 100-odd total recorded tracks were for Four Star; at the expiration of the Four Star contract in 1960 she signed with Decca, which had already provided recording facilities and distribution for the songs assigned to her by Four Star to record. Patsy first sang on the Grand Ole Opry, a lifelong goal, in 1955, the same year her first recordings were released. She became an Opry regular only in 1960. Her first major success was the 1957 release of *Walkin' After Midnight*, produced by Owen Bradley, with whom she worked throughout her recording career, and a man largely credited with what came to be known as the Nashville Sound.[3] Patsy recorded

1 The most comprehensive survey of the history of female country singers is by Mary A. Bufwack and Robert K. Oermann, *Finding Her Voice: Women in Country Music, 1800–2000* (Nashville: The Country Music Foundation, and Vanderbilt University Press, 2003), incorporating an extensive and well-designed bibliography on individual artists; for a capsule account of Cline's life and career, see pp. 215–22. There are several biographies available. The most detailed by Ellis Nassour, *Patsy Cline* (New York: Leisure Books, 1981); see also by the same author a briefer account, *Honky Tonk Angel: The Intimate Story of Patsy Cline* (New York: St. Martin's, 1993), based on the 1981 volume; Margaret Jones, *Patsy: The Life and Times of Patsy Cline* (New York: HarperCollins, 1994); Mark Bego, *I Fall to Pieces: The Music and the Life of Patsy Cline* (Holbrook, MA: Adams Publishing, 1995); and Doug Hall, *The Real Patsy Cline* (Kingston, ONT: Quarry Music Books, 1998). Each of these volumes provides a discography; the most detailed are those in the volumes by Jones and Bego.

Several DVD releases are available concerning Cline's life and career: *The Real Patsy Cline* (White Star D1744), 48 minutes; *Patsy Cline: Remembering Patsy (The Authorized Video Biography)* (White Star D3084), 60 minutes; and *Patsy Cline: Sweet Dreams Still: The Anthology* (MPI DVD7738), 55 minutes. Although each of these DVDs incorporates a variety of clips of Cline's performances, virtually all from television broadcasts, the most comprehensive is the last, which includes seventeen songs, performed in whole or part.

2 The contract details are spelled out by Nassour, *Patsy Cline*, pp. 68, 73–4.

3 Bufwack and Oermann, *Finding Her Voice*, p. 218: The so-named Nashville Sound, characterizing Patsy's later recordings (especially those from 1961 and thereafter), is largely credited to Decca's A & R man and Patsy's producer, Owen Bradley, as well as Don Law (Columbia), Chet Atkins (RCA), and the freelance arranger/singer Anita Kerr. See further Joli Jensen, *The Nashville Sound:*

only four LPs: *Patsy Cline*, 1957; *Showcase (With the Jordanaires)*, 1961; *Sentimentally Yours*, 1962; and *The Patsy Cline Story*, 1963, released after her death.

Her life was troubled. She grew up poor and poorly educated. Her father abandoned the family (Patsy had two siblings) when she was fifteen, after which she gave up schooling to work in a drug store in Winchester, Virginia, where her family was then living, in order to help provide support. She was twice married and had two children by her second husband, Charlie Dick. Her marriage to Dick was complicated, rife with arguing and sometimes worse, apparently in large part due to his heavy drinking. Earlier in her career she had an abortion. During her marriage to Dick, and earlier, she had affairs and some one night stands with fellow musicians, most commonly the result of long weeks on the road without her family, and experiencing extreme loneliness. Like many musicians at the time, she used

---

Authenticity, Commercialization, and Country Music (Nashville: The Country Music Foundation Press, and Vanderbilt University Press, 1998), which includes a chapter on Patsy Cline, pp. 89–117; and by the same author, "Patsy Cline, Musical Negotiation, and the Nashville Sound," in *All That Glitters: Country Music in America*, ed. George H. Lewis (Bowling Green, OH: Bowling Green State University Popular Press, 1993), pp. 38–50; and Paul Hemphill, *The Nashville Sound: Bright Lights and Country Music* (New York: Simon and Schuster, 1970). Jones, *Patsy*, p. 268: The Nashville Sound aimed to broaden the audience for country music by introducing into its sonorics the sounds of mainstream pop, in response to the economic challenges of emerging rock 'n' roll, amplified not least by the success of Elvis. The effort worked. In 1961 only 80 stations were devoted to country music playlists; by 1967 there were 328, and by the decade's end 500. Notwithstanding Patsy's role in the success of the Nashville Sound, throughout her career she insisted that her music was country, not pop; indeed, she quite consistently resisted the moves to turn her into a crossover artist—which she unquestionably became, and which largely defined her late-career success.

On Cline's resistance to pop, see Nassour, *Patsy Cline*, p. 133; and p. 116, remarks by songwriter Don Hecht, who wrote *Walkin' After Midnight*: "Patsy was stubborn in that any material performed by her under any circumstances had to be pure Country, 'or else,' she said, 'I would feel like a whore." See also Joli Jensen, "Patsy Cline: The Search for a Sound," *Journal of Country Music* 9 no. 2 (1982), 33–46. Jones, *Patsy*, p. 194: The Nashville Sound "eschewed the corn, the twang, the nasal singing, the yodeling [which Patsy loved but was consistently steered away from], the weepy sound of the steel guitar and the whine of the fiddle—in other words, just about everything that made country country." See further Hall, *The Real Patsy Cline*, p. 143.

The Nashville Sound downplayed, or outright abandoned steel guitar and fiddle in favor of a small string section and back-up vocals provided, variously, by the Anita Kerr Singers and the Jordanaires; both groups accompanied Patsy's late recordings. (The Jordanaires are well known for their background vocals on numerous recordings by Elvis Presley.) Cline's early work (1955–60), by contrast, employed a then-standard ensemble as accompaniment: piano, drums, steel guitar, bass (acoustic or electric), fiddle, and guitar (acoustic and/or electric). Overdubbing of the lead vocal was common to the Nashville Sound; the obvious benefit was voice-matched harmony. The technique was occasionally used for recordings by Cline. See, for example, *The Patsy Cline Collection*, 4 CDs (MCA MCAD4–10421), released in 1991: *Yes, I'll Understand* (1959), CD 2, track 9; *How Can I Face Tomorrow* (1960), CD 2, track 14; *Crazy Dreams* (1960), CD 2, track 16; and *Who Can I Count On* (1961), CD 3, track 2. This now shopworn technique, while hardly initiated for Patsy (Patti Page, for example, had already used double tracking), stands out from most of her recordings, which, whether taped in mono or, later, in both mono and stereo, were single-takes.

amphetamines; uppers helped get her through the rigors of endless nights of performing followed by car rides to the next gig.[4] In 1961 she was nearly killed in a car accident, which left her face badly scarred; she disguised the scars with wigs and makeup. But whatever the trials and tribulations, she never long left off performing (even after her two children were born), and the same is true of her recording sessions, thirty in all.

For most of her brief professional career she had very little money to show for her efforts, due in part to the Four Star contract. Indeed, her frenetic performance schedule, taking her for weeks on end from the east coast to the west, from the deep South to Canada, including Carnegie Hall (one group Opry gig in 1961), the Hollywood Bowl (1962), and Las Vegas (five weeks around Christmas, 1962 at the Mint Casino Lounge), sometimes performing in as many as four shows per night, left her exhausted but not a lot better off economically until near the end of her life. According to Charlie Dick, the highest single-date fee she ever earned was $1,200.[5] Though Patsy Cline was, for all intents and purposes, a professional singer fully half of her short life—including on the honky-tonk bar circuit early on—her recording career was brief, from 1 June 1955, to her last sessions, 4–7 February 1963, less than eight years in all. Despite the brevity of her career, the mark she made on country music, and also on pop, is undisputed. She has long been credited with opening doors for many female singers who followed her, Loretta Lynn perhaps the most prominent among a distinguished list. Patsy Cline marked the moment when women country singers began to break free from a long-held role as little more than window dressing for country music and its institutional performance venues that were dominated by men. Beyond that, and at least as important, she introduced new ways of singing songs, even (perhaps especially) when the songs themselves continued all too often to reflect tired clichés about women and their relationships to the men they putatively loved.

In this essay, I will be particularly interested in Patsy Cline's voice and what she did with it. What I am after is an exploration of the gender in her voice; specifically, I hope to suggest ways that Patsy's singing effectively repositioned some of the well-established conventions of country music and pop alike used to define women's identities. Her singing brushed across the grain of the voice then sanctioned for female performers, and did so smartly and invariably musically. Her voice, considered as a cultural phenomenon, was saturated in

4 See Jones, *Patsy*, p. 185.

5 Brian Mansfield, *Remembering Patsy* (Nashville: Rutledge Hill Press, 2002), p. 18. Concerning Cline's perennial money shortage, see her letters to her young fan and the de facto "manager" of Cline's fan club, Treva Miller, in Cindy Hazen and Mike Freeman, eds., *Love Always, Patsy: Patsy Cline's Letters to a Friend* (New York: Berkley Books, 1999), unpaginated: postcard dated 17 January 1957; undated letter immediately following a postcard dated 31 July 1957; 31 July 1957; letter dated 15 June 1958 ("I've got $1050.00 that's got to be paid before the end of the month or I'll lose every-thing [sic]); letter dated 18 April 1958 ("I'm down to my last $10.00 and I owe every body [sic] including you."; and 22 October 1958. On what seems to be a fairly regular basis, Cline sent Miller small amounts of money to defray the costs of maintaining the fan club, typically $10 a month. Cline seems to have managed her own financial affairs, evident for example in a letter to Treva dated 7 March 1957, when she discusses her compensation and complains of mistreatment; she states what her salary demands will be for agreeing to perform on a weekly television program on CBS: $700 per week for Monday through Friday morning shows, plus $200 for Saturday nights (still below union scale, she notes). See further Jones, *Patsy*, p. 208, 272.

personal experience, just as it was invested in the larger history of 1950s America and the South in particular. That history, to be sure, is manifested indirectly in her performances; the results were very direct indeed. Her voice struck listeners' ears with force, conviction, and authority. The question is: how, by what means?

Kitty and Patsy. Kitty Wells's signature hit, *It Wasn't God Who Made Honky Tonk Angels* (1952), was an answer-song to Hank Thompson's *The Wild Side of Life*. Perhaps the most famous answer song in country music, it provides an apt means of distinguishing between the gender-reflexive work of Wells, a duly respected and slightly earlier (b. 1919) contemporary of Patsy, and Cline's take on men-women relations, and all of it determined by the difference in their vocal delivery.[6] The song's lyric throws the charge back at men: honky-tonk (i.e., loose) women were made not born, and made (degraded) by men. Mary Bufwack has aptly encapsulated what is historically at stake:

> The popularity of Wells's lament about male victimization of women indicates a conscious knowledge of women's discontent in post-war America and an interest within the country audience in a dialogue about male-female behavior. ... The men cried of their loneliness and of their betrayal by women, but they also celebrated a freer lifestyle. Although men also expressed guilt and regret about their rowdy ways and often blamed their losses on themselves, their real anger was reserved for the woman who chose 'Dim Lights, Thick Smoke (And Loud, Loud Music)' over a husband and children. Non-traditional women were a convenient scapegoat for men's post-war depression. ... Women's frustrations received no mass legitimacy."[7]

All this is to the well and good, but there is a serious disjunction between the song's text, on the one hand, and both the tune and Wells's performance, on the other. Wells's lament complains more than it protests. Vocally, she does not so much stand up to an injustice as she simply marks it, and with more than a hint of emotional fatigue. Her singing underscores the lack of agency inscribed in the tune itself, fundamentally a simple, folklike minor mode ballad, principally defined by falling melodic lines that collapse at phrase endings, all of it governed by four-square rhythms that work to keep the complaint firmly in its place. The melody itself is old, possibly rising from British-American folk tradition; moreover, it had been used for earlier country songs: by the Carter Family's *I'm Thinking Tonight of My Blue Eyes*, recorded in 1929, and by Roy Acuff's *The Great Speckled Bird*, recorded in 1936.[8] A listener's recognition of the previous usage can diminish the impact of the otherwise more

6 For a brief summary of her career, see Bufwack and Oermann, *Finding Her Voice*, pp. 150–4. For a longer account, see A. C. Dunkleburger, *Queen of Country Music: The Life Story of Kitty Wells* (Nashville: Ambrose Printing, 1977).

7 Mary Bufwack, "The Feminist Sensibility in Post-War Country Music," *Southern Quarterly* 22 no. 3 (Spring 1984), 138–9. See also Bufwack and Oermann, *Finding Her Voice*, pp. 141–4, for a brief history of the gap between post-war happy-couples/domestic-bliss suburban imagery and the realities of fundamental cultural and social upheaval taking place—the toll charged against human relationships.

8 Robert K. Oermann, "Honky-Tonk Angels: Kitty Wells and Patsy Cline," in *Country: The Music and the Musicians*, Paul Kingsbury and Alan Axelrod, eds. (Nashville: The Country Music Foundation, and New York: Abbeville Press, 1988), p. 328.

or less newly insistent insight delivered by the text. That is, the tune's familiarity, as well as its style, pushes back hard against the lyrics, and not least because the pre-used tune does not quite fit the narrative. Kitty makes the best of it and follows along; Patsy, as I will later suggest, tries a different approach. To be sure, *It Wasn't God Who Made Honky Tonk Angels* does not give Wells much to work with, though the same holds true for many of the songs Patsy Cline was handed by Four Star Records. In any event, on balance there is little distance between the song's fundamental conservatism and Wells's delivery. The result, so far as concerns a successful assertion of one's identity in the face of a demonstrable wrong, is to project resignation. The performance lacks even a hint of the kinetic energy embedded in the lyrics, however absent any forcefulness is apparent in the melody itself.[9] Nonetheless, Wells's protest was new to country music. Despite the song's commercial success—it went #1 on the Billboard charts—it was initially considered so controversial that the Opry refused to permit Wells to perform the song, in perfect reflection of the extreme conservatism marking what was thought appropriate to women country singers. The recording established Wells's country music stardom.

Robert Oermann describes the differences between Kitty and Patsy as follows:

> On the one hand there is Wells, the wife and mother who faced modern problems in her songs with tight-lipped intensity. On the other is Cline, the beer-drinking, goodtime gal who bared her soul with open-throated fervor. Wells wore gingham, Cline wore lamé. [Cline once showed up at the Opry to perform in a pants suit; she was made to change the outfit before being permitted to go on stage.] Wells modernized traditional country music and women's place in the country music world. Cline broke with country's musical and cultural traditions, and created new ones.[10]

Wells marks tradition and convention with her distinctive nasal twang, an effect that has little place in Patsy's singing. Indeed, her vocal sound, quite apart from her phrasing and other elements of her delivery, clearly responded to a sonic and historical barrier that she was insistent to cross, acknowledging thereby both an awareness of a tradition and the desire to move beyond it. That is, the sound of Cline's voice reclaims the very agency that many of the songs she sang, still duty bound to "traditional" values, eschew. In particular, Patsy's tendency, if not outright to leave the gender straightjacket in the dust of her performance, was to push hard against the established boundaries that so many of the songs she was handed otherwise so commonly observed.

Whereas Wells's singing is anchored in gospel tradition, Cline's musical experiences were distinctly secular and underscore an adolescence of considerable privation, street learning, and road life in the honky tonks while she was very much still a kid. A good deal of the difference between the two singers is evident from Patsy's cover of the Wells hit preserved in a recording thought to date from around August, 1954.[11] The debt to Wells is evident in the

9 Concerning the cash benefits of answer-song responses to previous hits, a potential not lost on the recording industry, see Paul Kingsbury and Alan Axelrod, eds., *Country: The Music and the Musicians* (Nashville: The Country Music Foundation, and New York: Abbeville Press, 1988), p. 326.

10 Oermann, "Honky-Tonk Angels," p. 315. On the down-home virtue, simple-housewife image that defined the official Wells publicity, see pp. 328, 330. For a photograph of the sun-bonnet outfit, see p. 322.

11 *The Patsy Cline Collection*, CD 1, track 2.

legato phrasing and, early on, the more or less plaintive hint this phrasing delivers. But the differences are what matters most. The performance is rough around the edges, aesthetically unfinished (Cline, just shy of her twenty-second birthday, was far less experienced than Wells); but on balance, Patsy's performance is considerably more insightful, despite its rough edges—or perhaps on account of them. Her singing suggests someone willing to talk back, refusing to be confined to a dispirited lament. There is both uncertainty and inconsistency in her unpolished performance, qualities that—however inadvertently—lend the result its distinctive energy. Particularly evident in this very early recording is Cline's sense of herself: not precisely confident but clearly unapologetic—and so far as performance style is concerned by no means aping her forbear in this cover. Indeed, when Patsy sang covers, she fearlessly made them her own, including—and maybe even especially—the best established hits.[12] She was in no sense deferential to any "authorized" or "authentic" original.

In *Honky Tonk Merry Go Round* (1955), one of four songs taped during her very first recording session, the honky tonk in Patsy herself comes out proudly: the singer enjoys the life—*and* she's no angel. Her singing is rhythmically punctuated. At times she flings out words, even growling on some of them (her justly famous growl).[13] In *It Wasn't God Who Made Honky Tonk Angels*, she projects not one emotion, as was the case with Wells's original, but several and in quick succession. Like Wells, she laments, but she also vents frustration and even anger. Above all, she is unresigned. Wells's performance borders on prettiness; vocally, it is skilled. But by comparison with Patsy, her performance is predictable to the edge of being dull, and not least on account of its incipient sweetness. Cline's performance, if less obviously "skilled," is musically considerably more imaginative. At times as "pretty" as Wells, Cline's delivery constantly alternates mood, duly expressive of her untenable position within the gender dyad that the narrative describes. Patsy, in brief, is not sitting still for history perpetually to wash over her. Her man, so says the text, has put her on the merry go round of ill repute and she wonders if she'll ever be get off. The text suggests "no"; the voice suggests something else. Avoiding any hint of the strident (the anger of the wronged woman), Patsy's voice projects the sense of her own identity. Two vocal qualities suggest as much; first, the degree to which she plays with the foursquare rhythms of the tune. Simply stated, she is not bound by the beat, but moves to its flow in something approaching her own time. Put differently, unlike the rhythmic lockstep of Kitty's version, Patsy rhythmically implies that she is someone quite able to strike out on her own. Still more, the rather lugubrious tone of Wells's delivery is almost entirely absented. Indeed, it is quite apparent that Patsy is enjoying herself. That is, the very pleasure she takes in singing trumps the cultural rules organized to make her into an angel of whatever sort. In Patsy's world, honky tonks are sites of more than occasions for domestic turmoil; they are a terrain for liberation. She has not forgotten how to have fun on this merry go round.

---

12 For example, her cover of Hank Williams's *Lovesick Blues* (1960), or the extraordinary cover of Bing Crosby's signature hit, *True Love* (1961), in *The Patsy Cline Collection*, CD 2, tracks 13 and 24, respectively.

13 *The Patsy Cline Collection*: Cline's growl is best heard on her earlier recordings like *Honky Tonk Merry Go Round* (1955), CD 1, track 5; the rhythm and blues flavored *Don't Ever Leave Me Again* (1957), CD 1, track 18; *Hungry for Love* (1957), CD 1, track 25; and *Got a Lot of Rhythm in My Soul* (1959), CD 2, track 10.

The difference in vocal delivery between these two artists carried over to the look each adopted. Early on, Wells's costume included a Little-Bo-Peep-like sunbonnet; Patsy would have none of this, remarking on a girlie ("ruffles and crinolines") outfit foisted upon her she looked like a "damn butterfly."[14] Cline's first outfits (her mother was her seamstress) were strictly cowgirl, decorated with long fringe and rhinestones, and completed with boots. This changed, reflecting the profoundly different pop dynamic driving the Nashville Sound. She worked hard, if ultimately unsuccessfully, to hold to the cowgirl look, something her producers and employers long discouraged and sometimes simply rejected out of hand.[15] By the end of her career, she characteristically wore highstyle cocktail and lounge dresses, knee length to floor length, and high heels: not standard country. Whatever the outfit, she wore it tight, accentuating the curves of her body and attracting notice. Indeed, she looked good—sexy good—in anything she wore. And she never looked like the dutiful farm wife projected by the costumes worn by Kitty Wells early in her career.

Hank and Patsy (and Elvis). Kitty Wells, like Hank Williams before her, by the early 1950s was an established icon of country music. It is worthwhile noting the correspondences and, especially, the differences between Hank Williams's songs of failed love and those of Patsy Cline, particularly in some of her early efforts, recorded between 1955 and 1959, coming only a few years after Williams's death on 1 January 1953.[16] The semiotic impact, apparent in many of Hank's songs about failed love, are often overdetermined. Lyrics, tune, and delivery work in tandem to produce an uncharacteristically honest admission of male shortcomings, while accepting blame without excuse. Patsy, as a woman, therefore commonly assigned blame in country music culture, takes a different tack, while still recognizing the realities of both loss and culpability. Her slow-moving *If I Could Only Stay Asleep* (1958) underscores the sense of loss inscribed by a vocal line repeatedly leaping to high notes only to slide back as if in defeat—echoing what is characteristic of so many of Williams's songs about disastrous relationships. In a similar vein, *I'm Blue Again* (1959) registers the vocal "tear"—perfected by Williams—to help mark a text entirely about loss, though this affect acts in tension with the song's upbeat tempo, and to Cline's overall vocal delivery that breathes an air of confidence seriously undercutting the text's projection of defeat. Indeed, time and again in Patsy's work, discrepancies occur between the putative subjects of the lyrics and her delivery of them. Among the reasons she is such an exciting singer is that, like Hank Williams, she stepped over the margins of musical convention, stretching affective possibilities by introducing contradictions and unexpected tensions. Thus the loss of a man may be getting her down, so her words go, but she won't be down for long, so her voice insists. She subscribes to the potential joys of men and women relating to each other but she refuses (not textually but vocally) to be overwhelmed by the absence or failure of the experience. It is very difficult to listen to *I've Loved and Lost Again* (1956) and really believe that the pain will be permanent. She will be up and dancing soon, playing a profoundly (vocally) liberated role of the sort apparent from the vocal gutteral growls that spice her recording of the upbeat *Gotta Lot of*

14 Jones, *Patsy*, p. 103.

15 On her fashion interests, see ibid., p. 256.

16 The songs discussed in this section are from *Patsy Cline: Today, Tomorrow & Forever*, LP (MCA–1463), a 1985 reissue of a disk originally released in 1964.

Rhythm (In My Soul) (1959), which echoes the celebratory affects heard commonly in early rock 'n' roll.

There is concordance between Patsy's performing look and that of both Hank Williams and Elvis Presley. Patsy projected confidence not least by how freely she moved about the stage during performances, freely: like a man, one might say, owning the space. How she looked and moved worked closely in tandem with the emotional force with which she sang, and which was reflected in her physical presence and, indeed, physicality—unfortunately little evident in the archived television performances, where active movement could not be accommodated; in this surviving footage she comes off as less forceful in this respect than was typical.

Whereas Patsy (at about 5'6" and 135 lbs or more) was full figured, and her body tucked into formfitting attire, Hank Williams (at 6', and he seemed taller given the ubiquitous hat he wore to cover his thinning hair about which he was selfconscious, and 140 lbs) by contrast was rail thin—and towards the end of his life haggard, gaunt and essentially wrecked, the opposite to prevailing imagery of male heroics and cultural dominance mirrored by physical appearance. Neither the Superman of contemporaneous comic books, nor the Charles Atlas of comic book advertising, his clothes hung loosely on him; there was little underneath to fill them out. However different, the two "looks" coincided in their effects. Hank's impact on audiences was as electric and sexy as Patsy's. In the words of Minnie Pearl, "He had a real animal magnetism. He destroyed the women in the audience."[17] Knowing well how to use his body,[18] he displayed a sexuality that was exciting precisely because of the contradictions it contained—Minnie Pearl suggests that Williams appealed to women's maternal instincts; others suggest a far more sensual dimension. The apparent contradictions evident in the performance styles as well as the messy personal lives of these singers engender an ambiguity of a simultaneously exciting and culturally provocative sort. At the least, the contradictions constitute a partially masked refusal to adhere to standards of propriety established for a postwar culture of re-domestication, a culture built on self-contradictory and increasingly complex erotic economies of controlled role playing. Patsy and Hank—like Elvis—spoke a language of difference and demand running counter to expectations of decorum and practice.[19]

17 Roger M. Williams, *Sing a Sad Song: The Life of Hank Williams*, 2nd ed. (Urbana: University of Illinois Press, p. 144.

18 Ibid., p. 74, Frank Page: "He was just electrifying on stage. ... He had the people in the palm of his hands from the moment he walked out there." See also George W. Koon, *Hank Williams: A Bio-Bibliography* (Westport, CT: Greenwood Press, 1983), p. 28.

19 Concerning Patsy's love of Elvis, see Jones, *Patsy*, p. 101; and Nassour, *Patsy Cline*, p. 322. For more on gender issues in America in relation to country music, see Rebecca Thomas, "The Cow That's Ugly Has the Sweetest Milk," in *The Women of Country Music: A Reader*, ed. Charles K. Wolfe and James E. Akenson (Lexington: University of Kentucky Press, 2003), pp. 131–47; Oermann, "Honk-Tonk Angels," pp. 314–41; and Andrew C. Hager, *The American Songbook: Women of Country* (New York: Friedman/Fairfax, and Liberty Express, 1998). Regarding Hank Williams, see Richard Leppert and George Lipsitz, "'Everybody's Lonesome for Somebody': Age, the Body and Experience in the Music of Hank Williams," *Popular Music* 9 no. 3 (October 1990), 259–74; regarding Patsy Cline's attraction to Elvis, see Jones, *Patsy*, p. 101; and Nassour, *Patsy Cline*, p. 322. Regarding Elvis, see Sue

Voicing Difference. Patsy liked a good joke, dirty ones especially, and she was good at telling them. By all accounts she had a boisterous laugh.[20] In this regard and in numerous other ways, she easily fit in with musicians of both sexes. She was supportive of other women, and she was entirely comfortable as one of the boys,[21] who—the buddy-ness notwithstanding—have many times remarked on her sexiness. She was plainspoken, and much concerned with daily minutiae—life at home, shopping, decorating—all of which she liked talking about. She had a way with homespun vernacular, the language of rural metaphor (of the sort: "busier than a cow's tail in fly season").[22] The humor and the sexiness alike are evident in two recordings of *Bill Bailey, Won't You Please Come Home* (1961, 1963).[23] The first is an essentially conventional reading, upbeat and fast tempo throughout, and marked by the energized delivery typical of the fast numbers she performed. The second is distinctly different. Here she divides the song into two distinct parts. The first half is transformed into a slow moving torch ballad, sorrowful and pleading for Bill's return. The second half, in sharp contrast, is fast and highly energized, just as one expects for this tune; it is also distinctly sexy, which one does not expect. What Patsy seems to encode after the break is less a plea and more a promise backed by confidence in her allure: "Come back; I'll make it well worth your while." But the delivery is more complex than this suggests to the extent that, despite the apparent confidence, she likewise voices a sexual hunger bordering on desperate frustration.

In the slow first half, she lingers over each word of the song's opening line, the seemingly "important" and unimportant words alike. She alters rhythm slightly so that barely perceptive delays are evident at the start of each beat, while her voice gives a slight crescendo, followed by fast decay, to each note. The result is a slow sexualized pulse that takes control of each word. What matters is less what little the words say and more what drives her to speak them in the first place: unquenched desire. In the second half, Patsy tries a different appeal, pleading and asserting at one and the same time. What she shows Bill Bailey here, while acknowledging again that it is her fault that he's gone, is the sort of energy that likely attracted him to her in the first place.

This performance aptly represents the two sides to Patsy's voicing of gender: a kind of A-side/B-side. But what matters most is the skill with which so many of her performances represent both sides simultaneously: pain, uncertainty, and loss, on the one side, and, on

---

Wiseman, "Sexing Elvis," in *On Record: Rock, Pop, and the Written Word*, ed. Simon Frith (New York: Routledge, 2000), pp. 390–8.

20 Friend Jan Howard: "I loved her laugh. Her laugh came from deep. She had a deep laugh. When she laughed, she really laughed. She didn't just smile or giggle. That giggle was not Patsy. She laughed, and it was a hearty laugh." And Bill Anderson: "I remember Patsy riding in the back seat of my car from Nashville to North Carolina. ... I remember her getting so tickled she would slide off of the seat and into the floorboard of the car. When she laughed, she laughed from the top of her head to the tip of her toes." Quoted in Mansfield, *Remembering Patsy*, pp. 54 and 66, respectively. Buddy Killen: "If you were in a room just loaded with people, you would hear her laughter above the whole thing. She laughed real loud and laughed a lot." Quoted in Jones, *Patsy*, p. 184.

21 Bill Anderson: "She was one of the boys. She was just one of the guys. You didn't have to watch anything you said or did around her, because chances are she said or did it first." Quoted in Mansfield, *Remembering Patsy*, p. 38.

22 Jones, *Patsy*, p. 98.

23 *The Patsy Cline Collection*, CD 3, track 13, and CD 4, track 17, respectively.

the other, confidence, absence of self-pity, and refusal of sentimentality—even, maybe even especially, in the most sentimental of the many ballads she recorded. Even early in her career, when she was so commonly faced with inferior material, she possessed an uncommon ability to articulate the contradictions of late modern life. Patsy Cline had a quite beautiful voice; she made it "do" many things, only some of which came off as conventionally beautiful. But whatever the sound she produced, the grain of her voice was as impressively sensitive to the various demands of her songs as was the consistent intelligence and nuanced musicality evident in her best work.

Lighting the Torch. She was at her best singing torch songs: typically slow to moderate tempo, ballad-like tunes about failed relationships, lost lovers. The sentimentality common to the genre—conducive to saccharine lyrics and melodies alike—was rarely an impediment to her ability to sing something memorable.[24] *I Fall to Pieces* (1960), one of Patsy's most commercially successful songs, is typical. The instrumental ensemble, standard country, is augmented by the Jordanaires gospel quartet. The entire song is sung within a narrow dynamic range, never rising above mezzoforte and most of it falling within gradations of piano. Spanning over an octave and a major third, most melodic movement is stepwise, though the tune dramatically exploits Cline's extraordinary legato on slowly executed octave leaps, of which she was a master. The expressive effects are principally accomplished through extremely skilled phrasing heavily dependent on playing with the beat via nuanced rubatos, all of it without deviating from what seems to be an effortless floating quality, achieved in part by extremely subtle variation in dynamics on single words and notes—slight crescendos, slight decrescendos.[25] None of her delivery forces the words, exactly what is appropriate to a song whose sentiment is so muted. The impact of her performance comes from understatement. The emotional effect projects vulnerability—one contributing factor being Patsy's tendency, here and in many other torch songs, to hum at phrase endings when the lyric permits (on words like "agai*n*," "so*m*eone," "wi*n*," etc.—but without projecting self-pity. The impact of her singing always seems direct; its effect hinges on what seems to be the artlessness of her unquestionably artful delivery. And this is the case whether she is singing torch songs, at one extreme, or honky tonk tunes, delivered fast paced and loud (reflecting the practical necessity of singing above the bar noise), on the other extreme.

Patsy Cline had a special way with lyrics. Harlan Howard, who co-wrote her hit *I Fall to Pieces*, explains: "She understood that certain lines in a song are just there to be sung. They're not emotional lines. Patsy had a knack of being able to hold back on those lines,

---

24 See, for example, *The Patsy Cline Collection*: *Three Cigarettes in an Ashtray* (1957), CD 1, track 22; *I Fall to Pieces* (1960, one of Cline's greatest hits), CD 2, track 20; *Crazy* (1961, another of her major hits), CD 3, track 1; *I Love You So Much It Hurts* (1961), CD 3, track 4; *She's Got You* (1961), CD 3, track 14; *That's My Desire* (1962), CD 3, track 19; *You're Stronger Than Me* (1962), CD 3, track 25; *So Wrong* (1962), CD 3, track 28; *Why Can't He Be You* (1962), CD 4, track 1; *When You Need a Laugh* (1962), CD 4, track 3; *Faded Love* (1963), CD 4, track 10; and *He Called Me Baby* (1963), CD 4, track 18.

25 For other examples demonstrating these techniques with particular effectiveness, see *The Patsy Cline Collection*: *Why Can't He Be You* (1962), CD 4, track 1; and, especially, *Sweeet Dreams (of You)* (1963), CD 4, track, 14.

then when she got to the really juicy part of the song she would give it everything she had."[26] For the opening line of *I Love You So Much It Hurts* (1961),[27] what really matters is less the love and the hurt, and more the intensity driving both. It is the word "so" that receives its due from her. The other words are like passing notes. "So" is lingered over, vocally caressed, variously attacked and swooned upon, hit square, the pitch slid from and then regained, and all the while via an extended rubato. Just that one word defines the song. Everything else she does is ancillary by comparison. Indeed, "so" is the song's last word; she breaks off the final phrase completely after the penultimate note, takes a short breath, and one last time gives out the word and the deep feelings it encapsulates. In the apt insight of Aaron A. Fox, "Subtle shifts in vocal articulation encode knowledge about and intervention in every dimension of 'ordinary' life."[28] Patty Griffin, in sync with this comment, draws attention to the history (personal and beyond) sedimented in the voice: "Since I know a little bit about growing up poor, I think [that Patsy's voice has] an incredible beauty. It's like a really elegant wildflower." Trisha Yearwood links this to her delivery: Patsy's voice ... is very emotional. You hear the breath. It's like she's standing in the room with you, singing. You hear her voice catch, the little lick that she does."[29]

Patsy's singing betrays no break between her low chest voice and her high head voice. The low and middle range is richly colorful, the high range crystalline. But always what matters is how she puts her voice to use, and that varies tremendously between the extremes of the songs she performed and recorded. Thus whatever the similarities between torch songs and her slow moving gospel numbers, differences are notable. In particular, the gospel songs are sometimes sung at extremely slow tempos,[30] which provides Patsy with the opportunity to lavish attention on individual words and phrases, drawing them out with a kind of reverence that gives these performances their notable power. The songs of worship seem to require the need to show by her performance a care for the Lord that is best demonstrated by the employment of her most accomplished musical skills: nothing else will suffice, and particularly on key words ("Jesus," "Thee").

At the other end of life, turning from the spirit and toward the flesh, lies the life-sustaining sexuality that Patsy adeptly projected. Repeatedly, this is the case with the torch songs. Occasionally, and by quite different means and to a different effect, the same is true of upbeat and even rockabilly-flavored tunes, like *Don't Ever Leave Me Again* (1957) recorded at a

26 Nassour, *Patsy Cline*, p. 241.

27 *The Patsy Cline Collection*, CD 3, track 4.

28 Aaron A. Fox, *Real Country: Music and Language in Working-Class Culture* (Durham: Duke University Press, 2004), p. 317. Fox's remark is made with regard to people living in and around Lockhart, Texas, whose lives and musical culture are the subject of his book. He continues, "'Ordinary' categories of self, person, identity, place, space, time, memory, knowledge, gender, and feeling are emergent from the close attention these Texans pay to the speaking/singing voice, and critical elaborations of these categories can be discerned in the smallest details of speaking and singing. The interpenetrated tropes of country songs and beer-joint talk open onto a world of social and individual experience."

29 Mansfield, *Remembering Patsy*, pp. 20, 24, respectively.

30 See, for example, *The Patsy Cline Collection*: *Life's Railway to Heaven* (1959) CD 2, track 11; and *Just a Closer Walk with Thee* (1959), CD 2, track 12, and, in particular, another performance of this song (undated), CD 4, track 22.

public performance.[31] Patsy delivers the tune with an urgency that growls, pleads, half sings/half speaks, and near the end incorporates what can best be described as *Sprechstimme*. Some of it has a Mae West character, lending a tinge of humor alongside the pain described by the lyrics. The beat, and even more the percussive backbeat, is on the edge of burlesque-house pulsing, in a word, almost "dirty." What we hear on balance is a song expressing a degree of acute horniness that *almost* takes itself seriously. The fun of it results from the foot-tapping energy of what is not quite what it claims to be, a lament.

Don't Ever Leave Me Again stands as an apt metaphor for the work of a rare singer who through her voice articulated the late-modern experience that life *is* what it seems: that is, that life is anything but what we are so commonly told it is. Patsy Cline had the courage to state a truth that many people, whether in her own time or in ours, are made to wait too long to hear. Consistently, she gave voice to her own humanity, and to a shared humanity, through sounds that project optimism about life, despite the odds. In sum, the voice of Patsy Cline is defined by the good faith of art that defines, and results from, her use of it, as well as by her self-reflexive awareness of art's necessity: the acute need to *do* it.

31 *The Patsy Cline Collection*, CD 1, track 18.

Part Two

Visuality

CHAPTER 5

The Prodigal Son: Teniers and Ghezzi

The parable of the prodigal son (Luke 15:11-32) first appears as a subject in the visual arts in Byzantine manuscripts from the second half of the eleventh century. In the West representations occur in twelfth-century sculpture, in manuscript illumination and stained glass (Chartres, Bourges, Sens, Poitiers, and Auxerre) in the thirteenth century, and in a number of tapestries dating from the fifteenth and sixteenth centuries.[1] In painting, the prodigal son enjoys particular popularity between 1500 and 1700, especially among — though not confined to — northern artists, after which the number of representations steadily declines.[2] The differences in treatment of this ostensibly common theme in Western art provide an index of class attitudes, artistic styles, religious and cultural tendencies. The subject of this article concerns two paintings of the prodigal son in The Minneapolis Institute of Arts which are significantly untraditional in the manner in which the parable is treated.

From the early days of the Church and throughout the Middle Ages, the parable was the subject of intense exegesis. Its explications, such as those found in late medieval visionary poems of the various *Pélerinages*, typically present it as a cosmically broad and complex allegory, the ultimate meaning revolving around man's redemption through repentance and the mercy of God. Allegorically, for example, the "certain man" St. Luke refers to was said to be God the Father, while his "two sons" were the Jews and the Nations. The inheritance they shared represented man's life on earth governed by free will. The prodigal son—variously understood as Everyman or Adam—squandered his wealth with "riotous living." The proportion of his sin was specified by the resultant "mighty famine in that land," explained as the intense spiritual hunger caused by a life of vice and the consequent separation from God. Filled with repentence he eventually returns to the house of his father, who, seeing him still a long way off, runs to him, "falls on his neck, and kisses him." This gesture was held to represent the forgiveness and compassion of God, ultimately manifested in the birth and passion of Christ, whose resurrection gave hope for eternal happiness—the "fatted calf," which, in the parable, the father orders slaughtered for a feast to celebrate his son's return, was said to signify the crucified Christ.[3]

In paintings, the prodigal son is usually treated in the medieval manner: combining in a single picture the most salient aspects of the story, but showing only one scene in detail and close up—the other incidents usually being placed in the background.[4] However, the complex allegory developed through medieval exegesis—which is visually reflected in a number of tapestries, including the one in Minneapolis—gradually disappears in pictures from the sixteenth century. Instead of representing a complex, indirect statement about Man's fall from grace and his redemption through the Incarnation, these pictures tend to reduce the substance of the parable to a general warning against luxury in the broadest sense and against sexual dissipation in particular. This change is reflected in the fact that perhaps the single most popular part of the story illustrated by northern artists was the prodigal's "riotous living" among the courtesans (the scriptural source is the brief remark made by the elder brother who, reacting negatively to his father's planned celebration for his brother's return, reminds his father that the young man "hath devoured thy living with harlots" [Luke 15:30]). Furthermore, in a number of representations the medieval allegorical impact of the parable is further eroded by the treatment of the dissipation scene among the prostitutes with such inviting gusto and elegance that a viewer might easily miss the subsidiary scenes clarifying the wages of these sins. As the century progresses, many such depictions move very close to the essentially secular. Considered in this light, the subject proves extremely important to the development of northern

---

RICHARD LEPPERT is Assistant Professor of Humanities at the University of Minnesota. He is author of *Musical Instruments and Performing Ensembles in Flemish Paintings of the Seventeenth Century*, 2 vols. (Munich: Katzbichler Verlag, 1976). A musicologist, he is engaged in musico-iconographical research.

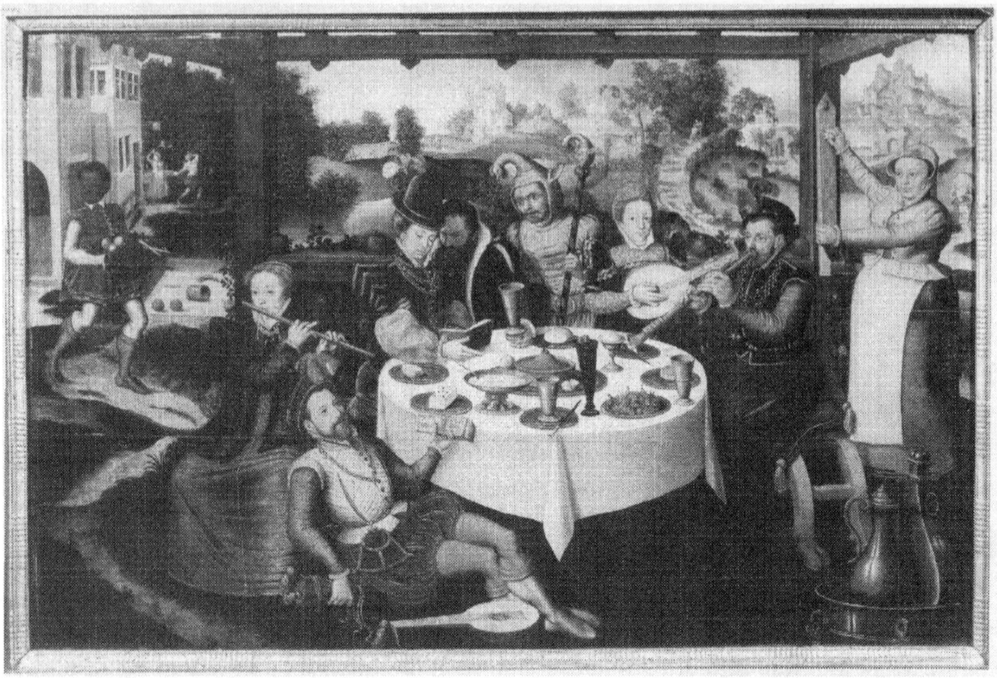

1. Frans Pourbus the Elder, attr.
Flemish, 1545-1581
Prodigal Son among the Courtesans
oil on canvas, 61.5 cm. x 98.2 cm.
Antwerp, Museum Mayer van den Bergh, cat. no. 27
(Photo: Copyright IRPA-KIK, Brussels)

2. Frans Francken the Younger
Flemish, 1581-1642
Prodigal Son among the Courtesans
oil on wood, 67.5 cm. x 110.5 cm.
Karlsruhe, Staatliche Kunsthalle, inv. no. 171
(Photo: Copyright IRPA-KIK, Brussels)

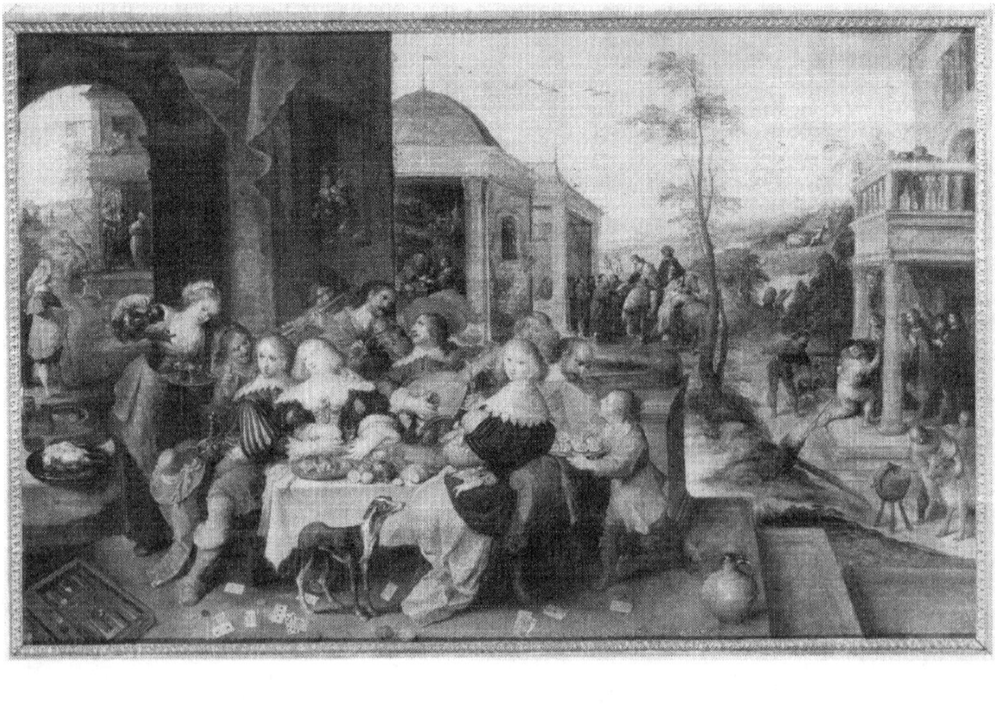

3. David Teniers the Younger
Flemish, 1610-1690
Prodigal Son among the Courtesans
oil type on copper, 22.5" x 30.5"
The William Hood Dunwoody Fund
45.8

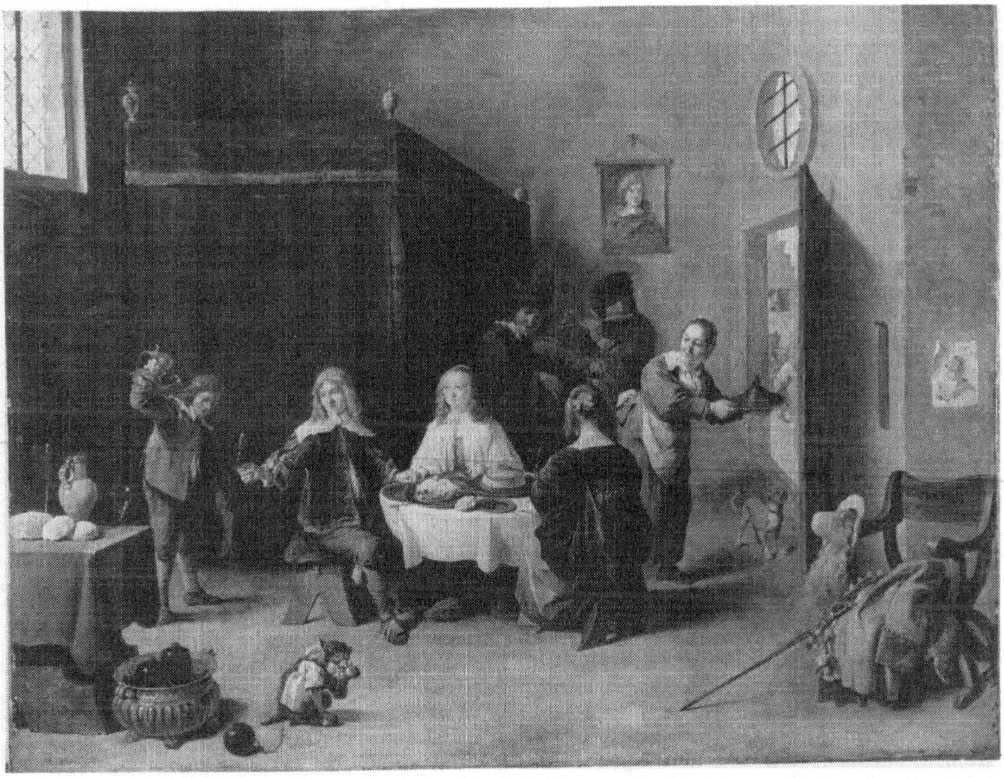

genre painting. The dissipation scene, often portrayed as a contemporaneous banquet, gave artists the chance to depict the "things" surrounding them in everyday life: food, tableware, flowers, costumes, animals, playing cards and parlor games, as well as architecture and landscape. In point of fact, it "was a subject often used by circumspect artists desirous of making genre pictures yet not wanting to be held impious or unmannerly."[5]

The *Prodigal Son Among the Courtesans* attributed to the sixteenth-century Flemish master Frans Pourbus the Elder (1545-1581) is typical (*figure 1*). The story moves in circular fashion, starting on the right where (in a tiny scene above the head of the male musician) the son takes leave of his father, whose rich estate occupies the upper right corner. At the extreme right edge of the picture he appears on his "journey into a far country" (Luke 15:13) where his final decline will occur. That ultimate spiritual debacle occupies the central portion of the panel, where the prodigal wastes his inheritance among the courtesans. In the upper left, penniless and in his underclothes, he is driven off by a harlot wielding a broom. Continuing the circle across the top center, he competes at the trough for "the husks that the swine did eat" (Luke 15:16). Finally, at the upper right, the circle is completed. The prodigal is welcomed back by his father who comes out of his estate to meet him on a bridge, the crossing of which presumably signals his transmission from a life of sin to one of grace. In other words, the basic message of the parable remains intact, if the viewer wants to squint for it. But the moral is not really what has occupied the attentions of the artist. On the contrary, Pourbus has done little more than pay lip service to it in tiny subordinate scenes. Instead, it is the possibilities for genre inherent in the central scene that have received almost all the emphasis.

Joining together with the others around a lavishly spread table,[6] the prodigal makes music as he reads from a partbook held by an elegant courtesan. With one hand he caresses her breast, while with the other he balances a goblet filled to the brim with wine (the innkeeper at the right keeps the tab). A fool stands behind the young man and probably serves a double function: he signals to the viewer the folly of the prodigal's behavior, and at the same time he very likely picks his pocket—the sinner being duly distracted by the woman, the music, and the drink.

Among seventeenth-century painters treating Bible stories as genre was Frans Francken the Younger (1581-1642). In his *Prodigal Son among the Courtesans* (*figure 2*), dated about 1630, the story is told in a manner similar to that of Pourbus, although the composition is so lavish that it possesses a fairytale quality. The *objets* have increased almost geometrically. The primary scene among the harlots is virtually overflowing with food (note the cooked bird stuffed back into its feathers!), tableware, musical instruments, and drapery. A knife rests precariously on the table edge, ready to tumble to the floor which is already littered with spilled playing cards and discarded oyster shells. Francken, apparently wanting an excuse to paint even more little objects, has even chosen to include a subordinate scene in the upper center showing the prodigal in the well-stocked pawn shop of a money lender—there is no scriptural basis for the inclusion of such a scene.

This painting, like the *Prodigal Son* by Pourbus, is entirely typical of the treatment afforded this subject by northern artists during the sixteenth and seventeenth centuries. This leads us to a most interesting picture in the collection of The Minneapolis Institute of Arts, a *Prodigal Son among the Courtesans* (*figure 3*) by the Flemish painter David Teniers the Younger (1610-1690), which deviates significantly from the established norm.

Teniers' setting is highly atypical, if not unique, among Flemish representations of this subject.[7] Here there is none of the lavishness or elegance seen in Pourbus and Francken. Instead of a palace terrace and a background filled with richly decorative architecture, Teniers presents a sparse interior, at best *petit bourgeois*. There is little that is fanciful. Unlike the painting by Francken where the architectural details are a mixture of the renaissance and the imaginary, Teniers gives us a northern setting, clearly hinted at by the view through the open door where the ubiquitous step-gable of a Flemish house is identifiable. Inside, a reckoning board on the wall to the right of the open door signals a public house and that a tab is being kept of the food and drink. On a table to the left are a pitcher, two glasses, and loaves of crusty, round bread. A wine cooler stands below the table. In the center the prodigal holds out his glass to be filled, while two courtesans wait to join him in a cake for dessert. The less-than-appetizing remnants of their chicken dinner remain on the table. A serving woman with a rather knowing look on her coarse face exchanges a word with the harlot with her back to us while, at the rear, two poorly dressed musicians perform for the assemblage. No one seems to be enjoying the proceedings in the least; an atmosphere of boredom pervades. The prodigal, dressed in a somewhat frazzled but formerly elegant costume, is about to lose the last of his possessions. Already having placed his outer garments, including his sword (the last measure of his defense?), on the chair in the right foreground, he is in effect but half-dressed or, if considered in terms of medieval exegesis, in the process of squandering the last measure of the garments of innocence and immortality. Through the open door a little vignette confirms the outcome: left with only his underwear, he is driven off with a shoe by one harlot who has robbed him, while a second empties what is probably a chamber pot on his head from a second story window.[8] It remains unclear whether or not he made use of the discreetly curtained bed looming in the background of the main scene.

A few other pictorial details probably deserve a word of explication, although almost all of the objects in the scene can be understood as pure and simple genre. The dog, for example, an age-old attribute of fidelity, may well be used here in an ironic sense. Standing near the doorway, he seems ready to flee—in the same manner that the "love" enjoyed by the major participants is ephemeral.[9] With a similar comment in mind Teniers has decorated the legs of the dinner table with the heads of dolphins, significantly, an attribute of love,[10] although here, judging from their slightly sagging lower jaws, the passion may well be exhausted. Significantly, one dolphin points toward the prodigal son and the other toward the courtesan whose back is to us, perhaps emphasizing the anonymity and detachment of it all. Finally, dressed as a human, is a little monkey, chained to a ball and eating an apple. Teniers, who painted pictures entirely "peopled" with these little characters, usually in the act of parodying human endeavors, most surely intended by the animal's presence an oblique—although not very subtle—comment on the proceedings. The monkey is an ancient symbol of luxury and vanity. Often depicted with a mirror in hand and fascinated by what he sees, he becomes a slave of his senses, losing himself in self-love. That he is a slave, that is, bound, is emphasized by Teniers in his use of a ball and chain. What he is slave to is made clear by the apple, an attribute of Venus and of love, which he unenthusiastically eats.[11] What we have, then, is the prodigal son as a slave to the vanity of venal love.

The last subject to be discussed in terms of the visual content of Teniers' painting is music. Iconographically speaking, it is in several respects the most interesting thing about the picture. The two musicians furnishing entertainment with a flute and violin without doubt represent poor itinerants, such as typically traversed the countryside in Teniers' own time, moving from village to village and quite literally playing for their dinners. They were among the few really fulltime and "professional" musicians of the period, aside from those retained by the Court (who themselves were considered no more than servants), and they were roundly and universally despised. Two points of particular significance can be made here: the first explicating the symbolism of the instruments; the second explaining why Teniers chose lower-class musicians for this scene—aside from the obvious fact that they "fit" the rather tawdry setting.

The symbolism attached to the flute was direct. Wind instruments in general, at least since the Greeks, have been associated with sex, whether on the basis of their shape (phallic), their sound (the arousing Dionysian winds, as opposed to the soothing Apollonian strings), or both.[12] That the sexual connotation of these instruments was not lost on the seventeenth century is clear from the fact that rarely — even in straightforward, more or less documentary genre scenes—does one find any kind of wind instrument in the hands of a woman. It was considered undignified for a lady to use them. Thus, in the painting by Frans Pourbus, where the woman on the left is shown not only holding but actually playing a flute (although he has mistakenly made her hold it backwards), the licentious significance was immediately made clear to his viewers, however innocent it may appear to us. The sexual symbolism of the shawm played by the male on the right in the same picture is even more obvious. The phallic shape of the instrument itself, together with the puffed-out cheeks of the male playing it, describes rather graphically the male genitalia. In this respect, it is noteworthy that one of the first northern artists to depict the prodigal son among the courtesans, Johannes De Hemessen (c. 1500-after 1563),[13] included a mouth-blown bagpipe which, with its chanter pipe and large wind sack, explicitly alludes to the male sex organs. (Both the shawm and the bagpipe are double-reed instruments—the shawm is the forerunner of the modern oboe—and thus are related to the Dionysian *auloi* of ancient Greece.)

Francken, a painter who influenced Teniers, in another representation of this subject[14] includes a man playing a pipe and tabor. In one hand he fingers the one-hand flute, while with the other he beats a small drum suspended from his waist. The little pipe carries the sexual allusion, but the combination of the two emphasizes the vanity of the whole undertaking by visually representing a popular Flemish proverb: "*Met het trommeltje gewonnen, met het fluitje verteerd*" ("What is gained with the drum is lost with the flute"). Finally, the lutes included by both Pourbus and Francken allude to sex by the nature of their shape—their vaulted backs replicate the bulge of the womb—as well as to a popular proverb of the time which stated that the beautiful sound of the lute helped one gain favors. The presence of these instruments in such settings is not merely symbolic; it has a basis in fact. Music provided an atmosphere conducive for the preliminaries to prostitution. Gosson in his *Schoole of Abuse* (1579) points out that harlots, gathering in taverns where they were welcomed because they brought in customers, "placed beside them a musical instrument in order to pretend that men who frequented the house came 'like children, to be taught.'"[15]

What remains to be considered is Teniers' use of lower-class professional musicians in this scene, something of an iconographical anomaly. Biographical data helps explain his choice. Born at Antwerp in 1610, Teniers became a member of the painters' Guild of St. Luke at age twenty-two; he later became its dean. Consciously upwardly mobile, he had the good fortune to marry the

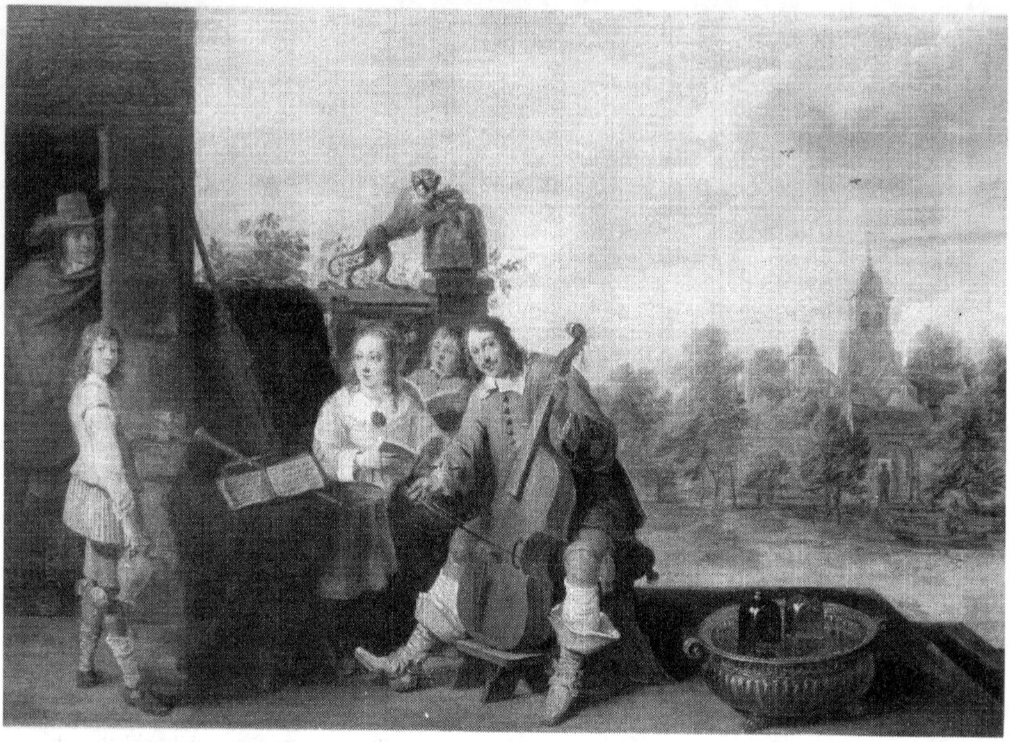

4. David Teniers the Younger
Flemish, 1610-1690
Portrait of the Painter and His Family in a Park
oil on wood, 38 cm. x 58 cm.
Formerly Berlin, Staatliche Museen, cat. no. 857
(Photo: Copyright IRPA-KIK, Brussels)

daughter of painter Jan Breughel the Elder, who, since the death of her father in 1625, had been the ward of the great Rubens. Teniers made it a point throughout his career to align himself with men of wealth and position, and this association with Rubens, who witnessed his marriage and took him into his circle, significantly advanced him in this objective. In 1651 Teniers moved to Brussels where he accepted an appointment from the Court to serve as its painter, as well as the keeper of and purchasing agent for Archduke Leopold William's extensive art collection. His success at Court and as a painter to a wealthy audience was so great that he was able to achieve a long-term goal by acquiring a country estate and becoming a landed gentleman.[16]

It has been called surprising that Teniers, being something of a social climber, "should have applied himself to scenes of low life in view of his ambitions."[17] In point of fact, it is not surprising at all. Teniers understood that his upperclass patrons sought in art an idealized representation of their own way of life—or, equally pleasant, art which reproduced in amusing manner the spectacle of the little people. His genre pictures of low life, in other words, were consciously designed for the diversion of *l'homme de goût*. They were realistic but not shocking. Essentially decorative and recreative, these pictures supplied reassurance of social status, for in their visual anecdote they reaffirmed class distinctions, with the viewer-patron on the top looking down. The audience for this sort of representation was enormous, so much so that a whole export trade developed in Flanders during the period. (The demand for Teniers' own pictures was so great that he employed numerous assistants, which may account for the decline in quality of his late works.) Among the genre artists in Flanders interested in low life scenes, Adriaen Brouwer (1605-1638), who for a brief time may have served as Teniers' teacher, stands practically alone in bluntly representing the lot of the common man. While in Brouwer there is sympathy, in Teniers and a host of painters like him there is satire. Not surprisingly, Teniers was the more successful of the two.[18] Thus, while the musicians —like the rest of the characters populating the prodigal son painting—have the look of dishevelment and bad times about them, they are painted in a way that inspires the viewer to smile more than to frown in contemplation of their condition.

In addition to the fact that amusingly painted lower-class types generally pleased his audience, one other factor in particular helps explain Teniers' musical choices in the painting. Like many of the bourgeoisie and nobility for whom he painted, Teniers was an amateur musician, which is not surprising in light of the fact that to be considered a gentleman it was virtually *de rigueur* that one play an instrument. Music was so much a part of the daily activity of the wealthy that, if they could afford it, they set aside a room in their houses expressly for this purpose. Gonzales Coques (1618-1684) and other painters who specialized in society portraits, often show well-placed families with their collections of instruments (or stage-prop instruments in cases where the sitters were not actually musicians but, understanding the convention, wanted posterity to think they were!). Unlike the lower-class "professional" musicians in Teniers' painting who—distastefully—made their living by music, the upperclass amateurs enjoyed it as recreation. Well-to-do amateurs found professional musicians so disconcerting, as well as vulgar, that they even disdained their instruments. The most significant example of this discrimination is the violin, such as that played by the poor itinerant in Teniers' painting. Because this instrument was associated with the lower classes, the nobility and upper bourgeoisie would have no part of it. Instead, they preferred the viols. The undeserved bad reputation of the violin persisted in this musically conservative region until near the end of the seventeenth century. Even in the eighteenth century, visual documentation exists to suggest that the old prejudices died very slowly.[19]

Secular music for some time had been considered by the churches a waste of time, a vanity, and an occasion of sin. Amateur musicians, enjoying secular music in their homes—public concerts were virtually unknown at the time—clearly resented this unsavory association attached to one of their chief modes of recreation. In view of this it is interesting that a very popular theme in Flemish art between about 1550 and 1650 was that of concerts of the muses with Apollo, all of whom play precisely those instruments commonly used by musical amateurs of the time. Both Apollo and the host of muses were chaste in reputation and thus offered the musical amateurs who commissioned these paintings comforting reassurance that their music-making was imitative of the activities of gods.[20] Prodigal son paintings such as those by Pourbus and Francken, on the other hand, were clearly distasteful to them, since these pictures seemed to suggest that the instruments they themselves played were instruments of the devil.

Teniers, understanding the musical tastes of his patrons and being a musician himself, very likely shared their attitudes about secular music. He also understood the social prestige of owning instruments—their very possession denoted both wealth and taste. Not leaving such things to chance, he painted at least two portraits of his family at music, including himself in one (*figure 4*).[21] Placed in a rather elegant outdoor setting, Teniers holds a violoncello, telling his viewers that he actually *plays* as well as possesses the instrument (in his other family portrait the same instrument rests unused against a table). The other instruments in the scene are a *tromba marina*, leaning against the wall at the back, and what is probably an *oboè d'amore* resting on the table. His wife and child sing from open partbooks.

Thus, by painting poor *musiciens ambulants* in his prodigal son picture, Teniers avoided offending his clientele by visually reminding them of the immoral significance of secular art music. Instead, the viewer sees only two rather downtrodden, comical characters whose music, as they themselves were, was generally dismissed without regard. Hence, if *they* are used to represent immorality no one is the worse for it. The *Prodigal Son among the Courtesans* by David Teniers the Younger is both genre and allegory, but it is also a compromise executed with a healthy respect for the interests of his patrons and, quite likely, with some degree of regard for his own rather well-developed musical sensibilities as well.

Before leaving the subject of the prodigal son, a few words should be said about another, considerably later treatment of the subject in a painting recently acquired by The Minneapolis Institute of Arts. The work in question is the *Return of the Prodigal Son* (*figure 5*) by the Italian artist Pier Leone Ghezzi (1674-1755).[22] Ghezzi shares a number of biographical details with Teniers. Like his Flemish predecessor, he had an important patron (the pope); he was a picture restorer and an art dealer; he moved with a socially important crowd, and—not surprisingly for someone in his position—he was a devoted musical amateur, even to the point of maintaining a weekly musical academy in his house. He had a penchant for humor and satire, most obvious in the caricatures for which he is particularly renowned. Finally, like Teniers, when saddled with biblical projects he was inclined to treat them as excuses to paint genre.

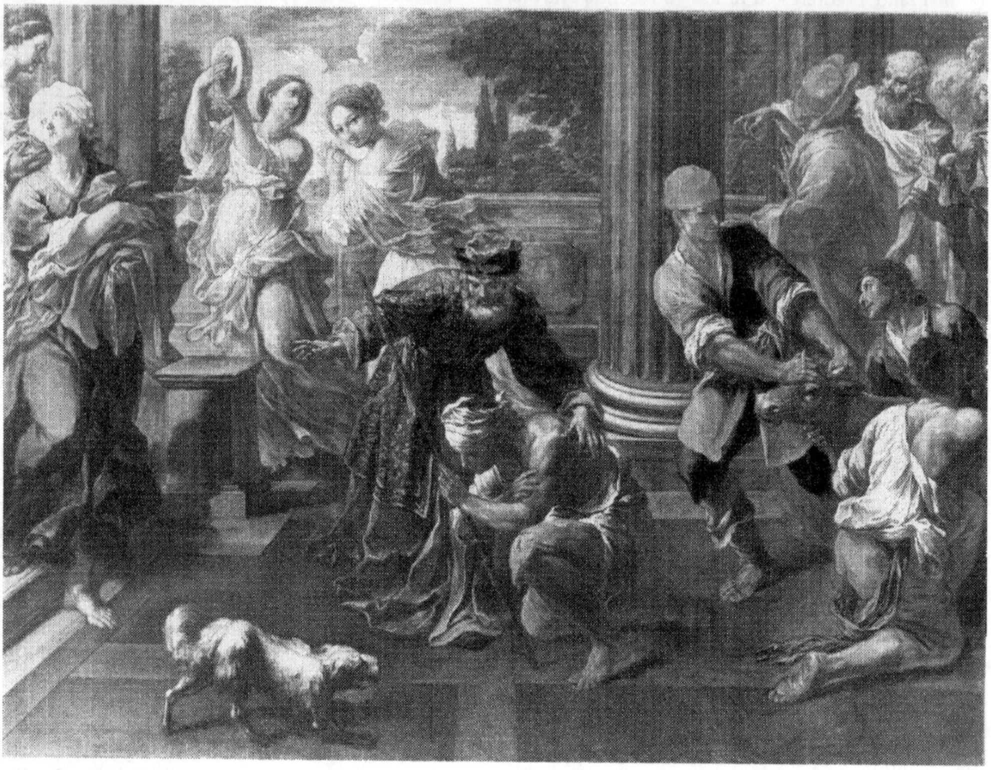

5. Pier Leone Ghezzi
Italian, 1674-1755
Return of the Prodigal Son
oil on canvas, 38.75" x 52.87"
The Putnam Dana McMillan Fund
71.23

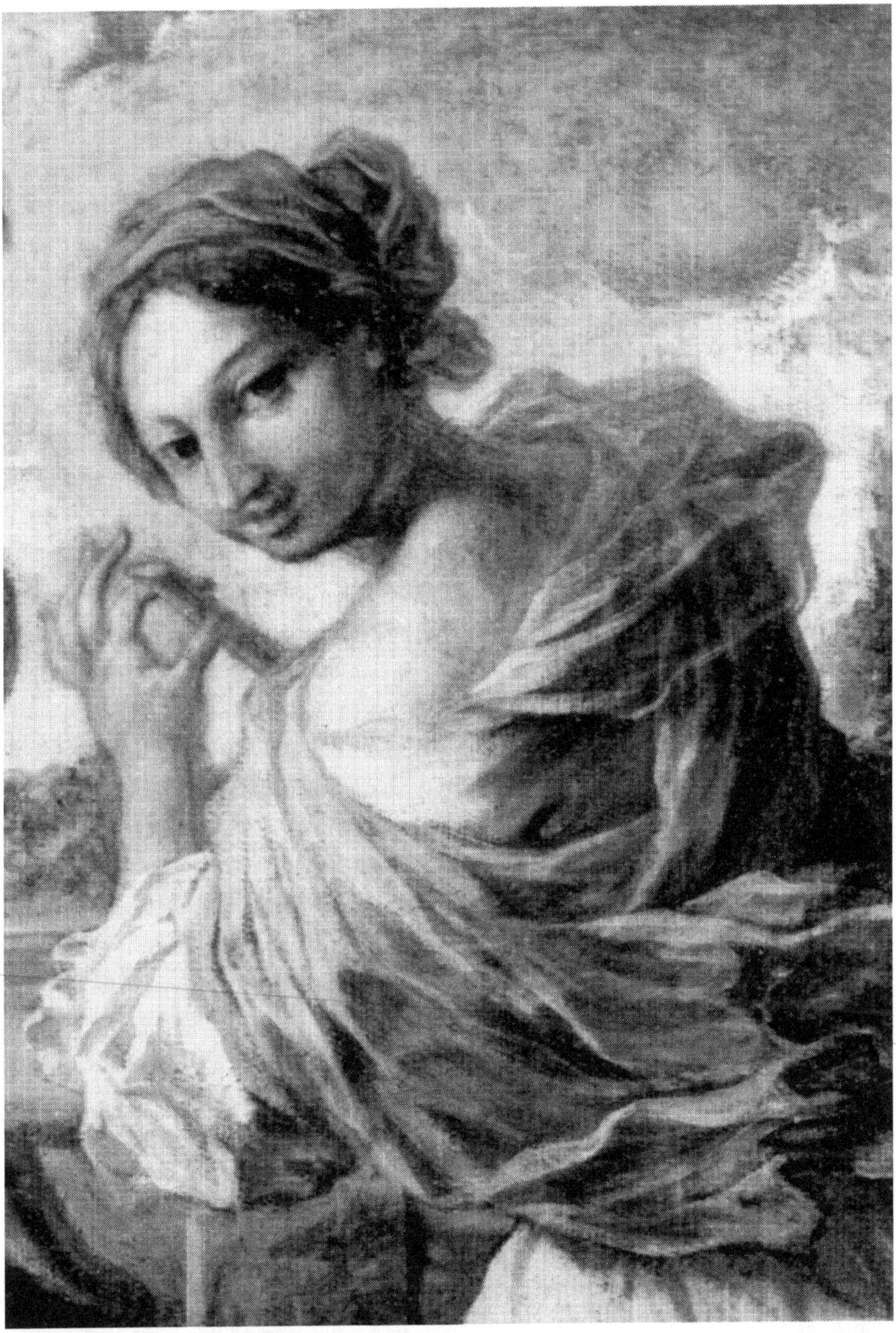

6. Detail: female musician with recorder

His *Return of the Prodigal Son* is set in an Italianate landscape with appropriate references to classical architecture. In the foreground the father welcomes home his ragged son. To the right a servant tugs at a reluctant yearling soon to be sacrificed for the feast of celebration. A woman coming down the stairs on the left brings a set of fresh and elegant clothes for the returnee. In the foreground the faithful family dog crouches and seemingly snarls, not recognizing the prodigal. As Anthony Clark points out, the drama of the subject "is poised in a very Italian way: it does not occur in the profound psychological subject (which is shown in an almost frivolous manner) but in its relieving natural aftermath, in the glowing celebration of the event."[23] This celebrative mood is reflected in the attitude of the two female musicians standing left of center at the rear, but their significance involves more than that of minor characters filling a spatial void in a rather dressy genre scene. On the contrary, evidence suggests Ghezzi may have employed them as vehicles for his wry sense of humor, perhaps dressing up a scene and subject that he might otherwise have found tiring (Clark points out that Ghezzi "was not a devoutly involved painter: he could out-think his painting hand consequently it somewhat bored him to paint").[24]

It seems to me that his choice of instruments was not arbitrary. The woman on the left holds a tambourine, an instrument frequently shown in the hands of bacchantes, as in numerous paintings by Rubens. The instrument is, in fact, an attribute of sensual pleasure, as opposed to virtue.[25] The profane sense of Ghezzi's intentions, however, is best clarified and strengthened by an examination of the second woman,who holds in her hand a small recorder (*figure 6*). Compared with the flute, the sexual significance of this instrument is if anything even more explicit; unlike the transverse flute which is played by holding it perpendicular to the mouth in order to blow across the air hole, the recorder is placed directly into the mouth. The manner in which the woman holds the instrument betrays an obvious sexual allusion: she does not play it but rather holds it *delicately* between her thumb and first finger in a way that has nothing to do with the way the instrument is held for producing sound (neither her thumb nor finger covers any holes). It is safe to conclude that Ghezzi, being a musician, produced this anomaly on purpose. His intention is confirmed by the woman's face. While holding the instrument/phallus sensually between thumb and finger and *with her back to us*—as if her action required privacy—she turns her head, looks over her shoulder and, with an eager, wide-eyed stare, focuses on the prodigal. Ghezzi has given us a little vignette, a caricature of human nature, which recalls the dissipations of the prodigal and, it might be said, the artist's own interpretation of the longevity of the sinner's return to grace.

NOTES:

1. See "Late Gothic Tapestry Acquired for Institute," *Minneapolis Institute of Arts Bulletin*, 27, no. 6 (1938), pp. 26-30.
2. See *Ikonographie der christlichen Kunst*, ed. Karl Künstle (Freiburg: Herder, 1928), vol. 1, pp. 400-401), *Lexikon der christlichen Kunst*, ed. Engelbert Kirschbaum (Freiburg: Herder, 1968), vol. 4, cols. 172-174; Louis Réau, *Iconographie de l'art chrétien* (Paris: Pressus universitaires de France, 1957), vol. 2, part 2, pp. 333-338; A Pigler, *Barockthemen* (Budapest: Ungarische Akademie der Wissenschaften, 1956), vol. 1, pp. 360-364.
3. See further Philippe Verdier, "The Tapestry of the Prodigal Son," *Journal of the Walters Art Gallery*, 18 (1955), pp. 20, 24-25. The major studies of the prodigal son theme in art are those by Kurt Kallensee, *Die Liebe des Vaters: das Gleichnis vom verlornenen Sohn in der christlichen Dichtung und bildenden Kunst* (Berlin: Evangelische Verlagsanstalt, 1960); Ewald Vetter, *Der verlorene Sohn*, Lukas-Bücherei zur christlichen Ikonographie, no. 7 (Düsseldorf: L. Schwann, 1955); and W. Witwitzky, "Das Gleichnis vom verlorenen Sohn in der bildenden Kunst bis Rembrandt," Diss. Heidelberg, 1930.
4. Occasionally artists have produced cycles of prodigal son paintings, each picture being devoted to a separate scene. Perhaps the most famous is that by Murillo in the Prado in which the parable is divided into six pictures.
5. Gordon Washburn et. al., "Genre and Secular Subjects," *Encyclopedia of World Art* (New York: McGraw-Hill, 1962), col. 89.
6. Most of the objects on the table and about the room, while representative of northern artists' affection for everyday things, are not chosen completely arbitrarily. They symbolize various vanities. See Guy de Tervarent, *Attributs et symboles dans l'art profane: 1450-1600*, Travaux d'humanisme et renaissance, no. 29, 2 vols. plus supplement (Geneva: Librairie E. Droz, 1958-1964).
7. Teniers himself produced at least two others. A picture now in the Louvre (reproduced in the study by Édouard Michel, *La peinture du Musée du Louvre: École flamande* [Paris, 1929], pp. 102-103) duplicates the Minneapolis work in its essentials, except that the setting has been moved to the street and the main characters increased from seven to ten. The rather tawdry nature of the scene is, if anything, more emphatically expressed than in the Minneapolis

picture: it includes a clearly-visible prodigal kneeling before hogs at their trough. On the other hand, in a picture reproduced by Adolf Rosenberg, *Teniers der Jüngere*, Künstler Monographien, no. 8 (Bielefeld: Verlag von Velhagen & Klassing, 1901), pl. 2, Teniers uses a setting rather more in keeping with the main stream of elegant prodigal son representations.

It has been suggested ("The Prodigal Son by Teniers the Younger," *Minneapolis Institute of Arts Bulletin*, 34, no. 9 [1945],p. 30) that the Minneapolis and Louvre pictures, together with one in the Dulwich Gallery, may have been intended as part of a series. I find this extremely unlikely, since the Minneapolis and Louvre pictures both represent the same theme—the prodigal among the courtesans. Furthermore, the Dulwich Gallery painting depicts the prodigal eating with the swine, a theme which, as I have just noted, is already present in the Louvre picture.

8. In the *Bulletin* article referred to in n. 10, this vignette is incorrectly described as "an irate woman . . . clouting a boy thief while a man flings water on him from a window above." John Smith, in his monumental *Catalogue Raisonné of the Works of the Most Eminent Dutch, Flemish, and French Painters* (London, 1829-1842), vol. 3, p. 307, does worse. He describes the exterior vignette as taking place in an "adjoining room" (!) where "are seen two persons quarrelling, and a third throwing water on them." Neither of these accounts has anything to do with prodigal son iconography. (The water-throwing motive is also used by Pourbus and Francken in the upper left in each.)
9. In the painting by Francken the ironic sense is on surer ground, since the dog—rather ill-fed and downtrodden—peers up at a courtesan who pays him not the slightest heed. Not surprisingly, the dog is male. Cf. Tervarent, *op. cit.*, vol. 1, cols. 93-96, on the meaning of dogs as attributes.
10. The source is Ovid. See Tervarent, *op. cit.*, vol. 1, cols. 143-144.
11. Tervarent, *op. cit.*, vol. 2, cols. 311-313, 352-355. The association of apples with Venus and love comes from the story of the judgment of Paris, who awarded the apple inscribed "For the fairest" to Venus, after she offered him the fairest woman in the world as his wife for choosing her over Juno and Minerva. Verdier, *op. cit.*, pp. 19 and 29, points out that the apple in Renaissance iconography could be used in an overtly sexual sense. In a tapestry in the Walters Art Gallery, "Eve holds the apple after the Fall in such a way that it exactly takes the place of her left breast." On a more abstract level, the apple alluded to the fruits of the Tree of Knowledge and connoted spiritual hunger.

There can be little doubt that Teniers was cognizant of the symbolic potential of objects and animals, judging from his numerous depictions of the temptation of St. Anthony, an iconographically rich and often surrealistically treated subject, previously popular with Bosch. In a similar vein, Teniers even painted a few *vanitas* pictures, a genre much more popular in Calvinistic Holland than in Catholic Flanders, in which, typically, ordinary everyday objects are gathered together in carefully arranged compositions of considerable iconographical complexity. The themes revolve around the transience of life and the ultimate uselessness of worldly pursuits, pleasures, and possessions.
12. See further on this point Emanuel Winternitz, "The Knowledge of Musical Instruments as an Aid to the Art Historian," *Musical Instruments and Their Symbolism in Western Art* (London: Faber, 1967), p. 48.
13. Brussels, Musées royaux des Beaux-Arts, inv. no. 2838. Dated 1536.
14. Oil on wood, 62 cm. x 86 cm. Paris, Musée du Louvre. Dated 1633. The painting represents the entire cycle of the parable in nine separate compartmentalized scenes.
15. François Lesure, *Music and Art in Society*, trans. Denis and Sheila Stevens (University Park: Pennsylvania Univ. Press, 1968), pp. 30-31.
16. On the life of Teniers, see the articles in Thieme-Becker, the *Niederländisches Künstler-Lexikon*, and the *Encyclopedia of World Art*.
17. "The Prodigal Son by Teniers the Younger," *Minneapolis Institute of Arts Bulletin*, 34, no. 9 (1945), p. 33.
18. See further F. C. Legrand, *Les peintres flamands de genre su XVIIIe siècle, Les peintres flamands du XVIIe siècle*, no. 8 (Brussels: Éditions Meddens, 1963), pp. 15-16, 128, 240; W. R. Valentiner, "Teniers and Brouwer," *Art Quarterly*, 12. no. 1 (1949), pp. 90-91, clarifies the difference between the two artists in a comparison between Teniers' *The King Drinks* in the Los Angeles County Museum and Brouwer's *The Smoker* in the Metropolitan Museum. Teniers borrows a number of details from Brouwer's work—some literally, some with changes. One of the more significant and telling of the alterations occurs in his use of a grotesque figure who, in Brouwer's painting, blows smoke out of one of his nostrils. Teniers makes him "into a more mannerly fellow, holding his pipe, in a 'refinement' characteristic of the artist who sought to tone down Brouwer's more extreme interpretation.... Teniers, in simplifying the composition and omitting some of the bold, forceful and boisterous qualities of the original, has left a painting of more appeal to those unaccustomed to life at a hectic pace in smoke-filled taverns, and who prefer a version of realism that is conceived at a lower pitch of intensity."
19. See further on this point A[lbert] P[omme] de Mirimonde, "Les sujets de musique dans la peinture Belge du XVIIIe siècle," *Jaarboek van het Koninklijk Museum voor Schone Kunsten* (Antwerp: n.p.,1967), pp. 199-274.
20. See Mirimonde, "Les concerts des muses chez les maitres du nord," *Gazette des Beaux-Arts*, Ser. 6, 63 (1964), pp. 130-132.
21. Oil on wood, 38 cm. x 58 cm. Formerly Berlin, Staatliche Museen, cat. no. 857. The other portrait, depicting his wife and son (oil on wood, 32 cm. x 42 cm.), is in Turin, Galleria Sabauda.
22. Oil on canvas, 38.75 x 52.87 in. The Putnam Dana McMillan Fund, 71.23. Anthony M. Clark, "Three Ghezzis," *Minneapolis Institute of Arts Bulletin*, 60 (1971-1973), p. 65, dates the work to the 1720s.
23. Clark, *op. cit.*, p. 65.
24. "Pierleone Ghezzi's Portraits," *Paragone*, 165 (1963), p. 13.
25. See Tervarent, *op. cit.*, vol. 2, col. 369.

CHAPTER 6

Concert in a house

Musical iconography and musical thought

Probably no types of art are of more interest to those concerned with instruments and performance practice than portraiture and naturalistic genre pieces appearing to mirror everyday activity. Both are often judged trustworthy in their musical content on the assumption that the portraits are of *real* people and the figures in genre works are at least characteristic types. Presumably, the activities portrayed are those people actually engaged in, or at least those they considered respectable. Although musical instruments in a portrait may only function as studio props, their very presence is taken to reflect preferences of musical taste, if not necessarily musical skills of the sitters themselves.

We can be fairly confident about the respectability of instruments in portraits for the reason that no sitter would want to be captured on canvas holding an unfashionable or disparaged instrument, any more than he would want to be preserved in other than his best attire. Sitters choose a milieu which signals success, wealth and refinement. Thus we recognize that even the interiors may well have been created for the occasion by the artist to give the required 'tone', sometimes made especially obvious by lavish drapery invading the architectural background. Yet tampering with reality at this level does not seriously affect the validity of the content for the musicologist. The potential insight to be gained from portraits and genre works need not be confined to organology and performance practice unless we look only for the most tangible evidence of musical activity. Additional content revolves around what can be called musical thought, expressed indirectly in the use of visual metaphor and analogy—through symbols. The study of musical thought is fundamentally, though not exclusively, the study of the perceived role or function of music in a given culture. It is the observation of music as a human and social activity, the examination of attitudes towards it.

None more perfectly typify the apparent realism of portrait and genre pictures than the works of the Flemish and Dutch masters of the 17th century. I have chosen a work often attributed to the Antwerp portrait painter Gonzales Coques (1618-84) representing a *Concert in a house* (illus. 1) precisely because it seems that what is recorded can be taken at face value. Yet, however convincing this portrait-like picture may be, a good deal more emerges than immediately meets the eye.[1] I hope to show that the painting's trustworthiness as a window on contemporary performance practice is highly questionable: this one work will thereby serve to emphasize the need for a cautionary approach to musico-iconographical research.

There are eight musicians present; an unusually large ensemble for *Hausmusik* in 17th-century Flanders. Four of the eight are singing (one woman, two men, and a child). The instruments (left to right) include virginal, violino piccolo (with its characteristically scalloped outline), theorbo-lute, and bass viol. The performers on the latter two read from partbooks, which suggests that they are doubling or substituting vocal lines. On the other hand, the violino piccolo player has no music, so we might assume that his part involves some improvisation rather than doubling. Curiously enough, the same holds true for the virginalist.

Clearly, there is no reason why the virginalist absolutely *must* have music, but there is a reason in this case why she should not. A sheaf of music would obliterate at least part of the inscription decorating the lid of her

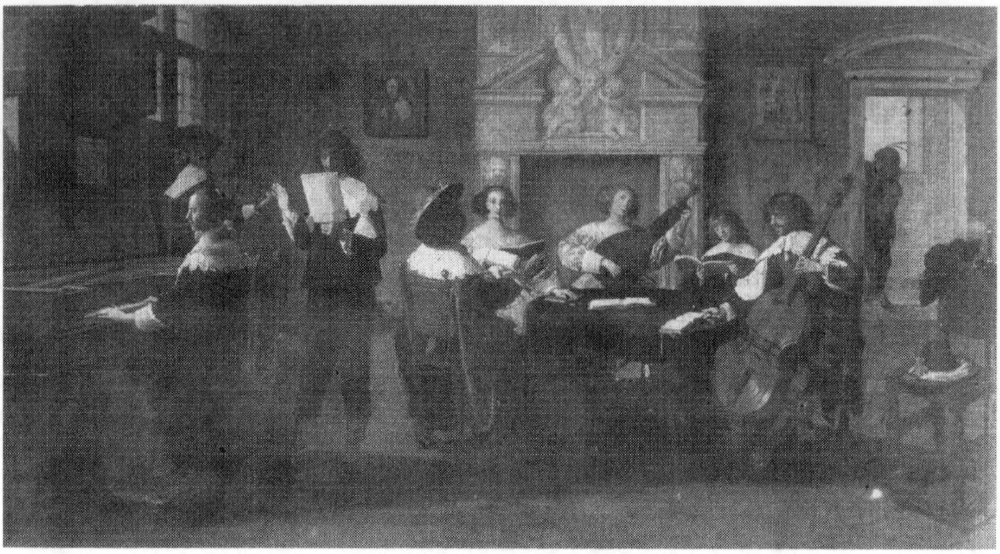

1. Concert in a house, *Franco-Flemish School (17th century), formerly in the Janssen Collection, Brussels*

instrument, an inscription which gives the first sign that more is intended here than the mere recording of a musical event. The Latin motto, typical of those appearing on Ruckers instruments made at Antwerp,[2] reads 'Musica letitiae comes medicina dolorum' [Music is the companion of joy, the healer of sadness]. Here the artist's concern with expressing an attitude towards music takes precedence over the realities of performance practice. The suggestion that leaving the inscription visible is not accidental, is strongly reinforced by several decorative details on the back wall of the room: specifically the stone fireplace, with its relief carvings on the over-mantel, and the two paintings flanking it (illus. 2). None of these is innocent decoration to fill an otherwise empty space; at least two represent specific, identifiable subjects, which seem so distinctly unsuitable for the ornamentation of a bourgeois interior that they must have been placed there for some other reason. In fact, they function only as symbolic, veiled commentaries on the main scene itself and, since this is musical, we can surmise that they purposefully provide amplification of the musical events.

The painting at the far right (next to the open door) unquestionably represents the sacrifice of Isaac, familiar through Genesis 22:1-19. The intervening angel stays Abraham's hand the instant before he would have killed his son. The painting at the left, seemingly less specific in subject, shows a young man with Flemish features, serious and pensive looking. One cannot be certain whom he represents, if in fact anyone particular is intended. The picture-within-the-picture is so small that tell-tale details are difficult to discern, but there can be little doubt that the character is biblical. A cloak covers part of his torso but his left shoulder is bare, a common pictorial means of alluding to such characters. Furthermore, he holds a chalice to his lips, as if about to drink. The chalice signified acceptance of the Lord through the Eucharist and even in the *Old Testament* a similar meaning applied: 'I will take the cup of salvation, and call upon the name of the Lord' (Psalm 116:13).[3]

4

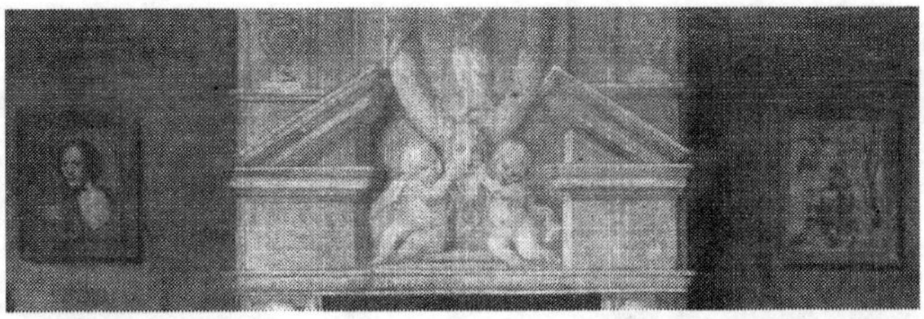

2. *Detail of illus. 1*

How do these two pictures function? Their purpose, I believe, is to associate the musicians in the concert scene with godliness. Through the religious art on the walls we recognize them as believers, and, by analogy, we associate their music making with that which is either pleasing to God, or at least upstanding. The two pictures reinforce the inscription on the virginal claiming secular music a positive force for good.

In the story of Isaac's sacrifice, the angel tells Abraham as he stays the old man's hand, 'Now I know that thou fearest God' (Genesis 22:12), a phrase which provides a *clavis interpretandi* to the painting as a whole; a painting of a concert yet also a lightly veiled defence of secular music-making. The question of why it would be necessary to draw such a connection between music and morality is not difficult to answer. The belief that performances of secular music might be uplifting was by no means universally held in the Low Countries in the 16th and 17th centuries. Opinions differed on whether such activity served God or the devil: a considerable amount of literature and art claimed the latter.

Suspicious attitudes towards music's relationship with morality were not, of course, new. Plato's warnings in *The Republic* and the Church's position from its inception attest to this. But in the 16th and 17th centuries these entrenched attitudes were once more disturbed by the voices of both the Reformation and the Counter-Reformation. The recommendations of the Council of Trent (1545-63) were concerned in part with ridding the liturgy of 'lascivious or impure' music,[4] a distinct reference to certain secular genres. On the Protestant side, the Calvinists in particular looked suspiciously on secular music, even though secular tunes found their way into their psalters, and even though Zwingli, Calvin's religious forebear, was himself an amateur musician. (On the other hand, Zwingli also took to hacking organs to pieces.)

Calvin's scruples about secular music are specified with considerable directness in the famous preface to the *Geneva Psalter* of 1543. He draws a clear distinction between what he calls 'the music one makes to entertain men at table and in their homes, and the psalms which are sung in the Church in the presence of God and His angels'. 'God knows', he says, 'how much we are inclined to delight in vanity. Just as our nature, then, draws us and induces us to seek all means of foolish and vicious rejoicing, so, to the contrary, our Lord, to distract us and withdraw us from the enticements of the flesh and the world, presents to us all possible means in order to occupy us in that spiritual joy which He so much recommends to us.' In the 1545 edition, Calvin amplifies these thoughts: 'Music should not be the occasion of our giving free rein to dissoluteness or of our making ourselves effeminate with disordered pleasures and ... it should not become the instrument of lasciviousness or of any shamelessness.'[5]

5

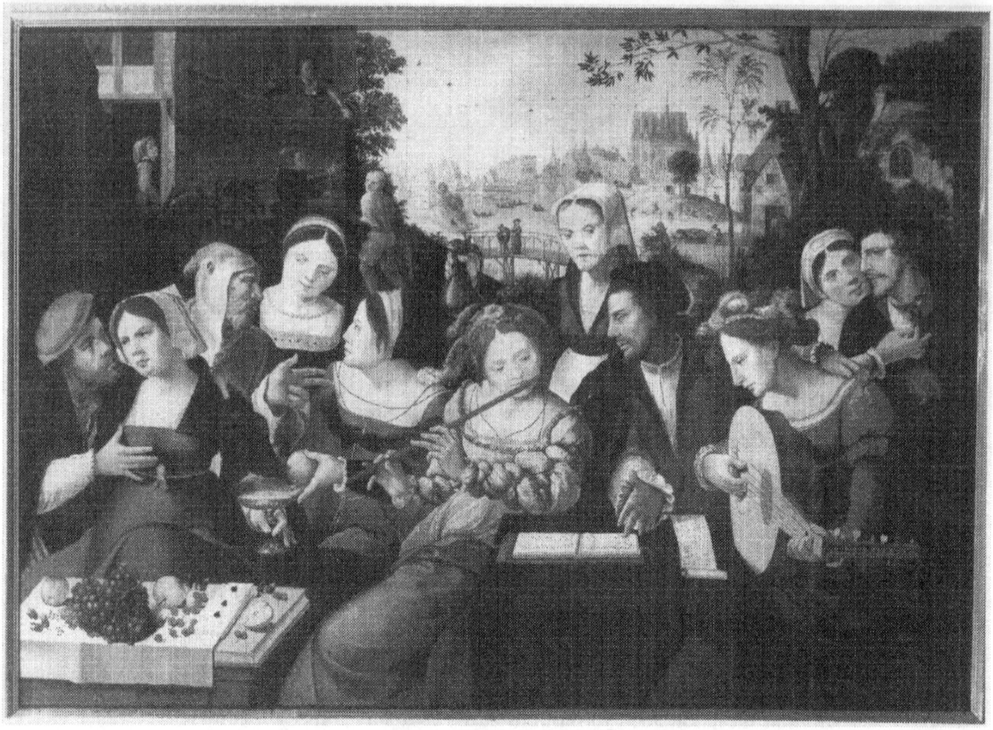

3. Prodigal Son among the courtesans, *Franco-Flemish School (16th century). Paris, Musée Carnavalet (P619)*

Calvin's musical conservatism is reflected in his general suppression of instruments. More important, his stringent views negatively affected the art music of the Low Countries, where the Calvinists formed a religious majority after the successful separation from the Spanish government (which retained control of the southern areas). All of this is not to suggest, however, that in this region the distrust of secular music was absolute. *Concert in a house* is one document testifying to the number of highly placed, talented musical amateurs educated in the best liberal, humanistic tradition who found all of this hard to accept.

Not surprisingly, the arts reflect both sides of this conflict.[6] I want now to mention several pictorial subjects which in one way or another have connections with Scripture or the lives of the saints, suggesting that these 'unimpeachable' sources could be used to prove the correctness of either attitude towards music.

One of the most popular subjects to emphasize the connection between music and lasciviousness—to use Calvin's word—is the *Prodigal Son among the courtesans* (illus. 3), drawn from St Luke 15:13. In visual representations of this story, music is almost always a part of the Prodigal's spiritual debauch, his 'wasting his substance with riotous living'—music is explicitly associated with evil. In this anonymous 16th-century Franco-Flemish painting, music simply serves as a preliminary to sexual encounter; music is seductive; it weakens the Prodigal, who according to medieval exegesis symbolized Everyman.[7]

There is a link between Prodigal Son pictures and the so-called 'Merry Company' scenes often painted by 17th-century northern artists. In typical 'Merry Companies' painters depicted aristocratic types in contemporary dress and local—if elaborate—settings, enjoying feasting and music along with easy courtship, just as in the Prodigal Son pictures. But to a moralist, the 'Merry Companies' may have been more disturbing, since allusion to a Bible story was essentially dispensed with, except perhaps for discreet lip service, so that the viewer was confronted with debauchery of a very immediate and undisguised kind. What a moralist would judge as sin, in 'Merry Companies' was celebrated with the slenderest apology to the Ten Commandments.

In the example (illus. 4) by Sebastian Vrancx (1573-1647), the moralistic relation to the Prodigal parable is evident only in a tiny vignette in the background which shows a man running away from a woman wielding a broom. This is a conventional visual reference suggesting that after the Prodigal had squandered his wealth among the harlots, he was driven off penniless, and half-clothed, to compete at the trough for 'the husks that the swine did eat' (St Luke 15:16). The other sexual allusions in the picture include the two dogs about to mate (in the left foreground) and the ugly woman near them who surely represents a procuress.

As a subject, the parable of the wise and foolish virgins (St Matthew

4. Merry company, *or* Prodigal Son among the courtesans *by Sebastian Vrancx. Brussels, Laurent Meeus Collection*

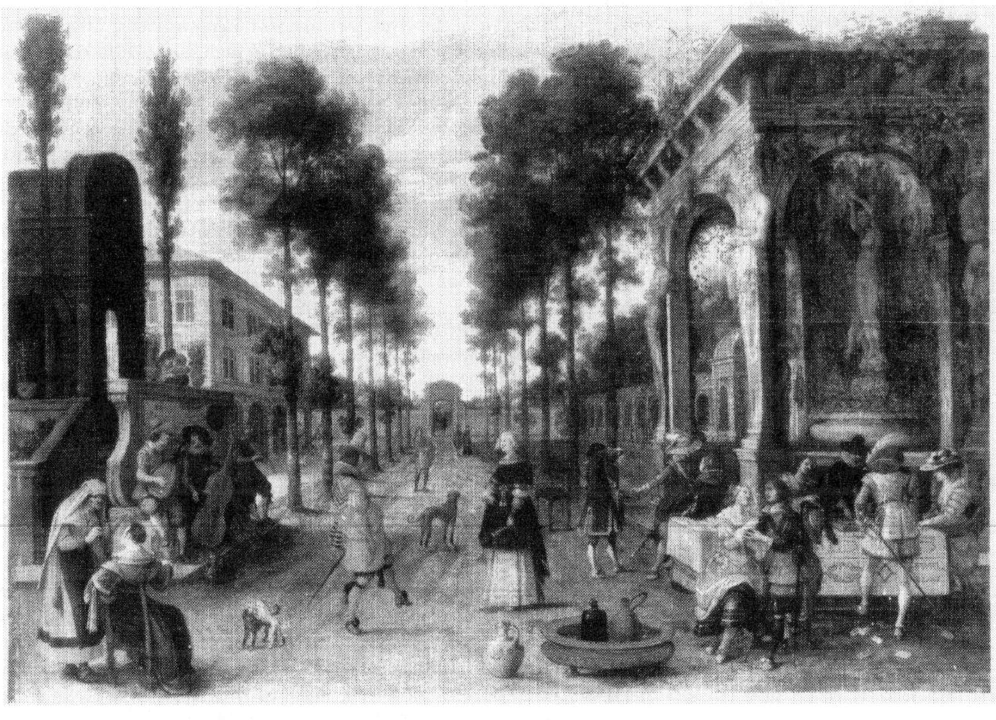

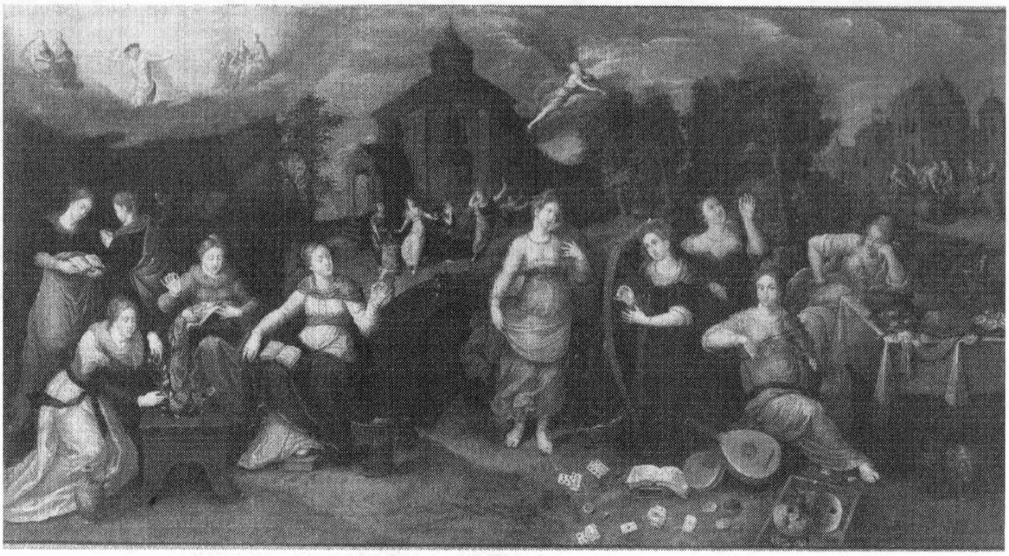

5. Parable of the wise and foolish virgins *by Pierre Lisaert (17th century). Seville, Sacro Imperio Collection*

25:1-13) allowed artists a fine opportunity to disparage music. An obscure painting (illus. 5) by the virtually unknown Fleming Pierre Lisaert (dates uncertain), shows the wise women tending to their domestic tasks, the most important of which, from an exegetical point of view, is the filling of the oil lamps which will light their way when they are called to meet the mystic bridegroom. On the opposite side of the picture the foolish women enjoy all the pleasures of the senses. They literally idle away their time with cards, in balls or masquerades (judging from the masks, age-old symbols of decadence),[8] in feasting and music. The pursuit of love also preoccupies them, evident not only from their immodestly draped bosoms, but also from the oyster shells, oblique allusions to Venus. In all this activity music stands out. Moreover, the instruments depicted are those considered respectable in the art music performed by upper-class amateurs of the period. Even the harp, universal noble attribute of King David, is shown, as if it too is in moral disrepute.

Several popular 17th-century subjects reduce music to parody and imply that it gives little pleasure, and even pain. Three stories come quickly to mind: the temptation of St Anthony, the rich man being led to Hell, and the trials of Job. In all three of these music is associated with torment. The usual technique of belittlement, following the tradition of Bosch, involves distorting the shapes of instruments, placing them in the hands of grotesque monsters (frequently more amusing to us than terrifying), grafting wind instruments onto the beaks or snouts of fantastic animals, or positioning them extraordinarily in body cavities. *The temptation of St Anthony* by David Teniers the Younger (1610-90), shows a host of mocking, noisesome rogues intent on disturbing the prayer of the hermit-saint, while Lust haunts him with erotic visions (illus. 6). On the left a man-monster plays on his shawm-like snout while his partner sings. At the right a man plays a pocket fiddle which, considering the usual function of the

8

instrument at the time, is probably an allusion to the 'disreputable' dance. In Teniers' *The rich man being led to Hell* (after St Luke 16:23) the selfish miser is met at Satan's gate by a hideous fanfare, a crazy-quilt mixed consort of *haut* and *bas* instruments, including snout-shawm, bagpipe and a lute played by a mouse with a woman's head (illus. 7). The singers include a fish-headed man next to the lutenist.

In *The trials of Job* (illus. 8), attributed to the 16th-century Antwerp master Pieter Huys (*c* 1519-*c* 1581), music has degenerated into aural torture, which the good man suffers stoically with the sores and boils covering his body. Job is mocked by his friends for the continuing strength of his faith. The use of musical instruments in the mocking scene itself has no precise scriptural source but is thought to originate in medieval mystery plays.[9] However, at one point (in Job 21:12-13) Job himself refers to evil people who endure nothing, but turn away from God and 'take the timbrel and harp, and rejoice at the sound of the organ. They spend their days in wealth, and in a moment go down to the grave'. There seems to be an oblique reference to the mocking musicians when Job denounces those deriding him: 'Among the bushes they brayed; under the nettles they were gathered together. They were children of fools, yea, children of base men: they were viler than the earth. And now I am their song, yea, I am their byword' (Job 30:7-9).

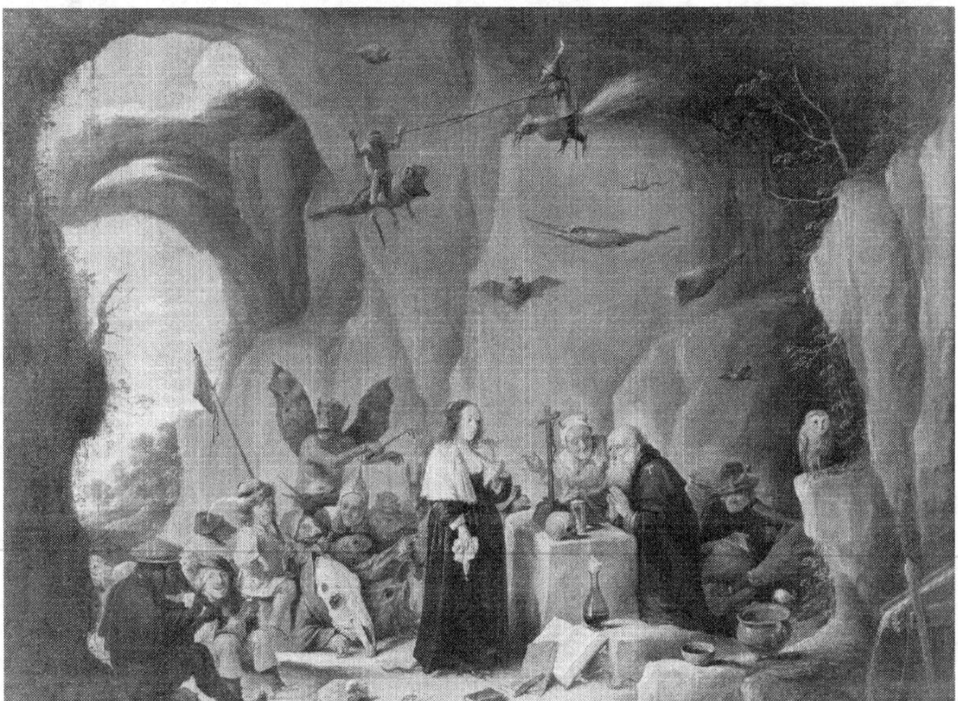

6. The temptation of St Anthony *by David Teniers the Younger. Antwerp, Koninklijk Museum voor Schone Kunsten (1970 no. 859)*

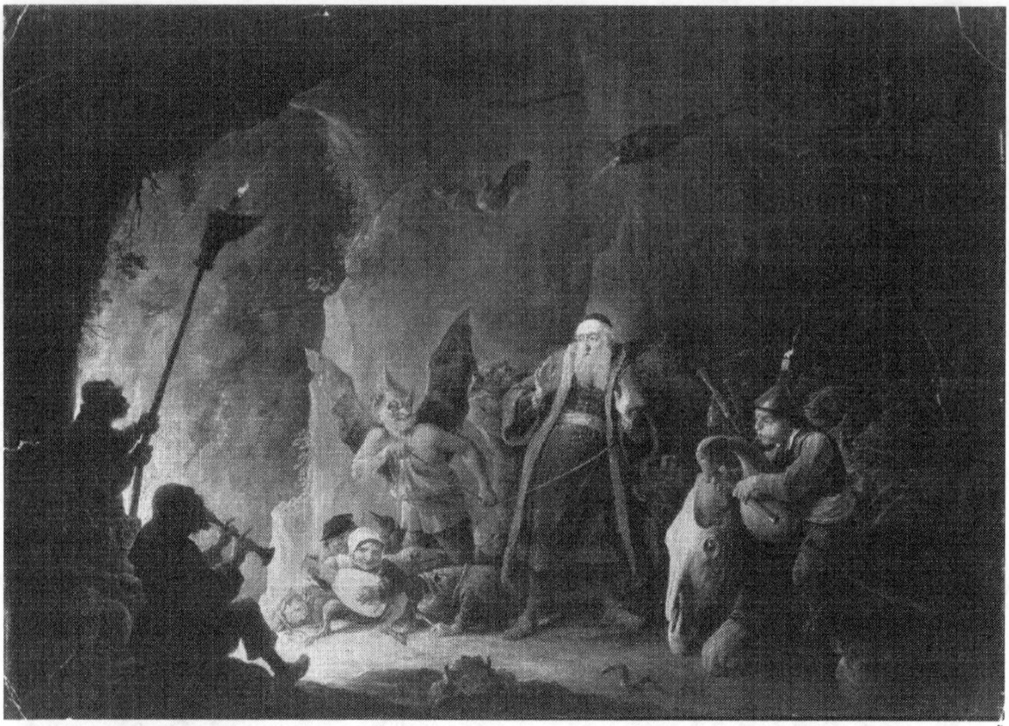

7

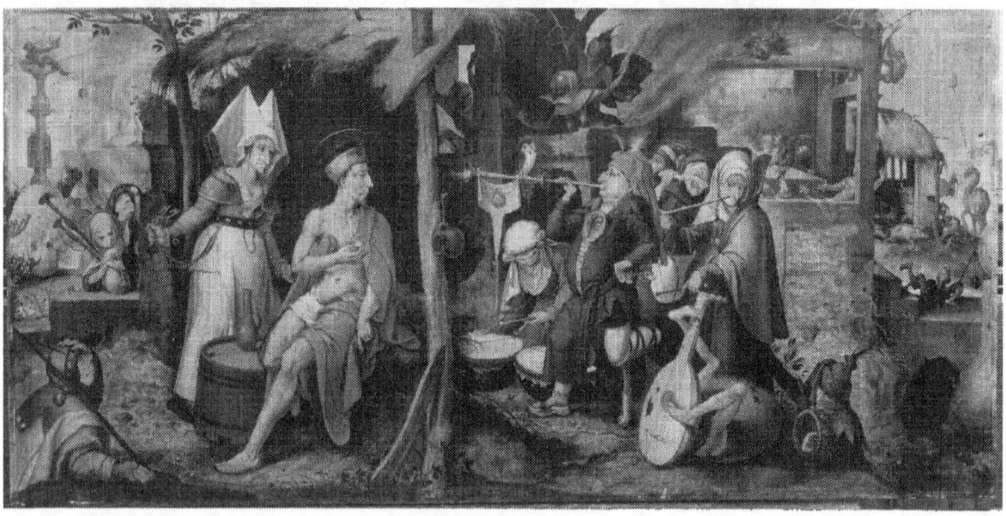

10

8

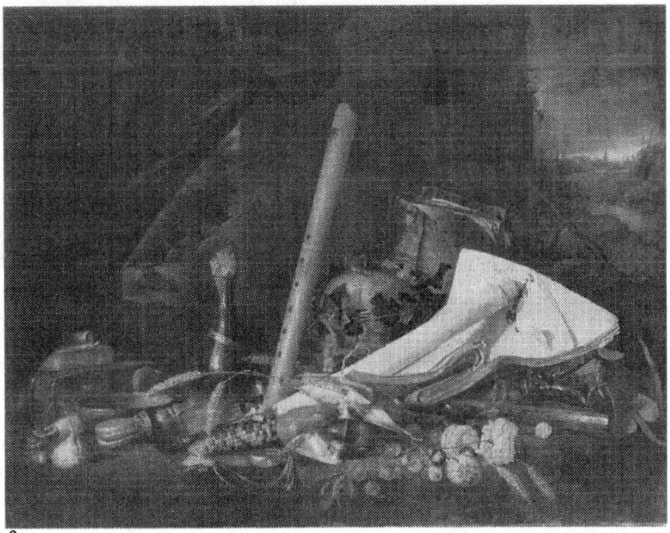

9

9. Vanitas (1664) *by Jan Davidszoon de Heem the Elder. Brussels, Musées Royaux des Beaux-Arts (208)*

But of all the subjects which in one way or another denigrated secular music making, none was so popular in the Low Countries (especially in the north) as the so-called 'Vanitas Still-Life', taking its title from Ecclesiastes 1:2. Music is at best a waste of precious time, at worst an occasion for sin. The impetus for this genre, which transforms textual allusions into emblems and attributes, came from scholars active at the University of Leyden, a Calvinist stronghold.[10] Every object was intended to make the observer contemplate the brevity of life and the frailty of man. Human skulls, instruments for measuring time, candles burning or just extinguished, flowers at the height of their bloom and hence about to fade, all suggest transience. Musical instruments, along with playing cards, dice, goblets, and smoking pipes, symbolize the tastes and pleasures, the *vita voluptuaria*, the vanity of all worldly things. The role of individual objects in such paintings is not always obvious to the untrained eye. Preferably, the sense should be somewhat obscure rather than immediately obvious, to compel the reader to ponder.[11]

7. The rich man being led to Hell *by David Teniers the Younger (c 1647), London, National Gallery (863). Reproduced by the courtesy of the Trustees*

Nevertheless, the gist of the message is explicit enough in the Still-Life (illus. 9) by Jan Davidszoon de Heem the Elder (1606-83/4). To cite the most important allusions: the Bible on the left represents both the word of God and the key to salvation. The book above is inscribed *Navolging Christi*, that is *The Imitation of Christ*, ascribed to Thomas à Kempis (1380-1471). A section of this book, admired by both Catholics and Protestants, deals contemptuously with the vanities of the world. At the opposite side of the picture stands a ledger marked 'Reckenigh', alluding either to the account of life's deeds or to the pursuit of worldly wealth. In the middle are objects referring to worldly endeavours, to life's temptations and pains (note the leper's clapper on the left). Other objects touch on the promise of salvation (the corn and the wheat of St John 12:24), and immortality is suggested by the evergreen ivy ironically wound around the skull. The one-piece recorder leans directly against the skull, a powerful allusion to death.

8. The trials of Job, *attributed to Pieter Huys. Musée de Douai (145) (Copyright ACL, Brussels)*

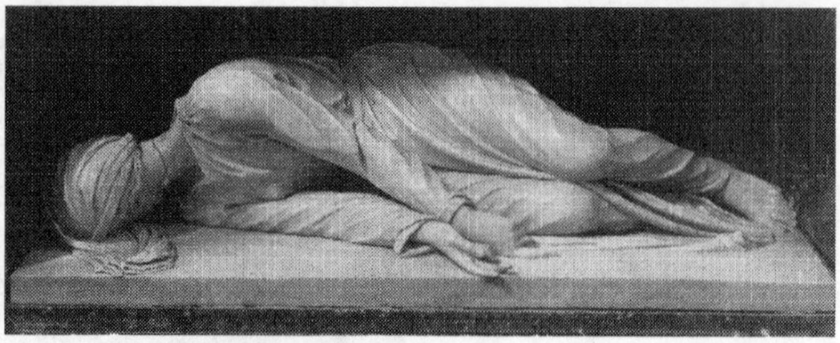

10. St Cecilia *by Stefano Maderno. Rome, Santa Cecilia in Trastevere (Photo: Scala/Art Resource, New York)*

Frequently, artists even placed the skull on top of a recorder, as if to clamp the instrument in its jaws.[12] The image seems designed to place music in the worst possible light. Even the phallic shape of such instruments carries extra-musical references—musical instruments in Vanitas pictures often evoking debauchery.[13]

In short, I suggest that the relation between music and degeneracy is explicitly stated in such works, and that it is precisely this kind of visual slander that the painter of *Concert in a house* probably sought to counter. Of all the demeaning views of music, the strongest are those which connect it to sexual sins, obliquely in some Vanitas pictures and explicitly in those of the Prodigal Son. This brings me full-circle to the vignette on the over-mantel in *Concert in a house* (illus. 2), which, in my view, forms the crowning counterargument to that connecting music with evil. The upper portion of the mantel-piece is not visible but enough remains to allow almost certain identification.[14] The figure enclosed in the medallion is, I think, none other than St Cecilia, the Roman virgin-martyr and patroness of music, here standing in ultimate testimony to music's 'heavenly connection'.

Cecilia was martyred by a sword, but her executioner, in attempting three times to behead her, managed only to wound her in the neck. Cecilia lived three days before succumbing, during which time she gave all her wealth to the poor. Her cult was revived in 1599 when, on opening the coffin in which the relic had been placed by Pope Pascal I in 821, her body was found intact, lying on its right side with the head half severed. Pope Clement VIII immediately commissioned the sculptor Stefano Maderno to produce a statue (illus. 10) faithfully to reproduce the exact appearance of the saint's body. This work became one of the most popular images of Cecilia, and influential in her iconography.[15]

Why is the figure on the over-mantel likely to represent this saint? Several factors weigh in her favour. She holds what appears to be a sword, the means of Cecilia's martyrdom. However, many female saints died by the sword and sword-wielding women often serve as non-religious allegorical figures in art, as a glance at Cesare Ripa's *Iconologia* (3rd edition, Rome, 1603) will confirm. Far more compelling is the unusual arm and hand gesture, precisely painted in this tiny detail—a comparison with Maderno's sculpture (illus. 10) shows a perfect concordance. The left hand crosses her body to line up roughly with her right knee and she points with her first finger. This famous gesture would have been instantly recognized by an educated 17th-century audience.

Two additional factors weigh on Cecilia's behalf. The first lies in the sculptural relief below the enclosing medallion. Two putti hold aloft a

12

mask with a turban-like wrap such as often appear in 16th-century Italian paintings—Raphael for example popularized their use. Such a mask, a simple grotesque borrowed from ancient Roman art, could here serve to remind us that Cecilia herself was a Roman and her head was found wrapped in a turban when her coffin was opened. Secondly, Cecilia as patron of music is a logical character to occupy the central location in a painting of a concert scene. Thus, notwithstanding all the contemporary negative associations between music and morality, these musicians seem to have a heavenly auspice smiling on them. And why not? No one could reasonably suggest that the secular music being performed here is evil: the decorum of the assembly, the very reserve of their behaviour, testifies to the opposite.

Put another way, the act of making music itself takes on allegorical qualities of virtue: it is a regulated activity, the embodiment of *mesure*. The group constitutes an ensemble which must carefully regulate itself if harmony is to result. The man by the virginal even beats time with his hand, as does another singer seated at the table with his back to us. It is not clear whether the picture frame on the wall in front of the virginal holds another picture or a mirror but the latter would allow the keyboard player to follow the rest of the ensemble. Furthermore, in the emblem books of the period, stringed instruments, especially lutes, were commonly used as attributes of the cardinal virtue of temperance or moderation.

Other paintings produced in the region centre on the same theme and use music in the allegory, one notable example being on a *Music party* by Jan Miense Molenaer (1609/10-68) (illus. 11). P. J. J. van Thiel has convincingly demonstrated[16] that, while at first glance the picture appears to be a simple music party of Dutch burghers, it is in fact a rather complicated allegory of fidelity, using music as the central metaphor for marital temperance. Again, the musical ensemble is an example of measure and regulation, visually stressed by the young woman sitting in the middle, with partbook in lap, singing and keeping time with her right hand. As van Thiel suggests, figuratively speaking she is acting with moderation and self-restraint, keeping her 'temper', behaving according to the requirements of temperance.[17] That virtue is reiterated by the man standing directly behind her. In a spectacular gesture borrowed from a temperance emblem,[18] he waters down wine held in a glass at his side by pouring from a jug held high above his head—an arresting image.

Molenaer reinforces his central theme of moderation by including visual reminders of antithesis; as we shall see, this identical technique is used in *Concert in a house*. In Molenaer's picture, two men on the left, stabbing each other with knives, provide rich and vivid contrast to the predominant virtue of temperance. They represent the corresponding cardinal sin of anger. In similar fashion, the painter of *Concert in a house* has hung a sword rather prominently on a chair in the right foreground. Its presence is not likely to be either accidental or merely decorative, as the sword is particularly rich in potential meanings. Most obviously, it is an attribute of war, an association which would surely have been recognized by any Fleming from the troubled 17th century.[19] It is thus the poignant antithesis of the peaceful and ordered musicmaking in the painting. It may also serve to point out that it is only when the sword is banished that the arts can flourish—a popular visual allegory of the period involved Mercury

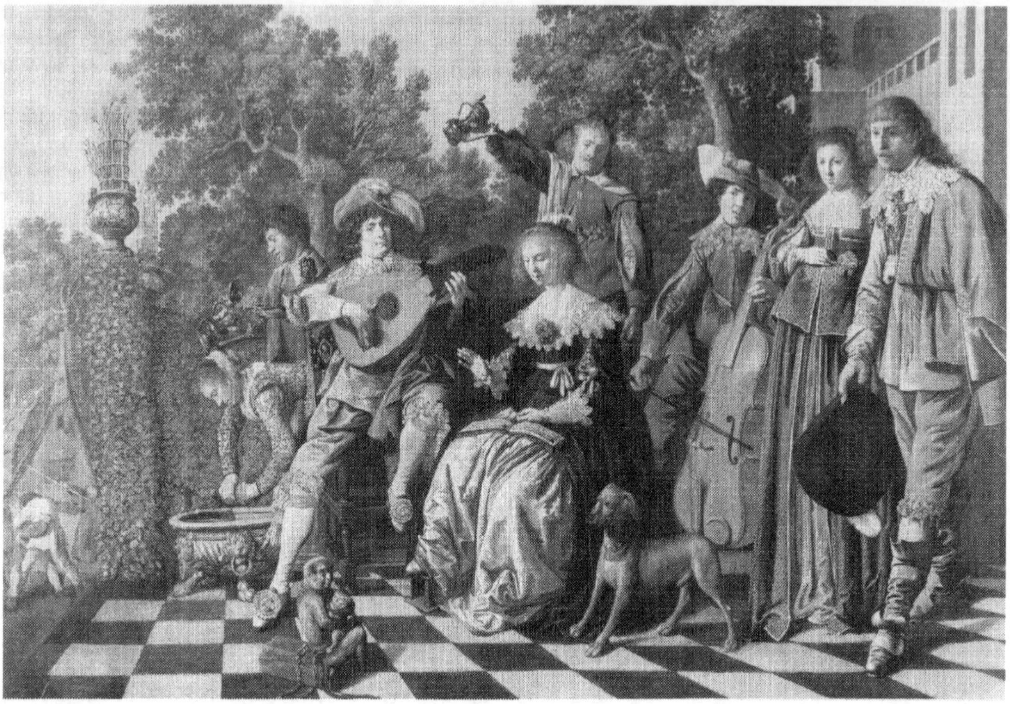

11. *An Allegory of Marital Fidelity* (1633) by Jan Miense Molenaer: Virginia Museum of Fine Arts, Richmond. The Adolphe D. & Wilkins C. Williams Collection. Photo: Ron Jennings. © Virginia Museum of Fine Arts.

awakening the fine arts from the slumber imposed on them by armed conflict.[20] Beyond this the sword could also serve as a symbol of temperance, if sheathed with its hilt bound.[21] This is exactly how it is depicted in *Concert in a house*.

In Molenaer's picture there is an additional vignette emphasizing another kind of immoderation, 'sinful, sensual love';[22] the chained monkey in the left foreground ridiculously embracing a cat. It represents enslavement to the senses and to pleasure, a meaning strengthened by the fact that the cat is a common symbol of libidinous temperament. On the right the married couple witnessing this sexual immoderation is guarded by a dog, a universal symbol of fidelity, standing between them and the stupid monkey. Molenaer's picture thus provides what van Thiel calls a 'Mirror of virtue' for the husband and wife: it is a 'key to an harmonious married life'.[23]

In *Concert in a house* the same matter is treated, less obviously, in the figure of the knavish youth peering round the door on the right. He is dressed in a flashy costume of the Italianate dandies painted by 17th-century northern Caravaggists, even down to his sporty, differently coloured leggings. In such paintings music is not so much an art as a dalliance or an accompaniment to sexual debauchery. It is not surprising that here he has a look of wonderment on his face. In the Caravaggist paintings, where he might well have been at home, the associations between music and venal love are blatantly Dionysian. Our artist seemingly meets that association head on, by using this man's presence as an outsider to remind us of what the musicians here are *not*.[24]

Now for a cautionary conclusion and a return to the question of this picture as a document in the history of performance practice. The painting is not trustworthy at all, even though its naturalism is compelling. There are two musical anomalies which attract our attention. To begin with, the musicians break into two separate groups: the one gathered around the table and the other around the virginal. They are arranged in such a way that one group cannot readily follow the other, each having its own leader regulating the beat with his hand. Secondly, there is a possible discrepancy in the music they are playing. The ensemble at the table performs from partbooks, but the trio at the left follows a score held by the standing leader-singer. Surely this signals two discrete musical events. Furthermore, on the basis of my study of 17th-century Flemish paintings with music, I can say with some confidence that this ensemble, taken as a whole, is one of the largest ever depicted by an artist from the region.

We seem to have here some kind of pastiche, a joining together of pictorial elements from more than one visual source. The central group is borrowed almost intact from a famous engraving by the French print-maker Abraham Bosse (1602-76) (illus. 12).[25] This piece is one of a series on the five senses executed *c* 1635 and representing *Hearing* (as is announced by the verses in both Latin and French, and by the large, rather comical pair of ears framing the engraved title).[26] Yet, if the *Concert* was modelled directly on Bosse's engraving the artist was not copying blindly, for important changes have been made in the two instruments. Bosse's lute has been updated to a theorbo-lute, an instrument very popular in the Low Countries, and the viol also conforms to the model generally found in the region.[27] In addition, the playing techniques—especially that of the viol player—are very well handled. As Emanuel Winternitz has pointed out: 'The representation of a player's hand and fingers is a delicate task, requiring absolute fastidious exactness and scrupulous observation; even a slight deviation in the design may result in functional nonsense.[28] The painter of this picture knew a lot about music.

Finally, the decorations on the wall have not been arbitrarily chosen—quite the opposite. They too enhance the role of music in this society, for it would seem that the artist was more concerned with expressing an idea than with the literal correctness of the musical event itself. From one side to the other the picture is wholly taken up with music in the same way that some medieval and renaissance paintings of the glorification of the Virgin include a veritable instrumentarium of the time. In such pictures, the purpose is not to realize any actual ensemble, but rather to give an allegory of the loudest and richest possible sound, as Winternitz has convincingly shown.[29] This may be true here. While obviating the picture's usefulness as documentation of performance practice, it in no way affects its value for the history of musical thought.

Ernst Gombrich suggests[30] that: 'Reading a picture is a piecemeal affair that starts with random shots . . . followed by the search for a coherent whole.' The search can lead us past the indisputably valuable 'hard evidence' visual art provides about performers and their instruments; it can lead us into what has been termed the 'invisible world of ideas'[31] (in this case about music). These are embodied, however obtusely, in the

This article is based on a lecture given to the American Musicological Society. Richard Leppert is Associate Professor of Humanities in the University of Minnesota, Minneapolis. His most recent book is Arcadia at Versailles *(Amsterdam and Lisse, 1978).*

symbolic images, and can be just as revealing to the music historian as the surface evidence. In this respect visual art is a far more valuable resource to study than photographs of early musical performances would be—were they available—because, unlike the 'real' world captured in a snapshot, in art the world is *constructed*, not real literally but symbolically so, for it represents the world view of an artist (and perhaps also of his patron). Not only do we see images of the past as in a photograph, but we grasp the ideas that governed that past and which are fundamental to historical understanding. Thus through *Concert in a house* we absorb some of the social attitudes, the moralistic and religious prescriptions which affected musical practices. Here the judgment is a happy one: 'Musica laetitiae comes medicina dolorum', but that, as I have shown, was a view by no means universally held.

[1] I have written about this painting before, but from a substantially different point of view. See *The Theme of Music in Flemish Paintings of the Seventeenth Century* (*Musik und Musiker im Bild* 1, Munich, 1977), 1, 138-41. See also Albert Pomme de Mirimonde, 'Les sujets de musique chez Gonzales Coques et ses émules', *Bulletin, Musees Royaux des Beaux-Arts de Belgique*, 16 (1967), pp. 179-208. Mirimonde points out (p. 197) that in the sale catalogue of the Janssen collection (Brussels, 1923, no. 35) the painting is simply listed as French School. It reappeared *c* 1940 in an Amsterdam sale where its older attribution to Coques was reinstated.

[2] These virginals are easily identified by the characteristic designs decorating the case: they were printed in black on white paper, then glued on the instrument and varnished. See further Raymond Russell, *The Harpsichord and Clavichord* (London, 1959), pp. 50-2.

[3] Biblical quotations throughout are from the Authorized Version. Were one to suggest a specific identification for this figure, John the Evangelist would be a strong contender. The depiction here conforms to the usual convention of showing him as young and clean-shaven and holding a chalice. John would have been a good choice for this subject—he was of course the apostle most loved by Christ, according to popular tradition. See further Louis Réau, *Iconographie de l'art chrétien* (Paris, 1955-9), 3:2, 712, 717-18. On the chalice as a symbol of faith and as an attribute of saints, see James Hall, *Dictionary of Subjects and Symbols in Art* (London, 1974), p. 63; see also George Ferguson, *Signs and Symbols in Christian Art* (New York, 1961), p. 163.

[4] Gustave Reese, *Music in the Renaissance* (New York, *R* 1959), p. 449.

[5] Quoted from *Source Readings in Music History: The Renaissance*, ed. O. Strunk (New York, 1965), pp. 156-7.

[6] Allegories of hearing, music personified, Orpheus charming the animals, and concerts of the Muses with Apollo were among the most popular defences of secular music in the northern art in the 17th century, along with pictures illustrating the Seven Liberal Arts and the Fine Arts. *Concert in a house* differs from these 'defenses' in that it is the only one given a contemporary setting and treated more or less as a genre scene. The others are either mythological or blatantly allegorical. See further, Pomme de Mirimonde, *L'iconographie musicale sous les rois Bourbons* (Paris, 1975), 1: 17-34, 62-82, and Leppert, op cit, 1: 95-114, and 2: 233-43, plates 15-25.

[7] H. Colin Slim discusses this painting in his monograph, *The Prodigal Son at the Whores': Music, Art, and Drama* (Irvine, 1976), pp. 13-16, as does Daniel Heartz, '*Au pres du vous*—Claudin's Chanson and the Commerce of Publisher's Arrangements', *Journal of the American Musicological Society*, 24 (1971), pp. 214-22. The musical inscriptions depicted in the picture have been identified by Heartz as a chanson by Claudin de Sermisy (*c* 1490-1562). See also Leppert, 'The Prodigal Son: Teniers and Ghezzi', *The Minneapolis Institute of Arts Bulletin*, 61 (1974), pp. 80-91.

[8] See Guy de Tervarent, *Attributs et symboles dans l'art profane, 1450-1600* (Geneva, 1958-9), cols. 261-4.

[9] See Reau, op cit, 2:1, 317.

[10] Charles Sterling, *Still Life Painting*, trans. J. Emmons (New York, *R* 1959), p. 52.

[11] Ingvar Bergström, *Dutch Still-Life Painting in the Seventeenth Century*, trans. C. Hedstrom and G. Taylor (London, 1957), pp. 155-6. See further Leppert, op cit, 1: 74-84.

[12] See, for example, a *Vanitas* by Cornelis-Norbertus Gijsbrechts (in a private collection), reproduced in Pomme de Mirimonde, 'Les peintres flamands de trompe l'oeil et de natures mortes au XVIIe siècle, et les sujets de musique', *Jaarboek, Koninklijk Museum voor Schone Kunsten* (Antwerp, 1971), p. 235, fig. 8.

[13] For a discussion of the emblems and attributes in this painting see Pomme de Mirimonde, 'Musique et symbolisme chez Jan-Davidszoon de Heem, Cornelis-Janszoon et Jan II Janszoon de Heem', *Jaarboek, Koninklijk Museum voor Schone Kunsten* (Antwerp, 1970), pp. 251, 272. Also, Ingvar Bergström, 'Disguised Symbolism in "Madonna" Pictures and Still Life: II', *Burlington Magazine*, 97 (London, 1955), p. 346.

[14] The whole top of the painting may have been cut down which would explain the apparently arbitrary truncation of the fireplace figure and also the rather narrow rectangular shape of the whole piece.

[15] Were the entire relief of the saint visible we could expect to see her neck wound and her usual attributes of roses and lilies. On the iconography of St Cecilia, see Réau, op cit, 3:1, 278-84, and Pomme de Mirimonde, *Sainte-Cécile: Métamorphoses d'un thème musical* (Geneva, 1974).

[16] 'Marriage Symbolism in a Musical Party by Jan Miense Molenaer', *Simiolus*, 2,2 (1967/8), pp. 90-9. For citation of a number of other allegories of temperance, see p. 91, note 2. On the lute as an emblem of temperance, see Tervarent, op cit, col. 255 (Luth V).

[17] van Thiel, op cit, p. 91.

[18] See the one by Jacques de Ghyen the Younger, showing this same gesture, reproduced in van Thiel, ibid, p. 92, fig. 2.

[19] It is worth noting that the region even produced a group of painters who specialized in battle pictures. See F.-C. Legrand, *Les peintres flamands de genre au XVIIe siècle* (Paris and Brussels, 1963), pp. 189-226, and Leppert, *Theme of Music*, 1, 201-23.

[20] Music often figures in such pictures. See the study by Pomme de Mirimonde, 'Les allegories de la musique. II. Le retour de Mercure et les allegories des beaux-arts', *Gazette des Beaux-Arts*, 6, 73 (1969), pp. 343-62.

[21] Hall, op cit, p. 295.

[22] van Thiel, op cit, p. 95.

[23] ibid, p. 99. See further pp. 95-8, where associations between the monkey and pictures on the Fall of Man are discussed in detail.

[24] The taste for images laden with meaning, as evident in these two paintings, was particularly strong in the 16th and 17th centuries. Perhaps the most eloquent testimony to this fashion is Cesare Ripa's famous *Iconologia*, first published in Rome in

1593, reprinted (often enlarged) and translated many more times during the succeeding century. The book is arranged in dictionary format, and provides a code to the depiction of literally hundreds of allegorical personifications, from those on the virtues and vices to every conceivable human sentiment and passion and their moral implications. Each allegory is endowed with a highly detailed list of its attributes, with an equally detailed commentary on the appropriateness of each, clarifying the purposeful mystery of the personifications. See further Erna Mandowsky's introduction to Ripa, *Iconologia* (1603, *R* Hildesheim and New York, 1970), pp. iii-v.

[25] The costumes are basically French as are the facial types and hair styles (except for the distinctly Low-Countries virginal player). The lace-like collars occur generally in northern Europe in the 1630s and 1640s, but in Dutch and French paintings more than in Flemish.

[26] The texts read as follows: 'Pulsa placet digitis mire mihi lyra peritis./ Cantibus et miris me philomela rapit;/ At mihi concentus numquam jucundior ullus./ Quam laudes docta qui canit arte meas' [The lyre plucked by my nimble fingers delights me wonderfully, and the nightingale enraptures me with its sweet songs. But to me no harmony is ever more pleasing than the one which sings my praises with skillful art.] and 'A bien considerer la douceur infinie/ Des tons de la Musique et leurs accords divers./ Ce n'est pas sans raison qu'on dict que l'Harmonie/ Du mouvement des Cieux entretient l'Univers' [Considering the infinite sweetness of musical sounds and their various harmonies, it is not without reason that it is said that the Harmony of the spheres sustains the Universe.]

[27] Pomme de Mirimonde, 'Les sujets de musique chez Gonzales Coques et ses emules', *Bulletin, Musees Royaux des Beaux-Arts de Belgique*, 16 (1967), p. 197, is the first to point out the borrowing from Bosse. He also reproduces an anonymous 17th-century French School painting copied from Bosse. This picture, an almost exact replica, is in the Musée des Beaux-Arts, Tours (ibid, p. 199, fig. 25).

[28] 'The Knowledge of Musical Instruments as an Aid to the Art Historian', *Musical Instruments and their Symbolism in Western Art* (New York and London, 1967), p. 47.

[29] 'On Angel Concerts in the 15th Century: A Critical Approach to Realism and Symbolism in Sacred Painting', ibid, p. 141.

[30] 'Illusion and Visual Deadlock', *Meditations on a Hobby Horse and Other Essays on the Theory of Art* (London, 1963), pp. 155-6.

[31] Ernst H. Gombrich, *Art and Illusion: A Study in the Psychology of Visual Perception*, Bollingen Series, 35, 5, 2nd edition (Princeton, *R* 1969), p. 9.

The author wishes to acknowledge the iconographical assistance of Professor Norman Canedy, University of Minnesota, and the valuable advice and criticism of Professors Howard Mayer Brown, University of Chicago, and John G. Suess, Case Western Reserve University.

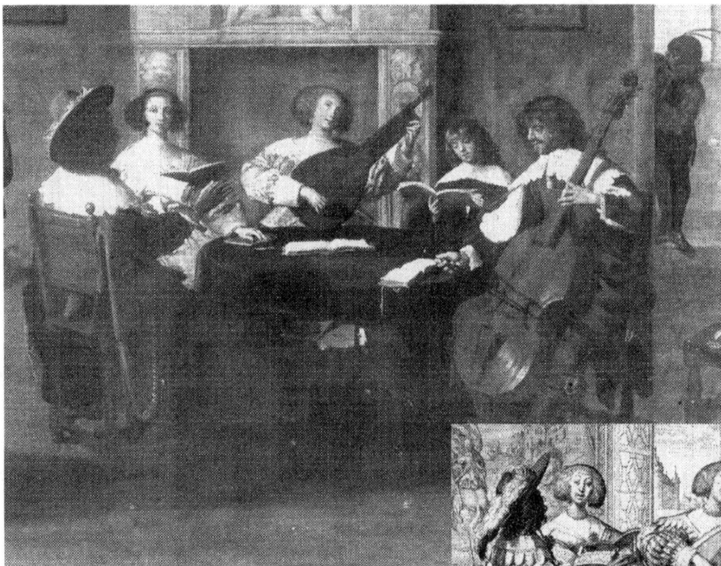

12. *(Left) Detail of* Concert in a house. *(Below) Detail of* Hearing *by Abraham Bosse. Paris, Bibliothèque nationale. (For a complete engraving, see* EM *6/4, p. 637)*

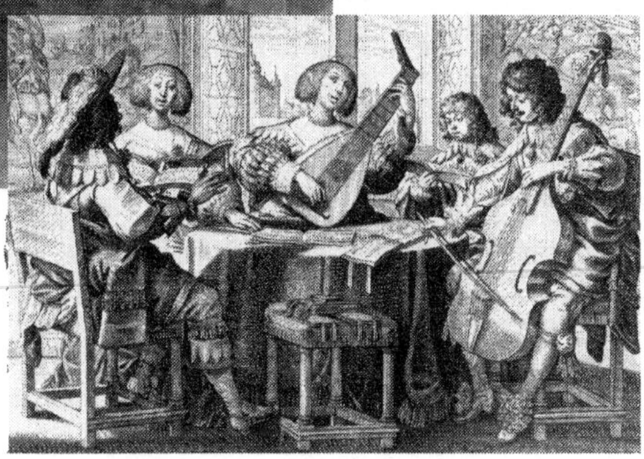

CHAPTER 7

Imagery, musical confrontation and cultural difference in early 18th-century London

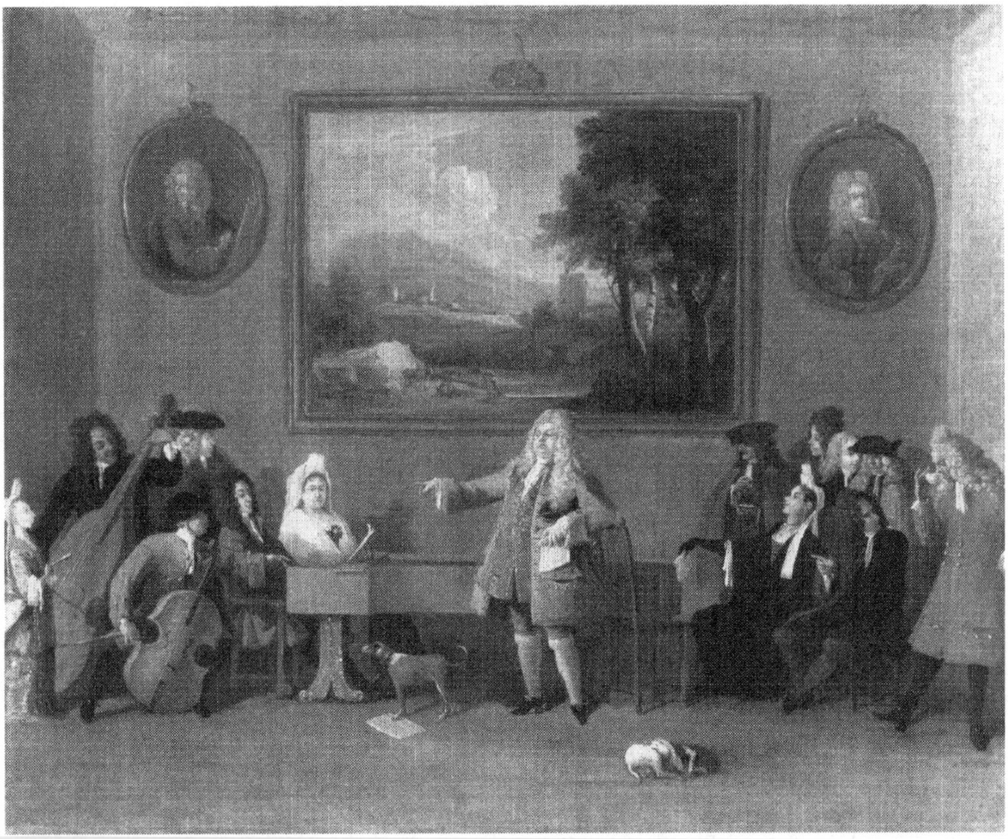

1 Rehearsal of an Opera (?) (c1709). **Painting by Marco Ricci (1676–1730) (London, Eric Charles Graham Coll.)**

The Italian painter Marco Ricci (1676–1730) came to England in late 1708 with fellow artist Giovanni Antonio Pellegrini in response to an invitation from Charles Montagu, 4th Earl and later 1st Duke of Manchester, then serving Queen Anne as Her Majesty's Ambassador Extraordinary to the Venetian Republic. The invitation was probably issued in order for the Italians to paint scenery for the opera at the Queen's (later King's) Theatre, Haymarket. While in England, Marco Ricci also painted several pictures (some slightly caricatured) said to represent the *Rehearsal of an Opera*. It is these images which will be examined here, together with their relationship to opera and English musical life in general as seen through the eyes of a foreigner. As far as I have been able to determine, nine such pictures are now known to exist, the first eight of which I have examined in reproduction. Several of these paintings have labels stuck on the back, all of which were written long after the pictures were produced. For the most part, these provide the identification of some of the sitters—if the labels can be believed—who were among the most notable performers on the contemporary London stage. Whether correct or not, discussion of the paintings to date has been completely dependent upon the assumption that much of the information given by these labels can be trusted. Indeed, the very claim that the images represent opera rehearsals is based on one of these labels.[1]

The paintings are immediately noteworthy for two reasons. Firstly, their subject matter is unique in British art of the period. They represent one of the earliest examples produced in this country of the so-called 'conversation piece'—the informal group portrait. Secondly, the images are fundamentally different from Ricci's own other known work in subject matter and style. Thus while he produced numerous caricature drawings throughout his life, the caricature quality evident in some of the Rehearsals is not repeated in other paintings, and among his published paintings there are virtually no other interior settings. Despite repetitions of this single subject the paintings remain strikingly unusual, which implies that Ricci was responding to something that mattered deeply to him or his patrons.[2] In the course of this essay I shall focus in particular on the possible reasons for there being so many versions, who may have commissioned them and how they may have been understood by contemporaries.

Ricci's work at the opera consisted of producing scenery, in part or whole, for three productions of well-known works. In collaboration with Pellegrini, he probably painted sets either for Francesco Conti's *Clotilde* or Alessandro Scarlatti's *Pirro e Demetrio* (*Pyrrhus and Demetrius*), parts of which were reused for Giovanni Bononcini's *Il trionfo di Camilla*, both in the 1708–9 season. In the following season, this time on his own, Ricci produced the scenery for Francesco Mancini's *Idapse fedele* (*Hydaspes*). (See Appendix (1).)

In 1710 or 1711 Ricci briefly returned to Venice, following a quarrel with the more famous and better established Pellegrini. He was back in London by 1712, this time with his uncle Sebastiano, a well known painter with whom Marco had previously collaborated. Both Riccis remained in England until 1716, when they returned via Paris to Italy where Marco died in 1730.[3]

The paintings

There is considerable agreement among scholars that Marco Ricci was responsible for the various versions of this subject (all except illus.8 have been previously studied) and that all, with the possible exception of illus.3 and 4, were painted during the artist's first visit to England, *c*1709.[4] Furthermore, it is generally concluded that the original among the Rehearsals is the version once owned by Horace Walpole (see illus.1). Like all the others, the size is small, 21″ × 24.5″; it is painted on canvas. On the basis of two labels glued to the back, part of the painting's provenance is known: before belonging to Horace Walpole, the picture was owned until 1760 by Charles Stanhope and later by John, Duke of Argyll, from whom Walpole bought it in 1771. But the individual for whom the canvas was painted is not known, and there is no reason to connect it to Stanhope's family prior to Charles's own time.[5]

The sitters are divided into two groups: six individuals on the left, at least five of whom are musicians, to whom a man standing at the centre gestures, and seven people on the right, all but one of whom appear to constitute an audience. By means of the label (written long after the canvas was painted) Horace Walpole names those supposed to be musicians, all of whom were famous singers associated with opera at the Haymarket during the time of Ricci's involvement there: '[Nicola Grimaldi] Nicolini [the celebrated castrato] stands in front, Mrs [Catherine] Toft[s, the celebrated English soprano] is at the harpsichord, [Francesca] Margarita [de l'Epine, an Italian soprano] is entering in black' (corrected in the catalogue for the sale of Walpole's estate in 1842 to read 'Margarita is sitting in black', that is on the right).[6] Finally among those tentatively identified (though not by Walpole) is a somewhat obscure singer known at the time as the Baroness, Johanna Maria Lindelheim, the small woman at the far left holding a closed fan.

Two dogs appear in the foreground; one sleeps, the other, standing on music, looks towards the musicians. On the far wall of the room hang three paintings: in the centre a very large Italianate landscape, flanked on the sides by two oval portraits. One of these represents an artist sketching while standing by an easel; the man on the other side is older, and holds a book of some sort, perhaps looseleaf. Oddly, the two figures face out of the painting; one would expect them more typically arranged to face inward and thus unify the composition. The young painter on the left has been tentatively

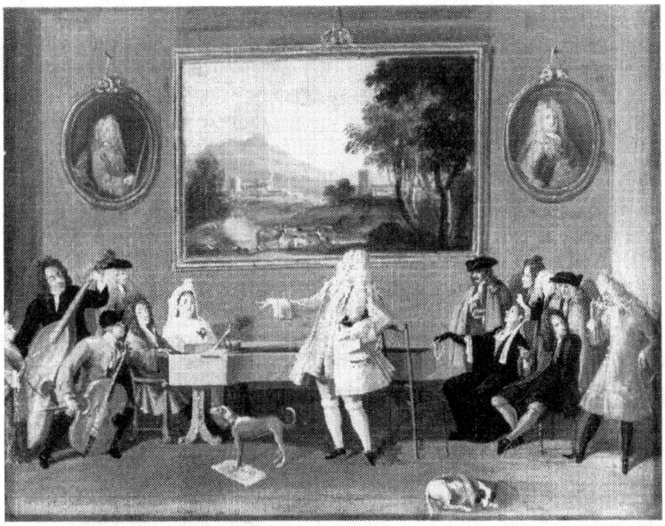

2 Rehearsal of an Opera (?) (c1709). **Painting by Marco Ricci (1676–1730) (Watford, Viscount Knutsford Munden Coll.)**

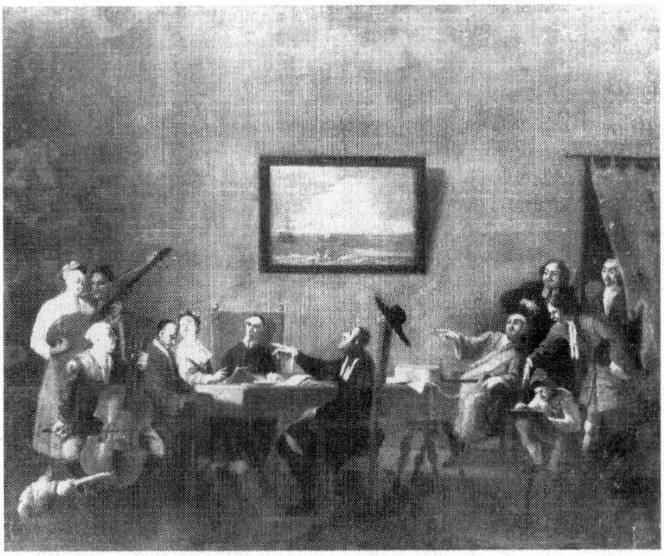

3 Rehearsal of an Opera (?) (c1709). **Painting by Marco Ricci (1676–1730) (current whereabouts unknown; Formerly London, A. W. Holliday Coll.)**

identified as Marco Ricci himself, an assertion I believe is likely; the man opposite as his uncle Sebastiano, which I think extremely unlikely, given that he was in Italy for the period during which these pictures were probably produced.[7]

This picture exists in another version (see illus.2) painted in gouache on thin leather, a medium often employed by Marco Ricci, though all the other Rehearsals are on canvas; its diminutive size (only 8″ × 10″) is anomalous as well. But its visual differences with illus.1 are minor, except that the oval portrait at the right represents a different individual. Alternatively, there is a version that is compositionally similar but is in most other ways very different (see illus.3). Here the sitters are still arranged into the same two groups, performers to the left, audience to the right (the instruments are the same, except that the bass viol is here replaced by an archlute, played by a woman). A flat-backed guitar can be seen resting face downwards on the end of the harpsichord. The sitters appear in most respects to be Italian. Though nothing is known about this painting to help clarify its history, its predominantly Italianate style places it outside the primary concern of this essay.[8]

Two other versions exist that appear as much Italian as English, although I have seen a reproduction of only one of them (see illus.4),[9] in which performers and audience appear once again, though in an opposite arrangement to those in illus.1–3. An Italianate landscape, similar to that in illus.1–2, features at the centre. However the flanking oval mounts now hold a harbour scene and a seascape. The costumes and facial types seem to be a mix of Italian (or Continental) and English, but that the majority of the musicians seem Continental could simply reflect the influx of foreign performers into contemporary London.[10] Judging from his inclusion of the woman identified in other versions as Mrs Tofts (right of centre, resting one hand on the harpsichord), Ricci may have intended the setting to be English. Equally possible—and in my judgment more likely—is that the work was produced a few years later than the rest, after Ricci's return to Italy; Mrs Tofts retired there and Ricci became a friend of her husband Consul Smith. The mixture of Italian and English faces among the audience would be explained by the presence of many Englishmen who lived in or visited Venice during the period. If I am correct, this would indicate that Mrs Tofts continued to sing after leaving England. The woman so identified in this image also appears older than in the other version of the subject. (See Appendix (2).) The woman standing next to her may be the Baroness, with whom Mrs Tofts sang a duet in *Pyrrhus and Demetrius*.[11]

One Ricci Rehearsal (illus.5) remains in the family of its original owner Charles Howard, 3rd Earl of Carlisle (1674–1738), a Whig nobleman who with his friend Lord Manchester was responsible for Ricci's arrival in England. Howard, like Manchester, was one of the 29 known subscribers to Vanbrugh's Haymarket theatre project.[12] He was also the owner of Castle Howard, North Yorkshire, Vanbrugh's first palatial house and his first architectural commission[13] (in which he was helped by the professional architect Nicholas Hawksmoor). Pellegrini, who received the bulk of the commission to decorate the house, was assisted by Ricci who painted the overdoors and overmantles. The first indications in the Castle Howard accounts of Ricci's work are two payments of £20 each, recorded during November 1709; he ultimately received a total of £125 15s.[14] Given the modest size of the Rehearsal painting, it must have been ordered independently from the house's decorative scheme. The two labels on the reverse of the painting both postdate 1791. The first identifies Nicolini at the harpsichord, and 'Margaretta in black with a muff'; the second provides further identification, naming 'First Violin Festini', 'Violoncello Corporali' and three 'attendants': Margaretta's mother, Mrs Tofts and Pepusch.[15] The Howard version has a strong resemblance to three further examples (illus.6–8), apart from the difference in the back wall, on which the central painting-within-the-painting (appearing in all other versions) is replaced by a view through an open window, and the flanking oval pictures (appearing in all but illus.3) have been eliminated. But what is especially noteworthy in comparison with the versions previously described is that the 'audience' has disappeared; here all but two or three are clearly involved in music making.[16]

It seems appropriate here, leaving aside illus.3, to summarize what is either known or speculated about the identification of the various sitters. One figure, identified as Nicolini, appears in all the paintings (except illus.4) standing by the harpsichord at the centre and gesturing with his right hand. Mrs Tofts also supposedly appears in all of the paintings: as a svelte, standing figure in illus.4–8 and perhaps (but less convincingly) in illus.1–2, where she is seated next to the harpsichordist and appears to be quite heavy. In turn, all three different representations of 'Tofts' position her differently: seated and only partly visible (illus.1–2), standing full height, facing forward (illus.4) and standing in profile (illus.5–8). Moreover, both dress and hair are different in each of these representations. Francesca Margarita de L'Epine is said to appear in illus.1–2, 5–8. In all cases she has a *fontage* on her head and wears a dark dress. In illus.1–2 she is seated in profile and the caricature presents her as relatively ugly, as was said to be the case. In Illus.5–8, she stands between the characters identified as Nicolini and Tofts holding the fan she was said always to have carried, half over the face; perhaps the artist's discretion? Given what remains visible, it is difficult to draw the conclusion that the two women depicted in these paintings are one and the same.[17]

Of the remaining characters the Baroness may be represented in illus.5–8 as the woman toward extreme right holding a muff (the label on illus.5 calls her Margarita). The Baroness has also been tentatively

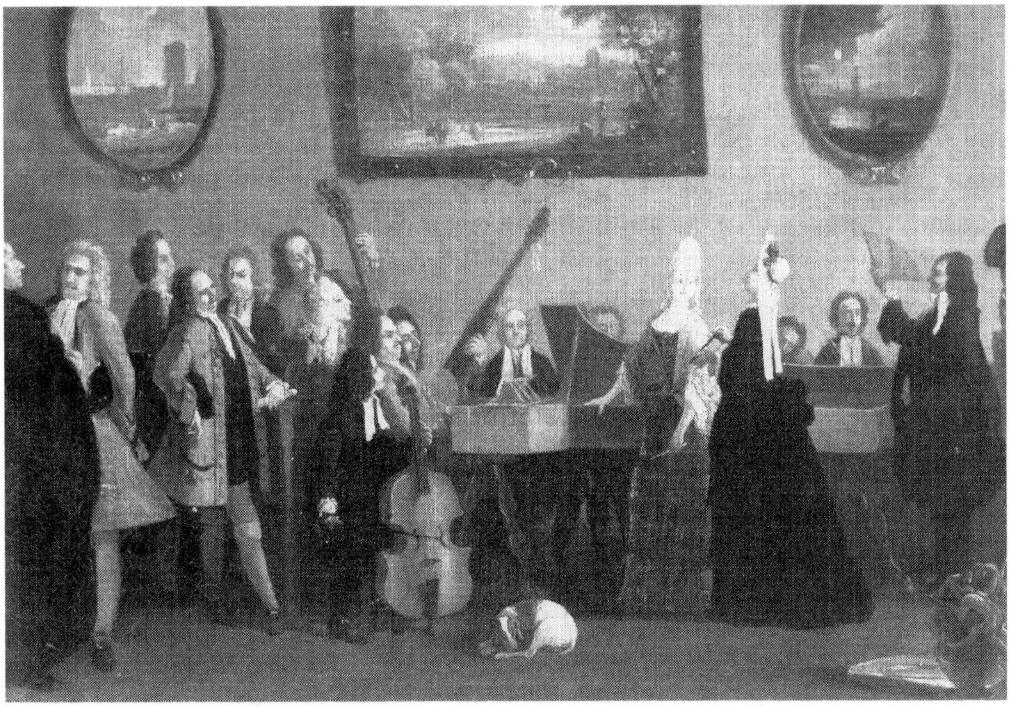

4 Rehearsal of an Opera (?) (c1709?). **Painting by Marco Ricci (1676–1730) (New Haven, Yale Center for British Art, Paul Mellon Coll.)**

given as a possible identity for the woman seated near the harpsichordist in illus.1–2.[18] According to the label the man seated and following a score, on the extreme right of illus.5–8, is Heidegger, and next to him Pepusch. Heidegger—who 'won a bet that Lord Chesterfield could not produce a more hideous face in London'—certainly was ugly.[19] Though the man Ricci has painted is homely, it is difficult from these paintings to sustain the opinion of his having a 'hideous face'. The otherwise unidentified man in profile (between the bass violist and cellist) appears to be this same individual. There is no obvious resemblance between Ricci's representation of 'Pepusch', and the portrait of him in the National Portrait Gallery, London.[20]

Finally, a word should be said about the string players in illus.5–8. The label on the reverse of illus.5, as previously mentioned, identifies Caporale as the cellist and Festing as first violinst. Presumably on this basis the *New Grove* identifies them as the Festing brothers, from left to right, John, James and Michael, with Haym at the harpsichord.[21] The men do not appear to be portrayed in the other paintings. These attributions seem to be incorrect—the Haymarket documents contain no reference to Caporale or the Festings, and for good reason. Andrea Caporale only came to England in 1734; the earliest known reference to a performance by John Festing is in 1721; Michael Festing's public début came in 1724, though he may have been born as early as 1680.[22]

Without labouring the complex issue of identification, and nothwithstanding White's careful detective work and his apparent logic as to the possibilities involved, I believe that all of this must ultimately remain highly speculative. Almost all the evidence is based on labels on the reverse of several of the paintings, all of which postdate the works and for the most part by at least several decades. Resemblances between the characters represented by Ricci and any other known likenesses seem mostly unconvincing. The identities suggested for the instrumentalists are spurious. Since no other representations are known to exist of either Margareta or the Baroness, written accounts are the only source (from which all we know is that Margareta was homely).

In my view only the identification of Nicolini is

secure, and there is even disagreement among the labels regarding Tofts (that on illus.1 cannot be correct). As to Heidegger and Pepusch, the best evidence is not pictorial: simply, they were involved in the Italian opera, and Pepusch is recorded (along with others) as having been paid fees for rehearsals.

Do the paintings represent opera rehearsals?

Eric Walter White suggested that illus.1–2 and 5–7 (and by implication illus.8, which was unknown to him) represent the rehearsal of scenes from *Pyrrhus and Demetrius*, and assumed that two specific parts of the opera may be shown: the first a duet between Nicolini and Mrs Tofts, the second a duet between the Baroness and Tofts (the only duet for the two women in the opera).[23]

It was the practice for the public to be admitted, usually for a fee, to full dress rehearsals just prior to the première of a new production. Thus on 6 March 1710 the *Daily Courant* carried an advertisement for 'a Practice of the new Opera [*Hydaspes*] in Form', which received its première on 23 March.[24] Records also exist of the many private rehearsals necessary to prepare an opera. Such practices would obviously not be carried out 'in form'; they would be informal, and involve only limited accompaniment, rather than full orchestra. Thus a document probably of January 1708, estimating the fees for all musicians and dancers includes a line (though failing to list an amount) for 'The Practices of 2 New Operas'. Next to the names of three musicians (an entry separate from the orchestra list) is written '25 shilling a Time [per performance], 5 shillings per Practice'; the implication is that for rehearsals only these musicians were used. If indeed Ricci's paintings represent rehearsals, surely they are of this kind.[25]

A Haymarket orchestra list from December 1710 alludes to a dispute over rehearsal space for either *Hydaspes* or *Pyrrhus and Demetrius*. The text reads: 'Mr Hill complains that Nicolini when he had apointed ye Practice att ye Chocolate house which was taken for that purpose he sent to them to come to his house & ye other Musicians take exceptions att coming to him. Mr Hill desires it may be att a Neutrol place & proposes to take ye Room in York buildings not taking ye Cloaths they would provide for him'.[26] This document indicates that at least some contemporary opera rehearsals occured in buildings rented for the purpose. The pronoun usage may render the statement ambiguous, but I take it to mean that Hill rented rehearsal space in the Chocolate house and that Nicolini's preference, to which the other musicians objected, was to rehearse in his own personal quarters. Hill then requested that the rehearsal be moved to York buildings, referred to as 'ye Room', which may indicate the concert room there. (The meaning of the last phrase seems unclear.)

It is conceivable, if unlikely, that Ricci portrayed a

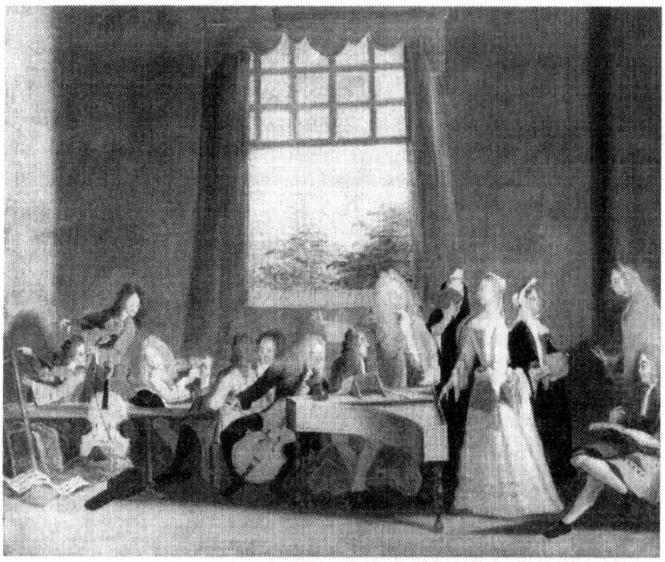

5 Rehearsal of an Opera (?) (c1709). **Painting by Marco Ricci (1676–1730) (Castle Howard, Yorkshire,** From the Castle Howard Collection.)

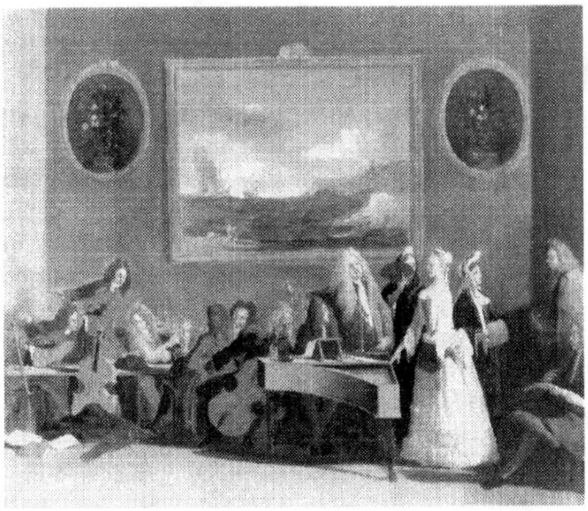

6 Rehearsal of an Opera (?) (c1709). Painting by Marco Ricci (1676–1730) (New Haven, Yale Center for British Art, Paul Mellon Coll.)

specific place: the room represented in each case is very neutral. White's suggestion, with which Mollie Sands concurs, that the practice room within the Haymarket itself is represented suggests that a specific event may have triggered the original commission for the paintings: an apparently unadvertised rehearsal of *Pyrrhus* on 9 December 1708, two days before the première. Sands's argument is based on a letter, written on 10 December 1708 by Isabella, Lady Wentworth, which reads: 'Yestirday I had lyke to have been ketched in a trap, your Brother Wentworth had almoste parswaded me to have gon last night to hear the fyne musick, the famous Etallion sing att the rehersall of the Operer, which he asured me it was soe dark none could see me.' She goes on to relate that she was happy not to have gone as 'thear was a vast deal of company and good light', how Nicolini initially refused to sing, how the Duchess of Shrewsbury set off in her own coach to fetch him, and how Mrs Tofts resenting Nicolini's refusal herself declined to sing, much to the criticism of Lady Wentworth.[27]

Sands asserts the opinion (one that I am not inclined to accept) that the scene may represent this very occasion, namely, Nicolini singing and (as Lady Wentworth put it) 'Mrs Taufs huft'. Though it would be appropriate for wealthy patrons to commemorate the arrival and performance of their most celebrated acquisition (Nicolini), to record a singers' row would be to trivialize the event. There is a more cogent objection. Though Sands depends on the letter for her argument, she omits those details which relate to the size of the company and the lighting of the rehearsal venue which do not support her case.

It would seem that the rehearsal for what was, as Sands suggests, almost certainly *Pyrrhus and Demetrius*, actually took place 'in Form', hence in the Haymarket auditorium, not a practice room. This is evident from Lady Wentworth's presumption that the place would be so dark she could not be seen. A rehearsal would hardly be kept dark, but even if it were the room would still be sufficiently lit to allow the identification of those present. Moreover, Lady Wentworth quickly confirms this by saying that the (well lit) space had 'a vast deal of company', clearly implying a room larger than a typical rehearsal venue. Moreover, there is no apparent reason for the final *Pyrrhus* rehearsal to have been held outside the main auditorium of the Haymarket, since the season opened with *Pyrrhus*: the theatre was otherwise not needed.[28]

All of this raises a larger question that unfortunately cannot be answered with any degree of certainty: is Ricci's subject really the rehearsal of an opera? Others before me have raised this question, and while the prevailing wisdom has been in favour of the traditional title, it has been suggested more than once that 'more probably' the paintings depict 'a private concert in which various personages connected with the Italian opera in London in the early part of the 18th century are taking part'.[29] Indeed, it is arguable that the setting, a richly appointed room, is typical of a great house, thus suggesting a private musical evening. Perhaps more to the point, were this an opera rehearsal, one might expect the singers to simulate positions and gestures more obviously associated with an actual production. An example of such an event, though from later in the century, does exist: *Musical Rehearsal* by Nathaniel Dance-Holland (1735–1811) set in a library–music room (see illus.9, p.332). The most that can be said is that Ricci painted a scene related to his experience with Italian opera in London, and perhaps with Nicolini in particular. But I believe that the paintings exist for reasons that are not specific to *Pyrrhus and Demetrius* and that, while Nicolini may have been the impetus for the paintings, Ricci himself used the opportunity for his own ends.

An interpretation

All of the nine Rehearsal paintings are small, on average about 18″ × 22.5″. Their modest size, especially given the large number of sitters represented, suggests that the paintings were intended for private viewing. If any of the non-musicians depicted in illus.1–4 commissioned the pictures (which to me seems plausible), the domestic nature of the paintings is supported, given the element of caricature. Caricature, as a humorous genre, runs counter to the expectations of portraiture, which is an inherently serious, more 'public' art. In point of fact, caricature was far more common in drawings, which typically were stored in cartons or folders, to be taken out and shown only to a selected audience of equals and friends.

This said, we can speculate about the identity of the individuals who, one after another, may have commissioned Ricci to repeat himself so many times. It seems logical to look for a small group of people who both knew each other and were directly concerned with (or at least interested in) Italian opera in London. One clue exists in the fact that illus.5 alone still remains with the family of its original owner, Charles Howard, 3rd Earl of Carlisle. As already indicated, he was one of the 29 original subscribers to Vanbrugh's Haymarket theatre project, of whom 11—Howard included—belonged to the famous Kit-Cat Club, along with Lord Manchester and Vanbrugh himself (see Appendix (4)). It is my suspicion that some of these 11 men, or perhaps some of the larger, original, 29 commissioned the paintings.[30]

It is reasonable that some of these men would have patronized Ricci in order to commemorate their involvement, but not simply because they made a modest financial investment in Vanbrugh's undertaking. Instead, I think that the explanation lies in the fact that the introduction of Italian opera in London was a matter of considerable controversy. As a cultural phenomenon it was something of a *cause célèbre*, the debate over which was discussed largely in terms of the political differences between some Tories, who were against it, and some prominent Whigs, who were its supporters (see Appendix (5)). For Tories Italian opera provided the evidence for a decline in national virtue and an excuse to proclaim a chauvinistic brand of patriotism. The political opportunity was provided by two facts: that Italian opera was foreign in every notable regard (its music, language, design, and performers), hence automatically suspicious, and that Italy was Roman Catholic. Tory antagonism exploited the British sense of cultural insularity which they trumpeted with pride. (Ironically, it was commonplace for young men on the Tour to behave with chauvinism while in Italy, and once home to deride anything not Continental.)

But the Whig sponsors had scored a popular victory among audiences, in part evident from the many slurs directed at opera from the legitimate stage, voiced by actors and playwrights who felt their livelihood threatened and in whom Tories found a group to reflect their views perfectly. Opera, at least in London, represented something akin to popular culture; a box office success to some extent indicated the political ascendancy of the Whigs, fully realized on George I's accession in 1714. However much a financial failure Italian opera may have been, due to the costs of production, its success with audiences may have been seen as politically worthwhile. In this sense Ricci's paintings represent the private acknowledgement of a political and cultural position, whether actual or

7 Rehearsal of an Opera (?) (c1709). **Painting by Marco Ricci (1676–1730) (London, Major Christopher Turnor Coll.)**

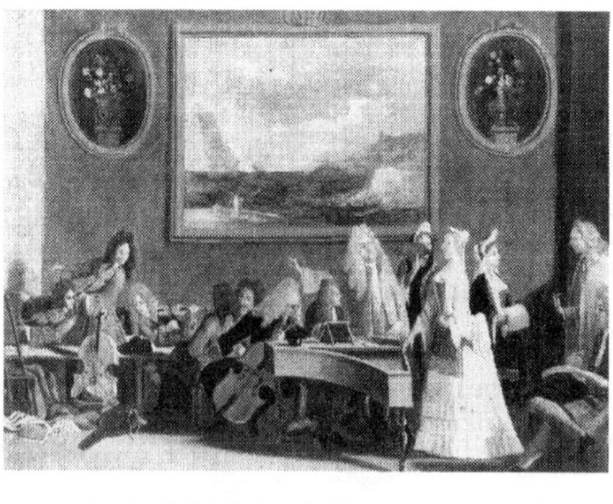

8 Rehearsal of an Opera (?) (c1709). **Painting by Marco Ricci (1676–1730) (Private Coll.)**

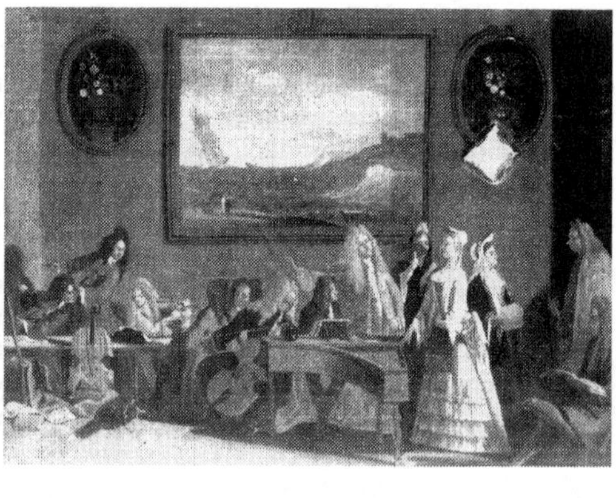

merely hoped for. To the average member of the English social and economic élite, the arts were taken less seriously for themselves than for their power to confirm status. Hence it is extremely unlikely that anyone would have commissioned the subject Ricci painted merely because of zeal for opera. However much a man liked music, either as a listener or an amateur performer, social prohibitions usually prevented these activities from being proclaimed.[31]

It is appropriate that Nicolini—the first (alto) castrato to perform in England—be represented at centre stage, because in him the terms of the debate are focussed. He was Italian, paid an extraordinary fee far in excess of that given to English singers, and made his first appearance—in *Pyrrhus and Demetrius*—singing in his native language, the English members of the cast singing in theirs. He was lauded for both his voice and his stage presence. But to the English mind he was also demeaned (if for the most part indirectly) notably by his exotic voice, and the Italian practice of castration: living evidence of the cultural gulf separating the two countries. In the opinion of some English, the castrati were the epitome of Italian–Continental degradation, or what Lord Chesterfield was later to refer to as 'that foul sink of illiberal vices and manners'.[32] Even Addison, who greatly admired Nicolini, allowed *The Spectator* a satirical reference to an English 'Squire *Squeekum*, who by his Voice seems (if I may use the Expression) to be cut out for an *Italian* Singer'.[33] Italian origin notwithstanding, Nicolini, a strikingly popular entertainer, could promote the Whig cause almost single-handedly, and this accounts for his compositional placement in Ricci's paintings.

The paintings-within-the-paintings are noteworthy for the amount of space they occupy (excepting illus.3, which falls outside my discussion, and illus.5, where there is none), though their importance seems not to be specifically related to the subjects they represent. What is most immediately striking is their Italian character, which, intentionally or not, further advertizes the foreign culture. More importantly, these images are actually 'Riccis-within-Riccis', being typical in both style and subject of the kind of work he was accustomed to produce. Perhaps by means of these paintings Ricci advertised himself to his patrons in the hope of realizing other commissions on a scale far exceeding anything he could hope to gain from these small pictures. He was an artist needing work and these pictures presented an early opportunity for him to show his work at its best. While in England Ricci worked very much in the shadow of the more famous and successful Pellegrini, who moved around country houses, and whose fees at Castle Howard, for example, exceeded those of Ricci eightfold—£852 5s. to Ricci's £125. 15s.[34]

In illus.4 (whenever and wherever it was painted) Ricci provided a sampling of subjects: a central landscape, flanked by two harbour scenes, one by day, the other by night. The harbour scenes were replaced with vases of flowers in illus.6–8; his heart does not seem in them, for in each instance they are handled in a cursory manner lacking the attention devoted to the central seascape. By contrast, there are no such paintings in the Castle Howard painting (illus.5). Instead there is only a view through an open window, exposing in a quickly painted, sketchy manner, some trees or parts thereof. The lack of self-advertizing here may be explained by the fact that Charles Howard, having ordered overdoors and overmantles at Castle Howard, was already his patron.[35]

The portrait in the oval mount on the left of illus.1–2 would seem to be Ricci himself holding the tools of his trade; by one gesture 'signing' the Rehearsal and promoting himself. No certain identification is possible with regard to the (two different) men represented in the oval to the right: the man represented in the oval of illus.1 could be Pellegrini; it bears a strong resemblance to a known self-portrait;[36] that in illus.2 may be Charles Howard (see illus.10, p.337). Ricci here may be singling him out for his generosity, and as an example to other wished-for patrons. This brings us back to the fact that these two men look 'out' of the picutre. This atypical arrangement may be explained by Ricci's attempt to strike out on his own, visually separating himself from the more successful Pellegrini while at the same time trading on Pellegrini's name. That the image of 'Pellegrini' appears only in the prime original supports this claim. Commissions to repeat these little paintings may have emboldened Ricci first to thank his first patron, the Earl of Carlisle (illus.2), and then simply to paint the primary subject—the musical event. It is possible that these pictures may have influenced the decision to employ Ricci as sole set designer for *Hydaspes*.[37]

All this notwithstanding, the Rehearsals constitute more than mere self-advertizing. As a scene painter and as an Italian, Ricci must have been aware of the controversies surrounding Italian opera. Working in the theatre, undoubtedly seeing performances and reading the reviews, he would have been aware of the

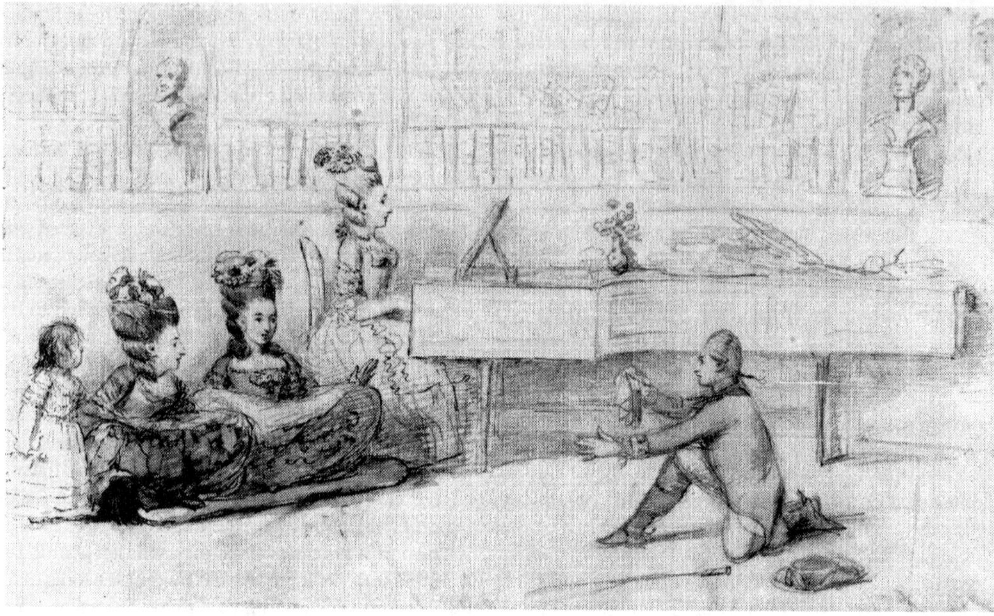

9 Musical Rehearsal. **Drawing by Nathaniel Dance-Holland (1735–1811) (London: British Museum)**

chauvinism directed against his compatriots (with whom we can presume he conversed in the privacy of their native language). As an artist he would have sensed the conflict between the preference for native over foreign talent; in some circles there was open resentment against Continental painters: Ricci's uncle, Sebastiano, later experienced this directly.[38]

Ricci is said to have been a neurotic and to possess a volatile personality. (By some accounts he died by his own hand, though that is now largely discounted.)[39] Thus in his early twenties in Venice he was involved in a tavern brawl with a gondolier who died after Ricci broke a jug over his head; he then fled the city and only returned several years later.[40] Likewise, after his well documented though unexplained quarrel with Pellegrini, Ricci took the considerable trouble to return to Italy, presumably to fetch his uncle Sebastiano who, significantly, had been Pellegrini's teacher and as such might be expected to put him in his place. Ricci had an acute sensitivity to his position and was therefore undoubtedly very aware of the fragility of his position in England. Marco Ricci, like his compatriot Nicolini and even, for that matter, the English musicians with whom he came into contact, found himself in a curious position. While he undoubtedly enjoyed some financial benefits made possible by the substantial wealth of the Whig noblemen, he would also have quickly discovered that his ability as an artist gave him no special status among the upper classes. Working in the opera he would have been intimately sensitive to the fact that his colleagues not only had often to suffer bitter satirization, equally often they had trouble getting paid—for him an irony given the very apparent wealth of his social superiors (*see* Appendix (3)). The Rehearsal paintings allude to a variety of these discriminations.

In Ricci's first group (illus. 1–2) the spatial separation between performers and audience is exaggerated; there is no interaction between the two groups. The audience is bunched up into the corner, unnaturally so, as if warily observing a group of exotics. Indeed, two of the six males talk and two sip tea. Two men, and a third at the opposite side, wear hats and cloaks as if they come and go as they please. Opera (or whatever is being portrayed) is treated as casual entertainment, demanding much less than full attention, even in the presence of one of Europe's great singers. This is arrogance, captured cautiously by Ricci in the slight caricaturing of some (but not all) of the 'audience'.

The two dogs included by Ricci inform on this matter. The one nearest the musicians stands in rapt attention, reinforced by Ricci's placing one of the dog's legs atop a music book. By contrast, the other dog lies asleep near the 'audience'. The polarity in the situation requires me to return momentarily to the question of who is represented in the audience. If these observations are correct, it is possible that the audience does not represent any specific group of individuals (who might object to being so depicted unless completely certain of their position), but rather types, some attentive to varying degrees, others not. But the fact that Ricci dispenses with them as a group in all the other examples may indicate that this part of the composition constituted a major obstacle for his patrons. The same is true of the dogs, except in illus.4 where one animal appears, this time more neutrally located precisely in the middle of the events.

Some of the musicians (illus.1–2, 4) are themselves caricatured: Nicolini gestures with an exaggeratedly curled forefinger; the harpsichordist wears a haughty expression; his plain female companion is ostentatiously adorned with beauty marks; the woman standing at the extreme left appears dwarfish. Ricci may have felt that to caricature one group it was necessary to caricature both. This may be supported by illus.5–8, from which the audience has disappeared, hence there is little if any caricature evident. What comes across instead is the seriousness of the music making. The instrumentalists play with intent, bending over their instruments with urgency; the harpsichordist watches Nicolini, who both sings and gestures to the band, at the same time intently watching Mrs Tofts as they perform in duet. Here one senses real rehearsal, rather than performance. The overall neatness of the first examples is in contrast to illus.5–8 where we see considerable clutter (especially to the left): the instrument case, music books and sheets, and musicians' outer wear, a folded cloak atop the table serving as a music stand. The scene is one of spontaneity, a working session of professionals.[41] Thus the man at the extreme right identified on the label as Heidegger follows a score. In these paintings Ricci has in effect moved his position nearer for a close up of the musicians, setting them very close to the picture plane and thereby leaving no room for the audience. By contrast in illus.1–2 the figures appear in the somewhat distant middle-ground.

Marco Ricci painted images which illustrate the cultural dialectic of his time. The Rehearsals of the first group (illus.1–2, 4) attempt at once to acknowledge and mediate the division between performers and audience; that is, the division between production and consumption which increasingly dominates the history of Western music from late Renaissance to the present. In the second group (illus.5–8) the division is visualized as unbridgeable, for here the musicians play by themselves, the audience now constituted only by the paintings' viewers standing in real space before the canvases. Put differently, in the Rehearsals music is either exploited as a mark of social position (illus.1–4), or it is made by musicians for their own purposes (illus.5–8), as self-communication separated from the larger realms of human affairs. This constitutes the history of music's gradual commodification, and its ironic partial silencing as a means of human communication—at least in the realm of high art. The classically peaceful Italianate landscape in illus.1–2 belies the tension evident between the groups of sitters. The storm-tossed sea in illus.6–8 tells the oblique truth, in the same way that the open window in the Castle Howard painting promises no egress from this reality: it seems to lead to nothing.

Appendix

(1) Ricci's scenery for London opera

Alessandro Scarlatti's *Pirro e Demetrio* received its première in Naples in 1694. *Pyrrhus and Demetrius* opened in London on 14 December 1708, though apparently not with the Ricci—Pellegrini scenery which was to come some months later. For the London production Owen Swiney translated the text and Nicola Haym arranged the music. It was to be one of the last operas to be performed bilingually in London, Nicolini singing in Italian, the rest of the cast in English.[42]

The first direct reference to the work of Ricci and Pellegrini appeared in an advertizement for *Pyrrhus* in the *Daily Courant* on 2 April 1709: 'With an entire set of new Scenes, Painted by two famous Italian Painters (lately arriv'd from Venice), and all other Decorations that were represented in the Opera of Clotilda.'[43] The author of *A Critical Discourse upon Operas in England*, thought to be Nicola Haym, states that Francesco Conti's *Clotilde* (*Clotilda*) was in competition with *Pyrrhus*, in so far as its producer, Johann Heidegger, had engaged '*Venetian* Painters to make a new Scene'.[44] As a principal player in these events Haym would have been in an excellent position to know the truth; this text may clarify what is otherwise ambiguous in the advertisement, namely that Ricci and Pellegrini were originally engaged for *Clotilda* (which opened on 2 March 1709 and had seven performances), and that its sets were taken over for *Pyrrhus*, the scenery for which was apparently unsatisfactory. The new sets must have been a success, for they were advertised again, only three days later (in the *Daily Courant* of 5 April

1709) as being used in the revival of Bononcini's *Camilla*.[45] And on 31 May 1709, the same paper advertised a benefit concert by Nicolini 'including music by Scarlatti, Bononcini, and other Italian composers' with 'the new Scene from *Pyrrhus*'[46] (implying, probably incorrectly, that Pellegrini and Ricci were responsible for only a single new scene). This set was obviously sufficiently popular with audiences to have commercial justification for its use as a backdrop for a recital. It is possible that Ricci and/or Pellegrini were responsible for a still later addition to the production: 'a new Cascade Scene after the Italian Manner', advertised several times in the *Daily Courant*, from 16 December 1710. However, if this is the case, and presuming the success of their earlier work on the production, it seems odd that the same painters were not credited directly in the advert. The 1708–9 production was replaced whole or in part for the 1716 revival.[47] *Pyrrhus* received six performances in 1708, 30 in 1709 (of which 13 preceded the performance with Ricci–Pellegrini scenery on 2 April), eight in 1710, five in 1711, 10 in 1716 and two in 1717.[48] The text was published in two quarto editions in 1709 and 1710.

Il trionfo de Camilla, with music by Giovanni Bononcini to a libretto by Silvio Stampiglia, was first produced at the Teatro di S Bartolomeo in Naples in 1696. The first London performance, in English, was at Drury Lane in 1706, where it was performed 34 times during 1707, as well as twice at Dorset Gardens in 1706. The Haymarket took it over for 10 performances in 1708, followed by 18 in 1709. It was 'the first full-length, heroic Italian opera mounted in London' and, as such, was enormously successful.[49] As far as I have been able to determine, Ricci's association with this opera was accidental. That is, some of his and Pellegrini's sets intended for *Pyrrhus* (and/or *Clotilda*?) were used to replace those of an earlier *Camilla* production. Judging from the librettos, perhaps four scenes from *Pyrrhus* would transfer easily to *Camilla*, where no fewer than eight and possibly as many as 10 different scenes are required. *Camilla* was revived at Lincolns' Inn Fields Theatre in 1717, 1719, 1726 and 1727. Quarto editions of the text appeared in 1706 and 1707, octavos in 1709, 1717 and 1726.[50]

The première of Francesco Mancini's *Idaspe fedele* (*Hydaspes*) was given at the Haymarket on 23 March 1710 and was one of the first operas in London to be performed entirely in Italian. Ricci alone was responsible for the scenery. Zacharias Conrad von Uffenbach, in his memoir of travels to London in 1710, commented on his impressions of Ricci's work: 'The scenery and properties had all been made expressly for the opera and were very fine, though not as costly as those in Italy; but the costumes were of the finest and the performances were in all things most natural and uncommonly elegant'.[51]

Judging from the libretto, he would have been required to paint eight separate sets, only one of which, a prison scene, would have been repeated. The popularity of the production with audiences was no doubt increased by Addison's famous essay in *The Spectator* on the strangling of the lion by Hydaspes (Nicolini).[52] Between the opening night and May 1712, 38 performances were staged; the opera was revived again in the 1714–16 seasons and given eight performances. On 27 August 1715, the opera was advertised to be performed 'With the Cloaths and several Scenes belonging to Amadis; with the Fountain Scene';[53] presumably either the audiences were growing tired of it or the old scenes were tattered. In any event, this proved to be the penultimate performance: *Hydaspes* appeared only once more during the next season. The text was published in a quarto edition in 1710 and an octavo in 1712.

That Ricci may have made something of a name for himself by the time of this production, or by means of the production itself, is evident in the fact that the 1710 edition of the libretto contains a specific reference to his contribution at the foot of the list of *dramatis personae*: 'The Scenes Painted by Signor Marco Rizzi of Venice'. This may be the first time such a reference is made to a scene painter in either a libretto or play text in England.[54] It is difficult to know what a scene designer-painter was paid. Some specific figures exist for the general period in question, but not so many as to allow generalization. Thus in 1699 Robert Robinson was hired to paint 'Several Sets of Scenes, & Machines' for a new opera by Elkanah Settle at a total sum, paid in instalments, of £130. Records exist of payments for improvements of one sort or another to existing productions.[55] One surviving account for the Haymarket from the 1707–8 season indicates a total outlay for '2 New Operas Cloaths & scenes' at £1275 (more than 17 per cent of the season's total expenditures), though a considerable amount of this sum would have gone for costumes and machines as well as the raw materials for scenery.[56]

(2) The singers

Nicolini [Nicolo Grimaldi] (1673–1732), an Italian alto castrato, was particularly associated with the operas of Scarlatti which he had often performed in his native Naples. His first appearance in London was apparently in Haym's arrangement of Scarlatti's *Pirro e Demetrio* on 14 December 1708. His first season thus coincided with Ricci's. Nicolini was the darling of the press[57]—even writers like Addison and Steele who otherwise satirized Italian opera praised him—though Nicola Haym is attributed with a comment that the applause Nicolini received in London 'be extraordinary, yet it is far short of what he has met with in *Rome, Venice* &c'.[58] Nicolini performed in all three productions with which Marco Ricci was associated.

Catherine Tofts (*c*1685–1756) was an outstanding English soprano who after joining the Drury Lane company had been singing in opera in London since about 1705. She sang opposite Nicolini in both *Pyrrhus* and *Camilla*.[59] She was the subject of satire in *The Tatler* (26 May 1709) shortly after her retirement from the stage at the height of her career. As

Richard Steele had it, Mrs Tofts so identified with her roles that she was unable to get out of character after performances and continued to wear stage costumes in her own lodgings. She had moved to Italy by December 1711, where around 1716 she married Joseph Smith who was eventually to represent the British crown as Consul.[60] Ricci undoubtedly knew Mrs Tofts well while he was in England; when he returned to Venice he received the patronage of her husband.

Francesca Margarita de L'Epine (*c*1680–1746), a soprano, was among the first Italian singers to perform in London, and appeared in both *Pyrrhus* and *Hydaspes*. She shared Catherine Tofts's misfortune of seeing herself satirized, even pilloried in the press, particularly for her looks. Von Uffenbach mentions seeing her perform at a concert: 'on a near view her face was uncommonly ugly, especially in complexion'.[61] Burney comments that 'she was so swarthy and ill-favoured, that her husband used to call her *Hecate*, a name to which she answered with as much good humour as if he had called her Helen'.[62] (Indeed, the woman represented in Ricci's painting, illus.1, caricatured in profile, is distinctly homely.) She was referred to as 'Greber's Peg', supposedly an account of her having arrived in England with the German composer Jacob Greber, whose mistress she is thought to have been. L'Epine was a bitter rival of Mrs Tofts, and this was played out in both the theatre and the press from 1704. In this her foreignness was contributory, as in John Hughes's verse which set her against the 'British Tofts'; he grouped the English nobility according to whether they were Whigs (favouring L'Epine) or Tories (favouring Tofts). She was also the subject of gossip concerning her supposed relationship with Daniel Finch, Earl of Nottingham. She eventually married Pepusch, though the marriage documents remain unfound.[63]

Johanna Maria Lindelheim (fl.1703–17), a German soprano, who during her career in London was known almost exclusively as the Baroness. Burney seems enigmatic about her: 'There is something so mysterious in the title and history of the singer called the Baroness, that I am by no means qualified to be her biographer. All that can be said of her with any certainty is, that she was a German who had learned to sing in Italy . . .'.[64] She performed in both *Pyrrhus* and *Camilla*. After the 1710–11 season few references to her singing are known, all of which are concerts.[65]

(3) Singers' pay and pay disputes

The fees given to singers, especially Italians, who performed in London opera could be extraordinarily high—the most notable example being the season rate of £800 promised to Nicolini for 1708–9. But obtaining the agreed fee from the opera manager was often a matter of some difficulty, reflecting in part the continual financial problems of the enterprise. Indeed, numerous documents from the period record the frequent wranglings about the rates and collecting of pay. Consequently, Nicolini—whose position as a superstar gave him a considerable advantage over other singers—felt obliged to complain and eventually to sue over what he regarded as breach of his 1709 contract with Swiney, who had taken over management of the Queen's Theatre from Vanbrugh.[66]

Not only did the singers feel maltreated, but also—if they were foreigners—they sensed that cultural difference was part of the reason. Thus Nicolini, in filing his suit against Swiney, wrote (in French) to the Lord Chamberlain: 'I beg for your protection, and particularly to deliver me from a disturbing and shameful enslavement which one would not imagine outside England.' And in expanding on this theme he added:

> '. . . Chevalier Nicolino is asking that (considering the disgraces, discomforts, mortifications, and insults that he was subjected to, to the point even of making him ill for almost the whole duration of the last season, . . .) [that] the contract existing between him and Swiney for the two coming years be entirely broken so that he may be free and delivered from such a deplorable tyranny and bondage; and so that he may, with full peace of mind, serve the nobility on whom alone he wants to be dependent.'[67]

Nicolini's remarks, which were over payments associated with the production of *Hydaspes* (for which Ricci had designed the scenery) undoubtedly state the case in the most vivid terms. But however we temper the evaluation of the description of insult he claims to have suffered, it seems reasonable to believe that he felt dishonoured and even demeaned at having to sue, feeling powerless to achieve satisfaction otherwise. Mrs Tofts, who sang with Nicolini in the 1708–9 productions of *Pyrrhus* and *Camilla*, Margarita de L'Epine and the Baroness all had difficulties with managers over salary, dating back as far as 1706 and continuing up to the time of Ricci's residence in London.[68]

(4) The Queen's Theatre, Haymarket

Sir John Vanbrugh, sometime playwright and architect, designed the Queen's Theatre, Haymarket and was intimately involved in establishing Italian opera on its stage—indeed, he may have designed the theatre explicitly with opera in mind[69]—though he gave up his position as manager at the end of his second season.[70] Vanbrugh initiated his enterprise by selling subscriptions costing £100 each to 29 well established individuals, only two or three of whom were untitled.[71] The theatre opened in 1705 with a German opera to an Italian text: *Gli amori d'Ergasto* by Greber. From late 1707, after the drama company who also used the Haymarket returned to Drury Lane, only operas were performed (including the premières of all Handel's Italian operas up to 1734). Though the audience for Italian opera was wider than 'the Quality' (the visual spectacle alone guaranteed a high degree of popular entertainment), it was nevertheless 'exotic, expensive, and artificially sustained for the enjoyment of the leisure class'.[72] Among the most ardent supporters were Vanbrugh's friends and fellow members of the famous Kit-Cat Club. These were individuals who could not only afford to subscribe but also to attend performances on a regular basis; admission was more costly than for dramatic theatre.

Thus during the 1708–9 season the manager, Owen Swiney, raised prices for the pit and boxes to half a guinea after the début of Nicolini, a price that 'excluded all but the very rich from the better seats and established opera as the plaything of the nobility'.[73] Alterations to the theatre in 1709 resulted in audience capacity of around 340 in the pit, 192 in the side boxes, and 96 in the stage boxes—a total of 630 for these prestigious locales; the two galleries each held probably less than 300.[74]

(5) Opposition to Italian opera

In 1710 Charles Gildon published *The Life of Mr Thomas Betterton, the Late Eminent Tragedian*, something of a biography but mostly a critical discourse on theatrical method and the contemporary theatrical scene. Gilden ridiculed the prevailing taste of 'People of Figure' whose subscriptions for '*Squeaking Italians*, and cap'ring Monsieurs' (by the latter he means French dancing masters) seriously threatened the stability of legitimate theatre in London.[75] Gildon was neither first not last among critics of Italian opera—Italian singers had been performing in England since the early 1690s—his chauvinism against anyone foreign was typical. Thus Thomas Burnet and George Duckett in their satire *A Second Tale of a Tub* (London, 1715) refer to 'the tuneful warbling Pig of *Italian Race*' (p.219). For Continentals in general, Italians in particular, religious difference often increased English antipathy:

> *Britons*, who constant War, with factious Rage,
> For Liberty against each other wage,
> From Foreign Insult save the *English* Stage.
> No more th' *Italian* squaling Tribe admit,
> In Tongues unknown, 'tis Popery in Wit.[76]

The earliest, best known and most virulent attacks against Italian opera in early 18th-century London were those written by John Dennis, something of a poet, dramatist, political writer and critic, though not particularly successful in any of these. In 1706 he published *An Essay on the Opera's after the Italian Manner, Which are about to be Establish'd on the English Stage: With Some Reflections on the Damage Which They May Bring to the Publick*.[77] Dennis's first concern, one in which he had much support, was to defend the legitimate English theatre from its musical rival. But what is of interest for the present purpose is the particular way he framed his attack.

Dennis argued that music, which, ironically, he apparently loved, not only weakened men (hardly an original idea in England at the time) but also ruined them as good citizens:[78] 'And as soft and delicious Musick, by soothing the Senses, and making a Man too much in love with himself, makes him too little fond of the Publick; so by emasculating and dissolving the Mind, it shakes the very Foundation of Fortitude, and so is destructive of both Branches of the publick Spirit.' He further held that it is 'soft and effeminate Musick which abounds in the *Italian Opera*'.[79]

Though Dennis's remarks even at the time were taken to be highly overwrought, he continued to address this subject until as late as 1726, his most detailed account appearing in portions of *An Essay upon Publick Spirit* (1711),[80] in which he virtually accuses English supporters of Italian opera of being enemies of the state:

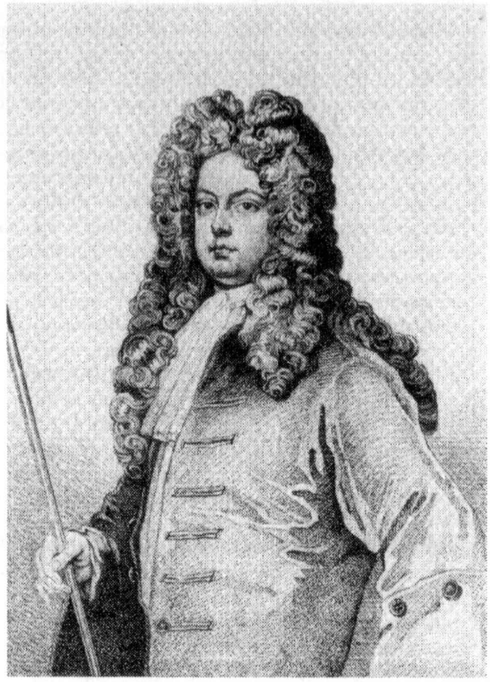

10 Charles Howard: engraving after a painting by Sir Godfrey Kneller, from [James Caulfield], Memoirs of the Celebrated Persons Composing the Kit-Cat Club **(London, 1821), opposite p.96**

> 'If they are so fond of the *Italian* Musick, why do they not take it from the *Hay-Market* to their Houses, and hug it like their secret Sins there? . . . Is there not an implicit Contract between all the People of every Nation, to espouse one another's Interest against all Foreigners whatsoever? But would not any one swear, to observe the Conduct of these Persons, that they were protected by *Italians* in their Liberty, their Property, and their Religion against *Britons*? For why else should they prefer *Italian* Sound to *British* Sense, *Italian* Nonsense to *British* Reason, the Blockheads of *Italy* to their own Countrymen, who have Wit; and the Luxury, and Effeminacy of the most profligate Portion of the Globe to the *British* Virtue?'[81]

Dennis later repeated and strengthened his attack against what he saw as the emasculating qualities of Italian music, suggesting that British women ought to discourage their men from opera, else risk their husbands becoming homosexual.[82]

The various critiques of Italian opera by Joseph Addison and Richard Steele in *The Spectator* and (to a lesser extent) *The Tatler* are well known. Though they couched much of their criticism in terms of aesthetics, like others I have cited, these authors were much concerned with the financial impact of Italian opera on the institution of the English stage.[83] Italian opera was a source of satire on the English stage itself, though usually by means of short reference. There is a single example of an extended satire, produced while Ricci was in London: *Prunella* (1708), a parody of *Camilla*, by Richard Estcourt, an actor and co-manager at Drury Lane.[84] *Prunella* was inserted as an after-piece in a performance of a play by George Villiers, Duke of Buckingham, called *The Rehearsal*, first produced in 1671.[85] An advertisement for the production claimed, with typical bluster, that the work was to be mounted 'at the Request of many of the Nobility (who have taken Tickets)', urging that servants be sent by 2 o'clock p.m. with tickets in hand in order to occupy the choice seats for their masters and 'to prevent any Disappointment'.[86] In fact, the work seems to have received only one performance, though its text was printed in the same year of the production. It consists of 26 song texts with text incipit indicating the musical score to which the new words are to be applied. *Camilla*, which had been performed in London 41 times up to the appearance of *Prunella*, is the source for 14 of the 26 songs: the tunes would have been well known. The texts are suitably ridiculous, as in '*Prince Prettyman's* Air to fall asleep with':

Constant Weeping, want of Sleeping,
Makes me weary as a Dog,
Sighing, Reaching, Gaping, Stretching,
Throws me down like any Log.
Ah, that any honest Fellow
Wou'd bring here a good soft Pillow,
Then, instead of a Fair Lady's Lap,
You'd quickly see me fall in a Gape, Gape, Gape.[87]

Richard Leppert was trained in musicology and art history at Indiana University. He is Professor of Humanities, University of Minnesota.

[1]A detailed study of some of these images was made some years ago by Eric Walter White, 'The Rehearsal of an Opera', *Theatre Notebook*, xiv/3 (1960), pp.79ff (with 6 plates); White then knew of seven versions. He carefully analyzed the information on the labels, wrote biographical sketches of the singers who seemed to be involved, and tried to establish not only the dates of the paintings but also the particular operas whose rehearsal(s) may be represented. I am interested in a set of questions this earlier article did not raise.

[2]The Royal Library, Windsor Castle, contains numerous drawings by Ricci for stage designs, though none belongs to his time in England; see A. Blunt and E. Croft-Murray, *Venetian Drawings of the XVII and XVIII Centuries in the Collection of Her Majesty the Queen at Windsor Castle* (London, 1957), p.42. Consul Smith's album of drawings, also now at Windsor, contains 141 images by Ricci. But according to Blunt and Croft-Murray, they 'doubtless all belong to the period following the artist's final return to Venice in 1716', though many of them represent operatic figures. By contrast Milkovich claims (I believe incorrectly) that 'many preparatory drawings still exist' for Ricci's work at the Haymarket in the Windsor collections; see M. Milkovich, *Sebastiano and Marco Ricci in America* [exhibition catalogue] (Lexington, Kentucky, 1966), p.11.

[3]On his first trip Ricci (with Pellegrini) decorated Castle Howard in Yorkshire for Charles Howard. Ricci also worked for Richard Boyle at Burlington House, Piccadilly, London. It is easy to guage England's attraction for the painter. As an artist working in Venice the opportunities were few: the Venetian nobility was not only impoverished, it also 'had never encouraged the arts on a large scale' (Milkovich, *op cit*, p.8). Indeed, in Venice it was foreign patrons, and especially the English, who provided commissions. While few records survive to document Ricci's financial affairs in England, Sebastiano succeeded admirably. When the two men left England in 1716, Sebastiano was 'laden with so much money that he had to pay a special tax in order to export it' (*Works by Sebastiano Ricci from British Collections* [exhibition catalogue], introduction by J. Daniels (London, 1978), p.4). For details of Marco's time in England, see R. Pallucchini, *Marco Ricci, Catalogo della Mostra* [exhibition catalogue] (Venice, [1964]), pp.xviii–xxi. George Vertue's period 'Notebooks' on artists contain only passing references to Marco Ricci's work in England: in a discussion of Sebastiano—where Vertue derisively describes his penchant for claiming as original, and for a high price, his own copies of masterworks—he alludes to Marco as Sebastiano's 'nephew of the same stamp, tho' both skilful painters in different manners'. Vertue elsewhere refers to Marco as a 'Landskip painter who painted Landskip very well as may be seen in several Noblemen & Lovers Collections': see 'The Vertue Notebooks', *Walpole Society Journal*, xviii (1929–30), p.39; xxiv (1936), p.82. Horace Walpole, who at one time owned illus.1, says of Marco that his works 'are still admired, though there is little excellence in them; his colouring is chalky, and without force' (H. Walpole, *Anecdotes of Painting in England*, i (Strawberry Hill, 1763), p.142).

[4]White makes this assertion on internal visual evidence, especially costume (*op cit*, p.82). With regard to attribution see *idem*, pp.89f, and Blunt and Croft-Murray, *op cit*, p.143.

[5]See Pallucchini, *op cit*, pp.44–6. However, the version reproduced in Pallucchini's catalogue (p.47) is actually (and mistakenly) the painting belonging to Viscount Knutsford Munden (illus.2). In the catalogue to the Royal Academy winter exhibition '*Italian Art and Britain*' (London, 1960), pp.176f, most of the painting is assigned to Sebastiano, Marco's contribution being the landscape painting-within-the-painting. More recent exhibitions and monographs, however, continue to assign the work wholly to Marco: among others, see *La Peinture italienne au XVIIIe siècle* [exhibition catalogue] (Paris, 1960–61), no.366, and J. Daniels, *Sebastiano Ricci* (Hove, Sussex, 1976), pp.61f. Daniels quotes Francis Watson's observation that a collaboration on so small a canvas is unlikely: 'The inclusion of Katherine Tofts, who left England for Venice in 1709 [the exact date of departure is not known] . . . adds further weight to this attribution, since Sebastiano did not arrive in England until 1711 at the earliest.'

[6]See *The Works of Horatio Walpole, Earl of Orford*, ii (London, 1798), p.498. For the full details of the labels, see White, *op cit*, pp.79f. This label also identifies: 'The gentleman in blue, with a patch on one eye, sitting by the Margarita, is Sir Robert Rich, father of Elizabeth Lady Lyttelton' (White, p.79), but the 1842 sale catalogue comments that 'the gentleman in blue, with a patch on one eye, standing next her . . .' which as White points out makes it unclear which figure is intended. The woman Walpole names as Mrs Tofts looks much heavier and coarser than the character so identified in other versions of the painting (illus.5–8); cf. White, *op cit*, pp.83f, especially the reproduced caricature-drawing on p.86. White (p.88) disputes this identification and suggests other possibilities, thereby contradicting Walpole.

[7]See M. Levey, 'The Eighteenth-century Italian Painting Exhibition at Paris: Some Corrections and Suggestions', *Burlington Magazine*, ciii (1961), p.140, and Pallucchini, *op cit*, p.45. The landscape is largely similar to two by Ricci representing a *View of Belluno* (see the reproductions in Pallucchini, no.81, reproduced p.109; no.138, reproduced p.147).

[8]Blunt and Croft-Murray, *op cit*, p.143, suggest that the provenance 'as far as one can make out, is English; indeed, there would have been nothing to prevent Ricci from painting Venetian subjects in England'. See also Pallucchini, *op cit*, p.44.

[9]The second example is mentioned (but not reproduced) by White, *op cit*, p.81; painted in oils on a canvas measuring 18" × 23", it is almost identical in size to the painting reproduced as illus.4. White knows of no label or inscription on either painting to leave us any written information about the possible identity of sitters (see White, *op cit*, p.82).

[10]The Haymarket documents of the period contain a single reference to 'Mr Sagione a Theorbo . . .', further references appear to this musician, though not to the theorbo; see J. Milhous and R. D. Hume, eds., *Vice Chamberlain Coke's Theatrical Papers, 1706–1715* (Carbondale, Illinois, 1982), p.77. Saggione is known to have been a composer and to have played the bass viol (idem, p.67), it is unclear whether he also played the theorbo. The fact that 'a Theorbo' appears on the following line may indicate the hiring of another, unnamed individual, but if that is the case a separate payment should have been recorded. Saggione was apparently first engaged to play in the 1708 production of *Pyrrhus*; thus it is possible that it is he who is depicted playing either the bass viol or archlute in illus.1, 2, 4. Musicians' rosters are given by Milhous and Hume on pp.33, 68, 127, 133, 151, 158f; for the names of other Continental instrumentalists who played at the Haymarket up until the 1711–12 seasons see pp.30–33, 38f, 69, 76–9, 118f, 127, 133, 151, 158f, 179f.

[11]White, *op cit*, p.87

[12]See J. Milhous, 'New Light on Vanbrugh's Haymarket Theatre Project', *Theatre Survey*, xvii/2 (1976), p.157.

[13]For further information on Castle Howard, see M. Bingham, *Masks and Façades: Sir John Vanbrugh, the Man in His Setting* (London, 1974), pp.143–9, N. Nicolson, *The National Trust Book of Great Houses in Britain* (Boston, 1978), pp.194–201, and especially L. Whistler, *The Imagination of Vanbrugh and His Fellow Artists* (London, 1954), pp.26–82, in particular pp.34–62.

[14]Whistler, *op cit*, p.56, and E. Croft-Murray, *Decorative Painting in England, 1537–1837*, ii (Feltham, Middlesex, 1972), p.265. Most of Ricci's work at Castle Howard (see Croft-Murray, figs.8, 9, for reproductions of two Ricci overdoors) was destroyed in the fire of 1940. See also F. J. B. Watson, 'English Villas and Venetian Decorators', *Journal of the Royal Institute of British Architects*, lxi (1953–4), p.172.

[15]White, *op cit*, p.82. For further comment on this painting, see: R. Pallucchini, 'Studi ricceschi (II) contributo a Marco Ricci', *Arte Veneta*, ix (1955), p.179; T. Borenius, 'Venetian Eighteenth Century Painters in England', *Fine Art (Studio)* [special issue] (Spring, 1931), pp.51, 53; Pallucchini, *Marco Ricci* [catalogue], p.48; T. Borenius, 'Two Venetian Pictures of Queen Anne's London', *Apollo*, iii (1926), pp.207–9.

[16]For general comments on illus.6–8 see White, *op cit*, pp.80f. Whereas I have divided the paintings into two groups, White on different grounds has divided them into three. Illus.8 was unknown to White, Blunt and Croft-Murray. Illus.7 is further discussed in Pallucchini, 'Studi ricceschi', p.178, and A. Morassi, 'Pitture Veneziane del Settecento in una Mostra a Londra', *Emporium*, cxiii (1951), p.220. Much of the information given by the label on the reverse of this version—which postdate the painting—is demonstrably wrong: in particular the identification of the 'conductor' as Senesino, who only came to England in 1720, long after Ricci's painting was produced, and 'the lady in white' as the soprano Anastasia Robinson, whose career began after Ricci's picture was painted. The label is quoted in full in White, *op cit*, p.81. For comment on the marine landscapes in illus.6–7, see Pallucchini, *Marco Ricci* [catalogue], pp.45f.

[17]White (*op cit*, p.87) suggests that the woman identified—on the label—as Margarita's mother is actually Margarita herself, and that the woman identified as Margarita is the Baroness! This conflicts with the identifications in the *New Grove*, 'L'Epine, Margherita de'.

[18]White, *op cit*, p.88

[19]The *New Grove*, 'Heidegger, Johann Jakob'; for a known likeness, cf. *idem*, 'Cuzzoni, Francesca'.

[20]The portrait is reproduced in the *New Grove*, 'Pepusch, Johann Christoph'. White (*op cit*, p.88) sees 'no need to query the identification' of these two sitters. While both individuals could logically be expected to be in the scene, the visual evidence seems very shaky. White also suggests that the man identified on the label as Sir Robert Rich (illus.1) ought instead to be taken as Christopher Rich, manager of Drury Lane. He also mentions that Owen Swiney, manager of the Haymarket, may be among the individuals otherwise not identified. This has some merit in that Marco and (later) Sebastiano were both friends of Swiney; see E. Croft-Murray, *op cit*, p.42.

[21]No explanation is given for these identifications which appear in the *New Grove*, 'L'Epine, Margherita de'.

[22]See P. H. Highfill, jr., *Biographical Dictionary of Actors, Actresses, Musicians, Dancers, Managers and other stage personnel in London, 1660–1800* (Carbondale, Illinois, 1973–), iii, pp.49f [Caporale], v, pp.235–8 [the Festings], and *The New Grove*, 'Festing, Michael'. There was a Mr Festing who as a violinist gave a benefit concert at York Buildings in 1707; despite reservations, it is conceivable that this individual, about whom little is known, is represented in Ricci's painting. Better choices could probably be made on the basis of the lists of orchestra personnel from the Haymarket for the period in question, see fn.10.

[23]White, *op cit*, pp.87f

[24]See M. Tilmouth, 'A Calendar of References to Music in Newspapers Published in London and the Provinces (1660–1719)', *RMA Research Chronicle*, i (1961), p.75; E. L. Avery, ed., '1700–1729', *The London Stage, 1660–1800: a Calendar of Plays, Entertainments & Afterpieces* (Carbondale, Illinois, 1960), pp.clvi, 214. There was probably a previous public rehearsal on 2 March.

[25]See Milhous and Hume, *op cit*, pp.68f. The financial account for the Haymarket dating from March 1708 details the costs for a new production of *Love's Triumph* including the 'Practices for it'; the rehearsals cost a total of £42 (*idem*, pp.91, 93f, 159). The three individuals named are: 'Mr Diopar', 'Mr Heyams' and 'Mr Papuch'; that is, Charles Dieupart (who appears in a list for 1707 as a harpsichordist), Nicola Haym (appearing on the same list as a bass player, and on one for December 1710 as a violoncellist) and John Christopher Pepusch (appearing on the first list as a harpsichordist, on the second as a violinist). All three were also composer-arrangers. According to John Hawkins, Dieupart and Haym played harpsichord and cello respectively in *Camilla* and *Pyrrhus*: *General History of the Science and Practice of Music*, ii (London, 1776, 2/1873/*R*1969), p.822. In January 1706 Haym had contracted with manager Rich 'to provide copies of the score and parts [of *Camilla*] using an English translation made at Rich's expense, advise Rich on casting the opera and help rehearse it, and provide and perform other Italian music' (Milhous and Hume, *op cit*, p.2). He also worked on the adaptation of *Pyrrhus*. White (*op cit*, p.88) suggests that Haym is the harpsichordist in illus.1, 2, 5–8, and perhaps the bass viol player in illus.4. This is a reasonable conjecture; the individuals represented in these two groups—the harpsichordist in six pictures and the bass violist in one—have a resemblance.

[26]See Milhous and Hume, *op cit*, pp.159f. Aaron Hill, together with William Collier, served as joint managers at the Haymarket for the 1710–11 and 1711–12 seasons.

[27]Lady Wentworth is quoted in J. J. Cartwright, ed., *The Wentworth Papers, 1705–1739* (London, 1883), p.66; the letter also appears in Avery, *op cit*, p.180. See also White, *op cit*, p.89, and M. Sands, 'The Rehearsal of an Opera', *Theatre Notebook*, xix (1964–5), pp.30f.

[28]See Avery, *op cit*, p.180

[29]*Eighteenth Century Venice* [exhibition catalogue], introduction by F. J. B. Watson (London, 1951), p.31 (repeated in *Italian Art and*

Britain, p.177); see also *La Peinture italienne au XVIIIe siècle* [catalogue], no.366, given as 'Répétition de Chant'.

[30]The audience in illus.1–2, and to some extent illus.4, could possibly include some of these patrons; Ricci's caricaturing of his sitters makes certain identification difficult. For example none bears a convincing resemblance to any of the 48 Kit-Cat portraits by Sir Godfrey Kneller, executed around the time of Ricci's paintings, c1702–17, and reproduced in J. Caulfield, *Memoirs of the Celebrated Persons Composing the Kit-Cat Club . . . Illustrated with forty-eight Portraits, from the Original Paintings by Sir Godfrey Kneller* (London, 1821).

[31]See R. D. Leppert, 'Men, Women and Music at Home: the influence of cultural values on Musical Life in 18th-century England', *Imago Musicae*, ii (1985), pp.51–133. Sir Joshua Reynolds was later to caricature young noblemen attempting to make music while in Italy on the Grand Tour. He produced these visual jokes for the very people he was satirizing, as may be the case with Ricci. Reynolds's caricatures, which were of course taken home to England among other souvenirs, reaffirm the subjects' Englishness amidst the temptations of the Continent. For further information see E. K. Waterhouse, *Three Decades of British Art, 1740–1770* (Philadelphia, 1965), p.27, and *British Artists in Rome* [exhibition catalogue] (London, 1974), no.99.

[32]S. L. Gulich, ed., *Some unpublished letters of Lord Chesterfield* (Berkeley, 1937), p.78

[33]D. F. Bond, ed., *The Spectator*, ii (Oxford, 1965), p.305 [no.205, 25 October 1711]

[34]Croft-Murray, *op cit*, ii, pp.254, 265. Ricci is known to have painted a landscape and a seascape or seaport for Richard Boyle, 3rd Earl of Burlington, Handel's patron. Burlington was not among the original 29 subscribers to the Haymarket project.

[35]There appears to be no relation between the various scenes Ricci painted in the Rehearsal pictures and those he may have produced for the operas on whose productions he worked. Only the libretto of *Camilla* calls for a scene that might bear resemblance to one of these pictures, namely the landscapes in illus.1, 2, 4: Act 1 scene i, 'A Champian Country with Plains and easie Hills, the End of a Wood on one Side, and Prospect of a City at Distance'. However, as I have previously pointed out, Ricci and Pellegrini did not work directly on this opera; that is, the pre-existant *Camilla* production only borrowed scenes which they had painted for *Pyrrhus* (or *Clotilda*).

[36]This was reproduced in the exhibition catalogue by A. Bettagno, *Disegni e dipinti di Giovanni Antonio Pellegrini* (Venice, 1959), no.112. However, the individual Ricci painted is not easily identified as an artist, given that he seems to hold a book, unless a sheaf of drawings is intended.

[37]Earning a living by this means could be precarious. During the 1712–13 season, when manager Owen Swiney absconded to the Continent, he left 'ye Singers unpaid ye Scenes & Habits also unpaid for'; see J. Milhous, 'Opera Finances in London, 1674–1738', *JAMS*, xxxvii (1984), pp.576ff.

[38]Thus Lord Halifax wrote on behalf of Thornhill (and against Sebastiano) for the commission to decorate the Prince of Wales's bedchamber at Hampton Court: 'Mr Thornhill our countryman . . . strove against all oppositions and difficulties and now had got near the very top of the Mountain and his grace would throw him down and oust all his endeavours, which would prevent and discourage all our countrymen ever after to attempt the like again'. Sebastiano lost the commission. See J. Hook, *The Baroque Age in England* (London, 1976), pp.49f, and Croft-Murray, *op cit*, i, pp.72–5; ii, p.266.

[39]Daniels, *op cit*, p.xvi

[40]Croft-Murray, *op cit*, ii, p.264

[41]From the impression given by illus.4 it is difficult to believe that more than one or two of the audience of six hears anything of the music.

[42]On Haym and his work on this opera, see Hawkins, *op cit*, pp.814, 819–22.

[43]Avery, *op cit*, ii, p.189; cf. C. Burney, *A General History of Music from the Earliest Ages to the Present*, iv (London, 1789, 2/1935/R1957), pp.209–11

[44]F. Raguenet, *A Comparison Between the French and Italian Musick and Opera's. Translated from the French; with Some Remarks. To Which is Added A Critical Discourse upon Operas in England, and a Means Proposed for Their Improvement*, with introduction by C. Cudworth (London, 1709/R1968), pp.80f. The first part of this is an English translation of Raguenet's *Paralèle des italiens et des français, en ce qui regards la musique et les opéras* (Paris, 1702, 3/c1710; Eng. trans. repr. in *MQ*, xxxii (1946), p.411). The facsimile reprint of the 1709 translation contains valuable marginal comments by an unknown 18th-century hand. On Haym's supposed authorship of the *Discourse* see p.2 of the introduction, and C. Price, 'The Critical Decade for English Music Drama, 1700–1710', *Harvard Library Bulletin*, xxvi (1978), p.22.

[45]See Avery, *op cit*, ii, p.189

[46]Tilmouth, *op cit*, p.73

[47]*Ibid*, pp.74, 77, 93; Avery, *op cit*, ii, p.cix. A performance of *Pyrrhus* on 21 March 1710 had been advertised 'With all the Scenes and Decorations of the last new Opera of Almahide'; Giovanni Bononcini's *Almahide* received its première at the Haymarket on 10 January 1710 (see Avery, *op cit*, pp.208, 216).

[48]*Ibid*, pp.180–439, *passim*

[49]See Price, *op cit*, p.49

[50]The 1706 edition is reprinted in facsimile, together with the 1696 Naples edition, in H. M. Brown, gen. ed., *Italian Opera Librettos 1640–1770*, x (New York, 1979). See also A. Nicoll, 'Early Eighteenth-century Drama', *A History of English Drama, 1660–1900*, ii (Cambridge, 3/1952), pp.227f, 274f. The most detailed study of *Camilla* appears in L. E. Lindgren, *A Bibliographic scrutiny of Dramatic Works set by Giovanni and his brother Antonio Maria Bononcini* (diss. Harvard U., 1972); see especially vol.i, pp.165–227, 686–8 for details on the London productions and the opera's reception in England. Burney, *op cit*, pp.201–3, 210, gives *Camilla* brief mention; Hawkins, *op cit*, pp.810, 860, discusses its success but concentrates on the later rivalry between Bononcini and Handel. For further discussion of the common practice of re-using sets from one production to another, see Nicoll, *op cit*, p.32.

[51]W. H. Quarrell and M. Mare, trans. and ed., *London in 1710, from the Travels of Zacharias Conrad von Uffenbach* (London, 1934), p.18. Raguenet (*op cit*, pp.55f) provided a lengthy description of Italian set design which he greatly admired:

'you'll find among their Decorations Statues of Marble and Alabaster, that may vye with the most celebrated Antiques in *Rome*; Palaces, Colonades, Galleries, and Sketches of Architecture, superior in Grandure and Magnificence to all the Buildings in the World; Pieces of Perspective that deceive the Judgment, as well as the Eye, even of those that are curious in the Art; Prospects of a prodigious Extent, in Spaces not thirty foot deep; nay, they often represent on the Stage the lofty Edifices of the ancient *Romans*, of which only the Remains are now to be seen . . . so that these Decorations are not only entertaining but instructive.'

That this text appeared in London just after the beginning of Ricci's first visit reinforces the importance attached to the importation of Italian scene painters, among whom Ricci and Pellegrini were the first. On this last point, see S. Rosenfield, 'Scene Painters at the London Theatres in the 18th Century', *Theatre Notebook*, xx (1965–6), pp.114f.

[52]See Bond, *The Spectator*, i, pp.55–59 [no.13, 15 March 1711]; this essay appeared nearly a year after the first performance. Steele took up the satire as well, as in a letter from 'Toby Rentfree' who wrote of his annoyance at having his shouts to encore the scene ignored by Nicolini (*idem*, iii, pp.138f [no.314, 29 February 1712], i, p.60 [no.14, 16 March 1711]). For a letter regarding a satirical puppet show in

which 'Punch most heroically kills a pig and sings an *Io Pean* in Italian music, this has affronted Nicolini and he threatens to tread the stage no more', see i, p.64, n.3. More details of Lady Mary Montague's reaction to seeing Nicolini kill the lion are given in R. Halsband, ed., *The Complete Letters of Lady Mary Wortley-Montagu*, i (Oxford, 1965), pp.22f, fn.3; see also Hawkins, *op cit*, p.814, and Burney, *op cit*, pp.212f.

[53]Avery, *op cit*, p.365; also given in Tilmouth, *op cit*, p.91

[54]See Nicoll, *op cit*, p.34; Hawkins, *op cit*, p.814, acknowledges Ricci's contribution as well, though undoubtedly from having read the libretto.

[55]See Avery, *op cit*, pp.cviii, lxv, and S. Rosenfield, 'An Opera House Accunt Book', *Theatre Notebook*, xvi (1961–62), p.88

[56]Milhous and Hume, *op cit*, p.77. Thus Mrs Tofts sought reimbursement for 80 guineas she had personally spent on her *Camilla* costumes, see *idem*, pp.29f, 46.

[57]For examples, see Bond, *The Spectator*, iii, pp.513f [no.405, 14 June 1712], and G. A. Aitken, ed., *The Tatler*, iii (New York, 1899), pp.5–7 [no.115, 31 December 1709–3 January 1710]. For further accounts of Nicolini, see Raguenet, *op cit*, pp.18f, fn.13, 40f, fn.26; Hawkins, *op cit*, p.809 (who states that Nicolini first performed in London in *Camilla*); B. R. S. Fone, ed., *C. Cibber: An Apology for the Life of Colley Cibber* (London, 1740/*R*1968), pp.209–11; G. Hogarth, *Memoirs of the Musical Drama*, i (London, 1838), pp.254–7; W. D. Montagu, ed., *Court and Society from Elizabeth to Anne*, ii (London, 1854), pp.352–3, 384f.

[58]Raguenet, *op cit*, pp.28f, fn.18

[59]Colley Cibber lauds her singing: see Fone, *op cit*, pp.211f, cf. Burney, *op cit*, pp.215–19, which includes musical examples of her vocal divisions; Hawkins, *op cit*, p.816. See also Hogarth, *op cit*, pp.249–52.

[60]See Aitken, *The Tatler*, i, p.171 [no.20, 24–6 May 1709]; for the date of her marriage to Smith, see M. Levey, 'Marco Ricci and "Madama Smit"', *Burlington Magazine*, civ (1962), p.352. See also Bond, *The Spectator*, iv, pp.55f [no.443, 29 July 1712] purported to be a letter from Mrs Tofts in Venice indicating that she is still performing. For the most detailed account of her life and career, see M. Sands, 'Mrs Tofts, 1685?–1756', *Theatre Notebook*, xx (1965–66), pp.100ff.

[61]Quarrell and Mare, *op cit*, p.67

[62]Burney, *op cit*, p.219

[63]For detailed accounts of her career, see D. F. Cook, 'Françoise Marguérite de L'Epine: The Italian Lady?', *Theatre Notebook*, xxxv (1981), pp.58ff, 104ff; and E. L. Moor, 'Some Notes on the Life of Françoise Marguérite de L'Épine', *Music and Letters*, xxviii (1947), pp.341ff. See also Hawkins, *op cit*, pp.816f, 884f; Burney, *op cit*, pp.197f, and Highfill, *op cit*, iv, pp.292–6.

[64]Burney, *op cit*, p.220

[65]For a biographical sketch, see *The New Grove*, 'Lindelheim, Joanna Maria' and Highfill, *op cit*, i, pp.298–301.

[66]Milhous and Hume, *op cit*, pp.139–42

[67]*Ibid*, pp.139, 141

[68]See *ibid*, pp.29f, 45–9, 56f, 67–71, 76–80, 99, 109; Price, *op cit*, p.62; Nicoll, *op cit*, pp.288–91

[69]See D. Nalbach, *The King's Theatre, 1704–1867* (London, 1972), pp.10f.

[70]Price, *op cit*, p.76, which, however, conflicts with the view stated by Nalbach, *op cit*, pp.1ff, and Milhous, 'New Light', pp.147, 150.

[71]Price, *op cit*, p.76

[72]Nalbach, *op cit*, p.14

[73]*Ibid*, pp.26–7; on the general early history of the Haymarket theatre and the establishment of opera there, see *idem*, pp.1–17; on the cheaper tickets, which went for as little as two shillings in the third gallery, see *idem*, p.25. Information regarding ticket prices and gate receipts for the 1710–11 productions of *Pyrrhus* and *Hydaspes* is given by Milhous and Hume, *op cit*, pp.156f, 160–66. For general information on opera finances during Ricci's time in England, see Avery, *op cit*, pp.lxf, lxviii–lxxiii, and Milhous, 'Opera Finances', pp.571–7, 590–2. These various accounts clarify the extent of the difficulty in maintaining Italian opera in England; more often than not it was an institution on—or over—the brink of financial disaster.

[74]Milhous, 'New Light', pp.156–9, provides a complete list together with basic biographical details and association, if any, with the Kit-Cat Club. Vanbrugh obtained pledges more easily than the fees associated with them (*idem*, p.145). In 1708 Vanbrugh corresponded with his patron Charles Montagu in Venice; some of this correspondence concerns Vanbrugh's work as architect for the rebuilding of Kimbolton Castle, Montagu's ancestral home. But many of the letters discuss music and the Haymarket, including the procurement of Italian singers: see Milhous and Hume, *op cit*, pp.85, 97, 106f, 112f; G. Webb, ed., 'The Letters', *The Complete Works of Sir John Vanbrugh*, iv (Bloomsbury, 1928), pp.16–21, 24, 26; Montagu, *op cit*, pp.289–91, 354–6, 377, 383f. See also P. Olleson, 'Vanbrugh and Opera at the Queen's Theatre, Haymarket', *Theatre Notebook*, xxvi (1971–72), pp.94ff. My source on seating capacity is Nalbach, *op cit*, p.26.

[75]C. Gildon, *The Life of Mr. Thomas Betterton, the Late Eminent Tragedian* (London, 1710/*R*1970), pp.142–4, 158–67.

[76]From an anonymous epilogue to Richard Steele's play *The Tender Husband* (1705), quoted from Nicoll, *op cit*, p.231; cf. Sands, 'Mrs Tofts', p.103. See also F. C. Petty, *Italian Operas in London, 1760–1800* (Ann Arbor, 1980), pp.3–17, 69–85; resistance to foreign musicians continued throughout the century. For an account of the effects of English chauvinism on foreign music teachers, many of whom were also professional performers, see R. D. Leppert, 'Music Teachers of upper-class amateur musicians in Eighteenth-century England', *Music in the Classic Period: Essays in Honor of Barry S. Brook*, ed. A. W. Atlas (New York, 1985), pp.133–58.

[77]E. N. Hooker, ed., *The Critical Works of John Dennis*, i (Baltimore, 1939), pp.382–93 [with editorial remarks on pp.520–24].

[78]Leppert, 'Men, Women and Music at Home . . .', see fn.31.

[79]Hooker, *op cit*, i, pp.389 and 384, respectively.

[80]The passages dealing with opera are reprinted in Hooker, *op cit*, ii, pp.393–6.

[81]*Ibid*, p.395; cf. Richard Steele in Bond, *The Spectator*, ii, pp.284f [no.200, 19 October 1711]

[82]Hooker, *op cit*, ii, p.396; cf. R. Steele in Bond, *The Spectator*, ii, p.82 [no.148, 20 August 1711], p.305 [no.205, 25 October 1711]

[83]For a general discussion of this subject, see S. A. Betz, 'The Operatic Criticism of the *Tatler* and *Spectator*', *MQ*, xxxi (1945), pp.318ff. The most important of these essays are those appearing in [Bond] *The Spectator*, i, pp.22–7 [no.5, 6 March 1711], 78–82 [no.18, 21 March 1711].

[84]For a discussion of theatrical satire on Italian opera, see D. I. West, 'Italian Opera in England (1660–1740), and some of its relationships to English Literature' (diss. U. of Illinois, 1937), pp.78, 113–35; most of the discussion focuses on the period after Handel's arrival in 1710. Also valuable, though primarily concerned with works postdating *The Beggar's Opera* (1728), is D. F. Smith and M. L. Lawhorn, *Plays about the Theatre in England, 1737–1800, or, The Self-Conscious Stage from Foote to Sheridan* (Lewisburg and London, 1979), pp.119–31.

[85]Lindgren, *op cit*, p.213, indicates that Estcourt wrote Prunella's passages as replacements or supplements for passages in *The Rehearsal*; most of my secondary information on this piece comes from this source, pp.212–23.

[86]Avery, *op cit*, p.166

[87]R. Estcourt, *Prunella* (London, 1708), p.12. No other parody opera was given in London until the 1719 production of *Harlequin-Hydaspes*, a satire on *Hydaspes* which had been most recently revived in 1717–19; on this piece see Lindgren, *op cit*, pp.222f and West, *op cit*, pp.142–7.

You cannot paint or sing yourselves into being good men; you must be good men before you can either paint or sing, and then the colour and sound will complete in you all that is best.

John Ruskin,
"The Relation of Art to Morals"

CHAPTER 8

MALE AGONY: AWAKENING CONSCIENCE

A MAN AND A WOMAN, alone in a gaudy Victorian room, have been at music (Fig. 91),[1] just now seemingly interrupted as the woman rises awkwardly from her seated position. The picture is richly narrative; its story is governed by music. Yet its musical situation is demonstrably "wrong." What might this mean? How, for example, can the man play the piano from a tilt-backed easy chair whose seat is too low for him properly to reach the keys? How can he play the instrument while a woman sits in his lap? His mouth is open, and he gestures as if expressing a song's words. We might reasonably think she is singing as well; her lips are parted, and her hands are held together as if in recital pose. Yet there is no audience for her performance except the unseen viewer; thus her formality is gratuitous. Perhaps she is wringing her hands (people wring their hands in opera, in the theater, and in paintings as a conventionalized indication of grief).[2] She stands bent forward at the waist, not a singer's stance. Nor do singers perform while dressed in nightgowns like hers,[3] except in operas, and then only when they have committed a crime (Lucia) or are about to die for a (supposed) crime (Desdemona). Operatic transgressions of this sort are invariably linked both to desire and sexuality.

Is she singing, or is she crying out in horror—at what he sings? The music on the piano rack begins, "Oft, in the stilly night." It is a song about love, loss, and memory; it is not a proper love song. Why is he singing to her a tale to evoke sadness and, in this instance, the moral revulsion attested to by the painting's title? The song cannot address his interests. She is, after all, his illicit lover. The song is only going to cause him problems; indeed, it already has. Although the

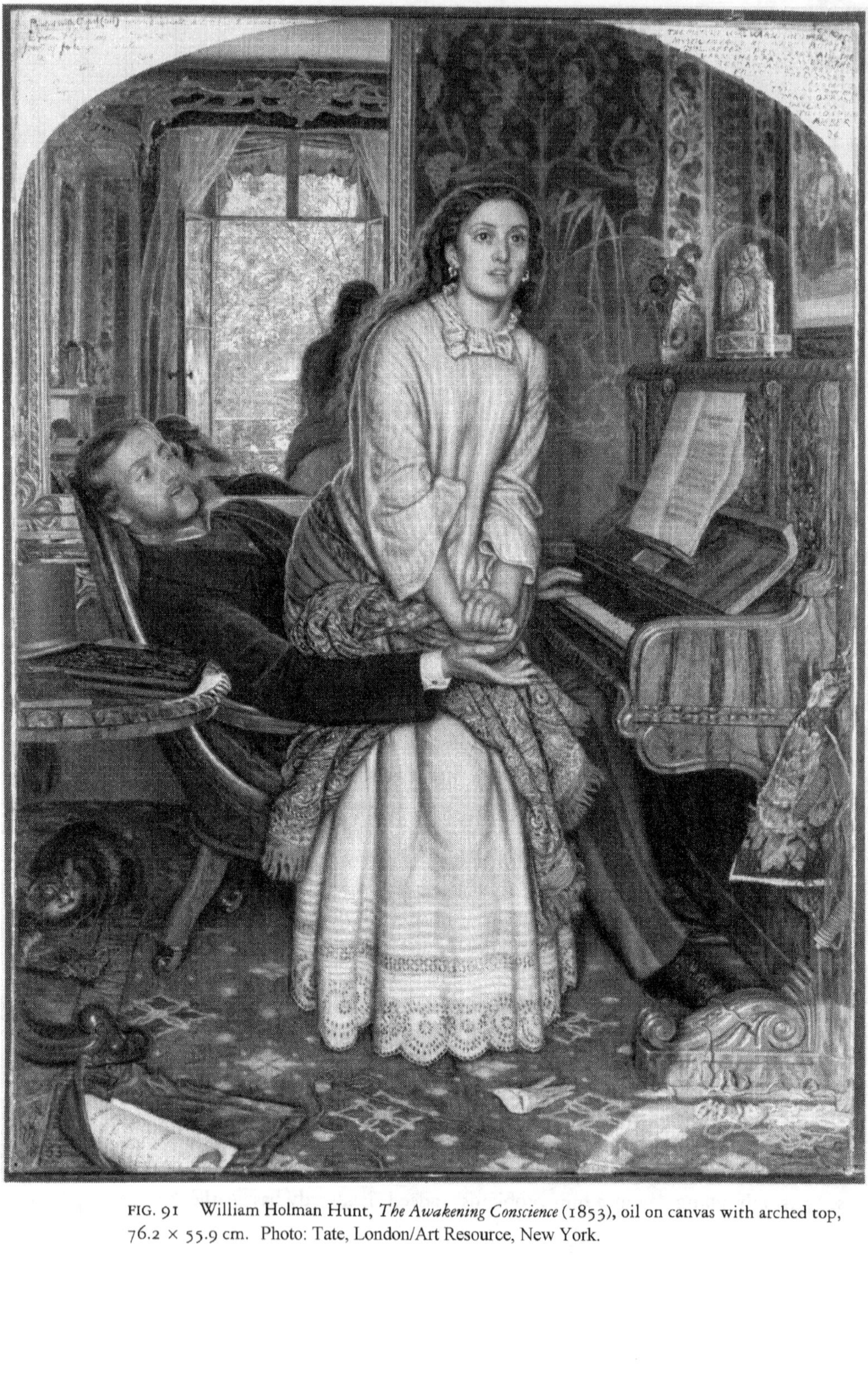

FIG. 91 William Holman Hunt, *The Awakening Conscience* (1853), oil on canvas with arched top, 76.2 × 55.9 cm. Photo: Tate, London/Art Resource, New York.

painting concatenates sex with music and music with a woman, the representation is contradictory as regards both music and woman.

In opera a scene like this would occur at night, the "time" for sex, and sometimes death. Not so here. The sun shines brightly in the garden at the back, and the room is bathed in light, accentuating the garish colors of the carpet. In the light of day things are clearer. Objectivity triumphs like an ancillary to science. Light vanquishes darkness and puts on display, almost clinically, the dark urges of the flesh. In Victorian culture sexuality was the urgent concern of medicine, psychiatry, law, and public morals, invariably focused on the illegalities of the night involving the bodies of prostitutes,[4] among whom painters commonly found their female models, including this one.[5] William Holman Hunt "discovered" her when she was fifteen.

> Child prostitution was a booming industry; virgins were particularly prized by gentlemen as "green fruit," and some parents, made heartless by desperation, sold their daughters' maidenheads for as little as five pounds or as much as twenty pounds—more money than some working-class people made in a year. (To salve everyone's conscience, the child was sometimes given chloroform during the defloration.)[6]

Hunt's interest in his model, whose name was Annie Miller,[7] was more than professional. He wanted her for his wife, provided he could get her made over into a proper bourgeois.[8] At age twenty-six he was himself a virgin, unlike his artist friend(s) who became her lover(s) after Hunt's temporary departure, following the completion of this very painting, for (where else?) the Holy Land to paint biblical scenes. Hunt's image of her "proper" self proved of little interest to Annie Miller.[9] In the end, Hunt married someone else and eventually had his literary revenge; in his end-of-life thousand-page autobiography he suppressed Annie Miller's name entirely, though her memory continued to haunt him. In *The Awakening Conscience* he also completely obliterated her face with repainting; it is not Annie Miller whom we now see. The original, incorporating the look of a woman fully realizing her sexual sin—as Hunt had imagined it—was called *The Awaken<u>ed</u> Conscience*, and it proved too much to bear for the man who had bought the picture.

Had she not risen from the man's lap, a second tune, just out of its wrapper and lying on the floor, might have been sung. Its too-blue cover opens to reveal the title page of Edward Lear's setting of Tennyson's 1847 verse "Tears, Idle Tears." (This was a bit of artist-to-artist commercial solidarity: Lear was Hunt's friend, whose tune had just been published.) Why did the man bring her this song (his hat is on the table; he is the visitor and gift-bearer)?

> Tears, idle tears, I know not what they mean,
> Tears from the depth of some divine despair
> Rise in the heart, and gather to the eyes,
> In looking on the happy autumn-fields,
> And thinking of the days that are no more.

What on earth could Hunt be thinking? This tune is even sadder than the other one. The painted pair are lovers; we know that. She is his mistress, his whore. He is a young man about town, a seducer, and a man of money. He has fine clothes. The apartment is hers, but he pays for it. It is at Woodbine Villa, No. 7, St. John's Wood, the suburb fashionable in those days for apartment-based assignations; Hunt rented the space and posed his model there, presumably so he could get it all just so—he did not know about these things firsthand.[10] A contemporary observed sarcastically that "if Hunt had wanted to paint Everton toffee, he would have felt obliged to take a studio in Everton."[11] There is more. "On the same principle that induced Hunt to boil a horse to produce a skeleton on which to base an accurate portrayal of its outward appearance, he invariably painted his models in the nude before adding their clothes."[12] All this—just to get it "right"? Surely there was another reason as well, one Hunt did not acknowledge in his memoirs. Hunt the virgin, obsessed with his beautiful model, about whose beauty everyone agreed, drew her again and again: as Lady Godiva and as the Lady of Shalott with flowing hair, or lying in bed, or, small irony, kneeling by the bed for *Morning Prayer.*[13] He painted his model as the icon of piety, but naked and sexually ravishing and stationed by furniture whose use, as conventionalized in painting, was not for sleeping but for sex. Yet if Hunt was only aiming to get his paintings' details "right," might we not ask, What kept woman, and what man who keeps a woman, would decorate the site of their pleasures with a print, the one over the piano, of *Christ and the Woman Taken in Adultery?* We have two songs, neither likely to elicit a mood conducive to lovemaking, and an interior image warning of the moral consequences of the act, all in a painting nonetheless virtually overwhelmed by "correct" detail appropriate to the residence of a kept woman. We have here an infusion of allegory into a painting of modern life.

She "grants" him her favors; it beats starvation. He is like the cat, under the table at the left, toying with the little songbird (did it fly in through the open window?). The cat is sneaky, crouched down, eyes glaring satanically. The man's glove, soiled, lies at her feet on the floor. Is it a sign of his passionate carelessness; or is it a gauntlet thrown down, a device for slapping, for waking someone to a new reality; or does it forewarn of her own fate, to be cast off; or is it none of these? Why is the glove, so prominently without its companion and half turned inside out—turned back so as to show that it was once clean but is now filthy? Why does the man wear the other glove, and on the hand with which he touches the piano's keys? What is the connection: naked/clothed, bright/dark, unclean/clean? Or has Hunt framed, instead of a binary, a conjunction: music and prostitution?

MONEY AND THE BODY

Is there not too much to look at? Is not the reality overwhelming, vulgar, too much of a visual feast? The painting is governed by excess. Surely Hunt knew that. Is the man's effort to secure regulated, steady sex with a whore-made-mistress not an *economic* scandal as well as an ethical one? Are the two not related, money and women's bodies?[14] Access to a woman's body cost money; in Victorian culture such an expenditure was conventionally regarded as waste, a condition that produced moral panic in men.[15] Indeed, men commonly spoke of both women and music in the discourse of contagion. By the close of the seventeenth century music in English culture was held a waste of time and money, an enervation of a young man's substance.[16] Sex, like music, is a momentary pleasure that vanishes but leaves its trace: physical and moral disease and weakness—the signs of women and the signs of death.

The painted conscience in the state of awakening takes no account of the material body, as if her found morality exists outside the realm of the physical and, closely related, the economic. Moreover, whereas men's sexual misadventures were readily forgiven and forgotten, no reciprocal pardon and amnesty were available to women. I speak here of the bourgeoisie, those who defined the official rules. Her refusal of his advance, money for sex, now promises the future life of her soul, but it will come at the expense (money again) of her body. How will she eat? No matter; she is saved. The "real" Annie Miller managed better than most; Hunt's phantasmagoria about saving her soul, like that of nearly every other Victorian painter of the very popular fallen-woman theme, was not hers. She had her own image of what she was after.

What gives the picture its moral charge? Is it the man's scandalous sexual spending or the scandalous spending of his money, as on garish furniture, for his mistress? The anonymous Victorian author of *My Secret Life* wrote in his voluminous sexual-accounts journal that he liked the "mercantile business" of buying the prostitute. (Until the laws and the police began to regulate "the trade," prostitution was commonly part-time work—hardly a "profession"—for poor women, who were typically married and had hungry children to feed.[17]) As he tells the tale, on two occasions he made his women's vaginas the literal bank to receive his presex shillings.[18] Nevertheless, the vaginal receptacle for both the flow of cash and, later, semen produces *his* loss, specifically of embodied energy. In the economy of power, his domination of his whore, a sign and self-confirmation of his strength, is maddeningly also the sign and confirmation of precisely the opposite. This confounding produces desire but also rage. A man giving in to sex showed a weakness of body over mind and—not coincidentally—resembled a man giving in to music: "I heard one of [two gentlemen] exclaim,—'I hate to see a *man* at the Harpsichord!' I had never before annexed the idea of effeminacy to that instrument; but from that moment, I began to be of that gentleman's opinion."[19] The sex act itself for men, so the medical authorities had it, exhausted the "vital force," life itself—Foucault has shown that this reading was already authorized by the ancient Greeks[20]—thus the obsessive Victorian fear of masturbation and thus the fear of prostitution, made worse by the threat of bacterial infection.

John Ruskin, Hunt's apologist for *The Awakening Conscience,* on art: "A maiden may sing of her lost love, but a miser cannot sing of his lost money. And with absolute precision, from highest to lowest, *the fineness of the possible art is an index of the moral purity and majesty of the emotion it expresses*" (Ruskin's emphasis).[21] Ruskin implies that the relation of song, love, money, art, and morals stakes out the difference between good and evil. The woman who can sing of love is she who has not embodied it in sex (else she could not remain a "maiden"). She who has embodied sex is like the miser whose money is spent and cannot be recovered. Proper art, like *The Awakening Conscience,* is an index of proper purity. Proper art is an economy of hoarding.

Is the vulgarity of too much carpet and too much rosewood and gilt—all of it, in its *newness,* purposely and appropriately shocking to the picture's original apologist, John Ruskin[22]—an easy out, a condemnation of the new bourgeoisie whose monied circumstances the painter did not share but among whom he wanted nonetheless to be (after all, he had to eat)? None of the decor is appropriate to the family parlor; this is furniture from Rent-a-Room. No wife and children will ever gather at this flat's imagined hearth. This unsettling picture is the dark reverse image of the cult of domesticity. The room and its furnishings mark the scandalous misuse of money for illicit sexual pleasures, an abhorrent waste the Victorian bourgeoisie preferred to associate with the aristocracy, their class enemy, and not with themselves, though they were in fact quite as guilty.[23] The painting's moral tale depends on articulating a prophylactic difference: the seducer is not middle class. Hunt's friend Fred Stephens, who advised Hunt on how to exact revenge for Annie Miller's blackmail (involving love letters and drawings, presumably nudes) following their breakup, interpreted the picture in describing the seducer's gesture: "One of his *patrician* arms surrounds the victim of his passions" (emphasis added).[24] Stephens condemns the sexual sin of an aristocrat. This is the irony: prostitution was all the rage among the urban bourgeoisie. Indeed, solicitation of prostitutes was medically explained, even justified, as the safety valve of the middle-class man, who had to confront the supposed sexual purity (read: frigidity) of the good bourgeois woman, deemed—by men—uninterested in sex. This painting is about a woman and her soul, but the device that governs everything is music—a piano and two songs, though only one is performed. It is about harmony, duet, and coming together but also about music and decay, death, and damnation. It is about pleasure and pain: our pleasure at her pain; our pleasure at his comeuppance, his softness, his smooth skin and perfect hands. Not like us, he is more of a dandy. He has no right to look as he does; his looks are altogether too much like those of a women. Small wonder that it is, unquestionably, he who sings.

TIME AND DETAIL

Music is time that draws attention to itself. On top of the piano rests a clock, encased in a bell jar: gilded time attended to by small classically garbed figures who lean over the clock face—over time—and embrace it, watch it, fetishize it. Does such a clock keep time or remind us of it? Does it keep time with the music, or the reverse? Music is time; time is life; here both are mechanical. Time is a machine that keeps watch on the young woman's life. Time keeps her date with her "lover," on whom she waits and depends: he feeds her. Time sits lavishly on top of the piano, and time acts itself out in the musical order of the song. This is the age of industry ("Be on time"), recently, for the first time, regulated by Greenwich mean time, and also the age of music regulated by the metronome ("Keep in time"). Time as we now know it, as though our time were somehow "natural," was defined in the nineteenth century on account of the same money force that underwrote the psychologies of timely pleasure in Hunt's picture. Our "time" was invented for the railroad *schedule*—so that raw materials could be gotten to the factories, to keep them running, ostinato fashion, and get goods to the towns, cities, and ports for consumption.[25] Music in Hunt's painting, like time, is order, *an* order; it is imposed. It is a harmony that makes demands, and in this instance does so "Oft, in the Stilly Night." To regulate time in Victorian factories was to regulate the one weak link in the production process, the human bodies that operated the machinery. The worker's body came to be defined by time. Annie Miller is a worker; in Hunt's painting, wherein music and time are concatenated, time regulates, defines, and organizes her body for sex; music aestheticizes the oppression and offers some compensation for her pain.

That this picture has too many details,[26] that everything seems to be shown, precisely drawn and brightly lit, is not accidental. "For the English painters of the middle of the century, moral truth and material fact, relentlessly pursued down to the last stitch in the last antimacassar, seem to be absolutely equated."[27] But can we "see" the antimacassar for the stitches? Can or will Hunt? This is a modern painting, or rather a modern discourse. It comes to us rich in data, clinically lighted, its contents seemingly inventoried. Ruskin claimed that the objects force themselves on us with a "ghastly and unendurable distinctness, as if they would compel the sufferer to count, or measure, or learn them by heart."[28] The non-modernist element, by contrast, is the intentionality of the allegory, a bit old-fashioned, like Hunt himself. The image is a paradise of consumption; it is very much "about" goods. Ruskin claimed horror at the room's vulgarity, to him an appropriate moral commentary on the illicit relationship Hunt depicted, though his charge rings a bit false. Part of the painting's "problem" is that it provides too much to consume. As in vanitas paintings of yore, its putative moral competes with an "extra," possibly contradictory, discourse about the pleasures of possession. In the process, the sin governing Hunt's vision is at once lost sight of and otherwise made to *appear* quite attractive, even bourgeois. After all, to the Victorian bourgeoisie material goods spelled success, and success itself was a sign of grace. On this score, Hunt seems to have confused his first viewers: "The effect was to generate demand for more and more doses of the scopic."[29] Ruskin explicitly sought to clear up the confusion: "People gaze at it in a blank wonder, and leave it hopelessly."[30] The *Athenaeum* reviewer reported that "innocent and unenlightened spectators suppose it to represent a quarrel between a brother and sister,"[31] confirming that the picture was not so different from scenes of proper family life. All these distractions notwithstanding, our eyes are eventually led back to her face projecting outward from the picture plane. It is the painting's focal point, despite the intrusive commentary of object data.

HER FACE

"The author of 'The Bridge of Sighs' could not have conceived a more painful-looking face."[32] The investment is too much to bear; it pricks the conscience. It was not pretty: "an ugly woman in the incipient stage of a hysterical attack."[33] The buyer lived with her face only briefly. In 1856 he returned the picture to Hunt and paid him to do it over; Hunt obliged. What survives of the original exists only in written text. Thus Lady Trevelyan wrote in her diary (13 May 1854), having seen the picture on exhibition: "The half insane horror in her eyes is marvelous."[34] Hunt, ill with fever, was dissatisfied with his repainting, but he soon sent the work back to the owner for an exhibition, where the title was changed. What that change admits is a progression, the passage of time. The frozen image is momentarily unfrozen, the film set in reverse a few frames—ironically, in this new age of progress, forward motion is halted, too much to bear. Now the conscience is not awakened but awaken*ing.*

In 1857 the picture was again back in Hunt's studio. This time he thought he had improved it: "Lately, I have had the 'Awakening Conscience' on my easel for a week, in the spring I had worked on the head of the girl before sending it to

Birmingham, when I was suffering from fever, which defeated my attempt to improve it. I think that I have materially bettered it now."[35] Annie Miller's face passes back and forth between two men somehow obsessed by it; one of them refashions it to the other's better pleasure. Artist as pimp? In the end, Annie Miller's face is gone, cut off, replaced by the hand of male creative authority, a new face sutured in, beautiful but Frankenstein's monster nonetheless, object of the paintbrush/scalpel.[36] The fussed-over face is the product of Victorian phrenology: "The very reading of Victorian faces itself was fostered by the restraints of Victorian social life and obsession with propriety. The constriction of behavior necessitated acute attention to emotional signs."[37]

John Ruskin, Hunt's champion, "read" her original face in a letter about the painting printed in the *Times* (25 May 1854):

> I suppose that no one possessing the slightest knowledge of expression could remain untouched by the countenance of the lost girl, rent from its beauty into sudden horror; the lips half open, indistinct in their purple quivering, the teeth set hard, the eyes filled with the fearful light of futurity and with tears of ancient days.[38]

One change we can be sure of: her teeth are no longer set hard. Her jaw is relaxed. Her parted lips, no longer "purple" or "quivering," might even be given over to song. No horror remains. But what is her recital? What is the "tune" Hunt has given her to sing, he who attempted to script her life, who saw her as a once-dirtied tabula rasa on whose soul's surface he desired to write his own response to the Woman Question?

THOMAS FAIRBAIRN

The man who bought *The Awakening Conscience* was Thomas Fairbairn from Manchester,[39] an established art patron and an industrialist—his father was the "founding father of mechanical engineering"[40]—whose family firm first had a hand in supplying machinery to textile mills but expanded into making steam engines, boilers, patent riveting machines, and iron steamboats.[41] Why did Fairbairn buy the picture? What did he see in it? How might it have functioned for him? The beginnings of an explanation can be located in his role in industrial worker relations, his perception of the family, and the connection between the two.

Carolyn Arscott has sorted out these issues very well.[42] She tells us that Fairbairn was a leader among Manchester industrialists, just as he was a leader in the formation of the city's cultural life. He established his position in the community in 1852–53 by helping put down, via a four-month lockout, a major labor strike by workers against local engineering firms. Under the name Amicus, Fairbairn published a series of letters in the *Times* that stated the position of the employers and attempted to discredit the union organizers by exaggerating the workers' demands; the effectiveness of his writings was acknowledged by people on both sides of the issue. These letters urged workers to abandon the strike so as to preserve home and family from undue suffering, the family being projected as the foundation for social morality. The ideology of domesticity, which Fairbairn in effect urged on the workers, was the basis on which he hoped to secure his own financial position.

The woman in *The Awakening Conscience,* purchased just one year after these events, occupies a middle ground between wife/mother and worker/whore. As a kept woman she is positioned above the streetwalker, but because she is hired for sex just the same, she is a prostitute.[43] In Hunt's painting, however, she literally rises from her position, via music, toward the goal (for her, unrealizable) of wife/mother. Her physical rising governs the entire image and probably governs as well Thomas Fairbairn's response, his desire to have the painting, to look at it/her at will. Her rising projects a dynamism that might be located in the mutually supporting economy of morality and the profit motive of capitalism; it is ideologically charged and culturally affirmative. She is the reformed worker who internalizes the cult of domesticity as the promise of her salvation. She is music to Fairbairn's ears.

Hunt's painting is about the possibility of improvement and accumulation, in which all sorts of things might be converted into "capital" and in which space itself is treated as distinctly developmental, not static. The moral charge and the charge of pleasure encoded in *The Awakening Conscience* are registered in Annie Miller's body—and not by the face, not hers, that rises so abruptly, like the line on the growth chart of the annual report. It is her *movement* that excites the viewer, Thomas Fairbairn, because that movement is an investment in both power (the power to make her over, in his own image, "better") and sex (a fantasy that he can enjoy while remaining morally insulated from it). But one small detail failed to work its charm on Thomas Fairbairn: Annie Miller's face had to go; its horror worked as the equivalent of an unannounced visit from the auditors. The face is *of* the body; it registers the sensation of pain. The "replacement" face is conventional, interchangeable with those from countless other Victorian moral narratives. Thomas Fairbairn is not hurt by looking at it. This one "fits" him better; his purchase is now satisfying. Thus the painting is like other consumer goods; if unsatisfactory, it may be exchanged. The buyer trades in Annie Miller for another woman—a simulacrum of prostitution. Did Hunt hire a different model off the streets to provide the "new" face? His autobiography is silent on this score.

The Awakening Conscience should be seen in conjunction with a later picture Hunt painted for Thomas Fairbairn, an 1865 portrait of Fairbairn's wife and five youngest children known as *The Children's Holiday* (Fig. 92)—the title, ironically,

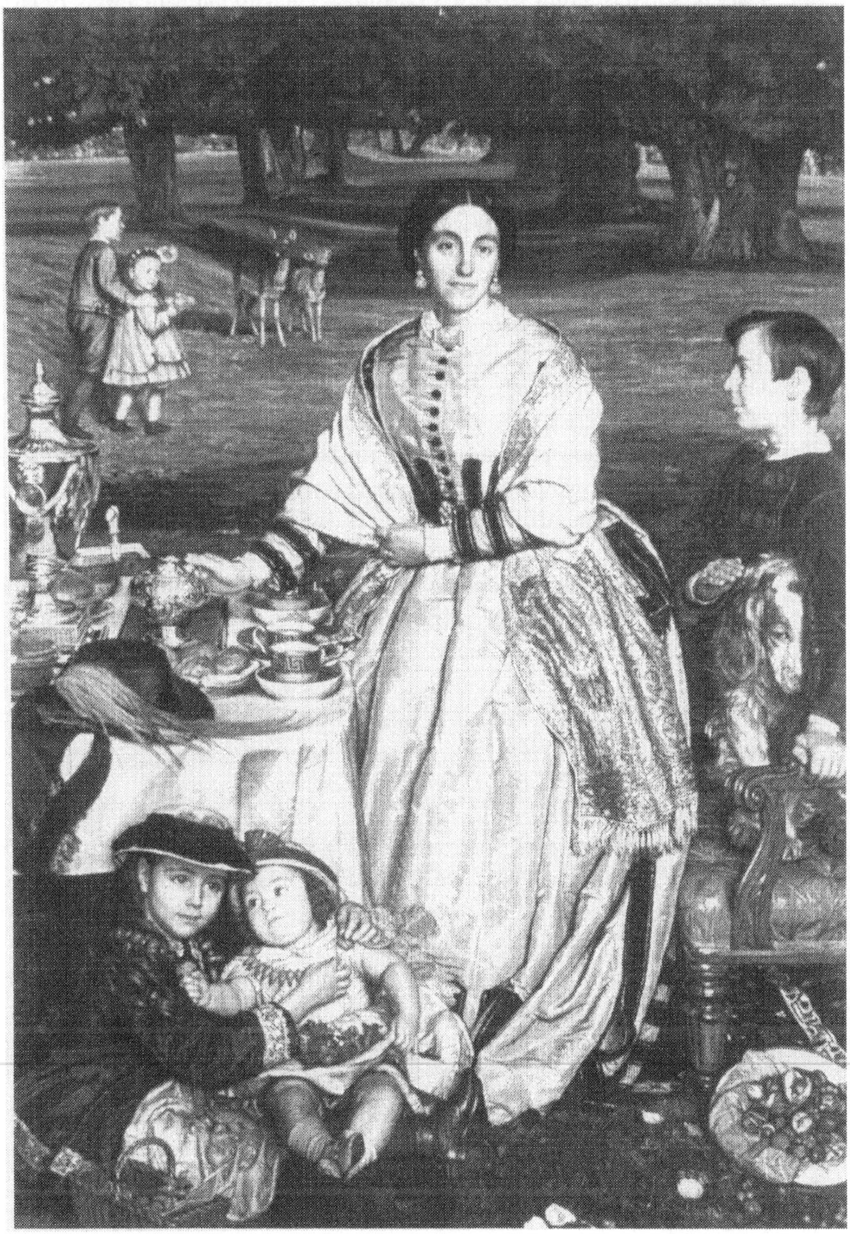

FIG. 92 William Holman Hunt, *The Children's Holiday* (1864), oil on canvas, 213 × 146 cm. Torquay, Torre Abbey.

was suggested to Hunt by Lewis Carroll.[44] The two paintings were in fact exhibited together in 1865.[45] Although the setting is outdoors, the image serves as a repository of domestic virtue and harmonious domestic life. In effect, the tranquillity and fundamental moral goodness of the scene both explain and justify the social order imposed by the industrialist in his public life. I want to describe and compare two details with their counterparts in *The Awakening Conscience.* The first is the shawl worn by Allison Fairbairn. In *The Children's Holiday* the adult woman wears it around her shoulders and indeed pulls it modestly together at the waist as she pours tea for her children on the lawn. In the earlier image, a similar shawl has been removed from the woman's shoulders and is tied around her hips, emphasizing their curvature; here the painting repeats the primary effect seen in *An Attentive Pet* (Fig. 83). In dressing her Hunt discloses what the garments hide. This single object in the two paintings, both overburdened with iconic signs, registers a difference in two ways: by color (Allison Fairbairn's shawl is cream and brownish gold) and by the position of the bodies. The "good" woman's shawl is in place; the "other" woman's emphasizes her sexuality. The large knot securing the shawl around Annie Miller's hips, together with the shawl's deep red color, which is set off by the neutral nightgown, attracts our gaze; in the painterly vocabulary of the time, the effect is orientalist, suggesting the odalisque, the harem. The second detail involves rings. Mrs. Fairbairn wears a wedding band on the hand that clutches her shawl. Annie Miller wears many rings, the overdetermined sign of her many "husbands."[46]

FRAME AND TEXT, AUTHORITY AND PAIN

The Awakening Conscience is surrounded by a frame designed by Hunt. He painted chiming bells and marigolds, emblems of warning and sorrow,[47] and a single star, perhaps a reference to Christ or truth.[48] (The reproduction here shows the picture removed from its frame; the writing visible in the upper corners, normally hidden by the frame's arched top, is Hunt's and indicates details about his retouchings of 1864 and 1886.) The frame also carries an inscription from Proverbs: "As he that taketh away a garment in cold weather, / so is he that singeth songs to a heavy heart"; by Hunt's own account these words provided guidance for the development of the picture.[49] The 1854 Royal Academy exhibition catalogue entry cited scriptural verses from Isaiah (Bishop Lowth's translation) and Ecclesiastes (14:18), the former giving courage to the timid ("Strengthen ye the feeble hands, and confirm ye the tottering knees; say ye to the faint hearted: Be ye strong; fear ye not; behold your God"), the latter developing a metaphor for moral rise or decline ("As of the green leaves on a thick tree, some fall and some grow, so is the generation of flesh and blood").[50]

Proverbs: to sing songs to someone with a heavy heart effects the reverse of what we might expect; it offers not comfort but *cold* cruelty, intentional meanness. Hunt in his autobiography offers this reading:

> These words, expressing the unintended stirring up of the deeps [*sic*] of a pure affection by the idle sing-song of an empty mind, led me to see how the companion of the girl's fall might himself be the unconscious utterer of a divine message. In scribbles I arranged the two figures to present the woman recalling the memory of her childish home, and breaking away from her gilded cage with a startled holy resolve, while her shallow companion still sings on, ignorantly intensifying her repentant purpose.[51]

Music and sin; sin as voice of salvation: the ambiguity is striking. The piano,[52] what Edmond de Goncourt called the "lady's hashish,"[53] foremost fetish of domesticity, marriage, the good wife, is in a house of ill repute, but *not* a home, so Ruskin informs us—that "fatal newness" again: "Nothing [is] there that has the old thoughts of home upon it, or that is ever to become a part of home." The piano's case, so precisely inscribed, "painted even to the last vein of the rosewood," given a "terrible lustre,"[54] is the visual source of Ruskin's horror. It is the is-not of domestic purity, of bourgeois identity. Yet it *is* that which it is not. In its "terrible lustre," it serves metaphorically as a terrible swift sword, for the tunes emanating from it strike to the depths of her soul, to her heart, and she is purified. Reborn, she leaps up, and remains forever rising, as if in resurrection from death, decay, contagion. What horrors might ensue were she to sit back down?[55] There is a catch. Is it the tune (music) or the text that reaches her conscience? Hunt tries to separate the two; he speaks of "words" yet he acknowledges that what stirs things up is not simply text but sonority. In a sense he attempts to transpose song into melodrama that operates, as Peter Brooks has shown us,[56] by displacing word: music at war with language.

Music functions within the image as the pretext for passion. To explain, I must digress briefly to consider *Music Hath Charms* (Fig. 93), painted four years after *The Awakening Conscience.* In the later work it is spring; the early flowers are blooming, and the willow (variety: weeping, never an accident in "love" pictures) is leafing out. A young man sits on the banks of a brook and sings, and a young woman hears him and comes—furtively? Or do the two of them play a game, act out a ritual? His sidelong glance will catch her at the earliest moment. He knows she is there.

But something is not right; there is a mistake. The young man is following a script; he reads his song from a sheet of music, a text. Worse: he beats time with his right hand. He conducts, like a leader or maybe a pied piper. Perhaps she, like the rats in the fairy tale, cannot resist his tune. The "victims" of this springtime story are several but among them count spontaneity. The young man may have all

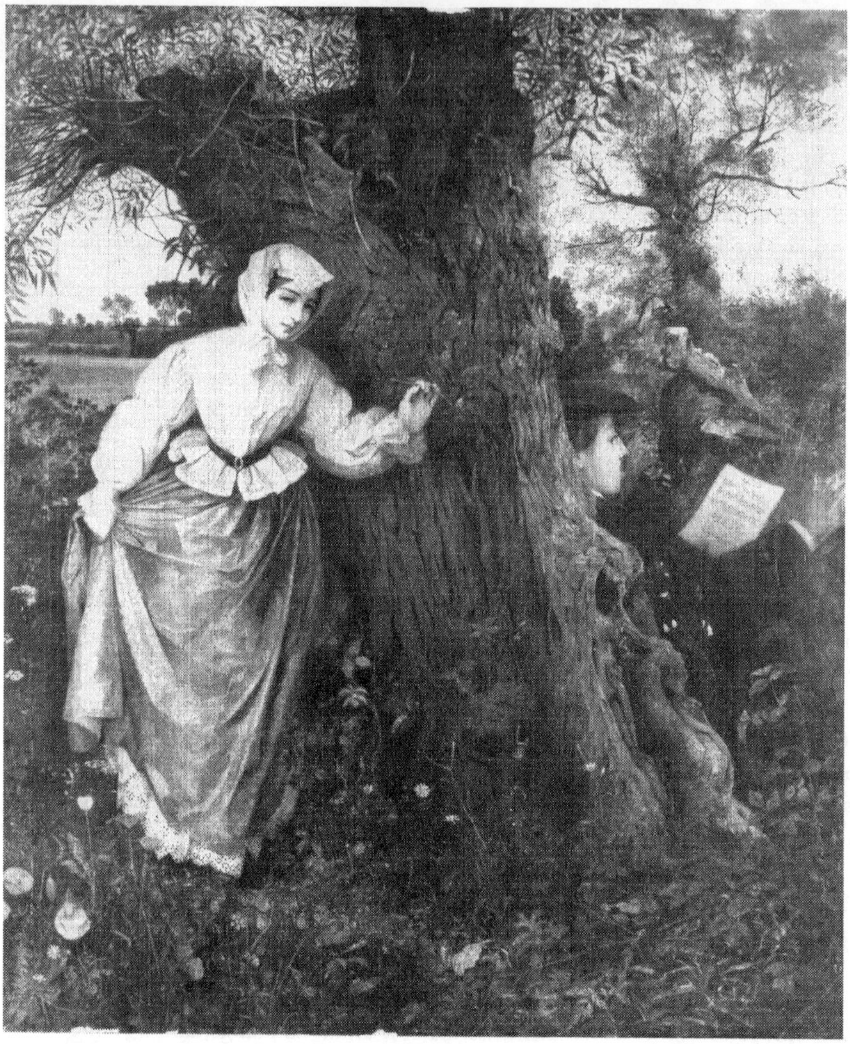

FIG. 93 George Adolphus Storey, *Music Hath Charms* (1857), oil on canvas, 75 × 62.2 cm. Private collection. Photo courtesy of Christie's, London.

the right moves as a would-be lover, but he is leaving nothing to chance. The sheet in his hands, an abbreviated sonoric love manual, recommends: make it musical, get all the notes, keep in time, inflect properly; then you'll get the girl. The scene projects music as a calculation. One buys it, for surely he did not write it out himself, and puts it to use. Music, indeed, hath charms but things have gotten a bit clinical, and loving has become a bit of a bore. I use *clinical* advisedly, so as to invoke a related trope:

> The dangerous affective power of music was a current commonplace in medical literature. Thomas Laycock, in *A Treatise on the Nervous Diseases of Women* (1840) quoted a Dr. J. J. Johnson's comment that "the stimulus of music is of a very subtle and diffusible nature, and the excitement which it produces in the nervous system is of a peculiar character, by no means generally understood" (p. 141).[57]

Hunt intended to pair *The Awakening Conscience* with *The Light of the World* (1851), destined to become the most famous religious painting of the Victorian age (Hunt painted three versions of the picture, and it was engraved in 1858 and again in 1865).[58] The paintings were exhibited together at the Royal Academy in 1854. Hunt addressed the question of the pairing as an intertextuality: "It occurred to me that my spiritual subject called for a material counterpart in a picture representing in actual life the manner in which the appeal of the spirit of heavenly love calls a soul to abandon a lower life."[59] The two images employ light differently. Unlike the stark brightness of the *maison* in St. John's Wood, *The Light of the World* is an outdoor night scene. It shows Christ in flowing robes carrying a lantern and knocking at a cottage door. Embedded in the putative sanctity of this subject is a curious fact: the two original models Hunt used for the Christ figure were both women. Did he first paint them in the nude, as was his ordinary practice with female models? Was Christ first sexed female?[60]

As Annie Miller's conscience awakens, she rises from her lover's lap, in moral transformation.[61] But her physical movement is itself transformed into something between a gesture and a tableau. The improbability of her pose translates her into a text about discipline. The pose required of Annie Miller to affect this rising would produce backache, leg strain, and general fatigue. It marks the visual-physical punishment for the transgression of being poor, a woman, and sexual. Discipline-punishment pays off; discipline *produces*—what? Marriage to the aspiring Hunt. But *only* if she can be "preached" to. She must listen—the ears again, music to his ears, apparently, but not to hers. Is it accidental that Hunt began speaking to Annie Miller about marriage at the same moment he undertook the picture?[62] He wanted to make her a lady; send her to school; correct thereby her "wretched false pride" and her "fatal indolence,"[63] as he put it.

Hunt framed Annie Miller in text, but she likewise framed him—and not only by blackmail. Hunt's obsession was not confined to paint. He excised her name from his writings, offering nothing about their stormy relationship, though in his autobiography he discussed the picture itself in some detail.[64] The excision notwithstanding, he spoke obsessively of her in the company of others in the summer of 1880, more than two decades after their breaking up, avoiding, it seems, all mention of her name:

> A very simple story, but recited in so vivid a minuteness as to hold the hearers spellbound; the reciter's wonderful memory supplying the actual conversations between the artist and his model. . . . It began in the afternoon, it went through dinner to bedtime, it was finished the next morning.[65]

The witness recounts Hunt's obsession, flowing through time, seemingly stopping time. Hunt's story about the unnamed Annie Miller is like music—in time, but taking his auditors beyond time in its pleasure.

BOOKS

On the table at the left are three books, together with a man's top hat, which rests against two of them. Ruskin remarked on their presence: "Those embossed books, vain and useless—they also new [i.e., like the furniture]—marked with no happy wearing of beloved leaves"[66] (thus the antithesis of domesticity). One book's title is sufficiently clear to permit identification; it is Henry Noel Humphries's *Origin and Progress of the Art of Writing* (1853), a text that traces "the forms of hands from hieroglyphics to modern scripts."[67] How might one account for Hunt's choice of this book, Ruskin's tacit "explanation" aside? We know of the artist's infatuation with Annie Miller and of his concern to make her sufficiently respectable to be his wife. To this end and at his own expense he placed her in the care of a governess charged with softening her rough edges. At one level, I think *The Art of Writing* references Hunt's personal obsession with both his own and Annie Miller's identity as would-be bourgeois. Hunt, however, need not have included any books in the picture; having decided to include some, he need not have rendered any of their titles identifiable. What was it about *this* book that moved him to draw it to our attention, especially given the obscurity of its subject, which includes the study of both hieroglyphics and paleography?

Humphries's book is fundamentally "about" the *visuality* of textuality: script. Hunt draws attention to writing but also to its connection both to privilege and to men. I take this to be the import of the man's top hat set against the books. The world is *written* in script, and writing, in the sense I am after, is and always has

MALE AGONY: AWAKENING CONSCIENCE 205

been an act of men. I am reminded of the medieval, chiefly monastic, scriptorium, wherein sanctioned discourse was given permanence and authoritative status as (true) knowledge. In this context writing is "about" power. In Hunt's world it is also about money, about which he was self-conscious, for his own resources at the time were limited, and money was the sine qua non of his own desire for bourgeois status and respectability. Humphries himself on the first page of his book unambiguously connects writing to money and the merchant class.

> Indeed, carelessly viewed, [the study of the art of writing] would merely seem to consist in the minute examination of the inscribed entries in the ledger of some London merchant, and accurately noting their superiority in flowing freedom and general neatness over those in the account-books of his ancestor, written a century ago.[68]

Annie Miller is the text Hunt himself at the time was attempting to "write," or get rewritten. In a bitter comment about his failure, he wrote: "If she cannot be preached to from the texts of her own bitter experience, then she cannot be awakened at all."[69] Thus he invoked his own painting (by the word *awakened*), conflating its model and subject with Annie Miller; he likewise invoked the authority of the scriptorium ("preached") and Annie Miller herself *as* writing ("the texts of her own bitter experience," a striking image). Hunt's comments present a difficulty, for they lead to his own conflation with the seducer who plays the piano.

I want to pursue the conjunction between writing and money to incorporate women and, specifically, prostitution, via Giuseppe Verdi's opera *La Traviata,* which premiered in 1853, the date of Hunt's *Awakening Conscience.* It is also about the working girl, though not a working-class girl, as in Hunt's painting. Like Mimi nearly a half century later (*La Bohème,* 1896), Violetta spends the opera's final act interrupting her own speech to cough blood, her mouth now an oracular wound, and thereby to trigger in her lover that delicious agony of regret.

Shortly after the opening of the last act, Violetta takes from her bosom a letter from her lover's father. In a striking gesture, she reads—rather than sings—it aloud, in the opera's only moment of true melodrama. It is nothing like a love letter, or even like a letter from a friend; indeed, it reads like a newspaper account or, perhaps, a telegram. It is mostly just facts. It is a businessman's text, the writing of the "perfect" bourgeois:

> Teneste la promessa—la disfida
> Ebbe luogo! Il barone fu ferito,
> Però migliora. Alfredo
> È in stranio suolo; il vostro sacrifizio
> lo stesso gli ho svelato;
> Egli a voi tornerà pel suo perdono;

Io pur verrò. Curatevi—mertate
Un auvenir migliore.

(You kept your promise. The duel has taken place! The Baron was wounded, but is recovering. Alfredo has gone abroad; I myself revealed your sacrifice to him; he will return to ask your pardon; I too shall come. Take care of yourself. You deserve a happier future.[70])

Verdi gives these words special status *as* words; he makes Violetta break character as an *operatic* heroine to speak a man's words, acknowledging in the process that this text controls her very reason for being. The words' power momentarily drives music from her lips and, indeed, off the stage. The music that survives, however, in the orchestral accompaniment to her reading, preserves the trace of textuality, in that it reprises the initial love melody sung to Violetta by Alfredo in his act 1 aria ("Di quell'amor ch'è palpito"). Violetta's world is overdetermined by two unseen men: one whose writing she *sees* and reads aloud and another whose once-sung sonorities she *hears* in the orchestra. The sight and sound overwhelm her; she puts the letter down and asks God's forgiveness.

CODE AND CODA. TWO TUNES

It is time to reconnect sight to sound. To us as viewers "everything" within the image is within sight, none of it left to chance, given the painting's intense lighting and precise detail. Inside the picture, however, glances do not meet: we know of the woman's awakening (we have Hunt's title to confirm it); but her "keeper" knows nothing, because he cannot see what is visible to us. He is blind, without insight. He sees instead something else, a script, "Oft, in the Stilly Night." He plays it for her to sing; maybe he sings along, or maybe he sings it to her. She has insight; she sees beneath and beyond that text. But what is it that she sees beyond, for the lyrics are suitably innocent, perfectly respectful of bourgeois domestic ideals?

Music functioned variously in Victorian society; today we may be inclined to think of it principally as art, but the parlor song, like those incorporated in Hunt's painting, did not enjoy the status of art. Indeed, far from transcending the mundane world of capital, as required of true Art under the terms of contemporaneous aesthetics,

> the bourgeois "popular song" was the first product which showed how music might be profitably incorporated into a system of capitalist enterprise. It is in the production, promotion, and marketing of the sheet music to these songs (and the pianos to accompany them) that we witness the birth of the modern music industry.[71]

Thus while the songs themselves are "innocent," they reference commerce, and not incidentally the commerce of the body. As I have been at pains to establish throughout this volume, music under the conditions of modernity was concatenated with woman (especially with her dangerous sexuality) and sometimes with the body of the prostitute, the woman for sale, on the market, like music—for prostitution was also a major industry in Victorian England in ways never previously actualized, involving the attention, concern, and profit of medical, psychiatric, judicial, and law enforcement institutions, paralleling the rapid and complex development of the music industry and its legal regulation.[72]

From the start popular music was a product, a sign, and a material-immaterial test case for an emerging consumer culture. In buying music, one bought "nothing," for thus had music in general been widely theorized in England by men for nearly two centuries.[73] The enterprise of profitably selling mere "sound" could hardly be a greater testimony to the heady implications of capitalism. Indeed, it seems to me that the bond being forged between music and money accounts in part for the implicit social antagonism in the ideological foundation of much nineteenth-century aesthetics—the protest of artists against an emergent condition they not only recognized but increasingly depended on for their economic well-being.

Nonetheless, one must acknowledge that the musical text itself may exceed its function to produce profit. To produce a song by itself does not respond to the demands of capitalism; the song must ultimately be consumed (sold) to produce profit. To be consumed, the music must in some sense "speak" to its auditor-performer. It seems safe to assume that the man in Hunt's painting bought the songs so as to engineer a sex act or, afterward, to serve as balm to the conscience and hence the pretext for the sex act next time. (The songs *must* drive the picture's primary narrative; otherwise there is no reason to incorporate a musical theme and to give it primary place in the composition. Hunt's own words on the matter establish as much, as I have already shown.) Accordingly, there is something in the tunes that she is supposed to hear, yet that sound must act against the texts, to the extent that they tell a story quite different from the one I am outlining; textually, the songs are far from sexual turn-ons. Is Hunt's patrician seducer thus a fool when it comes to buying music for his mistress? Is the tunes' textual propriety intended to serve both man and woman as a veneer of romantic love, a disguise for the truth of their relation?

Here is the song that brings him grief and her salvation:

> Oft, in the stilly night,
> Ere Slumber's chain has bound me,
> Fond Memory brings the light
> Of other days around me;

The smiles, the tears,
Of boyhood's years,
The words of love then spoken;
The eyes that shone,
Now dimm'd and gone,
The Cheerful hearts now broken!
Thus, in the stilly night,
Ere Slumber's chain has bound me,
Sad Memory brings the light
Of other days around me.

When I remember all
The friends, so link'd together,
I've seen around me fall,
Like leaves in wintry weather;
I feel like one,
Who treads alone
Some banquet-hall deserted,
Whose lights are fled,
Whose garlands dead,
And all but he departed!
Thus, in the stilly night,
Ere Slumber's chain has bound me,
Sad Memory brings the light
Of other days around me.[74]

And here is the song on the floor, still partly in its wrapper—the backup, so to speak:

Tears, idle tears, I know not what they mean,
Tears from the depth of some divine despair
Rise in the heart, and gather to the eyes,
In looking on the happy autumn-fields,
And thinking of the days that are no more.

Fresh as the first beam glittering on a sail,
That brings our friends up from the underworld,
Sad as the last which reddens over one
That sinks with all we love below the verge;
So sad, so fresh, the days that are no more.

Ah, sad and strange as in dark summer dawns
The earliest pipe of half-awaken'd birds

MALE AGONY: AWAKENING CONSCIENCE 209

To dying ears, when unto dying eyes
The casement slowly grows a glimmering square;
So sad, so strange, the days that are no more.

Dear as remember'd kisses after death,
And sweet as those by hopeless fancy feign'd
On lips that are for others; deep as love,
Deep as first love, and wild with all regret;
O Death in Life, the days that are no more![75]

Hunt chose his tunes carefully, and not only to help his composer friend Lear peddle the second song. There are connections between the two texts that I can evoke with a list of words encountered in other chapters of this volume: sleep, dreams, love, death, memory, silence, sorrow; and in the first, winter, in the second, autumn. The texts inscribe the reverie of loss, the pleasure of bankruptcy, the self-loathings over missed opportunities—even a self-loathing of self-loathing: *idle* tears, not productive ones.

In his autobiography a half century later, Hunt, an old man who even then could not forget Annie Miller, though pretending to, engaged in a bit of spin control:

> I spoke freely of this intended subject, but, while cogitating upon the broad intention, I reflected that the instinctive eluding of pursuit by the erring one [Annie Miller] would not coincide with the willing conversion and instantaneous resolve for a higher life which it was necessary to emphasize.[76]

Contaminated, she is incapable of self-redemption; yet the mouth and hands of her seducer, twin agents of an "empty mind," produce the music that supplies her salvation. Are we thus to understand that the man's own performance is little more than a pathetic self-remonstrance over his own dissolute life, a nostalgic ecstasy of self-directed abuse and sentimental sing-song idling? Both tunes narrate devolution, in the imputed story of the man who sings them, stupidly, with a grin on his soft, effeminate face and the so-soft hands (Hunt is careful to represent this detail), one still gloved. Nonetheless, the ballad he sings about bygone boyhood years reforms the erring woman—not its lyrics but the *sonorities;* were mere words sufficient to Hunt's purpose, he might have gone with a poetry reading—certainly the Tennyson verse, still in its wrapper on the floor, might have done nicely.

If it is the tune that awakens her conscience, what does Hunt think she hears? Tom Moore's *Irish Melodies* setting of "Oft, in the Stilly Night," piano arrangement by the church musician Sir John Stevenson, is (pseudo-) folklike, its C-Major melody, spanning no more than a major seventh, structured in uniform 4-bar phrases: $AA_1BB_1AA_1/AA_1BB_1AA_1$; its scale is entirely diatonic, without chromatic inflection; it is rhythmically square, except for an occasional syncopation; the harmonies are sweetly consonant but for the mildest occasional spice provided by a suspension—the chords employed never exceed tonic, subdominant, and dominant seventh; its dynamics range between piano and pianissimo—to be sung "With Melancholy Expression." In short, the tune is devoid of musical surprise. It is the music of parlor domesticity, more so in light of the text, to the extent that the words narrate boyhood memories and the innocence of first love, in conjunction with an implied maternal protection. The song's sonoric "purity"—ironic, given the occasion—evokes the angel in the house. That is, the male voice, recalling childhood, "reverts" to the rhetorically feminine so as to recall loss: the music is Oedipal; as such it must be cast off. The musical text, briefly taken up, is feminine and, in effect, castrating. It may save her—thus what Annie Miller is made to hear is Hunt's self-described sing-song vision of the wife—but in the same moment it condemns him. Little wonder that Hunt exaggerated the seducer's corporeal softness—and in his own words belittled the tune.

Had Hunt given the seducer "Tears, Idle Tears" to sing, a difficulty would have ensued, not on account of the text, which would do nicely, but because of the musical setting. While strophic, Lear's tune is considerably more complex, musically more interesting, sonorically and rhetorically more slippery and uncertain than "Oft, in the Stilly Night." With a melody far less repetitive than the other song, midway through it modulates from D Major to G Major and remains there. This shift is likewise reflected in the song's other musical parameters. Thus the accompaniment changes from struck to arpeggiated chords; and its tempo moves from larghetto to allegretto. In effect, the tune musically turns its back on the past, via the shift in key, accompaniment, and tempo, never to look back, even while textually invoking the past. Chromaticism, with its shifts and momentary uncertainties, plays a significant, if already clichéd, role throughout the song; moreover, the general harmonic vocabulary is richer, just as the ambitus is wider, spanning nearly two octaves. By comparison with the tune on the piano, this one seems almost dangerously passionate, for it plays off generic male self-pity more than male constructions of feminine self-control and nurture.

In Hunt's painting there are two open mouths, his and hers. He is singing, that much seems certain, but what of her? She no longer has a look of horror, and her lips are no longer quite so purple, but Hunt still invests in her mouth. Why is it open? What leads him to this repainting? She does not scream—no mouth from Munch here by a long shot—but perhaps, instead, merely half smiles, or shows something of open-mouthed shock. But it *could* as well be that her mouth opens to sing. To replicate the shape of her mouth, the upper lip must be pulled upward so as to expose the teeth as she does. This mouth shape is characteristic

MALE AGONY: AWAKENING CONSCIENCE 211

not of speech, not really of smiling, but of song. Once song is evoked, so also is the body. Hear Roland Barthes:

> The singing voice, that very specific space in which a tongue encounters a voice and permits those who know how to listen to it to hear what we can call its "grain"—the singing voice is not the breath but indeed that materiality of the body emerging from the throat, a site where the phonic metal hardens and takes shape.[77]

And Kaja Silverman:

> The voice is the site of perhaps the most radical of all subjective divisions—the division between meaning and materiality.[78]

At some level both the painting's actors engage speech. The quotation from Proverbs on the picture frame characterizes the man's; hers remains ambivalent. All speech, or would-be speech, in the painting asks the Woman Question, to a necessarily musical accompaniment. Hunt responds to the question in a chain of contradictions involving hatred and love, loathing (also self-loathing) and desire, and painful embodied pleasure. My interest in the sight of sound—in this (still our) age of visuality, when every human phenomenon is invested in by being looked at—hinges on the link between music's sounds and the human bodies that produce them, and in the perfect reciprocity by which each defines the other. Hunt's own attempt to locate the terms of this reciprocity failed in both art and life because Annie Miller refused; she chose her own song: Annie Miller took to "composing" her own self. It is hardly accidental or surprising that Hunt's chosen tunes are male products, literally and discursively. That Annie Miller's recital of men's songs was short-lived offers primary hope for what awakening is all about, though this is nothing like the wakefulness Hunt imagined, and it is quite different from the effect of men's speech on the fate of Verdi's Violetta. The social-musical future, measured from the real, not obliterated, Annie Miller, is very much up for grabs, though it has been hopefully suggested that the utopia she advanced in rejecting Hunt's tune is already in the making and recognizable as such. Notwithstanding the pleasure of contemplating such a prospect, I ask indulgence for a last word, to confront not the sight of sound, but the sight of silence.

CHAPTER 8

1. William Holman Hunt's *Awakening Conscience* is perhaps the most written-about English painting from its decade; indeed, few other Victorian pictures to the end of the nineteenth century have attracted as much scholarly attention—a description of the picture serves as the opening paragraph of the recent, rather sensational, study by Bram Dijkstra, *Idols of Perversity: Fantasies of Feminine Evil in Fin-de-Siècle Culture* (New York: Oxford University Press, 1986), p. 3. In addition to the sources cited throughout this essay I must mention one study that was not available to me: Anne J. d'Harnoncourt, "*The Awakening Conscience:* A Study in Moral Subject Matter in Pre-Raphaelite Paintings," master's thesis, Courtauld Institute of Art, University of London, 1967. On visual antecedents to this painting see Susan P. Casteras, "Down the Garden Path: Courtship Culture and Its Imagery in Victorian Painting," Ph.D. diss., Yale University, 1977, pp. 433–44.

2. Cf. Roland Barthes, "Diderot, Brecht, Eisenstein," *Image, Music, Text,* trans. Stephen Heath (New York: Hill and Wang, 1977), pp. 73–74, concerning what he calls "social gest": "It is a gesture or set of gestures (but never a gesticulation) in which a whole social situation can be read. Not every gest is social: there is nothing social in the movements a man makes in order to brush off a fly; but if this same man, poorly dressed, is struggling against guard-dogs, the gest becomes social."

3. Diana Holman-Hunt, *My Grandfather, His Wives and Loves* (New York: Norton, 1969), p. 113.

4. Michel Foucault, *The History of Sexuality,* vol. 1, *An Introduction,* trans. Robert Hurley (New York: Pantheon Books, 1978). On the general topic of prostitution, much researched, see Judith R. Walkowitz, *Prostitution and Victorian Society: Women, Class, and the State* (New York: Cambridge University Press, 1980); E. M. Sigsworth and T. J. Wyke, "A Study of Victorian Prostitution and Venereal Disease," in *Suffer and Be Still: Women in the Victorian Age,* ed. Martha Vicinus (Bloomington: Indiana University Press, 1973), pp. 77–99; Steven Marcus, *The Other Victorians: A Study of Sexuality and Pornography in Mid-Nineteenth-Century England* (New York: Basic Books, 1966).

5. Lise Vogel, "Fine Arts and Feminism: The Awakening Consciousness," in *Feminist Art Criticism: An Anthology,* ed. Arlene Raven, Cassandra Langer, and Joanna Frueh (Ann Arbor: UMI Research Press, 1988), p. 51: "In the milieu of the pre-Raphaelite painters, no real distinction existed between modeling and prostitution." Regarding Pre-Raphaelite photography and the sexual relationships involving artists' models see also p. 57. Hunt, as we know, did not behave in this manner. See also Holman-Hunt, *My Grandfather,* pp. 66–68.

6. Gay Daly, *Pre-Raphaelites in Love* (New York: Ticknor and Fields, 1989), p. 112.

7. Credit for the identification of Annie Miller as Hunt's model for *The Awakening Conscience* goes to Oswald Doughty, *A Victorian Romantic: Dante Gabriel Rossetti* (London: Muller, 1949), pp. 258–59. A great deal has recently been written about Annie Miller and her relationship to Holman Hunt, though much of it repeats from one text to another. Many of the details in this chapter are drawn from these studies. See especially Holman-Hunt, *My Grandfather,* the principal source of information; Daly, *Pre-Raphaelites in Love,*

pp. 101–08, 113–26, 132–37; Jan Marsh, *The Pre-Raphaelite Sisterhood* (New York: St. Martin's Press, 1985); G. H. Fleming, *That Ne'er Shall Meet Again: Rossetti, Millais, Hunt* (London: Joseph, 1971).

8. Holman-Hunt, *My Grandfather,* pp. 97–99, 113–14; and James H. Coombs et al., eds., *A Pre-Raphaelite Friendship: The Correspondence of William Holman Hunt and John Lucas Tupper* (Ann Arbor: UMI Research Press, 1986), p. 53 n. 1.

9. Regarding the slow deterioration of their relationship see Holman-Hunt, *My Grandfather,* pp. 173–80, 188–89, 194–210. Annie Miller died at age ninety in 1925, having spent her adult life financially secure, happily married to Sir Thomas Ranelagh Thomson, first cousin to Lord Ranelagh, to whom she had been, like her defaced self in *The Awakening Conscience,* mistress after leaving Hunt's employ-embrace. From Holman-Hunt, *My Grandfather,* pp. 228–29. Concerning her husband, see p. 166; see also pp. 223–29 and 245–49 regarding her blackmail of Hunt—at the instigation of her future husband! Regarding the blackmail see also the lucid commentary by Daly, *Pre-Raphaelites in Love,* pp. 135–37.

10. Daly, *Pre-Raphaelites in Love,* p. 135; on the relation between Hunt's "reputation for Christian purity" and the successful sale of his paintings, see p. 134.

11. Quoted in Jeremy Maas, *Holman Hunt and "The Light of the World"* (London: Scholar Press, 1984), p. 46.

12. Holman-Hunt, *My Grandfather,* p. 205.

13. Ibid.

14. See Georg Simmel, *The Philosophy of Money,* trans. Tom Bottomore and David Frisby (1900; reprint, London: Routledge and Kegan Paul, 1978), p. 383.

15. On the moral panic surrounding prostitution and its relation to political crises, see Lynn Nead, "The Magdalen in Modern Times: The Mythology of the Fallen Woman in Pre-Raphaelite Painting," in *Looking On: Images of Femininity in the Visual Arts and Media,* ed. Rosemary Betterton (London: Pandora, 1987), pp. 82–83.

16. See Richard Leppert, *Music and Image: Domesticity, Ideology, and Socio-Cultural Formation in Eighteenth-Century England* (Cambridge: Cambridge University Press, 1989), pp. 16–27.

17. See Jeffrey Weeks, *Sex, Politics, and Society: The Regulation of Sexuality since 1800,* 2nd ed. (London: Longman, 1989).

18. Marcus, *Other Victorians,* p. 159.

19. John Berkenhout, *A Volume of Letters from Dr Berkenhout to His Son at the University* (Cambridge, 1790), vol. 1, p. 189. I have further addressed this issue in *Music and Image,* pp. 22, 24, 127, 129.

20. Michel Foucault, *The History of Sexuality,* vol. 2: *The Use of Pleasure,* trans. Robert Hurley (New York: Vintage Books, 1990).

21. John Ruskin, "The Relation of Art to Morals," in *Lectures on Art, Lectures on Landscape, Aratra Pentelici,* vol. 14 of *The Complete Works* (New York: Thomas Y. Crowell, n.d.), p. 46. Concerning Ruskin's views on the use and moral value of art, see George P. Landow, *The Aesthetic and Critical Theories of John Ruskin* (Princeton: Princeton University Press, 1971), pp. 53–68. See also William J. Gatens, "John Ruskin and Music," *Victorian Studies* 30 (1986), pp. 77–97.

22. For a commentary on Ruskin's reading of Hunt's painting, see James Thompson, "Ruskin and Hunt's 'Awakening Conscience,'" *Victorian Institute Journal* 8 (1979), pp. 19–29.

23. Regarding the economic constitution of the Victorian middle class, including population tables and occupations, see Patricia Branca, *Silent Sisterhood: Middle Class Women in the Victorian Home* (Pittsburgh: Carnegie-Mellon University Press, 1975), pp. 38–45, and, for comparison, domestic servants' incomes, pp. 54–55. See also the excellent thorough study by Leonore Davidoff and Catherine Hall, *Family Fortunes: Men and Women of the English Middle Class, 1780–1850* (London: Hutchinson, 1987).

24. George P. Landow, *William Holman Hunt and Typological Symbolism* (London: Yale University Press for the Paul Mellon Centre for Studies in British Art, 1979), p. 48; Nead, "Magdalen in Modern Times," p. 89; and Caroline Arscott, "Employer, Husband, Spectator: Thomas Fairbairn's Commission of *The Awakening Conscience*," in *The Culture of Capital: Art, Power, and the Nineteenth-Century Middle Class*, ed. Janet Wolff and John Seed (Manchester: Manchester University Press, 1988), p. 186.

25. See Donald M. Lowe, *The History of Bourgeois Perception* (Chicago: University of Chicago Press, 1982), pp. 37–38.

26. For a fuller accounting of the myriad objects in the painting and their potential iconographical significance see Ronald Parkinson, "The Awakening Conscience and the Still Small Voice," in *The Tate Gallery Illustrated Biennial Report and Catalogue of Acquisitions [1976–1978]* (London: Tate Gallery Publications, 1978), p. 26; Susan P. Casteras, *Images of Victorian Womanhood in English Art* (London: Associated University Presses, 1987), pp. 140–42; and Landow, *Hunt and Typological Symbolism*, pp. 51–52.

27. Linda Nochlin, *Realism* (Harmondsworth: Penguin Books, 1971), p. 201; see also Nead, "Magdalen in Modern Times," p. 79.

28. William Holman Hunt, *Pre-Raphaelitism and the Pre-Raphaelite Brotherhood* (New York: Macmillan, 1905), vol. 1, p. 419.

29. Arscott, "Employer, Husband, Spectator," p. 181.

30. Hunt, *Pre-Raphaelitism*, vol. 1, p. 418.

31. Review of *The Awakening Conscience* published as part of a longer essay on the 1854 Royal Academy exhibition in *Athenaeum* (6 May 1854), pp. 559–61, and reprinted in John Charles Olmsted, ed., *Victorian Painting: Essays and Reviews*, vol. 2, *1849–1860* (New York: Garland, 1983), p. 289. On the problem of "reading" the picture, then and now, see the first-rate essay by Kate Flint, "Rereading *The Awakening Conscience* Rightly," in *Pre-Raphaelites Re-Viewed*, ed. Marcia Pointon (Manchester: Manchester University Press, 1989), pp. 45–65.

32. *Athenaeum* (6 May 1854), pp. 559–61, reprinted in Olmsted, *Victorian Painting*, vol. 2, p. 288.

33. From an 1856 exhibition review, quoted in Arscott, "Employer, Husband, Spectator," p. 185. Arscott provides a consistently brilliant reading of Annie Miller's face in *The Awakening Conscience*, pp. 180–84, focusing on psychoanalytic questions of scopophilia, the male gaze, and sexual desire. She points out that Ruskin's reading of the picture "converts the dangerous scopophilia offered by the picture into a safe sadistic voyeurism" (p. 184).

34. Judith Bronkhurst, "Fruits of a Connoisseur's Friendship: Sir Thomas Fairbairn and William Holman Hunt," *Burlington Magazine* 125 (October 1983), p. 588 n. 24.

35. [Bennett,] *Hunt,* p. 37. Holman-Hunt, *My Grandfather,* p. 134: "I think that Hunt did more than change the expression, I believe he scraped out most of the head, instead of overpainting. X-rays show nothing underneath. The new face does not resemble Annie Miller in the least." Hunt retouched the picture again in 1864, 1879–80, and finally 1886, though in these instances he apparently did not repaint the face of Annie Miller. See Bronkhurst, "Connoisseur's Friendship," pp. 588, 594–95; and the exhibition catalogue *The Pre-Raphaelites* (London: Tate Gallery/Harmondsworth: Penguin Books, 1984), no. 58, p. 120. See Hunt's own comments on the repainting in his *Pre-Raphaelitism,* vol. 1, p. 418 n. 1, which suggests that he reworked the face only once; avoiding Annie Miller's name, he acknowledges only that "the woman's head in its present condition is not exactly what it was when Ruskin described the picture."

36. Cf. Marcia Pointon, *Naked Authority: The Body in Western Painting, 1830–1908* (Cambridge: Cambridge University Press, 1990), p. 43, concerning Thomas Eakins's painting *The Gross Clinic.*

37. Julie F. Codell, "Expression over Beauty: Facial Expression, Body Language, and Circumstantiality in the Paintings of the Pre-Raphaelite Brotherhood," *Victorian Studies* 29 (1986), p. 273. For more on the massive interest of Victorians (including Hunt) in phrenology, physiognomy (both involved reading the body as a map of permanent character traits), and pathognomy (reading the body as a map of momentary emotion) and an interpretation of the central figure in *The Awakening Conscience,* see pp. 272–79. See also the excellent study by Mary Cowling, *The Artist as Anthropologist: The Representation of Type and Character in Victorian Art* (Cambridge: Cambridge University Press, 1989); and Patricia Magli, "The Face and the Soul," trans. Ughetta Lubin, in *Fragments for a History of the Human Body,* ed. Michel Feher (New York: Zone, 1989), vol. 2, pp. 86–127.

38. Hunt, *Pre-Raphaelitism,* vol. 1, p. 418. Regarding the early reception history of the painting see Fleming, *That Ne'er Shall Meet Again,* pp. 2–4; Holman-Hunt, *My Grandfather,* pp. 133–34; and especially Arscott, "Employer, Husband, Spectator," pp. 170–87, who provides a thoughtful, detailed account not only of Ruskin's gloss on the painting but also of the responses to his reading; she also reprints Ruskin's letter.

39. Janet Wolff and Caroline Arscott, "'Cultivated Capital': Patronage and Art in Nineteenth-Century Manchester and Leeds," *History Today* 37 (March 1987), pp. 22–28. See also Arscott, "Employer, Husband, Spectator," pp. 159–90.

40. Bronkhurst, "Connoisseur's Friendship," p. 586.

41. Ibid., p. 587. For additional biographical information see William Pole, ed., *The Life of Sir William Fairbairn . . . Partly Written by Himself* (London, 1877); and Arscott, "Employer, Husband, Spectator," pp. 162–63.

42. See Arscott, "Employer, Husband, Spectator," pp. 163–68.

43. On the subject of the fallen woman, much studied, see especially (1) Linda Nochlin, "Lost and *Found:* Once More the Fallen Woman," *Feminism and Art History: Questioning the Litany,* ed. Norma Broude and Mary D. Garrard (New York: Harper and Row, 1982), pp. 220–45. The subject of the fallen woman reached a peak in mid-nineteenth-century

England and "perhaps received its characteristic formulation in the circle of the Pre-Raphaelites and their friends. . . . [Indeed, it] interested Dante Gabriel Rossetti almost to the point of obsession" (p. 221). Nochlin's essay concerns Rossetti's painting *Found,* which she suggests "may be considered in some ways a paradoxically contradictory pendant" (p. 222) to Hunt's *Awakening Conscience;* (2) Nead, "Magdalen in Modern Times," pp. 73–92. This essay provides an excellent discussion of the "way in which paintings and other forms of cultural representation participated in the definition of sexual behaviour and 'respectability' during the nineteenth century" (p. 73); (3) Lynda Nead, *Myths of Sexuality: Representations of Women in Victorian Britain* (Oxford: Blackwell, 1988); (4) Helene E. Roberts, "Marriage, Redundancy, or Sin: The Painter's View of Women in the First Twenty-Five Years of Victoria's Reign," in *Suffer and Be Still: Women in the Victorian Age,* ed. Martha Vicinus (Bloomington: Indiana University Press, 1973), pp. 45–76; (5) Casteras, *Images of Victorian Womanhood,* pp. 131–43; and (6) Eric Trudgill, *Madonnas and Magdalens: The Origins and Development of Victorian Sexual Attitudes* (New York: Holmes and Meier, 1976), pp. 101–28, 277–306.

44. Bronkhurst, "Connoisseur's Friendship," p. 594. The painting is illustrated in color in Wolff and Arscott, "Cultivated Capital," p. 25. See also the discussion of the painting, pp. 27–28.

45. Bronkhurst, "Connoisseur's Frienship," p. 594.

46. Arscott, "Employer, Husband, Spectator," pp. 168–71, offers additional valuable insights in a comparison of the two paintings.

47. [Mary Bennett,] *William Holman Hunt* [exhibition catalogue] (Liverpool, Walker Art Gallery, 1969), p. 36.

48. Landow, *Hunt and Typological Symbolism,* p. 51.

49. See Hunt, *Pre-Raphaelitism,* vol. 2, pp. 429–30.

50. See [Bennett,] *Hunt,* p. 35, for the full texts; and Arscott, "Employer, Husband, Spectator," p. 178, for an interpretation of the verses. Hunt later disclaimed the scriptural passages printed in the Royal Academy catalogue; see Nochlin, "Lost and *Found,*" p. 244 n. 32.

51. Hunt, *Pre-Raphaelitism,* vol. 1, p. 430.

52. For more on the role of the piano in the home and the music played, see Derek Scott, *The Singing Bourgeois: Songs of the Victorian Drawing Room and Parlour* (Milton Keynes: Open University Press, 1989); and Mary Burgan, "Heroines at the Piano: Women and Music in Nineteenth-Century Fiction," *Victorian Studies* 30 (1986), pp. 51–76. From p. 51: "The sacrifice of her piano is one of the harshest elements of the woman's share in the economic disasters portrayed in nineteenth-century fiction. Without a piano, women with pretensions to gentility are deprived of the exercise of their special training, of any leading role in family recreation, and of one of their few legitimate channels for self-expression." Burgan has some excellent things to say about what she terms women's "demonic affinity with music" (p. 69). Danièle Pistone, *Le Piano dans la littérature française des origines jusque vers 1900* (Paris: Champion, 1975), has located references to the domestic piano in two thousand scenes in nineteenth-century novels.

53. Quoted in Michelle Perrot, ed., *A History of Private Life,* vol. 4, *From the Fires of*

Revolution to the Great War, trans. Arthur Goldhammer (Cambridge: Belknap Press of Harvard University Press, 1990), p. 531.

54. Ruskin in the *Times,* quoted in Hunt, *Pre-Raphaelitism,* vol. 1, p. 419.

55. See Dijkstra, *Idols of Perversity,* p. 65.

56. Peter Brooks, *The Melodramatic Imagination* (London: New Left Books, 1983); see also the discussion in Laura Mulvey, "Melodrama inside and outside the Home," in *Visual and Other Pleasures* (Bloomington: Indiana University Press, 1989), pp. 63–77.

57. Quoted from Flint, "Rereading *The Awakening Conscience* Rightly," p. 59.

58. For detailed information see Maas, *Holman Hunt and "The Light of the World,"* primarily a study of the later version painted between 1900 and 1904, especially the history of its exhibition tour and reception in Canada, Australia, New Zealand, and South Africa prior to its installation in St. Paul's Cathedral, London, where it has hung since 1908. See also Mark Roskill, "Holman Hunt's Differing Versions of *The Light of the World,*" *Victorian Studies* 6 (1962/63), pp. 329–42.

59. Hunt, *Pre-Raphaelitism,* vol. 2, p. 429. See further, re Hunt's intentions, George P. Landow, "Shadows Cast by *The Light of the World:* William Holman Hunt's Religious Paintings, 1893–1905," *Art Bulletin* 65 (1983), p. 481; the essay studies the impact of this painting on Hunt's life's work, and his virtual obsession with the subject of conversion and illumination.

60. Nina Auerbach, *Woman and the Demon: The Life of a Victorian Myth* (Cambridge: Harvard University Press, 1982), p. 77.

61. Codell, "Expression over Beauty," p. 264: the depiction of bodies in "transitional postures" is characteristic of Pre-Raphaelite Brotherhood art.

62. Holman-Hunt, *My Grandfather,* p. 98.

63. Marsh, *The Pre-Raphaelite Sisterhood,* p. 108.

64. Hunt, *Pre-Raphaelitism.* Principal references to the picture, so far as I can determine in this sprawling, unindexed two-volume book, are in vol. 1, pp. 347–48, 405, 418–19; vol. 2, pp. 428–31.

65. Remarks by Edward Clodd, published in his *Reminiscences,* p. 200, as quoted in Fleming, *That Ne'er Shall Meet Again,* p. 134.

66. Quoted in Hunt, *Pre-Raphaelitism,* vol. 1, p. 419.

67. Flint, "Reading *The Awakening Conscience* Rightly," p. 49.

68. Henry Noel Humphries, *The Origin and Progress of the Art of Writing,* 2nd ed. (London: Day and Son, 1855), p. 1.

69. Quoted in Vogel, "Fine Arts and Feminism," p. 21.

70. Giuseppe Verdi, *La Traviata,* act 3, English translation by Dale McAdoo (Angel Records: 3545 B/L, 1956), p. 14.

71. Scott, *Singing Bourgeois,* p. x. Regarding the success of Tom Moore, in whose collections "Oft, in the Stilly Night" appeared (without the comma in its title), see pp. 25–26. See also Maurice Disher, *Victorian Song: From Dive to Drawing Room* (London: Phoenix House, 1955); and Jacqueline S. Bratton, *The Victorian Popular Ballad* (Totowa, N.J.: Rowman and Littlefield, 1975).

72. See Jacques Attali, *Noise: The Political Economy of Music,* trans. Brian Massumi (Minneapolis: University of Minnesota Press, 1985), pp. 51–62, 77–81.

73. This matter is dealt with in detail throughout Leppert, *Music and Image.*

74. *The Poetical Works of Thomas Moore, Collected by Himself,* vol. 4, *Irish Melodies, National Airs, Sacred Songs* (London, 1853), pp. 167–68.

75. *Tennyson's Poetry: Authoritative Texts; Juvenilia and Early Responses; Criticism,* ed. Robert W. Hill, Jr. (New York: Norton, 1971), p. 114. For a good analysis of this poem see Graham Hough, "Tears, Idle Tears," *Hopkins Review* 4, no. 3 (1951), pp. 31–36.

76. Hunt, *Pre-Raphaelitism,* vol. 2, p. 429.

77. Roland Barthes, "Listening," in *The Responsibility of Forms: Critical Essays on Music, Art, and Representation,* trans. Richard Howard (New York: Hill and Wang, 1985), p. 255.

78. Kaja Silverman, *The Acoustic Mirror: The Female Voice in Psychoanalysis and Cinema* (Bloomington: Indiana University Press, 1988), p. 44; see also pp. 67–68. Cf. the chapter "Chant / Song," in David Appelbaum, *Voice* (Albany: State University of New York Press, 1990), pp. 85–97: "The sung voice introduces quantity. . . . Quantity in voice transmits the basal vibration of the body, calling an awareness of its condition and the condition of the world surrounding. Its *telos* is activation, address, and embodiment" (p. 94).

CHAPTER 9

The Musician of the Imagination

Opportunity and Necessity

I'd like to explore the representation—including self-representation—of the musician and/or composer during the emergence and development of modernity in the eighteenth and, principally, nineteenth century. This was when professional musicians and composers confronted for the first time the realities of market economies transforming or supplanting patronage systems, which musicians both recognized and learned how to exploit as necessary corollaries to their livelihoods. If musicians necessarily operated as opportunists under market conditions, it is obvious that their appeal to the market was anchored in something beyond their talent to produce musical sonorities in an aesthetically pleasing fashion. My remarks are intended to examine this issue by considering the position of the audience—the collective auditor-viewer of music and musicians.

To state the obvious: Opportunism succeeds only where an opportunity exists. The opportunities available to nineteenth-century musicians were considerable not least because musicians functioned as embodiments of a rich—and, to be sure, highly dialectical—cultural imaginary concerning music. Specifically what interests me is the perceived need to *imagine* the musician, and in direct regard to the larger phenomenon of Western modernity. I hope to trace the parameters of this, as well as what the imagined figure of the musician might represent for music history in particular, and cultural and social history more generally.

Consider, for example, Franz Liszt. As a suitable, if hyperbolic, archetype of the star-quality musician, he was more than a man or a performer; he also was a psychological projection produced by his auditor-lookers, the "ordinary" bourgeois and aristocratic publics and published critics alike. As such, Liszt was a consumer product in the early history of modern consumption and he was much consumed, thereby convincingly demonstrating virtuosity's cultural utility. And true to the necessity of capitalist production driven by the requirements of the consumer economy, he repeatedly reinvented himself—and was by others reinvented—throughout his long professional life. This reinvention received its public due: Liszt the virtuoso, the composer, and indeed the man, for decades was continually reevaluated in music journals in an exercise that represents the aesthetic correlative of new-model product reviews that we might read today in magazines such as *Consumer Reports.* Put simply, Liszt was a linchpin in the formation of the nineteenth-century's cultural imaginary.

The virtuoso anchored a broad range of paradoxical, often contradictory, meanings: artist and businessman; inspired superhuman Genius, and sonority-producing machine; utterly sincere in character and calculatingly manipulative; authentic and fake; masculine and feminine; Byronic hero possessing militaristic stamina and strength but, ironically—as regards Liszt—in the body of a pale, thin, and sometimes fainting aesthete. These polarities to no small degree not only define the obsessive fascination with the virtuoso in the nineteenth century but also mark the virtuoso at the epicenter of the cultural and social issues that characterize modernity itself.[1]

It's not by accident that so many images produced during the course of the nineteenth century permit us to see musicians at once as real and imagined; their very reality in part is determined by the imaginary. The nineteenth century produced a great many images that affirm the need to look at the representation of looking at musicians (Fig. 1)—some suggesting, through satire, that a love of looking, a scopophilic experience attached to music (Fig. 2), was engaged in to the point of emotional catharsis in the form of apparent stupefied exhaustion (Fig. 3). The "visual turn" that marks modernity, increasingly ubiquitous after 1800, enjoyed a longer genealogy stretching back at least to the early seventeenth century; this visual record provides a distinct and distinctive trace of the epistemic change marking the musician of the imagination. If, for the

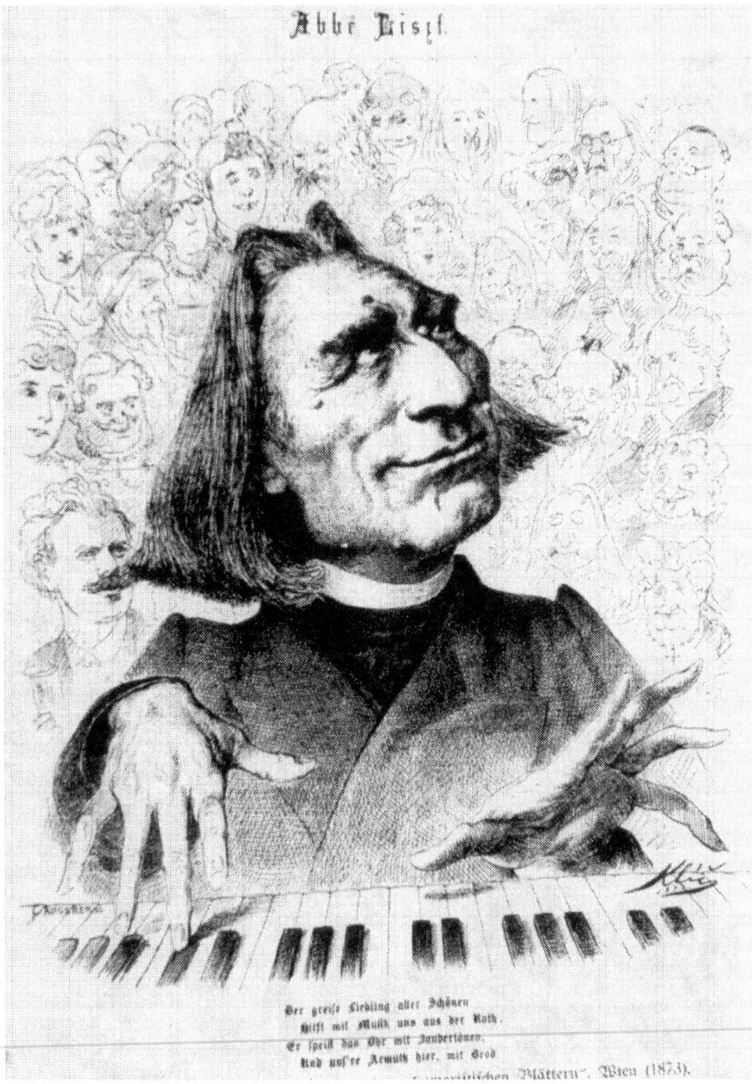

Figure 1. Karl Klic, *Abbé Liszt* (1873). *Humoristische Blätter* (Vienna).

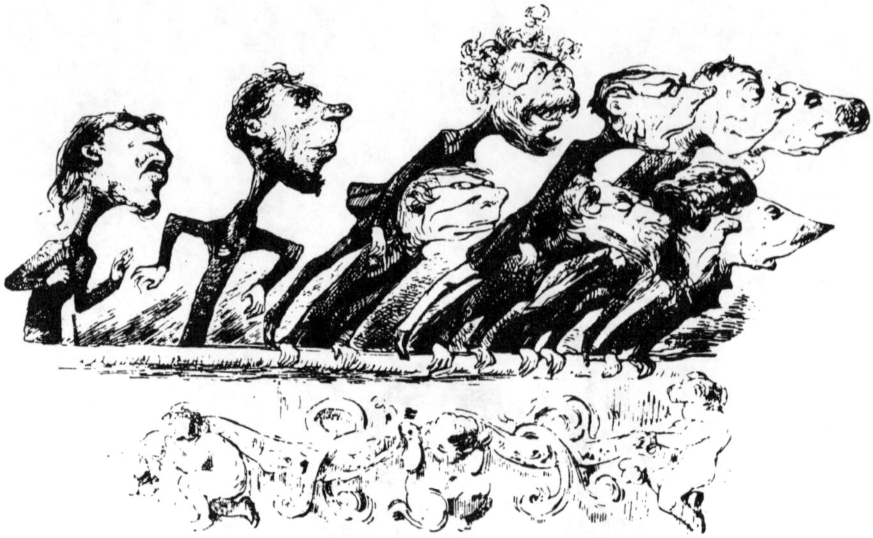

Figure 2. Gustave Doré (1832–83), *Those Who Are Carried Away* (1849). From *Grotesques*.

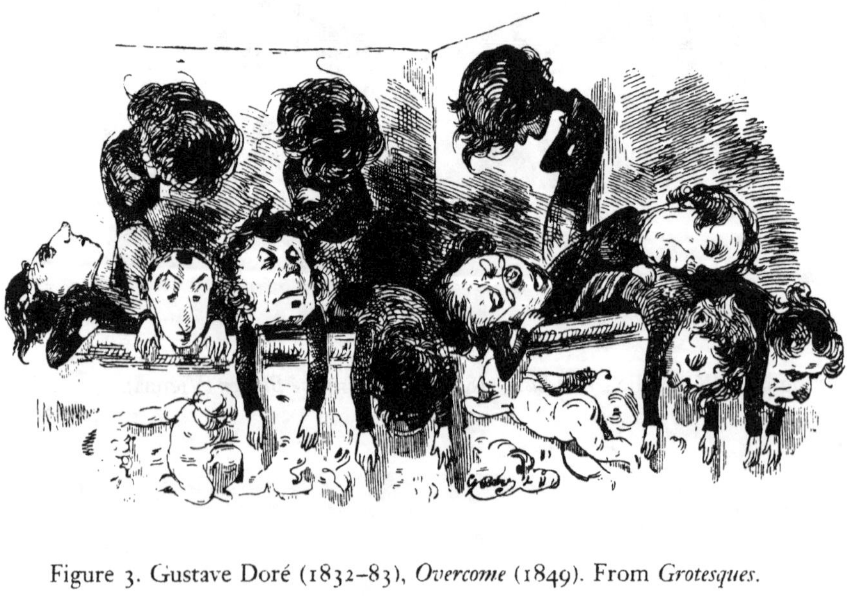

Figure 3. Gustave Doré (1832–83), *Overcome* (1849). From *Grotesques*.

sake of convenience, we simply follow the representational record from the advent of the eighteenth century forward into the nineteenth, a couple of critical ruptures become apparent in the visual field—ruptures that delineate something about a more general disturbance in the cultural and social arena.

Identity Claims

Portraits in oil mark the most prestigious form of visual representation to which any professional musician living during the early decades of modernity might hope to attain. The cultural stakes of the oil portrait were higher than for other media. Portraits were expensive, intended for more than private viewing (even when hung in more or less private surroundings), and in some instances served as the matrix for mass-produced copies via the various reproductive technologies of the time: engravings, mezzotints, and, later, lithographs. The portrait's function, in other words, was not merely decorative, and not least because of its own visibility or the visibility of the images for which it served as a model. The portrait not only helped to anchor the sitter's claims to identity and social station but also served to establish the very means by which such measures could be determined in the first place.

By definition, portraits flatter. But that's not what makes them interesting for my purposes. Their significance resides in the particular ways that they constitute in two dimensions the abstract qualities of the musician, at a given time and in a certain place. What I'm after is not the visual datum that, say, Marin Marais with his bass viol da gamba (Fig. 4), or Robert Lindley (Fig. 5) with his violoncello, were virtuosi, but how that data, visually represented, served to locate these musicians in the cultural (hence social) imaginary of their own times. What I'd suggest—and speaking pretty generally—is that both portraits situate these professionals in a musical and social world that's at once established and settled. Marais, who spent most of his professional life in royal service, reminds us of that fact, sitting idly as if waiting for his summons, dressed in appropriate court regalia while perhaps practicing a bit (the music on the floor) or perhaps composing (the manuscript, quill, and ink stand on the desk), but anyway at the ready. Marais is imagined as the dutiful keeper of the king's sonoric prestige.

Robert Lindley, painted exactly one century later, was active in London, where he performed as principal cellist in the Italian Opera orchestra and in Philharmonic concerts, among a host of others. Lindley,

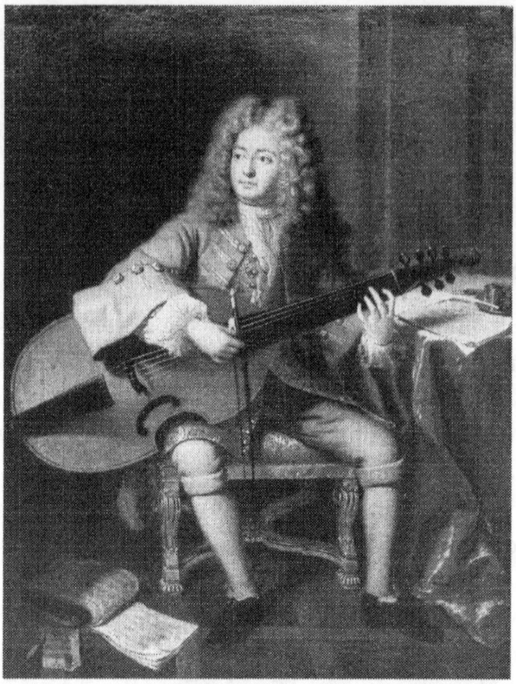

Figure 4. André Bouys (1656–1740), *Portrait of Marin Marais* (1704). Paris, Bibliothèque Nationale de l' Opera. Photo: Réunion des Musées Nationaux; Art Resource, New York.

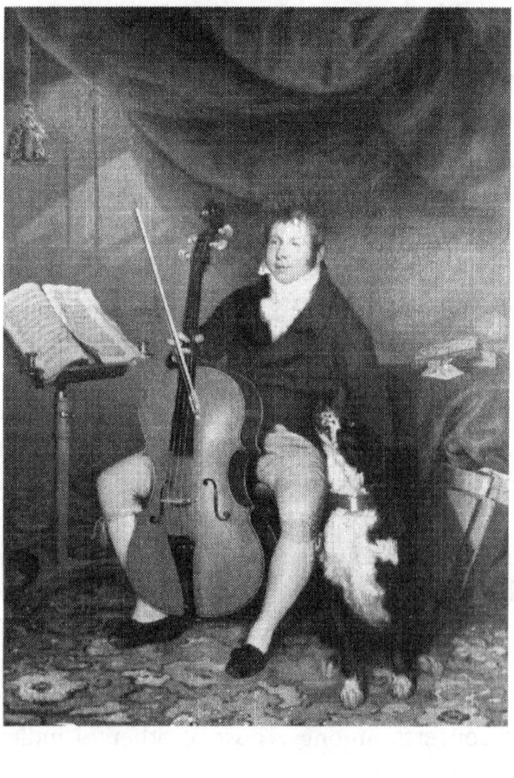

Figure 5. Sir William Beechey (1753–1839), *Robert Lindley* (c. 1805). Hanover, N.H., Dartmouth College Collection, Hood Museum of Art, Gift of Irving S. Manheimer.

attired simply, albeit as a bourgeois gentleman (of no special means), affirms his social position by absent-mindedly petting his dog rather than playing his cello. The visual vocabulary marks not only his status as a professional but also his claim to upward class mobility defined by the incorporation of leisure—the rhetorical function of the dog. Critical to the semiotics of the image, Lindley—quite unlike Marais—commands his *own* time, just as he commands his own *space* (here the improbable space marked by theatrical drapery, itself a visual hold-over from decades' worth of aristocratic portraiture, and, accordingly, a visual clue to class prestige, whether real or merely fantasized. Not by accident is Marais's spatial enclosure devoid of such drapery; the room he inhabits is pointedly utilitarian, in essence a practice space, with only the somewhat excessive table covering replicating the drapery conventions of contemporaneous portraits of the French nobility.

Two musician portraits (Figs. 6–7) from the last third of the eighteenth century reiterate, although by means quite different from the Marais portrait, the established position of professional court players, in this instance in Bavaria. The sitters are virtually swallowed up by the courtly architectural backdrop. In the first example, the musician waits in a fashion similar to that of Marais, but in this instance in lavish surroundings more common to contemporaneous operatic stage sets than actual court buildings. In other words, the space isn't his; there are quite a number of crucial visual clues to overdetermine a culturally correct reading provided. The musician, sitting as if interrupted from practicing, is situated in a quasi-public space, at the base of a large stairway and in the archway of a colonnade: He, together with the instruments piled akimbo, is rather in the way. He's there for someone else. Furthermore, his spread-legged pose, perfectly ordinary and unremarkable in life, is indecorous for a portrait. No aristocrat would ever sit so posed—and that, of course, is precisely the point, a matter not left to chance.

In the second example, the musician seems only to be passing through as he catches us looking. Furthermore, the considerable inventory of instruments practically swallows him. Indeed, the overwhelming nature of the architectural enclosure and the instrument inventory together render him almost—but not quite—superfluous. While the musician enjoys the status afforded by a clearly specific, personalized portrait head, duly framed by an archway, everything else about him and the image places him in the role of staffage: He is there not for himself, but to serve. And the lavishness of the palace and its orchestral inventory together help make very clear that he is part of someone else's property.

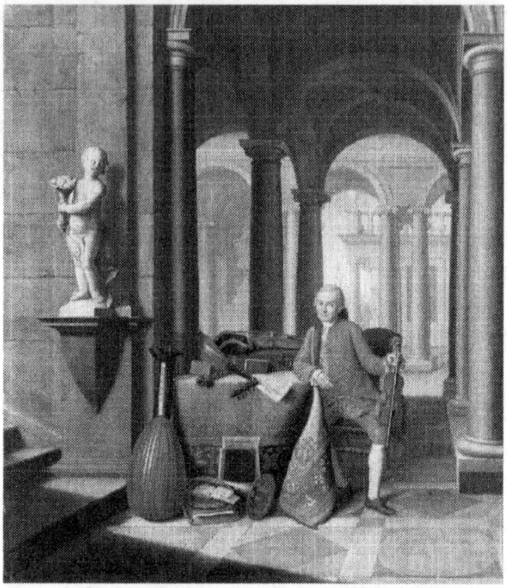

Figure 6. Peter Jacob Horemans (1700–76), *Portrait of Violinist Johann Georg Holzbogen* (1774). Munich, Bayerische Staatsgemäldesammlungen.

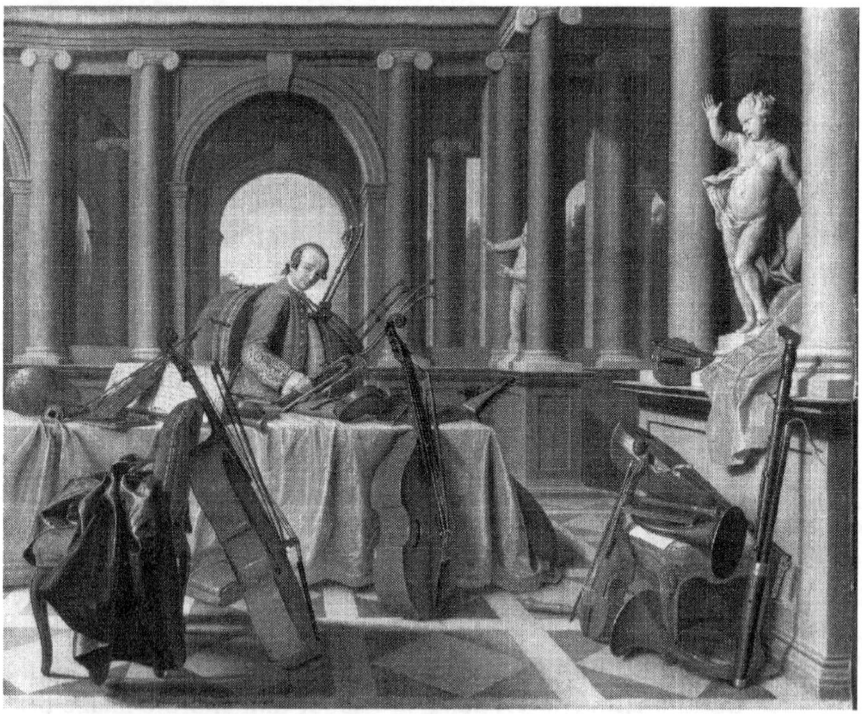

Figure 7. Peter Jacob Horemans (1700–76), *Portrait of the Bassoonist Felix Reiner* (1762). Munich, Bayerische Staatsgemäldesammlungen.

These musicians exist in the imagination of those who employ them—those who, in short, commissioned the images. The commentary the portraits provide, overdetermined by virtually everything represented in them, repeatedly affirms the command over time claimed by those on whose walls the pictures were intended to hang, and affirms as well the distinctive role that music generally, and these musicians in particular, perform in the aestheticization of the time owned—that is, the aestheticization of history itself. The high precision with which the instruments are painted, to a degree that is visually virtually fetishistic, confirms the fact that prestige formation and its maintenance is serious business. The musician thus imagined is no mere figment of the idle mind but, rather, a player given an important supporting role in a social drama wherein the imagination and the imaginary served quite specific social demands rather more distinctly socially instrumental than socially utopian.

The visual representation of the manner in which these musicians account sonorically for their world—the full century separating the portraits of Marais and Lindley—marks, at least on the surface, a more or less orderly social evolution, although dramatic changes were of course afoot; it's these changes that especially interest me. The portraits I've mentioned so far represent time contiguous to when they were painted. That is, they constitute a claim to the future by locating themselves in the same moment of their execution. Their current temporality characterizes most such images from the eighteenth century. Not so those from the nineteenth.

The nineteenth century, more than any preceding period of Western history, was obsessed with and by time, which served as the experiential parameter through which progress, like capital, flowed—ideally, if seldom in actuality—solely by positive forward movement. Ironically, the obsessive requirement to have time at one's back led to a great deal of looking back. Stated differently, Walter Benjamin's elegant and deeply ironic metaphor of the angel of progress being blown backward, hence blindly, into the future[2] delineates the reality of the enormous degree of troubled time consciousness against which the present operated. The pastness of the past became an issue of striking importance, not least in light of the overwhelming disruptions to culturally embedded ordinary life experiences now rapaciously challenged by time advancing with a determination that seemed to promise universal colonization of everything within modernity's considerable grasp.

Enter the musician, thoroughly reimagined (Fig. 8). To make my point most efficiently, I've leapt ahead to the later decades of the nine-

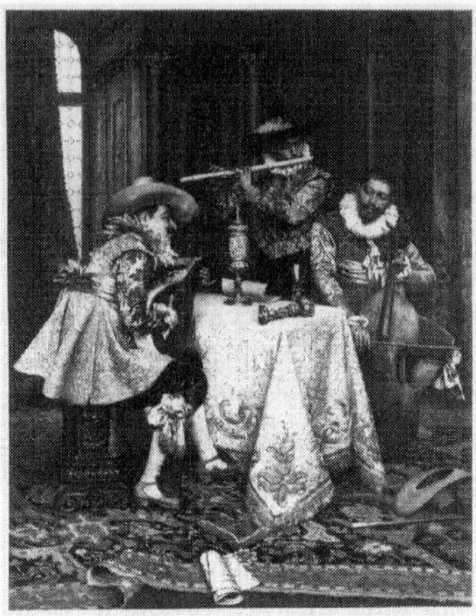

Figure 8. Adolphe Alexander Lestrel (1839–after 1865), *Musicians* (1887). Private Collection.

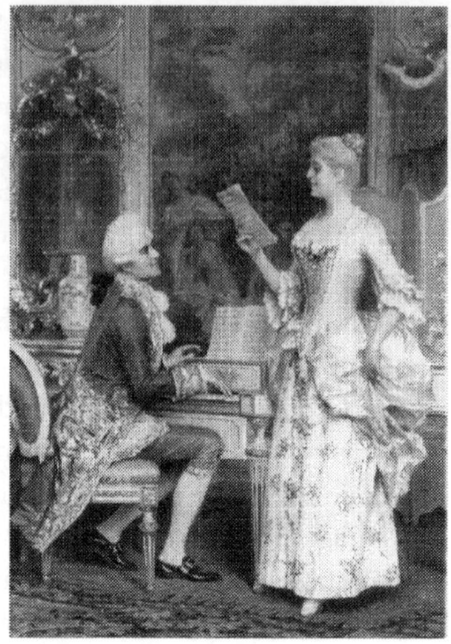

Figure 9. Arturo Ricci (b. 1854), *The Singing Lesson.* Private Collection.

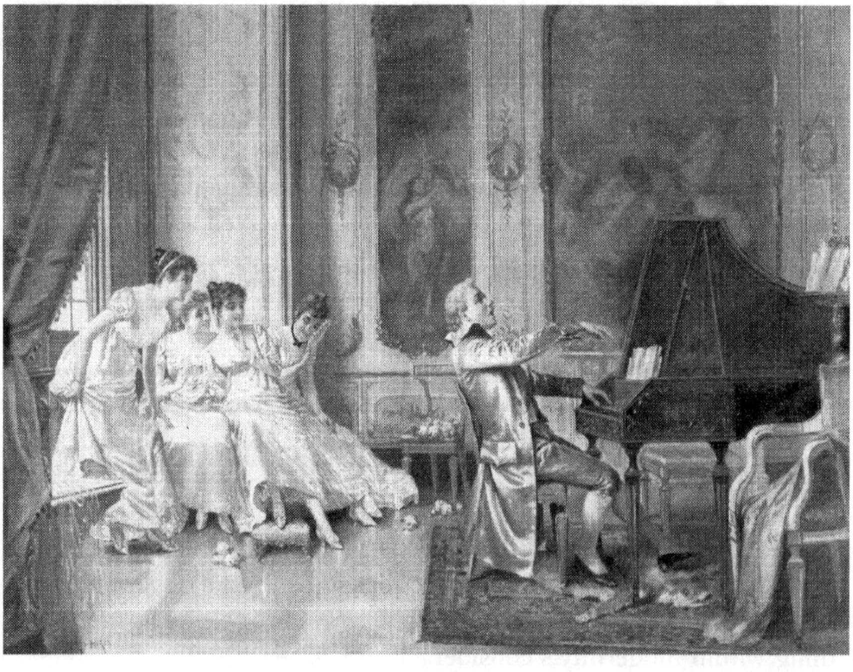

Figure 10. Edward Percy Moran (b. 1862), *The Recital.* Private Collection.

teenth century, as it were into the realm of the full-blown modernity of the European Industrial Revolution—only to find three freeze-frames of past history (and these examples are entirely typical of a large repertory of similar representations). The first, set the Dutch seventeenth century, reimagines, via a musical metaphor, the incorporation of a sociality at odds with social structures defined by economic competition and social Darwinism. Here men cooperate, rather than compete, a wholly fictional reenactment of an otherwise abandoned ideal. Nostalgia for the *ancien régime* likewise flourished (Figs. 9–10), in a kind of infantile reversion that preferred a misremembered past to the awesome potentialities and implications of 1789 or 1830. Both images, saccharine in the extreme, display not the slightest trace of irony. Most striking are the faces, male and female alike: equally pretty, equally feminine. Both pictures provide visual pleasure by articulating, and indeed valorizing, a normally repressed eroticism operating within male homosocial desire.[3] These paintings, one by an Italian and the other by an American, evoke an erotic fantasy involving men *not* acting like men.[4] The men in both images dress like women, gesture like women, are set in elaborate domestic surroundings, and in effect engage in women's "activities." Thus imagined—and these representations are nothing if not imaginative—music constitutes the agent in the feminization of men, which is simultaneously held at bay while at the same time made the subject of scopophilic desire of viewing. In both images, the erotic charge is produced by the males insofar as they are constituted as aberrant, whereas the females by comparison are treated conventionally.[5] Music provides the ether for the return of the repressed. But more to the point, the gendering of music and musical practice has moved from the sociocultural background (common to pre- and early modernity) to the foreground of social consciousness. Indeed, the gendering of music marks a nineteenth-century obsession, which fundamentally reshapes the musical imaginary—from the elevated realm of aesthetics to the more mundane history of musical reception.

Return of the Repressed

Not the least reason for the intense public interest in nineteenth-century virtuosos, Liszt, for example, was their paradoxical, often contradictory relation to the bourgeois social and cultural revolution swirling around them, in which they were active participants. Not the least source of excitement for audiences viewing male virtuosos resides in the fact that their performances often contradicted, or at least challenged, the increasingly rigid boundaries organizing gender difference.[6] Indeed, the terrain of gender distinction constituted fertile ground upon which the specifically visual components of virtuosity could at once be tested, developed, and profitably marketed, precisely to the extent that music generally, and physically manifested male virtuosity in particular, traversed with such seeming ease the increasingly demarcated territories assigned either to the female or the male, but not to both. Simply stated, virtuosity was literally marketable as a display mechanism for the return of the repressed.

A nineteenth-century watercolor by the English artist Henry Stock entitled "A Musician's Reverie" (Fig. 11), representing aesthetic inspiration, helps clarify the paradigmatic sociocultural dialectics of the musician reimagined—erotically. In a world fast being rid of traditional patrons, the new patron is the market that (ideally) demands the product that musicians produce. And yet the product that's culturally needed in this brave new world is one that sells itself, so to speak, on the basis of its non-material (spiritual), or anti-market, marketability. Is it any wonder, in the first age in which language itself achieves the dubious distinction of its thorough instrumentalization, that there appears on the scene the purposeful fiction of absolute music: music, that is, wholly spiritualized (and, of course, marketed as such)?

Stock's watercolor constitutes something of a discourse on the contradiction I've just described, but in this instance the contradiction is transferred from music (which cannot be represented directly) to an embodiment in an imaginary musician who dreams his music, just as we are invited in turn to dream him—or, better, to see the dream materialized into an objective reality, a fantasy come true. The musician realizes himself through his violin. That is, music realizes the imagination; and the imagination is the mark of identity. The cost of imagination, however, is isolation and narcissistic self-absorption, visually conjured via a virtually autoerotic fantasy—an unremitting and solitary passion—of Watteauesque nudes, not to mention Goyaesque nocturnal demons, dimly visible in the background. The paradox of this excited scene lies in the degree to which it deviates from established social norm, except, of course, to the extent that one role anticipated for artists is to play the part of transgressors, the carnivalesque safety value that ironically helps guarantee the hegemony of the status quo.

What does this suggest about music? In this male reverie, music operates on two levels. Visually it is a bit of a sideshow, like modern-day amusement rides that simultaneously promise the thrill of a lifetime and

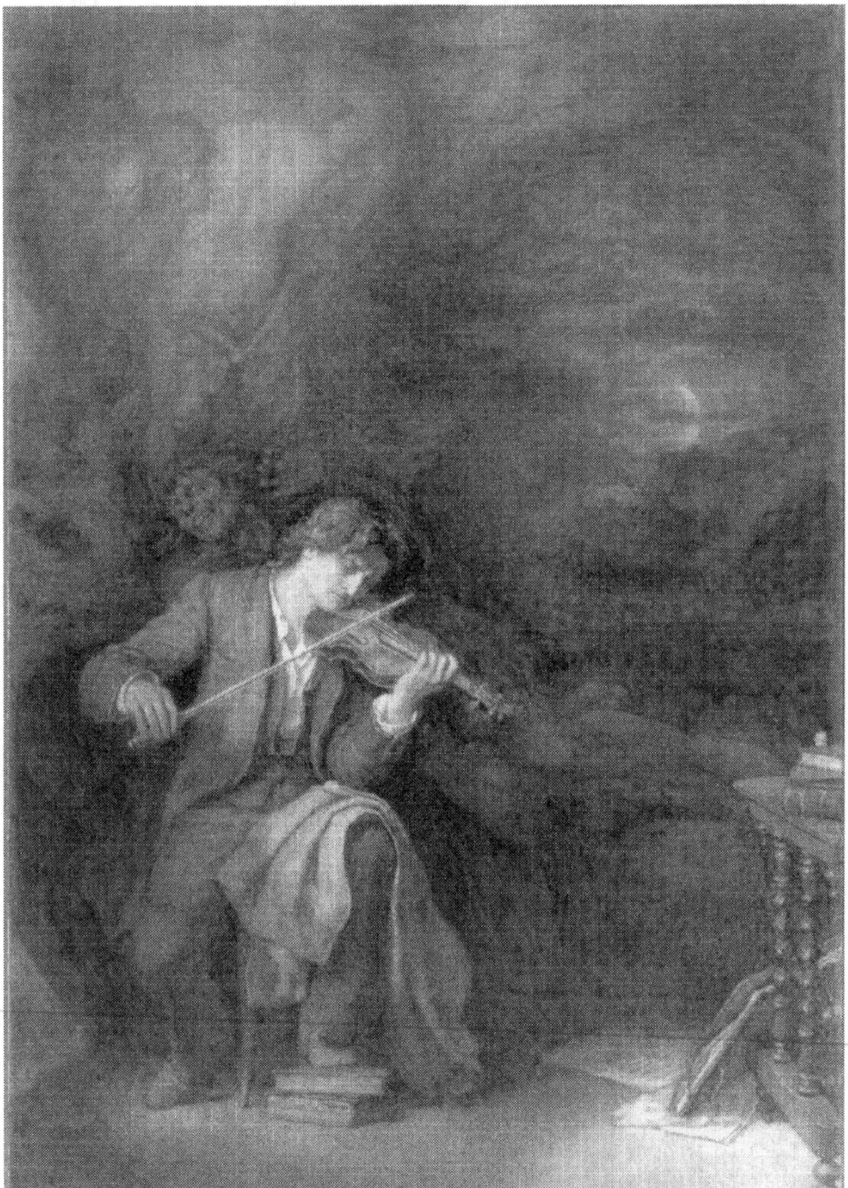

Figure 11. Henry J. Stock (1853–1931), *A Musician's Reverie* (1888). Harrow (Greater London), Harrow School Collection, The Keepers and Governors of Harrow School. Photo: Photographic Survey, Courtauld Institute of Art.

an utterly predictable, completely safe sixty-second experience, a kind of assembly-line excitement: We have it, we walk away from it. Music operates as the analogical manifestation of the thrill (and not coincidentally the climax), as such extraordinary yet peripheral and inevitably momentary. The socioerotics of music established by these private-public dichotomies, wherein the visual inscription of music serves as a substitute for both emotion and sensuality, operate also as momentary compensation and consolation for the fracturing that defines modernity's increasingly competitive, class- and gender-separated social and economic order. And a corollary: Compensation and consolation are salable commodities.

Contradictions of Difference

Let's back up a bit, to Beethoven (Fig. 12), and to an image that graces the cover of Tia DeNora's book on the construction of genius. What's striking about this fictional scene, produced years after the composer's death, is less the representation of Beethoven and more the apparent impact of his music on others. Each of the four auditors is posed uniquely; each reacts to the music in a personally unique manner. Beethoven, Beethoven's playing, and Beethoven's music together momentarily at once isolate and spiritualize each auditor, as each appears to experience emotions akin to those of the Burkeian sublime. In the process, the four men are shown to lay claim to their own subjecthood by means of the singularity of their reaction to music's ineffability. The decentering loss of self to music redeems the self from the mundane—and Beethoven is "there" to fill the need. An image of this sort plays both sides of modernity's street to the extent that the redemption from instrumentality, carefully delineated, is simultaneously marketed as a fantasy, and evident not least in the extent to which the fictional nature of the scene so amply announces itself to the viewer whose own life experiences could necessarily bear only the most distant relation.

The unstable social position of actual musicians challenged efforts to represent appropriately musicians of the imagination. Indeed, even Beethoven, the archetype of the musician in the nineteenth-century imaginary, was subjected to the complicated dialectics of social difference, especially evident when taken away from his music and set onto the street (Fig. 13). In this non-aesthetic space, musically silent, the composer performs an ambiguous cultural role, less Artist-Genius, more Viennese

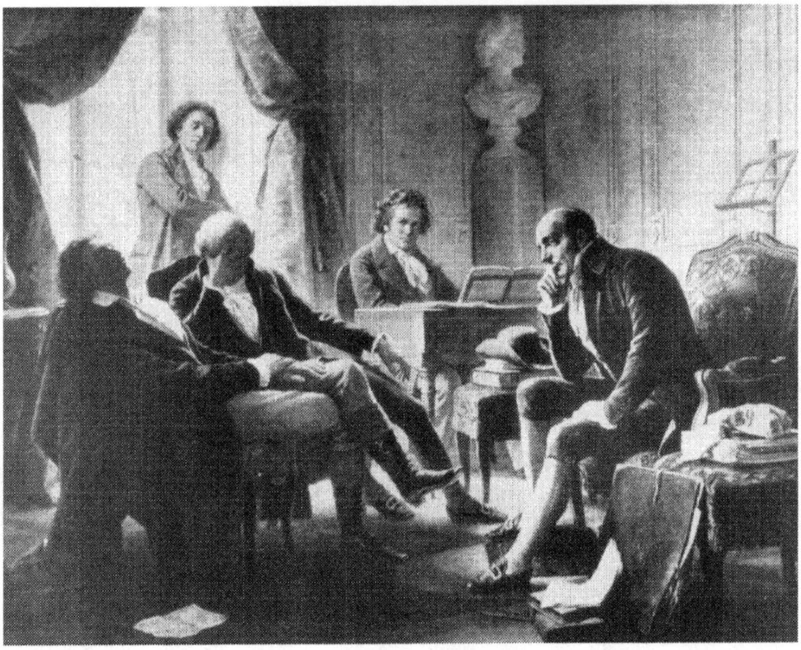

Figure 12. Albert Graefle (1808–89), *Beethoven's Intimates.* Private Collection.

bourgeois, if of the middling sort, and as though sent from Central Casting in full regalia, a veritable fashion plate, intended for the wide distribution made possible by engraving. But, in other images, canonization by appearance is distinctly muted, if not altogether absent (Fig. 14); Beethoven in these instances takes on the look of physiognomic atavism, a man at the lower fringes of the class to which his aesthetic accomplishments have gained him, providing the composer with the profiled face later in the century conventionally assigned to the criminal element. And the same may be said for Wagner. If Wagner, perhaps the most caricatured musician in Western history, commonly enjoyed visual apotheosis, the compliment often was anchored in deep resentment whose foundation was planted firmly in the ground of class conflict and differential pedigree (Fig. 15), whose visual authorization came from the well-established pseudo-sciences of physiognomy and phrenology that functioned to naturalize and embody social relations structured on class

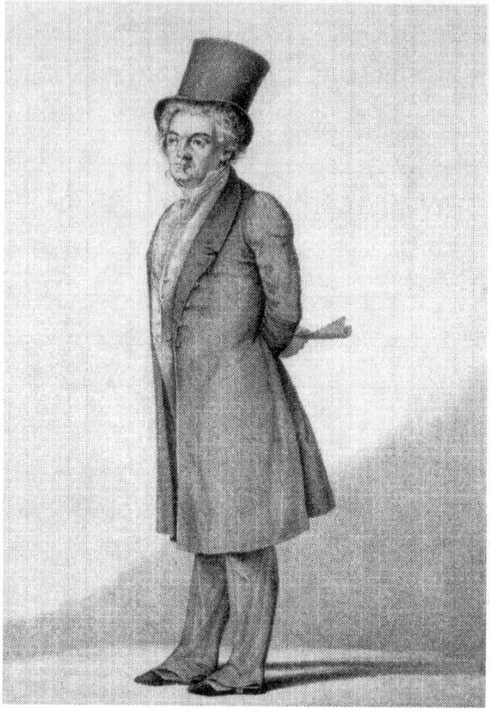

Figure 13. *Beethoven in Street Attire* (1823), engraving after a drawing by Martin Tejcek. Vienna, Museen der Stadt Wien.

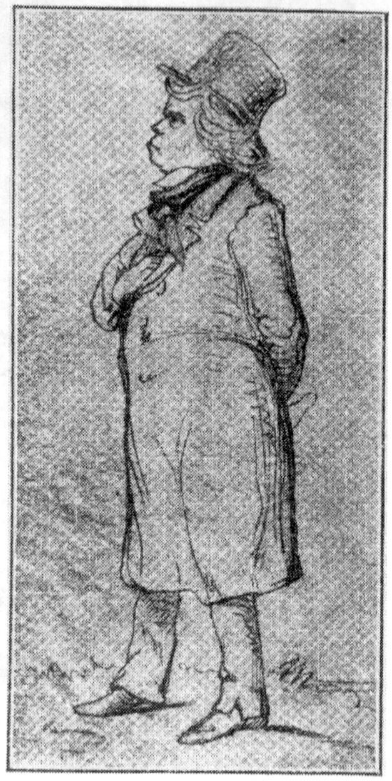

Figure 14. Joseph Daniel Böhm (1794–1865), *Beethoven in Profile* (c. 1820). Bonn, Beethoven-Haus, H. C. Bodmer Collection.

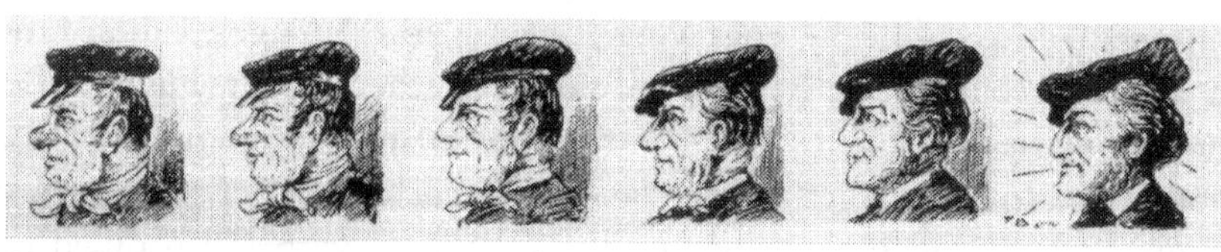

Figure 15. F. Boscovits, *Physiognomic Transformation into Wagner. Nebelspalter* (Zürich).

difference.[7] In this instance, Wagner quickly morphs from the lower orders in an evolutionary regeneration up the social and physiognomic ladder—the image nonetheless serving principally to affirm precisely the opposite.

Machines, Warriors, and Gender Uncertainty

The musician of the nineteenth-century imagination was a paradoxical concatenation of transgression against, and aesthetic affirmation of, prevailing social, cultural, and capitalist-industrial economies of Western Europe. The piano virtuoso, beginning with Liszt, and the conductor, ending with Gustav Mahler, embody one thread of this paradox. It's not a cultural accident that Liszt and Mahler, whose musical careers precisely span the eighty-year history of high capitalism, serve to mark the energy of the Industrial Revolution in the cultural imaginary. The look of frenetic performers (Fig. 16), and equally frenetic conductors together with their disciplined orchestras (Fig. 17), constituted via sight the aesthetic transformation of human mass labor, and, via sound, the aesthetic manifestation of the results of work: namely, artistic Production. Not for nothing do cartoons of Hans von Bülow (Fig. 18) and Mahler conducting remind us of things to come, the high-speed motion of modernity captured in early industrial films celebrating ever-more-efficient Taylorist technologies of material manufacture. The comedy immanent to the cartoons reflects not just derision but, in equal measure, the disquieting awe demanded by Supermen, in which actions—borderline militaristic—speak much louder than words (or, for that matter, music). No small irony, the (anti-bourgeois) indecorous lack of physical reserve exercised by numerous prominent nineteenth-century orchestra conductors was as much admired as it was derided; not least, conductors' physical histrionics also were clearly marketable, serving as an aestheticized imago of male authority and power—an aesthetic simulacrum of social authoritarianism that Adorno had the ill-grace, and insight, to diagnose as a "Führer complex."[8] To be sure, the exaggerated motions of the gesturing and gesticulating bodies of conductors, and virtuosos, vastly exceeded the boundaries of contemporaneous notions of male decorum, and on that score their behaviors transgress convention. But to repeat: The principles of bourgeois decorum violated by such movement nonetheless paradoxically inscribed and validated the bourgeois idealization of industry's ceaseless energy and also its disciplining of the body to the demands of the machine and the highly regulated work day—one of the best send-ups of which is Charles Chaplin in *Modern Times.*

Outside of opera, women played only a small role as professional musicians in the cultural imagination. This made it all the more significant that men, who dominated this fantasy, played extreme roles, on the

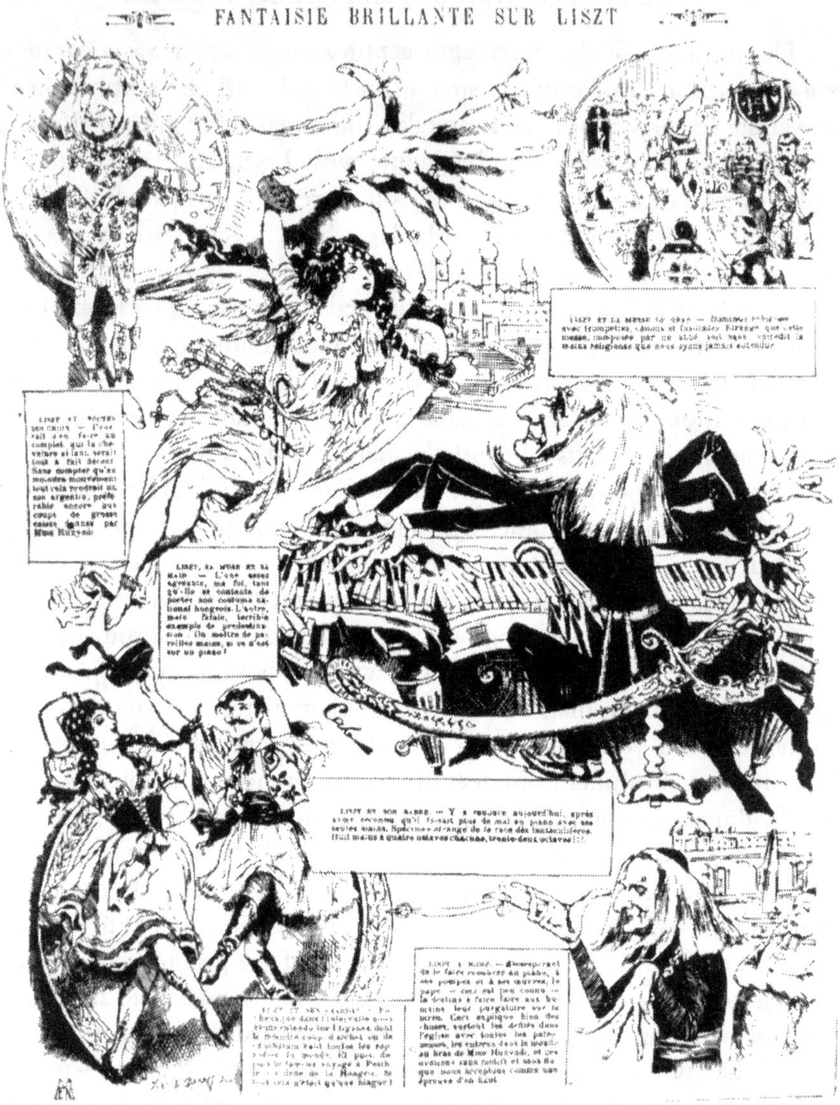

Figure 16. Anonymous, *Liszt-Fantaisie. La Vie Parisienne* (Paris, April 3, 1886).

one hand as effeminized aesthetes (Figs. 9–10), and on the other as warriors, as if in recovery of a masculinity otherwise at threat from its association with music. In 1839, Liszt, for example, was likened by a critic

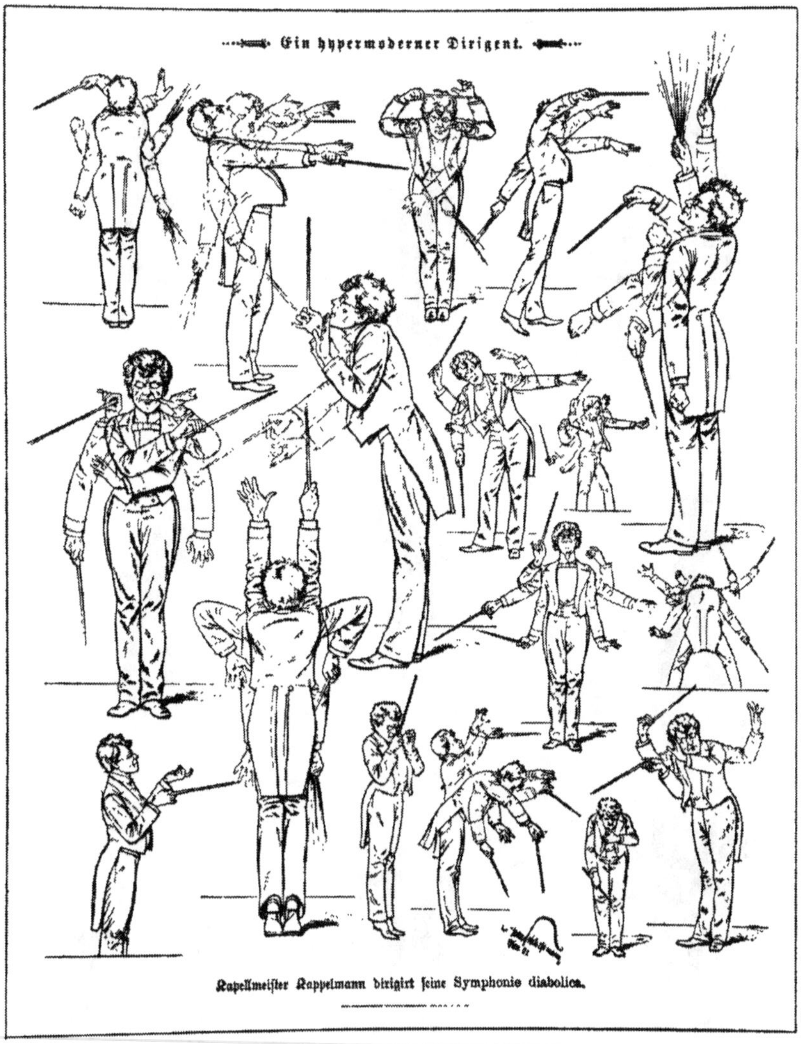

Figure 17. Hans Schliessmann, *A Hyper-Modern Conductor* (caricature). *Fliegende Blätter* (March 1901).

to "this musical Byron,"[9] and virtuoso pianists and their concerts were commonly linked, respectively, to warriors and warfare. The imagery of battle is apparent in many accounts of Liszt's playing. No less a critic than Robert Schumann was caught up in it:

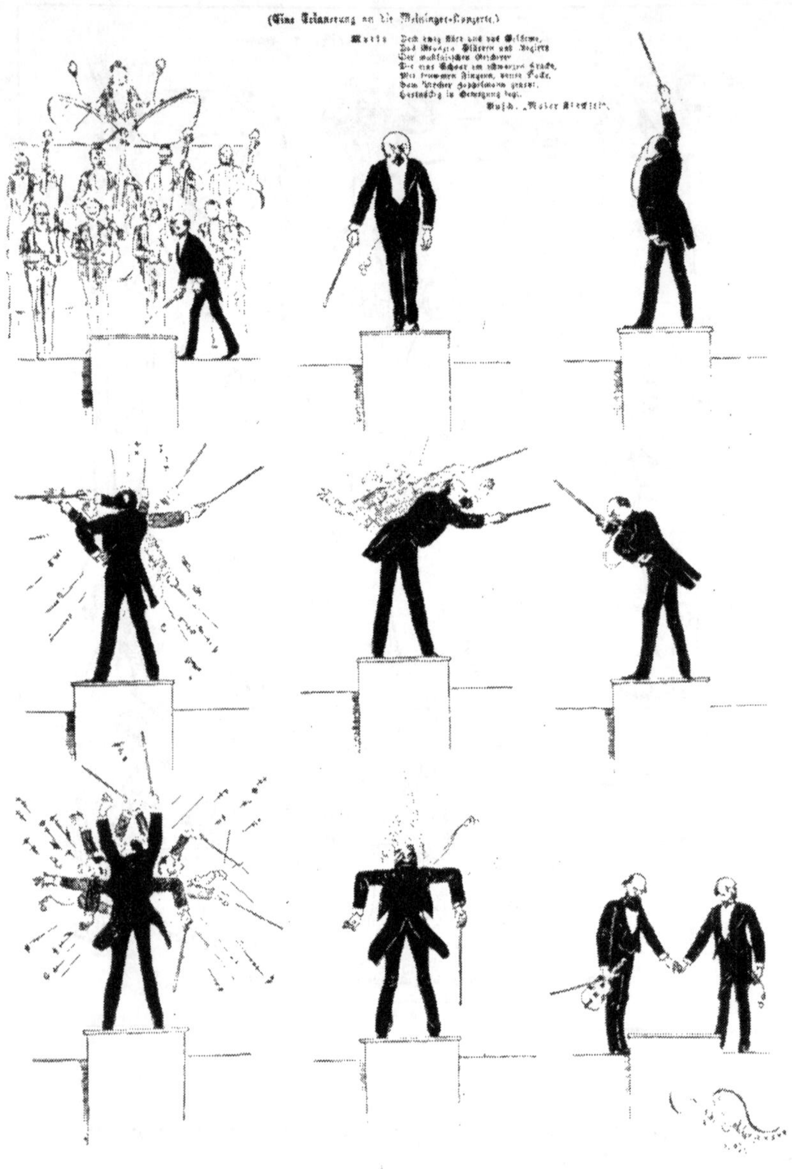

Figure 18. Hans Schliessmann, *Hans von Bülow Conducting* (caricature). *Le Figaro*, Paris (1884).

> And how Liszt went at the piece, with a strength and grandeur as if it concerned a battlefield manoeuvre. . . . As this moment he seemed, indeed, that field commander to whom, in outward appearance, at least, we have previously compared him [Napoleon], and the applause was mighty enough to have been a *Vive l'Empereur*![10]

Accordingly, it's hardly surprising that Beethoven who, more than any other musician of his time, remasculinized music—to the extent that was culturally possible—was represented as a classical hero.[11] But for every textual and visual reference grounding music and masculinity in a military discourse, there are competing representations using the same discursive vocabulary to dismantle such claims on grounds of its patent absurdity. Thus Berlioz may conduct with the appropriate props, but he can't pull off the charade (Fig. 19). As lieutenant-general, in other words, he appears to be cross-dressing, with the gestures and body shape of a French fop, a kind of Percy Blakeney from *The Scarlet Pimpernel* in reverse, that is, where the would-be masculinized hero is actually a hopelessly effeminate aesthete.

Although Liszt, in imagery, sometimes fares no better than Hector Berlioz,[12] Liszt's playing unquestionably overwhelmed the commonplace associations and uncertainties revolving around the piano and masculinity—at the same time his success benefited directly from exploiting the tensions evident in bourgeois concern. By the eighteenth century, musical instruments were commonly appropriated to one or the other gender, and keyboard instruments, as is by now well established, were commonly, if not universally, deemed feminine.[13] The association of music in general with femininity, and the assignment of masculine or feminine traits to specific musical instruments in the course of the eighteenth and nineteenth centuries underscores not only the uneasy uncertainty about music's role in the promotion of masculinity but also about the extremely uncertain ground on which masculinity itself was built during this period.[14]

Romantic artistic identity depends on the bridging of cultural gaps, of establishing a relation between opposites and holding them in productive tension. Thus the rationalized mechanization of the new Industrial Age, of which the piano itself was a perfect example,[15] is connected to its extreme opposite, the freewheeling, as it were, seemingly unpredictable improviser-composer virtuoso. It's hardly surprising that a visual—and also textual—discourse serving to recuperate masculinity in the face of music, perhaps more consistently effective than the use of the military metaphor, imagined the musician within the metaphor of the

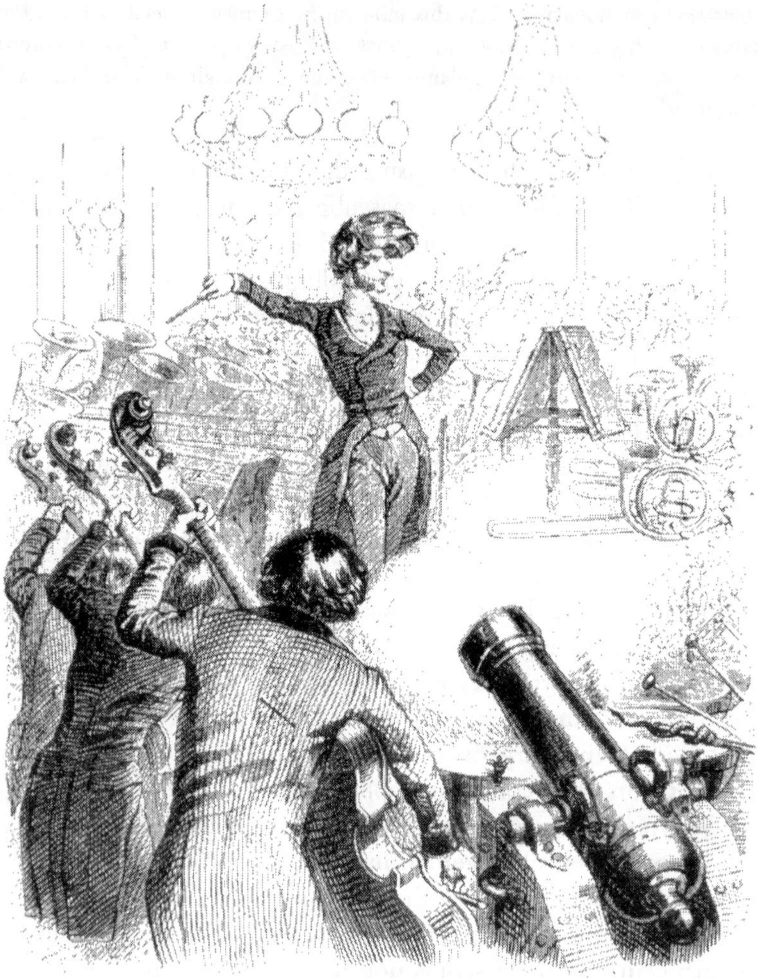

Figure 19. Andreas Geiger, *A Concert in the Year 1846* [Berlioz conducting in Vienna]. Private Collection.

machine. Whereas the movements of the steam engine's pistons and the factory gears driven by these engines are fully planned, the pianist performing on the machinery of the piano, itself the direct result of factory production, apparently escapes the instrumental rationality of the machine age—at the same time that the staggering numbers of performances given by virtuosi such as Liszt do exaggerated honor to the bourgeois work ethic upon which the Industrial Age depended for its success, the effect increased proportionally by the cultural value assigned to the difficulty of the music played. In other words, virtuoso performance constituted an aesthetic transformation of bourgeois appreciation for male heroics linked to overcoming obstacles. Thus, in the course of Liszt's most active years as a virtuoso performer (1839–47), he gave more than one thousand performances, one concert every three days on average.[16] Liszt's mystique in this regard continued long after his career as a frenetic traveling virtuoso ended, evident in a published caricature from 1876 (Fig. 20) representing an intent and somewhat demonic Liszt seated at the keyboard of his "Musical Steam Engine," a veritable one-man brass and percussion band, in addition to the odd woodwind, and replete with a steam whistle and bell, reminiscent of factory signaling devices. Ludwig Bösendorfer fires the furnace chamber of Liszt's instrument, while the steamy spirit of Richard Wagner rises from the bell of a French horn that does double duty as a steam stack.

The mystery of machines, and virtuosos performing on a musical machine, fed—and fed from—contemporaneous fascinations with and anxieties over the brave new industrial world. The saving grace of musicians in this respect was that they demonstrated a magical ability to out-machine the machinery, while at the same time aestheticizing—hence, helping to market—the capitalistic-bourgeois work ethic. The concatenation of artist qua machine demonstrates that romantic fantasies and desires, which in no small part help account for audience response to the virtuosi, were constructed out of the very mythologies of industry and modernity to which music and the other arts were ascribed as an escape from or an alternative to. More accurately, perhaps, music in general, and the performances of piano virtuosos in particular, served as an aesthetic analogue to economic, political, technological, and cultural modernity.

Modernity's musician of the imagination is assigned the task to reclaim a humanity that is remembered while being perceived as lost. The socially imagined musician's own imagination articulates a presence in the experience of absence, an absence that threatens to produce a perfect vacuum of dehumanization. Indeed, music itself is threatened to the extent that it is assigned the cultural task either as foil to the machine or as compensation for the social costs of the mechanization of life. It is, of course, no accident that the piano, one of the great success stories of capitalist industrial production processes, served as ground zero for the possibility of rendering the musician obsolete. Parenthetically, I take this

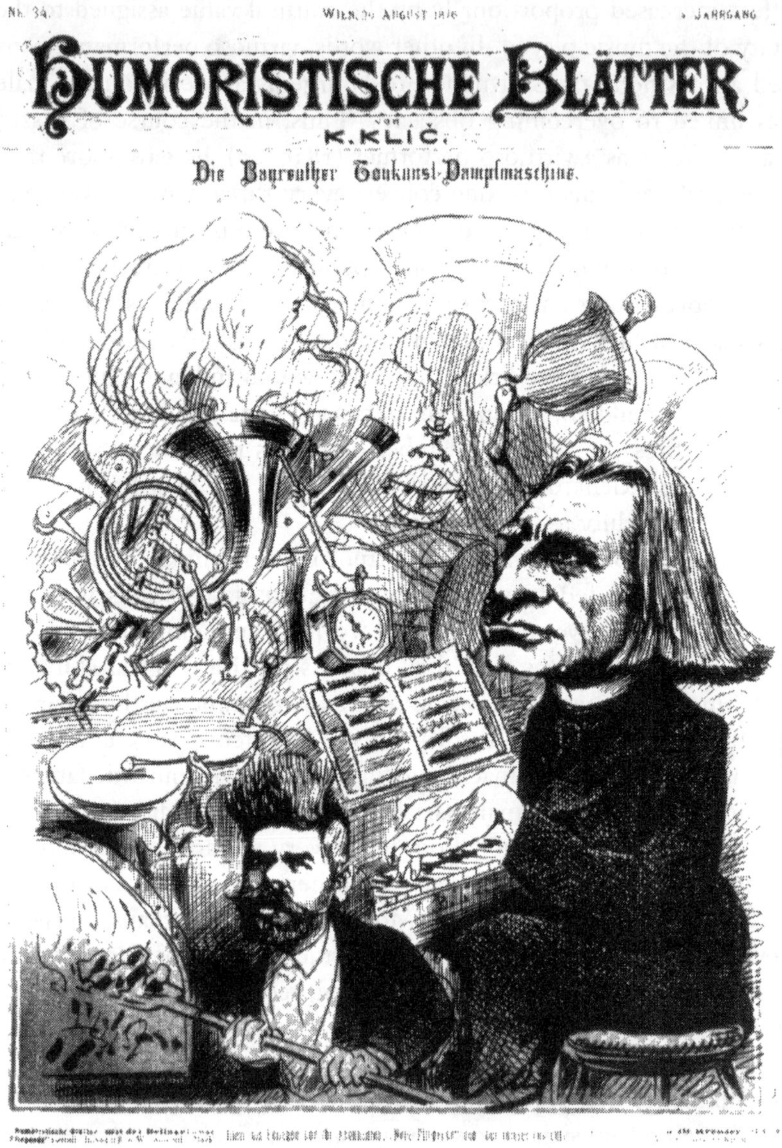

Figure 20. Karl Klic, *The Bayreuth Musical Steam Engine. Humoristische Blätter* (Vienna, August 20, 1876).

as one import, however unintended, of the 1922 Queen's Hall Orchestra concert, led by Sir Henry Wood, involving a Duo-Art Pianola that "performs" without a performer (Fig. 21), thereby necessarily abandoning the conventional dialogic relation between orchestra and soloist. Instead, conductor and orchestra align themselves precisely and wholly to the pace preestablished by the mechanical instrument. The live musicians, in order words, robotically respond to the command of machine.[17] The assembly line of the shop floor is transposed into the domain of aesthetics. (It's not a historical accident that this musical experiment was nearly contemporaneous with Fritz Lang's *Metropolis* [1926].)

Beethoven Alive, and Dead

I'd like to end by returning briefly to Beethoven, or, to state my intention more accurately, to Beethoven's body. The cultural place accorded Beethoven and his music[18] played out over a vast, varied, and ultimately complementary discursive frame that prominently included the visual, as traced in exhaustive detail by the art historian Alessandra Comini.[19] The mythic Beethoven was (and still is) dramatically overdetermined by the seemingly limitless efforts to represent the supposedly "actual" Beethoven. Indeed, the effort to get Beethoven *right* in representation was, by any standard measure, extraordinary, both during his life and afterwards, on flat surfaces and in three dimensions, in sculptural relief, free-standing sculpture, paintings, pencil drawings, crayon, pastel, and watercolor; via engravings, lithographs, silhouettes, and in cameos. Beethoven was drawn from the front, side, and even from the back. But by getting Beethoven "right" I am not principally nor even necessarily referring to any homology between how Beethoven really looked and how he was made to look in representation. As Comini, speaking of written texts concerning Beethoven's appearance, has aptly pointed out, "Surprisingly few contemporary descriptions of Beethoven stuck to the physical data; Beethoven's mannerisms, manners, and moods invariably color the facts of his physiognomy."[20] That is, Beethoven's physical appearance was made to match increasingly conventionalized perceptions of his character, artistic sensibility, and genius, both during his life and after his death—coterminous with the heyday of phrenology (no accident). Furthermore, the representational vocabulary developed for Beethoven quickly came to serve as the gold standard for visually imagining ideal music itself, or at least ideal German music.

One sort of representation in particular interests me, a visual type

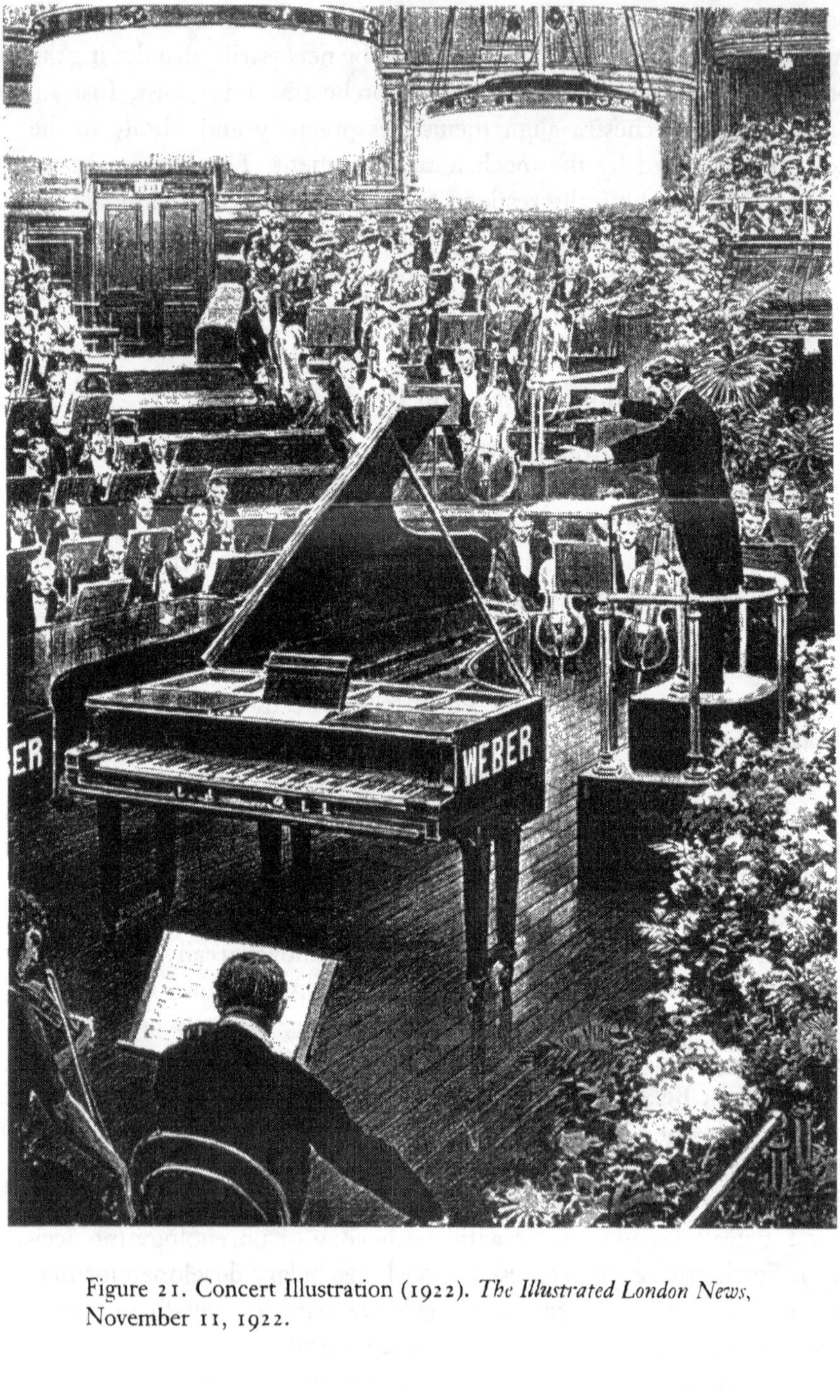

Figure 21. Concert Illustration (1922). *The Illustrated London News*, November 11, 1922.

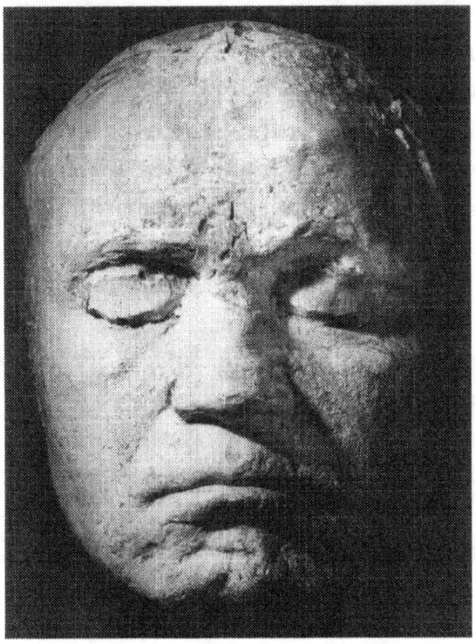

Figure 22. *Beethoven* (1812), life mask by Franz Klein. Bonn, Beethoven-Haus, H. C. Bodmer Collection.

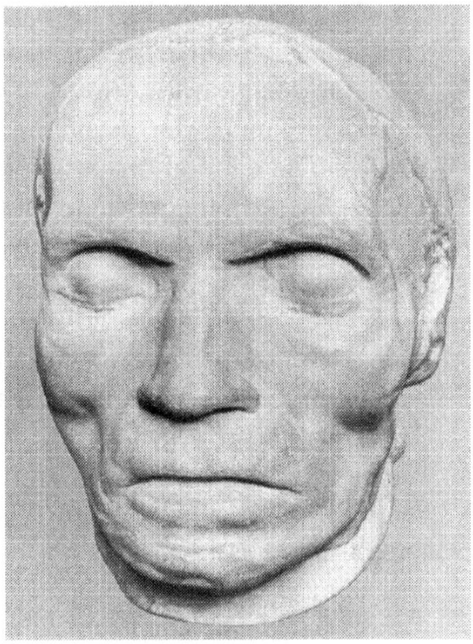

Figure 23. *Beethoven*, death mask by Josef Dannhauser (1827). Bonn, Beethoven-Haus.

that occupies the space between the embodied Beethoven and the Beethoven of the imagination, namely, the mask, taken in life (Fig. 22) and taken in death (Fig. 23)[21]—the latter an age-old practice dating to Roman times, although it wasn't often exercised with regard to musicians until modernity, and then usually only for the purportedly musically heroic (and/or romantically tragic) ones such as, besides Beethoven,[22] Liszt (whose hands also were cast several times during different periods of his life), Mahler, Wagner, and Hugo Wolf. The mask is the clearest possible confirmation of the desire to take the other to one's self, by taking from the embodied other the most self-confirming aspect of identity, the precise and three-dimensional visage. (In this respect, the mask is complementary to the fashion for clipping locks of hair from the deceased—and even the not-quite-deceased in the case of Beethoven: Schindler was there with his scissors waiting for an opportunity. Beethoven's hair, fetishized for its aesthetically unruly abundance—not the least result of the Beethoven iconography—attracted a small army of admirers paying homage to his corpse while wielding scissors.)[23]

The desire to take the mask confirms the ineffability of what the musician is culturally made to stand for. The musician of the imagination, in other words, cannot in the end be grasped, and remains a fantasy—very much the case in the vast repertory of the Beethoven iconography. The cultural desire to take over his embodiment seems to me to be no less than the reflection of that unanswered need. The mask, which by definition hides one identity, does so in order to proclaim another. Beethoven's death mask—quite different from the 1812 life mask that was taken so as to serve as the model for a marble bust—functions as a material and metaphorical means by which to imagine Beethoven—to fantasize him, by psychological transference—in a way and to a degree that mere representation cannot achieve. The death mask is Beethoven in incorruptible form.[24] Beethoven's mask can be put on, so to speak, but in the end, of course, it won't—indeed, can't—fit. In staring at Beethoven's mask, as in looking at his representations, as in performing and listening to his music, we confront that other that is, and is also not, ourselves: the unattainable Absolute. The death mask, in other words, constitutes a final, if somewhat desperate, effort to grasp a desire that, by being grasped, only reminds us of what's missing.[25]

Beethoven's death mask disappoints, and not least because, unlike Mahler's death mask, it doesn't much look like the Beethoven of the iconographical tradition already firmly established during the composer's lifetime, because of the disfigurations to his skull from the autopsy performed before the mask was taken.[26] Small wonder that it was the 1812 life mask that was commonly reproduced, as it looked like, and was indeed a source, for much subsequent iconography. Small wonder, furthermore, that the life mask was commonly taken to be the composer's death mask.

Even though the death mask presents the opportunity to capture the embodied essence of the composer at the moment when his life, and all that it adds up to, is complete, the Beethoven death mask fails the task, precisely because it simply doesn't look much like the Beethoven *of the imagination*. It's something like an imposter, forcing on us an image that our imaginations cannot sustain: The death mask deflates the myth. Better the now canonic, leonine idealizations reproduced after the several formal oil portraits, appropriately described by Comini as displaying "a determined effort to trace an anatomy of melancholy—genius incarnate—close to and still of this world, yet removed from the commonplace by transfiguring inspiration."[27]

But the best of the representations was life mask *serving as death mask:*

the life mask that most closely matches the imagined Beethoven—scowling (some say), Promethean, and, no small matter, inscrutable—the ultimate assignment for any mask, including the mask of affirmed Genius; and more than slightly at odds with the embodied Beethoven. Thus, the young Ludwig Rellstab recalled (to be sure seven decades later) about his audience with the composer in 1825, his reaction tinged with disappointment: "His features at first glance seemed lacking in significance: his face was much smaller than I had pictured it in accordance with the likeness which has forcibly constrained it to an appearance of powerful, genial savagery."[28] It's no accident that it was the life mask that anchored the visual, and indeed textual, tradition of the Beethoven mythology, precisely to the extent that the fiction of myth is by such obvious factual data transformed into truth. Still, what's most significant in all of this is why such transformations were culturally necessary in the first place—what role, in other words, they played in the imagination as a corrective to the reality that the fantasy worked to mediate. It seems to me that the musician of the imagination functioned to articulate the possibility of music's non-identity (as Adorno used the concept), just as modernity itself worked tirelessly to subsume everything under the sway of its universalizing and stultifying sameness.

A life or death mask records a single look, and that look must stand for everything that matters about the identity it records. Nineteenth-century death masks of artists were valued precisely to the extent that they supposedly recorded the absolute truth of a distinctly singular—and (ideally) sublime—individuality, anchored in the extraordinary, even unique aesthetic sensibility that was taken to mark the sign of difference from the brave new world of mundane experience. The incorruptible mask, permanent mirror of the musician-composer's impermanent and moldering body, was the single form of representation that replicated (rather than, as with visual art, merely imitated) the body itself and, at the same time, made the "sitter's" identity, in all its preciseness, available for personal possession through more or less mass marketed reproductions. As the "embodied" analogue to absolute music that helped authorize, promote, and sustain nineteenth-century art religion, the mask was a three-dimensional replica (and not merely a representation) of Absolute Genius itself, a tactile article of faith. As an *icon* suitable for hanging on the wall, it announced to others the sensibility of its viewer-owner by serving as a display item of personal identity; and all the while it silently reflected back to its owner his own imagined better self—his soul, as it were—in the memory of music as idealized sound.

Recall Schopenhauer on the question of musical affect:

> The inexpressible inner essence of all music, by virtue of which it flows past us so utterly comprehensible and yet so inexplicable, like a familiar but eternally distant paradise, is rooted in the fact that it reproduces all the movements of our innermost being but quite divorced from phenomenal life and remote from its misery.[29]

What Schopenhauer acknowledges is that the "condition" of music is less an aspiration of art and more a desire for an embodied happiness that resides only in the imagination. Schopenhauer's notion of "the inexpressible inner essence of all music" involves the decentering of the self, a letting go of mind. But it also requires joining a social group—an audience—that is disciplined (and immobilized). Desire is cultivated, but it is simultaneously transferred onto the spectacle of the Other; a projection of the self is cast into and onto the sight and sound of the musician, who enacts the desires imagined—and stage manages them as well, and not least in light of the stakes that, while concerned with aesthetics, are always already economic as well.

Notes

1. See Richard Leppert, "Cultural Contradiction, Idolatry, and the Piano Virtuoso: Franz Liszt," in *Piano Roles: Three Hundred Years of Life with the Piano*, ed. James Parakilas (New Haven, Conn.: Yale University Press, 1999), pp. 252–81.

2. Walter Benjamin, "Theses on the Philosophy of History," in *Illuminations*, ed. Hannah Arendt, trans. Harry Zohn (New York: Schocken, 1969), pp. 257–58.

3. Eve Kosofsky Sedgwick, *Between Men: English Literature and Male Homosocial Desire* (New York: Columbia University Press, 1985), pp. 1–2. Her study is based primarily on the study of English novels published between 1750 and 1850, and thus complements the period of my own concerns.

4. For a literary analogue, see Carol Christ, "Victorian Masculinity and the Angel in the House," in *A Widening Sphere: Changing Roles of Victorian Women*, ed. Martha Vicinus (Bloomington: Indiana University Press, 1977), pp. 146–62. She examines a similar phenomenon in Coventry Patmore's "The Angel in the House" and Tennyson's "The Princess," focusing on both poems' representations of masculinity that valorize male feminization. See also Richard Dellamora, *Masculine Desire: The Sexual Politics of Victorian Aestheticism* (Chapel Hill: University of North Carolina Press, 1990), which approaches the question in terms of homosexual desire.

5. I should add that such pictures are by no means unusual; similar examples exist in large numbers, although almost all are very small, thus semi-private—and

many are done in watercolor, rather than oil, which privatizes them the more, in that such images might be stored in folders and looked at out of sight of others.

6. Thus the recollection of Kurd von Schlözer (1822–1894) of Liszt performing in Göttingen in 1841, at the height of his public career, similar to many other accounts: "With it all you had to *see* him at the piano! Everything he did on the keys was mirrored in his features, flashed in his eyes and electrified all his movements. . . . It was divine!" Quoted from Adrian Williams, *Portrait of Liszt: By Himself and his Contemporaries* (Oxford: Oxford University Press, 1990), p. 172. Liszt's physical body is a text to be read. As a result, the music Liszt produced was doubly scripted, not only as a sonoric event defined by formal musical processes but also as an action in spectacle: the language of the soul, speaking through the language of the body. To be sure, both "languages" are subject to ambiguity, paradox, contradiction, and—inevitably—depend for their meaning on a complicated cultural hermeneutics.

7. See Mary Cowling, *The Artist as Anthropologist: The Representation of Type and Character in Victorian Art* (Cambridge: Cambridge University Press, 1989).

8. Adorno characterized the relation of conductor to orchestra as the Hegelian dialectic of master to servant, and as a microcosm of society, and in society's darkest hour: "The histrionics at the podium are easy to credit with the dictatorial capacity for frothing at the mouth at will," he wrote, adding hyperbolically that "It is astonishing that the Nazis did not persecute conductors as they did soothsayers, for competing with their own charisma." From T. W. Adorno, *Introduction to the Sociology of Music*, trans. E. B. Ashton (New York: Continuum, 1976), pp. 104, 106, respectively. Indeed, much of Adorno's scathing critique of conductors is anchored in the dystopian role he envisions them playing in the imaginations of their auditor-viewers, that is, the audience whose response he reads as a social-psychological pathology. Adorno's allusion to the militaristic resonances of conducting is uncannily echoed in the degree to which the visual caricatures of von Bülow and Mahler in turn concatenate to Foucault's description, in *Discipline and Punish*, of the instructional techniques in eighteenth-century Prussian military manuals, Taylorist to the nth degree, however Taylorist *avant la lettre*. See Michel Foucault, *Discipline and Punish: The Birth of the Prison*, trans. Alan Sheridan (New York: Vintage, 1979), p. 154.

9. Ernst Burger, *Franz Liszt: A Chronicle of His Life in Pictures and Documents*, trans. Stewart Spencer (Princeton, N.J.: Princeton University Press, 1989), p. 336.

10. *Neue Zeitschrift für Musik* 12 (April 1840): 118–20; quoted from Alan Walker, *Franz Liszt: The Virtuoso Years, 1811–1847*, rev. ed. (Ithaca, N.Y.: Cornell University Press, 1988), p. 350.

11. For illustrations of quasi-classical renderings of Beethoven, including Caesar-like busts in marble and ivory, and both front-view and profile medallions, see Robert Bory, *Ludwig van Beethoven: His Life and His Work in Pictures*, trans. Winnifred Glass and Hans Rosenwald (New York: Atlantis Books, 1960), pp. 176, 228. See also the excellent essay by Sanna Pederson, "Beethoven and Masculinity," in *Beethoven and His World*, ed. Scott Burnham and Michael P. Steinberg (Princeton, N.J.: Princeton University Press, 2000), pp. 313–31.

12. See, for example, a distinctly effeminized Liszt astride a horse, prominently displaying the Hungarian "Sword of Honor" given him in 1840 and that for a

time thereafter became part of his performance attire. Any potential heroic associations produced by the portrayal of Liszt as a mounted, sword-carrying warrior are rendered entirely ironic. For a reproduction, see Karl Storck, *Musik und Musiker in Karikatur und Satire: eine Kulturgeschichte der Musik aus dem Zerrspiegel* (Oldenburg im Grossherzogtum: G. Stalling, 1911), p. 333.

13. Richard Leppert, *Music and Image: Domesticity, Ideology and Socio-Cultural Formation in Eighteenth-Century England* (Cambridge: Cambridge University Press, 1988), pp. 122–25.

14. See Michel Foucault, *The History of Sexuality*, vol. 1: *An Introduction*, trans. Robert Hurley (New York: Pantheon Books, 1978).

15. See Wilhelm Seidel, "Olympia: Über die Magie der Herzlosigkeit," in *Die Mechanik in den Künsten: Studien zur äesthetischen Bedeutung von Naturwissenschaft und Technologie*, ed. Hanno Möbius and Jörg Jochen Berns (Marburg: Jonas Verlag, 1990), pp. 201–12; and Arthur Loesser, *Men, Women and Pianos: A Social History* (New York: Simon and Schuster, 1954), pp. 233–35, 367.

16. Walker, *Franz Liszt*, p. 285.

17. "Absent Pianists Play to an Enthusiastic Audience at Queen's Hall," *The Illustrated London News*, November 11, 1922, p. 769: "A remarkable concert was recently held at Queen's Hall, where a 'Pianola' Piano ('Duo-Art' Reproducing Model)—untouched by human hands—played Harold Bauer's interpretation of Saint-Saëns's Concerto in G minor, accompanied by the Queen's Hall Orchestra under the direction of Sir Henry J. Wood. It subsequently accompanied Miss Carrie Tubb in vocal numbers, and Mr. William Murdoch in a pianoforte duet. Pianoforte recordings by Paderewski, Madame Chaminade, Busoni, and Pachmann were also given, the latter listening to his own playing from a seat in the stalls."

18. Tia DeNora, *Beethoven and the Construction of Genius: Musical Politics in Vienna, 1792–1803* (Berkeley and Los Angeles: University of California Press, 1995); and Scott Burnham, *Beethoven Hero* (Princeton, N.J.: Princeton University Press, 1995).

19. Alessandra Comini, *The Changing Image of Beethoven: A Study in Mythmaking* (New York: Rizzoli, 1987).

20. Ibid., p. 10.

21. Alessandra Comini has devoted a recent essay to Beethoven's look, including his look as captured by masks. My remarks, while complimentary, follow a different tack. See "The Visual Beethoven: Whence, Why, and Wither the Scowl?" in *Beethoven and His World*, ed. Scott Burnham and Michael P. Steinberg (Princeton, N.J.: Princeton University Press, 2000), pp. 287–308. Concerning the death mask, see Comini, *The Changing Image of Beethoven*, pp. 72–73.

22. Cf. oil sketches of Beethoven after death by Josef Danhauser (who also took the death mask) of Beethoven's face and hands, reproduced in *Ludwig van Beethoven*, ed. Joseph Schmidt-Görg and Hans Schmidt (Bonn: Beethoven-Archiv, 1970), pp. 31, 256, respectively.

23. Christopher H. Gibbs, "Performances of Grief: Vienna's Response to the Death of Beethoven," in *Beethoven and His World*, ed. Scott Burnham and Michael P. Steinberg (Princeton, N.J.: Princeton University Press, 2000), p. 241; and Russell Martin, *Beethoven's Hair: An Extraordinary Historical Odyssey and a Scientific Mys-*

tery Solved (New York: Broadway Books, 2000), an entertaining, if more than slightly bizarre, history from 1827 to the present of the several hundred strands of Beethoven's hair clipped postmortem by fifteen-year-old Ferdinand Hiller.

24. The general literature on the death mask is notably thin. See, in particular, Ernst Benkard, *Undying Faces: A Collection of Death Masks*, trans. Margaret M. Green (London: Leonard and Virginia Woolf, 1929), pp. 17–40, a basic history of the death mask. The book, principally a picture book illustrating 112 masks from the fifteenth century to the early twentieth (most are from the nineteenth), also includes the contents lists of four collections. Brief biographies are included for each of the individuals illustrated, along with details of the making of each person's mask, when known. Eight composers' death masks are illustrated: Beethoven, Haydn, Liszt, Mahler, Mendelssohn, Max Reger, Wagner, and Hugo Wolf. Benkard, who made death masks, includes a description of the technique, and the timing (ideally not long after death), replete with purple prose ("Whether it is an old man or a child upon the bier, whether death has come easily or painfully, I must hasten; on every face is the smile of the soul released," p. 44).

See also Robert Wilkins, *The Bedside Book of Death* (New York: Citadel, 1991), pp. 184–85, mostly a basic account of the technical process of making the mask; Wilkins points out that, in the nineteenth century, phrenologists made many masks for use in their obsessive measurements of skulls as a means by which to gauge intelligence, personality traits, and moral qualities. Masks of this sort were commonly taken from criminals, whether pre- or postmortem; Christine Quigley, *The Corpse: A History* (Jefferson, N.C.: McFarland, 1996), pp. 42–44; and Bert Sliggers, "Dode gipsgezichten of het eeuwige gelaat," in the exhibition catalogue *Naar het lijk: Het Nederlandse doodsportret, 1500-heden*, ed. Bert Sliggers (Haarlem: Teylers Museum, 1998), pp. 178–93, containing information of the history of death-mask production in Holland, incorporating a chronological list of Dutch death masks made from the nineteenth to late twentieth centuries.

25. See the discussion in Comini, "The Visual Beethoven," p. 288, on the fetishization of Beethoven's life mask, which exists in numerous later copies. "To the uninitiated, the grimacing white or black Beethoven masks ubiquitously populating music and antique shops during the age of Romanticism were generally presumed to reflect the unhappy composer's facial expression as ghoulishly immortalized in death." Regarding the history surrounding the making of the 1812 life mask, see pp. 290–91; and Comini, *The Changing Image of Beethoven*, pp. 33–34. Comini attributes the "scowl" to the distinct unpleasantness commonly remarked by people having a life mask taken; the irony here, of course, is that this look became the trademark iconography of the Suffering-Beethoven/Genius-Hero myth, endlessly repeated in various representational media, from the graphic arts and painting to sculpture.

Benkard, *Undying Faces*, p. 18, points out that death masks were uncommon prior to the nineteenth century for any but the privileged classes, royalty especially; Philippe Ariès, *The Hour of Our Death*, trans. Helen Weaver (New York: Alfred A. Knopf, 1981), p. 263, dates the change to the eighteenth century.

26. See Martin, *Beethoven's Hair*, pp. 20–22.

27. Comini, *The Changing Image of Beethoven*, p. 46.

28. Quoted in ibid., p. 22.

29. Arthur Schopenhauer, *Die Welt als Wille und Vorstellung* (1819), excerpted and reprinted in *Music and Aesthetics in the Eighteenth and Nineteenth Centuries*, ed. Peter le Huray and James Day (Cambridge: Cambridge University Press, 1981), p. 330.

Part Three

Practice

CHAPTER 10

Music Teachers of Upper-Class Amateur Musicians in Eighteenth-Century England

In eighteenth-century England, upper-class boys were educated for a life in the world, girls for a life in the home. For both sexes education in music was a tangential concern. At best, music was looked upon as an "accomplishment," an outward sign of breeding and taste in an age very conscious of both. At worst, music was considered a waste of time or a step down the path to degradation. Although many children and adolescents (and even adults) of both sexes studied music for varying lengths of time, relatively few became proficient. More girls than boys took lessons; more girls made the effort to develop their talents. In other words, the situation of the young person taking music lessons in eighteenth-century England bears resemblance to the practice of our own time and place.[1]

My concern here, however, is not with the students but rather with their teachers. I want to suggest something about the life of the music masters who ministered to this social class, to indicate the kinds of social conventions at play between music teachers and their upper-class employers, and, in the process, to illuminate more clearly the general relation between musical life in eighteenth-century England and the social forces which in part controlled it.

Children were educated either at home by private tutors (for

[1] This subject will be treated in detail in my forthcoming monograph, in progress, a social history of amateur upper-class musicians in eighteenth-century England. I wish to acknowledge support received from the John Simon Guggenheim Memorial Foundation, the National Endowment for the Humanities, the American Philosophical Society, and the Graduate School, University of Minnesota. Special thanks are due my research associate, Mary Finn-Carlson.

From *Music in the Classical Period: Essays in Honor of Barry S. Brook*, ed. Allan Atlas, pp. 133–58. New York: Pendragon, 1985.

boys) and governesses (for girls) or at boarding schools. Some children were exposed to both types of education. Boys often continued studies thereafter at the university, where they matriculated in their early teenage years, and on the Grand Tour at the end of the teens and into their twenties. Most girls skipped anything posing as higher education and simply married; indeed, many upper-class girls were never educated outside their homes.

A girl's governess was paid a few pounds a year plus room and board to teach the requisites of housewifery and the rudiments of "accomplished" behavior. Families advertised for governesses in newspapers; the ad copy typically stressed the candidate's moral character and her religion and national origin. The curriculum for which she would be responsible was a secondary concern when compared with the qualifications of respectability. Thus, in an advertisement in the London *Gazetter and New Daily Advertiser* for 1768, the copy reads:

> WANTED to be A companion and a Go-ness to a Young Lady, a middle aged single lady, a native of England, and a protestant, of unexceptionable morals and character, attested by persons of undoubted credit and veracity; she must have had a virtuous and useful, as well as polite and ornamental education; must be mistress of the French tongue, and of her needle; if she is conversant in music, and drawing, still the more agreeable. Any such lady . . .[2]

When music is mentioned, as here, it tends to be taken lightly. More important, the governess is expected to be a generalist (to put the best light on it), to know a little about a lot. With regard to breadth of "curricular" expectations, an advertisement from the Bath newspaper, *The Sun*, from 1797 is typical:

> A GOVERNESS. A GENTLEWOMAN of middle age is wanted in a Private Family, as GOVERNESS, to have the Care of Two Children, one Eight, and the other Nine Years old, to instruct them in English and French grammatically, Geography, Arithmetic, Writing, Drawing, Plain and Ornamental Needlework (if in Music, the more agreeable). A moderate salary will be given, and will be treated as one of the Family. Address to Mr. Meyler, Bath.[3]

Only rarely do advertisements appear in which musical concerns

[2] Issue no. 12, 419: 21 December, p. 2, col. 4.

[3] Issue no. 1563: 27 September, p. 1, col. 1.

are more central, as in copy from London's *Daily Advertiser* in 1771:

> WANTED, A Governess in a Gentleman's Family, a Native of France, and a Protestant, who understands Musick perfectly, and to teach French grammatically. . . . None need apply unless well qualified and can have a good Character.[4]

In 1710 one candidate for a position in the household of Lady Thunderton announced her capacities as, "I can sow white and colourd seam; dress head suits, play on the Treble and Gambo, Viol, Virginelles and Manicords, which I can do, but on no other."[5] Mrs. Hannah Woolley, as an adult an author of several books on housewifery published in the 1660s and 1670s, began her career as a school mistress at age fourteen! By seventeen, now a governess in a noble household, she was charged with educating a child in Italian, dancing, singing, and on several instruments, along with some of the usual womanly household tasks.[6] When it came to music, few of these women could have possessed more than rudimentary skills. Virtually none could have instructed their wards in the "science" of music—an eighteenth-century term meaning basic music theory.

A boy's curriculum was broad but shallow. It included languages (at least French), arithmetic, geometry, algebra, geography, historical chronology, history in general (ancient and modern, domestic and foreign), rhetoric, a bit of Latin and sometimes Greek, perhaps logic, ethics, metaphysics, and a little natural science, theology, and law. A variety of physical exercises were *de rigueur*. Drawing and dancing preceded music in bringing up the rear as polite accomplishments.[7] Thus it is not surprising that advertisements for—or by—male tutors (typically young university graduates) to serve in households as instructors for boys seldom made

[4] Issue no. 12, 535: 27 February, p. 2, col. 2. Most governesses were expected to know French, whatever their own national origin. Here a native speaker is sought, so long as she is not a Catholic.

[5] Marjorie Plant, *The Domestic Life of Scotland in the Eighteenth Century* (Edinburgh, 1952), p. 14.

[6] George E. Fussell and K. R. Fussell, *The English Countrywoman: a Farmhouse Social History, A. D. 1500-1900* (London, 1953), pp. 87–88.

[7] George C. Brauer, Jr., *The Education of a Gentleman: Theories of Gentlemanly Education in England, 1660–1775* (New York, 1959), pp. 74–76.

reference to music. A notable exception appeared in *The General Remark on Trade* from 1707:

> A Gentleman, who through Misfortunes is now reduced, is very desirous to be a Tutor to any of the Nobilities, or Gentries Children; or any Service to Command by Pen or Book, with Musick on the Violin and Flute to be Taught, and of an extraordinary good Disposition; he can be well Recommended. Enquire at the Traders Exchange House.[8]

At boarding schools, even among many of the better ones intended for children of the middle and upper orders, the curriculum was haphazardly serviced. Music was common fare at most of them, especially at institutions for girls, and consisted of private or group lessons at singing or on instruments. Music lessons were not ordinarily provided in the basic price, but were paid for by surcharges.[9] The music masters were in most cases professionals, either in residence or, more commonly, brought in on a regular basis. At only a few of these schools was there outright devotion to music. Mrs. Perwich's school at Hackney in the middle 1660s offered lessons on a variety of instruments, maintained an orchestra, and included in the curriculum the study of theory and composition. The famous school operated by Josias Priest at the end of the same century, for which Purcell wrote *Dido and Aeneas*, likewise ran a strong music program. I know of no remotely comparable schools in England at any time in the eighteenth century.

The most common surviving written references to musical education in the eighteenth century represent complaints about and satires of the music masters. Playwright Thomas Shadwell was already poking fun at this subject in the late seventeenth century. In his *Epsom-Wells*, Mistress Jilt evaluates her musical education as being able to play on the virginals a few popular tunes and a psalm, and to be capable of six lessons on the viola da gamba.[10] In

[8] Issue for 9 July. Quoted from Michael Tilmouth, "A Calendar of References to Music in Newspapers Published in London and the Provinces (1660–1719)," Royal Musical Association, *Research Chronicle*, I (1961), 69. The man probably lost his hopes of income to an elder brother and primogeniture.

[9] Thus a boarding school in Hunter's Crost, Manchester, in 1763 advertised a basic curriculum for £16 16s. per annum. Music lessons were available for a £1 1s. surcharge. See *The Manchester Mercury and Harrop's General Advertiser*, issue no. 576:15 February, p. 4, col. 1.

[10] Thomas Shadwell, *The Complete Works*, ed. Montague Summers, 5 vols. (London, 1927), II, 138.

MUSIC TEACHERS OF UPPER-CLASS AMATEUR MUSICIANS 137

The Scowrers (1690), two of Shadwell's characters, Eugenia and Clara, belittle:

> for Musick an old hoarse singing man riding ten miles from his Cathedral to Quaver out the Glories of our Birth and State, or it may be a Scotch Song more hideous and barbarous than an Irish Cronan.

To which Eugenia responds:

> And another Music-master from the next Town to teach me to twinkle out "*Lily burlero*" upon an old pair of Virginals, that sound worse than a Tinkers kettle that he cries his work upon . . .[11]

Jane Austen, in 1815, wrote to her sister Cassandra complaining about a provincial music master, a Mr. Meyers, who "gives his three Lessons a week—altering his days & his hours however just as he chuses, never very punctual, & never giving good Measure."[12]

Most of the boarding schools were in the provinces; most of the music masters—like Austen's Mr. Meyers—were provincials. Those who were skilled were certain to be frustrated by their working conditions. Indeed, serious professional musicians looked upon school employment as desultory. In 1658 Richard Flecknoe wrote lamentedly of girls at boarding schools "learning to quaver instead of *singing, hop* instead of dancing, and rake the *Ghitar*, rumble the *Virginals*, and scratch and thrumb the *Lute*, instead of playing neatly and handsomely."[13]

None of this is surprising given the qualities sought in music masters. In 1771 at Ayr Academy in Scotland, the candidates for music teacher were in *some* cases asked to sing "a tune of music." By contrast, candidates for mastership of the Academy were required among their tasks to translate literally advanced Latin and Greek texts and also to translate from English into Latin.[14] Sir George Smart, the conductor, organist, and composer, as a young man of twenty-two in 1798, was recommended to teach music at the school of a Mrs. Cameron in London. Smart auditioned before a Mr. Twiss, said to be a "tremendous critic . . . [who] formed his

[11] Shadwell, *The Complete Works*, V, 98.

[12] Robert W. Chapman, ed., *Jane Austen's Letters to Her Sister Cassandra and Others* (Oxford, 1932), p. 440.

[13] *Enigmaticall Characters, All Taken to the Life, from Severall Persons, Humours, & Dispositions* (London, 1658), p. 44.

[14] John Kerr, *Scottish Education, School and University: From Early Times to 1908* (Cambridge, 1910), p. 169.

judgment on the performer's efficiency in sight playing." Smart continues,

> The first question put to me was: 'Can you play at sight?' I boldly answered 'Yes.' He then placed before me a very difficult sonata, and put his ear close to the pianoforte. I saw at once that the sonata was too much for me, but I dashed at it and rattled over the right and wrong notes. Mr. Twiss expressed his perfect satisfaction and reported to Mrs. Cameron that I must be a very capable teacher. With Mr. Twiss I was intimate for some years.[15]

In 1784 Samuel Wesley began his twenty-five-year teaching career at Oxford House, Marylebone, in an establishment run by a Mrs. Barnes. He spoke ill of the experience in a letter to his sisters, surmising that "The profits are inadequate to the slavery," which he defined as the "unworthy employment of teaching sound without sense, without honour, and without any real advantage but 'the meat which perisheth.' " He commented on another occasion that "I cannot bear the drudgery of more dunces assaulting my ear for six hours together," and again lamented "this contemptible, frivolous work of hammering sounds into blockheads."[16]

Several characteristics of the music teacher in eighteenth-century England can be defined. Most were specialists—omitting the governesses and generalist tutors attached to some households—

[15] H. Bertram Cox and C. L. E. Cox, *Leaves from the Journals of Sir George Smart* (London, 1907), p. 6. Another way of demonstrating the relative unimportance of music in the curriculum is to examine the place of professors of music at the universities. At Cambridge, for example, a chair of music was established only in 1684; it was the last professorship to be established at the university. Dr. Nicholas Staggins, who first held the position, enjoyed little prestige and, since he was dependent upon receiving fees from the candidates, earned little money. The inferiority of his position was reinforced by university protocol; a professor holding only a musical degree required special permission to enter the Senate House to present degree candidates. Once admitted, his academic robes were not his own but rather those of a doctor of law or of physics. See Denys A. Winstanley, *Unreformed Cambridge: A Study of Certain Aspects of the University in the Eighteenth Century* (Cambridge, 1935), pp. 77, 142–43.

[16] James T. Lightwood, *Samuel Wesley, Musician: The Story of His Life* (London, 1937; repr. New York, 1972), pp. 115, 117. However bad the pay and working conditions, some teachers were willing to bribe music sellers in exchange for recommendations, according to Charles Dibdin, a music teacher himself, though never an objective assessor of musical affairs. A music seller

though many claimed skills on several instruments. Many were professional performers who made names for themselves through concerts; others played in various theater orchestras. Musicians of these sorts lived mostly in London.[17] As for national origin, many were English (and it is from this group that most primary accounts survive), but the most sought after were Italian immigrants who veritably flocked to England in the later seventeenth century and throughout the eighteenth.

So ubiquitous were these individuals that it is difficult to find an eighteenth-century comedy of manners containing a music master who is English-born. Though satirized on the stage (where their dialogue was invariably in broken English), they nevertheless found the English receptive to their talents and willing to reward them financially to a degree making it worthwhile to stay. Stephen Penton, in a courtesy book from 1694, clarified a common English view of Italian music professors in a general comment on education:

> And what Nation in Europe need we envy the Professors in all Arts and Sciences, Divinity, Mathematics, Civil Law, Physick, Critical and Philological Learning: So that let not our good Beef and Mutton be thought ill of, for the air impregnated with our Ignorance and Dulness: Unless in favour of Musick and Italian should put in a Caveat against all Tramontanes, and with a keener Judgment split our gross Sounds, and seem to want the delicate touch upon the drum which beats in his Climate.[18]

With regard to continental music masters, the commonplace and centuries-old scorn of the English towards anyone foreign was not confined to theatrical satires. English musicians for obvious reasons were undoubtedly dismayed by the competition brought by the

---

would recommend the teacher to a school "on condition that no other books are used at the school but those such music-seller publishes; and very often, though not always—for there are exceptions in music shops as well as in musicians—an additional contribution is levied on the teacher's profits." *A Letter on Musical Education Addressed to a Father* (London, c. 1791), pp. 14-15. By means of this pamphlet Dibdin hoped to advance his own compositions in the schools.

[17] See further, Eric D. Mackerness, *A Social History of English Music* (London and Toronto, 1964), pp. 88-89.

[18] *New Instructions to the Guardian, with a Method of Institution from Three Years of Age, to Twenty-One* (London, 1694), p. 76.

foreign invasion. John Playford, in the preface to his *Musick's Delight on the Cithren* (London, 1666), lamented that every mother in London was "ambitious to have her Daughters Taught by Mounsieur La *Novo Kickshawibus* on the *Gittar* . . ." (p. i).

Hannah More, at the close of the eighteenth century, likewise complained about the ubiquitous presence of numerous music masters attending the female children of London parents, though her judgment is based on the time music takes away from other, more worthy endeavors. However exaggerated her account, it nevertheless reflects the social acceptability of music as an upper-class female accomplishment.

> The science of music, which used to be communicated in so competent degree to a young lady by one able instructor, is now distributed among a whole band. She now requires, not a master, but an orchestra. And my country readers would accuse me of exaggeration were I to hazard enumerating the variety of musical teachers who attend in the same family; the daughters of which are summoned, by at least as many instruments as the subjects of Nebuchadnezzar, to worship the idol which fashion has set up. They would be incredulous were I to produce real instances, in which the delighted mother has been heard to declare, that the visits of masters of every art, and the different masters for various gradations of the same art, followed each other in such close and rapid succession during the whole London residence, that her girls had not a moment's interval to look into a book . . .[19]

As More suggests, music masters—mainly Italian—active in London tended to specialize in one or perhaps two instruments. (Harpsichord teachers would commonly teach thorough-bass; others claimed to instruct in "composition"—generally meaning rudiments of music—in addition to teaching an instrument.) Outside London, demand was apparently insufficient for music masters to survive with pedagogical skills on a single instrument. Most provincial advertising copy suggests that "country" music masters had acquired—or at least claimed—competency on several instruments, as in an advertisement from the *Bath Advertiser* from 1758:

> Walter Claggett, Musician and Dancing-master, At Mr. Paget's near the Theatre, in Orchard-street, Waits on Ladies and Gentlemen at their

[19] *Strictures on the Modern System of Female Education with a View of the Principles and Conduct Prevalent Among Women of Rank and Fortune* (Charlestown, Mass., 1800; first published in London, 1799), p. 49.

> Lodgings, To instruct them in DANCING, And the Use of the following Instruments, viz. The Violin, Violoncello, Guitar, German-Flute. Likewise Tunes, Harpsichords, and Spinetts.[20]

In the same year an advertisement appearing in Aberdeen, Scotland, announced the new arrival from Germany of a Mr. Roche who "proposes to teach the following instruments, viz., the Fiddle, the German Flute, Hautboy, Bassoon, Violoncello, French Horn, etc. He likewise teaches Singing and the [English] Guittar."[21]

Others advertised a variety of academic skills in addition to music. In London's *The General Advertiser* from 1779, an individual made known his availability as a kind of non-resident generalist:

> PRIVATE EDUCATION. LADIES and Gentlemen taught in Writing, Arithmetic, and the Harpsichord or Spinnet at their own habitations, in an easy and familiar method, by J. Cadman . . .[22]

In Leeds in 1786, a Mr. H. Hamilton advertised his teaching on the harpsichord and English guitar, mentioning that he also tuned and repaired the instruments of his students.[23]

The social position of music masters was not enviable. Not only were they satirized on the stage, they were also made to suffer indignities at the hands of their employers or even their students. Charles Burney, himself a famous and successful teacher through most of his life, related an incident suffered by his own tutor (for French and the violin), Nicola Matteis. The young daughter of

[20] Issue no. 159: 28 October, p. 3, col. 2. There were two common ways that a music teacher could advertise his services, either by distributing handbills at the houses of fashionable people, or by advertising in the newspapers and advertisers published throughout the country. Considering the highly ephemeral nature of handbills, it is not surprising that very few have survived. Eighteenth-century newspapers and advertisers, on the other hand, are more readily available and provide considerable information on the subject. (Virtually all were printed on both sides of single or double sheets; very few exceeded four pages. Most were printed three or four columns per page.) The majority of advertisements are for music masters who teach only music and who visit individual homes to give private lessons.

[21] Henry George Farmer, *A History of Music in Scotland* (London, 1947; repr. New York, 1970), p. 325.

[22] Issue no. 586: 16 January, p. 1, col. 2.

[23] Emily Hargrave, "Musical Leeds in the Eighteenth Century," *The Publications of the Thoresby Society*, XXVIII, *Miscellanea*, IX (1928), 342.

Sir John Astley, later Lady Tankerville, upon discovering Matteis a timid man, "helpless at the slightest distress or danger," insisted on taking her violin lesson with both of them seated in an

> old and lofty oak tree, placing there a seat and a desk, adroitly well arranged for her accommodation; while another seat and desk, upon a thick but tottering branch, was put up for poor Matteis, who was so terrified, that he could not stop a note in tune; yet so fearful, that he could not bring himself to resist her orders.[24]

The indignities suffered by Matteis, if true, seem unusually demeaning. Yet they are reflective of the social stature of musicians in general, even the famous and successful. Burney's career as a music master at a boarding school in Queen Square, Bloomsbury, run by a Mrs. Sheeles, was apparently considered sufficiently injurious to the dignity of his memory that Fanny Burney "did her best to delete every reference to it in her father's 'Memoirs' and other papers."[25] (Indeed, Burney participated in the indignity of capitalizing on the performing skills of his ten-year-old daughter Esther in order to advance his own career. In April 1760, shortly after Burney returned to London from nine years at King's Lynn, she played in a concert with other child prodigies. Her success brought him many students.)[26]

No totally reliable source exists for establishing the numbers of music masters active in England at any one time. However, two directories survive which provide useful information. The first is *The Universal Director; or, The Nobleman and Gentleman's True Guide to the Masters and Professors of the Liberal and Polite Arts and Sciences; and of the Mechanic Arts, Manufactures, and Trades, Established in London and Westminster, and their Environs*, com-

[24] The anecdote comes from Burney's *Memoir*, which was heavily edited by his daughter, Fanny D'Arblay, 3 vols. (London, 1832), I, 9.

[25] Roger Lonsdale, *Dr. Charles Burney: A Literary Biography* (Oxford, 1965), p. 54. In examining Burney's letters in the Osborn Collection, Beinecke Library, Yale University, I found very few references to his teaching. Those that survive are mainly complaints. Daughter Fanny, who had her hands on many of these letters, obliterated those portions which she apparently felt did no service to her father's memory. Many of the letters are more than half censored.

[26] Lonsdale, *Burney*, pp. 54–55.

piled by Thomas Mortimer and published in London in 1763.[27] At the end of his list of "Masters and Professors of MUSIC," Mortimer states that he has taken care to include only those masters and professors residing in London and its environs who actually teach; there are ninety-five in all. He indicates that retired individuals have been omitted, as have a few whose addresses could not be ascertained. The list is arranged alphabetically by name and includes the musical instrument taught. Some of the masters are well known—William Boyce, Charles Burney, Jacob Cervetto, Felice Giardini, James Nares—but the majority remain obscure. Among instruments played by amateurs, the harpsichord is listed with the names of seventeen masters, the violin with twenty-one, the transverse flute with six. Only two voice teachers are mentioned, confirming the directory's lack of comprehensiveness. Only one guitar master is given—the rise to popularity of the English guitar among amateurs was yet to come (see further, below). About three quarters of the individuals listed played or instructed on a single instrument. Among those who knew two instruments, the combinations suggest that they played one professionally but gave instructions on the other. Thus six are listed as organists who teach on the harpsichord—for which there was real demand. Similarly, Charles Jones played the French horn and Jacob Neilson the kettledrums, but both taught the German flute.

The second source is the *Musical Directory* for the year 1794 compiled by J. Doane, comprising eighty-eight pages, and containing names and addresses of "Composers & Professors of Music, with a number of Amateurs, Vocal and Instrumental," in addition to music sellers, instrument makers, etc. Doane's list covers musicians throughout England and totals about one thousand three hundred. Of these only twenty-nine are identified specifically as music teachers, two thirds of whom are from London and its environs. Sixteen of the total group are recorded as dancing masters, all of whom in the London area (thirteen) also claim to be teachers of the violin. A few teach piano (the harpsichord having been supplanted) or organ; as many as three may be voice teachers, though the listings are unclear. Only J. Wragg is given as a teacher of winds, specifically the flute and oboe (Wragg was the author of one of the most successful flute treatises, *The Flute Preceptor*,

[27] One copy is known to survive, in the Guildhall Library, London. The sections on music were reprinted in the *Galpin Society Journal*, II (1949), 27–31.

first published in 1792). Outside London, the only instruments represented on Doane's list of teachers are the piano, harpsichord (the instrument held its caste in the provinces longer than in London), organ, and violin.[28]

Whatever their numbers, the supply of teachers, especially in London, seems to have exceeded demand. Evidence of competition for students abounds, judging in particular from advertising copy. One example will suffice. In December 1755 London's *The Public Advertiser* carried copy for two different teachers–in the first a Mr. Call, in the second a Mr. Alexander–seeking students for instruction on the English guitar, an instrument only beginning to attract the attention of amateurs. In both advertisements, the masters cite a Miss Macklin,[29] who performed on the instrument on the stage, apparently with great success. In different ways each instructor plays off her name.

> LADIES or Gentlemen who are desirous of learning to play on the Instrument, commonly call'd the Citter, otherwise Guittar, otherwise Lute or Pandola: this being the very identical Instrument which is play'd on in the Chance and in the Englishman in Paris [i.e., two plays]; Mr. Call, the Teacher of this Instrument, begs Leave to inform such Ladies and Gentlemen, that he is to be heard of at Mr. Bennet's,

[28] In the Advertisement, Doane says that he intends to publish his *Directory* annually, soon after each Christmas (presumably so as to coincide with the beginning of the season), though the work seems to have appeared only once. Doane further comments that he possesses the names of several hundred musical persons not inserted in this present edition for lack of sufficient information (p. vii). Thereafter follow seventy-two pages of names, addresses, and musical interests of individuals. The "interests" are mostly musical organizations–choirs, theater orchestras, etc.–to which individuals belong, many of which are from outside of London in the other large towns of the country.

The list of musicians includes both vocal and instrumental performers and dancing masters and teachers. As with Mortimer's *Director* it is safe to assume that many of the professional musicians gave music lessons. Unfortunately, it is difficult–and often impossible–to distinguish between amateur and professionals in Doane's *Directory*. Obviously, those individuals playing in theater orchestras would have been professionals, whereas amateurs constituted most of the membership of the choral societies. Unfortunately, Doane's mixing of amateurs with professionals makes his *Directory* of limited value for my present purposes.

[29] She played the original Mrs. Subtle in Foote's *Englishman in Paris*. Her husband was the playwright Charles Macklin. She died in the season of 1758/9. See the *Dictionary of National Biography*.

> Staymaker, in Little Wild-street, ... he having had the Honour of teaching many Ladies and Gentlemen of Rank; and also is the only Person who has and still continues to teach Miss Macklin this, and other Particulars relating to the Grounds of Musick. As this Instrument is so portable, its Sound so acute, and yet withal so soft and sweet; it is of itself a proper Recommendation. Instructions are also given how to play it in Concert, with the Harpsichord, Violin, German Flute, &c. Also if any Lady should fancy to play it a different Way of tuning than what is common, they might be instructed in five or six Ways.[30]

The advertisement was repeated on 24 December; on 30 December it elicited a competitive response from Mr. Alexander:

> Any Nobleman, Ladies, Gentlemen, or others, that are desirous to learn to play on the Instrument upon which Miss Macklin plays on the stage, may be instructed therein in an elegant, concise, musical Manner, by a proper Master of upwards of thirty Years Experience on the said Instrument. He has had the Honour to teach of several of the Nobility and Gentry, who after trying other Masters have declared that his Method both of teaching and playing, was much superior to any of the others. He is ready to wait upon Gentlemen or Ladies to perform for their Satisfaction, upon directing a Line, or enquiring for Mr. Alexander, at Mr. Bailey's Organ Builder . . .[31]

Music masters, always eager to attract new students, promised quick results and ease of effort. Advertising copy, such as the following from *The Gazetteer and New Daily Advertiser* (1768), consistently carries these claims:

> MUSIC. THE Guittar, Harpsichord, and Singing taught in a most easy and elegant manner, by an eminent master of undoubted character and abilities, who engages to teach any person unacquainted with music to play ten tunes the first month, and in three months to be so far accomplished on the [English] guittar as to be able to play any common piece of music at sight on the low terms of half a guinea a month, and the same entrance by sending their names and places of abode in a letter directed for A.B. to be left at Mr. Sutherland's, peruke-maker and hair-dresser, in Queen-street, Westminster.[32]

[30] Issue no. 6583: 3 December, p. 2, col. 3.

[31] Issue no. 6600, p. 3, col. 1.

[32] Issue no. 12,409: 9 December. Claims of quick success had a long life in the history of English advertising. On 30 December 1661, for example, *The Kingdom's Intelligencer* carried an "Advertisement concerning a new Method for teaching the knowledge of Musick to persons of age in 6. or 7. hours (so

Many teachers published tutor books for particular instruments, the title pages of which almost always make the same claims evident in advertising. Even tutors intended for serious students often promise that "the knowledge and execution of Music is attainable in a few months, by a study not only easy but entertaining . . ."[33] Throughout most of the century, tutor books sold for only two or three shillings; authors' earnings could not have been great. However, an additional incentive for writing a method book was undoubtedly the hope of attracting new students by its sale. Judging from the repetition from one book to another—often involving outright piracy—many authors (or booksellers) did not expend much effort on the task. Yet out of self interest, each author conventionally claimed his book as the best in the field. Finally, while many were designed for "self instruction," most required the "aid of a master," though this need was not always openly stated in the text. My main point is that the hope of financial gain encouraged the false claims of easy success in both advertisements and tutor books.

Music masters also gave "benefit" concerts (that is, for their own benefit), following which they sometimes advertised to attract new students.[34] Masters/performers who normally resided in London would, after playing in provincial towns, sometimes linger several weeks to take pupils—and reported their intentions to local papers.[35] Music masters of greatest renown also took apprentices to be trained as professional musicians. Of the ninety-five music masters included in Thomas Mortimer's 1763 directory, discussed above, twenty-two were listed specifically and only as teachers. This suggests that only a quarter of the total could sup-

as they shall be able, by a little practice, to sing any aire or song, and keep their part in a Consort; and the skill of singing the most curious songs) by the help of one word, which the Author calls the MUSICAL WORD, which comprehends the whole grounds of the Science . . ." Quoted from Tilmouth, "Calender of References to Music," p. 1.

[33] Giffard Bernard, in the prefatory "Advertisement" to his English translation of a treatise by Anton Bémetzrieder, *Music Made Easy to Every Capacity* (London, 1778). The text of this ambitious harpsichord (and general music) tutor, written in the form of a dialogue, covers more than 250 pages. By and large, tutor books made slight technical demands on the amateur. The collections of popular (often stage) songs anthologized in them confirm the very modest ambitions of their purchasers.

[34] See Hargrave, "Musical Leeds," p. 351.

[35] See Hargrave, "Musical Leeds," p. 352.

port themselves by teaching alone. Most of the remaining individuals were professional performers (and, in some cases, composers) as well. Those listed solely as teachers instructed on the most popular amateur instruments: sixteen of the twenty-two on the harpsichord (one of these also offered lessons on the violin and another in singing); four individuals taught the transverse flute.

As a group, music masters were often accused—sometimes by one another—of puffing up and otherwise encouraging students with no talent, in order to keep the lessons going as long as possible. William Turner added a charge of incompetence to his particular indictment:

> Nay, I have a particular Knowledge of some, who have taken extream Delight in being complimented with the Title of *Masters* of *Musick*, when they know not so much as the *Gamut*; just the same, as if a Man should acquire the Name of an experienced *Sailor*, who cannot say his *Compass:* A *Ship* would be well steer'd by such a *Pilot*. But, which is worst of all, these People, by such an unmerited Reputation, gain *Proselytes* too, under the Pretence of teaching them to sing (miserably enough) and so pick their *Pockets*, as it were, of their *Money*. Pity it is, that such a lamentable *Disease* should want a *Remedy*. But this not being the only Grievance that wants redress, we must content ourselves with it, as well as we can; and those who Part with their *Coin* to purchase meer *Air*, we may blame, but not Pity; though they wasted even their whole Substance, on such *Trifles* of *Tutors.*[36]

Parents, of course, wanting their daughters in particular to acquire "accomplishments," were only too happy to hear and believe the flattery provided by the teachers. Many parents were in no position to make judgments on the issue, in any event. (Henry Fielding, in *Tom Jones*, did not create Squire Western—who when drunk liked to hear his daughter play on the harpsichord—out of whole cloth.[37]) James Fordyce in his *Sermons to Young Women* wrote that

[36] *Sound Anatomiz'd, in a Philosophical Essay on Musick* (first published 1677; London, 1724), pp. 2–3.

[37] "It was Mr. *Western*'s Custom every Afternoon, as soon as he was drunk, to hear his Daughter [Sophia] play on the Harpsichord: For he was a great Lover of Music, and perhaps, had he lived in Town, might have passed for a Connoisseur; for he always excepted against the finest Compositions of Mr. *Handel*. He never relished any Music but what was light and airy; and indeed his most favourite Tunes, were *Old Sir* Simon *the King*, St. George, *he was for* England, *Bobbing* Joan, and some others.

you will readily allow, that for a young person who has no turn for the study I am speaking of, to be condemned both to mortify herself, and to punish her acquaintance, by murdering every lesson put into her hands, is a very aukward [*sic*] situation, however much her master may, for the sake of his craft, flatter her or her friends; assuring them, perhaps with an air of great solemnity, that he never had a better scholar in his whole life . . . But how does a judicious hearer blush for the poor beginner, when set down by the command of a fond parent to entertain perhaps a large company, as we have often seen, with performing that of which she scarce knows the very rudiments; while all is disappointment on their part, and, if she have any understanding, confusion on hers![38]

In 1743 Horace Walpole complained about such a girl in a letter written to his friend in Florence, Sir Horace Mann. Walpole's sister, Lady Mary, had just been visited by a Norfolk heiress, a young gentlewoman, who after less than three hours in the house—and visiting for the very first time—

notified her talent for singing, and invited herself upstairs to Lady Mary's harpsichord; where with a voice like thunder, and with as little harmony, she sung to nine or ten people for an hour . . . We told her, she had a very strong voice—'Lord, Sir, my master says 'tis nothing to what it was.'—My dear child, she brags abominably; if it had been a thousandth degree louder, you must have heard it to Florence.[39]

Lack of musical talent is a recurring subject in fiction from the period. Thus in Jane Austen's *Northanger Abbey*, young Catherine Morland's

mother wished her to learn music; and Catherine was sure she should like it, for she was very fond of tinkling the keys of her old forlorn spinnet: so, at eight years old she began. She learnt a year, and could

---

"His Daughter, tho' she was a perfect Mistress of Music, and would never willingly have played any but *Handel*'s, was so devoted to her Father's Pleasure, that she learnt all those Tunes to oblige him." Ed. by Sheridan Baker (New York, 1973), Book IV, chapter 5, p. 128. The novel was published in 1749.

[38] 2 vols. (London, 1771), I, 258–59.

[39] Horace Walpole, *Correspondence with Sir Horace Mann*, Ed. by W. L. Lewis, Warren H. Smith, and George L. Lam (New Haven, 1954–71), XVIII/2, 316–17.

> not bear it;–and Mrs Morland, who did not insist on her daughters being accomplished in spite of incapacity or distaste, allowed her to leave off. The day which dismissed the music-master was one of the happiest of Catherine's life.[40]

To sum up the complaints: Thomas Worgan wrote in his *The Musical Reformer* (1828):

> What a wealth of time is wasted in the desperate efforts of unqualified aspirants to soar to this empyreum! What havock does fashion make with the hours, days, months, and years of thousands, and tens of thousands, from whose education music ought to have been wholly excluded: nor can it be denied that, in the conquest of practical difficulties, the mental labour bears no proportion to the mechanical; and ultimately the vocal organs or the fingers move, while the mind is either asleep, or wandering in the fields of irrelevant cogitation.[41]

Occasionally, writers express sympathy for the teacher who, probably by financial necessity rather than gratuitous dishonesty or money-grubbing, suffered through the musical plunderings of the least talented of students–and all the while lied through the teeth about his ward's progress–for fear of losing an account. Ambrose Pitman in 1815 published a little book in verse called *The Miseries of the Musick-Masters.* In part it is a "Serio Comick Didactick Poem" about ill-talented children and hopelessly hopeful parents, in part a tutor book on the rudiments of music explained at the keyboard. (The book's 954 lines of rhyming couplets in iambic quatrameter are incongrously interrupted by numerous musical examples.)

> But when compell'd his *hour* to stay, 13
> And teach Miss *Play-ill* how to play–
> *One hour!* the usual courtesy
> And limit of his *Misery!*
> . . . .
> For when she sings, Miss *Play-ill* squalls 19
> Certain, unlike *Celestials.*
> Yet though *discordant* sounds may shock,
> *One* hour his time is–by the clock;

[40] Ed. Anne H. Ehrenpreis (Harmondsworth, 1973), p. 38. The novel first appeared in 1818. Similar examples are almost legion.

[41] P. 44. See also pp. 36–37.

Which is to *Masters*, horrid meed!
The first of *Miseries* indeed!
. . . .
That frequent instances as these 628
Occur to *Masters* of the *Keys*,
Who daily are oblig'd to sit
Their *hour* to teach some *petted chit*,
Or some *Adult* of larger size
The mysteries of Harmonies,
Many a woe-worn wight can tell
That here they are depicted well;
And well the Author's time were spent,
If the exposure should prevent
One Misery the less to those,
Who're hourly subject to such woes.[42]

Music teachers worked very hard during the season from January to June. Charles Burney and Sir Frederick William Herschel are notable examples. Burney kept to the task until he was seventy-eight, by which time he had been at it for no fewer than fifty-five years, with few interruptions.[43] In 1767, when he was forty-one, he claimed to have taught fifty to sixty students a week, in addition to those at the boarding school referred to previously.[44] In 1775 Fanny Burney confided to her father's friend Samuel Crist that "He teaches from nine to nine almost every day, and has scarce time to write a page [of his *History*] a week." Years later Burney himself recalled having taught twelve to fourteen hours a day during this period.[45] Indeed, Burney's *History*, published in four volumes between 1776 and 1789, was in large part so slow in being completed precisely because of his heavy seasonal teaching obligations. He complained in a letter to his friend Thomas Twining in 1775 that "It is only in the broken-stick way that I can now say a word to you:—out before 9, & hardly ever at home before 11."[46]

[42] On Pitman and contemporaneous reactions to his book, see Jamie Croy Kassler, *The Science of Music in Britain, 1714–1830: A Catalogue of Writings, Lectures and Inventions*, 2 vols. (New York and London, 1979), II, 843–45.

[43] Lonsdale, *Burney*, pp. 408, 421–22.

[44] Lonsdale, *Burney*, p. 75.

[45] Lonsdale, *Burney*, p. 159.

[46] From the Twining Letterbook, No. 2 (1773–75), Osborn Collection, Beinecke Library, Yale University. Dated 28 February.

In 1780 an astonished Samuel Johnson told Mrs. Thrale that Burney had taught fifty-seven lessons in one week.[47] In December 1783 Burney complained in a letter to his daughter Susan Phillips that he had to pay four guineas a week for a coach, plus seven shillings for the driver, to rush him from lesson to lesson ("my back aches at the Idea of the number of hours I must fag [to pay] for this" [convenience]).[48] Lady Tankerville, mentioned earlier, returning to England after spending many years abroad, sought Burney as a teacher. Told that his day was completely taken with students from eight in the morning, she requested his services at seven, a request acceded to by Burney twice a week.[49]

Sir Frederick William Herschel (1738–1822), the famous English astronomer and son of a professional musician from Hanover, spent many years of his life as a professional organist and music teacher—he studied astronomy informally and only as an adult. A series of memoranda dated between 1768 and 1781 (the latter date corresponds to the year in which he discovered Uranus) contains references to his career as a private music master. Thus in 1769 he noted that "Besides public business I attended four, five or six private scholars every day"; from 1771, "New furnished my house. Sometimes seven scholars per day"; from a memorandum dated 28 March 1772, "This week gave 39 lessons to ladies, the following week 38, other weeks little less." In 1773, during which he bought two books on astronomy and rented a reflecting telescope, he "Attended private scholars as usual," one week forty, another week forty-six. In January 1774 he notes that he "Gave 6, 7 and 8 private lessons every day." In the same year he began his astronomical journal and was busy casting mirrors for a telescope. At the end of September 1777, he noted that "Musical business [was] carried on as usual." But by January 1779 he had given up "so much of my time to astronomical preparations that I reduced the number of my scholars so as seldom to attend more than three or four per day." In 1782, when his reputation as an astronomer was already recognized, he continued "Attending scholars by day and astronomical observations at night," though of his students he remarked that "Some of them made me give them astronomical instead of musical lessons"![50]

[47] Lonsdale, *Burney*, p. 254.

[48] Lonsdale, *Burney*, pp. 293-94.

[49] D'Arblay, ed., *Memoirs of Doctor Burney*, I, 135–36.

[50] *The Scientific Papers of Sir William Herschel*, 2 vols. (London, 1912), I, xxi-xxiii, *passim*.

The cost of music lessons varied considerably over time, as well as by teacher and the social standing of the clientele. In 1653 Anthony Wood employed a teacher named Charles Griffith, one of the Oxford city musicians, and paid him a 2s. 6d. entrance (a start-up fee) and 10s. quarterly.[51] Samuel Pepys wrote in his diary on 25 June 1661 that he had hired Theodore Goodgroome to teach him to sing. Pepys paid Goodgroome a 20s. entrance and agreed to an additional 20s. monthly ("And so we begun and I hope I shall come to something in it").[52] Goodgroome was still on the scene at the end of August 1667 when Pepys wrote that "being dissatisfied with my wife's learning so few songs of Goodgroome, I did come to a new bargain with him, to teach her songs at so much, *viz*., 10s. a song; which he accepts of and will teach her."[53] For the vast majority of the population, however, such fees were not small sums; in the 1660s curriers, shoe makers, and turners from Middlesex earned between £6 and £10 per annum, depending on their skills. [54] Goodgroome likely made more than the larger of the two figures from Pepys alone.

Eighteenth-century English parents tended to place greater value on their children than had been the case in previous centuries[55] –a reflection of which is the sums of money they spent educating their children. Music lessons, especially among the higher social orders, formed one component of these expenditures. The demands of social respectability required that the upper classes–and especially the nobility–admit into their homes only those music masters of the best character and musical reputation. Thus the wealthy aristocrat Fulke Greville, wanting a musician who was also a gentlemen, chose the cultivated Charles Burney. Those teachers at the pinnacle of musical success (as teachers, performers, or–occasionally–composers) could demand very large

[51] Andrew Clark, ed., *The Life and Times of Anthony Wood, Antiquary, of Oxford, 1632-1695, Described by Himself*, 5 vols. (Oxford, 1891-1900), I, 181. Elsewhere Wood states the quarterly fees as "5s. or 10s. quarterly," having forgotten which. See p. 181, n. 7.

[52] *The Diary of Samuel Pepys*, ed. Robert Latham and William Matthews, 9 vols., in progress (Berkeley, 1970–), II, 126.

[53] *The Diary of Samuel Pepys*, VIII, 411.

[54] Leslie A. Clarkson, *Pre-Industrial Economy in England, 1500–1700* (London, 1971), p. 223.

[55] See Lawrence Stone, *The Family, Sex and Marriage in England, 1500–1800*, abridged ed. (New York, 1979), pp. 254–65, 285–99.

salaries. In 1728 Handel was paid £200 to instruct the daughters of the Prince of Wales, Princesses Amelia and Carolina.[56]

In the early 1700s, John Hervey paid large fees for the musical education of his daughters, as his account books reveal.

	£	s	d
1702, 28 May. Paid Mr Ralph Courtivill in full for teaching my daughter Bell [Isabella], ...	7	10	6
1709, 2 Jul. Paid Dieupart for teaching Bell and Betty on the harpsichord last winter, ...	25	1	6
1711, 6 Dec. Paid Mr Dieupart for teaching Bell and Betty to sing and play, ...	10	15	0
1713, 25 May. Paid Francis Dieupart in full for teaching Betty on the harpscord [*sic*]	21	0	0
1716, 25 Jan. Paid Dieupart in full for teaching my daughter Betty on the harpsycord, ...	15	11	9
1735, 10 May. Paid Joseph Kelway, Nanns musick master in full, ...	9	5	6[57]

In 1775 records of payment to Vicenzo Ciampi, the music master for Lady Caroline, twelve-year old daughter of the Duke of Bedford, indicate that he received £22 3s. 6d. for fifty-six lessons; the total represented a rate of £3 3s. for each set of eight lessons plus 2s. 6d. per song learned. Between 7 April and 10 May of the same year, Ciampi received £11 0s. 6d. for singing lessons and harpsichord lessons (twenty-eight lessons at three guineas per eight).[58]

Charles Burney, between the years 1776 and 1782, was involved in the circle of the wealthy Thrale family at Streatham; his first contact came as the harpsichord teacher to the eldest Thrale

[56] Otto E. Deutsch, *Handel: A Documentary Biography* (London, 1955), p. 231.

[57] Michael Tilmouth, "Chamber Music in England, 1675–1720." (Ph.D. diss., Cambridge Univ., 1960), p. 139.

[58] In 1757 Caroline was apparently having lessons on the English guitar. Her father paid John Branson £3 7s. for an instrument. Gladys Scott Thomson, *The Russells in Bloomsbury, 1669–1771* (London 1940), pp. 204–05.

daughter, the twelve-year-old Hester Maria, "Queeney." According to Mrs. Thrale's own account, Burney was employed to attend to the daughter once a week, but he made such an impression on the family, both personally and intellectually, that he soon became an intimate acquaintance. The lessons themselves were no great success. Mrs. Thrale enjoyed Burney's conversational abilities (she was also an intimate of Johnson) and, according to Fanny Burney's edited *Memoir* of her father, continually interrupted the lessons in order to converse.[59] But Burney was nevertheless fortunate; the Thrales decided to keep him on retainer, so to speak, for £100 per annum for weekly visits which included a music lesson, supper, and a stay as an overnight house guest. Burney gladly acceded to this plan which was carried out until Henry Thrale died.[60]

Burney's normal fees—higher than most at the time—are evident from a surviving receipt for music lessons and music, dated 30 September 1779, from Burney to the account of Miss Hoare. The total sum was £40 5s. 6d., of which £6 3s. was for music (Schobert, Eichner, and J. C. Bach sonatas, Vauxhall overtures, harpsichord duets, and a blank music book) and £4 4s. as the entrance. The charge for fifty-seven lessons came to £29 18s. 6d., or 10s. 6d. per lesson. Burney's arrangement with the Thrales thus paid him at nearly thrice his normal rate.[61]

Samuel Wesley, writing about fees charged by music masters in the late eighteenth century, claimed that

[59] D'Arblay, ed., *Memoirs of Doctor Burney*, II, 76. On the Thrales and Burney's experiences with them, see Percy A. Scholes, *The Great Doctor Burney*, 2 vols. (London, 1948), I, 316–26. After Henry Thrale's death, his wife married the Italian singer Gabriel Piozzi, creating a field day for gossip, much of it printed and some of it put on the stage in the form of a play. See James L. Clifford, *Hester Lynch Piozzi (Mrs. Thrale)*, 2nd ed. (Oxford, 1952), pp. 204–23, 326ff.

[60] Lonsdale, *Burney*, p. 234.

[61] Osborn Collection, Beinecke Library, Yale University. Also cited in Lonsdale, *Burney*, p. 234. On the rate of pay, see also p. 272. Years earlier, in 1764, he lost an annual payment of £100 (for how long he had been receiving it is unclear) with the death of a Sussex banker and member of Parliament named Fraser Honeywood. The fee was apparently for the benefit of having Burney's conversation, though nominally it was for harpsichord lessons. Though Burney admitted that neither man much amused the other, he could not afford to lose the fee—and he counted the loss thereof at Honeywood's death a catastrophe. Honeywood at the time of his death could barely play the harpsichord. See further Lonsdale, *Burney*, p. 60, and Scholes, *The Great Dr. Burney*, I, 106, and II, 307.

> The inferior masters were used to receive two guineas for eight lessons, and two guineas entrance also. Three guineas for eight lessons was a very usual price with masters of the higher order, and four for those of the highest.[62]

Thus entrance fees increased from the 1660s, when Pepys and Anthony Wood paid 20s. and 2s. 6d., respectively (a wide variation), to at least twice the higher figure a century of so later—four times for someone of Burney's stature. Individual lessons in Pepys's time may have cost only two or three shillings at the cheapest (Pepys himself paid more), whereas, as Wesley suggests, even "inferior" teachers could demand better than five shillings a lessons towards the end of the eighteenth century.

As for relative costs involved in musical education, in 1720 Charles Sanderson estimated the expenses of a (financially secure) student at the Middle Temple to be £178 17s. per annum. Of this about seventeen guineas went to a music master. Eating cost £45 7s., and room rent £22 10s.[63] In other words, Sanderson contrived his estimate with a serious musical amateur in mind—a man willing to spend on music and dancing lessons half of what it cost to eat. To put this matter in a different light, the seventeen guineas spent on music constituted the better part of a typical wage-earner's total annual income. For example, "Journeymen stocking-weavers in London in the 1740s earned no more than nine or ten shillings a week."[64]

The financial condition of music teachers in eighteenth-century England is ultimately difficult to assess. If we are to believe the Italian expatriot, literary critic, and verbal defender of his homeland, Joseph Baretti—complaining in his *An Account of the Manners and Customs of Italy* (1769)—Italian musicians in England were far from getting rich from their labors.

> As to the fiddlers and other Italians, who come here to play or to teach music, foolishly attracted by the great renown of English riches, they perform at the Opera at Madam Cornelys's, and trot about from house to house every morning, to give lessons for two or three guineas a dozen, while the winter lasts: but scarcely one in twenty has found himself

[62] Lightwood, *Samuel Wesley*, p. 114.

[63] Edward W. Hughes, *North Country Life in the Eighteenth Century*, 2 vols. (London, 1952-65), I, 82.

[64] Clarkson, *Pre-Industrial Economy*, p. 224.

twenty pounds the better at the year's end for these twenty years past.[65]

In trying to determine a range of salaries gained from teaching amateur musicians in London, I have made four calculations based on statements cited above and dating from the late 1760s to the 1780s (Table 1). I am assuming the average number of lessons taught per week to be fifty (Burney and Herschel), the season to be twenty-four weeks long, and half the students (twenty-five) new to each teacher and hence charged the entrance fee. Each student received one lesson per week.

TABLE 1

SOURCE	Entrance Fees x 25 students (assumes half are new to teacher)	Lesson Fees x 50 students x 24 weeks	Total Seasonal income from teaching
A. Advertisement, *Gazetteer and New Daily Advertiser* (1768), p. 145, above	(10s. 6d. each) £13 2s. 6d.	(10s. 6d. per month per student) £157 10s.	£170 12s. 6d.
B, Baretti, *Account of the Manners and Customs of Italy* (1769), p. 155, above	(assumes £2 2s. entrance) £52 10s.	(at £1 11s. 6d. per dozen lessons) £157 10s.	£210
C. Wesley (late 18th century), p. 155, above	(assumes £2 2s. entrance) £52 10s.	(at £3 3s. per eight lessons) £472 10s.	£525
D. Burney (1779-80), p. 154, above	(£4 4s. each) £105	(10s. 6d. per lesson) £630	£735

[65] Second ed., corrected, 2 vols. (London, 1769), I, 148.

As Barretti suggests, the work was seasonal. At least in London, it ex-

The final column represents total seasonal income. To earn these monies the teachers would have worked a six-day week and averaged slightly more than eight lessons per day.[66] In other words, all four totals must be taken as high estimates; they assume very successful teachers with full complements of students. The discrepancy in earnings between a Charles Burney (Column D) and the unnamed teacher of the English guitar, harpsichord, and voice (Column A) is obviously wide.

What kind of living was possible on incomes of £170–735? Unfortunately, only a very general answer can be given, but it confirms that even the least paid of the teachers from the table would have lived substantially above the level achieved by the lower social orders. For London wage earners, yearly income, based on a three-hundred-day working year, has been estimated at £25 in 1700, rising slowly to £30 in 1750, and remaining at that figure until 1790—the figures are less for the West and North of England.[67] A craftsman's day wage in London in 1700 started at 2s. 6d. In 1661 Pepys, as I have shown, paid his teacher twenty shillings per month for singing lessons. Presuming these lessons lasted an hour and were given once a week, Pepys's Mr. Goodgroome could take home £2 per day from eight students.[68]

The most successful music masters seem to have had incomes within the range of the ten thousand to twenty thousand landholders, best described as "modest gentlemen," whose annual earnings might have averaged £300 for a hundred acres of land, to upwards of £700 for larger estates. (In the 1790s English landholders whose annual incomes exceeded £1000 numbered perhaps five thousand; the greatest had incomes averaging as much as £10,000.) Such incomes allowed one to live "a genteel but re-

tended from January to June, though the "schedule" was by no means rigidly adherred to. (Of the fifty-odd lessons that Miss Hoare had from Burney in 1778-79, perhaps a dozen fell outside the "normal" period.)

[66] Lessons seem to have lasted an hour. Masters taught in the homes of their students. Between teaching and commuting, the work day must have been at least ten hours for a teacher giving fifty lessons per week. Indeed, Burney's experiences seem to indicate an even longer day. See p. 150- 51, above.

[67] Elizabeth W. Gilboy, *Wages in Eighteenth Century England* (Cambridge, Mass., 1934), p. 220.

[68] These figures presume, of course, that Mr. Goodgroome and those who followed him had as many students as they could handle. I assume that this held for the most successful, like Burney.

stricted life."[69] As for the buying power of £300, Arthur Young "remarked in 1789 that in France the cost of living was so low that a nobleman with as little as £300 a year could keep two men, two maids, three horses and a cabriolet; but only a fool, he said, would attempt to do it on the same income in England."[70]

Teaching has never been a profession of great social distinction in England. But that is not to say that it has always been unprofitable. Unquestionably, the provincial music masters of little renown and small talent must have been poor all their lives. Those in London, on the other hand, seem to have done reasonably well —especially when compared with simple laborers—Joseph Barretti's comments notwithstanding. And the few of Burney's stature did very well, indeed. Burney taught until he was seventy-eight, not, in my judgment, because he was obliged to "fag" it (to borrow his verb), but for the substantial financial rewards.

Nevertheless, the job was not easy. The hours were long; competition for students could be stiff. The profession was commonly satirized; a teacher's social position was never very high. Moreover, masters were usually condemned to suffer mediocrity in their students and to pretend they liked it. Few masters with real talent or musical taste could have found satisfaction with their amateur clientele, the majority of whom were proud dabblers expecting to receive compliments, whether deserved or not.

[69] G. E. Mingay, *English Landed Society in the Eighteenth Century* (London, 1963), p. 22. See further pp. 20–26.

[70] Mingay, *English Landed Society*, p. 21, from A. Young, *Travels in France* (1793), I, 270.

CHAPTER 11

Music and the body: dance, power, submission

EIGHTEENTH-CENTURY courtesy and conduct writers addressed dancing in the same breath as music. And while many opposed the study of music at least by men, most clearly favored dancing for both sexes of the well-born. Briefly, men and women were encouraged to pursue dancing for two primary reasons – both simply stated, the second ideologically packed. First, as vigorous exercise it was considered beneficial to health; second, it promoted the development of good body carriage. With respect to the latter I will argue that dancing promoted a certain *sight*, both on (and more important) off the dance floor, a visual affirmation of social position, accomplished by means of the way one stood and moved. But, as I will show, the subject of dance and its practice by men and women alike was viewed with confusion, contradiction and ambivalence throughout the century, for reasons that touch on central perceptions of cultural, social and gender identity, and even politics. And in regard to all of these, dancing's intimate relation to music mediated the way in which both forms of expression operated within the society among this social group. My purpose ultimately is to define an ideology of social dancing, relying primarily on dancing's visual presentation of the body – or more specifically, of its presentation of one body in relation to others.

In 1722 John Essex suggested that the knowledge of few if any of the arts and sciences were so necessary or advantageous as dancing, especially under the tutelage of a good dance-master, both as a diversion and as an essential exercise. In these remarks, in which dance instruction is recommended to begin as soon as children (of the well-born) "can well Walk," Essex acknowledged the art as a means of correcting or minimizing the *appearance* of birth "defects," literal or metaphorical, misfortunes that were not confined to the less fortunate classes but which nevertheless were highly articulated *signs* of lower-class standing. In this way Essex perhaps inadvertently encapsulated the essential function of dance as the presentation – and ritualization – of status through grace of body, accomplished by careful attention to a rule or the imposition of a particular order. Essex understood that dance was culture, not nature, ideally to be "naturalized" in children at the tenderest age for the purpose of visually representing social position and thereby helping preserve a status quo. His remarks in other words constitute the (partly hidden) essence of my topic:

> I reckon those who are crooked or ill shap'd, Splay-footed, Baker-kneed, or of an aukward Gate, ought to be the first Persons who should learn to Dance; not because they are aukward only, but because it is high time to correct the Misinformation of Parts, and acquire such a Habit of Body from Dancing, and the Master's Rules of Position, as shall cure, or at least make their Defects less visible. Children should be taught to Dance as soon as they are capable of learning, that is as soon as they can well Walk; the Advantage whereof is this, that it strengthens the Fibres, confirms the Tone of the Parts, and fashions the whole Body to a graceful and becoming Carriage: So much therefore of Dancing as belongs to the Behaviour, and handsome Deportment of the Body, is not only useful, but absolutely necessary.[1]

PHYSICALITY, SEXUALITY AND IDENTITY

John Playford's *The English Dancing Master: or, Plaine and Easie Rules for the Dancing of Country Dances*, first published in 1651 (in print well into the eighteenth century; an eighteenth edition appeared in 1728), was easily the best-known dance collection of its time. As such its short opening address to the reader is significant given its defensive tone:

> The Art of Dancing called by the Ancient Greeks *Orchestice*, and *Orchestis*, is a commendable and rare Quality fit for yong Gentlemen, if opportunely and civilly used. And *Plato*, that Famous Philosopher thought it meet, that yong Ingenious Children be taught to dance. It is a quality that has been formerly honoured in the Courts of Princes, when performed by the most Noble *Heroes* of the Times![2]

(He continued the paragraph by mentioning the health benefits of dance and its aid in teaching gentlemen proper carriage.) Playford published his little book only two years into the Commonwealth and its official recognition of Puritanism, the position of which against public music and dance is well known, though both activities continued of course under prohibitions that were never made absolute. Yet Playford's sensitivity to the ambivalent position of dance in English society carried through the next century and a half, long after the short-lived Commonwealth, and his defense was in many ways characteristic of those that followed him. He cited the authority of the ancients – placing the appropriate words in italics to rivet the eye: he mentioned Greek names for the dance (therefore the Greeks danced) and named the philosopher who approved of it. He asserted the appropriateness of dancing as an upper-class activity ("fit for yong Gentlemen"), one manly in aspect ("*Heroes*"). Playford acknowledged dancing as recreation, yet the pleasures it provided were as such devalued: dancing's worth, as defined by a man presumably keen on profiting from the sales of his dance collection, was not dancing itself, but what accrued from it. At least that was the stance that he felt compelled to adopt for his potential buyer.

The concerns that informed Playford's particular apology for social dancing had their tap-roots anchored in the politics of morality, especially in the relation of moral virtue to human sexuality. Even by the time Playford was writing, these issues had long been the subject of debate, one that continued throughout most of the eighteenth century, though in somewhat altered form. A pamphlet from 1603 voiced the topic in a way that not only identified sexuality as a watchword, but at the same time marked the connection between music and dance as twin components of immoral leanings which together – and through women – contrived to destroy men's virility; misogyny thus entered the equation. Dance was dangerous to the spiritual purity of men who might be (even physically) polluted by women in physical motion:

> For, amongst the frivolous pleasures, which, as I may so term it, ravish men's senses with delight, not any one is more coveted than that of dancing; from which nothing proceedeth, but that which favoureth of lust, hateful to every honest man, and ought, in general, to be a disgrace to all . . . Besides, what can be more absurd, than for a man, not hearing the musician's instrument, to be leaping and skipping amongst a company of foolish women, and men worse than they? . . . Dancing is the voluntary, which is plaid before a passage is made to unlawful desires.[3]

Physical motion here is at issue; it is culturally contested. Women inflamed men through movement (beginning with Eve's *gesture* of handing Adam the apple); women should therefore be contained, immobilized (I shall discuss this in detail in a later chapter). Among such writers, women who danced moved for ill purpose, to arouse the passions of men and thereby enslave them: Samson and Delilah. For men, by contrast, dance was movement for no purpose (it accomplished nothing), hence dance was by nature unmanly, for a man's physical actions distinguished him from women. Movement was the tool of his empowerment, of enacting his will. But a man leaping and skipping among women acted only to unman himself, either through debauch or effeminacy.

Simon Eccles, the rigid Quaker convert, in 1667 repeated all this, placed blame on musicians and dance teachers, and indirectly called down Scriptual wrath on them for the ruination of God's English kingdom. At this point the personal nature of sexuality and gender identity was made tacitly political by means of its claimed threat to natural order:

> O ye Fidlers and Dancing-Masters, let this President break you off from your filthy practice; Why do you dance without the Ark? Where is your

Ark? What President have you in Scripture for your Danceing? You set up the Devils Kingdom by your proud Calling: You set their Bodies in postures to enflame and take with the lustful Nature in men, and with your proud Apparrel, and Spots on their Faces.[4]

By the eighteenth century few writers condemned dancing with the virulence of those from the 1600s, and indeed most sanctioned social dancing. If this moderation reflected the fact that dancing was a firmly established general practice, it nevertheless remained true that dancing's cultural standing remained uncertain. The ideologies informing Eccles and his anonymous forebear were still operative, if more ambiguously and indirectly stated; often the grounds for criticism shifted from the issue of "morality" per se to that of the social order which presumably depended upon morality's foundations. The dialectic that characterized attitudes toward dancing during this period is evident in the oddly contrary opinions expressed within individual texts. Thus the Rev. John Bennett, writing in 1789 to a female audience, affirmed dancing's usually acknowledged benefits of graceful carriage and health through exercise, but then cautioned that dancing's popularity had grown to immoderate proportions, politely restating Eccles' position: dancing might therefore inspire "too great a fondness for dissipating pleasures, and proportionably abate the ardour for more retired virtues." He saw a passion for dancing as a distraction from domestic responsibilities and closed with a warning: "Besides dancing is not, at *certain* moments, without its temptations. An elegant, illuminated room, brilliant company, the enchanting powers of musick, admiring eyes, obsequious beaus, attitude, &c. are apt to transport the mind a little beyond the rational medium of *gentle* agitation."[5] Bennett focused on protecting female virtue. That in itself reflected considerable change over a century; yet the protection of female virtue was, after all, essentially fueled by the need to preserve male virtue – and position – as confirmed in virtually all courtesy and conduct literature of the time, except for that written by feminists. The real issue was female sexuality and its power to (re-)shape society,[6] an inherent acknowledgment that physicality in women presented a social danger. That is, female sexuality threatened the hegemony of men within the gender hierarchy upon which society was itself structured. Women's capacity for passion, enlivened by dance, might subvert the bounds of "*gentle* agitation" that Bennett recognized as necessary to women's sense of well-being. Dance offered women at least the appearance of empowerment through physical action and the emotions that physicality enlivened. (Women increasingly demanded more freedom which in itself triggered endless amounts of male-authored prose as to why men were divinely intended to dominate them.) Dance was a valve that might release the pressure women's urgings engendered. The problem was that the very presence of a release valve constituted an acknowledgment of pressure and might thereby actually contribute to the increase of that which it sought to dissipate. "*Gentle* agitation", in the metaphor of temperature, was the first sign of approaching boil.

John Locke, not favoring music for gentlemen, nevertheless found dancing acceptable on grounds of its teaching "graceful motions" and "above all things, manliness and becoming confidence." Locke perceived that dancing taught a man how better to control his body and by so doing to instill visually on the spectator of that body an impression of power and status. Yet Locke, like Bennett and others both before and after him, immediately acknowledged that this issue was more complex, for he also identified dance as a potentially destructive source of the very manliness he claimed dance promoted. His concern with the loss of virility, however, was not the sexuality of women but the pollution of a foreign culture embodied in dance-masters. Locke warned that, however necessary dancing might be to the making of a gentleman, "natural unfashionableness [was] much better than apish, affected [read 'foppish'] postures," adding "I think it much more passable to put off the hat, and make a leg, like an honest country gentleman, than an ill-fashioned dancing-master."[7] National identity was built on the preservation of cultural difference, and the purity of this difference for Locke was threatened by dance-masters, the most sought after of which in England were French, presumably the group Locke had in mind. The pollution of cultural purity for Locke was of an especially dangerous sort, because it was rendered visible, and even celebrated or paraded, via the body movements of the social elite and in public (if a public restricted to society's upper orders). All of this will need further discussion here.

John Weaver in 1712, acutely conscious of the ambiguous position of social dancing early in the century, established its pedigree in a *tour de force* of erudite citation of ancient and scriptural sources favoring the practice. He repeatedly acknowledged dancing as a social activity of high civilizations, and further pointed out that dance "fits and qualifies Men to put forth those Endowments, and Embellishments, which would else be obscure, and buried in a bashful Rusticity, and offensive Negligence, extremely prejudicial to every Man's Interest and Reputation." He later added that dancing gained a man the assurance or "*handsome Confidence*" that is "an absolutely necessary Qualification, with regard to the *Fair.*"[8] He hyperbolically warned that the man who could not dance would not enjoy love. Like others before and after him, Weaver acknowledged "rusticity" as an accompaniment to Britain's insularity, a cross-class national trait both lamented as a fault and trumpeted as a virtue. As a cultural marker of Englishness rusticity was read as "lack of pretension, openness," but as a social marker it ran the danger of also being read as "oafish," hence lower class or without class distinction. Dancing, among other activities and means, could alleviate rusticity's vice easily enough; the trick was not to destroy its inherent virtue at the same time. Thus Lord Chesterfield heartily recommended dancing to his son, then abroad on the Tour, as one of the "Graces" necessary for a man of the world.[9] But to acquire the skill, Chesterfield suggested a dance-master from Leipzig. That is, Chesterfield accepted the training of a foreigner, but only on the comparatively (culturally) neutral territory of Saxony and not France, though even a Saxon dance-master almost certainly would have been trained by a Frenchman.

One learned to dance from a dance-master. London especially, but also the provinces, had many. The most sought-after were indeed French who in some cases enjoyed considerable status and also became wealthy: "At balls in great houses they [led] out high-born ladies with an air of insolent confidence; favours were heaped on them and substantial fees enabled them to live in luxury and ride in their own coaches."[10] But in England not even financially successful – hence much sought-after – French dance-masters could depend on attaining social respectability, especially because respectability itself was culturally defined by men. Male antipathy ran deep, not only on account of national difference, but also due to the potential threat that English men recognized in dance-masters' activities. Already in 1658 Richard Flecknoe in his *Enigmaticall Characters* described the French dance-master as one who "makes all dance after his *Fiddle*," by which Flecknoe seemed to mean more than the musical instrument, as he combined xenophobia with misogyny by reference to sexual liaison: "He has the *Regimen* of your Ladies Legs, (nay little *Montague* pretended higher yet) and is the sole pedagogue of the Feet, teaching them not onely the French *pace* but the French *language* too, as *Coupéz, passéz, levéz &c.*"[11] In fact, the particular foreignness taken to be most fundamental to French dance-masters was sexual license, with respect both to their own gender identity and to the virtue of English women. That is, the French were seen as characteristically effeminate, foppish, less than men. Yet their effeminacy was not equated with homosexuality; quite the opposite. Instead, they were consistently represented as womanizers and seducers – the loss of female virtue to seduction was easier for the English male to bear than the prospect of an assignation between a déclassé French steward and one's daughter or wife. In fact, the consistent representation of dance-masters as foppish may have rested largely on the fact that they chiefly attended women (upon whose support they depended for their livelihood); such attendance unmanned them in the eyes of English men. But this assessment naturally only reaffirmed that dance-masters' attentions to English women potentially unmanned English men by making them cuckolds, or so the fear ran.

In literature such fears were more easily expressed with respect to female children – a worthless daughter was less damaging than a faithless wife. For example, Thomas D'Urfey's play dating from 1691, *Love for Money*, demonstrated the lust of three male teachers in a girls' boarding school. Here children, without parental guidance or protection, are introduced to Mr. Semibrev, the music teacher, Mr. Coopee, the dancing master, and M. Le Prate, the French teacher, all of whom are sexually aggressive. Le Prate is described in the *Dramatis Personae* as "an impertinent, noisie, singing, dancing, prating, French Fop, perpetually gabling in Company, and crying up for Actions of the French King." This is interesting precisely in that the characterization is never spoken upon the stage, but appears only in the character list. So stated, the description is naturalized (how else would a Frenchman appear?) – and also politicized: a foreigner on English soil forever trumpeting the virtues of French absolutism under Louis XIV.[12]

When made to speak through English authors, French dance instructors were rarely treated sympathetically. Charles Dibdin in his *Musical Tour* introduced a Frenchman on the subject of dance:

> *Monsieur* – *Sare* – look all over de varld, every ting depend pon larn to *danse*. *Sans cela* vidout larn to *danse* you cannot vat you call see life – you cannot know noting. De younk chentelmen *danse* away vid dere money before dey come to dere estate; de lofer *danse* away vid de laty to Scotland [that is, elope to Gretna Green]; de *marchand* clerk *danse* away vid the English bank note. Ven de housband find chentelman little too kind to his wife, he don't quarrel, make no noise, he make one very low bo – *serviture Madame*. Vat de devil you call dis but larn to *danse* . . . *Enfin* – in short, if you vould go vit great *eclat* troo de varld, you must do *comme en France* – vare de *pauvre danse* avay dare *misere*, de *riche danse* avay dare *conscience*, de *general dance* avay from de *enemy*, and all the rest of de varld *danse* away from dare friend, *ma foi*.[13]

Ironically in the very voice of French dance-master, Charles Dibdin thus reaffirmed every argument against dancing that English society had developed. French masters produced social disruption: gentlemen squandered their inheritance before they had it, clandestine marriages occurred, class ranks were disturbed. While clerks robbed to pay for their dance habits, thus aping activities better reserved for their social superiors, wives cheated on their husbands, husbands – emasculated – no longer cared. The poor danced to forget, the rich to forget their morals, and men deserted the field of responsibility. All of these faults Dibdin laid at the doorstep of the foreigner (whose successes he, as a native-born music teacher, deeply resented). Dance here functioned both as a barometer and as a metaphor of the nation's well-being: the grotesque chauvinism of Dibdin's broken-English discourse betrays more than vulgar comedy, for it depends implicitly on the fact that social dancing in England served, for better or for worse, as the ritual re-enactment of various fundamental components of the social and cultural order, here described in a state of advanced dissolution.

78

MUSIC AND IMAGE

In visual representation, as in literature and on the stage, the French dance-master was ugly, thin-waisted and effeminate, a man who seldom stood straight and never still, his form and posture embodying cultural degradation conflated with cultural difference (Fig. 18). In art the very denial of bodily substantiality to French dance-masters (commonly linked to their opposites, very John Bullish natives, Fig. 19) undoubtedly also delineated, simultaneously, their inherent weakness and the irony of their ability to seduce a nation on the very basis of their physical insubstantiality. The weak can subdue the strong, just as the bear-leader can subdue the bear (Fig. 19, the picture-within-the-picture).

DANCE, CLASS AND SELF-REPRESENTATION

It is difficult to overstate the importance of dancing among the upper classes in England during the eighteenth century. Jane Austen noted that it was possible for people to do without it entirely, that some instances were recorded where young people

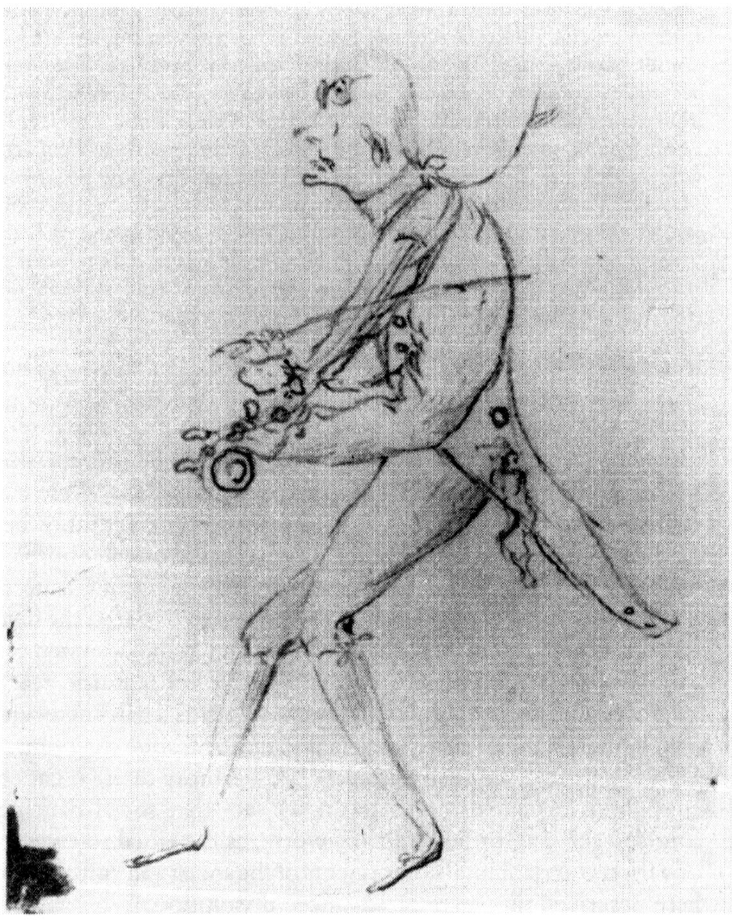

18 British School (late eighteenth century), *French Dance-Master*. pencil drawing, 15.2 × 10.2 cm.; Whereabouts unknown

survived for many months without dancing with no apparent damage done to body or mind. But, as she put it, "when a beginning is made – when the felicities of rapid motion have once been, though slightly, felt – it must be a very heavy set that does not ask for more."[14]

Children among the upper orders were often taught dancing from an early age – according to Richard Steele's ironic comment, a

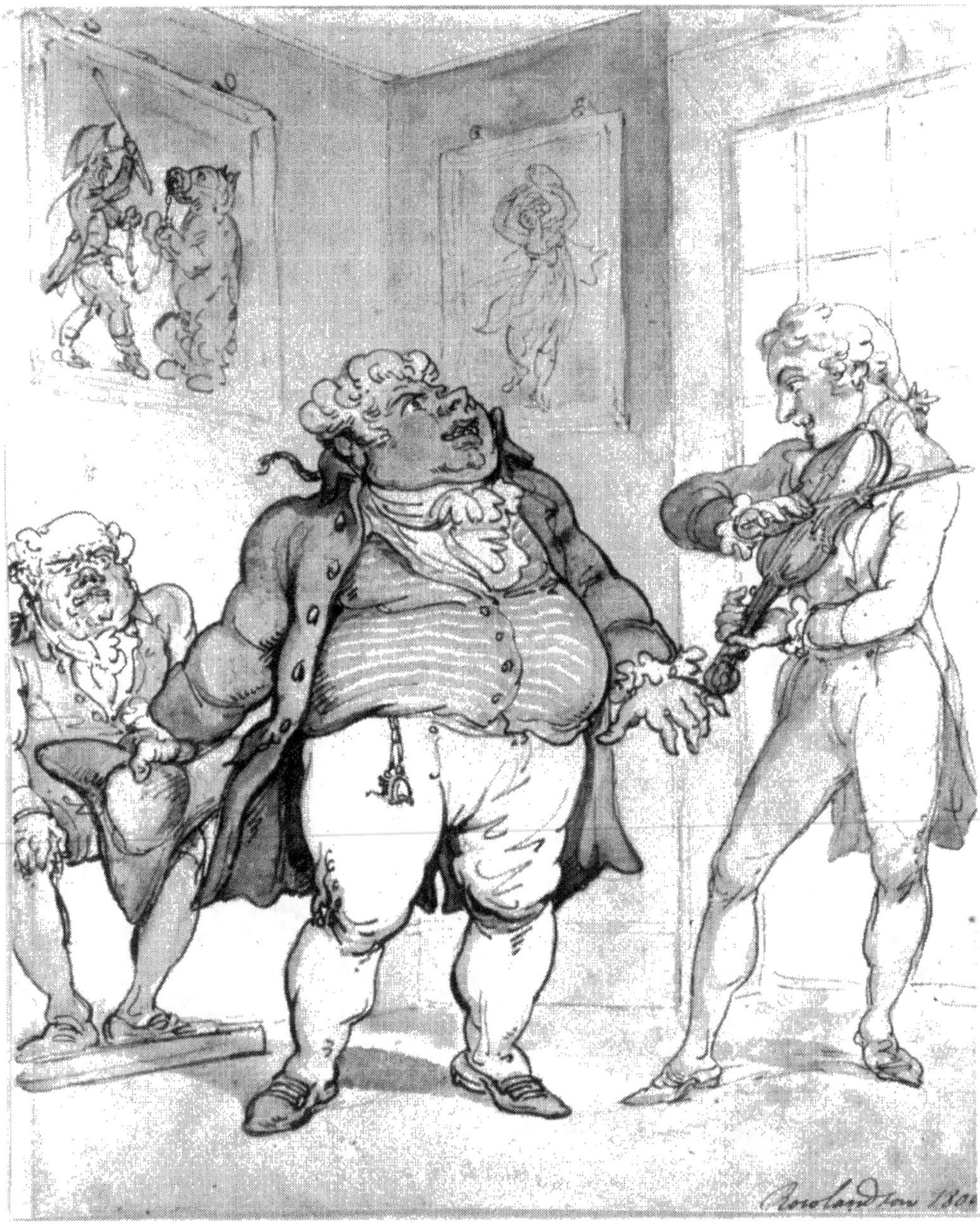

19 Thomas Rowlandson (1756/7–1827), *The Dancing Lesson* (1800), drawing; Whereabouts unknown

girl was "delivered to the Hands of her Dancing-Master" as soon as she was weaned, "before she is capable of forming one simple Notion of any thing in Life."[15] Dance instruction often took place at schools, where children were taught in groups. In 1786 Sophie von la Roche visited such an institution run by four sisters; her account documented the somewhat grim determination of dance instruction approximating military drill. The hall was an amphitheater where more than a hundred girls, aged six to sixteen, took their turns, six couples at a time, for minuets and country dances. Sophie commented that "all the parents subscribe to it and dress up their children, sit all round as spectators, and are either amused or annoyed, according to the amount of applause their children receive."[16] This is the subject of a Rowlandson drawing (Fig. 20), wherein the parents observe the performances with attention and smug satisfaction. What gives everyone pleasure, presumably, is the dancing to the tune, literally and metaphorically, of a very Frenchified instructor. It is through the medium of contrasted body types that Rowlandson ironicizes the event and critiques the participants. The dance-master, pencil-like, towers over not only the children but also their relatives, whether seated or standing. He completely dominates the scene, flitting about on thin legs and pointed toes, the extreme opposite of the thick, stationary gentleman, his foil, on the opposite side of the image. Rowlandson here retells the tale of the Pied Piper. The children, represented as miniaturized adults, to be sure are more attractive than their generally fattened, even grotesque forebears. But it is not accidental that

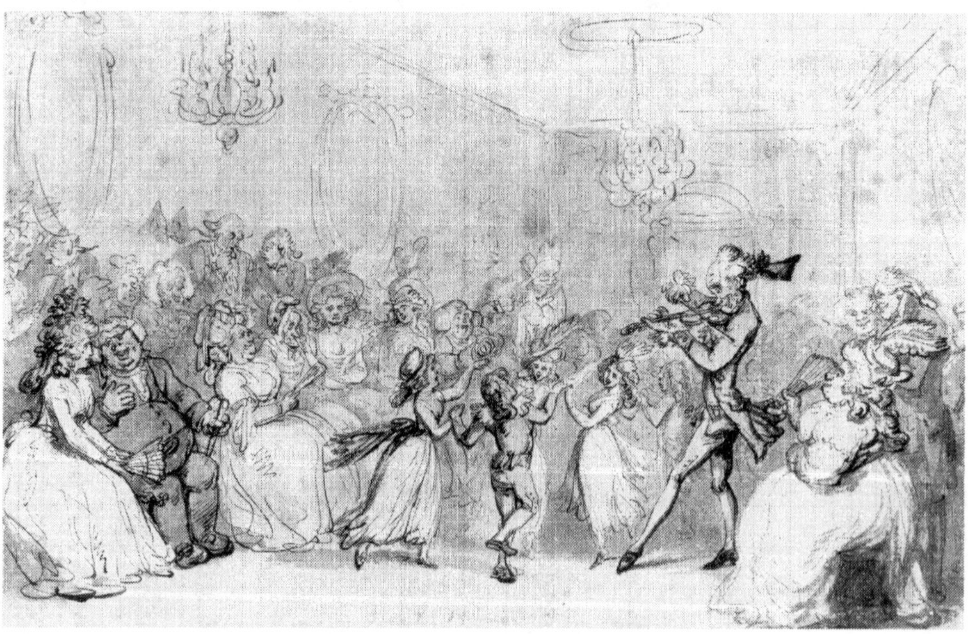

20 Thomas Rowlandson (1756/7–1827), *The Children's Dancing Lesson*, watercolor over pencil, 22.9 × 37.1 cm.; Boston, MA. By courtesy of Boston Public Library, Print Department

their bodies most closely approximate that of the dance-master in whose image they are being fashioned.

In 1736 a (presumably fictional) letter appeared in *Gentleman's Magazine* from a person describing himself as a man from the country, thirty years old, educated at Eton and Cambridge and now in London, who had never been taught to dance, his father thinking it folly and beneath the dignity of a man of learning. Among company going dancing he was soon asked by a beautiful lady to be her partner in a country dance, but not knowing how, he confessed his ignorance, whereafter "she left me with a Disdain which shew'd her Contempt of me." He asked the editor whether dancing was a reasonable recreation and if "it wou'd not betray my *Folly* too much to learn this Diversion in the 30th Year of my Age." (He wanted another chance with the lady.) The editor responded with citations from biblical history and the ancients favoring dancing and recommended that the man attain the skill so as not to be "either an *ill-natur'd Stoic*, or *ill-bred Pedant*. All that is [n]ecessary for a Gentleman is just so much as will give him a Kind of *Carelessness*, as if it was rather a *natural Motion* than a *laborious* and *artificial Acquisition*."[17]

Not knowing what to do, the gentleman had the good sense to stay off the dance floor. But others more boldly plunged in. Indeed, it is clear that dance-instructors earned considerable sums from adult, rather than juvenile, pupils. The demand for instruction from adults reflected a changing cultural and social climate. In the case of the former (cultural climate), social dancing, in particular for men, became increasingly *de rigueur* rather than optional (women apparently had more consistently been given dance instruction), and this meant dancing mediated through French traditions. In the case of the latter (social climate), it reflected social climbing and the blurring of class distinction, as the middle orders aped the behaviors of the upper.

Literary and visual representations of galumphing dancers, usually men, were common throughout the century and are worth examining for more than their intended humor. Thomas Gordon, for example, described a "country entertainment" in which "the Majority made such a Rattle on the Boards, as quite drown'd the Musick. This made me call to Mind your mettlesome Horses, that dance on a Pavement to the Musick of their own Heels." Gordon described the local squire's eldest son, a bachelor and captain of the militia, who on the dance floor "not only threw down most of the Women, and with abundance of Wit hawled them round the Room, but gave us several farther Proofs of the Sprightliness of his Genius, by a great many Leaps he made about a Yard high, always remembring to fall on somebody's Toes."[18]

Both this account and that from *Gentleman's Magazine* tell tales about gentlemen, but for an audience of others. That is, the fictive anti-heroes come from the country; the readership is primarily from the city (London). The social class critiqued in these satires, was the same as that of the presumed reader. The humor was nevertheless achieved by the common technique of establishing and valorizing socio-cultural difference, in this instance that of town versus country. Dancing thus constituted a mark of urban sophistication, together with a Continental air, unavailable in its pure form to provincials. In these instances French intrusions, however else they may have been problematic, were positive forces as signifiers of subcultural difference, hence status. This phenomenon helps explain why French dance-masters succeeded in London and the other major centers. Indeed, the triumph of French dancers came apart from – even in spite of – political realities. (Thus in the season of 1780–1 two Frenchmen, father and son, named Vestris, lately come from Paris were all the rage on the London stage, despite the fact that the two countries were at war – even the King attended their performance at Covent Garden.)[19]

Nevertheless, the ambivalence of reception of French dance-masters (and what they taught) was never overcome in eighteenth-century England. And this is best borne out, significantly, by *visual* means in satirical drawings and especially prints, the latter mass-marketed cheaply. The one subject that recurred more than any other in this regard was the dancing lesson for adult learners (Figs. 19, 21–23). In some cases these prints played off the problems of men and women whose childhood education did not include dancing (provincials, parvenus). But apart from an audience of rank beginners, there were two other important reasons that French dance-masters were employed by adults: the popular social dances of the century were extraordinarily complicated, especially by comparison with almost all of the dances of our own time, and they were constantly changing. This is to say that anyone willing to put themselves on public view at a ball or assembly required constant instruction and practice simply in order to know the latest dances and to be able to execute them properly. Needless to say this fact forced adult English men and women into permanent subservience to their French instructors, compounding the problem of cultural pollution with that of a perpetual teacher–pupil relationship in which the "natural" social order was reversed.

21 John Collett (c. 1725–80), engraved after, *Grown Gentlemen Taught to Dance* (1768), engraving, 31.4 × 24.8 cm.; London, British Museum. By courtesy of the Trustees Photo: © Copyright the Trustees of the British Museum.

Rowlandson's dancing lesson (Fig. 19) encapsulates the visual conventions of these satirical representations. Most notable, again, is the difference in body types of the two men in the foreground, the English gentleman depicted as overstuffed, almost furniture-like (and as difficult to move), the French master thin and taller than his student. At the back a second gentleman waits his turn, seated in misery with his feet stuck in a hollowed-out wooden device employed to stretch the leg muscles. But his pain is emotional as well. Perhaps harder to bear than his aching legs is the fact that he is being made to wait until his own "employee" can attend to him. This is more than role/class reversal; it is gender reversal as well. The fat, immobile man adopts the waiting aspect culturally assigned to women; as such he is entirely comic and pathetic.

"Grown Gentlemen Taught to Dance" (Fig. 21) repeats much of

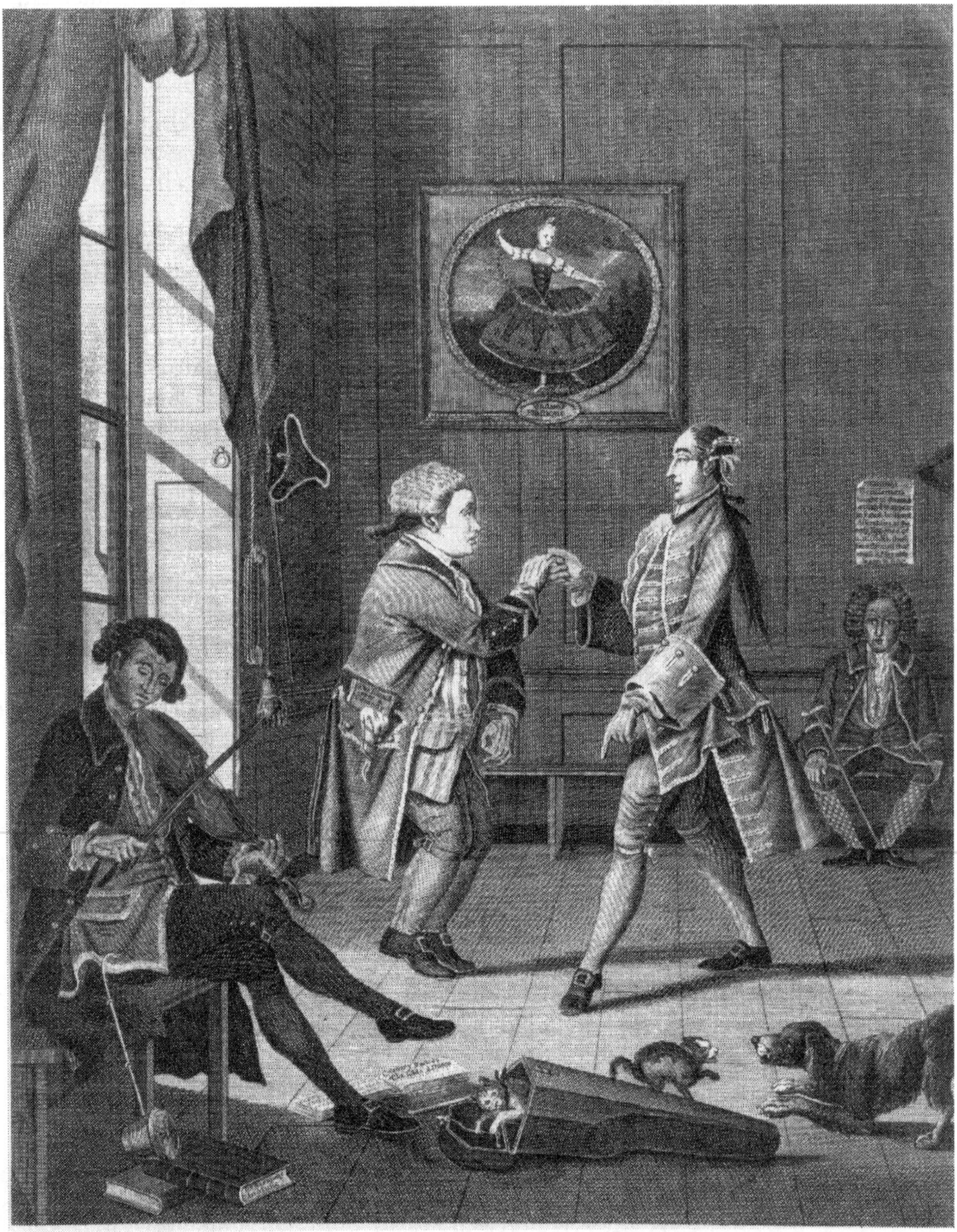

this imagery, though this dance studio may be of a higher order in that the master has employed a separate fiddler for the occasion. (He plays with one broken string; he is both blind and deaf – his ear trumpet rests at his feet.) The man at the back sits with his feet in proper dance position (but without the leg board), the unnaturalness of the self-imposed constraint perfectly evident. (A sheet tacked to the wall just above his head reads: "Grown Gentlemen taught to dance, & qualify'd to appear in y^{e} most brilliant Assemblies, at the easy Expense of 1$^{£}$ 11^{s} 6^{d}. NB. those Gentlemen that chuse it May also learn to sing.") The two central characters are powerfully differentiated, and in such a way that the very tall master in every sense commands his adult ward. The English gentleman (with a copy of *The Blunderer A Comedy* in his pocket) virtually cowers to his master's gestural instructions. He bends his kness to execute a dance step, and at the same time affirms his inferiority. His face is rendered not simply as fat, but as baby-fat, a physical metaphor of his reversion. Additional commentary is provided by the little dance book at the feet of the fiddle player, *Country Dances, The Lad's a Dunce*, and by the scrapping cat and dog: a mixing of "species" that cannot produce a happy end. What the image emphasizes more than anything else is role reversal, where the real master abrogates his social position to become a servant to a foreigner, waiting like a servant to be summoned by his servant, a transposition made more damning in that the affair is entered into willingly. England surrenders to France; the elite cave in to the rabble. This episode echoes a scene in Edward Ravenscroft's *The Citizen Turn'd Gentleman*, a translation-adaptation of Molière's *Le bourgeois gentilhomme* (1670), in which Mr. Jordan calls for instruction in the minuet and his dancing master obliges with the following: "Come, Sir, begin; your hat Sir; so now your honour la, la . . . not to fast, la la . . . keep your leg straight, la la . . . don't hunch your shoulders so, la la . . . you carry your arms as if they were broken, la, la . . . hold up your head, keep your toes out . . . don't loll out your tongue, la la . . . and make such faces, as if you were on the close stool, la, la."[20]

The violation of sexual taboo (men dancing together) delineates the central paradigm of this socio-cultural perversion. The portrait of a graceful and nimble "Madame Elastique" hanging above the dancers shows that their success depends upon their replicating the gestures of a woman. Her image finalizes the scene's absurdity by the additional implication that English men degrade themselves in this fashion essentially to please their would-be female dance partners. This is subservience of the worst kind, based on the loss of gender hierarchy and as equally disruptive to cultural order as abetting the imposition of a foreigner's will.[21]

Representations of women alter this visual formula to produce quite different results (Figs. 22–23).[22] "Grown Ladies &c. Taught to Dance" (Fig. 22), the companion print to the one just discussed,

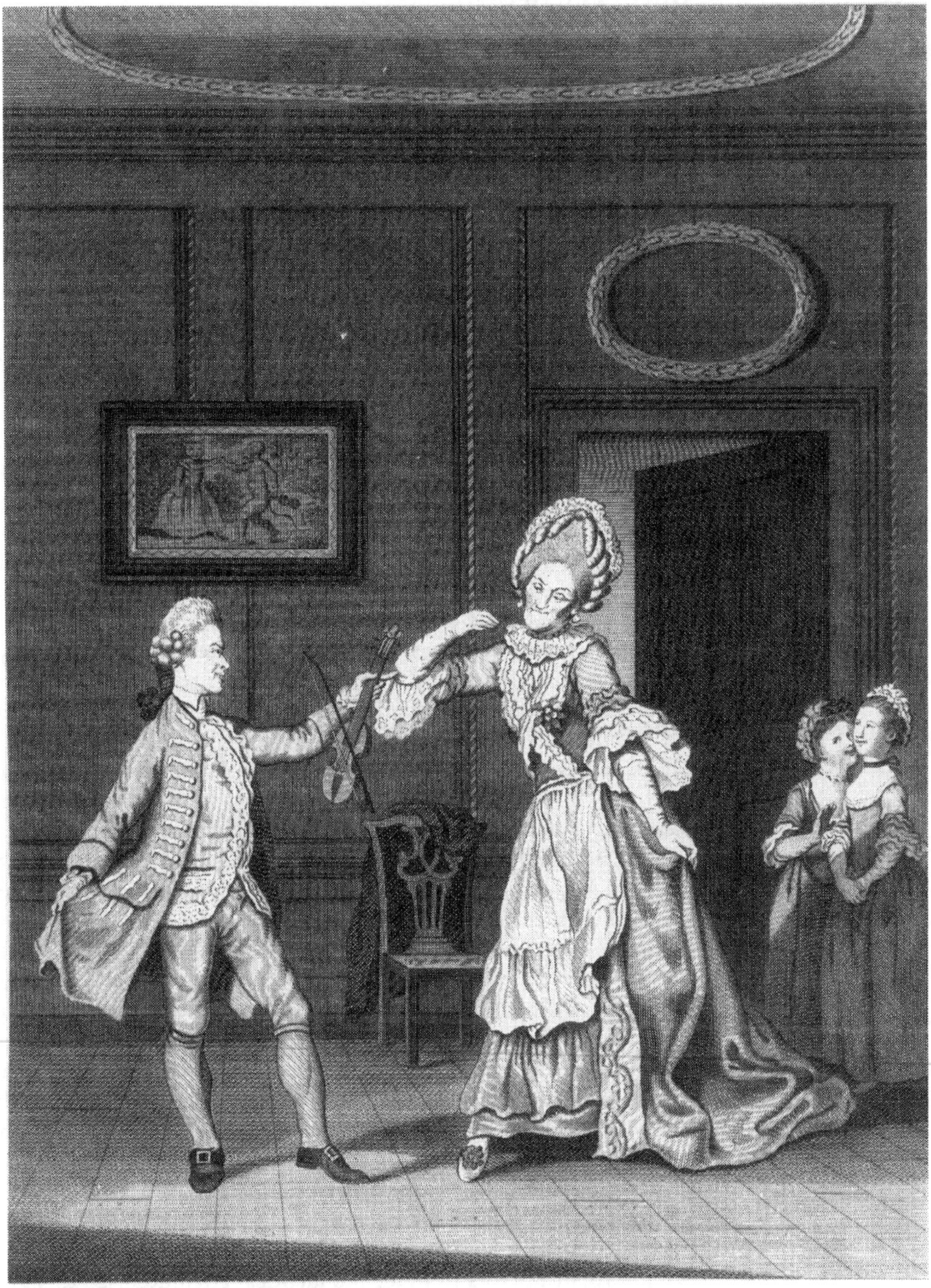

22 Rennoldson (act. 1760s), after John Collett, *Grown Ladies &c. Taught to Dance* (1768), engraving, 32.7 × 23.8 cm.; London, British Museum. By courtesy of the Trustees Photo: © Copyright the Trustees of the British Museum.

addresses neither role reversal nor cultural difference. Instead, the image constitutes fairly straightforward misogyny built on the cultural cliché of female vanity. In the background two attractive girls (they embody the "&c." of the print's title) whisper of the absurdity of the old woman's youthful pretension as she accepts the flattery – and hand – of her French master, over whom she towers, a physical difference that mocks both of them, at once making him less of a man and turning her into a kind of grotesque scarecrow, accentuated of course by her wrinkled face framed by a highly inappropriate wig. The old woman is mocked both by the girls, and by the master whose flattery she both compels as part of their financial arrangement and heartily swallows, as we see by means of the girlish gestures of daintiness and modesty signified by her arm and hand gestures. That she is being led around by the nose is evident from the picture-within-the-picture on the back wall, where a monkey leads a be-gowned cat.

In another print of similar title (Fig. 23) Vanity's monkey still holds court, now holding a lady's fan. On the back wall we have the dialectic of two images, a Watteauesque couple gracefully dancing, on the right, and the bear-leader, on the left. Since gracefulness is nowhere evident in the scene below the pictures, the difference-by-analogy is clear. The same waiting seen earlier still prevails, but the level of grotesquerie is increased. The parameters of the feminine are ironically presented: tall, skinny and old (a dried-up stick), short, fat and young (a bovine creature with enormous hands and with legs that appear not to reach the floor), stupid and uncomprehending. The only intelligence evident is in the face of the French master whose business sense is astute, though his only dance success in these chambers will be with the little dog standing between the two women. Again, in both images the satire is redirected away from the overriding socio-cultural and even political issues evident in the representations of men and toward the easy and perennial target of women qua women whose supposed vanity precludes their being ideal examples of their sex.

All this relates closely to another subject for which a number of visual and textual satires exist, "Boarding School Education, or the Frenchified Young Lady" (Fig. 24). Here again misogyny and vanity make the argument, via the anecdotal metaphors of a monkey instructing a puppy, and a mirror on the back wall. (In European culture monkeys had long been held as libidinous and vain. In art the association of monkeys with vanity was often signified by giving them mirrors to hold, the identical attribute used to signal the vanity of women. The conflation of monkeys with women thereby represented women as less than human, as irrational, vain and dangerously sexual.) Two new elements also operate in this image. First, it is noteworthy that the young woman at the left is relatively attractive at least in body, though her face is unintelligent.

She is slim and moves with grace, and hence contrasts utterly with her piglike companion, profiled to exaggerate her bulk. Both are analogues to the puppy in the foreground, innocently being taught "to dance" by the French "monkey." They are fruit ready for harvest: the Frenchman's ogling of the slim one is satirically evident from his exaggerated eyebrows that seem to leap out toward her. The conquest-by-gaze is already complete, though she herself is (necessarily) totally uncomprehending of the fact. The second new feature of the print is the matter of class rank and social position-

23 Artist Unknown (Crochet), after Daniel Dodd, *Grown Ladies Taught to Dance* (1768), engraving, 26.1 × 22.4 cm.; New Haven, CT, Yale Center for British Art, Paul Mellon Collection

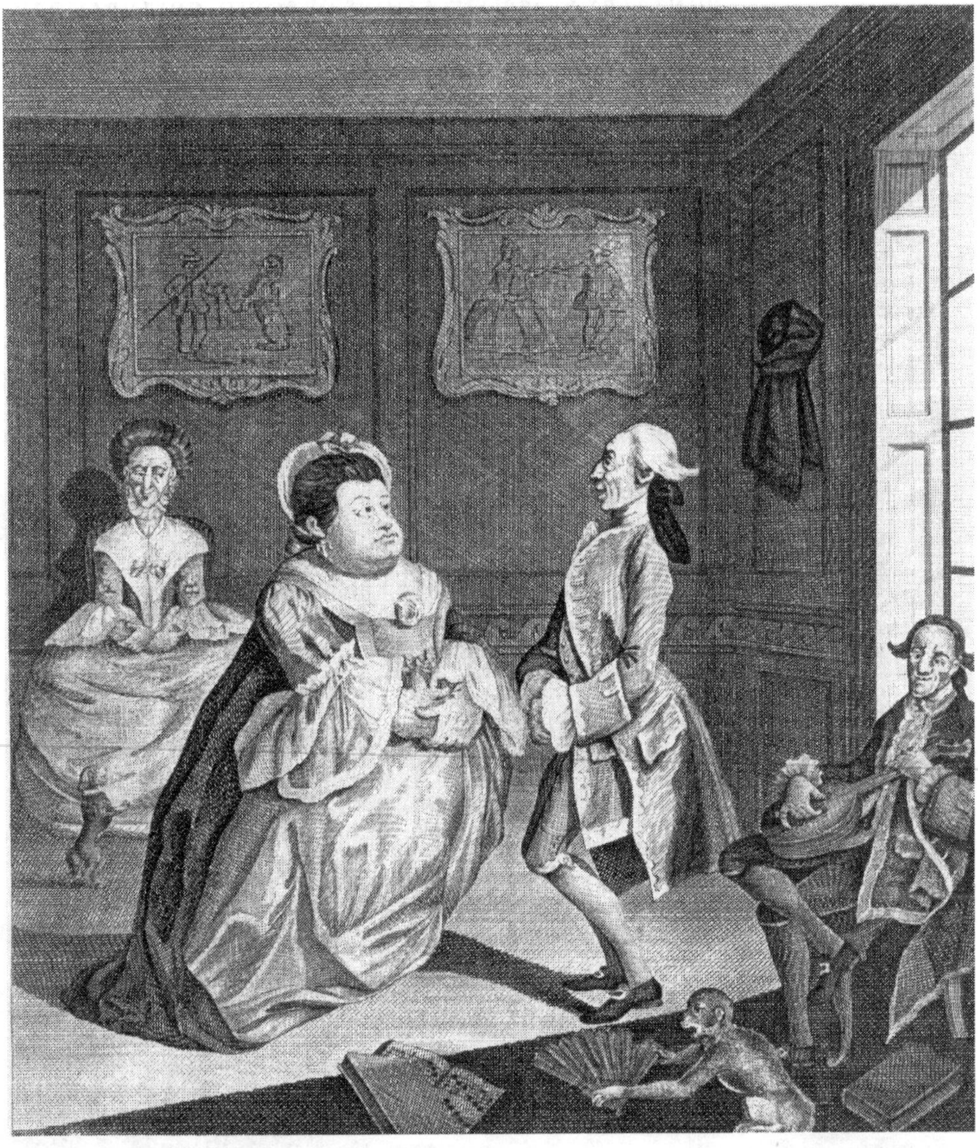

via-geography. The fat dancer is the daughter of a country gentleman, the thin one of a farmer; they are provincials. We are told this via the images on the back wall, country scenes with dwellings appropriate to each. In other words, the French dance-master plays wittingly for a seduction and unwittingly for the crossing of class and social boundaries (these females ought to be milking cows), the anger over which this engenders I have discussed in a previous chapter.

CONTRARY REPRESENTATIONS OF SOCIO-CULTURAL ORDER

At this point I want to focus more directly on the types of social dancing practiced in England during the eighteenth century, starting with the minuet, in order to explore in greater depth contemporaneous perceptions of dancing in its relation to social order.

Though the precise origins of the minuet are somewhat obscure, the dance was established at Versailles under Louis XIV in the 1650s and 1660s, and fast became the predominant dance of the French aristocracy. By the early eighteenth century it had crossed the Channel, where it remained in vogue until c. 1750 (though it did not entirely disappear until the nineteenth century). Two issues concern me here: how the dance looked and, on account of its look, how the dance functioned ideologically and hence socially.

The minuet's aristocratic bearing, enshrined by its formality,

24 Mary Darly (act. 1762-72), *Boarding School Education, or the Frenchified Young Lady* (1771), engraving, 24.5 × 34.9 cm.; New Haven, CT, Yale Center for British Art, Paul Mellon Collection

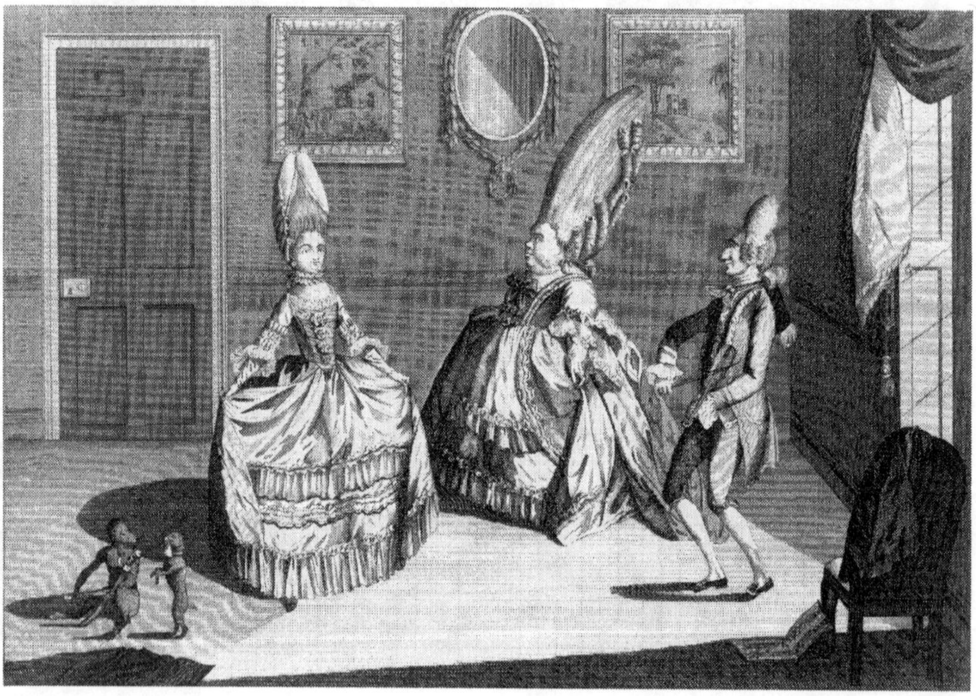

exaggerated grace and complexity of structure, grew from its use at Versailles as one of the means by which Louis XIV exercised control over the courtiers forced against their will to live months at a time under his roof. At Versailles the minuet (in fact, like other dances) was begun by the King and his partner, with all other couples following his lead. But once Louis had initiated the dance, he withdrew to the sidelines the more carefully to watch his semi-permanent guests perform their routines *for his benefit* as proof of their loyalty.[23] In the King's perception of dancing's function, a courtier who failed to perform well might be devoting his time to tasks impinging on the King's stately powers. To commit a *faux pas* under Louis' surveillance (literally, in the policing sense of the word) was sufficient to cause temporary banishment from Court and a cut-off of financial support. The astute courtier, in other words, stayed entirely out of state politics, devoting instead many hours a week pent up with his dance-master in order to learn and rehearse for each evening's entertainments.

The minuet was a ritualized microcosmic social order, exactly replicating a real one. It demanded an exactingly prescribed behavior. The dance was extraordinarily complicated, not because its steps in themselves were so difficult, but because it involved precise control over the entire body, from the carriage and turn of the head to the position of the arms, wrists, hands, legs and feet. By dancing the minuet in the prescribed manner (the only way permissible), the French aristocracy nightly affirmed *visually and formally* their submission to the King – and, equally important, they did so *silently*, moving without speech in time to the music and under the King's watchful eye.

The minuet began with a bow, a mutually acknowledged deference to one's partner as well as to the dominance of the King who watched and waited. As such, in the Versailles minuet, the bow was not a simple (or natural) gesture. Its form, like all else, was highly articulated and self-conscious – best evidenced by the dance treatises of the time which devoted enormous amounts of space to describe its correct execution – two chapters in one text, sixty pages in another, and the entire book in the case of a third.[24] The dance itself reiterated submission and control at literally every step, for, as the name of the dance itself asserts, the individual steps were invariably tiny (*menu*), hence unnatural, constrained, all the more because the constraint had to be performed effortlessly, as if it were natural movement. The dance's tempo was slow to moderate, that is, deliberate, rationalized, non-spontaneous. Actual climax was prevented, for no energy was allowed to build: the individual dance-units were only two bars long. Nearly every step ended with the dancers' weight concentrated on the balls of the feet, a highly unstable stance that affirmed their weakness, especially by comparison with that of the very stable, seated King. Similarly, the dance ended with couples turning several circles, always in elaborate step patterns, in anticlimactic gestures of graceful stasis.

Throughout, the body's carriage was expected to be "*douce.*" Yet this did not signal naturalness, but actually its oxymoronic opposite: naturalized control. The grace of the body in the minuet was the signifier of total submission of the de-individualized courtly society, the surrender of bodily power to an order imposed from without. Submission was of course masked in beautiful gesture, in the smooth textures of an imposed calm. In sum, the minuet constituted the visual affirmation of French politics and state authority; it represented discipline imposed from above and outside the self. Not necessarily danced voluntarily, the minuet was required in order to retain one's personal status and prestige. (Later in the century, and after the death of Louis XIV, in France and England alike the minuet was replaced by the infinitely more energetic *contredanse*/country dance; yet balls and assemblies continued to pay it lip service by starting with a single minuet, then abandoning it for the newer, freer forms. By preserving the minuet for the start of balls, rather than simply dropping it, it is possible that the dancers took pleasure in ritualistically "killing" it anew, over and over again, thus re–celebrating liberation by temporarily reinstituting the authority of that which was overthrown.) But, as so far described, all this concerns issues internal to France. What of England?

The minuet's introduction into England came not only through dance-masters but also by way of translations of French treatises, and also by texts first published in England. These books served a capacity similar to self-tutors for musical instruments. In the first part of the century the minuet received much attention. Kellom Tomlinson's *The Art of Dancing Explained by Reading and Figures* (London, 1735), for example, devoted nearly forty pages to the minuet, along with sixteen plates illustrating steps and gestures. (He devoted only three pages to country dances.) The subscribers' list to Tomlinson's book contains nearly 170 names of men and women from the aristocracy and gentry, as well as those of dance-masters, including a number of names of individuals living outside London.

However the upper-class English learned the dance, the minuet signified to them nearly everything I have already suggested, and something more: it represented France – a state, a political system, a religion and a culture at once profoundly familiar and foreign, both admired and despised. The introduction of the minuet into England was severely complicated and compromised by these contradictions which were in fact never overcome. Yet the issues that surfaced were fundamentally, if not altogether exclusively, class specific. They did not go much beyond the concerns of the upper orders of English society. That is, the minuet engendered deep concerns about self-definition and national identity only among those who were in social positions allowing them to define the latter and worry about the former. (What the minuet's introduction into England did *not* specifically introduce were questions of social class and class blurring, except as regards the class pretensions related to boarding school education and the like discussed earlier, an issue that would have existed without French dancing. This issue did arise with respect to country dances, as I shall discuss presently.)

English ambivalence toward the minuet can be examined through visual representations, notably in an unusual family portrait by Zoffany (Fig. 25), where the minuet itself constitutes the subject occupying the center of the picture space via embodiment in the gracefulness of the daughter's form. The girl's weightlessness achieved through dance contrasts sharply with the weighty stasis of the other family members to the right, in particular the girl's mother sitting stiffly and staring off into space (in fact, neither parent looks at the girl). To be sure, it is an odd painting, but this is not due to any lack of skill on Zoffany's part. It is because he has a socio-culturally impossible task to perform. The daughter is to be shown accomplished. We know she played the piano – Zoffany

25 Johan Zoffany (1733–1810), *A Family Party, The Minuet*, oil on canvas, 99 × 124.5 cm.; Glasgow, Glasgow Art Gallery and Museum, McLellan Bequest Photo: Glasgow City Council.

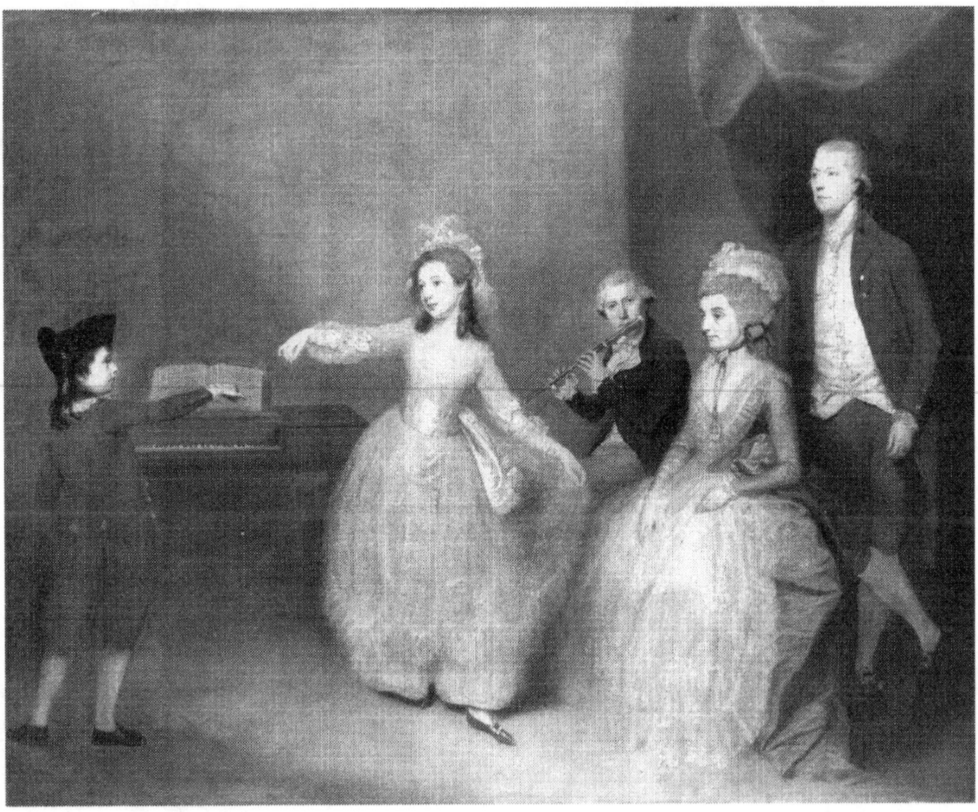

includes it in silent witness to her musical skills – but that by itself apparently was not enough. She also danced (here with her little brother as temporary partner). Yet to show her off as a dancer was to distract from other family members who were, of course, more important. Here they essentially serve only to frame that which is visually much more interesting and they suffer on account of it. Zoffany compensated for this by making them uninvolved. The mother sits as though she were in another portrait where none of the distractions of the dance occur. The father adopts the usual cross-legged pose of easy assurance, his dominance somewhat preposterously asserted by means of the conventional baldachino-like drapery incongruously floating over his head. (The eldest son accompanies on the flute – though badly, judging from the way he holds the instrument, and takes a back-seat to his sister, in itself a profound upheaval of family hierarchy otherwise demanded by the narrative: dancers require accompaniment.) I am suggesting that the very form of the image is disrupted by allusion to the minuet – it is the minuet's gestures that the girl executes. Indeed, Zoffany painted her with the air of Watteau, whose work he admired. But what resulted was a visual dissonance, literally a French intrusion into English space, both formally (how Zoffany painted) and liter-

26–29 W. Dickenson (act. 1787), after Henry William Bunbury, *A Long Minuet as Danced at Bath* (1787), stipple engraving, 21.7 × 214.9 cm.; London, British Museum. By courtesy of the Trustees
Photo: © Copyright the Trustees of the British Museum.

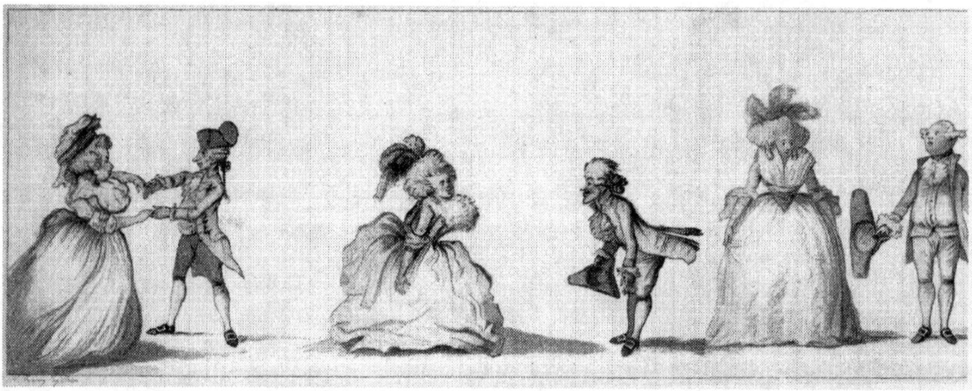

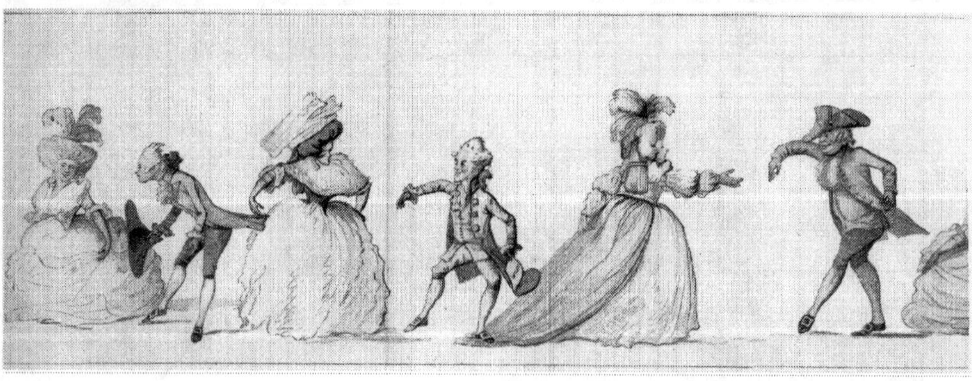

ally (what he painted). As a result the image denied itself the easy affirmative qualities the conversation piece normally produced, and as such subverted the Englishness of the sitters. The French intrusion, centered around an event, a French dance, interrupts a visual order otherwise functioning to affirm an English socio-cultural order. (Zoffany concentrated all his attention on the sitters themselves, on their body types and gestures. This lends greater impact, hence meaning, to them than commonly occurred in his portraits, where the settings themselves were highly decorative and distracting.)

In a quite different way precisely the same is true of a satirical print called "A Long Minuet as Danced at Bath" (Figs. 26–29). Most striking is the form of the image, an extraordinarily rectangular print (actually a strip sequence of four prints, since its extreme rectilinarity could not be contained on a single plate of a standard press). The print, well known in its time, comically problematized the minuet not only by its literal content – what is represented – but also by its form. In content, Bunbury represented the minuet via a series of ten couples, each of whom executes a different gesture of the dance. Some dancers are attractive and accomplished, others are homely and graceless (the seventh man steps on the dress of the

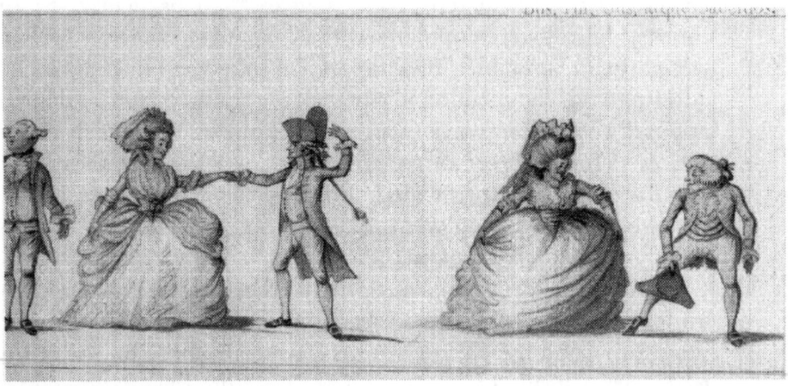

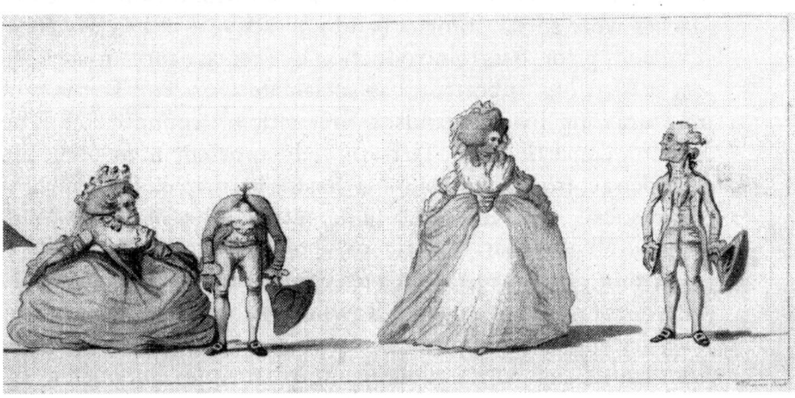

eighth woman, not his partner, thus making his ineptitude worse). One is confused (the third man), others apprehensive (last couple) and so on. There is much to laugh at, since two essential components of the minuet are either missing altogether or are effectively made absent by their occasional presence (whereas they should be everywhere manifested), namely, decorum and, especially, grace. The minuet, in a sense, has been Englished, in a peculiar, quasi-anarchic way. But of course the minuet's adaptation into English society has not so much been de-Frenchified as its proponents have rendered themselves absurd. At this juncture the prints' form plays a crucial role, for by violating pictorial conventions via extreme rectilinearity, it powerfully articulates the cosmetic absurdity of the minuet's French formalism. These dancers simply do not get it, and make fools of themselves for pretending that they do.[25]

In order to make better sense of my analysis thus far concerning the minuet, it is necessary to consider country dances, which increasingly gained the attention of the English during the same period. The history of the country dance is lost in the obscurity of folk dancing. But by the mid seventeenth century and the publication of Playford's treatise they were already accepted by the upper strata of English society. Around the beginning of the eighteenth century they became popular on the Continent, though they could no longer be considered "folk" dances.[26] In particular, English country dances were popularized and adapted in France, where they were called *contredanses*. In altered form they were introduced back into England, the cotillion in particular, a round or square dance, as opposed to the longways form more common to English country dances.[27] In whatever form, country dances were extraordinarily popular on the Continent and in England alike, and the reasons why are directly reflected in what may be termed the politics of movement associated with them.

Country dances were, essentially, the opposite of the stately minuet. In tempo they were fast and in spirit gay. Their meters were duple and the phrase lengths four times those for the minuet, eight bars instead of two. By comparison with the minuet, country dances were social, informal and interactive – in its early form in England, prior to its reintroduction by French dance-masters, steps per se were less important than social interchange.[28] This is evident in a drawing by Rowlandson illustrating a round dance type of country dance (Fig. 30). To be sure, the apparent intent of the image is to detract from any stateliness that the participants may imagine is their social due, an ironic undercutting of which Rowlandson achieved by his characteristic juxtaposition of opposing body types – fat-thin, short-tall, as well as strong-profile caricature and the like. Yet on a political level Rowlandson undercut himself by the fact that his visual opposites interact so happily. Men and women join hands and with childlike enthusiasm move about the floor, each to her or his own highly varied skills and concerns. Indeed, as was typical of English country dances, at least in their earlier history, social interaction was more important than individual steps or gestures, so long as things kept moving. The beautiful hold hands with the ugly, the young with the old. Rowlandson created a visual community (all of one social class) – toward which he was sympathetic, given that nearly half of the dancers are represented as physically attractive (the three young women and the older man in the center at the back).

In the most common longways form of country dancing couples lined up in a row, men on one side, women on the other. Usually there were at least three couples, but very often the instructions, as in Playford's *English Dancing Master*, call for "Longwayes for as many as will." Unlike the Versailles minuet, where one couple danced at a time to public scrutiny, the country dance was, at least in spirit, all-involving: as many could join in as the room (ideally rectangular) would accommodate. The dance's pattern was shared by all, passing from one couple to another, each couple moving gradually to the head of the line. To be sure, it was a dance type of considerable order – each person having to execute the dance steps properly otherwise chaos resulted – but each person shared equal status with the others (and a different couple started each dance). This contrasts with the Versailles minuet where movement per se was everything and social interaction essentially irrelevant. Under Louis XIV the minuet was less a social dance than a test which, successfully passed, allowed one to retain membership in courtly

30 Thomas Rowlandson (1756/7–1827), *Round Dance*, watercolor, pen and ink, 19 × 31.8 cm.; Honolulu, HI, Honolulu Academy of Arts

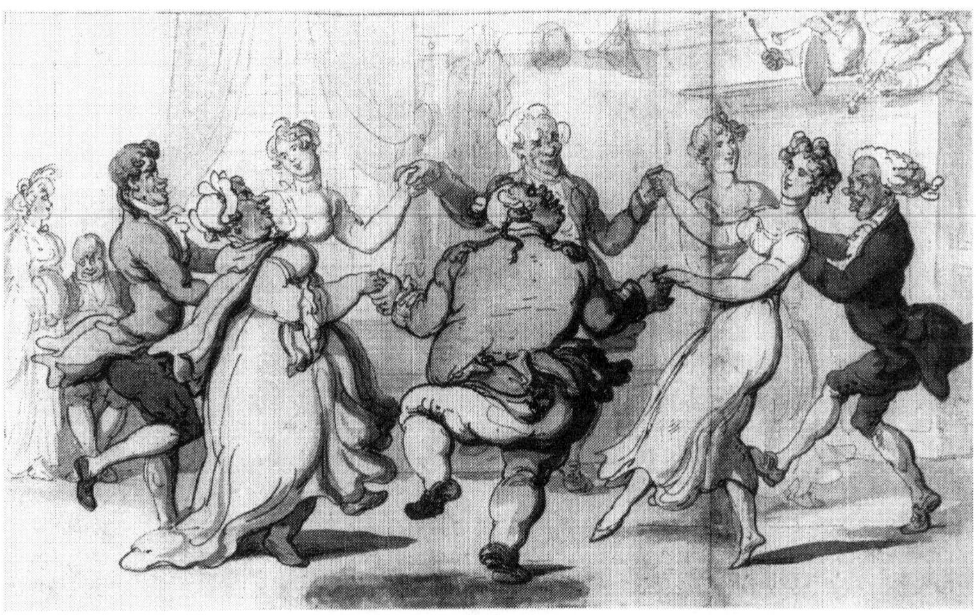

society. But as regards the way it was danced, one couple at a time before the King, the minuet belied the nature of the society its function underwrote: the minuet inherently announced itself as a coercive device.

There was in effect a single minuet, whatever the accompanying music. There were by contrast as many country dances as there were tunes: endless variety was the most essential component. Each country dance tune required the learning of new combinations of movements (a boon to dance-masters). Thus Playford's *English Dancing Master* contains one dance per page, each consisting of one or two lines of melody beneath which are brief textual instructions for the dancers. In the first edition (1651) there were 104 dances in all (about seventy-six of which are the longways type). By the 1728 eighteenth edition, the anthology swelled to 900 dances, each with separate instructions!

What is striking about these numbers is the social politics that informed them. At Versailles the minuet's form, in its seemingly timeless unity, constituted a statement of orthodoxy, a kind of loyalty oath on the part of the dancers and an assertion of power on the part of the King. But with 900 country dances in a single collection no individual could hope to possess control. Indeed, the variety of dances was so great and the speed of change in popularity so fast that dancers employed crib sheets to help them get through an evening's entertainment. Most common were ladies' fans (Fig. 31) printed with the latest tunes and brief instructions on the movements to be used for each. In a word, the politics of the country dance, by comparison with the minuet, was democratic (within the

31 Dance Fan (1793), hand-colored stipple-engraving; London, British Museum. By courtesy of the Trustees
Photo: © Copyright the Trustees of the British Museum.

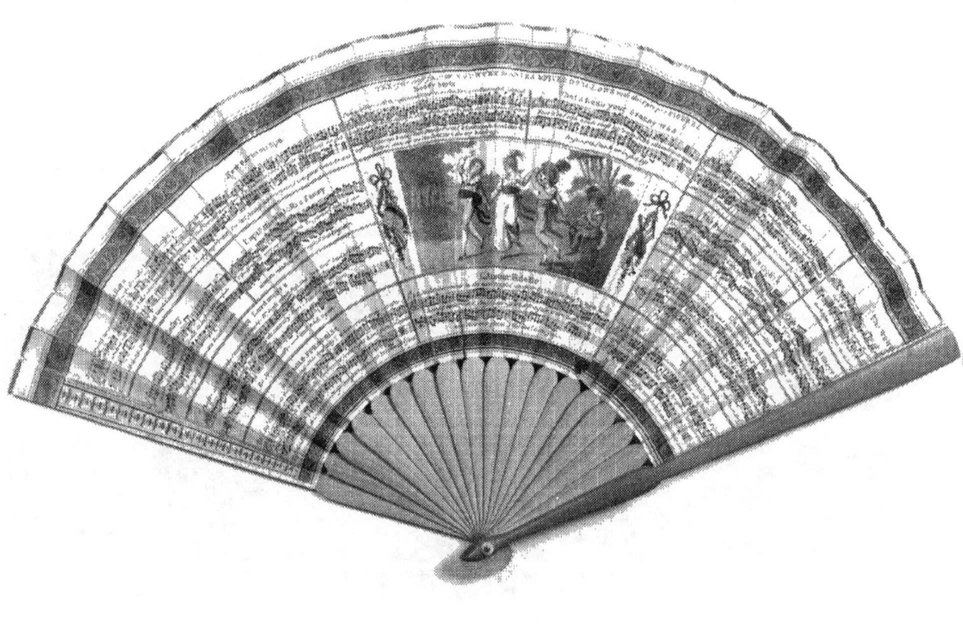

confines of the upper class). This is not to suggest that the English Court, even in its condition of diminished power, was incapable of exerting influence. It did, but in a way that only confirmed its political weakness. In the annual celebration of the "King's Birthnight Ball" a new dance was composed and notated by the court dance-master, then printed and distributed for sale. Individuals hoping to attend had to know the dance.[29] Yet this royal dance could not dominate the evening in the way of the minuet at Versailles. Its status was momentary – and needless to say, failure to dance it well could not result in anything worse than gossip.

The country dances' progressive movement, where each couple in turn took each position in the hierarchy of couples, where gaiety and speed overwhelmed formality, where each dance was different from the last, together expressed the fetishization of change itself. The negative dialectics inherent in this taste for change, and specifically in the semiotics of the dances themselves, however, suggested that such change might not be confined solely to the dance floor. It might spill over into the social structure. That is, within the class domains of society's upper strata the country dance, even in its French-influenced versions, activated and problematized historical memory of the dance's popular origins. This memory, constructed from the semiotics of physical movement, heralded and mirrored fundamental social restructuring. As Sachs described the phenomenon, "The advance of the *contre* is analogous with the rise of bourgeois society and the decline of the aristocratic culture."[30] Country dances in Elizabethan times presumed the mixing of the entire household, servants taking their places alongside their masters, villagers alongside local gentry.[31] Yet in this instance the dances confirmed not change but stasis, the eternity of feudal order, a secure, seamless social hierarchy. It confirmed its own correctness. In the eighteenth century by contrast, country dances were performed in class-specific groups, as was common to all social dancing, and this affirmed not stasis but change. The physical exclusion of the lower classes from upper-class balls and assemblies normally was a sign of hierarchical superiority. But the introduction into these balls and assemblies of the (rather de-rustified) music and dance of the lower classes contradicted exclusivity; the lower classes intruded in spite of themselves – without knowing it, so to speak – as present absences.

Occasionally these concerns found expression in visual form. My examples (Figs. 32–33) are nominally comic, though the comedy is recessive in favor of what can only be called pastoral "charm." Here two country dances have been moved back outdoors, in a visual embodiment of historical memory which in no sense reflected eighteenth-century practice among the upper orders (it is clear the individuals involved are people of status). In the first instance (Fig. 32) professional musicians provide accompaniment, the little band obviously having followed the revelers into the landscape. The dancers all but constitute a Maypole group, if we accept the large tree's function in that light. But more noteworthy are the physical gestures of both couples signaling an unself-conscious abandon and joy, especially in the men who have uncharacteristically, presumably temporarily, allowed emotion to take control over their conventional reserve. Most of the same applies to the second image (Fig. 33) but with three essential differences. First, the musicians are "rustics," in Watteauesque fashion playing the hurdy-gurdy and shawm. Second, the dancers now appear in the costumes of a

32 George Dance (1741–1825), *Country Dance*, pen and wash, 29.4 × 50.8 cm.; San Marino, CA, Henry E. Huntington Library and Art Gallery

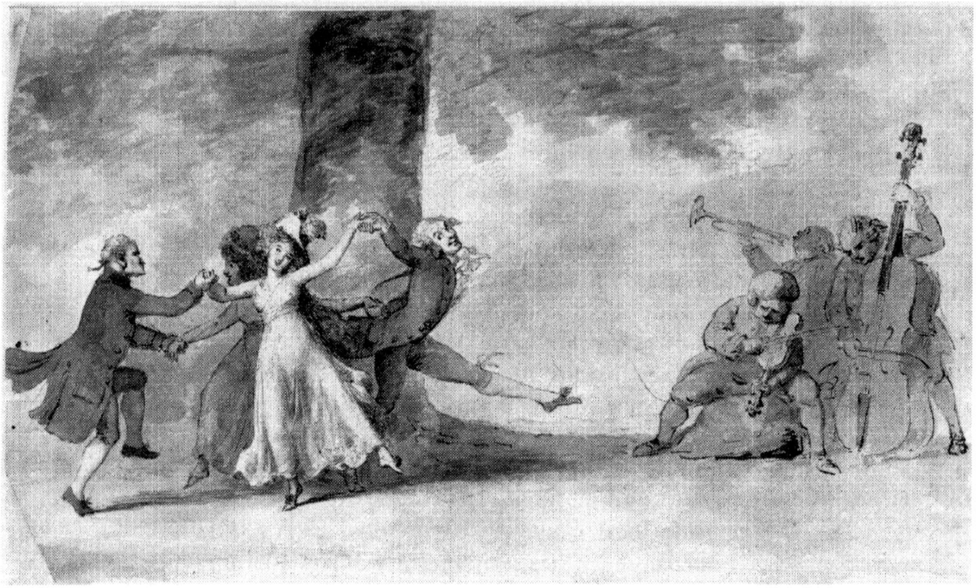

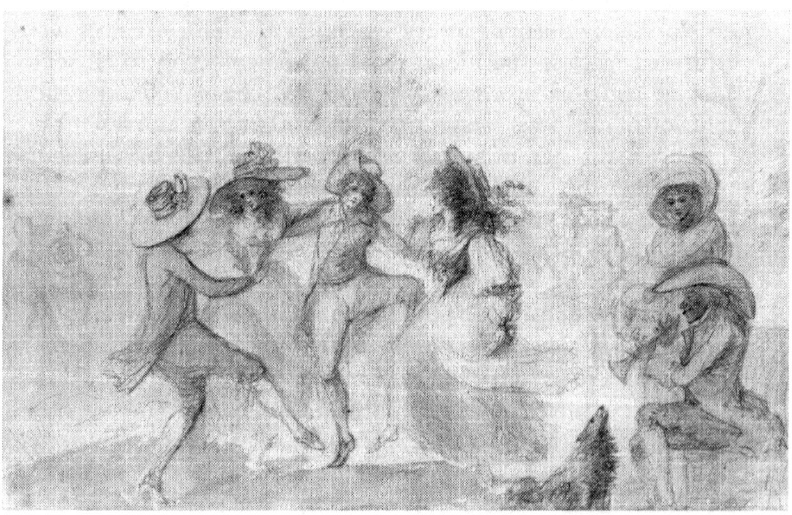

33 Henry William Bunbury (1750–1811), *Ladies and Gentlemen Dancing*, watercolor, 35.4 × 58.7 cm.; Toledo, OH, Toledo Museum of Art

French *fête champêtre*, albeit anachronistically. Third, they have an audience. All present, except perhaps for the musicians, are from the upper classes. Those looking on, far in the background and off to the side, are themselves almost like shadows, de-emphasized to benefit the two couples at the frontmost picture plane. But they clearly look on, all of them at full attention, and from the positions of their heads, especially those of the women, there is a scent of melancholic nostalgia in the air.

At this point the two images sharply diverge. For in the first what is celebrated is the momentary – and fictional – freedom of a frolic outside the bounds of the assembly rooms, a semi-private revel. But in the second the image is troubling, as nostalgia always is, in its utterly false reconstruction of history, an aristocratic Arcadia: Bunbury gives us the gardens of Versailles in England, in effect, a reality that never was. Memory as lie; memory coping with a (deteriorating?) present.[32] The remainder of my comments on country dancing will consider this issue.

DANCE AND THE DIALECTIC OF ENLIGHTENMENT

At this juncture I want to consider more directly the relations between dancing's physicality and social order, as constructed around a paradigm of rationality versus irrationality. In *The Tatler* Addison wrote a comic letter describing supposed events occurring next door to his rooming house. He told of how he was awakened by a sudden shake of his building several times repeated, followed by his landlady coming to him for help. Her nextdoor neighbor had let rooms to a youngish, genteel man a few days earlier but now feared that the man was mad. Addison approached the man's door, rapier at the ready, and looked through the key-hole:

> there I saw a well-made man look with great attention on a book, and on a sudden, jump into the air so high, that his head almost touched the ceiling. He came down safe on his right foot, and again flew up, alighting on his left; then looked again at his book, and holding out his right leg, put it into such a quivering motion, that I thought he would have shaken it off . . .
>
> After this, he recovered himself with a sudden spring, and flew round the room in all the violence and disorder imaginable, till he made a full pause for want of breath.[33]

The man turned out to be a dance-master. After conversing with him a while Addison returned to his own quarters, so the story ends, "meditating on the various occupations of rational creatures."

To be sure, the letter is focused on the comic, yet the particular way Addison structured the story brings to account metaphors that represent order and disorder on a socio-cultural level. The dancer's gyrations are hyperbolically described, the effect of which is to make the man appear possessed (upon entering the dancer's room Addison is surprised to find him cogent, which he attributes to the dancer's being in a mere "lucid interval"). In other words, the dancer's extreme physicality stands in as a metaphor for irrational behavior. Further, his movements shake not only his own dwelling but also Addison's next door. Now clearly this is a literal impossibility, which the reader understands, thus shifting Addison's story into metaphorical gear: the man's actions have import beyond himself; the effects of his actions are played out in the community. The order of both the immediate community (the dancer's own building) and a surrounding one (Addison's) is disturbed. The nature of the disruption is described in terms of extreme physicality, more animal-like than human (and threatening: "I got up as fast as possible, girt on my rapier"). In closing, Addison underlined this comparison by reference to rationality and its absence. What was given in *The Tatler* as entertainment was at heart, like all satire, serious, the concerns revolving around national identity and, above all, social order.

In the first-act aria "Se vuol ballare" from Mozart's *Le Nozze di Figaro*, Figaro (a servant) expresses anger over his master the Count's designs on Susanna, to whom Figaro is engaged. Figaro pledges revenge. But as far as the text is concerned, he does so only comically, in an apparent contest of wits pretty much literary standard fare in servant–master relationships. What Figaro *says* is that if the Count wants to cut capers, Figaro will call the tune. What underscores the socio-political sentiment of these words is Mozart's music, specifically his use of two opposing metric patterns associated with dance: what is absent, or at least highly sublimated, textually, is present musically.

The "dance" to which Figaro "invites" the Count begins with a 3/4–time minuet: courtly, aristocratic. However, Mozart soon ruptures the conventional stateliness of the dance by surprising off-beat rhythmic punctuations that would cause chaos on the dance floor (all this is in an aria, not an actual dance). First he mocks the minuet, then he simply replaces it. Halfway through the aria Mozart abruptly changes both tempo and meter, as Figaro becomes more assertive, moving to an aggressive 2/4 presto *contredanse*. Now Mozart's combination of minuet–*contredanse* echoes the common practice of beginning a ball with a single minuet to be followed immediately by country dances, but with an essential difference. In *Figaro* the minuet is not simply succeeded but interrupted, overthrown. The change is sudden, unexpected. It is a musical revolution carried out beneath a tame, unthreatening text. The musical order heralds a new social order, all of librettist Da Ponte's efforts to neutralize Beaumarchais' original highly political play notwithstanding.[34] In Mozart and in Addison alike (from one end of the century to the other), dance is implicitly understood as an expression of order/

competing order, stability/instability. As the people dance, so to speak, so goes the nation.

In all their popularity, country dances, whether English or French-inspired, demanded the imposition of mechanisms to control their meaning in ways that supported the socio-cultural ideologies of the upper classes. This was notably achieved in contemporaneous dance treatises which consistently atttempted to preserve in all social dancing the aristocratic air of the minuet via the careful articulation of body carriage and gesture. Kellom Tomlinson in his *The Art of Dancing* (1735, though written in 1724) thus provided minute directions to achieve proper standing, walking and bowing (eleven pages to the last) – all prior to one's setting foot on a dance floor; and he described the body, part by intricate part, as regards the function of each in dancing, from the nose (which "points out the graceful Twists or Turns the Head makes") down to the joints of the toes.[35] Pierre Rameau's treatise devoted nearly fifty pages to the proper movements of the arms and wrists in various dances, and likewise provided an acutely detailed account of the proper manner to doff one's hat, replete with engraved illustration.[36] Only men of leisure could hope to have sufficient time available to learn such skills of self-definition as given in John Essex's amended 1710 English translation of a famous treatise by Raoul Auger Feuillet, where no less than six pages of notational signs were required to account for the requisite hand gestures and foot movements proper to social dancing.[37] Ironically, the precision of decorum demanded by these treatises could hardly be maintained in a country dance, but this in fact undoubtedly only heightened concern therewith. In any event, there can be no question that dance and dance gesture, as well as body carriage not strictly part of but appropriate to the dance (standing, etc.), were self-consciously perceived as a principal means of establishing a class hierarchy of the human body. As Giovanni-Andrea Gallini, one of the most famous dance-masters of his time, put it:

> When once an habit of easy dignity, with an unaffected air of portliness, has been sufficiently familiarised, it will constantly shew itself in every even the most indifferent gesture or action of the possessor . . . Does he come into a room? His air immediately strikes the company in his favor, and gives a prepossessing idea to his advantage.

Gallini was specific as to what he meant by contrast to this portrait, as when he described a young woman lacking in all such skills. Failing to execute a correct "curtesy," she "hangs her head, and makes her obeisance with her eyes fixed on the ground, or pokes out her head, sticking back her arms, *like one of the figures in Hogarth's dance* [my italics]." In a word, such a lady gave the appearance of an urban peasant.[38]

It is significant that Gallini would refer to a printed image by which to make his point. He did so precisely because the memorable/memory image is what his prescribed gestures were intended to create, the failure to do so threatening instead to result in a grotesquerie from the Hogarthian pantheon. It is important to point out that the convention of gesture as outlined for the social dancing carried over into imagery, in particular – for my concerns – to portraiture, by which the same class-specific, class-defining meanings were commonly achieved by artists and described by artist-theoreticians.[39]

John Weaver in his *Anatomical and Mechanical Lectures upon Dancing* (1721) explicitly outlined the class distinctions delineated by body carriage and physical motion. In his politics of motion, the upper classes moved with seamless smoothness, at once natural(ized) and ordered. The lower classes by contrast moved haltingly, without grace. Without question Weaver's paradigm is true as regards a peasant's execution of the minuet, but it is patently false with respect to the rhythms laboring people establish in the routines of their work. Conversely, persons unused to working with their hands immediately display clumsiness when required to take up an unfamiliar tool. This says something quite obvious: as long as one group defines the rules (in this case, ones outlining the means by which bodily grace is measured) only they can win the game:

> From the Regular or Irregular Position, and Motion of the Body, we distinguish the handsome Presence, and Deportment of the fine Gentleman, from the awkward Behaviour of the unpolish'd Peasant; we discover the graceful Mien of a young Lady, from the ungainly Carriage of her Maid; and this Regulation even stamps Impressions on the Mind, which we receive from the outward Figure of the Body; for as the Soul is inform'd from the external Objects of Sensation, how careful ought we to be, to give the most agreeable Impressions, which cannot be affected without this Regularity; and how commendable, how advantageous is it, for a Gentleman, or Lady, to be *Adroit* at every Step, and, that every Motion, and Action of the Body, be consonant to Symmetry and Grace.[40]

It is tempting to explain these gestural intricacies to French influences of the early eighteenth century and to the minuet in particular: all very unEnglish. But such an explanation fails when we examine a book by Thomas Wilson on English country dancing published at the end of my period in 1820. What is striking about this treatise is evident in its title, *The Complete System of English Country Dancing*. That is, country dancing was here *rationalized.* What this text established was an order, a scheme of classification, one presuming its opposite, disorder. What I suggest here is not a false accusation; to be sure, from Playford onwards country dances were passed on through instructions, either verbally or with choreographic notation – but in Playford, as in dance fans, these instructions were normally very cursory. By contrast, what

Weaver had in mind was something very different. He opened his lengthy book (over 300 pages) with the following:

> A COUNTRY DANCE, As it is named, is almost universally known as the national Dance of the English, and as correctly known, is constructed on mathematical and other scientific principles, clearly displayed in its operative effect, when properly and well performed.[41]

Wilson thus established at the outset two significant premises: first, that country dances were national in character, and second (in fact as corollary to the first) that they were constituted on rational grounds ("mathematical and other scientific principles"). That is to say that country dances were quintessentially English precisely because they were highly rationalized. I am suggesting that by the early years of the nineteenth century in England the *contredanse*, represented in Mozart as revolutionary, had been completely subsumed by the dominant culture (though to be sure that was a culture reformulating itself within boundaries that now also encompassed the wealthy sectors of the middle class).

Toward the end of the book Wilson appended a previously published chapter on ballroom etiquette as it related particularly to country dances, and to more recently introduced species such as quadrilles and waltzes. With respect to country dancing, Wilson outlined a code of behavior dependent on (self-)policing, all in an effort to control spontaneity:

> No person during a Country Dance, should hiss, clap, or make any other noise, to interrupt the good order of the company.
>
> No Lady or Gentleman must, during a Country Dance, attempt at Reels, or any other Figures, in the same room.
>
> Snapping the fingers, in Country Dancing and Reels, and the sudden howl or yell too frequently practised, ought particularly to be avoided, as partaking too much of the customs of barbarous nations [in part he makes reference here to the Scots, whom the English essentially considered ungovernable].[42]

And if disputes arose they must be referred to the Master of Ceremonies "and his decision abided by." The Master of Ceremonies, playing the twin role of king and chief justice, was himself to wear a sash "or some conspicuous ensignia" to distinguish him from the rest. And in this metaphorical nation, whose citizens ideally moved only to prescribed order, there was even to be a written constitution: "To preserve greater order, and to prevent disputes, it is advisable, that the proprietors, or the conductors of Public Balls and Assemblies, should have the foregoing Etiquette, particularly so much of it as relates to the company, written and hung up in some conspicuous part of the room, during such evenings as the Balls or Assemblies may be held."[43] The resemblance to the systematized behavior at Versailles under the Sun King is not difficult to recognize.

104 **MUSIC AND IMAGE**

DANCE AND THE METAPHOR OF FAMILY HIERARCHY

The rage for dancing of all kinds, especially among the young, caused other sorts of social disruptions, the most interesting of which were familial, since the family was considered the hull to society's ship. Essentially dancing raised questions about every possible combination of intra-familial relationship, that is, between spouses, and between parents and their children of both genders. The characters in Hannah More's novella, "The two wealthy farmers; or, the history of Mr. Bragwell," provided a parable formulization of these concerns. The rich Bragwells, including their two dreadful daughters, are *au courant*, frivolous, arrogant and selfish. Hannah More opposed them with a family headed by Mr. Worthy, alike in numbers and wealth, but different in every other way. Daughter Betsey Bragwell showed her true colors at a dance, at the expense of her foil, the young, good, basically simple Mr. Wilson who made the mistake of asking to be her partner. As the elder Bragwell related:

> But when he asked what dance they should call, miss drew up her head, and in a strange gibberish [French], said she should dance nothing but a *Minuet de la Cour*, and ordered him to call it. Wilson stared, and honestly told her she must call it herself; for he could neither spell nor pronounce such outlandish words, nor assist in such an outlandish performance . . . Seeing her partner standing stock still, and not knowing how to get out of the scrape, the girl began by herself, and fell to swimming, and sinking, and capering, and flourishing, and posturing, for all the world just like the man on the slack rope at our fair. But seeing Wilson standing like a stuck pig, and we all laughing at her, she resolved to wreak her malice upon him; so, with a look of rage and distain, she advised him to go down country bumpkin, with a dairy maid, who would make a much fitter partner, as well as wife, for him, than she would do.[44]

In this story, told by a woman, several violations of social order ensue as a direct result of the allowance of a French minuet. Betsey Bragwell herself is displayed as a foreigner whose language the natives do not speak. As such, and because of her behavior throughout, she dishonors her father by making herself an object of ridicule to the entire assembly. Bragwell *père* has squandered money on her, given the results attained, and degraded himself into the bargain. By contrast, Mr. Wilson, the good Englishman, whose simplicity and natural unaffected goodness registers against Betsey's artificiality, is rendered impotent by Betsey's outburst. Unable to lead her in the dance, he is left to stand helplessly (or, more appropriate no doubt, slump) on the sidelines, a "stuck pig": metaphorically bleeding – and by the hand of a woman. Betsey meanwhile further violates convention by dancing alone. She becomes instantly androgynous by this act, for she subsumes the role of her male partner together with her own. Her gestures on the floor are whorelike; they also break class rank, being likened to those of a circus performer. By attempting to assert power over a man she considers stupid and beneath her she destroys herself unawares. Her final insult to Wilson, telling him to go marry a dairy maid, constitutes the last straw. Indeed, a similar challenge laid at Wilson's feet by another male would have required public retraction or retribution. Betsey Bragwell expresses an uncontrolled individuality (totally out of keeping with the ideology informing Wilson's dance treatise), particularly unacceptable on account of her gender. Her violations of social order cannot be tolerated; hence the audience derides her through laughter.

THE WALTZ AND THE BOURGEOIS ORDER

The country dance, supplanting the minuet, triumphed through most of the century, though its socio-cultural meaning (less so its form) evolved in the direction of an increasingly rationalized conservatism. But near the century's end country dances themselves gave way to a new dance, the waltz, the ascendancy of which defined the advance of a new social order, the emergent bourgeoisie, that would come fully into its own in the nineteenth century. Edward Francis Burney, c. 1800, illustrated this new dance in a way that perfectly captured the profound social changes it both engendered and mirrored (Fig. 34).[45]

In one sense his image is bitterly nostalgic, for what it recalls by a

34 Edward Francis Burney (1760–1848), *The Waltz* (c. 1800), watercolor drawing, 47.5 × 68.6 cm.; London, Victoria and Albert Museum. By courtesy of the Board of Trustees

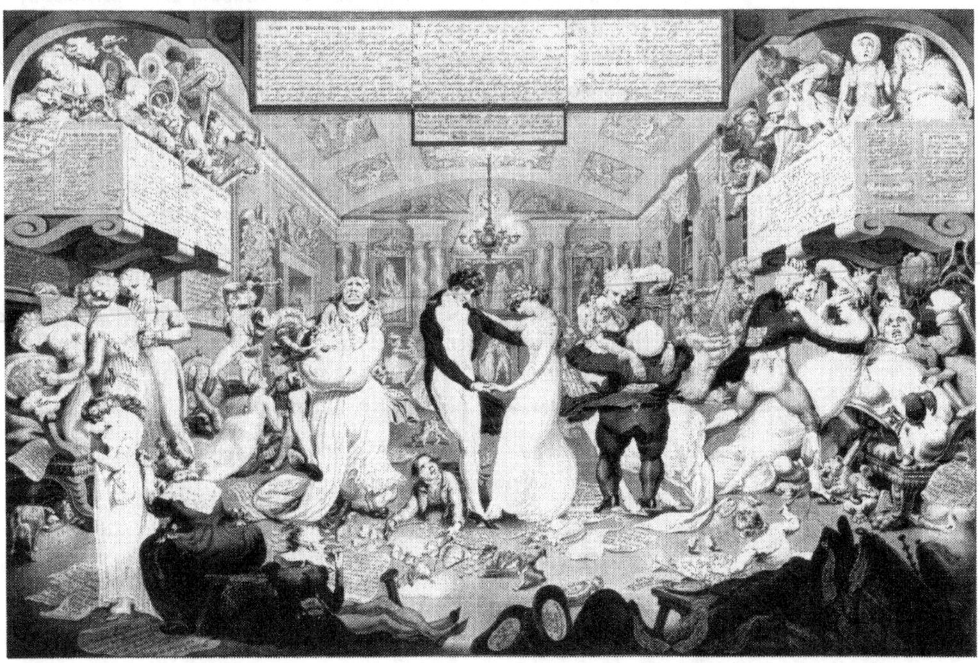

present absence is the social-dance world of the century just past, the assembly hall of Bath's Beau Nash where decorum itself was fetishized. The floor rules for Burney's gathering, like those at Bath and in Thomas Wilson's aforementioned book, are also written out in elaborate detail (at the top center), sixteen in all, appropriately signed by "Solomon Wiseman." But each is silly, a mockery of former rules which a man at the extreme left in the background is destroying with a stick. The dancing that Burney illustrates is either ridiculous or vulgar; it degrades the upper-class people performing it – and scandalizes the morally superior lower-class witnesses standing in the balcony at the right (one lower-class mother forcibly carries her daughter away from the temptations she watches). In a related vignette a sheet affixed to this same balcony draws attention to a missing dog, in fact described as a woman: "STRAYED, A Grown Pug Bitch, answered to the name of Dreary, was missing after the WALTZ was danced last Assembly night. Anyone bringing her [here the sheet is 'torn' by Burney] good . . . no questions will be asked." At the back of the room, unobserved, hang royal portraits, including one of Elizabeth I looking on in all her stateliness; the glorious past they represent is forgotten. Just above these portraits, hence just above the dominant couple at the center of the image, is the Latin reminder of vanity: *Sic transit gloria mundi*, pointedly flanking both sides of a ticking clock.

But it is the central couple that is most important, for they are marked by Burney as the hub and key to the entire assembly. They are characters in a state of languorous collapse, self-contained, not social (no longways dance here), their twin shapes forming a sort of circle. The woman is represented well within the traditions I have elsewhere described, as a passive but most willing inducement to sex and hence the ruination of a man. The man, on whom Burney concentrates his most pointed satire, is physically womanized in every way imaginable: his hair in its abundance, gloss and curl; his body in shape, especially his hips which are distinctly female; his feet in their daintiness; and his face in its utter androgyny. This is a world come apart, the reasons for which are not of course the result of dancing but which, in Burney's hyperbolic representation, are nevertheless perfectly reflected therein and replicated thereby. It is for him a new world wholly negative, and an adjustment of the social order that will permit no happy return.

5 MUSIC AND THE BODY: DANCE, POWER, SUBMISSION

1 Essex, *Young Ladies Conduct*, pp. 82–3. Though addressed to females his remarks are actually more typical of those intended for males.

2 John Playford, *The English Dancing Master: or, Plaine and Easie Rules for the Dancing of Country Dances* (1651; reprint. ed. London, 1933), ed. Hugh Mellor and Leslie Bridgewater, p. [i]. For information about the publishing history and contents of later editions, see "England," *New Grove*, vol. 6, pp. 188–9.

3 I. H. Æ., *The Mirrour of Worldly Fame* (London, 1603), reprinted in *Harleian Miscellany*, vol. 2, p. 525.

4 Eccles, *Musick-Lector*, p. 14.

5 Bennett, *Letters to a Young Lady*, vol. 1, pp. 235–6.

6 In this regard see George, *Catalogue of Satires*, vol. 7, pp. 508–9, no. 9299, a print entitled "Ecclesiastical Scrutiny – or the Durham Inquest on Duty" (1798) reflecting contemporaneous debates about women, dress and morals, with reference to dance thrown in.

7 Locke, *Some Thoughts Concerning Education*, pp. 190–1.

8 John Weaver, *An Essay towards an History of Dancing* (London, 1712), pp. 6, 25, respectively; see further to p. 27. This text constituted "the first apology for dancing *per se* in English," according to Richard Ralph, *The Life and Works of John Weaver: An Account of his Life, Writings and Theatrical Productions, with an Annotated Reprint of his Complete Publications* (New York, 1985), p. 101. On the *Essay towards an History of Dancing* see pp. 115–43.

9 Stanhope, *Letters to his Son*, vol. 1, pp. 114–15 (letter no. 51, dated 20 September O.S. 1748).

10 Gardiner, *English Girlhood at School*, p. 248. For example, on the wealth of the famous master Giovanni-Andrea Gallini – and of his parsimony – see Henry Angelo, *Reminiscences of Henry Angelo* (London, 1828–30), vol. 2, pp. 38–40.

11 Richard Flecknoe, *Enigmaticall Characters, All Taken to the Life, from Severall Persons, Humours and Dispositions* ([London,] 1658), p. 59.

12 Thomas D'Urfey, *Love for Money, or the Boarding School* (London, 1691).
13 Dibdin, *Musical Tour*, p. 309, from letter no. 75.
14 Austen, *Emma*, Chapter 29, p. 253.
15 *The Spectator*, ed. Donald F. Bond, 5 vols. (Oxford, 1965), vol. 1, pp. 282–3 (issue no. 66, 16 May 1711).
16 Sophie von la Roche, *Sophie in London, 1786: Being the Diary of Sophie v. la Roche*, trans. Clare Williams (London, 1933), pp. 247–50; the quotation is from pp. 249–50.
17 *Gentleman's Magazine*, 6 (1736), pp. 131–2 (the letter was reprinted from *Universal Spectator*, 6 March 1736, issue no. 387).
18 Thomas Gordon, *The Humorist: Being Essays upon Several Subjects*, 3rd ed. (London, 1724), pp. 23–4.
19 For more on the two Vestris, see George, *Catalogue of Satires*, vol. 5, pp. 532–3, no. 5903, a print by Paul Sandby, "Bass Relief Found at the Opera House" (1781).
20 Edward Ravenscroft, *The Citizen Turn'd Gentleman* (London, 1670?), Act I.
21 See further Frederic G. Stephens and Edward Hawkins, *Catalogue of Prints and Drawings in the British Museum. Division I. Political and Personal Satires* (London, 1883), vol. 4, pp. 493–4, no. 4250 (1768). The advertisements placed by dance teachers typically stressed four complementary features: ease of learning (a fabrication), the latest dances (always a necessity), teaching in the studio or in the client's home and, as a corollary to the last, privacy of instruction (to avoid public embarrassment or acknowledgment that one did not already know how to dance). The ads were common in both London and provincial papers. One example will suffice, from *The Public Advertiser* (London) (issue no. 4168, 8 August 1752, p. 2), an ad placed by N. Dukes, Dancing-Master: "Grown Gentlemen or Ladies may be taught . . . in so private, genteel and expeditious a Manner, as to render them very soon capable of performing in any polite Company or Assembly whatever. And on Monday and Wednesday Evenings there's a compleat Set of Gentlemen only, which assembles for the learning and practicing of Country Dances."
22 See further Stephens and Hawkins, *Catalogue of Satires*, vol. 4, p. 494, nos. 4251, 4252 (1768).
23 This arrangement is preserved in an engraved image in a treatise by Pierre Rameau, *The Dancing-Master: or, The Art of Dancing Explained*, trans. J. Essex (London, 1728), opposite p. 30, an oversized foldout. The extraordinarily precise regimen of the Versailles ceremonial, especially that following the King's retirement to watch each couple present themselves to him in turn, is described on pp. 28–30.
24 See Curt Sachs, *World History of the Dance*, trans. Bessie Schönberg (New York, 1937), p. 398. See also pp. 397–402 for additional information on the minuet upon which some of my comments are based, and also "Minuet," *New Grove*, vol. 12, pp. 353–4; and Frances Rust, *Dance in Society: An Analysis of the Relationship between the Social Dance and Society in England from the Middle Ages to the Present Day* (London, 1969), pp. 59–62.
25 See also the description given in George, *Catalogue of Satires*, vol. 6, pp. 444–5, no. 7229, including an explanation of the parodic citation from Horace. The original drawing upon which the print was based is in the Paul Mellon Collection, Yale Center for British Art, New Haven, no. B1975.4.1894.
26 Sachs, *World History of Dance*, p. 420.
27 See further ibid., pp. 423–5. For a comic print (1771) illustrating this dance, see *New Grove*, vol. 4, p. 829.
28 "Contredanse," *New Grove*, vol. 4, p. 704.
29 Rust, *Dance in Society*, p. 59.
30 Sachs, *World History of Dance*, p. 398.
31 Rust, *Dance in Society*, p. 58. For comments on the continuation of this practice in the eighteenth century in country houses, see p. 61.

32 See further Richard Leppert, *Arcadia at Versailles: Noble Amateur Musicians and their Musettes and Hurdy-Gurdies at the French Court (c. 1660–1789)* (Amsterdam and Lisse, 1978).

33 *The Tatler*, ed. George A. Aitken, 4 vols. (New York and London, 1899), vol. 2, pp. 273–6; the quotation is from p. 274 (issue no. 88, 1 November 1709).

34 The analysis of "*Se vuol ballare*" is in part from Wye J. Allanbrook, "Metric gesture as a topic in *Le Nozze di Figaro* and *Don Giovanni*," *Musical Quarterly*, 67 (1981), pp. 106–7; and Wye J. Allanbrook, *Rhythmic Gesture in Mozart: "Le Nozze di Figaro" and "Don Giovanni"* (Chicago and London, 1983), pp. 79–82; see also Frits Noske, "Social tensions in *Le Nozze di Figaro*," *Music and Letters*, 50 (1969), pp. 45–62.

35 Kellom Tomlinson, *The Art of Dancing Explained by Reading and Figures* (London, 1735), p. 22.

36 Rameau, *Dancing-Master*, pp. 14–15, 113–50.

37 Raoul Auger Feuillet, *For the Further Improvement of Dancing*, trans. John Essex (London, 1710), pp. 7–12.

38 Giovanni-Andrea Gallini, *Critical Observations on the Art of Dancing; to Which is Added, a Collection of Cotillons or French Dances* (London, n.d.), pp. 126, 128–9.

39 Thus see Thomas Page, *The Art of Painting in its Rudiments, Progress, and Perfection* (Norwich, 1720), passim. See also Alastair Smart, "Dramatic gesture and expression in the age of Hogarth and Reynolds," *Apollo*, 82 (1965), pp. 90–7, especially pp. 94–5; and D'Oench, *Conversation Piece*, pp. 15–18.

40 John Weaver, *Anatomical and Mechanical Lectures upon Dancing* (London, 1721), pp. viii-ix. I first came upon this passage through the dissertation by Shirley Spackman Wynne, "The charms of complaisance: the dance in England in the early eighteenth century (Ohio State Univ., 1967), p. 126.

41 Thomas Wilson, *The Complete System of English Country Dancing, Containing All the Figures Ever Used in English Country Dancing, with a Variety of New Figures and New Reels . . . Elucidated by Means of Diagrams* (London, 1820), p. 1.

42 Ibid., p. 267.

43 Ibid., pp. 268–9. In a footnote Wilson added that if the printed etiquette were put on public view, the pronouncements of the Master of Ceremonies would stand less chance of being disputed "and his authority consequently treated with contempt." On the maintenance of decorum see also Walter Besant, *London Life in the Eighteenth Century* (London and New York, 1903), p. 404. Weaver may have had "Beau" Nash, Master of Ceremonies at the Bath assemblies from c. 1703 until his death in 1761, as a model for his own ajudicator. As Goldsmith described, Nash was famous for maintaining ritual-like order at the proceedings. See Oliver Goldsmith, *The Life of "Beau" Nash* (1762; reprint. ed. San Francisco, n.d.), pp. 22–31, but especially pp. 28–9, "Rules to be observed at Bath," according to Goldsmith written by Nash himself. The rules were posted in the Pump Room and rigidly observed.

44 Hannah More, "Rural tales. The two wealthy farmers; or the history of Mr. Bragwell," *Village and Other Tales* (New York, 1851), pp. 43–5; the story was originally published by 1795.

45 The Yale Center for British Art, Paul Mellon Collection, New Haven, CT, possesses a sketch (B1975.4.1045) and a preparatory drawing (B1975.4.1046) for this print. In characteristic Burney fashion, the image is so overladen with bits of text and separate vignettes that a separate study would be required to piece them together. My interests do not justify attempting that here.

Part Four

Utopia

CHAPTER 12

Nature and Exile: Adorno, Mahler and the Appropriation of Kitsch

In *Minima Moralia,* Adorno's exile monograph subtitled *Reflections from Damaged Life,* written in California between 1944 and 1947, the German Jew emigré confronted the vast American interior (profoundly different from anything he knew in Europe) in a single, aphoristic paragraph—which, not coincidentally, he titled *"Paysage"*, not the worst clue to the foreignness of what filled his visible horizon on what must have seemed like a very long drive from New York to the Pacific in 1941. Famous (or perhaps infamous) for paragraphs that commonly stretch pages on end, Adorno's account of the American landscape merits only a couple of dozen lines—and this from a man who was as sensitive to nature as Mahler, a composer whose works Adorno admired in large part for what he perceived as their aesthetic confrontation with humankind's fractured relation to nature, precisely the point of his landscape paragraph.

Adorno's account begins about as one might expect of a European intellectual: "The shortcoming of the American landscape", he wrote, "is not so much, as romantic illusion would have it, the absence of historical memories, as that it bears no traces of the human hand. This applies not only to the lack of arable land, the uncultivated woods often no higher than scrub, but above all to the roads" (Adorno 1978:48). And here, for Adorno, the road turns, and in a direction that sheds light on the more general, and indeed important, part of the exile experience.

Adorno is not in the least put off by the seeming—and undoubtedly strange—emptiness of the American interior, but by what he perceives as the way that its human inhabitants relate to it, namely, with a degree of indifference that shocks him. It's the roads. "These", he says, "are always inserted directly in the landscape, and the more impressively smooth and broad they are, the more unrelated and violent their gleaming track appears against its wild, overgrown surroundings".

Adorno is almost certainly reacting to the transcontinental highways that systematically parallel the railroad tracks across the Great Plains. These roads, he laments, are "expressionless. Just as they know no marks of foot or wheel, no soft paths along their edges as a transition to the vegetation, no trails leading off into the valley, so they are without the mild, soothing, un-angular quality of things that have felt the touch of hands or their immediate implements". Adorno then provides a striking metaphor of the unreconciled separation of subject from object, of man from nature, his most persistent encapsulation of dystopian modernity: "It is, he says, "as if no-one had ever passed their hand over the landscape's hair. It is uncomforted and comfortless" (Adorno 1978:48).[1]

Adorno's work is tightly focused on the history of Western modernity from its ascendancy in the late eighteenth century to its end phase in the aftermath of World War II and the Cold War. His social and sociological concerns were principally defined by the history and impact of the bourgeoisie, from the class's dramatic emergence in the early decades of the nineteenth century and its foundation in economic and cultural capitalism, to its saturation and colonization of the subject and subjectivity during and after the same period. Adorno saw modernity as a period of more or less permanent crisis as regards the deeply ironic relation between, on the one hand, the general possibility for human happiness and emancipation as a result of the highest ideals of the Enlightenment and the technological advancements beginning with the Industrial Revolution, and, on the other, the actual general failure to realize either. Adorno saw modernity as a long history of lost opportunity in the face of myriad catastrophes. In the late essay "Why Still Philosophy" (1962), he summarized the urgency that stubbornly drove his practice in the face of this reality: "Philosophy", he said, "must come to know, without any mitigation, why the world—which could be paradise here and now—can become hell itself tomorrow. Such knowledge would indeed truly be philosophy" (Adorno 1998b:14).[2]

Adorno's experience as an "exile in paradise" (a phrase in play among the German émigrés at the time) suggested what would follow the defeat of fascism: a world increasingly dominated by technologically accomplished forms of mass culture first and foremost organized by the principles and functions of entertainment and advertising. As he saw things, happiness and emancipation would devolve to little more than publicity slogans and, of course, advertising's near cousin, political propaganda.

Minima Moralia consists of 153 numbered fragments (shattered writing about shattered history), aphoristic in design, many not more than a single brief paragraph, and none more than a few pages in length. *Minima Moralia* is a book of memory and experience—not by accident is the first aphorism entitled "For Marcel Proust" (Adorno 1978:21).[3] *Minima Moralia* reflects life as

[1] The aphorism concludes: "And it [the landscape] is perceived in a corresponding way. For what the hurrying eye has seen merely from the car it cannot retain, and the vanishing landscape leaves no more traces behind than it bears upon itself."

[2] Cf. the opening of *Negative Dialectics* (Adorno 1983:3): "Philosophy, which once seemed obsolete, lives on because the moment to realize it was missed".

[3] Cf. p. 166, the aphorism "All the little flowers", in which Proust is invoked again: "Just as no earlier experience is real that has not been loosed by involuntary remembrance from the deathly fixity of its isolated experience, so conversely, no memory is guaranteed, existent in itself, indifferent to the future of him who harbours it; nothing past is proof, though its translation into mere imagination, against the curse of the empirical present". The deep history embedded in language use may return to haunt, pp. 110–11: "One evening, in a mood of helpless sadness, I

damaged, its condition articulated through the traces of a European culture left behind, a fractured totality whose long history can only appropriately be recapitulated by a writing process which itself preserves the abiding sense of radical disruption and loss. *Minima Moralia* is a scathing critique of modernity whose fragmented structure abandons historicism's linearity in favor of a list, a kind of empirical anti-empiricist grab bag of cultural detritus, which Adorno variously treasures and abhors: from Goethe and Hegel, to cookie-cutter bungalows and refrigerators; from Mozart and Beethoven, to rudeness and insincere friendliness, early signs of things we take for granted, and in stride: discount store greeters, and "Have a nice day". (As any reader of *Dialectic of Enlightenment* knows, this text, written in the looming shadow of Hollywood, is permeated by the presence of kitsch culture—and not only the book's best-known chapter on "The Culture Industry".) And not coincidentally, in *Minima Moralia*, Goethe and Beethoven are subjected to as rigorous a dialectical critique as the various manifestations of cultural kitsch and mundane insincerity. Thereby, Adorno acknowledges his considerable debt to his friend Walter Benjamin, who insisted that cultural treasures are to be viewed by the historical materialist "with cautious detachment", their origin not to be contemplated "without horror"; as Benjamin famously put it, "There is no document of civilization which is not at the same time a document of barbarism" (Benjamin 1969:256). Nothing brought Benjamin's insight more directly to Adorno than his American exile. And therein his own crisis, founded on the insight that the present catastrophe reached well beyond the criminality of a few European heads of state.

Throughout his life's work Adorno pursued Benjamin's insight framed by the question of suffering in specific relation to modernity, and to the shared social responsibility of both philosophy and aesthetics. Above all, "it is the sufferings of men that should be shared", Adorno wrote in *Minima Moralia* (Adorno 1978:26), a responsibility, not coincidentally, that constituted for him a principal function of art, as he later pointed out by way of a rhetorical query: "But then what would art be, as the writing of history, if it shook off the memory of accumulated suffering" (Adorno 1997:261). (This is the last sentence in Adorno's last, and unfinished, major work, *Aesthetic Theory*.) Nearly a quarter century ago, Harvey Gross, assessing *Minima Moralia*—and its author's exile—referred to what he named Adorno's "unremitting moral intelligence mediated through a subdued, sometimes almost inaudible 'form of hope'"; Gross suggested that what was revealed in Adorno's writing above all was "the

caught myself using a ridiculously wrong subjunctive form of a verb that was itself not entirely correct German, being part of the dialect of my native town. I had not heard, let alone used, the endearing mis-construction since my first years at school. Melancholy, drawing me irresistibly into the abyss of childhood, awakened this old, impotently yearning sound in its depths. Language sent back to me like an echo the humiliation which unhappiness had inflicted on me in forgetting what I am."

perplexed clarity of a mind struggling in uncertainty" (Gross 1979: 348)—precisely, that is, the one certainty marked by the condition of exile.

Adorno regarded art as the repository for the faint semblance of a social happiness otherwise unavailable, at the same time he insisted that art could not provide what society denied. Among all the arts, music for Adorno was the most important; indeed nearly one third of his massive written corpus concerns music, his interest in which was almost entirely confined to the Western music of the previous 150 years—that is, the music of modernity. And like modernity itself, modern music, in Adorno's regard, was in a state of crisis, concerning which I'll focus my remarks on a single manifestation: kitsch—which, perhaps surprisingly, interested him a great deal—and its reappropriation by Mahler.

Clement Greenberg, in his famous essay "Avant-Garde and Kitsch", first published in 1939, provided the classic account of the relationship between the terms invoked in his title, much of which resonates with Adorno's own position. Both understood kitsch as commercial, mass-produced, formulaic, standardized, and aesthetically and politically rear-guard ersatz culture, which feeds off genuine culture but only for the purpose of enjoying the profits that might accrue from the recognition and/or patina of prestige and comfort that such culture might provide—of enjoying what Greenberg called "vicarious experience and faked sensations". Kitsch, as he put it, "pretends to demand nothing of its customers except their money—not even their time" (Greenberg 1957:102).[4]

On the whole, Adorno's account is notably more interesting and, not least, more nuanced than Greenberg's, despite the similarities of their positions. For starters, Adorno insisted that kitsch and art share common ground—too much so for comfort. Both "escape" reality: art through its autonomy, kitsch through the reification that attends commodity fetishization. Both are permeated with history, but whereas art seeks to invoke history, specifically to engage it, the history to which kitsch responds is one that kitsch either erases or, more likely, seeks to make palatable. Further, as Adorno suggests in *Minima Moralia*, both

[4] See Jachec 1998, which considers each man's aesthetic theory in relation to political liberalism. See also Huyssen 1986:55–58, for a discussion and comparison of Adorno and Greenberg on mass culture. Adorno himself refers to Greenberg's essay (Adorno 1985:10).

In another aphoristic essay, "Is Art Lighthearted?" (Adorno 1992b:249, Adorno attempted to define kitsch, again by comparing it to what he regarded as the authentic art work: "Though attempts to define kitsch usually fail, still not the worst definition would be one that made the criterion of kitsch whether an art product gives form to consciousness of contradiction—even if it does so by stressing its opposition to reality—or dissembles it. In this respect seriousness should be demanded of any work of art. As something that has escaped from reality and is nevertheless permeated with it, art vibrates between this seriousness and lightheartedness. It is this tension that constitutes art."

kitsch and the art work celebrate "freedom from nature". That is, art and kitsch alike seek to dominate that which dominates us; by mimetically recreating what we fear we symbolically break the compulsion to adapt. In both art and kitsch "freedom from nature is celebrated, yet remains mythically entrapped"—not really overcome but seemingly so (Adorno 1978:225). Kitsch lavishly relishes in imitation; art hides the fact but utterly depends on it. Kitsch, art's bad conscience, reminds art of the imitation that underlies art's every effort, and also art's privilege—class privilege notably.[5] "In the end", Adorno insists, "indignation over kitsch is anger at its shameless reveling in the joy of imitation, now placed under taboo, while the power of works of art still continues to be secretly nourished by imitation". Put differently, he suggests that kitsch "incurs hostility because it blurts out the secret of art and the affinity of culture to savagery" (Adorno 1978:225–26). Further, and more scandalously, he argued in the *Aesthetic Theory* that "Kitsch is not, as those believers in erudite culture would like to imagine, the mere refuse of art, originating in disloyal accommodation to the enemy; rather, it lurks in art, awaiting ever recurring opportunities to spring forth" (Adorno 1997:239).

Adorno insisted that "every great, authentic piece of musical kitsch . . . is capable of acting as the accompaniment to imaginary catastrophes" (Adorno 1992e:16). His telescoped sentence is semantically slippery. Adorno's claim expresses the seriousness which he accords it: kitsch comes in varieties of greater and lesser, authentic and inauthentic, and it semiotically underscores danger. Moreover, he posits a kind of authenticity in kitsch, as it were, "authentic kitsch", a phrase reminiscent of an advertising campaign in the 1980s for shopping-mall art emporia selling expensive "authorized Authentic Reproductions", duly copyrighted, of masterwork paintings from "The Nelson Rockefeller Collection". Selling, in other words, Real Fakes—a current variation of which is the Thomas Kinkade Galleries industry of reproductions which can be transformed, before the buyer's eyes, into ersatz "originals", by traveling assistants who, for the extra price, will paint tiny highlights onto one's reproduction (as many as can be done in fifteen minutes, the actual time allotted), and thereby literally render it a painting, and not coincidentally something weirdly reminiscent of Duchamp's moustache and goatee on Mona Lisa, absent any trace of Duchamp's bitter-comic irony. Adorno is eliciting the reality of the truth in the lie, that is, that the truth of kitsch is its falseness, which every "authentic" example thereof represents before all else.

In an aphoristic essay titled, simply, "Kitsch" (c. 1932), Adorno suggested that kitsch has the "quality of being unrealized, merely hinted at". In music it has the character of a model, that is, the "outline and draft of objectively compelling, pre-established forms that have lost their content in history". And yet kitsch is also a form of remembering, however distorted and illusory, of what

[5] Adorno 1997:240: "Fidelity to the noble in art should be maintained, just as the noble should reflect its own culpability, its complicity with privilege".

Adorno terms "a formal objectivity that has passed away" (Adorno 2002a:501). It is the moment of objectivity of kitsch that constitutes its justification. In Adorno's late collection *Quasi una fantastia*, an essay called "Commodity Music Analysed" opens with a send-up of Gounod's *Ave Maria*, a piece Adorno regarded as unmitigated kitsch. Here's how it goes: "Gounod's *Ave Maria:* an Englishman has proposed this formula for music hall: Put three half-naked girls on a revolving stage. Then play the organ." The *Ave Maria*, he notes, is "a piece of sacred pop music featuring one of those Magdalens notable equally for their penitence and their seductiveness (...) Thus saccharined religion becomes the bourgeois cloak for a tolerated pornography" (Adorno 1992a:37). And yet: Adorno took such music seriously, and not simply as an aural proof of a culture in decline, à la Spengler. Adorno commented that "kitsch contains as much hope as is able to turn the clock back. It is the depraved reflection of that epiphany which is vouchsafed only to the greatest works of art". And he adds the critical proviso that: "Kitsch only forfeits its right to exist when it enters into a parasitical relationship to history, mimics its verdicts and finds itself forbidden to reverse them" (Adorno 1992a:43). Kitsch, that is, evokes a future utopia but only by looking back at a past that is selectively (mis)remembered, thereby helping to stabilize the present towards which kitsch is otherwise deeply antagonistic. Great art, by contrast, Adorno suggests, stares history directly in the face and speaks the unspeakable—and sometimes the unbearable. By contrast, as he bitterly wrote, "the positive element of kitsch lies in the fact that it sets free for a moment the glimmering realization that you have wasted your life" (Adorno 1992a:50).

Kitsch, for Adorno, fundamentally evokes the momentary self-imposition of exile from the present. Yet in the effort by kistch to forget the present, the past is remembered: history is evoked, but misleadingly. Hence, the progressive element in kitsch in its insistence that the past matters—despite the claims authorized by modernity's mantra of Progress that the past is irrelevant. Were the present less painful, the lie of kitsch would be less insistent. Put differently, the aporia of modernity leads us to seek consolation in place of what appears to be the impossibility of reconciliation with the otherness—the condition of general estrangement—that we at once ironically desire and abhor.

Adorno addressed all of this in a brief and extraordinary essay he called "Music in the Background" (1934), which constitutes a striking counter-discourse to the unrelenting, undialectical, albeit nearly canonic critique, of kitsch by Clement Greenberg. Adorno's subject is the everyday, utterly ordinary—indeed clichéd—live entertainment music typical to European cafés and pubs in the 1930s, and, at least in this country much later, even into the 50s and 60s in fancy supper clubs whose entertainment was supplied by large string orchestras with names like The Living Strings. The aphoristic text provides an apt conclusion to Adorno's take on musical life under the pervasive conditions of modernity as defined by mass culture and, more particularly, the Culture

Industry. His concern, in essence, is musical ruins, whose sounds he pursues with both determination and sadness.

He opens the essay with a series of hyperbolic images of music now-silenced in the administration and bustle of modern life, concluding: "If you are looking for music, you have to step outside the space of immediate life, because it no longer is one, and find the lost immediacy where it costs the price of admission, at the opera, at a concert". Modern life, that is, is unmusical—despite music's inescapable ubiquity—and the only way to recoup the loss is to see that life re-staged, on historical display, and in the elevated fashion of high art. The exceptions only serve to prove the rule.[6] Here Adorno makes an unexpected turn to the extent that he identifies places where ordinary musical life holds on and which he clearly valorizes: the café and the bar. Here music still "belongs". It lives in the background—you don't have to bother listening—but it maintains a presence nonetheless as accompaniment to conversation. The crowd does not constitute an audience; they treat the music simply as "an objective event". And yet the music does something: Music and people are "caught up and bound together" (Adorno 2002c:506–07).

Adorno hears in live-performance café music the remnant of a musical life, without the self-consciousness of formal art or, for that matter, the administered goods variously distributed through the reach of the Culture Industry. Well, not quite. Musically, there's nothing original, just pared down arrangements of stuff likely first intended for an orchestra. Light-classical kitsch.

As Adorno explains, the music's not much. But it's something. As he puts it: "The café arranges bouquets of dead flowers". What we will hear, should we choose to listen to the background, are acoustic ruins, yet ruins awakened to "new, ghostly life". The music-in-ruins "lights up" those who hear it, even though its glow is "netherworldly". When café music falls silent, its loss is instantly apparent: "It sounds as if a miserly waiter is turning off a couple of electric bulbs". The sad state of the late-modern transformation of Enlightenment ideals is allegorized as paltry electric illumination: "Background music", he says, "is an acoustic light source". In other words, it illuminates, however dimly, what might have been (Adorno 508-09).[7] Or, as he puts it elsewhere, "In art we can read off clearly the ambivalence of all progress" (Adorno 1998a:76). Adorno defines a social utility for musical kitsch, less as a sign of total reification, and more as a sonoric ruin that permits fractured remembrance.

[6] In Adorno 1988:129, written nearly three decades after this essay, Adorno pointed out that nowadays music in no longer exceptional but instead is ubiquitous and a "part of everyday life", principally the result of mass cultural production. Nonetheless, he posits that music of substance retains its exceptional character.

[7] See Edström 1989.

Richard Leppert: Nature and Exile

I 'd like now to turn from kitsch to say a few words about nature, after which I'll connect kitsch and nature, as well as exile, to Adorno's read of Mahler.

Throughout *Dialectic of Enlightenment,* Adorno and Horkheimer address the fractured relationship between human subjects and nature, which, not coincidentally, is a trope that for Adorno was fundamental to the music of Mahler. Adorno and Horkheimer argued that the fundamental forms of domination organizing modernity had their roots in the primordial efforts of human beings to survive in a nature—primordial totality—which they feared. Ultimately, as they put it, "What men want to learn from nature is how to use it in order wholly to dominate it and other men" (Horkheimner and Adorno 1972, 4). The alienation of the subject from nature was doubly articulated; that is: the othering of nature othered as well the self, since human beings are not only always already *in* nature but also always already *of* nature. As they put it:

> As soon as man discards his awareness that he himself is nature, all the aims for which he keeps himself alive—social progress, the intensification of all his material and spiritual powers, even consciousness itself—are nullified, and the enthronement of the means as an end, which under late capitalism is tantamount to open insanity, is already perceptible in the prehistory of subjectivity. Man's domination over himself, which grounds his selfhood, is almost always the destruction of the subject in whose service it is undertaken. (Horkheimer & Adorno, 1972:54).

In the end, subjects lament the separation from nature upon which their damaged subjectivities are ultimately grounded. In *Aesthetic Theory* (1969), Adorno stakes out his position on natural beauty, which he regards as the defining issue of aesthetics and a good deal more besides. Our longing for nature—for example, ecological regard, wilderness preservation, but also art, in Adorno's argument—is a projection of a lack that develops alongside our separation from and domination of nature.[8] As he put it, "The concept of natural beauty rubs on a wound" (Adorno 1997:61–2).[9] Art is called upon to answer for natural beauty, in effect to substitute for it; art—wholly artifactual, that is, literally unnatural—perpetuates the attack on nature. And yet art does more, for it acknowledges the natural beauty that the human subject has otherwise degraded yet nonetheless desires in its non-extant "perfect" state; art reflects on this fact. Art, Adorno says, "want(s) to keep nature's promise (...) What nature strives for in vain, artworks fulfill" (Adorno 1997:62, 65–6).[10] Natural beauty, he insists, is "the trace of the nonidentical in things under the spell of universal identity" (Adorno 1997:73).[11]

---

[8] Adorno is thus bluntly positioning himself against Hegel, whose disregard for nature is well known. On this point, see Adorno 1997:63, 75–77; and Wolin 1990:42.

[9] See also Paetzold 1997:213-35.

[10] Adorno 1997, 71: "Under its optic, art is not the imitation of nature, but the imitation of natural beauty". See also Behrens 1997.

[11] Cf. composer-philosopher David Dunn (Dunn 2001:95). Alluding to a lengthy passage in James Agee's *Let Us Now Praise Famous Men* describing the meanings and intelligence audible in late

Kantspel

Adorno heard Mahler's music, caught between late Romanticism and modernity, as the sonoric engagement of history as well as the utopian echo of something better, read through the lens of nature and—not least—by self-reflexive appropriation of kitsch, rubbed against the grain. Fundamentally, Adorno's Mahler is a progressive, but one who looked backward and wrung from the increasingly worn-out musical language of the nineteenth century the contradiction of its confrontation with history—Adorno once noted that Mahler "has absolutely nothing in common with the idea of originality" (Adorno 1992c:84). The truth of Mahler, the character of his greatness, is located in his ability to imagine something different, paradoxically by using the detritus of an exhausted musical vocabulary, as it were, against itself. In Mahler, Adorno hears the acoustic trace of hope's realization.[12] The society immanent to the music assures that the music will ultimately remain tied to that against which it protests—an entanglement that art would escape, if it could. Thus Mahler's works "are rooted in what music seeks to transcend" (Adorno 1992d:6). Formally, as Rose Rosengard Subotnik has pointed out, Mahler's invokes Beethovenian totality but negatively—as an "as-if", a totality irretrievably lost—by "constructing enormous symphonic patterns out of elements too discontinuous to effect any large-scale unity" (Subotnik 1991:208).[13] Adorno hears Mahler's protest in his works' perpetual motion, what he terms their "aimlessly circling, irresistible movements [which] (…) are always images of the world's course" (Adorno 1992d:6). Simply put, Mahler renders problematic the supposed forward motion of frenetic modernity, trapped in activity, the "vain commotion" of a general unfreedom. Adorno

night calls of two foxes, Dunn comments: "We hear in the world talking to itself a sense of otherness that simultaneously mirrors our deepest sense of belonging"; and (p. 97) "Perhaps music is a conservation strategy for keeping something alive that we now need to make more conscious, a way of making sense of the world from which we might refashion our relationships to nonhuman living systems".

[12] Adorno 1992d:6: "It is music's nature to overreach itself. Utopia finds refuge in its no man's land."

[13] Subotnik 1991:208. The phrase "as-if" is Adorno's own (Adorno 1988:108). Art works for Adorno provide an illusion of truth. Their illusory character emerges from the demand for structural unity or wholeness, which in turn defines the art work's autonomy from society, that is, art's determinate negation of society. In art, however, unity is usually feigned rather than fully achieved, and in any event unity runs the risk of disguising social antagonism. The semblance or illusory nature of art works carries with it an element of (necessary) deceit as a precondition of its protest. Part of art's truth, of course, is its own guilt.
Schoolman 1997:61–62: "Art is ambiguous. As the image of reconciliation, art creates an illusion. As the subtle articulation of the nonidentity of being, art exposes the illusion and reveals an insurmountable barrier to reconciliation and the violence to nature and difference met out by the quest for reconciliation (…) Paradoxically, Adorno is saying that art 'achieves reconciliation', provides an idea of what our relation to nature ought to be, only by showing through the history of artworks that every image of reconciliation is a lie." See also Zuidervaart 1991:168–69, 178–80.

suggested that: "Hope in Mahler always resides in change", a struggle against "blind functioning (...) Mahler's symphonies plead anew against the world's course. They imitate it in order to accuse" (Adorno 1992d:7), and in the end decline to offer a counterfeit reconciliation.

Mahler's utopia is "the forward motion of the past and the not-yet-past in becoming". It looks back in order to discern a better future, which can only come about if the past is faced squarely. Mahler seeks out Otherness, whose conventionally-hidden presence he brings forward into view" (Adorno 1992d, 14). Nowhere does Mahler's pursuit of otherness come more significantly into play than in his incorporation of the musically banal and vulgar: in kitsch. (As Adorno noted, "[Mahler's] symphonies shamelessly flaunt what rang in all ears, scraps of melody from great music, shallow popular songs, street ballads, hits") (Adorno 1992d, 35).

Adorno long lamented the social causes and effects of musical division, the increasingly absolute separation of light or popular music from its "serious" twin. Both high and low, stigmatized by capitalism, were but the sundered fragments of a whole, now extant only as an "unresolved contradiction" (Adorno 2002d:293, Adorno 2002e:395).

Mahler sets these musics against each other, and in extreme tension, producing for the effort, in Adorno's apt phrase, "the scandal of all bourgeois musical esthetics" (Adorno 2002f:314).[14] It's the tension between the musics that matters, not simply the incorporation of the banal and vulgar (Adorno's words) with the supposedly elevated. As a result, both musics are changed: "nothing sounds as it was wont to; all things are diverted as if by a magnet. What is worn out yields pliantly to the improvising hand; the used parts win a second life as variants" (Adorno 1997:41). Or, as he elsewhere remarked: "In his musical vagrancy [Mahler] picks up the broken glass by the roadside and holds it up to the sun so that all the colors are refracted. (...) In the debased and vilified materials of music he scratches for illicit joys" (Adorno 1992d:36).

The scandal of Mahler's use of the banal and vulgar develops from his acknowledgment of the putative legitimacy of both. What conventionally goes unrecognized is not the otherness of banality and vulgarity but the fact of their worn-out character—precisely what Mahler preserves in order to reach his destination, defined by a utopia of truth that emerges from lies exposed.[15] And otherness arises from victims and victimization, the losers in "progress", with

[14] Cf. Adorno 1997:41: "Mahler's music is progressive just by its clumsy and at the same time objective refusal of the neo-romantic intoxication with sound, but this refusal was in its own time scandalous, modern perhaps in the same way as were the simplifications of van Gogh and the fauvres vis-à-vis impressionism".

[15] Adorno 1992d:17: "If the Other is not to be sold off, it must be sought incognito, among lost things".

Kantspel

whom Mahler identifies.[16] Desperately, his music holds onto what culture has cast off as unworthy, mutilated.[17]

Mahler is a dealer in detritus, one who picks from the scrap heap of the present; something of a naïve and visionary, he finds new ways of assembling the scraps so that they both retain the look of what they were when he found them and also gain a new essence, often profound and invariably meaningful, as he sets them in tension with the aesthetic principles of the art work, but not without affecting the formal "mold" into which they are put. Not least, the "vulgar and banal" in Mahler produce the tendency to re-materialize (or objectify) the reality which nineteenth-century musical aesthetics otherwise all too often worked hard to etherialize and, hence, ironically to reify. Mahler returns music to the here and now precisely to insist on the profound inadequacy of what is. In particular, the banal and vulgar, intruding into the aesthetic glories of the late-romantic language of self-affirmation, forcefully announces to the bourgeois audience just who has been left out of this equation, very much as if the servants insisted on helping themselves to the cornucopia laid out on the sideboard buffet, inserting themselves into line, plates in hand, alongside their social "betters".

Mahler knew the social semiotics of sound. And he knew the effects of sound intrusions. The Mediterranean, swarthy urban: the mandolin in the Seventh Symphony, as well as the guitar; and the multiple mandolins in the Eighth Symphony. The Austrian peasant: the cowbells in the Sixth and Seventh Symphonies. Rather like an accordion band on the White House lawn performing "Hail to the Chief". Yet it would be misleading simply to suggest that Mahler's music is principally a sonoric effort to scandalize smug urbanites by attacking haut-bourgeois solipsism and complacency. Mahler's setting in tension of high art and low functions as more than a sonoric comeuppance of privilege because the everyday itself is transformed, raised up, just as the high and mighty are taken to task—and maybe taken down a peg—by the presence of the otherwise suppressed Other. But the real point is that Mahler acknowledged and valorized difference without valorizing the current state of either

[16] Adorno 1992c:96: "The expression of suffering, his own and of those who have to bear the burdens, no longer knuckles under at the behest of the sovereign subject which insists that things must be so and not otherwise. This is the source of the offence he gives."

[17] Adorno 1992c:38: The art work, "chained to culture, seeks to burst the chain and show compassion for the derelict residue; in Mahler each measure is an opening of arms". Cf. p. 39: "Not despite the kitsch to which it is drawn is Mahler's music great, but because its construction untied the tongue of kitsch, unfetters the longing that is merely exploited by the commerce that kitsch serves". See further pp. 61–62. Adorno's admiration for Mahler is tempered by his consideration of the composer's weaknesses; see especially his critique of the Eighth Symphony, pp. 138–39, which he wryly names "the official magnum opus", and notes its "ostentatious cardboard, the giant symbolic shell", the "aborted, objectively impossible resuscitation of the cultic (…) The dogmatic content from which it borrows its authority is neutralized in it to a cultural commodity. In reality it worships itself".

the high or the low. Instead, his sprawling symphonies, for Adorno, hint of a utopia that develops both by articulating the inadequacy of the here and now and by positing an alternative—without however pretending that current reality has been rendered moot.[18] The lack of an organic totality that defines Mahler's musical structures acts to prevent such wishful thinking. Mahler, Adorno insists, works to reverse the direction of history's forward march: "He promises victory to the losers. His entire symphonic work is a reveille. Its hero is the deserter" (Adorno 2002b:617).[19]

What do Adorno's claims for Mahler amount to in sound? Permit me to concretize his argument by a single example, drawn from the Third Symphony (completed in 1896 and first performed in 1902). In six movements, incorporating a female solo, a boys' choir, and a women's choir, the Third was the composer's longest symphony (1:40) and, indeed, one of the longest in the history of the symphony (it's first movement is longer than the entire Fifth Symphony of Beethoven). I'll principally confine my remarks to the third movement, a scherzo.

The symphony has two parts. Part 1 is constituted by the gigantic first movement; part 2 by the succeeding five. The whole is shaped by a program, which Mahler, post-composition, discarded. Briefly stated, the symphony is a sonoric enactment of a progression towards enlightenment built on a foundation of love, and deeply informed in particular by reconciliation with nature. The third movement is titled "What the creatures of the forest tell me". Its extended opening defines a kind of animal paradise in raucous equilibrium. But at the height of the musical frenetics, a sudden silence is momentarily imposed, as if the creatures of the forest sensed a new, unnerving, and unseen presence. Immediately thereafter, and from offstage, a posthorn sounds. It announces history: the arrival of man—and by means of an instrument not commonly associated with high caste symphonic literature. Softly, it plays a distinctly simple, folklike, sentimental, and—as has often been suggested by scholars—nearly banal melody.

[18] What Adorno once said of Berg holds true for Mahler. Adorno 1999:79: "The greatest works of art do not exclude the lower depths, but kindle the flame of utopia on the smoking ruins of the past".

[19] Cf, Adorno 1992d:166–67, the final lines of this monograph; Adorno returns to the "Rewelge": "Mahler's music has sympathized with the social outcasts who vainly stretch out their hands to the collective (...) Only those cast from the ranks, trampled underfoot, the lost outpost, the one buried 'where the shining trumpets blow', the poor 'drummer boy', those wholly unfree for Mahler embody freedom. Bereft of promises, his symphonies are ballads of the defeated, for 'Nacht is jetzt schon bald' – soon the night will fall."

Kantspel

The structure of this movement is complex and nuanced, and I cannot do justice to it here. But I do at least want to make a couple of basic points relative to the larger theme of my paper.

Here is Mahler's program description:

> [The movement] illustrates the quiet, undisturbed life of the forest before the appearance of man. Then the animals catch sight of the first human being and, although he walks calmly past them, the terrified [animals] sense that future trouble will come from him. (Flores 1993:102)

What Mahler actually scores does not precisely follow this program. First Man or, in reality Modern Man, doesn't "walk calmly past" the animals; rather he approaches no closer than sufficient to make his aural presence known. He intrudes on nature from afar, sounding his posthorn, which the creatures of the forest read as a warning (in the orchestral score, at rehearsal numbers 14–16). This seems clear from the semiotics associated with the sonorities of the posthorn in the nineteenth century. The posthorn was a signaling instrument, a harbinger. As its name implies, it communicated the arrival of communication itself, the post. Its sound traveled through space to confirm the command of both space and time marked by rapid travel, the ultimate sign of and cliché for Modernity and Progress alike. Put differently, Mahler's posthorn communicates a notably particular message; it certifies change. The simple instrument and its equally simple folklike, almost childlike tune, is thus appropriated by Mahler not as a nostalgic remembrance of things past, but as the critical warning of what is to come, and indeed of what has already arrived. The posthorn fulfills, for Nature, the role of the canary in the coalmine, and the fauna know it. In other words, however distant its sound and innocent its tune, for Mahler's musical Nature the posthorn is at best ambiguous. (I should mention that the posthorn part is usually given to the flugelhorn, common to military bands at the time, since the music is essentially beyond the technical capability of the valveless posthorn.)

After the horn dies away the animals gradually return to their chatter, but now uneasily. And soon every instrument is expressing its concern in a cacophony of simultaneously sounding voices, whose panic is evident not least in Mahler's scoring the music at the extreme limits of individual instruments' ranges, which as a result sound strained (an effect Mahler often exploited). Then, quite suddenly, as though without warning, the posthorn makes a second (and last) appearance, though here more briefly (rehearsal numbers 27–29). Thereafter, and within a few seconds of the horn's last sounds, now at the movement's close, there follows an fortissimo *tutti;* the orchestra playing in identical rhythm, registering the unanimity of hysterical response, as if Nature had all at once figured out the stakes, for better or worse, of the arrival in Paradise of the human subject.

Mahler's "creatures of the forest" tell of fear and impending conflict. The seeming innocence of the posthorn solos, clichés of pseudo-folk simplicity, are the not-so-innocent foretaste of the dialectic of enlightenment aestheticized. And the fauna, so to speak, like Mahler, recognize it. The transformation of what we may hear as a fairly kitschy little tune, utterly pretty and utterly predictable, into something more comes not in Mahler's putative reappropriation of the tune itself, but in his appropriation of its reception in and by Nature, that is, by means of the music that follows the posthorn solos. But there's more. Mahler self-reflexively shares with us what he's learned, and places it in an aesthetic form that paradoxically rescues the aesthetics from its own dehistoricized aesthetciziation. In this movement he juxtaposes two distinctly different kinds of music, the symphonically High and the quasi-kitschy Low, both of which Mahler treats with equal honor. Neither music is the same as a result of the juxtaposition. That is, once the posthorn is first heard, the movement cannot continue as if the intrusion never happened. To be sure, the music of the opening attempts to reassert itself but it just won't work; it's forced to deal with the ghost of the posthorn, even though the posthorn's music is wholly absented. And just at the moment when "nature" seems to have overcome the intrusion, by a return to the formal disorder of a happy sonoric fecundity, the posthorn sounds again, after which, simply put, no recovery is possible. Any resolution of the aporia produced by these two oppositional sound masses can only be addressed in the movements that follow—precisely what happens: the ultimate move, towards which Mahler aims, is reconciliation between nature and the subject—what Adorno hears in Mahler's music generally.[20]

Adorno argued that authentic art works silently hail natural beauty, which, like nature, is not directly available to us to the extent that "nature" is both pre-determined and pre-structured by history. Art, Adorno claimed, "is the semblance of what is beyond death's reach" (Adorno 1997:27). Not coincidentally, kitsch, for Adorno, is modernity's signpost of death, and in this respect kitsch shares a common boundary with exile; but kitsch—like exile—used against its own bad intentions, can point in the direction of life, as Mahler's music, and Adorno's philosophy, persistently affirm.

[20] Cf. Solomon 1995:187–209, the chapter "Trouble in Paradise". "In several of Mozart's most characteristic adagios and andantes a calm, contemplative, or ecstatic condition gives way to a troubled state—is penetrated by hints of storm, dissonance, anguish, anxiety, danger—and this in turn is succeeded by a restoration of the status quo ante, now suffused with and transformed by the memory of the turbulent interlude" (ibid:187). Solomon ultimately reads this phenomenon via a psychoanalytic history of the composer.

Kantspel

References

Adorno, Theodor W. 1978. *Minima Moralia: Reflections from Damaged Life*, trans. E. F. N. Jephcott (London: Verso)

Adorno, Theodor W. 1983. *Negative Dialectics*, trans. E. B. Ashton (New York: Continuum)

Adorno, Theodor W. 1985. *Philosophy of Modern Music*, trans Anne G. Mitchell, & Wesley V. Blomster (New York: Continuum)

Adorno, Theodor W. 1988. *Introduction to the Sociology of Music*, trans. E. B. Ashton (New York: Continuum)

Adorno, Theodor W. 1992a. "Commodity Music Analysed", *Quasi una Fantasia: Essays on Modern Music*, trans. Rodney Livingstone (London: Verso), pp. 37–52

Adorno, Theodor W. 1992b. "Is Art Lighthearted?", *Notes to Literature*, ed. Rolf Tiedemann, trans. Shierry Weber Nicholsen (New York: Columbia University Press), vol. 2, pp. 247–53

Adorno, Theodor W. 1992c. "Mahler", *Quasi una Fantasia: Essays on Modern Music*, trans. Rodney Livingstone (London: Verso), pp. 81–110

Adorno, Theodor W. 1992d. *Mahler: A Musical Physiognomy*, trans. Edmund Jephcott (Chicago: University of Chicago Press)

Adorno, Theodor W. 1992e. "Motifs", *Quasi una Fantasia: Essays on Modern Music*, trans. Rodney Livingstone (London: Verso), pp. 9–36

Adorno, Theodor W. 1997. *Aesthetic Theory*, ed. Gretel Adorno & Rolf Tiedemann, trans. Robert Hullot-Kentor (Minneapolis: University of Minnesota Press)

Adorno, Theodor W. 1998a. *Beethoven: The Philosophy of Music*, ed. Rolf Tiedemann, trans. Edmund Jephcott (Stanford: Stanford University Press)

Adorno, Theodor W. 1998b. "Why Still Philosophy", *Critical Models: Interventions and Catchwords*, trans. Henry W. Pickford (New York: Columbia University Press), pp. 5–17

Adorno, Theodor W. 1999. "Alban Berg". *Sound Figures*, trans. Rodney Livingstone (Stanford: Stanford University Press), pp. 69–79

Adorno, Theodor W. 2002a. "Kitsch", *Essays on Music*, ed. Richard Leppert, trans. Susan H. Gillespie (Berkeley and Los Angeles: University of California Press), pp. 501–5

Adorno, Theodor W. 2002b. "Marginalia on Mahler", *Essays on Music*, ed. Richard Leppert, trans. Susan H. Gillespie (Berkeley and Los Angeles: University of California Press), pp. 612–18

Adorno, Theodor W. 2002c. "Music in the Background", *Essays on Music*, ed. Richard Leppert, trans. Susan H. Gillespie (Berkeley and Los Angeles: University of California Press), pp. 507–10

Adorno, Theodor W. 2002d. "On the Fetish-Character in Music and the Regression of Listening", *Essays on Music*, ed. Richard Leppert (Berkeley and Los Angeles: University of California Press), pp. 288–317

Adorno, Theodor W. 2002e. "On the Social Situation of Music", *Essays on Music*, ed. Richard Leppert, trans. Wes Blomster (Berkeley and Los Angeles: University of California Press), pp. 391–436

Richard Leppert: Nature and Exile

Behrens, Roger 1997. "On Music in Nature and Nature in Music", *Issues in Contemporary Culture and Aesthetics*, 5, pp. 17–26

Benjamin, Walter 1969. "Theses on the Philosophy of History", *Illuminations*, ed. Hannah Arendt, trans. Harry Zohn (New York: Schocken), pp. 253–64

Dunn, David 2001. "Nature, Sound Art, and the Sacred", *The Book of Music & Nature*, ed. David Rothenberg & Marta Ulvaeus (Middletown, CT: Wesleyan University Press), pp. 95–107

Edström, Olle 1989. "'Vi skall gå på restaurang och höra på musik': Om reception av restaurangmusik och annan 'mellanmusik'" ["'We Shall Go to a Restaurant and Listen to Music': About Reception of Music Played in Restaurants and Other 'Middle Music'"], *Svensk Tidskrift för Musikforskning*, 71, pp. 77–112

Flores, Constantin 1993. *Gustav Mahler: The Symphonies*, trans. Vernon Wicker (Portland, OR: Amadeus Press)

Greenberg, Clement 1957. "Avant-Garde and Kitsch", *Mass Culture: The Popular Arts in America*, ed. Bernard Rosenberg & David Manning White (Glencoe, IL: Free Press), pp. 98–107

Gross, Harvey 1979. "Adorno in Los Angeles: The Intellectual in Migration", *Humanities in Society*, 2/4, pp. 339–51

Horkheimer, Max, and Theodor W. Adorno 1972. *Dialectic of Enlightenment*, trans. John Cumming (New York: Continuum)

Huyssen, Andreas1986. *After the Great Divide: Modernism, Mass Culture, Post-modernism* (Bloomington: Indiana University Press)

Jachec, Nancy 1998. "Adorno, Greenberg and Modernist Politics", *Telos*, 110 (Winter), pp. 105–18

Paetzold, Heinz 1997. "Adorno's Notion of Natural Beauty: A Reconsideration", *In The Semblance of Subjectivity: Essays in Adorno's Aesthetic Theory*, ed. Tom Huhn & Lambert Zuidervaart (Cambridge: MIT Press), pp.213–35

Schoolman, Morton 1997. "Toward a Politics of Darkness: Individuality and Its Politics in Adorno's Aesthetics", *Political Theor*, 25/1, pp. 57–92

Solomon, Maynard 1995. *Mozart: A Life (*New York: HarperCollins)

Subotnik, Rose Rosengard 1991. "The Historical Structure: Adorno's 'French' Model for the Criticism of Nineteenth-Century Music", *Developing Variations: Style and Ideology in Western Music* (Minneapolis: University of Minnesota Press), pp. 206–38

Wolin, Richard 1990. "Utopia, Mimesis, and Reconciliation: A Redemptive Critique of Adorno's *Aesthetic Theory*", *Representations*, 32, pp. 33–49

Zuidervaart, Lambert 1991. *Adorno's Aesthetic Theory: The Redemption of Illusion (*Cambridge: MIT Press)

CHAPTER 13

FOUR HANDS, ONCE AGAIN

BY THEODOR W. ADORNO
TRANSLATED BY JONATHAN WIPPLINGER

That music we are accustomed to call classical I came to know as a child through four-hand playing. There was little symphonic and chamber music literature that was not moved into home life with the help of those oblong volumes, bound uniformly green in landscape format by the bookbinder. They appeared as if made to have their pages turned, and I was allowed to do so, long before I knew the notes, following only memory and my ear. Even violin sonatas by Beethoven were found among them in curious arrangements. Many a piece from that time in my life, such as Mozart's Symphony in G minor, became so imprinted in my memory that even today it seems to me as though no orchestra could ever produce the tension of the introductory movement of eighth notes as fully as the questionable touch of the second player. Better than all others, this music befitted the home. It was brought forth from the piano, a piece of furniture, and those who went at it without fear of faltering and false notes were part of the family.

Four-hand playing was the gift the geniuses of the bourgeois nineteenth century placed at my cradle at the beginning of the twentieth. Music for four hands: that was music with which one could still interact and live, before musical compulsion itself commanded solitariness and secretive craft. Something is said by this not merely about performance practice but also about what is played. For the music that was available here as classical is from an era of less than a hundred years: itself predestined for four-hand playing. This period begins with Haydn and ends with Brahms. Bach is strangely unsuited to be arranged for four hands, and I cannot recall Bach being played in my childhood; the post-Brahmsian modern, already eliminated for its manual difficulty alone, is further excluded by the autocratic nature of its timbres. It is therefore the symphonic in the narrow sense that is, or was, accessible to four-hand playing. This period stems, however, from the era of authentic bourgeois musical practice. If Bekker's[1] theory of the community-forming force of the symphonic is correct, then this community is at the same time also one of individuals. That every individual finds himself reaffirmed in the great whole of the symphony is demonstrated to him by the fact that he can admit it into the family without surrendering any of the latter's binding quality, just as he hung pictures of his classics on the walls. Yet four-hand playing was better than the *Isle of the Dead*[2] hanging above the sideboard; at all times, he had to truly earn the symphony in order to own it: to play it. And he did not play it entirely in private. He was not allowed to modify the tempo and dynamics according to capricious inclinations, as he was accustomed to do with his lyrical pieces by Grieg. Rather he had to orient himself according to the text and the instructions of the work, if he did not want to "come out of it," to lose the connection to his partner. More than this: within the works themselves there appeared to dwell something of the secret of four-hand playing.

It is no coincidence that the literature of "original compositions" for four hands is limited to this period. Its true master is Schubert. The most important of his works for four hands, the Sonata 'Grand Duo,' the Fantasia in F minor, the Divertissement à la Hongroise, the Rondo in A major, and the military marches as well, are all stylistically close enough to the orchestra; perhaps written for piano simply due to a lack of orchestral performance possibilities or haste, these pieces clearly demonstrate that equivocal relationship between objective symphonicity and private musical practice, which on the whole may yield important rules for the compositional praxis of the nineteenth century. Conversely, if one plays four-hand reductions from the symphonies of Schumann and Brahms, one will be amazed at how well this form seems to suit them: all too well; even a piece as compositionally rich as the first movement of Brahms's Fourth feels so self-evident to four hands that I cannot escape the feeling that it was only retrospectively elevated from the realm of the monochrome, tragically intimate duet to instrumental multiplicity. At the same time, all four-hand playing is unreliable and fallible; the instantaneous sounding of the piano does not allow for the rhythmic compensation that the vibrating strings of the violin make possible. And two piano soloists with the highest rhythmical training will find it more difficult to play precisely than an average orchestra. Finally, listening to four-hand playing is hardly ever a joy. If, despite that, four-hand playing maintained its great role for a hundred years, it is because it alone guarded the musical tradition in living quarters, which have in the meantime also lost chamber music to the podium. In the age of strict division of labor, the bourgeoisie defended its last music in the fortress of the piano, which they vigorously maintained; inconsiderate, indifferent to how it sounded in the ears of the others, the alienated ones. Even their mistakes, which were unavoidable, preserved an active relation to the works that those who in an intoxicated state listened to perfect concert performances had long ceased to possess. For this, certainly, the four-handed player had to pay the price of entering into action archaically domestic, dilettantishly unschooled. Their dilettantism, however, is nothing other than the reverberation of the true musical tradition and the product of its decline. The question remains, for whom will the last artist meaningfully play when the last dilettante, who lives by the dream of being an artist, has died? No choral community will replace him.

It is anything but surprising, then, that four-hand playing has since fallen silent. Just as one now rarely hears of novels of abducted female piano students and abducting piano teachers at conservatories, so just as rarely, given the automobiles of the gramophone and the radio, will four-hand piano equipages trot or gallop, the heads of good horses nodding in rhythm, carrying their illustrious Mozart and their dignified Brahms, surely endangered, proudly to the finish line. Four-hand playing has become a gesture of memory, and few live, mostly musicians, who still practice this outmoded art. But it is possible to think that many a work, which in their orchestral grandiosity ring out in vain under mighty exertions, reveal themselves only to the timid gesture of memory, which shares with them the secret of participating as a humane human in the life of society. If the lonesome, who do not have to hope for listeners and have none to fear, were now and then to give four-hand playing a try, it would not necessarily be to their harm. In the end, a child might be found to turn the pages for them.

1933

Notes

This piece first appeared as "Vierhändig, noch einmal" in the *Vossische Zeitung*, December 19, 1933. It was reprinted in Adorno's *Impromptus* (Frankfurt am Main: Suhrkamp, 1968), and is now collected in Adorno's *Gesammelte Schriften*, Hrsg. Rolf Tiedemann, Bd. 17 (Frankfurt am Main: Suhrkamp, 1982), 303–6.

1. Frankfurt musicologist Paul Bekker (1882–1937).—Trans.
2. A reference to Swiss symbolist Arnold Böcklin (1827–1901) and the series of five paintings he did under the title *Die Toteninsel* between 1880 and 1886.—Trans.

"FOUR HANDS, THREE HEARTS": A COMMENTARY

A man cannot become a child again, or he becomes childish. But does he not find joy in the child's naïveté, and must he himself not strive to reproduce its truth at a higher stage? Does not the true character of each epoch come alive in the nature of its children?

—Karl Marx, *Grundrisse*

"*Noch einmal.*" Four-handed—again? Recurrence is invoked, but uncannily. The very ordinariness of what follows the comma, "*noch einmal,*" draws attention to what it modifies, *vierhändig*. Like a repeat sign. Do it again. The present-day cultural singularity of *vierhändig* is as oddly disconcerting as the *noch einmal* is insistent: let me say this again, not because it's already familiar like a tune that will sound nice on a second hearing and sound even better with more practice but because you haven't heard this in a while, so let me remind you. But why tell me at all? What are the stakes?

English refers to the practice as "four-hand(s)," as in Sonata for Piano Four Hand, or, simply, four-hand music; German renders it "four-handed," which doesn't parse well in literal translation. Either way, "*vierhändig*" nowadays conjures up something quaint—or, better, archaic, which, precisely, is Adorno's point, exclaimed in sadness. Standard piano music involves two hands; since the convention is well established, hands aren't mentioned on title pages. Ravel's *Concerto for the Left Hand* rightly insists on drawing attention to its notably exceptional self-limitation. Otherwise, it's only when more hands are added that hands get counted. More hands than two were often called for in the past, sometimes performing on multiples of the same instrument. Conversely, a few composers, while sticking to one keyboard, increased the players beyond the conventional upper limit of two—W. F. E. Bach: three players/six hands; Cécile Chaminade

(1857–1944): four players/eight hands—presumably attached to small bodies sitting on an extended bench, each set of hands responsible for only a couple of octaves.

In compositions involving more than one instrument, it's the specific excess of keyboards that gets title-page mention, not the additional hands required to realize the music. For a long time, duets for two keyboard instruments were quite common, reaching their apogee of popularity during the course of the nineteenth century. But as early as the eighteenth century the odd composer experimented with keyboards beyond two, though the results didn't add up to much more than being "worth the try." The best-known examples are by Bach: his concertos for two, three, and even four harpsichords. He went for two harpsichords three times, three harpsichords twice, and four once: clearly diminishing returns—the only logical move for five in this progression was zero. And in the good American tradition, according to which too much is nowhere near enough, there were Gottschalk's so-named monster concerts staged in Rio in 1869, one of which involved sixteen pianos and thirty-one pianists. (These monstrous events, together with malaria, proved to be the death of him.)[1]

There's a degree of terminological ambiguity in the history of the keyboard duet, since duet, while invariably referring to two performers, could designate either one or two instruments. The question of one piano or two defined distinctly different markets. A duet for two pianos (four hands, and sometimes eight, although then no longer a duet) pretty much meant a piece intended for concert performance, for the simple and obvious reason that very few people had either the domestic space or money to afford two such large instruments. Accordingly, there wasn't much of a market for two-piano music. Adoption of the term *vierhändig* in the course of the nineteenth century erased any ambiguity concerning performance requirements and did so as an advertising device intended to appeal to a very considerable niche market, that of the bourgeois amateur. In short, four-hand music, for the most part, was music for the home.

As the quintessential domestic instrument of the nineteenth-century bourgeoisie,[2] the piano played its part in the increasingly common hoarding behaviors of the emerging market economy. Industrially produced, by mid-century it was available virtually everywhere.

More to the point, and thanks to endless advertising, the piano was broadly perceived not simply as a desirable possession but as a socially necessary one—and entirely without regard to whether anyone actually ever touched the keys. The piano, as furniture, staked a highly visible claim for one's economic potential to consume, to lead a life defined by tangible accoutrement. If played, the instrument's relation to market-driven modernity was further overdetermined. There were lessons to be paid for; there was music to buy—torrents of it churned out for decades on end and made to help form, and then to suit, many different tastes.

Domestic piano music was the sonoric analogue to Victorian bric-a-brac. It acoustically decorated the parlor, the room that defined a transitional space between the private and public worlds whose conventional separation lay at the very heart of the nineteenth- and early-twentieth-century Western cultural imaginary. The parlor was an important locus within which to structure modern identity—identity incorporating in particular irreconcilable differences and attendant injustices associated with the increasingly sharp distinctions organizing gender and class. Put differently, the parlor was a principal site within which to define and help authorize some of most fundamental social contradictions shaping modern consciousness.

Unlike any other single instrument apart from the organ (far more expensive and uncommon to most homes), the piano was capable of realizing music originally intended for ensembles, ranging from the string quartet to the orchestra, by means of transcriptions—reductions, really. Music publishers rose to the challenge, producing vast quantities (indeed, many thousands) of transcriptions, including the dozens of Haydn symphonies, and those by Mozart, Beethoven, and Brahms; orchestral tone poems; and even opera—from *Fidelio* to *Tristan* and even the complete *Ring* cycle.[3] And many composers wrote original compositions for piano *vierhändig*, Schubert notably. All this was in addition to the vast amount of music published for piano solo. In short, if it was music, the piano could (re)produce it.

Four-hand piano transcriptions (leaving aside music first composed expressly for piano four-hand) were pitched to the bourgeoisie as a domesticated, and indeed privatized, version of what was originally intended for the public concert. This was music for pedagogy as well as fantasy; pedagogy to the extent that, even into the first decade of the gramophone, self-performance was the only mechanism by which to experience orchestral music outside the concert hall; fantasy in that piano transcriptions permitted amateurs to amass under their own control not only an imaginary orchestra but also the conductor's baton—rather in the way that music lovers (almost invariably male, so far as I know) sometimes stand in front of their stereo systems conducting, say, the Ninth Symphony, usually the fast and loud movements. Further to the matter of fantasy, four-hand music rose in popularity precisely alongside the rise of the solo virtuoso in the nineteenth century, with all the associations of demonic mastery: hundreds of notes at breakneck speed. It's no coincidence that myriad piano transcriptions, including operatic arias and entire symphonies, by Franz Liszt—the virtuoso against whom all others were conventionally measured—were in many instances precisely the same works made available for four-hand performance, though now requiring twenty fingers to Liszt's ten.[4]

Yet whatever the potential of four-hand music for evoking fantasies of virtuosity and control, Adorno connects with none of it. Indeed, he ignores it utterly; it wasn't part of his experience with the music. His memorial moves in a distinctly contrary direction, brushing the history of *vierhändig* firmly against the grain of its conventional history. To him, the piano provided more than mere acoustic decoration aestheticizing dystopian social realities—music in the parlor could permit one to hear, and indeed literally to perform, however momentarily, a sonic alternative to the way things were.

Three Hearts. "*Vierhändig*" signals one organism, a unity of substance and intent. In this respect, four-hand is analogous to the operatic duet evoking the harmony of love—all those unisons and octaves, parallel thirds and sixths, and, not least, voice crossings that together exceed in expressiveness what either voice can render on its own. The piano duet was long associated with something of the same sort, very much—if hardly always—a boy-girl affair. Four-hand duets were long a standard of piano pedagogy, exactly what young Teddie Wiesengrund experienced. They were also an apt occasion for libidinal exercise and, as such, produced endless parental anxieties—the instructors were usually youngish men and the pupils young(er) women. (The piano lesson-qua-seduction is much discussed in courtesy and conduct literature already by the eighteenth century and became a literary trope so common as to be virtually a running joke for many decades; it was also a common source of laughter in the theater as well as in visual art [Leppert 1988, 61–67]). Indeed, composers understood how to maximize the advantage presented by the occasion; hand crossing[5] between the two players was conventional. Bodies necessarily pressed against each other, repeatedly. And as the players' eyes moved from score to keyboard, there was plentiful opportunity for eyes to meet, however furtively, and perhaps more.[6] But, again, none of this is Adorno's concern, and that's precisely the point.

"Vierhändig, noch einmal" was published in the *Vossische Zeitung* on December 19, 1933, the conclusion of a momentous year in German history. Adorno reads this unhappy present, very much his own, against the treasured memories of a very different time, that of his childhood, spent in an upper-bourgeois house filled with music, piano music especially, and in the presence of two women, sisters, each of whom he called Mother, one biological and the other honorary, both musical.[7] Bio-Mother Maria sang; Mother-Auntie Agathe played piano—extremely well. And there was a third woman, Sanna Stoltze Drescher, his first piano teacher from outside the family. When Adorno's mother died in 1952, Frau Drescher wrote her onetime pupil a heartfelt note of sympathy: "Tief erschüttert hat mich die Todesnachricht Deiner lieben guten Mutter. Sie was eine seltene Frau unendlicher Güte und Selbstlosigkeit, stets besorgt, ihre Familie zu beglücken ["News of your loving, good Mother's death has deeply shaken me. She was an exceptional woman, endlessly kind and selfless, always concerned with her family's happiness"] (Ewenz et al. 2003, 19). Adorno would have wholeheartedly agreed, and not least on the account that his mother's love manifested itself in music. Indeed, Adorno's early experiences with music *vierhändig* led him to connect the very principle of music to belonging—as it were, to *being home*. In December 1933, home unquestionably felt distant; as would become ever thereafter increasingly apparent, the very principle of home, both broadly and narrowly conceived, seemed irretrievable—the realization of which virtually haunted Adorno throughout the rest of his life.

In 1965, in an essay called "On the Question: 'What is German?'" originally written as a radio talk, Adorno recalled his leaving home (homeland) in 1934 for England, thereafter back and forth to Germany now and again (initially possible for half-Jews by the terms of the Nuremberg Laws), to America in 1938, and finally returning to a Germany in ruins in 1949, and to stay for good only in 1953—by which time his immediate family was gone forever:

> At no moment during my emigration did I relinquish the hope of coming back. . . . I simply wanted to go back to the place where I spent my childhood, where what is specifically mine was imparted to the very core. Perhaps I sensed that whatever one accomplishes in life is little other than the attempt to regain childhood. (1998, 209–10)[8]

The happiness marking childhood for Adorno was literally musical; the meaning of the blessed childhood he experienced was purchased through sonority, and with two mothers. In the dark and cold of early winter 1933, Adorno, just thirty, looked back to what was already long gone, the *vierhändig*. And as if to confirm one loss, there'll soon be another. Aunt Agathe will die in 1935, and her loss Adorno will connect to Mahler, whose music he could hardly ever seem to get out of his head, not least because he perceived in Mahler a consistent engagement with the past in the name of a future that might be. In 1936, his thoughts on Mahler addressed death, specifically, the death of children. "Why Mahler, following those poems by Rückert, wrote the *Kindertotenlieder,* I understood the first time in my life when someone I loved died" (2002c, 612).[9] Aunt Agathe was an old woman, but her death gave insight into the death of children—and the end of childhood. Mahler's music, Ruckërt's poetry, the loss of Agathe, and the anniversary of Mahler's death (which the essay commemorates) together invoke the traumatic realization, faced variously by everyone past childhood, of all that cannot ever be again—but with the plea for a remainder:

> Du musst nicht die Nacht in dir verschränken,
> Musst sie ins ew'ge Licht versenken![10]
>
> [You must not grasp the night within you,
> You must drown it in eternal light.]

Adorno's citation of the *Kindertotenlieder* in his Mahler essay, like "Vierhändig, noch einmal," evokes personal history for purposes that reach beyond the self. In both texts, he grasps to recall what is otherwise lost—obliterated history: "The rescue of what is possible, but has not yet been—this is the aim of remembrance" (2002c, 612). In Mahler, Adorno hears the reconfiguration of the past into the hopes and innocent dreams of all those who have lived, and especially in the unselfconscious vitality, energy, and spontaneity of the very young.[11] Adorno perceives this not as a gesture of blind nostalgia and solipsistic melancholy but precisely as a promise unfulfilled: remembrance as a responsibility toward the dead on behalf of the living and those who have not yet been born. Much the same holds true for his personal memories of home, the personal state—and stakes—of a fortunate childhood, defined by harmony.[12] Not, however, the harmony of lovers at the keyboard but of a social harmony now disappeared. In "Vierhändig, noch einmal" the memory is at once specifically and unquestionably personal, but it is also at the same time deeply historical: 1933. The personal memory is likewise social, and the history is that of modernity, anchored to the profoundly mundane, the parlor piano—the only piece of furniture that Adorno ever spoke of with reverence (if hardly always)—and, presumably, a bench long enough for two bottoms, the child's and his mother's, either one of them.

The Wiesengrund-Adornos had a separate *Musikzimmer*. The piano was positioned in the center of this room (Müller-Doohm, 47), just as music, both figuratively and literally, defined the center for Adorno of the utopian longing invoked in the conjunction of childhood and belonging that under ideal circumstances appends to "home," that most heavily weighted of words. Again, Rückert/Mahler:

> Oft denk' ich, sie sind nur ausgegangen!
> Bald werden sie wieder nach Hause gelangen![13]
>
> [Often I think they have only gone out!
> Soon they will come home again.]

It's not lost on Adorno that the parlor, clichéd sign of bourgeois self-sanction, economic well-being, and cultural achievement, real or imagined, was defined by the still-more-clichéd piano gracing its space—what he called "a piece of furniture," in reference to the plain fact that, in the bourgeois catalogue of signs of the self, it was rather more essential to *have* a piano than actually to play it. Not for nothing does he sarcastically refer to the "fortress of the piano" (*die Festung der Klaviers*), in hardly veiled allusion to the absolute privacy of the private sphere, the home as inner sanctum, the holy of holies, wherein is celebrated the self-conscious *arrivisme* measured by money and its endless domestic trappings. The piano signaled a cultural sublime available for purchase and in a staggering multiplicity of models—materials, size, workmanship, and decoration to fit pretty much every pocketbook across a surprisingly wide swath of the social spectrum. Despite particular association with the middle class, the piano came in models appropriate to the European, and American, populations at large. For the well off, it was commonly encased in the visual—often excessive—splendor of the finest cabinetry; but affordable stripped-down models were very successfully marketed to the working class. As Adorno recognized, there were stark social truths standing in the shadows behind the very real beauty of the rare woods and ivory and the elaborately carved and inlaid cases of pianos built especially for the bourgeoisie. Indeed, no other musical instrument so effectively aestheticized the histories of imperialism, protoglobalization, alienated labor, class warfare, and, not least, the radical domestication of women (Leppert 1993, 134–87).

Benjamin, confiding to his *Moscow Diary*, once imagined a scene whose familiar reality embraced the dialectics of ordinary domestic life enacted in the parlor: "In my room we got to talking about the 'piano' as a piece of furniture that functions in the petit-bourgeois interior as the true dynamic center of all the dominant miseries and catastrophes of the household. Asja was electrified by the idea; she wanted to write an article on it with me which Reich would then turn into a dramatic sketch" (28).[14]

Adorno, writing about the same phenomenon a decade or so after "Vierhändig, noch einmal," and from the prospective of southern California, set aside his memories of a musical childhood among women in a bitter evocation of the Angel in the House, echoing Benjamin and then some:

> The planned cultivation of beauty was entrusted to women. . . . What was left of the fans, songs, and dances of Roman slave girls was definitively reduced in Birmingham to piano playing and other handicrafts,

> until the last residues of female wantonness had been entirely sublimated as emblems of patriarchal civilization. (Horkheimer and Adorno 2002, 207)

But in 1933 Adorno clung forcefully to the positive part of the piano's dialectical social equation.

Music for Adorno served to bridge a chasm separating the private world of relative privilege and the public world upon which privilege was constructed but commonly excluded. Music for Adorno was a sonoric simulacrum of a reconciliation between subject and object, nature and culture. Music did not make the world right, but it did give access to what that world might sound like.[15] Adorno experienced, indeed learned, all this as a child, making music with the women who first taught him to listen, and then to play—lessons he never forgot.[16] The symphony especially, the music of the concert hall, was domesticated, "moved into home life," transcribed and published in "those oblong [*Querformat*] volumes"—specially bound in matching green covers. Nicely bound, but not for show.[17] "They appeared as if made to have their pages turned," and turn them he did, receiving permission long before he had the notes in his fingers. Adorno's remembrance of his childhood playing accesses and valorizes the world of difference—the outside-of-oneself—of music that he realized with his own hands and those of his mother(s). The four-hand duet for the child Adorno was like a sonic embrace: part him, part another, one whole.

Adorno acknowledges that now he cannot hear the music he first played as a child *except* through (and weighed against) those early experiences. Even the full orchestra measures up poorly against the tension produced by the introductory eighth notes that set pace for what follows in the Mozart G Minor symphony when played on the piano; and not least because it's the second player—little Teddie —who's responsible. That is, when the transcribed symphony opens, sans conductor, it's the child, sitting in front of the keyboard's lower half, who determines the tempo and has to keep it going steadily, evenly, through all the chord changes, with even a little chromaticism. The child establishes the foundation for the opening theme in the treble handled by Mom. Even though his touch is "questionable," even though there will be "faltering and false notes," what matters is "an active relation to the works," something lost to the passive auditors in the concert hall who "in an intoxicated state listened" to the flawless playing of the professionals—what he would elsewhere and later refer to as the "barbarism of perfection," a form of fetishistic technocratic discipline and musical purity commonly under the reign of a conductor's steely, Führer-like (his word) control (2002d, 301).[18]

Young Teddie experienced the terror of doing, but also the excitement. Making music, not in subservience to familial authority as a rehearsal for life after childhood, but in equal partnership with his elders. What higher indication of mutual respect, indeed love, could a child imagine, and how better to understand the responsibilities that he enjoys? He knows full well the tightrope he's walking, given his musical fallibility, his small hands, short fingers, and uncertain technique. He plays on the brink of failure in order to give to what he loves: music, mothers. Making music, whatever the mistakes, sanctioned belonging; it was "the gift . . . placed at my cradle." (The earliest sounds Adorno recalled, even before those on the parlor piano, were tunes sung to him by his mothers, songs for sleep—Brahms, of course, the lullaby, and some others) (Müller-Doohm, 33).

The music Adorno played, most of it arranged from orchestral scores and some of it originally composed for four-hand, was the quintessential music of the bourgeois period, in all of its dialectical splendor. On the one hand, this was the music that all too nicely served to make the bourgeois auditor comfortable in the concert hall, to the extent that it seemed to repeat in sound, indeed to make pretty, the successful striving of modernity and its adherents: the sonoric-German version of all those Dickens heroes. But on the other hand, and put less crassly, some of it was the music in which Adorno heard the highest ideals of the Enlightenment: demand for emancipatory social change, for individual interests realized reciprocally with others—more wished than real, to be sure, but not poorer for the aspiration. Not accidentally in this context, Adorno, in the act of remembering his musical childhood in the dark circumstances of 1933, invokes Paul Bekker's "theory of the community-forming force of the symphonic,"[19] insisting that community and individuality can each ultimately survive only as a unit.

The reduction of four-hand music from the orchestral mass of perhaps eighty players to just two drives home the point. That is, Adorno hears a socially revealing relation between two forms of performance of the same music. The "community" of the orchestra submerges the individual voice in order to make possible the whole; the performance of the same music four-hand brings to the surface the voice of the individual while at the same time preserving allusion to the communal circumstances upon which the music depends. There is just one piano, one keyboard, but there are two players sharing it. Admitted "into the family," the symphony reaffirms "every individual" in its "great whole"—and, critically important, "without surrendering any of the latter's binding quality." For any of this to happen, the domestic-scene player has to "earn" [*erwerben*] the music, and that comes from playing it again and again—*noch einmal, immer noch einmal*—so as to learn it from the inside.

The musical community evoked by four-hand music is ultimately located in the specifics of performance practice. That is, Adorno's point is not simply about playing but about how one plays. The (musical) child in training for a life in the (musical) community is given his freedom to extend the rubato over the solo Grieg on the music rack; after all, with Grieg, rubato is sanctioned. But he is not permitted to play around with the tempo and dynamics of the four-hand transcriptions of symphonies. He owed his partner more, and he owed the music better. Connections to both needed to be maintained; this in effect is "the secret" of four-hand music: it demands much of the self in relation to the otherness of the partner, but also to the otherness of the music. The rubato, characteristic of self-willed expressiveness, would wrest from the symphony its insistence on its distinct difference from the child who brings it to life. Expressed differently, if there's to be a rubato, it has to be agreed upon with one's partner, and result from what the music requires.

The reward for any such self-sacrifice is considerable, and the reward exceeds matters of taste and stylishness: the aesthetics Adorno cares about is at once intimate and social at heart. Edward Cone suggests that the aim of four-hand music is to evoke oneness, as it were, an almost spiritual "harmony" at the unison. "Such a performance," he suggests, "is thus a peculiarly intimate affair, and when it is undertaken in public, the auditor may feel at best an intruder, at worst a voyeur." The performers perceive one another as extensions of themselves, "each participating fully and equally in the life of the persona they jointly symbolize" (Cone 1974, 135).[20]

Adorno never mentions any possibility other than performance; in particular, he's not interested in that other acoustic machine already competing for space in the parlor, the gramophone,[21] which graced his own family's living space, or, later, the radio. Winding the spring or turning the switch that activates the apparatus is not what he intends by musical doing.[22] Not for nothing does he therefore make deeply ironic allusion to Arnold Böcklein's grimly evocative *Die Toteninsel*, which, oddly enough, decorated many a Biedermeier dining room, including, apparently, his own family's (Müller-Doohm 2003, 47).[23] The original commission called for a picture to induce (day)dreams: hazy reverie while supine on the sofa (though dreaming in the dining room doesn't quite compute). Like 78 rpm shellacs, early storehouses of sonoric culture, and the vehicle for possessing permanently the labors of other people's music making, the mass-produced art reproduction offered instant access to "the beautification of life."[24]

> If you can afford good oil paintings, they will become the loveliest ornament in your home, a refreshment for your and others' eyes. If good oil paintings are too expensive for you, then prefer beautiful photographs, steel engravings, and similar reproductions of famous paintings that you can nowadays acquire in rare perfection and at small expense to poor paintings or worthless chromolithographs.[25]

Music shouldn't be instant culture that can be bought on shellac or like a print hung on the wall; music, Adorno says, "in order to be owned" has to be earned by *making* it. Nor is it for show, even if the bourgeoisie quite commonly bought pianos for their decorative value. The green-bound piano scores in the Wiesengrund household, however nicely matched, hence duly decorative, were there to be opened, read. Passively listening to four-hand playing, by contrast, Adorno acknowledged, "is hardly ever a joy." The pleasure, and the worth, was in the doing.

December 1933. Four-hand playing has already "fallen silent," traceable only in the recollections of lost childhood: "Playing four-hand has become a gesture of memory." Adorno hears the now-distant echo of whatever remains of the music's trace of humaneness, and in spite of the barbarism in which it too commonly participates as the price to be paid for its existence. Modernity, marked by the dark sublime of the *ew'ge Licht* extinguished, requires relief from itself, its capacity for so-doing in doubt. In this we may recognize the urgency of Adorno's insistent *"noch einmal."* The late-modern subject sitting at the piano with a partner, tackling Beethoven, Schubert, or Brahms, might find in this music—realized by this always-hybridized, and now mostly out-of-fashion means—a bridge to the severed connections that severely limit late-modern intersubjectivity. (Adorno, in any event, kept trying; an older friend of mine relates that as a young man—this would have been in the sixties—he played four-hand music with Adorno.) In a musical situation where the partners, musically intimate, must account for one another, they might discover in the process, however briefly, a semblance of a harmony that words—even Adorno's—fail to measure. And there might even be something more, and wholly unexpected: "a child might be found to turn the pages for them."

The closing line of Adorno's great, unfinished last book, *Aesthetic Theory,* asks rhetorically, "what would art be, as the writing of history, if it shook off the memory of accumulated suffering" (1997, 261). Adorno's 1933 aphoristic memory piece turns back a page of history to find a place for its better future. That, after all, defines the hope at the heart of having a child, and of being one. Those oddly shaped green volumes, printed oblong, one page for me and the other for you, which we will read together with sympathetic touch, connect Adorno to the loving touch of the history of his small self, the acute memory of the immeasurable happiness that fortunate children experience when unconditionally loved. Those odd-shaped music books, which on account of their format intrude in the goodly order of the library (where to put them, since they jut out unreasonably from any shelf?), cannot be ignored. The green covers and *querformat,* a duet of visual provocation, invite allegiance to the sounds they encode, for Adorno the cipher of an acoustic utopia. They wait for large hands and small hands; they wait to be touched, their contents sounded, given life *noch einmal.* "Ownership," Benjamin once commented, "is the most intimate relationship that one can have to objects. Not that they come alive in him; it is he who lives in them" (Benjamin 1969, 67).

Notes

1. More recently, there was a performance in Shenzhen, China, celebrating the one hundredth birthday on August 22, 2004 of Deng Xiaoping ("paramount leader"), involving two hundred pianos and pianists, ages eight to eighty-two, performing on twenty-eight grands of various sizes along with 172 uprights. The program included "Edelweis," "The Blue Danube," and, as one might anticipate these days, the "Ode to Joy." See Rockwell 2004.

2. Winter et al. 2001, 690: In Britain, France, Germany, and America collectively, it is estimated that the manufacture of pianos in 1870 numbered 85,000; in 1890, 212,000; in 1910, 590,000.

3. The best recent account of this music is by Christensen 1999.

4. Four-hand music was performed alike by men and women. For women, however, transcriptions of (commonly heroic) symphonic music in particular (Beethoven, say) would have resonated quite differently from the music deemed at the time "feminine"—Mendelssohn and Chopin, for example—hence, specifically appropriate for females. See Kallberg 1996.

5. Lubin 1976, 3: "Perhaps it is no more than a mere accident that so much piano duet music involves a crossing of the hands between the partners, even where it may not be absolutely required by the music itself."

6. Christensen 1999, 293: "Piano duet performances are arguably a doubly eroticized activity, for not only are there twenty fingers touching the keys, two bodies are coming into contact with each other—hands crossing over and interlocking; legs, hips, elbows, and shoulders rubbing and bumping into each other. Four-hand performances have the capacity to generate a sexual synergy whose potency has been recognized since the eighteenth century when piano tutors prescribed the proper etiquette and attire for playing duets." Regarding four-hand music, eroticism, and same-sex performers, see note 19, below.

7. Concerning the sisters' musical talents, and in particular Agathe's on the piano, see Müller-Doohm 2003, 32, 39–40.

8. Adorno is, of course, playing off the title of Wagner's essay "What Is German?" (Wagner 1966). See also Levin 1985; and Berman 1989, 184.

9. The essay was written on the occasion of the twenty-fifth anniversary of the composer's death, May 18, 1936; Agathe Calvelli-Adorno died on June 26, 1935.

10. From the first of the *Kindertotenlieder*, "Nun will die Sonn' so hell aufgeh'n," lines 5–6.

11. During the same period, Adorno was at work on the libretto for his never completed stagework *Der Schatz des Indianer-Joe: Singspiel nach Mark Twain*, based on *The Adventures of Tom Sawyer*. Adorno had shared the libretto with Walter Benjamin who, not much liking the piece, wrote Adorno (January 29, 1934) that he "should have much preferred to have congratulated you in detail upon your sketch of children in ["Vierhändig, noch enimal"]—the most recent thing of yours which I have read"; instead, Benjamin found himself saddled with the

unpleasant task of delivering a brief but—to Adorno's eyes—quite devastating critique. Not long thereafter Adorno abandoned the project, for which he had already written a small amount of the music. See further Adorno and Benjamin 1999, 23–28, which includes Adorno's reply to Benjamin. See also Tiedemann 2004, especially concerning Adorno's happy childhood in relation to the realities of the Nazi present and the future it promised set against the text of *Indianer-Joe*: "Here he faced the deathly fear of losing that which one believes to be secure to the very last: the continuing promise that seemed to guarantee a happy childhood" (383).

12. Adorno's childhood, in Martin Jay's words, "provided him a model of happiness whose memory served as a standard against which he would measure all subsequent disappointments" (Jay 1984, 25).

13. From the fourth of the *Kindertotenlieder*, lines 1–2.

14. Benjamin was in Moscow from December 6, 1926 to February 1, 1927. The reference to Asja is to Asja Lacis, whom Benjamin loved; Reich is Bernhard Reich, a director who previously had been with the Deutsches Theater in Berlin and who later married Asja.

15. In a brief memoir of Adorno, Peter von Haselberg (2003, 133–34) recalled having played four-hand music with his friend two years after "Vierhändig, noch einmal" was published. Adorno had returned to Frankfurt in 1935, staying on for several months, though he found the possibilities of seeing old friends severely reduced. Von Haselberg recalls the two men taking their pleasure instead in four-hand playing, including a piano reduction of Mahler's Seventh Symphony, which they played repeatedly. Much to von Haselberg's surprise, his landlady recognized it as Mahler. Adorno in turn wanted to invite her over to hear the piece the next time they performed it, an idea that von Haselberg rejected. The would-be invitation, Haselberg relates, grew from Adorno's conviction, misplaced in Haselberg's sense of the historical moment, that Mahler's music exercised a kind of moral imperative—something the times very much demanded. (Von Haselberg objected that in the culture of National Socialism Mahler's invocation of folksong was suspect.) My thanks to Jonathan Wipplinger for bringing this text to my attention.

16. Concerning music in the Wiesengrund-Adorno home, see Müller-Doohm 2003, 47–48.

17. Benjamin 1969, 60, citing Anatole France: "The only exact knowledge there is is the knowledge of the date of publication and the format of books."

18. See also Adorno 1999, 40–53.

19. Bekker 1936, 116, writing about the Beethoven symphonies and overtures, as well as the *Missa Solemnis* and *Fidelio*: "[The music's] spiritual attitude, linked with the ideology of liberty, fraternity, and the demand for individual responsibility, perfectly reflected the ideal of liberation of individuality through development of independence, the final goal being unification of all individualities into a free community."

20. See Brett 1997, 149–76, who considers this issue at length and with regard to personal experience playing the Andante from Schubert's Grand Duo in C Major with a male partner. The essay, as insightful as it is principled, was written in the larger context of recent debates concerning Schubert's sexuality.

21. See, however, three brief essays by Adorno that do consider the gramophone: Adorno 2002a, 2002b, 2002e, and related commentary (232–40); see also Levin 1990.

22. On this point, see also Christensen 1999, 292–93.

23. The painting, the artist's most famous, exists in five versions (1880–1886); the version in the Metropolitan Museum, New York, dates from 1880. A night scene, it represents a seascape with an islet of rock and tall cypresses, with a small grouping of cryptlike ruins as well as doorways cut into a rock face. A small boat approaches containing a figure in white, back to us, standing before a cloth-draped casket. The paintings were endlessly reproduced for home display; the island detail was also replicated in period advertisements for products as diverse as mouthwash and sparkling wine. Rachmaninoff's 1909 symphonic poem *Ostrov myortvikh* [The Isle of the Dead] was inspired by the painting. Finally, in our own time, Patrice Chéreau's Bayreuth *Ring* cycle (1976–80) based a set design on the *Toteninsel*. See further, Gay 1995, 293–96; and Zelger 1991.

24. Beta 1874, 521; quoted in Gay 1995, 289.

25. Franken 1977, 50; quoted in Gay 1995, 289.

Works Cited

Adorno, Theodor W. *Aesthetic Theory*. Ed. Gretel Adorno and Rolf Tiedemann. Trans. Robert Hullot-Kentor. Minneapolis: University of Minnesota Press, 1997.

———. "On the Question: 'What Is German?'" In *Critical Models: Interventions and Catchwords*, trans. Henry W. Pickford, 205–14. New York: Columbia University Press, 1998.

———. "The Mastery of the Maestro." In *Sound Figures*, trans. Rodney Livingstone, 40–53. Stanford, CA: Stanford University Press, 1999.

———. 2002a. "The Curves of the Needle." In *Essays on Music*, ed. Richard Leppert, trans. Thomas Y. Levin, 271–76. Berkeley and Los Angeles: University of California Press, 2002.

———. 2002b. "The Form of the Phonograph Record." In *Essays on Music*, ed. Richard Leppert, trans. Thomas Y. Levin, 277–82. Berkeley and Los Angeles: University of California Press, 2002.

———. 2002c. "Marginalia on Mahler." In *Essays on Music*, ed. Richard Leppert, trans. Susan H. Gillespie, 612–18. Berkeley and Los Angeles: University of California Press, 2002.

———. 2002d. "On the Fetish-Character in Music and the Regression of Listening." In *Essays on Music*, ed. Richard Leppert, trans. Wes Blomster, 288–317. Berkeley and Los Angeles: University of California Press, 2002.

———. 2002e. "Opera and the Long-Playing Record." In *Essays on Music*, ed. Richard Leppert, trans. Thomas Y. Levin, 283–87. Berkeley and Los Angeles: University of California Press, 2002.

Adorno, Theodor W., and Walter Benjamin. *The Complete Correspondence 1928–1940*. Ed. Henri Lonitz. Trans. Nicholas Walker. Cambridge: Harvard University Press, 1999.

Bekker, Paul. *The Story of the Orchestra*. New York: W. W. Norton, 1936.

Benjamin, Walter. "Unpacking My Library." In *Illuminations*, ed. Hannah Arendt, trans. Harry Zohn, 59–67. New York: Schocken Books, 1969.

———. *Moscow Diary*. Ed. Gary Smith. Trans. Richard Sieburth. Cambridge: Harvard University Press, 1986.

Berman, Russell A. *Modern Culture and Critical Theory: Art, Politics, and the Legacy of the Frankfurt School*. Madison: University of Wisconsin Press, 1989.

Beta, H. "Moderne Kunstindustrie." *Gartenlaube* 22 (1874): 521.

Brett, Philip. "Piano Four-Hands: Schubert and the Performance of Gay Male Desire." *19th Century Music* 21, no. 2 (Fall 1997): 149–76.

Christensen, Thomas. "Four-Hand Piano Transcription and Geographies of Nineteenth-Century Musical Reception." *Journal of the American Musicological Society* 52, no. 2 (Summer 1999): 255–98.

Cone, Edward T. *The Composer's Voice*. Berkeley and Los Angeles: University of California Press, 1974.

Ewenz, Gabriele, et al., eds., *Adorno: Eine Bildmonographie*. Frankfurt am Main: Suhrkamp Verlag, 2003.

Franken, Konstanze von. *Handbuch des guten Tones und der feinen Sitte*. 23rd improved ed. 1900; repr. Munich: Matthes und Seitz, 1977.

Gay, Peter. *The Bourgeois Experience: Victoria to Freud*. Vol. 4, *The Naked Heart*. New York: W. W. Norton, 1995.

Haselberg, Peter von. "Wiesengrund-Adorno." In *Adorno in Frankfurt: Ein Kaleidoskop mit Texten und Bildern*, Ed. Wolfram Schütte, 123–34. Frankfurt am Main: Suhrkamp Verlag, 2002.

Horkheimer, Max, and Theodor W. Adorno. *Dialectic of Enlightenment: Philosophical Fragments*. Ed. Gunzelin Schmid Noerr. Trans. Edmund Jephcott. Stanford, CA: Stanford University Press, 2002.

Jay, Martin. *Adorno*. Cambridge: Harvard University Press, 1984.

Kallberg, Jeffrey. *Chopin at the Boundaries: Sex, History, and Musical Genre*. Cambridge: Harvard University Press, 1996.

Leppert, Richard. *Music and Image: Domesticity, Ideology, and Socio-Cultural Formation in Eighteenth-Century England*. Cambridge: Cambridge University Press, 1988.

———. *The Sight of Sound: Music, Representation, and the History of the Body*. Berkeley and Los Angeles: University of California Press, 1993.

Levin, Thomas Y. "Nationalities of Language: Adorno's *Fremdwörter*, An Introduction to 'On the Question: What Is German?'" *New German Critique* 36 (Fall 1985): 111–19.

———. "For the Record: Adorno on Music in the Age of Its Technological Reproducibility." *October* 55 (Winter 1990): 23–47.

Lubin, Ernest. *The Piano Duet: A Guide for Pianists*. New York: Da Capo, 1976.

Marx, Karl. *Grundrisse: Foundations of the Critique of Political Economy (Rough Draft)*. Trans. Martin Nicolaus. London: Penguin, 1993.

Müller-Doohm, Stefan. *Adorno: Eine Biographie*. Frankfurt am Main: Suhrkamp Verlag, 2003.

Rockwell, John. "Reverberations: Like 76 Trombones, Multiple Pianos Make a Formidable Sound." *New York Times*, September 17, 2004, B3.

Tiedemann, Rolf. "Adorno's *Tom Sawyer* Opera Singspiel." In *The Cambridge Companion to Adorno*, ed. Tom Huhn, 376–94. Cambridge: Cambridge University Press, 2004.

Wagner, Richard. "What Is German?" In *Richard Wagner's Prose Works*, trans. William Ashton Ellis: vol. 4, 149–69. 1895; repr. New York: Broude Brothers, 1966.

Winter, Robert, et al. "Pianoforte." In *The New Grove Dictionary of Music and Musicians*, 2nd ed., ed. Stanley Sadie, vol. 19, 655–95. London: Macmillan, 2001.

Zelger, Franz. *Arnold Böcklin Die Toteninsel: Selbstheroisierung und Abgesang der abendländischen Kultur*. Frankfurt am Main: Fischer Taschenbuch Verlag, 1991.

CHAPTER 14

MUSIC "PUSHED TO THE EDGE OF EXISTENCE" (ADORNO, LISTENING, AND THE QUESTION OF HOPE)

That art stands as a reminder of what does not exist, prompts rage.

—Theodor W. Adorno, *Aesthetic Theory*

Hope is not confidence. Hope is surrounded by dangers, and it is the consciousness of danger and at the same time the determined negation of that which continually makes the opposite of the hoped-for object possible.

—Ernst Bloch [in conversation with Adorno], "Something's Missing"

PROLOGUE

These days it's often nearly as difficult to escape music as it is to close one's ears to sound generally. Or, to state the matter more directly, wherever there's commerce—and commerce is everywhere (in the public selling of goods, ideologies, subjectivities, identities)—there's music to help grease the skids of attraction. Music promises good times as you prepare to part with your coin, whatever you're buying or buying into. Given the virtually sacred nature of late capitalism's secular materialism, the ritual of selling is rampantly overdetermined, and here music plays a fundamental role, no matter the product and without regard to whether the consumers are presumed to be the de facto proles, on the lower end of the social spectrum, or the Quality, on the upper end. As it were, pretty much everyone has music in his or her ears throughout the exchange process. The ubiquity of music in commerce, broadly conceived—in a postindustrial world defined by commerce—engenders repetition on a vast scale, more and more of the same so long as it sells, like sitcom spin-offs gone cosmic: interchangeable music Clearly Channeled into a would-be mass consciousness, as though life were lived within the confines of a global elevator outfitted with surround sound. Positive social effects pretty much go begging, so the story goes. Decades ago, Theodor Adorno diagnosed and predicted all this, repeatedly, and to the considerable consternation of music lovers of nearly every bent.

But things aren't quite that simple, and in particular not for Adorno. Indeed, though Adorno is commonly (if carelessly) charged with unrelenting pessimism, at the very heart of his sustained and often bitter critique of modernity there lies fundamental hopefulness, if not precisely optimism, conceived within the context of art's role—music especially—in providing the wherewithal to imagine social utopia. But for Adorno to imagine a better reality, the actuality of the present dystopia must be directly confronted.

In about 1934 Adorno drafted an essay called "Music in the Background," so aphoristically brief that it might be taken almost as an afterthought. Anecdotal and (atypically) almost conversational in tone, the text hints at a foundation for hope, but indirectly. Adorno describes the everyday, utterly ordinary—and indeed clichéd—live entertainment music typical of 1930s European cafés and pubs, music that for the time served a similar function to the most ritualistically commercial musics of today. Adorno's concern, in essence, was music in a state of ruins, whose sounds he nonetheless pursued with both determination and sadness.

He opens the essay with a series of images of music—or, perhaps better, of musical life—now silenced in the administration and bustle of mundane existence. If one sings aloud on the street there's the risk of being arrested as a disturber of the peace; if one hums while in the car, the very lack of attention to the task of (hectic) driving may produce an accident. In short, "If you are looking for music, you have to step outside the space of immediate life, because it no longer is one, and find the lost immediacy where it costs the price of admission, at the opera, at a concert" (Adorno 2002b, 506). In the 1930s Adorno "heard" the silencing of music—except in the sanctioned venues of high bourgeois art—at a time when the phonograph and the radio were already well established as the foundation for musical mass culture. Modern life as he perceived it was unmusical, and the only way to recoup the loss was to see that life restaged, on museumlike historical display, and in designated, official-culture performance sites. The exceptions proved the rule.

Our present-day situation leaves us very little silence to "hear"; music in particular is virtually inescapable. And the effects at the heart of Adorno's concern are the same: repetition (a complement to ubiquity), as Jacques Attali reminds us, is a form of silence—and silencing (Attali 1985, 87–132).[1] At this point in his essay Adorno takes an unexpected turn, to the extent that he identifies places where ordinary musical life (a type of commerce-music) holds on, places which he clearly valorizes: the café and the bar. As he puts it, "exiled Music herself, pushed to the edge of existence, holds out loyally there: music as background" (Adorno 2002b, 506). Here (live) music still "belongs"; "it may have been shooed off the street, but not to the distant reaches of formalized art." It lives in the background—you don't have to bother listening—but it maintains a presence nonetheless as accompaniment to conversation. The people within the music's earshot do not constitute an audience; nor, for that matter, are they in what Adorno terms a "musical mood." Indeed, the music's "first characteristic" is that "you don't [even] have to listen to it." And yet the music does something; music and people are "caught up and bound together"; "it keeps the customers company" (507)—and perhaps momentarily happy.[2]

Adorno hears in live-performance café music the remnant of a musical life without the self-consciousness of Art (writ large) or, for that matter, the administered goods variously distributed through the reach of the culture industry. Well, not quite. Musically, there's nothing original, just pared down arrangements of stuff likely first intended for an orchestra. As music, its lifeblood is the cliché; it's been heard before, many times. As he explains, it's not much, but it's something, a something evident in the music's absence when the tune concludes or the set ends. When café music falls silent, its loss is instantly apparent; "It sounds as if a miserly waiter is turning off a couple of electric bulbs" (508).

The limits of what we're hearing are tightly circumscribed: "The café arranges bouquets of dead flowers" (508). In our own time, consider the potpourris of classic hits that interpellate would-be store customers—or "guests," in current deceitful business parlance—by invoking the imagined core of our identities via sonorically induced nostalgia and, no doubt, melancholy. Adorno minces few words on the nature of the appeal: "If our art music lingers in the comforting realm of Orpheus—here its echo sounds from Euridice's mournful region." In the café, Adorno suggests, what we will hear, should we choose to listen to the background, are acoustic ruins, yet ruins awakened to "new, ghostly life." The music-in-ruins "lights up" those who hear it, even though its glow is "netherworldly" (509).

Adorno encapsulates late modernity's sorry remnant of enlightenment ideals via the metaphor of paltry electric illumination: "Background music is an acoustic light source" (508). It illuminates, however dimly, what might have been.[3] For Adorno, the potential realization of "what might have been" marks the socially hopeful possibility (or threat) of conjuring from auditors a social critique, however vague, of the very conditions (antimusical to the core) that produce the musical ubiquity of Muzak and its aftermath in the first place. Let's be clear: the social critique that Adorno imagines carries minimal threat to the status quo, on account of the fact that listeners are not being introduced to the music as anything new: no demands are made on them and especially none necessitating conscious thought. What's given is simply the same-old; the music quoted connects to memory that it's there to soothe and stroke, eliciting the "emotional calm" characteristic of predictability. And, with luck, to encourage its auditors to fork over. There's no way around the conflicted nature of this dialectic of late-modern musical reception. Nowadays we may enter the Gap or Abercrombie and Fitch to buy a shirt, but if we cathect to whatever bit of the playlist that accompanies our movements—a playlist we're already likely to know—the CD compilation is available for purchase, seasonally adjusted to coincide with the merchandise that's offered, as part of the *Gesamtkunstwerk* of the shopping experience.

But there's more, as it were, a remainder. Whatever the grim reality of the metaphoric affinity between music and the myriad rhetorics of everyday life under the conditions defined by late capital, music, however debased—and indeed, however potentially debasing—still points to something better. This is what informs Adorno's insight that background music is an acoustic light source illuminating what might have been. Put differently, the presence of music—*any* music—references a lack. And lack, properly understood, is not an ontological condition but a social one. Lack, in other words, invites critique; critique in turn is the precondition for social change.

MUSIC AS SUCH IN MUSICAL THOUGHT

The social impact of music has been endlessly claimed since the dawn of Western history. In particular, as is very well known, social conservatives—from Plato to the neoplatonist Alan Bloom, among a substantially larger host—have looked with suspicion on music—all music. They insist that music is more than entertainment, that it shapes society. The trick, as they see it, is to make music effective principally as a (properly masculinized) agent of prevailing orders of power, the State especially. Plato's account of music's enervating force on the male (the female being of little interest to him), endlessly repeated by close paraphrase thereafter to the present, fundamentally equates musical "excess," for example, with masturbation —to borrow from the prevailing metaphor in Kubrick's *Dr. Strangelove,* the loss of "precious bodily fluids," the essence as it were of masculinity itself. Thus Plato (as the voice of Socrates):

> Then when any man lets music flute his soul away, and pour flooding into his mind through his ears, as through a funnel, those sweet and soft and mournful melodies which we have described, till he spends his whole life piping and cloying himself with sound, that man at first tempers the spirited element in him, as steel is tempered, and makes it useful instead of useless and hard; but if he continues without ceasing to beguile that element, after a time he begins to dissolve and melt it away, till he pours out his spirit in a stream, cuts as it were the sinews of his soul, and makes of it a "feeble warrior." (Plato 1957, 118)

And Bloom, who for good measure considerably outdoes Plato via a seething flow of images incorporating solo sex, cross-dressing, and parental murder, together the result of a kid having the wrong tunes in his ears:

> Picture a thirteen-year-old boy sitting in the living room of his family home doing his math assignment while wearing his Walkman headphones or watching MTV. He enjoys the liberties hard won over centuries by the alliance of philosophic genius and political heroism, consecrated by the blood of martyrs; he is provided with comfort and

> leisure by the most productive economy ever known to mankind . . . And in what does progress culminate? A pubescent child whose body throbs with orgasmic rhythms; whose feelings are made articulate in hymns to the joys of onanism or the killing of parents; whose ambition is to win fame and wealth in imitating the drag-queen who makes the music. In short, life is made into a nonstop, commercially prepackaged masturbational fantasy. (Bloom 1987, 74–75)

And so on.[4] These social conservatives, whatever their moral panic regarding the dystopian potential of music, got it distinctly correct that music matters at the level of social formation and its maintenance. Their concern, unlike mine, was to enshrine a status quo whose interests were, and continue to be, underwritten by something less than the "democracy" Bloom predictably invokes in his book's title. What I'm after develops from the same insight but leads in a different direction. My concern is the hope that music posits for a society that one now can only imagine rather than experience, a society, to use Ernst Bloch's characterization, perceived as "if only it were so" (Bloch and Adorno 1988, 3; and Adorno 1997, 105).[5] As Adorno succinctly put it, "The promise contained in the age-old protest of music [is] the promise of a life without fear" (1981b, 156);[6] and, as a corollary, "A priori, *prior to its works,* art is a critique of the brute seriousness that reality imposes upon human beings. Art imagines that by naming this fateful state of affairs it is loosening its hold" (Adorno 1992c, 248, emphasis added). I will develop my argument concerning music and hope not around any particular example but around a social philosophy of music *as such*—and with the understanding that music, to be understood, to be able "to speak" its protest, needs philosophy.[7]

My principal claim is that music is the Other, not the other of silence, but the other of the nonmusic and the antimusic of social relations. Music registers itself as a difference, as it were, as an alternative to nonmusical life—nonmusical life meant both as neutral fact of existence and, more to the present concern, as a dystopian reality in which music is, in ironic actuality, virtually inescapable. The stakes of the claim are high. To speak in general terms: Adorno suggests that "every artwork is an instant; every successful work is a cessation, a suspended moment of the process, as which it reveals itself to the unwavering eye" (Adorno 1997, 6). That is, art seemingly, momentarily, stops time. It interrupts the dystopian "progress," the backward march that incessantly claims forward movement.[8] This "moment" gives access to a time that does not yet exist but that someday might: utopia. In short, music *as such*, even in its own common ordinariness and inescapability, signals a difference from—more, an opposition to—what otherwise passes as the ordinary and the expected. Music posits the sonoric possibility of something better; "An 'it shall be different' is hidden in even the most sublimated work of art" (Adorno 1992a, 92).[9]

At the same time however, every instance of the artwork fails in its effort. It offers appearance, rather than the "real thing." "Art," Adorno points out, "is [only] the semblance of what is beyond death's reach" (Adorno 1997, 27). As a product of a world awry, the perfection it attempts will necessarily always elude it. But it is precisely in the attempt—exercised in hopeful desperation, one might say—to imagine something different that the reality of the illusion can be appropriately certified: "Artworks are afterimages of empirical life insofar as they help the latter to what is denied them outside their own sphere and thereby free it from that to which they are condemned by reified external experience" (Adorno 1997, 4). Yet artworks are caught in the very web whose bind they seek to transcend: "there is no artwork that does not participate in the untruth external to it, that of the historical moment" (Adorno 1997, 347). And this untruth marks the perpetual failing of art to attain the Absolute for which it nonetheless perpetually strives.[10]

Modernity is marked by the principle of accumulation—possession. Possession defines both subjectivity and identity, just as it serves as the organizing principle of the material economies through which subjects are realized. Within this context, music's sublime, the root of its utopian promise, lies in the materiality of its *im*material essence. That is, music is the result of social practice; it "happens" through (embodied) labor. And yet at heart music cannot be either grasped or held onto, despite its being "made," and despite its being made "tangible" as a product. In the most fundamental sense, *music resists being possessed.*[11] Music—ironically highly commercialized, fully incorporated into the exchange economy—refuses the very principal upon which modernity depends: ownership. Music invariably slips from reach. Literally. Our hold on it lasts only so long as its sounds remain audible. Its only permanence (the defining principle of possession) is its impermanence. Consider the dim regret we feel when a piece of music we love ends. We want to hear it again, even knowing that a rehearing will produce the same result. We will re-experience the regret that it's "over," and that its being over is so complete. Dissatisfied satisfaction.

Ironically, music evokes the very spirituality (immateriality) upon which modernity feeds as the loss leader for keeping things just the way they are. That is, music spiritualizes, but music also is given to play the game of spiritualiz*ing*—aestheticizing—the sanctity of possession, the very principle against which it proclaims its difference. But its co-opting is never complete. Music plays along, but under protest, which ever threatens to break into the open. Whatever the degree of music's sonic affirmation of society-as-it-is, music's otherness remains insistent, if often disguised. Music's soul stands in the shadows, ever ready for its moment to break through to the light. Plato knew all this. Plato feared music, and with good reason.

Adorno regarded art as the repository for the faint semblance of a social happiness otherwise unavailable; at the same time he insisted that art could not provide what society denied. "Art," as he put it, "is the ever broken promise of happiness" (Adorno 1997, 136). The faint trace of art's broken promise could be seen, if only as a shadow, *even in debased art*. Take kitsch. Adorno insisted that "every great, authentic piece of musical kitsch . . . is capable of acting as the accompaniment to imaginary catastrophes" (Adorno 1992e, 16). His telescoped sentence is semantically slippery, though his claim expresses the seriousness he accords to kitsch, which, as he understands it, comes in varieties of greater and lesser, authentic and inauthentic, all of it semiotically underscoring danger. Adorno is eliciting the reality of the truth in the lie, that is, that the truth of kitsch is its falseness, which every "authentic" example represents before all else. The precise truth of the lie is the actual catastrophe, which the kitsch-work accompanies, rather like the blindfold offered the man about to be shot: the blindfold visually confirms what the optics of the victim's masked eyes can no longer physiologically project onto the retina. The blindfold is felt on the skin as a preview of the absolute darkness into which its wearer is about to be transported.

Adorno commented that "kitsch contains as much hope as is

able to turn the clock back. It is the depraved reflection of that epiphany which is vouchsafed only to the greatest works of art" (Adorno 1992b, 43). Nor was kitsch precisely the antithesis of great art: "Kitsch is not, as those believers in erudite culture would like to imagine, the mere refuse of art, originating in disloyal accommodation to the enemy; rather, *it lurks in art,* awaiting ever recurring opportunities to spring forth" (Adorno 1997, 239, emphasis added).[12] Kitsch—even kitsch—evokes a future utopia, but only by looking back at a past that is selectively (mis)remembered, thereby helping to stabilize the status quo toward which kitsch is otherwise deeply antagonistic.[13] Kitsch, for Adorno, fundamentally evokes the momentary self-imposition of exile from the present. Yet in the effort by kitsch to forget the present, the past is remembered: history is evoked, but misleadingly.[14] Hence, the progressive element in kitsch is its insistence that the past matters (despite the claims authorized by modernity's mantra of progress that the past is irrelevant). Were the present less painful, the lie of kitsch would be less insistent. That is, the aporia of modernity leads us to seek consolation in place of what appears to be the impossibility of reconciliation with the otherness—the condition of general estrangement—that we at once ironically desire and abhor. "The positive element of kitsch," Adorno bitterly noted, "lies in the fact that it sets free for a moment the glimmering realization that you have wasted your life" (1992b, 50). *Even so,* this insight makes space for the principle of hope.

Ernst Bloch, whose influence on Adorno's thinking on art, kitsch, and hope was considerable, often discussed kitsch and a variant, colportage (in reference to itinerant booksellers or colporteur common in Europe from the seventeenth through nineteenth centuries who hawked a wide variety of books—bibles, cookbooks, medical books, fairy tales, what we would recognize as pulp fiction, and so on) (Bloch 1988d, xxxvii).[15] He recognized in kitsch and colportage what he termed "a yearning . . . that is itself not nonsensical, even though it is shrill and fraudulent, cheap and uncontrolled" (1988b, 181).[16]

I embrace Adorno's and Bloch's insistence that kitsch can function as a repository for hope (however faint), evinced from an awareness (however unreflexive and dim) of the truth of its lie, because I wish to insist on the significance of music *as such* to the delineation of its own otherness from mundane, nonmusical (ironically all-too-musical) life. My concern is music—period. That is, I am not building my argument about hope on the distinction between music high or low, nor of good music versus bad, however we might sort that out the latter, though the distinction is obviously important (Adorno more or less spent his entire life addressing the question). I am suggesting instead that the singular distinction of good or bad gains relevance precisely because the phenomenon of music as such is prior and fundamental alike to the real or imagined well-being of society and its subject-inhabitants: important, as it were, without specific regard to self-reflexive consideration of aesthetic or other "qualities." Thus, I do not believe that the potential social utopianism of music resides solely in what we might choose to call "socially engaged" or "socially progressive" music. However inadvertently, even the musically debased can lay some claim to social utopianism on account of the fact that it is, simply, music.[17] All music, that is, like art generally, constitutes what Bloch aptly terms "anticipatory illumination" [*sichtbarer Vor-Schein*] (1988e, 73; and 1988a), a phrase that resonates with Adorno's metaphor in "Music in the Background" likening music to the light from an incandescent bulb.

Adorno insisted on music's "theological dimension," which he located in music's relation to the absolute: "Its Idea is the divine Name which has been given shape. It is demythologized prayer, rid of efficacious magic. It is the human attempt, doomed as ever, to name the Name, not to communicate meanings" (1992f, 2).[18] Music, he suggests, "says" something, but what it says is at once revealed and concealed. This insight is critical to the social foundations of the argument I'm advancing. Late modernity, as a distorted by-product of the Enlightenment, is defined by the positivisms of instrumentalized reason, ubiquitously repeated in the fully naturalized parlance of everyday relations embedded in communications lingo: "headline news," "factoids," "sidebars," "get to the point," "the bottom line," "time is money," and the like.[19] What this interlocked web of presumed "objectivity" assumes is that everything worth knowing is available in quantifiable form: as fact ("information" in distinction from knowledge). What cannot be assigned the absolute status of facticity is ignored, deemed insignificant, or, alternately, denounced as significant only on account of the immanent danger arising from the "remainder" that cannot with certainty be contained or appropriated within the parameters of "pure" objectivity (which in reality is seldom either pure or objective). Music is a commodity, more now than ever before, at the same time music's commodification is incomplete. And it is precisely music's quality of possessing a remainder beyond its prevailing identity with the here and now—the beyond that Adorno called the nonidentical—that has rendered music suspicious since the ancients began worrying about it. Moreover, it is precisely the nonidentical nature of music's social situation that defines music's centrality to life lived under prevailing conditions of nonliving, as reflected, for Adorno, most obviously in the labors and products of the culture industry, in allegiance with the now-globalized economies and nation-states that run in parallel with its premises.

A corollary: the coercive pressures exerted on musicians throughout history to adhere to the established conventions have become increasingly ironic in late modernity. By definition, the modern artist must at least give the impression of subverting the rules in order to lay claim to the originality that lies at the very foundation of individuality. The artist defines—and is anticipated to define—the most individual of individualities, but in doing so lays claim to a subversiveness that may threaten the well-guarded boundaries of a society of other individuals whose "individuality" in fact is mass produced, and must be mass produced if the dominant ideological matrix is to perform its critically supportive role in the material economy.

My point, then, is this: virtually everything about music—the music "itself," the musicians who make it, and the myriad practices that Christopher Small aptly calls musicking (Small 1998)—possesses a distinctly real potential for subversion, however modest, of the status quo, and everyone knows it. To nail down, measure, and hence control music's potential for subversiveness requires a great deal of effort, effort all too willingly attended to by the highest levels of both government authority and industry, whether state-authorized composers' unions, congressional oversight committees, record companies' ever-nervous advertising departments, or what have you.

> [Theorists of totalitarianism] have all explained, indistinctly, that it is necessary to ban subversive noise because it betokens demands for cultural autonomy, support for differences or marginality: a concern

> for maintaining tonalism, the primacy of melody, a distrust of new languages, codes, or instruments, a refusal of the abnormal—these characteristics are common to all regimes of that nature. (Attali 1985, 7)

But also, in point of fact, common as well to now-dominant "liberal" market societies, where—small irony—the subversive, in the spirit of Bataille, all too easily is transformed into highly marketable "subversiveness," nowadays the sine qua non for virtually every imaginable marketing scheme, from fashion to automobiles, in addition to music itself.

PHILOSOPHY

Adorno often commented on the myriad failings of Western philosophy—this was the indictment of his *Negative Dialectics*—as part and parcel of modernity's more general failure to serve the human subjects on whose behalf it endlessly, if utterly falsely, proclaims its undying allegiance. As he put it in the late essay "Why Still Philosophy," "After having missed its opportunity, philosophy must come to know, without any mitigation, why the world—which could be paradise here and now—can become hell itself tomorrow. Such knowledge would indeed truly be philosophy" (Adorno 1998b, 14). Stating the matter more succinctly, he noted, "It is incumbent upon philosophy . . . to provide a refuge for freedom" (10). In this respect, music and philosophy share the same responsibility, just as each needs the other in order to realize its potential for truth.[20] The "language of music," that is, must "speak" through the voice given to thought.

In his 1956 essay on "Music, Language, and Composition," Adorno assigned profound significance to musical sounds: "They say something, often something humane" (Adorno 2002c, 114). Music is the (concrete) voice of yearning for happiness, which cannot otherwise be directly annunciated, let alone be realized. But as the expression of hope, which seeks to name the philosophical (and spiritual) Absolute that nevertheless is unnamable, music "speaks" indirectly.[21] Adorno stressed the similarities of music to language in order to outline how musical processes produce meaning—though he acknowledged that what music "says" cannot be abstracted from the music, as occurs with language, because music is not constituted by a referential sign system. Unlike language, music has no concepts, but like language it does possess a coherent and meaningful structure. As an "organized coherence of sounds" music is analogous to speech; it "has its sentence, phrase, period, and punctuation." Like language, music is "a temporal succession of articulated sounds." Its content is the "wealth of all those things underlying the musical grammar and syntax. Every musical phenomenon points beyond itself, on the strength of what it recalls, from what it distinguishes itself, by what means it awakens expectation" (Adorno 2002c, 113, 115).

Music is language-like, but it is not language. Music is riddle-like—enigmatical: it says something that the listener understands and yet doesn't. Like all art, music cannot be "pinned down as to what it says, and yet it speaks" (Adorno 2002c, 122). Richard Wolin points out that,

> Unlike philosophy, the language of art is sensuous. Art's mode of articulation relies on images, sounds, and colors rather than the clarity of discursive argument. Consequently as vehicles of truth works of art are inherently "enigmatic" (*rätselhaft*). And it is precisely this enigmatic quality that beseeches, implores, and requires the *philosophical interpretation* of art. In other words, this dynamic alone mandates the necessity of *aesthetic theory*. (Wolin 1990, 39, emphasis in original)[22]

Further to the same point, Adorno insisted that the enigmatical nature of art is bound up with history. "It was through history that [artworks] became an enigma; it is history that ever and again makes them such, and, conversely, it is history alone—which gave them their authority—that holds at a distance the embarrassing question of their raison d'être" (Adorno 1997, 120).

Adorno understood the enigmatical character of art not as its failure but as an essential component of its being art in the first place; he perceived the residue of the uncertain in art as all the more critical under prevailing historical circumstance to the extent that art's enigmaticalness constituted a resistance to its instrumental utilization. The enigmatical character of music, for Adorno, marked its connection to utopia.

During the long period of so-named common practice, conventions (already in place by the eighteenth century) increasingly served to make music's meanings appear self-evident; accordingly, music's enigmatical character was ever more concealed. Today, Adorno argued, when tradition no longer "prescribes anything for music," music's enigmatic character re-emerges, though it remains accessible only through attention to its historical characteristics and mediations (Adorno 2002e, 140–41). Music "speaks" through a process of mimesis, which in turn demands thought: reflexivity on music's immanence, production, realization (performance), and consumption alike.

Mimesis[23]—or mimetic expression—constitutes a central feature of Adorno's aesthetic theory. Mimetic activity occurs both in production (in music, both composing and performing) and in consumption (listening). Mimesis, as Adorno envisions its ideal realization, results from the rational manipulation of musical materials (form, melody, harmony, rhythm, timbre, and so on) in such a way as to engage and indeed to render problematic their conventional usage (to cite an obvious example, Mahler's use in several symphonies of déclassé and low-caste instruments whose sounds intrude into the sanctioned timbres of the late-Romantic orchestra). By this means, and however momentarily, convention releases its claim to the transcendental. That is, through mimetic engagement convention is denaturalized, returned to history, and rendered profoundly social. Put differently, through mimesis the contingency of the conventional can be exposed: no longer to be perceived simply as the way things *are*, but as the way things have been made to *seem*.

In a notably evocative, not to mention intellectually challenging, assertion, Adorno names mimesis "an assimilation of the self to the other" (Nicholsen 1997, 147).[24] That is, he regards mimesis as the enactment of reconciliation between subject and object. The subject comes to the object and reaches out to it, yet not as an act of domination but as one of regard, seeking the difference—the otherness—upon which it insists.[25] Through mimesis the difference otherwise hidden in the sameness of convention is given to speak: another possibility is admitted by means of a remembering of what had been forgotten.[26] The utopian quotient of artworks is reflected best in the dystopian actuality they hold up to the light. By insisting on history, artworks express the possibility of something different. Stated crassly, artworks' mimetic engagement with convention is one means by which subjects may gain the insight that it's *not* part of the natural order that "shit happens" (as the bumper-sticker slogan has it), it's that shit is caused.

Our individuality, our modernity (which Adorno and Horkheimer trace back to Homer), comes with a considerable bill attached. In *Dialectic of Enlightenment*, Adorno (with Max Horkheimer) argued that the human subject's historical relation to nature was one of conflict that turns the subject against others and, ultimately, against the self. They argued that the fundamental forms of domination that organize modernity have their roots in the primordial efforts of human beings to survive in a nature—primordial totality—of which they are at once a part yet deeply alienated from and fearful of. And yet human subjects lament the very separation from nature upon which their subjectivity is ultimately grounded. Thus, by the principle Adorno and Horkheimer articulate, the designation of national parks, which first occurred during the heyday of the industrial revolution—itself signaling a kind of final triumph over nature—directly responded to the fractured relation of the subject to nature; the setting aside of small and as-yet-"untamed" geographies signified less a nostalgic return to nature than a material acknowledgment of the permanence of the fracture, in the same way that salvage anthropology in essence picks among the graves and ruins to remember what "advanced man" has destroyed to become advanced.

Adorno recognized a critical relation between natural beauty and art beauty; indeed, he argued that the separation of human beings from nature and the consequences of this separation were the very subject of art. By denaturalizing this separation—he insisted that the separation was rooted in history—one could gain access to the progressive potential of imagining a reconciliation of the opposing terms in the subject-object and man-nature dyads. Finding a means of so imagining was necessary not least because the subject's separation from nature, self-imposed, produces a division within the self, caused by a rejection of the nature that defines our very own core.[27] As he put it, "The concept of natural beauty rubs on a wound." Art is called upon to answer for natural beauty, which we have degraded and yet nonetheless desire in its nonextant "perfect" state: art reflects on this fact. Art, Adorno says, "want(s) to keep nature's promise. . . . What nature strives for in vain, artworks fulfill" (Adorno 1997, 62, 65–66).[28] Composer-philosopher David Dunn recently said something similar in an allusion to a lengthy passage in James Agee's novel *Let Us Now Praise Famous Men* describing the meanings and intelligence audible in the late-night calls of two foxes. Dunn comments: "We hear in the world talking to itself a sense of otherness that simultaneously mirrors our deepest sense of belonging"; and "Perhaps music is a conservation strategy for keeping something alive that we now need to make more conscious, a way of making sense of the world from which we might refashion our relationships to nonhuman living systems" (Dunn 2001, 95, 97).

In *Philosophy of New Music,* Adorno refers to music as "a gestural art, closely akin to crying," calling it a gesture of "dissolving." Music, like crying, addresses the reality of sorrow and seeks to reach beyond it—music of whatever "quality."

> Music and crying open the lips and bring delivery from restraint. The sentimentality of inferior music recalls in its caricature what superior music is truly capable of shaping at the boundary of frenzy: reconciliation. The man who surrenders to tears in music that no longer resembles him at the same time allows the stream of what he himself is not—what was dammed up back of the world of things—to flow back into him. In tears and singing, the alienated world is entered. "Tears pour, the earth has taken me back"—this is the gesture of music. Thus the earth reclaims Eurydice. The gesture of returning, not the feeling of waiting, describes the expression of all music, even in a world worthy of death. (Adorno forthcoming)[29]

Ernst Bloch makes a complementary claim when, at the opening of his lengthy chapter "The Philosophy of Music" in *The Spirit of Utopia,* he lamented the separation of the subject from nature with a metaphor evoking self-isolation and audition: "We hear only ourselves. For we are gradually becoming blind to the outside." Bloch titled this opening "Dream," which is a recurrent motive in his utopian writing, serving here as the device through which to imagine a better world than the present one—with which he steadfastly refused to make his peace.

> But we walk in the forest and we feel we are or could be what the forest dreams. . . . We do not have it—all that this moss, these strange flowers, roots, stems and shafts of light are or signify—because we ourselves are it, and stand too near to it, this ghostly and ever so nameless

> quality of consciousness or of becoming-inward. But the note flares out of us, the *heard* note, not the note itself or its forms. Yet it shows us our way without alien means, shows us our historically inner path as a flame in which not the vibrating air but we ourselves begin to tremble, and throw off our coats. (Bloch 2000, 34)[30]

The metaphors in play in these citations are anchored in an imagined unity within the natural world, a utopian reconciliation of the most fundamental, if distant, sort, upon which any imaginable form of hope must build. Complementarily, Nietzsche, writing against Wagner, citing in one breath the bond between music and philosophy, likewise evokes hope—via emancipation—all of it with the imagery of a nature of the sublime:

> Has it been noticed that music liberates the spirit? gives wings to thought? that one becomes more of a philosopher the more one becomes a musician?— The gray sky of abstraction rent as if by lightning; the light strong enough for the filigree of things; the great problems near enough to grasp; the world surveyed as from a mountain. —I have just defined the pathos of philosophy.—And unexpectedly answers drop into my lap, a little hail of ice and wisdom, of *solved* problems.—Where am I?— . . . Whatever is good makes me fertile. I have no other gratitude, nor do I have any other *proof* for what is good. (Nietzsche 1967, 158)[31]

Adorno offers a succinct corollary of emancipation that lies at the heart of reconciliation with otherness: "Music says We directly, regardless of its intentions" (Adorno 1997, 167).

THUS FAR

I have drawn heavily on Adorno's *Aesthetic Theory*, a book which has relatively little to say about mass culture beyond its paradigmatic emergence from, and life within, the culture industry. *Aesthetic Theory* is foremost a text in which Adorno pursues what he understood to be the nature of the truth content of artworks, a truth rarely to be found *anywhere*, and not even in what, for better or worse, is commonly called "serious" art. Though Adorno evoked the extreme anti-aesthetic specter of kitsch only a few times in this complex and lengthy volume, he allowed that the shadow of utopian semblance is preserved even in "debased" art, though to be sure he did not make this argument as openly as did Bloch. I seek to push precisely this point, and for one strategic reason, which I can best explain by beginning with what will seem a digression.

Adorno long lamented the division of all art, but music especially, into the categories of high (classical, serious) and low (popular, mass culture); at the same time he recognized the specific social reality driving the separation. He recognized that the categories themselves mirrored social divisions—and helped keep the divisions in place. To cite a mundane example, the category arrangement of CDs in stores at once reflects and helps to perpetuate these now-naturalized—indeed rampantly overdetermined—divisions, as part and parcel of cultural marketing. Think twice before going near the classical because it's not the popular, and vice versa. Either way, the divisions help one past the uncertainty of the unknown, of stepping beyond the bounds of comfort, assurance, and predictability. In short, the labels help keep listeners in line. To argue that labeling is simply a matter of convenience is merely to reflect the dross that market culture only gives us what we already want. Musicians, as well as their listeners, learn early to present themselves within the terms of the division. To do otherwise runs enormous risks associated with not fitting in, and this translates all too easily into not having work and not being taken seriously. Only occasionally do we have the opportunity to denaturalize what for a long time has appeared as "just the way things are"—for example, the momentary dilemma regarding where in the store to look for CDs by an artist like Laurie Anderson, though the very denomination "crossover" carries the tinge of transgression (which can sometimes be marketable); too often it can work to define a location in nowhere.

To be somewhat perverse, in order to get to my main point, let's name Mahler a crossover artist. Adorno wrote extensively, but particularly in his Mahler monograph (Adorno 1992d), about the utopian semblance that emerges when the musical high and low meet in aesthetic reconciliation in Mahler's symphonies. However, Adorno's point is *not* that the former swallows (and therefore "betters") the latter, or that Mahler, in some Rodney King–like manner, brings the high and low together in such fashion that they "just get along." His point is that with Mahler a mutual transformation occurs, without either the high or the low disappearing. The sign of truth, however dim, however partial, *lies in each*, in essence as the raw material for a higher truth content; the one illuminates the truth of the other. I take from this that the debased (the low)—if you prefer, the already ruined—longs for the "something that's missing" (Bloch and Adorno 1988) no less, however less successfully, than does its "better" (the high). My concern, accordingly, is to argue for the hope that lies in all music, and not simply in the music where we might more easily assume it to reside (Great Works). Perhaps we might say that the often-irritating inescapability of music today is more than the result of marketing schemes in overdrive and as much the simultaneous reflection of the increasingly desperate longing for whatever musical sonority points toward: a *promesse de bonheur.* A promise defines the unrealized, to be sure; it results from an acknowledgment of unmet need. Stendahl, from whom Adorno borrowed the phrase "*promesse de bonheur,*" articulated this point. Music, he said, "as an art, suffuses the soul of man with sweet regret, by giving it *a glimpse of happiness*; and a glimpse of happiness, even if it is no more than a *dream* of happiness, is almost the dawning of hope" (Stendahl 1972, 347, emphasis in original).[32]

LISTENING

In the remarks that follow, I want to pursue in some detail the social stakes of listening that emerge within the assumed context of two paradigms of late-modern society: (1) the suspicion and surveillance that increasingly surrounds all cultural activity, and (2) the mechanisms of industrialization through which so much, though hardly all, music is realized. I wish to make three particular points. The first is that listening is a cultural, rather than natural, practice, and one of enormous social import. The second point, closely related to the first, is that listening has to be learned. The third, emerging from the first two, is that the hope immanent to music is manifest in sounds that are not merely heard but are listened to; I'm suggesting, that is, that the semblance of utopia in music becomes the more apparent when a reciprocal relationship exists between the object (music) and the listening subject. However, my point is not simply a reflection of the mundane instrumental reality that an active listener may have a better sense of what the music is "saying"; rather, it's that active listening itself enacts a form of subject-object reciprocity (or, if you wish, reconciliation) that lies at the heart of any imaginable form of social utopia. Active listening honors music; active listening acknowledges the otherness just as it seeks otherness and even merges with it.

Jacques Attali, Roland Barthes, Ernst Bloch, and Adorno have addressed the question of listening in ways pertinent to this essay, and I'll deal with each of them, though only with Adorno in detail. My purpose is to suggest that listening, by which I mean focused audition, is a path to knowledge, one that has the potential to complement Adorno's perception of the musical avant-garde's socially critical utopianism: "New music keeps reopening the wound, instead of affirming the world as it exists. . . . Above all, then, the goal of new music must be the complete liberation of the human subject" (1999b, 120–21).

In *Noise: The Political Economy of Music* (first published in 1977), the French economist Jacques Attali argued that "the world is not for the beholding. It is for hearing. It is not legible, but audible" (Attali 1985, 3). Music for Attali is a special kind of noise (noise in his formulation being the aggregate of all sound) that engages or confronts all other forms of sound/noise, whether naturally occurring or culturally produced, though it's the latter that principally interests him. His concern is not to theorize music in society but, contrarily, to theorize society through music. Listening receives primary attention. Attali hears in music the sounds of the past that shape the sounds, and, more to the point, the society, of the future. Accordingly, his focus is on late modernity and its historical roots, with respect to which one insight in particular, organizes his thinking: Music "makes audible what is essential in the contradictions of the developed societies: *an anxiety-ridden quest for lost difference, following a logic from which difference is banished*" (5, emphasis in original). In other words, he posits music's exposure of the social anxiety engendered by the radical separation of subject from object. Echoing Adorno's own utopian regard for art generally, Attali suggested that music is a "refuge for residual irrationality," which he set in opposition to the instrumentalized rationality organizing modernity, while nonetheless recognizing that music is at the same time commonly employed—as it were, against itself—as a force for shaping the increasingly administered late-modern dystopia; music's uses and its effects, not least the progressive ones, are anything but guaranteed (of which more later).

Listening necessarily means hearing much more around us than we might wish to hear, for the organ of hearing, unlike the eyes (which can easily look away), cannot so easily or conveniently be closed to sound. The fact that in late modernity sound, notably musical sound, is now fundamentally inescapable, articulates for Attali the stakes of his larger concern: "Listening to music is listening to all noise, realizing that its appropriation and control is a reflection of power, that it is essentially political" (6). Since noise (including the "noise" of music) is the source of power, "power has always listened to it with fascination. . . . [and] What is called music today is all too often only a disguise for the monologue of power (7–9).[33] Accordingly, Attali's argument hinges on the question not simply of listening but on listening *for*. And this brings me to Barthes.

Barthes points out that listening, at its most basic, defends against the unexpected; again, we listen *for*. His formulation invites reaction: listening "either reveals danger or promises the satisfaction of need" (Barthes 1985a, 247). But Barthes's interest is in something less obvious and more profound. He quickly turns to rhythm—in language, speech, music—through which, he suggests, is revealed not the *possible* (danger, satisfaction) but the *secret*. By secret he means something real but that can penetrate our consciousness only in code, "which serves simultaneously to encipher and to decipher that reality." Listening, in other words, involves hermeneutics: "to listen is to adopt an attitude of decoding what is obscure, blurred, or mute, in order to make available to consciousness the 'underside' of meaning (what is experienced, postulated, intentionalized as hidden)" (249). And though at this juncture Barthes associates the hermeneutics with religion ("To listen is the evangelical verb par excellence"), his point is larger and echoes Attali's: we listen in order to decipher the future; *and* we listen for transgression. But it's not Barthes's echo of Attali's evocation of listening for danger, transgression, and subversion that most interests me. Instead, it's his account of the utopian potential that arises from what could be called the intersubjectivity of listening that lends something more important to this discussion.

Barthes distinguishes between hearing, which he notes is a physiological phenomenon, and listening, which he describes as an intersubjective psychological act, which thus presumes reciprocity: "'I am listening' also means 'listen to me'" (246). In short, listening invokes the other: "The injunction to listen is the total interpellation of one subject by another: . . . it creates transference: *'listen to me'* means *touch me, know that I exist*" (250–51, emphasis in original). In order to radicalize the insight, Barthes organizes his comments around the specific form of listening associated with the telephone, a medium that radically diminishes the agency of every sense except that of hearing (no longer always the case, to be sure, given the newest technologies that permit the transmission of both voice and image).[34] His point is that the telephone concentrates the entire somatic self in the voice of the speaker and the ear of the auditor. Under conditions where the auditor is successfully interpellated by the speaker, a second, as it were, silent interpellation occurs. The auditor, through the silence of listening, intersubjectively answers back: *"listening* [thus] *speaks"* (252, emphasis in original).

Barthes's concern with the intersubjectivity of listening is fundamentally utopian, to the extent that the listening he invokes by means of a telephone conversation is, in essence, voluntary, even wished, hence not coerced. Under such circumstances, listening connects; it is, perforce, (re)conciliatory. The intersubjectivity he describes can occur as well, and at least as deeply (spiritually), with music, whether performed live or heard recorded. Barthes is keenly aware of this. His essay turns to music in order to invoke the singing voice, noting what he here and elsewhere famously termed the "grain of the voice" (Barthes 1977; and Barthes 1985a):

> The singing voice, that very specific space in which a tongue encounters a voice and permits *those who know how to listen* to it to hear what we can call its "grain"—the singing voice is not the breath but indeed that *materiality of the body* emerging from the throat, a site where the phonic metal hardens and takes shape. (Barthes 1985a, 255, emphasis added)

In the singing voice Barthes hears reconciliation of the subject-object binary antagonism. Music emerges from the body's muscles and spatial interiority in the utterly disembodied ethereality of its sounds; so doing, music bridges, even perhaps momentarily erases, the distinction between soma and spirit. And more, embodying the "corporality of speech, the voice is located at the articulation of body and discourse" (255). Barthes thus doubly articulates the connection between the seeming immateriality of the singing voice and the body's flesh—the metaphysical and the physical—both of which belong to history (discourse).

Barthes nonetheless recognizes that the utopian quotient he attaches to the intersubjectivity of listening must be qualified by the changed circumstances of modern listening. Nowadays, he suggests, listening functions under conditions of panic. "It is believed that, in order to liberate listening, it suffices to begin speaking oneself" (259). Think of *Crossfire* and similar television "news and opinion" shows, where the evening's guests commonly shout over one another, less to listen and more to silence their opponents. By contrast, Barthes suggests, "a free listening is essentially a listening which circulates, which permutates, which disaggregates, by its mobility, the fixed network of the roles of speech: it is not possible to imagine a free society, if we agree in advance to preserve within it the old modes of listening: those of the believer, the disciple, and the patient" (259).

The sounds of late modernity, including all too much music, commonly interpellate us less as subjects than as the subjected, and the subjection that's proffered is not uncommonly sadomasochistic. To cite a hyperbolic example, the better to make the point (though I would argue nonetheless for the example's socially paradigmatic qualities), take futurist Luigi Russolo who, with anticipated delight, charted among his "6 families of noises" to be realized mechanically in his would-be futurist orchestra, the "Voices of animals and people," which incorporate solely the sounds of distress and suffering: "Shouts, Screams, Shrieks, Wails, Hoots, Howls, Death rattles, Sobs" (Russolo 1986, 28). Yet even in Russolo's neofascist rant there lies a not-quite-silent oppositional and utopian prospect to the extent that the sounds he evokes are not only properly associated with suffering and abjection; they are also at heart pleas for life, against all odds. Bloch sensed as much. In *The Principle of Hope,* he commented that "music surpasses other arts in its ability to absorb the manifold griefs, wishes and rays of hope common to the socially oppressed. . . . It is inherent in the material of hope, even when the music is expressing sorrow at its times, society or world, and even in death" (Bloch 1985, 201).[35] Russolo, as if in spite of himself, has adopted Bloch's insight avant la lettre and cut directly to the chase.

Barthes concludes his essay on listening by noting that no law can oblige us to take pleasure where we don't want to, "no law is in a position to constrain our listening: freedom of listening is as necessary as freedom of speech. That is why this apparently modest notion . . . is finally like a little theater on whose stage those two modern deities, one bad and one good, confront each other: power and desire" (Barthes 1985a, 260). And this leads me, finally, back to Adorno.

DIALECTICS OF STRUCTURAL LISTENING

Adorno's commentaries on the social state of listening are several and oft-cited,[36] among which none has received as much attention, commonly hostile, as his insistence on the importance of what he duly termed "structural listening." I want first to rehearse briefly what he meant by the phrase, then précis the case against structural listening made by the most thoughtful of its numerous critics, Rose Rosengard Subotnik, and finally, and in some detail, suggest what of Adorno's concept bears relevance within the larger context of this essay. First, what does Adorno mean by "structural listening"?

In one simple sentence in his 1941 essay "The Radio Symphony" Adorno encapsulated both the meaning and the stakes of what he intended by the phrase. Addressing what he regarded as the locus classicus of musical idealism, he argued that, "structurally, one hears the first bar of a Beethoven symphonic movement only at the very moment when one hears the last bar" (Adorno 2002h, 255).[37] As Subotnik effectively parses Adorno, "This concept of structural listening . . . was intended to describe a process wherein the listener follows and comprehends the unfolding realization, with all of its detailed inner relationships, of a generating musical conception, or what Schoenberg calls an 'idea'" (Subotnik 1996, 150). Expressed negatively, and in light of what Adorno feared was the more common form of modern listening, music is not "about" any of its individual moments made to stand alone, and that particularly included those moments of apparent distinctive beauty or climactic drama—what Adorno witheringly referred to (writing in English) as music's "gustatory qualities" (Adorno 1945, 211), got at by what he termed "atomized listening" (Adorno 2002h, 261–62). Hearing music as little more than a series of disconnected episodes, he argued, produces a music that sounds like its own quotation: "Details are [thus] deified as well as reified" (Adorno 2002h, 266).

The centrality of the whole notwithstanding, Adorno fully recognized, and clearly valorized, the musical moment, the particular—even what he called, for example, beautiful passages (*schöne Stellen*).[38] More to the point, Adorno promoted the realization through listening of a reciprocal relation between part and whole, by means of which each would be the more fully realized. Heard atomistically, by contrast, the detail was rendered meaningless in its isolation, just as any sense of the whole was obliterated. Conversely, however, if the detail were heard *solely* as a building block of something larger, it would surrender any sense of its own spontaneity—which ultimately must be preserved if the whole is to express anything more than its own immanent structure. The relation between part and whole is radically reciprocal; each emerges and, indeed, lives from and through its other.

In musical details Adorno heard the subject speaking, willingly bending toward the musical object (the whole) in order to make possible the work, a whole larger than the sum of its individual parts. Something, in other words, like a utopian society. Musical details, bending and blending their expressive character toward the whole, while retaining their own specific character, permitted the re-enactment of reconciliation between subject and object, for Adorno the artwork's highest goal. He understood the stakes to be high. "Form," as he put it, "is the law of the transfiguration of the existing, counter to which it represents freedom" (Adorno 1997, 143). Form takes what is and refashions it into the semblance of what *might be*.

Engaging Adorno's concept of structural listening, Rose Rosengard Subotnik historicized the concept, locating it in bourgeois formalist (if not precisely positivistic) aesthetics—think Hanslick's *On the Musically Beautiful* at the historical beginnings, Stravinsky's *Poetics of Music* at the end. She aptly pointed out that very little music can actually lay claim to the (utopian) autonomy principle assumed by Adorno and critical to the demand for structural listening. This principle, Subotnik pointed out, cannot be applied to Western musical structures prior to the nineteenth century, to say nothing of the music produced elsewhere in the world. She further correctly noted that structural listening is fundamentally applicable only to instrumental music, not vocal. Moreover, Adorno—as well as Schoenberg (Schoenberg 1975), of course—stressed the point that structural listening is directed toward the discernment of development in musical structures, notwithstanding the fact that development is a foundation principle, as Subotnik states, of "very little music" (Subotnik 1996, 159).[39]

It's not the case that Adorno rejected all forms of listening other than structural; after all, not all forms of music demanded it, and neither did all occasions for listening. Music, for example, often served its purpose well "just" as entertainment, as, for example, music in the background (essentially passive listening), to recall an earlier trope. But entertainment, as he realized, could easily stand on its own, often without controversy attached to it, as something society wanted; it didn't need either him or philosophy to make its point or define its social worth. Its worth, which he regarded as genuine, was compensatory; it offered relief, however momentarily. But relief as such was insufficient to the social responsibilities music, like other art forms, needed to shoulder, were music to contribute to any future limitation on human suffering. Beyond relief, there was engagement. In turn, engagement for Adorno elicited the demand for a kind of music that, through its own internal processes, was capable of addressing the myriad complexities of modern life. "Tea for Two," whatever its genuine entertainment worth, was not assigned that task; Mahler's Third Symphony or Schoenberg's *Erwartung* were—and were up to the job: "Works become beautiful," Adorno noted, "by the force of their opposition to what simply exists" (Adorno 1997, 51).

One doesn't require structural listening, or for that matter Schenkerian analysis, to understand what's going on musically in "Tea for Two" or "Hail to the Chief"—just as one doesn't need to get soaked to figure out when it's raining. With Mahler and Schoenberg what might be gained from structural listening, by contrast, is amply demonstrated by Adorno's own studies of these composers. Nonetheless, as Subotnik appropriately insists, there is rather more to music, any music, than structure. Accordingly, it's crucial not to fetishize structural listening and thereby, however unwillingly, silence those parameters of sonic experience that cannot be understood simply as structure and as such are not subject to conventional musical-theoretical analysis. Indeed, Adorno was at once sensitive to this fact and at pains to acknowledge the point in his own musical-analytical writing (which depended foremost on his ears, rather than his eyes focused on a printed score), as evident, for example, in his Mahler monograph (Adorno 1992d), principally a study of the symphonies—which have elsewhere and often by others been subjected to the most intense (and sometimes stultifying) hard-core formal analysis—precisely what Adorno does not do.[40]

Adorno's concern for the *social* efficacy of structural listening depends less on the fact that it so aptly seems to "fit" the compositional processes of complex works, and more on the cultural duress under which such music (along with other musics) maintains its life. That is, the difficulty of difficult music is itself a reflection on the lamentable state of society and the subjects who inhabit it. Take that as a given. What matters is how that socially necessary difficulty can be made to speak. Adorno's point is that *it cannot speak on its own.* If it is to be more than sound and fury signifying nothing, the listener must make the conscious decision to do what's necessary to meet the music halfway, so to speak, in particular by coming to terms with the music's immanence, by means of which it "speaks." What happens thereafter has no guarantees—the listener's active stance engages the composition, not simply "receives" it under the terms Adorno describes; yet without such reciprocity between music and its auditor (or its performer, to be sure), the music is ironically "silenced." Put differently, and to borrow a phrase from Queens of the Stone Age, without this reciprocal "exchange," what remains is little more than "songs for the deaf."[41]

For Adorno, hard times demand hard music—and hard listening. Hard listening, however, is not its own end but a means by which to conjoin musical sound and philosophy.[42] The musical thinking congealed, like history, within music is released in the acts of interpretation that emerge from performance and reception, both of which are anchored in the act of focused listening. As he put it in *Aesthetic Theory,* "History is the content of artworks. To analyze artworks means no less than to become conscious of the history immanently sedimented in them" (Adorno 1997, 85). For Adorno, the ultimate "beauty" of music is its truth content; music's truth is in its sounds, which must be both heard and *thought.* One might be tempted to accuse Adorno of devalorizing musical sound in favor of thinking about music, as though the sounds of music were nothing more than a vehicle for philosophy. The accusation would be false. One might far more appropriately, and simply, "accuse" him of regarding music with as much seriousness and social significance as it deserved and of being willing to do whatever was necessary to elicit the music's aesthetic-social truth.

Finally, whatever the limitations of applicability as regards the sorts of music for which structural listening is most appropriate, Adorno's conception posits something eminently applicable to listening generally: Structural listening posits an active listener. That is, Adorno perceived active listening roughly analogous to what Barthes, speaking of performers, called musical doing (Barthes 1985b). What's central to Adorno is the intersubjective relation that active listening establishes between the subject (the listener) and the object (the composition), which object, at a minimum, sediments within itself history, which by definition is always already (dialectically) intersubjective. The humane quality of music emerges not simply from the fact that music is made by and for human beings; rather, music's humaneness develops from the specific fact that music mediates human longing into an acoustics at once part of the social and cultural boundaries marked by history and language and at the same time reaches well beyond what language can pin down, gain control over, classify, regulate, and, not least, help market, all of this the result of a history that recognizes language first and foremost for its instrumental potential.[43]

It is precisely through the act of listening *to* and listening *for* that music's utopian character, as Adorno understood it, could be made to appear. At first glance Adorno's position on structural listening may seem both unreasonable (who but trained musicians can hear music in the manner he prescribes?) and/or elitist (the likely high socioeconomic tier necessary to support the requisite musical training, not to mention the leisure time for listening). But the matter is not so simple. Adorno himself was keenly sensitive to the history of privilege that accrued to the history of art, but that fact by itself could not for him stand as good reason to disparage art—or to deny art's truth content. Put differently, if art's own (internal) resistance to the regressive nature of its origins was to be realized, the act of reception must meet the artwork's immanent demands for this to occur. The fact that the demand was likely not often actually met served as an indictment of the very social causes preventing its occurrence.

Adorno's well-known, and to some infamous, typology of listening characterizes eight types of auditor, the expert at one end of the spectrum, and the "anti-musical" at the other (Adorno 1988, 4).[44] None is perfect. Every station on the scale is rife with shortcomings: all forms of listening bear the marks of an antagonistic social totality. Type three, for example, the "culture consumer," Adorno associates with the "upper and uplifted" bourgeois symphony and opera crowd whose social prestige is reflected in and perpetuated by showing up—these are people who, as he puts it, "posture as elitists hostile to the mass"; they are the same group that "to a great extent determines the official life of music" (6–7). The point I'm after is that Adorno reads off this typology the social divisions of late-stage capitalism, which is to say that the critique informing the typology is not organized by elitism but by its extreme opposite: solidarity with the masses. Adorno, here as elsewhere, identifies not with society's victors but with its victims. "My point," Adorno concludes,

> is neither to disparage representatives of the described listening types negatively nor to distort the picture of reality by deriving judgments on the world situation from the present dubious state of listening to music. To posture mentally as if mankind existed for the sake of good listening would be a grotesque echo of estheticism, just as the converse thesis, that music exists for mankind, merely puts a humane face on the furtherance of thought in exchange categories—a way of thinking to which everything that exists is only a means for something else, a way that degrades the truth of the matter and thus strikes the very men it attempts to please (Adorno 1988, 18).[45]

Adorno's typology articulates precisely the fundamental social impediments to the very forms of listening he believes music has a right to expect from its listeners. The listeners he describes are wounded subjects whose ears are socially scarred. And yet, of course, listeners abound: however imperfectly they may hear, they recognize the nearly absolute necessity that the world's noise includes music, not simply as an accompaniment, but as an alternative.

CAVEAT

The true "magic" of music lies in the degree to which it mirrors in its material objectivity the spirit and spirituality that enlivens it (Adorno 1997, 86–94). Music makes audible the materiality of human spirituality and the spirituality of our materiality, not as forever separate and oppositional entities but as momentarily reconciled, a microcosm of society in a state of bliss.

And yet, as ever, the dialectical nature of spirituality itself must be factored. In 1937 Herbert Marcuse referenced the phrase "affirmative culture" to designate the role, pervasively assigned to cultural practices in late modernity, of cheering (by aestheticizing) for the status quo. By this means, culture (in the utopian sense of what might be, as opposed to what is) is neutralized. Affirmative culture, he suggested, insisted on the soul's nobility, but precisely because it cost very little to do so—and with the added advantage that appeals to the soul's nobility could serve as a safety valve to release social pressures demanding change. Locating humanity in the soul, in other words, all too conveniently leaves intact the material reality that debases the body. According to the operating principles of affirmative culture, "Humanity becomes an inner state. Freedom, goodness, and beauty become spiritual qualities. . . . [Affirmative] Culture speaks of the dignity of 'man' without concerning itself with a concretely more dignified status for men" (Marcuse 1968, 103).[46]

Society's invitation to music merely to affirm—to play the role of "tolerated negativity" or, worse, as a "lubricant for the system" as it exists—is writ large and accompanied by myriad enforcement techniques (Adorno 1991a, 102; Adorno 1997, 311). Playing its assigned role in the domain of domination, music puts on the costume of reconciliation and consolation. Its name tag reads "cultural decoration," and it moves about the floor to the tunes of the easiest of listening.[47] Yet even under these circumstances, the contradictions immanent to the truth of its lie—"The whole is the false" (Adorno 1978, 50)[48]—can all too plainly render the default "easiness" of listening into productively painful realizations about what stands behind the mask of the most culinary of sonorities. And this is so because, even in debased form, music's own otherness from mundane existence remains a pervasive reminder of something better that neither it nor we can properly name but that we can nonetheless imagine.[49] Bloch argued that "music's connection with this world means that it is nothing less than a seismograph of society. For it reflects any cracks beneath the social surface, expresses desires for change, and is synonymous with hoping" (Bloch 1985, 243, original emphasis).[50]

Hope aims for utopia. What Bloch named the "utopian function" has agency; it "knows about explosive powers since the utopian function itself is a condensed form of them: the utopian function is the unimpaired reason of a militant optimism" (Bloch 1988c, 107). And yet it is precisely the "better" to which music points that is used against what music otherwise aims toward. The neutralization of music's insistence on the truth regarding untruth is what the culture industry so pervasively works to mask under the guise of its entertainments. "Today," Adorno noted in 1945, "the terms ethereal and sublime have become trademarks" (Adorno 1945, 211).[51] The affirmative element of music, as Adorno reminded himself in the notes to his never-completed Beethoven monograph, lies "merely in the fact that it is *a voice lifted up*, that it is music at all." Accordingly, music can proclaim against its own and society's greater interests, that "all is well" (1998a, 6–7)—or, as I'm arguing, and despite all the claims to the contrary, that all is *not* well. Either way, no guarantees.

In 1990, during the academy's first-blush romance with postmodernism, Fredric Jameson mused about the continued relevance of Adorno's unrelenting dialectical critique of modernity. Recalling Adorno's famous lament that to write poetry after Auschwitz was barbaric, Jameson aptly, if bitterly, posed a question informed by the suburban imagery of the postmodern condition: he asked whether nowadays one could bear to read *Dialectic of Enlightenment* "next to the pool" (Jameson 1990, 248). Those who turn away from Adorno on account of the often-alleged unrelenting pessimism of the "news" he imparted would do themselves a considerable favor were they to connect his critique, unrelenting as it may be, to the sustained hope that informs it at heart.

Bloch, Adorno's older contemporary, with whom he shared a complicated friendship, gave music a pride of place in his extensive utopian writings, the gist of which is anchored in the power of music to point to something beyond itself, something better. Bloch offers a reason why music playing next to the pool, like reading Adorno there, might offer rather more than a distraction from the boredom of lying motionless in the sun:

> Thus music as a whole stands at the farther limits of humanity, but at those limits where humanity, with new language and *haloed by the call to achieved intensity, to the attained world of 'we,'* is first taking shape. And this ordering in our musical expression means a house, indeed a crystal, but one derived from our future freedom; a star, but one that will be a new Earth. (Bloch 1985, 243, emphasis in original)[52]

That mundane living is lacking life is an ordinary, indeed clichéd, experience. Music, at its best, engages precisely this lacuna, though not in such a way as to alleviate the lack but to make its reality at once undeniable and potentially productive of something better. Music is the stuff of insight, just as insight is the prerequisite for any substantive engagement with history and historicity. Music, at its best, does not decorate social antagonisms but highlights them; it helps to render the visibility of suffering insistent. The pleasures of music are to be had, Adorno argued, not in an untroubled prettiness that under better circumstances we might be better able to both sustain and to afford with a clean conscience; instead, the true pleasures of music are properly located in the means—whether "pretty" or ugly—by which music never lets us forget that the most beautiful artifact of human activity is the promulgation of universal justice.

Adorno's concluding aphorism in *Minima Moralia* opens with a remark, more than slightly similar to the one by Bloch just cited addressing philosophy, that he would unquestionably apply to music as well: "The only philosophy which can be responsibly practised in the face of despair is the attempt to contemplate all things as they would present themselves from the standpoint of redemption"

(Adorno 1978, 247).[53] Adorno's insistent invocation of hope, found here and elsewhere throughout his writing, hinges on the ordinary insight that the world as it is didn't just happen; it was made to happen. Our future isn't written in the stars but is to be written on earth. It's ultimately up to "us":

> The neon signs which hang over our cities and outshine the natural light of the night with their own are comets presaging the natural disaster of society, its frozen death. Yet they do not come from the sky. They are controlled from earth. It depends upon human beings themselves whether they will extinguish these lights and awake from a nightmare which only threatens to become actual as long as men believe in it. (1991b, 83)

In short, listen up.

Notes

I wish to express my gratitude to Berthold Hoeckner, Robert Hullot-Kentor, Martin Scherzinger, Jochen Schulte-Sasse, Rose Rosengard Subotnik, and Gary Thomas for their careful reading and thoughtful criticism of earlier drafts of this essay.

1. Despite Adorno's comments in "Music in the Background" about the silencing of music, he elsewhere (in 1953) acknowledged precisely the point made later by Attali: "While the ever-present and inescapable music installs itself as a piece of concrete daily life, as one producer-standardized consumer good among others, and divests itself of everything that might go beyond service to and betrayal of the consumer, it becomes comical" (2002e, 135–36); and also: "Music is no longer exceptional . . . rather, it has achieved an ubiquity that makes it part of everyday life" (1988, 129).

2. Compare Adorno 1997, 253: "If a work of authentic music strays into the social sphere of background music [as in a café], it may unexpectedly transcend that sphere by the purity that is stained by social function."

3. See further Edström 1989.

4. See Leppert 1988 for a variety of neoplatonist rants appearing in European courtesy and conduct literature.

5. To which Bloch added, concerning utopia, "But it is not something like nonsense or absolute fancy; rather it is not *yet* in the sense of a possibility; *that* it could be there if we could only do something for it" (Bloch and Adorno 1988, 3). Utopia, as he points out (4) is dependent on social conditions, just as "the essential function of utopia is a critique of what is present" (12).

6. This is the closing line of Adorno's monograph *In Search of Wagner.*

7. Adorno 1998a, 10: "Music can express only what is proper to itself: this

means that words and concepts cannot express music's content *directly,* but only in mediated form, that is, as philosophy"; and Adorno 1997, 262: "Every artwork, if it is to be fully experienced, requires thought and therefore stands in need of philosophy, which is nothing but the thought that refuses all restrictions."

8. Adorno 1997, 32: "The new is the longing for the new, not the new itself: That is what everything new suffers from. What takes itself to be utopia remains the negation of what exists and is obedient to it."

9. Adorno 1992a, 92: "No moral terrorism can control the fact that the face the work of art turns toward the viewer gives him pleasure, even if it is only the formal fact of temporary liberation from the compulsion of practical ends." Compare St. John Chrysostom (d. 407): "Nothing so uplifts the mind, giving it wings and freeing it from the earth, releasing it from the prison of the body, affecting it with love of wisdom, and causing it to scorn all things pertaining to this life, as modulated melody and the divine chant composed of number" (Chrysostom 1998, 123).

10. Painter Francis Bacon: "Of course what in a curious way one is always hoping to do is to paint the one picture which will annihilate all the other ones, to concentrate everything into one painting. . . . I've got an obsession with doing the one perfect image" (Hullot-Kentor 2004, 183). Compare Adorno 1997, 35: "The truth content of artworks is fused with their critical content. That is why works are also critics of one another. This, not the historical continuity of their dependencies, binds artworks to one another; 'each artwork is the mortal enemy of the other'; the unity of the history of art is the dialectical figure of determinate negation. Only in this way does art serve its idea of reconciliation" [the internal quote references a remark Adorno previously had made elsewhere].

11. The currently erupting legal and ethical controversies surrounding file sharing have brought the issue of possession a degree of renewed public awareness that far surpasses those of a generation ago over cassette-tape copying. The point I'm after, however, is entirely separate from concerns over the physical ownership of recordings (of whatever legality).

12. Adorno incorporated the critical proviso that "kitsch only forfeits its right to exist when it enters into a parasitical relationship to history, mimics its verdicts and finds itself forbidden to reverse them" (1992b, 43).

13. Great art, by contrast, Adorno suggests, stares history directly in the face and speaks the unspeakable—and sometimes the unbearable. And great art knows how to evoke kitsch for the utopia that inhabits its shadows—Mahler generally; Berg occasionally: "The greatest works of art do not exclude the lower depths, but kindle the flame of utopia on the smoking ruins of the past" (1999a, 79).

14. Elsaesser 1981–82, 115: "Kitsch is the gesture that embraces what once was product of a living tradition, covering the gap between past and present which only historical understanding could otherwise rescue with a desperately fake aura. Kitsch and myth are both historical attempts to live outside history." Berthold Hoeckner (in a personal communication) notes that both art and kitsch "share the fundamental experience of alternative realms of existence and hence

are pointers to a better world. . . . *Kitsch* does it through affirmation; *Kunst* through negation. Put differently, *Kitsch* evokes a lost past; *Kunst* projects a utopian future. Where *Kitsch* is concerned with the 'no longer,' *Kunst* is concerned with the 'not yet.' . . . *Kitsch* and *Kunst* exist (necessarily or mostly) in impure mixtures. One might say that the *Kitsch* portion of *Kunst* is its regressive component, while the *Kunst* portion of *Kitsch* is its progressive element. The extremes touch, paradoxically, where *Kitsch* is most authentic. Precisely where *Kitsch* is silent (or silenced) music, we hear its *Kunst*-voice."

15. Zipes (Bloch 1988d, xxxvii) points out that, by the nineteenth century, the colporteur's "materials catered to the dreams and wishes of lower-class readers who looked for something totally outside their ordinary routines. Though the works were of dubious ideological character—often sexist, militaristic, and sadistic—Bloch refused to dismiss them as reactionary because they addressed the hunger of the imagination of people whose wants he felt must be respected." Zipes adds, in this regard, that "the drive for the new [represented, for example, by the constant flood of pulp fiction] is obviously conditioned by fashion and market demands, but it also represents a constant hope for something more than the market can offer, something that exceeds society's limits." Speaking more generally about art, Zipes, echoing Bloch, later adds (xl), "To write, to compose, to paint. To read, to listen, to view. These are human acts of hope."

16. Bloch continues: "The dream of colportage is: never again to be trapped by the routine of daily life. And at the end there is: happiness, love, victory. The splendor toward which the adventure story heads is not won through a rich marriage and the like as in the magazine story but rather through an active journey to the Orient of the dream" (1988b, 183).

17. Adorno (1981a, 27–28) makes this point with regard to affirmative culture generally: "Just because culture affirms the validity of the principle of harmony within an antagonistic society, albeit in order to glorify that society, it cannot avoid confronting society with its own notion of harmony and thereby stumbling on discord. The ideology which affirms life is forced into opposition to life by the immanent drive of the ideal."

18. See similar remarks in Adorno 2002c, 114.

19. Compare Adorno 1991b, 74, concerning the separation of fact from value, and the positivism of "information": "As facts they are arranged in such a way that they can be grasped as quickly and easily as possible. Wrenched from all context, detached from thought, they are made instantly accessible to an infantile grasp."

20. Adorno 1988, 149: "Criticism is immanent to music itself; it is the procedure which objectively brings each successful composition as a force field to its resultant. Music criticism is required by music's own formal law: the historic development [*Entfaltung*] of works and of their truth content occurs in the critical medium" (translation modified).

21. See Zuidervaart 1991, 125–28; and Nicholsen 1997, 70–76.

22. On Adorno's concept of enigmaticalness in art, see Adorno 1997, 120–22.

23. See Leppert 2002, 89–90.

24. Nicholsen 1997 cites a number of passages in Adorno's *Aesthetic Theory* where the term is used in various contexts.

25. Adorno 1997, 53: "In art the subject exposes itself, at various levels of autonomy, to its other, separated from it and yet not altogether separated. . . . That art, something mimetic, is possible in the midst of rationality, and that it employs its means, is a response to the faulty irrationality of the rational world as an over-administered world." Georges Bataille addressed this matter in his account of eroticism: "Erotic activity, by dissolving the separate beings that participate in it, reveals their fundamental continuity, like the waves of a stormy sea" (Bataille 1992, 22). He regarded eroticism as what he called "the disequilibrium in which the being consciously calls his own existence in question. In one sense, the being loses himself deliberately, but then the subject is identified with the object losing his identity" (31).

26. Composer, performer, and listener each in turn make themselves aware of the music's mimetic comportment through the act of interpretation, which requires what Adorno perceives as philosophical engagement. Adorno 1992f, 3: "To interpret music means: to make music. Musical interpretation is performance, which, as synthesis, retains the similarity to language, while obliterating every specific resemblance. This is why the idea of interpretation is not an accidental attribute of music, but an integral part of it." Compare Adorno 1997, 128: "The need of artworks for interpretation, their need for the production of their truth content, is the stigma of their constitutive insufficiency." Although Adorno consistently speaks of a score in these discussions, the principle he invokes applies as well to nonnotated music and improvised music and is in no sense necessarily confined to high-caste artworks.

27. Adorno 1997, 62: "Wholly artifactual, the artwork seems to be the opposite of what is not made, nature. As pure antitheses, however, each refers to the other: nature to the experience of a mediated and objectified world, the artwork to nature as the mediated plenipotentiary of immediacy. Therefore reflection on natural beauty is irrevocably requisite to the theory of art."

28. Compare Adorno 1997, 71: "Under its optic, art is not the imitation of nature but the imitation of natural beauty"; natural beauty, he insists, is "the trace of the nonidentical in things under the spell of universal identity" (73). See further Paetzold 1997.

29. The internal quotation is from Goethe, *Faust* I, line 784.

30. This translation is based on the second edition, published as *Geist der Utopie: Bearbeitete Neuauflage der zweiten Fassung von 1923* (Frankfurt am Main: Suhrkamp Verlag, 1964). Written in 1915–16, that is, during conflagration and general trauma of World War I, the book was first published in 1918.

31. Adorno 2002e traces this same connection.

32. My thanks to Paul Chaikin for bringing this passage to my attention.

33. Attali 1985, 7: "Eavesdropping, censorship, recording, and surveillance are weapons of power. The technology of listening in on, ordering, transmitting, and recording noise is at the heart of this apparatus."

34. Rose Rosengard Subotnik, in a personal communication, points out that

cell phones "massively reinforce the image of phones as a medium for hearing only. Think even of the way they look: the mouthpiece doesn't extend anywhere near as low as the mouth. Thus, the only anchor for such phones is literally the ear, which still fits into the earpiece."

35. Compare Bloch 1985, 237: "If death conceived as an annihilating scythe is the hardest non-utopia, then music is pitted against it as the most utopian of all the arts. It contests it with a concern that is all the greater because precisely death's mysterious territory is filled with night, a generative force which seems so profoundly familiar to music within this world." This volume is based on a 1974 anthology of Bloch's musical writings. For an alternate translation, see Bloch 1986, 3:1063, 1097. *Das Prinzip Hoffnung* was written in the United States between 1938 and 1947 and was revised in 1953 and again in 1959. The book was first published in 1959.

36. See 1988, 2002a, 2002d, 2002f, 2002i. His principle argument is that listeners are socially made not born, that listening is a cultural practice, and that modernity has served the practice poorly, by turning music—all music, to every degree possible—into a thing, a market object. Listeners—and he means all listeners, whatever their social class or educational background—are in his words "betrayed," and the betrayal's cost is charged against their own subjectivity and identity.

37. In the subsequent discussion, Adorno amplifies his point in a discussion of the Fifth Symphony regarding the ways in which its musical processes are rendered inaudible through the limitations of 1941 AM radio.

38. Adorno 1984; see also Adorno 2002a, 318–22.

39. See also a more recent essay by Edström 1997.

40. See Adorno 2002g.

41. Queens of the Stone Age, *Songs for the Deaf* (Interscope Records, 2002), CD.

42. See further Goehr 2004.

43. Hoeckner 2002, 12–50, considers at length the issue of hope via the close analysis of a number of canonic nineteenth-century German compositions—*Fidelio*, for example. Particularly striking is a consistently insightful discussion of how Benjamin's image of the falling star, which he borrowed from Goethe, repeatedly reappears in Adorno's philosophy of Beethoven as a trope of transcendence. In Hoeckner's words: "Only at the moment of its fall does a star shine the brightest. Only then does it become a source of hope" (23).

44. The full typology is: (1) the expert listener; (2) the good listener; (3) the culture consumer; (4) the emotional listener; (5) the resentment listener; (6) the jazz expert and jazz fan (in fact, similar to type five); (7) the entertainment listener; and (8) the indifferent, the unmusical or the antimusical.

45. For an attempt to relate a portion of Adorno's typology to actual listeners, see Lindstrom 1986.

46. See also on this point Adorno 1988, 42–43.

47. Adorno 1997, 160: "Art's affirmative element and the affirmative element of the domination of nature are one in asserting that what was inflicted on nature was all for the good; by re-enacting it in the realm of the imagination, art makes it its own and becomes a song of triumph."

48. Adorno is, of course, reversing Hegel's famous dictum in *The Phenomenology of Spirit*, "The True is the whole" (Hegel 1977, 11).

49. Adorno 1988, 175: "If my conclusions are not premature, whatever the culture industry sets before people in their free time is indeed consumed and accepted but with a kind of reservation. . . . Apparently the integration of consciousness and free time has not yet wholly succeeded. The real interests of individuals are still strong enough to resist, up to a point, their total appropriation. . . . I think that there is a chance here for political maturity that ultimately could do its part to help free time turn into freedom." Compare with a similar remarks in Adorno 1991a, 113; and Adorno 1991b, 80.

50. The passage originally appeared in *The Principle of Hope* (Bloch 1986, 3:1088; different translation).

51. He continues (211): "Music has become a means instead of an end, a fetish. That is to say, music has ceased to be a human force and is consumed like other consumers' goods."

52. This text originally appeared in *The Principle of Hope* (Bloch 1986, 3:1103; different translation).

53. Adorno's debt here to Walter Benjamin is obvious. Adorno (1992c, 248) remarked that, were art not "a source of pleasure for people, in however mediated a form, it would not have been able to survive in the naked existence it contradicts and resists. This is not something external to it, however, but part of its very definition. . . . It embodies something like freedom in the midst of unfreedom. The fact that through its very existence it stands outside the evil spell that prevails allies it to a promise of happiness, a promise it itself somehow expresses in its expression of despair."

Works Cited

Adorno, Theodor W. 1945. "A Social Critique of Radio Music." *Kenyon Review* 7, no. 2 (Spring): 208–17.

———. 1978. *Minima Moralia: Reflections from Damaged Life*. Trans. E. F. N. Jephcott. London: Verso.

———. 1981a. "Cultural Criticism and Society." In Theodor W. Adorno, *Prisms*, trans. Samuel Weber and Shierry Weber, 17–34. Cambridge, MA: MIT Press.

———. 1981b. *In Search of Wagner*. Trans. Rodney Livingstone. London: Verso.

———. 1983. *Negative Dialectics*. Trans. E. B. Ashton. New York: Continuum.

———. 1984. "Schöne Stellen." In Theodor W. Adorno, *Gesammelte Schriften*, vol. 18, ed. Rolf Tiedemann et al., 695–718. Frankfurt am Main: Suhrkamp.

———. 1988. *Introduction to the Sociology of Music*. Trans. E. B. Ashton. New York: Continuum.

———. 1991a. "Culture and Administration." In Theodor W. Adorno, *The Culture Industry: Selected Essays on Mass Culture*, ed. J. M. Bernstein, trans. Wes Blomster, 93–113. London: Routledge.

———. 1991b. "The Schema of Mass Culture." In Theodor W. Adorno, *The Culture*

Industry: Selected Essays on Mass Culture, ed. J. M. Bernstein, 53–83. London: Routledge.

———. 1992a. "Commitment." In Theodor W. Adorno, *Notes to Literature*, vol. 2, ed. Rolf Tiedemann, trans. Shierry Weber Nicholsen, 76–94. New York: Columbia University Press.

———. 1992b. "Commodity Music Analysed." In Theodor W. Adorno, *Quasi una Fantasia: Essays on Modern Music*, trans. Rodney Livingstone, 37–52. London: Verso.

———1992c. "Is Art Lighthearted?" In Theodor W. Adorno, *Notes to Literature*, vol. 2, ed. Rolf Tiedemann, trans. Shierry Weber Nicholsen, 247–53. New York: Columbia University Press.

———1992d. *Mahler: A Musical Physiognomy*. Trans. Edmund Jephcott. Chicago: University of Chicago Press.

———. 1992e. "Motifs." In Theodor W. Adorno, *Quasi una Fantasia: Essays on Modern Music*, trans. Rodney Livingstone, 9–36. London: Verso.

———. 1992f. "Music and Language: A Fragment." In Theodor W. Adorno, *Quasi una Fantasia: Essays on Modern Music*, trans. Rodney Livingstone, 1–6. London: Verso.

———. 1997. *Aesthetic Theory*. Ed. Gretel Adorno and Rolf Tiedemann, trans. Robert Hullot-Kentor. Minneapolis: University of Minnesota Press.

———1998a. *Beethoven: The Philosophy of Music*, Ed. Rolf Tiedemann, trans. Edmund Jephcott. Stanford, CA: Stanford University Press.

———. 1998b. "Why Still Philosophy." In Theodor W. Adorno, *Critical Models: Interventions and Catchwords*, trans. Henry W. Pickford, 5–17. New York: Columbia University Press.

———. 1999a. "Alban Berg." In Theodor W. Adorno, *Sound Figures*, trans. Rodney Livingstone, 69–79. Stanford, CA: Stanford University Press.

———. 1999b. "Classicism, Romanticism, New Music." In Theodor W. Adorno, *Sound Figures*, trans. Rodney Livingstone, 106–22. Stanford, CA: Stanford University Press.

———. 2002a. "Little Heresy." In Theodor W. Adorno, *Essays on Music*, ed. Richard Leppert, trans. Susan H. Gillespie, 318–24. Berkeley and Los Angeles: University of California Press.

———. 2002b. "Music in the Background." In Theodor W. Adorno, *Essays on Music*, ed. Richard Leppert, trans. Susan H. Gillespie, 506–10. Berkeley and Los Angeles: University of California Press.

———. 2002c. "Music, Language, and Composition." In Theodor W. Adorno, *Essays on Music*, ed. Richard Leppert, trans. Susan H. Gillespie, 113–26. Berkeley and Los Angeles: University of California Press.

———. 2002d. "On Popular Music." In Theodor W. Adorno, *Essays on Music*, ed. Richard Leppert, 437–69. Berkeley and Los Angeles: University of California Press.

———. 2002e. "On the Contemporary Relationship of Philosophy and Music." In Theodor W. Adorno, *Essays on Music*, ed. Richard Leppert, trans. Susan

H. Gillespie, 135–61. Berkeley and Los Angeles: University of California Press.

———. 2002f. "On the Fetish-Character in Music and the Regression of Listening." In Theodor W. Adorno, *Essays on Music*, ed. Richard Leppert, 288–317. Berkeley and Los Angeles: University of California Press.

———. 2002g. "On the Problem of Musical Analysis." In Theodor W. Adorno, *Essays on Music*, ed. Richard Leppert, trans. Max Paddison, 162–80. Berkeley and Los Angeles: University of California Press.

———. 2002h. "The Radio Symphony." In Theodor W. Adorno, *Essays on Music*, ed. Richard Leppert, 251–70. Berkeley and Los Angeles: University of California Press.

———. forthcoming. *Philosophy of New Music*. Trans. Robert Hullot-Kentor. Minneapolis: University of Minnesota Press.

Attali, Jacques. 1985. *Noise: The Political Economy of Music*. Trans. Brian Massumi. Minneapolis: University of Minnesota Press.

Barthes, Roland. 1977. "The Grain of the Voice." In *Image – Music – Text*, trans. Stephen Heath, 179–89. New York: Hill and Wang.

———. 1985a. "Listening." In *The Responsibility of Forms: Critical Essays on Music, Art, and Representation*, trans. Richard Howard, 245–60. New York: Hill and Wang.

———. 1985b. "Musica Practica." In *The Responsibility of Forms*, trans. Richard Howard, 261–66. New York: Hill and Wang.

Bataille, Georges. 1992. *Death and Sensuality: A Study of Eroticism and the Taboo*. 1962; repr. Salem, NH: Ayer.

Bloch, Ernst. 1985. *Essays on the Philosophy of Music*. Trans. Peter Palmer. Cambridge: Cambridge University Press.

———. 1986. *The Principle of Hope*. 3 vols. Trans. Neville Plaice, Stephen Plaice, and Paul Knight. Cambridge, MA: MIT Press.

———. 1988a. "The Artistic Illusion as the Visible Anticipatory Illumination." In *The Utopian Function of Art and Literature: Selected Essays*, trans. Jack Zipes and Frank Mecklenburg, 141–55. Cambridge, MA: MIT Press.

———. 1988b. "Better Castles in the Sky at the Country Fair and Circus, in Fairy Tales and Colportage." In Ernst Bloch, *The Utopian Function of Art and Literature: Selected Essays*, trans. Jack Zipes and Frank Mecklenburg, 167–85. Cambridge, MA: MIT Press.

———. 1988c. "The Conscious and Known Activity within the Not-Yet-Conscious, the Utopian Function." In Ernst Bloch, *The Utopian Function of Art and Literature: Selected Essays*, trans. Jack Zipes and Frank Mecklenburg, 103–41. Cambridge, MA: MIT Press.

———. 1988d. *The Utopian Function of Art and Literature: Selected Essays*. Trans. Jack Zipes and Frank Mecklenburg. Cambridge, MA: MIT Press.

———. 1988e. "The Wish-Landscape Perspective in Aesthetics: The Order of Art Materials According to the Dimension of Their Profundity and Hope." In *The Utopian Function of Art and Literature: Selected Essays*, trans. Jack Zipes and Frank Mecklenburg, 71–77. Cambridge, MA: MIT Press.

———. 2000. *The Spirit of Utopia.* Trans. Anthony A. Nassar. Stanford, CA: Stanford University Press.

Bloch, Ernst, and Theodor W. Adorno. 1988. "Something's Missing: A Discussion between Ernst Bloch and Theodor W. Adorno on the Contradictions of Utopian Longing." In Ernst Bloch, *The Utopian Function of Art and Literature: Selected Essays,* trans. Jack Zipes and Frank Mecklenburg, 1–17. Cambridge, MA: MIT Press.

Bloom, Allan. 1987. *The Closing of the American Mind: How Higher Education Has Failed Democracy and Impoverished the Souls of Today's Students.* New York: Simon and Schuster.

Chrysostom, Saint John. 1998. "Exposition of Psalm XLI." In *Source Readings in Music History,* rev. ed., ed. Oliver Strunk, general ed. Leo Treitler, 123–26. New York: W. W. Norton.

Dunn, David. 2001. "Nature, Sound Art, and the Sacred." In *The Book of Music and Nature,* ed. David Rothenberg and Marta Ulvaeus, 95–107. Middletown, CT: Wesleyan University Press.

Edström, Olle. 1989. "'Vi skall gå på restaurang och höra på musik': Om reception av restaurangmusik och annan 'mellanmusik'" ["'We Shall Go to a Restaurant and Listen to Music': About Reception of Music Played in Restaurants and Other 'Middle Music'"]. *Svensk Tidskrift för Musikforskning* 71:77–112.

———. 1997. "Fr-a-g-me-n-ts: A Discussion on the Position of Critical Ethnomusicology in Contemporary Musicology." *Svenskt Tidskrift för Musikforskning* 79:9–68.

Elsaesser, Thomas. 1981–82. "Myth as the Phantasmagoria of History: H. J. Syberberg, Cinema, and Representation." *New German Critique,* no. 24–25 (Fall–Winter): 108–54.

Goehr, Lydia. 2004. "Dissonant Works and the Listening Public." In *The Cambridge Companion to Adorno,* ed. Tom Huhn, 222–47. Cambridge: Cambridge University Press.

Hanslick, Eduard. 1986. *On the Musically Beautiful: A Contribution towards the Revision of the Aesthetics of Music.* Ed. and trans. Geoffrey Payzant. 1854; repr. Indianapolis: Hackett.

Hegel, G. W. F. 1977. *Phenomenology of Spirit.* Trans. A. V. Miller. Oxford: Oxford University Press.

Hoeckner, Berthold. 2002. *Programming the Absolute: Nineteenth-Century German Music and the Hermeneutics of the Moment.* Princeton, NJ: Princeton University Press.

Horkheimer, Max, and Theodor W. Adorno. 2002. *Dialectic of Englightenment: Philosophical Fragments.* Ed. Gunzelin Schmid Noerr, trans. Edmund Jephcott. Stanford, CA: Stanford University Press.

Hullot-Kentor, Robert. 2004. "Right Listening and a New Type of Human Being." In *The Cambridge Companion to Adorno,* ed. Tom Huhn, 181–97. Cambridge: Cambridge University Press.

Jameson, Fredric. 1990. *Late Marxism: Adorno, or, the Persistence of the Dialectic.* London: Verso.

Leppert, Richard. 1988. *Music and Image: Domesticity, Ideology and Socio-Cultural Formation in Eighteenth-Century England.* Cambridge: Cambridge University Press.

———. 2003. "Introduction." In Theodor W. Adorno, *Essays on Music,* ed. Richard Leppert, trans. Susan H. Gillespie et al., 2003: 1–82. Berkeley and Los Angeles: University of California Press.

Lindstrom, Fred B., and Naomi Lindstrom. 1986. "Adorno Encounters Cu-Bop: Experimental Music as a Task for Critics and Their Audiences." *Sociological Perspectives* 29, no. 2 (April): 284–304.

Marcuse, Herbert. 1968. "The Affirmative Character of Culture." In *Negations: Essays in Critical Theory,* trans. Jeremy J. Shapiro, 88–133. Boston: Beacon Press.

Nicholsen, Shierry Weber. 1997. *Exact Imagination, Late Work: On Adorno's Aesthetics.* Cambridge, MA: MIT Press.

Nietzsche, Friedrich. 1967. *The Birth of Tragedy and The Case of Wagner.* Trans. Walter Kaufmann. New York: Vintage Books.

Paetzold, Heinz. 1997. "Adorno's Notion of Natural Beauty: A Reconsideration." In *The Semblance of Subjectivity: Essays in Adorno's Aesthetic Theory,* ed. Tom Huhn and Lambert Zuidervaart, 213–35. Cambridge, MA: MIT Press.

Plato. 1957. *The Republic of Plato.* Trans. A. D. Lindsay. New York: E. P. Dutton.

Russolo, Luigi. 1986. *The Art of Noises.* Trans. Barclay Brown. New York: Pendragon Press.

Schoenberg, Arnold. 1975. *Style and Idea: Selected Writings of Arnold Schoenberg.* Ed. Leonard Stein, trans. Leo Black. New York: St. Martin's.

Small, Christopher. 1998. *Musicking: The Meanings of Performing and Listening.* Hanover, NH: Wesleyan University Press.

Stendahl [Henri Beyle]. 1972. *Life of Rossini.* Trans. Richard N. Coe. Seattle: University of Washington Press.

Stravinsky, Igor. 1959. *Poetics of Music: In the Form of Six Lessons.* Trans. Arthur Knodel and Ingolf Dahl. New York: Vintage Books.

Subotnik, Rose Rosengard. 1996. "Toward a Deconstruction of Structural Listening: A Critique of Schoenberg, Adorno, and Stravinsky." In *Deconstructive Variations: Music and Reason in Western Society,* 148–76. Minneapolis: University of Minnesota Press.

Wolin, Richard. 1990. "Utopia, Mimesis, and Reconciliation: A Redemptive Critique of Adorno's *Aesthetic Theory.*" *Representations* 32 (Fall): 33–49.

Zuidervaart, Lambert. 1991. *Adorno's Aesthetic Theory: The Redemption of Illusion.* Cambridge, MA: MIT Press.

Index

www.ingramcontent.com/pod-product-compliance
Lightning Source LLC
LaVergne TN
LVHW080806011026
849160LV00015B/1550
* 9 7 8 1 1 3 8 3 8 3 5 4 8 *